The
AMERICAN
HERITAGE®

Guide to Contemporary Usage *and* Style

The
AMERICAN
HERITAGE®

Guide to Contemporary Usage *and* Style

HOUGHTON MIFFLIN COMPANY
Boston · New York

Visit our website: www.houghtonmifflinbooks.com

Library of Congress Cataloging-in-Publication Data

The American heritage guide to contemporary usage and style.
p. cm.
ISBN-13: 978-0-618-60499-9
ISBN-10: 0-618-60499-5
1. English language--Usage--Dictionaries. 2. English language--Style--Dictionaries. 3. English language--United States--Usage--Dictionaries. 4. English language--United States--Style--Dictionaries. I. Houghton Mifflin Company.
PE1464.A46 2005
423'.1- -dc22

2005016513

Manufactured in the United States of America

QUM 10 9 8 7 6 5 4 3 2 1

Contents

Editorial and Production Staff

Vice President, Publisher of Dictionaries
Margery S. Berube

Vice President, Executive Editor
Joseph P. Pickett

Vice President, Managing Editor
Christopher Leonesio

Senior Editors
Steven Kleinedler
Susan Spitz

Database Production Supervisor
Christopher Granniss

Editor
Catherine Pratt

Art and Production Supervisor
Margaret Anne Miles

Associate Editors
Erich Michael Groat
Uchenna Ikonné
Patrick Taylor

Editorial Production Assistant
Katherine M. Getz

Administrative Coordinator
Kevin McCarthy

Assistant Editor
Nick Durlacher

Intern
Tracy Duff

Contributing Editor
David Pritchard

Text Design
Catherine Hawkes, Cat & Mouse

Claudine B. Malone
Management consultant; former Associate Professor, Harvard Business School

Robert Manning
Writer; editor; former Editor in Chief, The Atlantic Monthly

Greil Marcus
Historian; essayist; critic

Suzanne R. Massie
Writer; lecturer on Russian history and culture; Fellow, Harvard Russian Research Center

Armistead Maupin
Author

Alice E. Mayhew
Editorial Director, Simon & Schuster

The Hon. Eugene McCarthy
Writer; poet; lecturer; former US Senator from Minnesota

Terrence McNally
Playwright

Leonard Michaels
Professor of English, University of California, Berkeley

Hassan Minor, Jr.
Senior Vice President, Howard University

Lorrie Moore
Writer; Professor of English, University of Wisconsin

Lance Morrow
Essayist, Time; *University Professor, Boston University*

Bharati Mukherjee
Professor; writer; recipient, National Book Critics Circle Award

Alice Munro
Author

Cullen Murphy
Managing Editor, The Atlantic Monthly

Thomas M.T. Niles
President, United States Council for International Business

Marsha Norman
Playwright

Mary Oliver
Poet; essayist

Cynthia Ozick
Novelist; essayist; member, American Academy of Arts and Letters

Margaret Sayers Peden
Translator

Ivars Peterson
Mathematics/Physics Editor, Science News

Steven Pinker
Johnstone Family Professor of Psychology, Harvard University; writer

Robert Pinsky
Poet; translator; former US Poet Laureate; Professor of English, Boston University

Robert S. Pirie
President and Chief Executive Officer, Rothschild Inc.

Katha Pollitt
Writer; Contributing Editor, The Nation

Alvin F. Poussaint, MD
Professor of Psychiatry, Harvard Medical School

Leah Price
Professor of English, Harvard University

Ellen F. Prince
Professor of Linguistics, University of Pennsylvania

Francine Prose
Writer

E. Annie Proulx
Novelist

Jane Bryant Quinn
Journalist; financial columnist

William James Raspberry
Urban affairs columnist and broadcast commentator; Knight Professor for the Practice of Journalism, Duke University; recipient, Pulitzer Prize

Robert Reich
Professor; former US Secretary of Labor; author; political economist

Richard Rhodes
Author; recipient, National Book Critics Circle Award, National Book Award, Pulitzer Prize, MacArthur Foundation Grant

Frank Rich
Writer and critic, The New York Times

John Rickford
Martin Luther King, Jr. Centennial Professor of Linguistics, Stanford University

Richard Rodriguez
Writer

Edward W. Rosenheim
Editor; writer; Professor of English Emeritus, University of Chicago

Judith Rossner
Novelist

Robert J. Samuelson
Columnist, The Washington Post, Newsweek

John Sayles
Film director; writer; screenwriter; actor

Antonin Scalia
Supreme Court Justice

Arthur M. Schlesinger, Jr.
Writer; historian; educator; former Special Assistant to the President of the United States; recipient, Pulitzer Prize

Lloyd Schwartz
Professor; poet; music critic

David Sedaris
Writer and humorist

Maureen Corrigan
Writer; book reviewer; professor

Robert W. Creamer
*Writer; biographer; former
Senior Editor*, Sports Illustrated

Gene D. Dahmen
*Attorney; past President, Boston
Bar Association*

Lois DeBakey
*Writer, lecturer, and consultant;
Professor of Scientific
Communication, Baylor College
of Medicine*

Frank Deford
Writer and commentator

Vine Deloria, Jr.
*Professor of Law, Religious
Studies, Political Science, and
History, University of Colorado*

Joan Didion
Author

Annie Dillard
Writer; recipient, Pulitzer Prize

Mark Doty
*Poet; Professor, University of
Houston*

Rita Dove
*Writer; Commonwealth
Professor of English, University
of Virginia; recipient, Pulitzer
Prize; Poet Laureate of the
Commonwealth of Virginia*

William K. Durr
*Professor Emeritus of Education,
Michigan State University; past
President, International Reading
Association*

Esther Dyson
*President, EDventure Holdings;
Chair, Electronic Frontier
Foundation; Member, US
National Information
Infrastructure Advisory Council*

Freeman J. Dyson
*Writer; Professor of Physics,
Institute for Advanced Study,
Princeton, New Jersey*

Anne Edwards
*Biographer; novelist; past
President, Authors Guild*

Gretel Ehrlich
Writer; Guggenheim Fellow

Louise Erdrich
Author

Carolly Erickson
Historian; writer

James Fallows
*Writer; national correspondent,
The Atlantic Monthly*

Frances FitzGerald
Writer; recipient, Pulitzer Prize

Maria Irene Fornes
Playwright

Elizabeth Frank
*Writer; Joseph E. Harry
Professor of Modern Languages
and Literature, Bard College;
recipient, Pulitzer Prize*

Reuven Frank
*Former President, NBC News;
former television news producer*

Ian Frazier
Writer

John Kenneth Galbraith
*Economist; writer; former US
Ambassador to India; Paul M.
Warburg Professor Emeritus of
Economics, Harvard University*

Catherine Gallagher
*Eggers Professor of English
Literature, University of
California, Berkeley*

Sara Garnes
*Linguist; Director of First Year
Composition and Associate
Professor of English, Ohio State
University*

Michael G. Gartner
*Language columnist; former
President, NBC News; past
President, American Society of
Newspaper Editors; past
Chairman, Pulitzer Prize Board*

Henry Louis Gates, Jr.
*W.E.B. DuBois Professor of
Humanities; Chair, Department
of Afro-American Studies,
Harvard University*

J. Edward Gates
*Lexicographer; editor; Professor
Emeritus of English, Indiana
State University*

James Gleick
Author; columnist

Philip Gourevitch
Writer

Francine du Plessix Gray
Writer

Georgia M. Green
Professor of Linguistics; writer

Stephen Greenblatt
*The Harry Levin Professor of
Literature, Harvard University*

Linda Gregerson
*Poet; critic; Frederick G.L.
Huetwell Professor of English,
University of Michigan*

Alma Guillermopricto
*Writer; staff writer, The New
Yorker*

Jessica Tarahata Hagedorn
Novelist; poet

Patricia Hampl
*Writer; Regents' Professor
of English, University of
Minnesota*

Liane Hansen
Radio correspondent

Robert Hass
Former US Poet Laureate

The Hon. Mark O. Hatfield
*Former US Senator from
Oregon*

William Least Heat-Moon
Writer

Mark Helprin
*Writer; editor; Senior Fellow,
Hudson Institute*

The American Heritage Dictionary Usage Panel

Harvey Shapiro
Poet; editor

Elaine Showalter
Professor of English, Princeton University

Leslie Marmon Silko
Author

John Simon
Drama and film critic; music columnist

Mona Simpson
Adjunct professor; novelist

David Skinner
Assistant managing editor, The Weekly Standard

Carlota S. Smith
Centennial Professor of Linguistics and Director, Center for Cognitive Science, University of Texas

Theodore C. Sorensen
Attorney; writer; of counsel, Paul, Weiss

Susan Stamberg
Special correspondent, National Public Radio

Margaret O'Brien Steinfels
Editor, Commonweal

Shane Templeton
Foundation Professor of Curriculum and Instruction, University of Nevada, Reno

Paul Theroux
Novelist; travel writer

Elizabeth Marshall Thomas
Writer

Nina Totenberg
Radio and television correspondent

Elizabeth C. Traugott
Professor of Linguistics and English, Stanford University

Calvin Trillin
Staff writer, The New Yorker

Anne Tyler
Novelist; recipient, Pulitzer Prize

The Hon. Stewart L. Udall
Writer; Chairman of the Board, The Archaeological Conservancy, Santa Fe, New Mexico; former US Secretary of the Interior and US Representative from Arizona

Helen H. Vendler
A. Kingsley Porter University Professor of English, Harvard University

Paula Vogel
Professor at Large, Brown University

Eugene Volokh
Professor of Law, University of California, Los Angeles Law School

David Foster Wallace
Writer

Barbara Wallraff
Author; columnist; Senior Editor, The Atlantic Monthly; *Editor in Chief, Copy Editor*

Douglas Turner Ward
Actor; playwright; recipient, Vernon Rice Award and Obie Award

Wendy Wasserstein
Playwright

Calvert Watkins
Professor-in-Residence, Classics and Indo-European Studies, UCLA; Victor S. Thomas Professor of Linguistics and the Classics (Emeritus); past President, Linguistic Society of America

Fay Weldon
Writer

Jacqueline Grennan Wexler
Writer; former college president

Tom Wicker
Author; journalist; newspaper editor

John Edgar Wideman
Novelist; Professor of English/Africana Studies, Brown University

Tobias Wolff
Writer; Ward W. and Priscilla B. Woods Professor in the Humanities

Alden S. Wood
Lecturer on Editorial Procedures, Simmons College; columnist on language and English usage

Richard A. Young
Writer; editor; lecturer; publisher; engineer; Executive Director, National Registry of Environmental Professionals

William Zinsser
Writer; editor; educator

We regret that the following members of the Usage Panel, who participated in the program for this edition, have died:

Elie Abel, Shana Alexander, Cleveland Amory, Sheridan Baker, Pierre Berton, Alton Blakeslee, The Hon. Daniel J. Boorstin, Paul Brooks, Heywood Hale Broun, Claudia Cassidy, Alistair Cooke, Roy H. Copperud, Michael Dorris, Andrea Dworkin, June M. Jordan, Alfred Kazin, Walter Kerr, Charles Kuralt, J. Anthony Lukas, William Manchester, Richard Curry Marius, David McCord, Kenneth McCormick, Mary McGrory, James A. Michener, Jessica Mitford, The Hon. Daniel Patrick Moynihan, Maurine Neuberger, David Ogilvy, Tony Randall, Leo Rosten, Vermont Royster, Carl Sagan, Robert Saudek, Glenn T. Seaborg, Susan Sontag, Eudora Welty.

Introduction

This book discusses current problems in English usage in an attempt to explain the effects that particular expressions are likely to have on readers of serious prose. The Guide covers the entire range of usage issues: traditional bugbears, emerging controversies, confused words, distinctions of meaning, differences between scientific and lay usage, words with controversial pronunciations, conventions of punctuation and style, and more.

The Guide examines the canons of traditional usage in light of the practice and attitudes of distinguished contemporary writers. Notions of beauty and decorum change over time, and the Guide shows how particular expressions are used in prestigious publications and how accomplished writers respond to these expressions in context. At the same time, the Guide looks back at the distinguished literary tradition of English for inspiring models, citing examples from exemplary writers to demonstrate effective usage and to clarify semantic distinctions among words. Citations of contemporary usage take their place against this background.

Many notes in this book also examine usage problems under the lens of linguistic and historical analysis. A number of tenets of traditional grammar were formulated in the 18th and 19th centuries by people who had little understanding of how language works and who saw Latin as the proper model for English grammar. The rationales for their directives often make little sense today, and writers confronted with making decisions about the correct form of words, grammatical agreement, parts of speech, and extensions of meaning should consider how the modern study of language can help them write more clearly and communicate more effectively. Many controversial usages can sometimes be justified by analogy with other words and grammatical constructions, that is, controversial usages sometimes function in much the same way as words and constructions that have been accepted as standard for many years. Arguments like these require some explanation of how words actually work, and linguistic analysis comes into play here.

Many other controversies reflect the conflict between ongoing language change and the conventions of publishing. English today, regardless of where it is spoken, sounds and looks different from the way it did even a hundred years ago. New words are constantly being created, and existing words are sometimes used in new and unexpected ways. Certain longstanding expressions, for reasons no one understands, fall out of use. Words with similar sounds or spellings get confused. The grammar of English has changed as well, slowly but relentlessly. People now use certain grammatical constructions (such as progressive tenses and attributive nouns) far more frequently than they did just two hundred years ago. Like words, some grammatical constructions simply drop out of the language, while others rise to take their place.

Publishing conventions, by contrast, are meant to be uniform and unchanging in the interest of clarity and decorum in expression. Today, writers take standardized spelling for granted, but English readers and writers of the past were accustomed to wide variations in spelling. The notion of "correct" spelling was unthought of. In contemporary publishing it is virtually impossible to write without using or being forced to use standardized spelling, and deviations from this practice are viewed either as errors or as deliberate breaks in convention. Similarly, the use of standard or traditional rules of punctuation and grammar are meant to make communication easier across a variety of communities and subjects and to enable a piece of writing to take its place as a serious contribution to the exchange of ideas in an open society. Ignoring these rules entails certain risks and has unavoidable consequences.

In some ways, the task of writing today is more complicated than it was in the past. Since the potential audience for most public discourse is so varied nowadays and encompasses a complex and dynamic society instead of a relatively small group of the educated and privileged, it is important for writers to be aware of the social sensitivities of readers (whether they share them or not) and to understand the hazards involved in dealing with gender in language and in discussing social groups. This book devotes many notes to words in these areas.

The Usage Panel and Usage Ballots

To help adjudicate controversies and to gauge how readers may react to specific words, the opinions of the American Heritage Dictionary Usage Panel, a group of about two hundred prominent writers, scholars, and scientists, are often invoked. The Usage Panel has been in existence since 1964, with new members taking their place beside longstanding veterans. Members of the Panel are periodically sent surveys containing questions on usage. The examples included in the questions are citations of actual usage or are adapted from citations of actual usage. Most questions are posed in a number of examples, so that a specific usage appears in a variety of different linguistic environments, and the Panel must cast judgment on each. Many usage issues have a number of faces, and experience has shown that the Panel's opinions about a usage can vary considerably depending on its setting and phrasing.

The surveys have become a valuable collection of information on many usage issues, covering more than forty years, and they provide a way of judging whether a controversy continues to have strength or is fading away, and whether a new linguistic development is likely to become incorporated into standard practice.

Acceptability

Most survey questions ask the Panelists whether they find a particular word or construction to be acceptable or not in formal Standard English. Acceptability does not mean that the Panelists necessarily use a particular usage in their own writing, but that the usage does not violate the propriety that the Panelists consider inherent to formal Standard English. Certain questions on the survey include the option of indicating acceptability in informal contexts. Sometimes Panelists are asked to indicate their own preferences or to provide alternative ways of saying something. When an overwhelming percentage of the Panel accepts a usage, this indicates that it has become standard and that it is likely to remain so. Usages that become standard may eventually fall out of use, but they are unlikely to return to nonstandard or unconventional status.

Acceptability is thus not really a matter of grammaticality but rather a broader notion of appropriateness. Judgments about acceptability can be based on aesthetics, as when a Panelist rejects a grammatical sentence for faulty parallelism. Judgments may also be influenced by a concern about pretentiousness, as when a Panelist rejects a term that has been borrowed from the technical vocabulary of a particular field of science. In some cases, a desire for social justice may motivate the Panelists' decisions about the acceptability of a word or construction, as when Panelists allow the pronoun *their* to refer to a singular noun in order to avoid using the masculine *his* to stand for both men and women. In this instance, these Panelists choose to supersede the dictums of traditional grammar in order to avoid perpetuating sexism in the language.

Levels of Usage

This book uses a number of terms to indicate different levels of usage and to provide guidance about the circumstances under which a given usage will be appropriate.

Standard English The term Standard English refers to both an actual variety of language and an idealized norm of English acceptable in many social situations. As a language variety, Standard English is the language used in most public discourse and in the regular operation of American social institutions. The news media, the government, the legal profession, and the teachers in our schools and universities all view Standard English as their proper mode of communication, primarily in expository and argumentative writing, but also in public speaking. As a norm, writers and editors look at Standard English as the model of language in which they work. Their decisions both are based on and help shape the rules and conventions of Standard English.

Standard English is thus different from what is normally thought of as speech in that Standard English must be taught, whereas children learn to speak naturally without being taught. Of course, Standard English shares with spoken English certain features common to all forms of language. It has rules for making grammatical sentences, and it changes over time. The issues of pronunciation discussed in this book mainly involve how to pronounce specific written words or written letters, such as *ch* or *g*, in different words. The guidance to pronunciation is not meant to standardize or correct anyone's naturally acquired form of spoken English.

Nonstandard English There are many expressions and grammatical constructions that are not normally used in Standard English. These include regional expressions, such as *might could,* and other usages, such as *ain't* and *it don't,* that are typically associated with varieties of English used by people belonging to less prestigious social groups. In this book an expression labeled *nonstandard* is thus inappropriate for ordinary usage in Standard English.

Formal English On many occasions it is important to adhere to the conventions that characterize serious public discourse and to avoid expressions that might be appropriate in more casual or intimate social situations. Formal writing and speaking are characterized by the tendency to give full treatment to all the elements that are required for grammatical sentences. Thus formal English will have *May I suggest that we reexamine the problem?* where both clauses have a subject and verb and the subordinate clause is introduced by the conjunction *that*. Of course, formal English has many other features. Among these are the careful explanation of background information, complexity in sentence structure, explicit transitions between thoughts, and the use of certain words such as *may* that are reserved chiefly for creating a formal tone. Situations that normally require formal usage would include an article discussing a serious matter submitted to an edited journal, an official report by a group of researchers to a government body, a talk presented to a professional organization, and a letter of job application.

Informal English This is a broad category applied to situations in which it is not necessary, and in many cases not even desirable, to use the conventions of formal discourse. Informal language incorporates many of the familiar features of spoken English, especially the tendency to use contractions and to abbreviate sentences by omitting certain elements. Where formal English has *May I suggest that we reexamine the manuscript?*, informal English might have *Why not give this another look?* Informal English tends to assume that the audience shares basic assumptions and background knowledge with the writer or speaker, who therefore alludes to or even omits reference to this information, rather than carefully explaining it as formal discourse requires. Typical informal situations would include a casual conversation with classmates, a letter to a close friend, or an article on a light topic written for a newspaper or magazine whose readership shares certain interests and values of the writer.

Of course, these functional categories are not hard and fast divisions of language; rather they are general tendencies of usage. People use language over a spectrum that shifts from intimate situations to public discourse, and a given piece of writing may have a mixture of formal and informal elements. It is important to remember that *formal* and *informal* refer to styles of expression, not standards of correctness. Informal English has its own rules of grammar and is just as logical as formal English. One can be serious using informal English, just as one can be comical using formal English. The two styles are simply used for different occasions.

As the ancient rhetoricians stated so compellingly, writing and public speaking are art forms that require close attention to one's subject, audience, and purpose. Each occasion presents a different set of challenges to the person choosing and arranging the words for it. This Guide is intended to make this often overwhelming task more manageable and less intimidating. My colleagues and I hope that readers approach this book critically and thoughtfully, in much the same spirit with which it was written.

Joseph P. Pickett
Executive Editor

Pronunciation Key

ă	pat		t	tight, stopped
ā	pay		th	thin
âr	care		*th*	this
ä	father		ŭ	cut
är	car		ûr	urge, term, firm, word, heard
b	bib		v	valve
ch	church		w	with
d	deed, milled		y	yes
ě	pet		z	zebra, xylem
ē	be, bee		zh	vision, pleasure, garage
f	fife, phase, rough		ə	about, item, edible, gallon, circus
g	gag			
h	hat			
hw	which			

Foreign

œ	French	feu
	German	schön
ü	French	tu
KH	German	ich
	Scottish	loch
N	French	bon

ĭ	pit
ī	pie, by
îr	dear, deer, pier
j	judge
k	kick, cat, pique
l	lid, needle
m	mum
n	no, sudden
ng	thing
ŏ	pot
ō	toe
ô	caught, paw
ôr	core
oi	noise, boy
ŏŏ	took
ŏŏr	lure
ōō	boot
ou	out
p	pop
r	roar
s	sauce
sh	ship, dish

The symbol (ə) is called *schwa*. It represents a vowel with the weakest level of stress in a word. The schwa sound varies slightly according to the vowel it represents or the sounds around it.

Stress is the relative degree of emphasis with which a word's syllables are spoken. An unmarked syllable has the weakest stress in the word. The strongest, or primary, stress is indicated with a bold mark (′). A lighter mark (′) indicates a secondary level of stress. The stress mark follows the syllable it applies to. Words of one syllable have no stress mark, because there is no other stress level that the syllable is compared to.

· A ·

a / an

In modern written English, the indefinite article *a* is used before a word beginning with a consonant sound, however it may be spelled (*a frog, a university, a euphemism*). *An* is used before a word beginning with a vowel sound (*an orange, an hour*). At one time, *an* was an acceptable alternative before words beginning with a consonant sound but spelled with a vowel (*an one, an united appeal*), but this usage is now entirely obsolete.

An was also once a common variant before words beginning with *h* in which the first syllable was unstressed; thus 18th-century authors wrote either *a historical* or *an historical*, but *a history*, not *an history*. This usage made sense in that people often did not pronounce the initial *h* in words such as *historical* and *heroic*, but by the late 19th century, educated speakers were usually giving their initial *h*'s a huff, and the practice of writing *an* began to die out. Nowadays it survives primarily before the word *historical*. It occurs occasionally in the phrases *an hysterectomy* or *an hereditary trait*. These usages are acceptable in formal writing.

pronouncing *a* and *an*   The indefinite article is generally pronounced (ə), as in *a boy, a girl*. When stressed for emphasis, it is pronounced (ā), as in *not a person was left*. The form *an* also has a variant that is unstressed (ən) and stressed (ăn).

a–

The basic meaning of the prefix *a–* is "not" or "without." For example, *abiotic* means "nonliving" and *achromatic* means "without color." Before vowels and sometimes *h*, *a–* becomes *an–: anaerobic, anhedonic, anhydrous.* The prefix *a(n)–* comes from Greek, and it is often found in the large number of scientific words in English that have been borrowed from Greek or coined in modern times using Greek elements, such as *aphasia, anoxia,* and *aseptic.* In newer scientific vocabulary, the prefix is also used to negate word-building elements taken from other languages, especially Latin. In the word *asexual*, for example, *a–* has been prefixed to *sexual*, a word of Latin origin. In fact, Greek *a(n)–* is the distant linguistic cousin of the native English prefix *un–*, also meaning "not," found in words like *unknown*. It is important not to confuse *a–* with other prefixes, such as *ad–*, that begin with the letter *a*.

abductor / adductor

Muscles that move body parts away from each other or from the trunk of the body itself are called *abductors*. For example, an abductor muscle moves your thumb away from your index finger, allowing the popular "thumbs up" salute. The word *abductor* comes from Latin *abducere,* which is built of the prefix *ab–,* "away," and the verb *dūcere,* "to bring."

Adductor muscles, by contrast, bring body parts together or bring them closer to the central axis of the body. It is a group of adductor muscles in the inner thigh, for example, that allows a rider to sit firmly astride a horse. Once the rider has dismounted, the same group of adductors works in concert with other thigh muscles to enable him or her to stand upright. *Adductor* comes from Latin *addūcere,* which combines *ad–,* "to," and the verb *dūcere.*

aberrant

Traditionally this word has been pronounced with stress on the second syllable (ă-bĕr′ənt). However, a newer pronunciation with stress on the first syllable (ăb′ər-ənt) has gained ground and is now equally acceptable. In 1992, 45 percent of the Usage Panel preferred the older pronunciation, and 50 percent preferred the newer one. A small percentage of the Panelists use both pronunciations. Perhaps one reason for the shift is the association of *aberrant* with *aberration* and *aberrated,* which are both stressed on the first syllable.

able

The construction *able to* takes an infinitive to show the subject's ability to accomplish something: *We were able to finish the project thanks to a grant from a large corporation. The new submarine is able to dive twice as fast as the older model.* Subjects to which we don't ascribe active roles tend to sound awkward in this construction, especially in passive constructions involving forms of the verb *be,* as in *The problem was able to be solved by using this new method.* Here, the use of the passive underscores the subject's not taking an active role, while the use of *able* suggests the opposite, creating a conflict. The conflict can be avoided by substituting *can* or *could: The problem could be solved by using this new method.* Another substitution involves using *capable,* which doesn't ascribe such an active role to its subject: *The problem is capable of being solved by using this new method.* Using a *get* passive, which ascribes a more active role to its subject, also avoids the conflict, but in such sentences the subject should be something or someone that naturally has such a role: *He was finally able to get accepted to a good school.*

–able

The suffix *–able,* which forms adjectives, comes from the Latin suffix *–ābilis,* meaning "capable or worthy of." Thus *a likable person* is one who is capable of or worthy of being liked. The suffix *–ible* is closely related to *–able* and has the same meaning, as in *flexible.* It is important to consult your dictionary when spelling words that end in these suffixes, since in many varieties of American English the two are pronounced exactly the same.

Note that there are a few words in which the difference in spelling corresponds to a difference in meaning. For example, *forcible* means either "characterized by force," as in the phrase *forcible arguments,* or "accomplished though force," as in *a forcible entry into the building. Forceable,* on the other hand, simply means "able to be forced."

The spelling of words like *forceable* occasionally poses another difficulty. In the past, when the suffix *–able* was added to a word ending in a silent *e,* the *e* was often kept in the spelling, as in *moveable* or *rideable.* Nowadays the silent *e* is often dropped. The *e* must always be kept, however, after a so-called "soft" *c* or *g,* in order to indicate their pronunciation as (s) and (j), respectively, as in *forceable* or *marriageable.*

See more at **forceful.**

aborigine / aboriginal

An *aborigine* or *aboriginal* is a member of the earliest known inhabitants of a region. The word *aborigine* ultimately comes from the Latin plural noun *aborīginēs,* which meant "original inhabitants" and in particular "the early ancestors of the Roman people." This word is usually said to derive from the Latin phrase *ab orīgine,* "from the beginning," but it may also have originated as the name of a local tribe in ancient Italy that the Romans reinterpreted and altered by association with the phrase *ab orīgine.* The Latin word had no disparaging or pejorative nuance, and the same is sometimes true of its modern English derivatives *aborigine* or *aboriginal,* which may sound natural and respectful in certain contexts or in reference to certain groups. In other situations, however, the terms may evoke unwelcome stereotypes. *Aborigine* is used primarily of the indigenous peoples of Australia, where it is generally capitalized as an ethnonym and accepted as inoffensive. In Canada the preferred spelling is *Aboriginal,* which is used respectfully both as a noun and an adjective in referring to native Canadian peoples, including First Nations, Inuit, and Métis. In the United States, however, these terms do not have the status of ethnonyms; they are uncommon today in reference to Native American peoples and, when used, are generally not capitalized.

See more at **native.**

abortion

For many people, the word *abortion* means one thing: the deliberate termination of a pregnancy. But the word is used in a number of ways, with important distinctions in its meaning, depending on context.

In medical communication, the term *therapeutic abortion* refers to a medically induced termination of pregnancy for any reason, in contrast to a *spontaneous abortion,* or miscarriage. Before abortion was legal in the US, the procedure was sometimes allowed under the law as "therapeutic" if proof of necessity was demonstrated. Today, *therapeutic abortion* is also used popularly to describe an abortion performed for known medical reasons, as in response to abnormal prenatal test results.

During a *spontaneous abortion,* the embryo or fetus is made inviable in the uterus by disease, genetic malformation, trauma, or other usually unintended causes. A *spontaneous abortion* that has not been detected is called a *missed abortion.*

See also **fetus.**

about

The preposition *about* is traditionally used to refer to the relation between a narrative and its subject: *a book about Cezanne, a movie about the Boston Massacre.* For some time this usage has been extended beyond narratives to refer to the relation between various kinds of nouns and the things they entail or make manifest: *The party was mostly about showing off their new offices. You don't understand what the women's movement is about.* This usage probably originates with the familiar expression *That's what it's all about,* but it remains controversial. In our 2001 survey, 62 percent of the Usage Panel rejected this use of *about* in the party example listed above, and 51 percent rejected *Their business is about matching people with the right technology.* This resistance appears to be holding strong, since 59 percent rejected a similar example in 1988. It is probably best to limit this use of *about* to more informal contexts.

not about to   When followed by an infinitive, *about to* means "presently going to, on the verge of," as in *I'm about to go downtown.* The construction *not about to* may be simply the negative of this, especially in response to questions: *I'm not about to go downtown. I'm about to go to the park.* But in most instances *not about to* expresses intention or determination, as in *We are not about to negotiate with terrorists.* This usage was considered unacceptable in formal writing to a majority of the Usage Panel in 1988, but resistance has eroded with familiarity. Fully 82 percent accepted it in our 2001 survey.

above

The use of *above* as an adjective or noun in referring to a discussion in the preceding text is a hallmark of business and legal writing, but it serves a useful purpose in other contexts as well. As far back as 1964, its use in general writing as an adjective (as in *the above figures*) was accepted by 72 percent of the Usage Panel. Here is a sampler of its use in varied contexts:

> While the above situation has never taken place, many industry experts say it could. In fact, they're somewhat surprised it hasn't already (Tom Regan, "When Terrorists Turn to the Internet," *Christian Science Monitor*)

> Mix all of the above ingredients together and pour into muffin tins lightly coated with nonstick cooking spray (Rhonda Gates and Covert Bailey, *Smart Eating*)

> Leland O. Howard was the author of the above quotations, which are taken from his report in the 1903 yearbook of the Department of Agriculture (Sue Hubbell, *Shrinking the Cat*)

In the same 1964 survey, only 44 percent of the Panel accepted the use of *above* as a noun (*read the above*), perhaps because the leap from adverb and preposition (the traditional roles of *above*) to noun seems too much of a stretch. Nonetheless, the noun is also used in a wide variety of contexts and should not be considered unorthodox:

> As the above already suggests, both Thucydides and Clausewitz laid very great emphasis on physical strength while at the same time suggesting that moral strength is, when everything is said and done, even more critical (Martin Van Creveld, "War," *The Reader's Companion to Military History*)

> The writer feels what it's like to be a player when the medium rules, when its constraints are also a free ride to unforeseen, unexpected, surprising destinations, to breaks and zones offering the chance to do something, be somebody, somewhere, somehow new . . . Given all the above, I still want more from writing (John Edgar Wideman, *Hoop Roots*)

> The exhibition comes with a 443-page catalogue including essays by 15 experts. They politely point out that the above is hogwash (William Wilson, "'Voodou' Works Unveil Triumphant Spirit," *Los Angeles Times*)

> At symposiums and writers' conferences, I've learned to duck and weave around the inevitable question "What do you look for in a short story?" I wish I knew! Heart? Soul? Truth? Voice? Integrity of intention and skill in execution? The answer is all of the above, and none of the above (Katrina Kenison, Foreword, *The Best American Short Stories 2001*)

Curiously, there has not been a parallel development with the word *below,* for which there would appear to be a similar need. Constructions like *the below instructions* meaning "the instructions listed below," and *The below explains . . .* are rare in comparison to the uses of *above.*

absolute constructions

Absolute constructions consist of a noun and some kind of modifier, the most common being a participle. Because they often come at the beginning of a sentence, they are easily confused with dangling participles. But an absolute construction modifies the rest of the sentence, not the subject of the sentence (as a participial phrase does). You can use absolute constructions to compress two sentences into one and to vary sentence structure as a means of holding a reader's interest. Here are some examples:

> *No other business arising,* the meeting was adjourned.
> *The paint now dry,* we brought the furniture out on the deck.
> *The truck finally loaded,* they said goodbye to their neighbors and drove off.
> The horse loped across the yard, *her foal trailing behind her.*

Constructions like these are used more often in writing than in speaking, where it is more common to use a full clause: *When the paint was dry, we brought the furniture out on the deck.* There are, however, many fixed absolute constructions that occur frequently in speech:

> The picnic is scheduled for Saturday, *weather permitting.*
> *Barring bad weather,* we plan to go to the beach tomorrow.

All things considered, it's not a bad idea.

See more at **having said that, that having been said.**

absolute terms

Absolute terms are words that supposedly cannot be compared, as by *more* and *most,* or used with an intensive modifier, such as *very* or *so.* The terms identified in many handbooks as absolute include *absolute* itself and others such as *chief, complete, perfect, prime,* and *unique.* Language commentators also like to list terms from mathematics as absolutes: *circular, equal, infinite, parallel, perpendicular,* and so on.

A great many adjectives in English cannot normally be compared or intensified. Adjectives from technical fields or with very narrow meanings often fall in this group. Think of *biological, catabolic, macroeconomic, millennial, online, retroactive, ultraviolet.* Statements like *These cells are more somatic* or *Our database is so online* simply do not occur. But sentences like *He wanted to make his record collection more complete* and *You can improve the sketch by making the lines more perpendicular* are very common.

People sometimes object to these constructions because they seem to violate the categories of logic. Something is either complete or it isn't. Lines are either perpendicular or they aren't. There can be no in-between. The mistake here is to confuse pure logic or a mathematical ideal with the working approximations that distinguish the ordinary use of language. Certainly, we all have occasion to use words according to strict logic. It would be impossible to teach mathematics if we did not. But we also think in terms of a scale or spectrum, rather than in distinct, either/or categories. Thus, we may think of a statement as either true or false according to rigorous tests of logic, but we all know that there are degrees of truthfulness and falsehood. Similarly, there may be degrees of completeness to a record collection, and some lines may be more perpendicular—that is, they may more nearly approximate mathematical perpendicularity—than other lines: *Is that picture frame more horizontal now, or have I made it even less? She has some of the most unique credentials I have ever seen on a resume.* Such examples are not less logical than their stricter counterparts. They simply represent a different way of using language to discuss a subject.

See more at **complete, equal, infinite, parallel, perfect,** and **unique.**

absorption / adsorption

Absorption indicates a process in which one substance is taken up by and accumulated in another, or one in which increasing amounts of the substance undergo a change of phase (as from water to ice): *The absorption of spilled juice into a paper towel occurs by capillary action. The ice absorbed the surrounding water vapor. Adsorption,* in contrast, describes the accumulation of a substance on the surface of a solid or liquid, without its necessarily becoming intermingled within the adsorbing solid or liquid: *The removal of dissolved gases from tap water is achieved by their adsorption onto a substance such as activated charcoal.*

access

The verb *access* is well established as a standard term in computer technology, as in *This program makes it considerably easier to access files on another server.* The verb has been extended in recent years to other contexts as well, and our surveys suggest that resistance to these usages is waning. When used to mean "to obtain something, especially by technological means," *access* was rejected by 82 percent of the Usage Panel in our 1988 survey, but by only 46 percent in our 2001 survey. Both surveys gathered responses to the same example: *You can access your cash at any of three hundred automatic tellers throughout the area.* In the 2001 survey the Panel showed less enthusiasm for using *access* to mean "to gain access to" in the example *Endovascular radiologists access patients' brain blood vessels through catheters.* So, although this term still strikes many readers as unsettling, it appears likely to become widely accepted as its uses proliferate.

accessory

Although the pronunciation (ə-sĕs′ə-rē), with no (k) sound in the first syllable, is commonly heard, it is not accepted by a majority of the Usage Panel. In the 1997 survey, 87 percent of the Panelists disapproved of it. The 13 percent that accepted the pronunciation were divided on usage: more than half accepted the (k)-less pronunciation for all senses. A few approved of it only in fashion contexts, and a few others approved of it only in legal contexts.

acclimate

Originally, the primary pronunciation of the verb *acclimate* received stress on the second syllable (ə-klī′mĭt). However, in recent decades, the preferred pronunciation has steadily shifted toward favoring a stress on the first syllable (ăk′lə-māt′). In fact, in a 2002 survey, the newer pronunciation was almost universally accepted, and four fifths of the Panel found the earlier pronunciation with stress on the second syllable to be unacceptable.

accompany

A traditional rule states that the preposition to use when *accompany* occurs in passive constructions should be *by* in the case of persons and *with* in the case of everything else. Thus the rule requires *The candidate was accompanied by six burly bodyguards,* and *The salmon was accompanied with a delicious salad.* However, *by* is quite commonly used in sentences of the second type, and the usage is grammatically defensible. The phrase introduced with *by* normally represents the subject of a related active sentence. Thus the passive sentence *The salmon was accompanied by a delicious salad* can be easily converted to its active counterpart *A delicious salad accompanied the salmon.*

accuracy / precision

In general use, the words *accuracy* and *precision* have close but distinct meanings. When we speak of the accuracy of a description, we are referring to how well it corresponds to the actual facts. When we speak of the precision of a description, we are referring to how much detail or specificity it provides. Thus we can describe a report as *accurate but sketchy,* but not as *precise but sketchy.*

In science, the accuracy of something is a measure of how close it is to what is known or acceptable. The result of an experimental measurement, for example, is considered accurate if it is consistent with a known or acceptable value for what is being measured. Similarly, a set of results is considered accurate if, taken as a whole (for example, taking their average value), they converge on a known or acceptable value. If a part of the measuring process can be shown to be flawed (as due to faulty equipment or a mathematical error), then the measurement will be considered inaccurate. In many cases scientists cannot know how accurate a measurement is until further work refines their knowledge of what is being measured.

The precision of a result, on the other hand, is an indication of how sharply it is defined. For example, an experimental numerical result is precise if it specifies a value that is many digits long; it is less precise if it specifies only a few digits or only an order of magnitude (leaving open a wide range of possible values). Similarly, a set of results is precise if they do not diverge greatly from each other.

Consider the calculation of pi by William Shanks. In 1853 he published a calculation of pi to 607 decimal places. Twenty years later, he published a result that extended this work to 707 decimal places. This was the most precise numerical definition of pi of its time and adorned many classroom walls. In 1949 a computer was used to calculate pi, and it was discovered that William Shanks's result was in error starting at a point near the 500th decimal place all the way to the 707th decimal place. Nowadays, with the benefit of a true value for pi to 100,000 decimal places, we can say that William Shanks's techniques generated a precise result, but the value he obtained was not accurate.

acquiesce

When *acquiesce* takes a preposition, it is usually used with *in: No government acquiesces in its own overthrow.* The preposition *to* is less common, but also acceptable: *She acquiesced to her parents' wishes. Acquiesced with* is obsolete.

act / action

The words *act* and *action* both mean "a deed" and "the process of doing." However, other senses of *act,* such as "a decision made by a legislative body," and of *action,* such as "habitual or vigorous activity," show that *act* tends to refer to a deed (i.e., something that has been completed), while *action* tends to refer to the process of doing something. Thus, one may want *a piece of the action,* but not *a piece of the act.*

The word *action* also tends to stress the vigor or intensity of the activity; thus, to be *a part of the action* suggests having a very active role, while to be *a part of the act* suggests simple participation. But subtleties of meaning, along with a large number of idioms involving these words, often demand one word or the other for unclear reasons. Thus people commit *sex acts* every day, but not *sex actions*. If they are seen, they are *caught in the act*, but not *in the action* (which would imply that they were unwittingly involved). In many cases, either word is acceptable, with no clear difference in meaning: *My act* [or *action*] *was premature.*

active voice   See **verbs, voice of.**

actor / actress   See **feminine suffixes.**

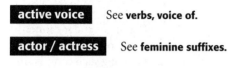

acumen

The pronunciation (ə-kyōō′mən), with stress on the second syllable, is an older, traditional pronunciation reflecting the word's Latin origin. The Anglicized pronunciation with stress on the first syllable, (ăk′yə-mən), was accepted as standard by the entire Usage Panel in the 1997 survey and was the preferred pronunciation of two thirds of the Panelists. The older pronunciation was considered unacceptable by 40 percent of the Panel, suggesting that eventually this pronunciation will fall into disuse.

AD / BC / CE

Traditionally in Western countries, events have been dated with reference to the birth of Jesus. In this system, the present epoch is designated by the letters AD, which stand for *anno Domini,* a Latin phrase meaning "in the year of the Lord." The epoch preceding the present epoch is designated in English with the letters BC, which stand for *before Christ.* The letters AD are usually put before the year number, but BC is put after, as in *The Roman Empire began in 31* BC *after the battle of Actium and ended, in the West, in* AD *476.* The foundations of this system were laid about 1,500 years ago by the monk and scholar Dionysius Exiguus. However, the determination of the year now known as AD 1 as the first full year of Jesus's life has turned out to be incorrect, and most scholars now accept that his birth probably occurred somewhat earlier. The traditional system has remained nonetheless.

As American society becomes increasingly diverse and awareness and respect for cultural and religious differences grows, many have felt the need for a new system that respects the beliefs of atheists and members of religious groups other than Christians. A growing number of writers now use another system of epoch names that contain no direct reference to Christianity. The current epoch is designated CE, standing for *common era,* while the epoch formerly designated BC is now designated BCE, standing for *before the common era.* Both CE and BCE follow the year.

The abbreviations BC, AD, BCE, and CE have traditionally been written with periods as B.C., A.D., B.C.E.,and C.E., but nowadays the periods are often omitted. Both styles are acceptable as long as consistency is maintained. The letters of all these abbreviations may be set in either small capitals or full capitals.

Many cultures have other epochs based on significant events in their religious history. For example, the era in Muslim societies is traditionally dated from the Prophet Muhammad's emigration from Mecca to Medina in the year 622 CE, an event called the Hijra. Dates reported in the Islamic system are given the abbreviation AH, short for Latin *anno Hegirae,* "in the year of the Hijra." Suleiman the Magnificent, for example, was born in AH 900, or 1494 CE. Writers should note that the year lengths in the Islamic calendar, based on the lunar, are shorter than those in the Gregorian calendar used in the West. Therefore, years in the Islamic calendar cannot be converted to years in the common era through simple subtraction. Writers should consult conversion tables or use computer programs when making such conversions. Conversion of dates from other calendars, such as the Jewish calendar, poses similar problems.

See more at **BP.**

ad–

The word element *ad–* is not a productive prefix in English; that is, it is not used to create new words, even though it can already be found in a very large number of words borrowed from Latin. It comes from the Latin preposition *ad,* meaning "to, toward, upon." In Latin, this preposition was also used as a prefix, and when it was followed by *c, f, g, l, n, r, s,* or *t,* it became *ac, af, ag, al, an, ar, as,* or *at,* respectively. The linguistic term for this kind of change, by which one sound becomes similar or identical to another sound found nearby within a word or phrase, is *assimilation.* In fact, the word *assimilation,* ultimately deriving from Latin *ad–* "to" and *similis* "similar" is a good illustration of the process—the prefix *ad–* has become *as–* before the *s* that follows it. Thus, Latin *ad–* is easy to see in English words such as *adhere, admit,* and *adverse,* but it is not so obvious in words such as *affix, apply,* and *attend.*

adage

It is sometimes claimed that the expression *old adage* is redundant, inasmuch as a saying must have a certain tradition behind it to count as an *adage* in the first place. But the word *adage* is first recorded by *The Oxford English Dictionary* in the phrase *old adage,* showing that this redundancy itself is very old. Such idiomatic redundancy is paralleled by similar phrases such as *young whelp.*

–ade

This noun suffix can be traced back through French, where it was found in a variety of words borrowed into French from Provençal, Spanish, Portuguese, and Italian.

Most English words ending with *–ade* were adopted from French with little or no change in spelling: *accolade, balustrade, charade, esplanade, façade, masquerade, serenade.* The many English words ending in *–ade* have been borrowed from French at different times over several centuries and under many different circumstances, and therefore the pronunciations of these words have been anglicized (made to conform to the sound pattern of the English language) in varying ways and to varying degrees. In a large number of words, the suffix is always pronounced as (ād). Many other words, such as *accolade,* have a variant with the pronunciation (äd), closer to the original French pronunciation. For some words, such as *esplanade* and *façade,* (äd) may be the most common or only acceptable pronunciation. Note that *comrade,* ending with the pronunciation (ăd), is unique. No one will have trouble pronouncing the words that are commonly used, but readers should consult their dictionaries when unsure how to pronounce a word ending in *–ade.*

ad feminam

The term *ad feminam* is a modern coinage patterned on *ad hominem.* Though some would argue that this neologism is unnecessary because the Latin word *homo* refers to humans generically, rather than to the male sex, in some contexts *ad feminam* has a more specific meaning than *ad hominem.* That is, *ad feminam* is often used to describe attacks on women as women or because they are women, as in *"Their recourse . . . to ad feminam attacks evidences the chilly climate for women's leadership on campus"* (Donna M. Riley).
    See also **ad hominem.**

ADHD / ADD

ADHD is an abbreviation for *attention-deficit hyperactivity disorder,* a common behavior disorder characterized by persistent inattention and poor concentration, often but not always with hyperactivity, that is present from early childhood. It has previously been called by other names including ADD (an abbreviation for *attention-deficit disorder*), and these names still commonly appear in print. ADHD, however, is the term that is used by medical and mental health professionals and is reflective of the most accurate and current knowledge about the nature of this condition.

ad hominem

As suggested by the principal meaning of the preposition *ad* ("to"), the *homo* of *ad hominem* was originally the person to whom an argument was addressed, not its subject. The phrase denoted an argument designed to appeal to the listener's emotions rather than to reason, as in the sentence *The Republicans' evocation of pity for the small farmer struggling to maintain his property is a purely ad hominem argument for reducing inheritance taxes.* This usage appears to be waning. In our 1997 survey only 37 percent of the Usage Panel found this sentence acceptable. The phrase now chiefly describes an argument based on the failings of an adversary rather than on the merits of the case: *Ad hominem attacks on one's opponent are a tried-and-true strategy for people who have a case that is weak.* Ninety percent of the Panel found this sentence acceptable. The expression now also has a looser use in referring to any personal attack, whether or not it is part of an argument, as in *It isn't in the best interests of the nation for the press to attack him in this personal, ad hominem way.* This use is acceptable to 65 percent of the Panel.

Ad hominem has also recently acquired a use as a noun denoting personal attacks, as in *"Notwithstanding all the ad hominem, Gingrich insists that he and Panetta can work together"* (*Washington Post*). This usage may raise some eyebrows, though it appears to be gaining ground in journalistic style.

See also **ad feminam.**

adjectives

Adjectives are words that modify nouns. While many adjectives are distinguished by their suffixes, such as *–able, –ous,* and *–ic,* many common adjectives, such as *good, hot,* and *young* have no distinguishing features that set them off from other parts of speech.

There are usually four criteria for judging a word to be an adjective:

1. It can appear before a noun or noun phrase and follow an article: *a good boy, the hot pavement.*

2. It can appear in the predicate following a linking verb like *be* or *seem: The boy has been good today. The pavement seems hot.*

3. It can be modified by *very: a very good boy, a very hot pavement.*

4. It can be used to make comparisons or gradations by means of the suffixes *–er* and *–est* or the words *more* and *most: A bigger house is at the end of the street. I can't imagine a more just settlement. That's the most ridiculous thing I've ever heard.*

Not all adjectives fulfill all four criteria. The adjectives *afraid* and *alive,* for instance, are not used before nouns (no one says *an afraid cat*). The adjective *utter* can only be used before a noun and does not meet any other criteria (no one says *That fool is utter* or *He's an utterer fool than you are*). In fact, a large number of adjectives cannot be compared at all. It is nonsensical to say *This book is more biological than that one,* for instance, or *This room is the most acoustic in the building.*

There are further exceptions to the four criteria. Adjectives can appear after the noun in the predicate of sentences like *She found the book boring. She made her parents proud. He pushed the door open.* A few adjectives normally appear after the noun, such as *proper* in *the population of Boston proper.* "Postpositive" modification also occurs when a clause has been truncated by omitting *that is* or a similar clausal construction. Thus it is acceptable to say *We could use something* [that is] *useful. The people* [who were] *present stood up and left. The surgeon,* [who is] *tall, dark, and handsome, walked confidently into the office.* Finally, certain adjectives, notably ones ending in –*able* and –*ible* can appear either before or after the noun in constructions like *That's the best answer possible* [or *the best possible answer*] and *That's the only seat available* [or *the only available seat*].

comparison of adjectives   An adjective in the comparative degree usually refers to two things (*The sequel is more daring than the original movie*), and one in the superlative degree refers to three or more things (*Her latest movie is the most daring of all three*). There are some simple rules for forming the comparative and superlative degrees of adjectives. Adjectives that have one syllable usually take –*er* and –*est*. Adjectives that have two syllables and end in *y* (*early*), *ow* (*narrow*), and *le* (*gentle*), can also take –*er* and –*est*. Almost all other adjectives with two or more syllables require the use of *more* and *most*. The rules are indicated in the chart below:

Number of Syllables	Unchanged	Comparative	Superlative
1	fast	faster	fastest
2	happy	happier	happiest
	complex	more complex	most complex
3	beautiful	more beautiful	most beautiful

The rules for spelling changes of compared adjectives are treated under **suffixes.**
English also has a few adjectives whose comparative and superlative forms are irregular:

Positive	Comparative	Superlative
good	better	best
bad	worse	worst
little	littler, less	littlest, least
far	farther, further	farthest, furthest

Adjectives can also be compared in a decreasing way by using *less* and *least: Jack is less skillful at carpentry than Bill is. Roberta is the least likely employee to have complained about working conditions.*

Aside from those adjectives (like *acoustic* and *reverse*) that cannot be compared, there are some adjectives (like *unique, parallel,* and *perfect*) whose comparison is controversial.

See more at **absolute terms.**

admission / admittance

Traditionally, *admittance* is used only to refer to achieving physical access to a place (*He was denied admittance to the courtroom*), while *admission* is used to refer to achieving entry to a group or institution (*her admission to the club, China's admission to the United Nations*). No harm can come from maintaining this distinction, though it may be lost on some readers since the terms have been largely interchangeable in speech for some time. The most common sense for *admission*, however, is "a fee paid for the right of entry": *The admission to the movie was ten dollars.*

admittedly   See **sentence adverbs.**

adopted / adoptive

Children are adopted by parents, thus we refer to an *adopted* child and to *adoptive* parents. By extension, *adoptive* can also refer to families and homes, or more generally to anything that actively accepts someone as a member. When describing places, writers can use either *adopted* or *adoptive*, but the difference in meaning is important: *She enjoys living in her adopted country* suggests that she has chosen to live there, taking it for her own; by contrast, *The refugees slowly settled in to their new lives in their adoptive city* implies that the city has taken in the refugees.

advance / advancement

When used as a noun, *advance* indicates forward movement (*the advance of the army*) or progress or improvement (*an advance in molecular biology*). *Advancement* is usually used figuratively to indicate promotion or movement beyond an established norm: *career advancement*. Unlike *advance, advancement* often implies the existence of an agent or outside force. Thus *the advance of science* means simply "the progress of science," whereas *the advancement of science* implies progress resulting from the action of an agent or force: *The purpose of the legislation was the advancement of science.*

adverbs

functions of adverbs   Adverbs can modify many different kinds of words: verbs (*They sang* beautifully), participles (*Singing* loudly *over the strings, she brought the song to an end*), other adverbs (*We will be arriving* fairly *soon*), whole sentences (Thankfully, *the concert ended before it started raining*), and even noun phrases (Nearly *the entire class came to the game*) and pronouns (Almost *everyone showed up*).

forms and comparison of adverbs   Many adjectives can be made into adverbs by adding the suffix *–ly:*

> We made a *conservative* estimate of the costs.
> We estimated the costs *conservatively.*

The monosyllabic adjectives *fast, hard,* and *long* do not change to form adverbs:

> He is a *fast* runner. He runs *fast.*
> She is a *hard* worker. She works *hard.*
> We waited for a *long* time. Have you been waiting *long?*

Some adjectives, like *close* and *high,* have two adverbial forms: one that is unchanged and one that ends in *–ly:*

We are *close* friends. Stay *close* to me. Look *closely* at the first chapter.
The platform is *high*. The bird flew *high*. The artist was *highly* praised.

It is best to check a dictionary to confirm the forms used by a specific adverb.

Similar rules to those for comparing adjectives apply to adverbs and are shown in the chart below:

Number of Syllables	Unchanged	Comparative	Superlative
1	soon	sooner	soonest
2 or more	early	earlier	earliest
	frequent	more frequent	most frequent
	comfortably	more comfortably	most comfortably

English also has some adverbs with irregular comparative and superlative forms:

Positive	Comparative	Superlative
good	better	best
bad	worse	worst
little	littler, less	littlest, least
far	farther, further	farthest, furthest

To compare adverbs to a lower degree, use *less* and *least:*

We rehearsed less often than the other actors. We rehearsed least often of all the actors.

position of adverbs   Because they have so many functions and they tend to modify the words they are closest to in a sentence, adverbs can cause a range of different problems, mainly by being ambiguous. This is especially true of certain adverbs like *also, just,* and *only,* where different positioning can imply drastic changes in the meaning of a sentence. Sentences with more than one verb also can pose difficulty. Which verb does *rapidly* modify in this sentence: *His insistence that the new sales plan should be implemented rapidly increased the company's profits?* Sentences that precede ones like this should establish a context that leaves no room for ambiguity, and it may be easier to rewrite the sentence to avoid ambiguity. Here are two possibilities for the previous example: *His insistence on implementing the new sales plan caused the company's profits to increase rapidly. Because he insisted on rapid implementation of the new sales plan, the company's profits increased.*

In initial position the adverb is usually followed by a comma: *Suddenly, the train started moving.* Many adverbs in initial position modify the entire sentence rather than the verb and usually express an attitude of some kind: *Fortunately, Higgins survived the ordeal. Admittedly, the city could use a new library.*

See more at **also, conjunctive adverbs, however, not, only, sentence adverbs, so, split infinitive,** and **transition words.**

adverse / averse

Averse normally refers to people and means "having a feeling of distaste or aversion," as in *As an investor I'm averse to risk-taking.* It is incorrect to substitute *adverse* for *averse* in these constructions with *to*. *Adverse* should not be used to describe people, but rather things that are contrary to someone's interests. Thus we say *We're working under very adverse circumstances* and *All the adverse criticism frayed the new mayor's nerves.* Indeed, most of us are *averse* to getting *adverse* reactions to our ideas.

advise

In its most common use, *advise* means "to give someone advice," that is, to make a recommendation about something. Thus one person advises another to do something, or advises on or about something, or advises against something: *The building contractor advised us to replace the roof. The financial expert advised the employees on how to save for their retirement. The nutritionist advises against eating fast food.* When *advise* in this sense is followed by a *that* clause, the clause implies obligation. Note in the following quotations the verbs *should* and *ought* expressing obligation:

> I see now little hope, if we do not soon vanish from sight for a while, and cover our trail. Therefore I advise that we should go neither over the mountains, nor round them, but under them (J.R.R. Tolkien, *The Fellowship of the Ring*)

> Who is there to advise him that it's not Hamlet on his father he ought to be quoting but Hamlet on his uncle, Claudius, Hamlet on the conduct of the new king, his father's usurping murderer? (Phillip Roth, *I Married a Communist*)

Advise is also used acceptably in the sense of "to inform, notify," and this usage has long been acceptable but tends to appear chiefly in business and legal contexts. Thus a sentence like *The suspects were advised of their rights* is utterly conventional, and *advise* is natural in a context like the following one, where the more formal word *apprise* would serve as a synonym. Note the absence of a verb of obligation:

> . . . in August he wrote a personal letter to Thomas Watson, with whom he had long worked to develop an automatic scorer . . . to advise him that his underlings were about to deep-six Johnson's machine (Nicholas Leman, "The Structure of Success in America," *Atlantic Monthly*)

But this use of *advise* is not common in general contexts, and a sentence like *You'd better advise your friends that the date of the picnic has been changed* may come off as pretentious or condescending.

aerate

The nonstandard pronunciation (âr′ē-āt′), with three syllables, is an example of *intrusion,* a phonological process that involves the addition or insertion of an extra sound for no obvious reason. The usual pronunciation of *aerate* has only two syllables, (âr′āt′).

See more at **intrusion**.

affect / effect

The words *affect* and *effect* are sometimes confused because they sound so much alike and have several related meanings. First of all, there are two words spelled *affect*. One is a verb meaning "to put on a false show of," as in *She grew up on Long Island but affected a British accent.* Its related noun is *affectation.*

The other *affect* can be both a noun and a verb. The noun, which means roughly "emotion," is a technical term from psychology that sometimes shows up in general writing, as in this quote from a Norman Mailer piece about the 1991 Gulf War: "*Of course, the soldiers seen on television had been carefully chosen for blandness of affect.*" Unlike the verb forms, which are pronounced with stress on the second syllable, the noun *affect* is pronounced with stress on its first syllable. As a verb, however, *affect* is far more common. In this role it means "to cause a change in, influence," as in *The Surgeon General's report outlined how smoking affects health.* Note that *affect* does not have a corresponding noun sense that means "an influence" or "a change resulting from an influence."

Effect can also serve as a noun or a verb. The noun means "a result." Thus if someone *affects* something, there is likely to be an *effect* of some kind, and from this may arise some of the confusion. People who stop smoking will see beneficial health *effects,* but not beneficial health *affects.* As a verb, *effect* means "to bring about or execute," as in these newspaper quotations:

> It is amazing that one year after the attacks of September 11, we are still hearing many usually progressive commentators complain that there is no public debate about the war on terrorism and George W. Bush's desire to effect a "regime change" in Iraq (Michael Bronski, "Brain Drain," *Boston Phoenix*)

> For sheer feigned agony, no athletes dive more extravagantly than soccer players, who make an art of the clutched ankle, the final-throes twitch and the incipient concussion headache. Soccer rules now mandate that a stretcher be rushed onto the field to cart off the bodies. Just the sight of the stretcher and the prospect of a few enforced minutes on the sideline are enough to effect a miracle cure (George Vecsey, "Art of Diving Should Stay in Olympics," *New York Times*)

Thus, the verbs *affect* and *effect* produce important differences in meaning. Using *effect* in the sentence *The measures have been designed to effect savings* implies that the measures will cause new savings to come about. Using *affect* in the very similar sentence *These measures will affect savings* implies that the measures will cause a change in savings that have already been realized.

affinity

When used as a simple synonym for *liking, affinity* can sometimes seem awkward or pretentious. Some 62 percent of the Usage Panel disapproved of it in our 1997 survey in the sentence *Her affinity for living in California led her to reject a chance to return to*

New York. This sentence was also rejected by a majority of panelists in 1981, so resistance is not waning. However, when *affinity* is used to indicate liking for a recurrent object or behavior, the Panel was more accepting. In 1997, 65 percent approved of it in the sentence *"Despite his affinity for coarse physical jokes practiced upon his courtiers, his moral views were more Victorian than Edwardian."* In such contexts, the more sophisticated tone inherent in the word can lend a certain archness.

prepositions with *affinity* *Affinity* has a variety of meanings, ranging from "relationship by marriage" (its earliest) to "a resemblance or similarity" and extending to "a natural attraction" and even "a chemical attraction." The meanings are clear enough, but it is not always easy to know which preposition to use for each of these senses, especially since other factors can affect the choice, such as the verb that is used. When affinity means "a natural attraction," *for, to,* or *with* are all standard: *They still feel a strong affinity for* [or *to* or *with*] *their old neighborhood.* Or, put another way, *There is a strong affinity between the old neighborhood and the people who once lived there.*

While all of these usages are acceptable, there are some restrictions on the choice of preposition. When *affinity* means "similarity or resemblance," the prepositions *with, to,* and *between* are standard, but *for* is less likely: *Birds have an affinity with dinosaurs. Pterodactyls have a closer affinity with reptiles than birds. There is an affinity between reptiles and birds.*

When affinity means "a feeling of kinship or sympathy," as in *I have an affinity for people in their situation, for* is perfectly acceptable. In some metaphorical uses, as in writing about food, *for* tends to predominate: *Lamb has a distinct affinity for red wines.* In chemical contexts, *for* is the preposition of choice: *the affinity of hemoglobin for oxygen; a dye with an affinity for synthetic fabrics.*

affirmative

The expressions *in the affirmative* and *in the negative* are thought to come from military aviation, where pilots use *affirmative* and *negative* as synonyms for *yes* and *no* in radio transmissions. The idea is that the longer words are less likely to get lost in static. But when used in ordinary contexts, such as *She answered in the affirmative,* these expressions almost always sound pompous. *She answered yes* would be more acceptable even at the most formal levels of style.

affixes

An affix is a word element, such as a prefix or suffix, that can only occur attached to a base form of a word. The meanings and applications of many affixes are discussed at entries for particular forms (such as *anti–* and *–ment*). Some affixes (such as *–ize*) have usage controversies associated with them.

Many hyphenation and spelling difficulties arise in connection with prefixes and suffixes, and rules for dealing with these problems are given at the entries **hyphenation** and **suffixes.**

affluence / affluent

Most people pronounce these two words with stress on the first syllable, (ăf′lōō-əns; ăf′lōō-ənt). The pronunciation with stress on the second syllable, (ə-flōō′ns; ə-flōō′nt), is a more recent development in American English. It is widely considered acceptable.

African American / Afro-American

During American Colonial and early national times, Black slaves and freemen alike were often referred to as *Africans,* even after several generations' residence in America. That this practice was common among Blacks as well as whites is obvious from the number of churches and institutions founded during this period with names such as the African Methodist Episcopal church and the Free African Society. With the end of the Atlantic slave trade, however, reference to Blacks as Africans gradually disappeared, and it was not until the Black Power movement of the late 1960s and early 1970s that Black Americans were again widely known by a name—*Afro-American*—that acknowledged their African heritage.

Together with *Black, Afro-American* gained rapid acceptance during this period as a self-chosen label expressive of ethnic and cultural pride. But in the following decades *Afro-American* lost some of its popularity, especially in referring to individuals, so that today a phrase such as *the election of two Afro-Americans to the board* sounds somewhat dated. To a large degree its place has been taken by the similar term *African American,* popularized in the late 1980s and far more widely used today, in all contexts and by people of all backgrounds, than *Afro-American* ever was.

Both as a noun and an adjective, *African American* may be spelled with or without a hyphen.

applicability of *African American* and *Afro-American* The terms *African American* and *Afro-American* could logically apply to people of Black African ancestry throughout the Americas, but, like *Native American,* they are strongly associated with the cultures and communities of the United States and are rarely used more broadly. In fact, these names do not always seem appropriate even for first-generation Black immigrants from Africa or the Caribbean, whose cultural and linguistic backgrounds are usually quite distinct from those of native-born Black Americans. It should be noted, too, that *African American* and *Afro-American* are inappropriate for Americans of North African ancestry or for white Americans who have immigrated to the United States from African countries. When used in these terms, *African* is understood to refer exclusively to the indigenous peoples of sub-Saharan Africa.

See more at **black.**

−age

This noun suffix appears in many words that are borrowed from French, such as *barrage* (a dam), *barrage* (heavy artillery fire; an outpouring), *damage, espionage, garage,* heritage, homage, language, manage, marriage, personage, reportage, sabotage, umbrage, usage, visage, voyage. The pronunciation of –age in these words can range from (äzh) to (äj) to (ĭj) depending on the degree to which the pronunciation has become Anglicized. In words formed in English on the same model, such as luggage, poundage, orphanage, parsonage, breakage, and wreckage, the pronunciation of –age is always (ĭj).

agenda

In Classical Latin, the word agenda was the plural form of agendum, which referred to an item of business placed before the Roman Senate. Borrowed into English, the singular form of this word became agend, now obsolete. In Modern English, agenda has taken the place of agend as a singular noun, and denotes the set or list of such items, as in The agenda for the meeting has not yet been set. If a plural of agenda is required, the form should be agendas: The agendas of both meetings are exceptionally varied.

The evolution of the word agenda as a singular noun thus anticipates similar developments that are now taking place with such words as **data** and **media.**

Agenda has additionally taken on an extended meaning, suggesting a plan or a set of intentions that underlie someone's behavior, especially a secret plan, as in the following quotation from the Sacramento Bee: "The story line is labyrinthine, full of conspiracies, double- and triple-crosses, hidden agendas, secret societies and everywhere a struggle for power and influence."

aggravate

Aggravate comes from the Latin verb aggravāre, which meant "to make heavier," that is, "to add to the weight of." It also had the extended senses "to burden" or "to oppress." On the basis of this etymology, it is claimed by some that aggravate should not be used to mean "to irritate, annoy, rouse to anger." But such senses for the word date back to the 17th century and are pervasive. In our 1988 survey, 68 percent of the Usage Panel accepted this usage in the sentence: It's the endless wait for luggage that aggravates me the most about air travel.

aggressive

Since the 1950s, the word aggressive has been applied to energetic activity or assertive behavior that is a product of inventiveness or necessity rather than aggression. The word sees much use in business, as in an aggressive sales campaign. In our 2002 survey, 78 percent of the Usage Panel accepted the word in The aggressive dumping of shares raised the specter that stock prices, which had rebounded in spring after a year-long slide, are on the verge of a new free fall.

Aggressive has recently been extended further into other uses, and the Panel accepts but is less sanguine about this, with 56 percent accepting the example The com-

pany issued an aggressive justification of its purchase of its major competitor, insisting that it had proved its doubters wrong in many previous acquisitions. There are plenty of synonyms available for these situations, including *assertive, vigorous,* and *forceful.*

The accounting scandals of 2002, in which a number of companies misstated their accounts to give a rosy impression of their performance, brought to the limelight *aggressive accounting,* which sometimes goes by another euphemism, *creative accounting.* Although this use of *aggressive* is common in business contexts, and can be used to humorous or satirical effect, a majority of the Panel sees it as unsuitable to standard communication. Only 39 percent accepted the example *Whatever is the most aggressive way to account for profits, that is the way the vast majority of companies report their numbers.*

agoraphobia

The pronunciation (ăg′ər-ə-fō′bē-ə) is the one most widely accepted in educated speech; it was the preferred pronunciation of two thirds of the Usage Panel in our 2001 survey. The variant pronunciation with a stressed second syllable (ə-gôr′ə-fō′bē-ə) is the preferred pronunciation of the remaining third of the Panel and is a more recent development that is quickly gaining acceptance. Likewise, the most widely accepted pronunciations of *agoraphobe* and *agoraphobic* are (ăg′ər-ə-fōb′) and (ăg′ər-ə-fō′bĭk); however, the variants (ə-gôr′ə-fōb′) and (ə-gôr′ə-fō′bĭk) are also gaining acceptance.

agreement

In grammar, agreement (sometimes called·*concord*) refers to correspondence in gender, number, case, or person between words. See more at **pronouns, agreement of** and **subject and verb agreement.**

ague

This somewhat old-fashioned word for a kind of fever usually resulting from malaria is properly pronounced (ā′gyōo), with two syllables.

ain't

By historical rights, *ain't* should be a contraction like any other in English. *Ain't* first appeared in English in 1778, evolving from an earlier form *an't,* which arose almost a century earlier as a contraction of *are not* and *am not.* In fact, *ain't* seems to have arisen at the tail end of an era that saw the introduction of a number of our most common contractions, including *don't* and *won't. Ain't* and some of these other contractions came under criticism in the 1700s for being inelegant and low-class, even though they had actually been used by upper-class speakers. But while *don't* and *won't* eventually became perfectly acceptable at all levels of speech and writing, *ain't* was subjected to a barrage of criticism in the 19th century for having no set sequence of words from which it can be contracted and for being "a vulgarism," that is, a term used by the lower classes. At the same time the uses of *ain't* were multiplying to include *is not, has not,* and *have not.* It may be that these extended uses helped provoke the negative reaction. Whatever the case, the criticism of *ain't* by usage commentators and teachers has not subsided, and the use of *ain't* has come to be regarded as a mark of ignorance.

But despite all the attempts to ban it, *ain't* continues to appear in the speech of ordinary folks, and it leads a vibrant life in song lyrics. Even educated and upperclass speakers see that *ain't* has no substitute in fixed expressions like *Say it ain't so, You ain't just whistlin' Dixie,* and *You ain't seen nothin' yet.* Educated speakers also use *ain't* in speech and informal writing when they want to suggest that the truth of an assertion should be obvious to anyone. The university dean who was quoted in *The Chronicle of Higher Education* as saying *"Any junior scholar who pays attention to teaching at the expense of research ain't going to get tenure"* successfully conveyed that his conclusion was based on ordinary common sense, not on a research report or specialized knowledge.

ain't I?   The stigmatization of *ain't* leaves no happy alternative for use in firstperson questions. The widely used *aren't I?*, though illogical, was found acceptable for use in speech by a majority of the Usage Panel as long ago as 1964, but in writing there is no alternative to saying *am I not?*

albumen / albumin

These two words are closely related in form, sound, meaning, and history. The word *albumen* comes from Latin *albūmen,* "egg white," from *albus,* "white" and was used in English to refer to the white of an egg as early as the 16th century. By the mid-1800s, chemists determined that the type of protein found in egg whites was part of a larger class of proteins that are chemically similar but have different functions. This group of proteins, also found in milk, blood, and various other plant and animal tissues became known as *albumin,* from a combination of *album(en)* with the suffix *–in,* which designates neutral chemical compounds. The *albumen* of an egg consists mostly of the protein *albumin.* All *albumins* dissolve in water and form solid or semisolid masses when heated, such as cooked egg whites.

Both *albumen* and *albumin* generally have stress on the second syllable, and, in fact, sound the same except for the final vowels, which may be slightly emphasized to preserve a distinction between the two. In British English, there is a variant pronunciation with the stress on the first syllable.

alga / algae

The term *alga* (plural *algae*) is often used as a convenient label to designate a very broad range of marine or freshwater organisms that have the photosynthetic pigment chlorophyll. Algae were once classified as part of the plant kingdom. However, the very comprehensiveness of the term limited its utility, since it could refer to anything from a microscopic bacterium without a cell nucleus to a sixty-meter-long kelp made of cells with a much more complex internal structure. Moreover, within the discipline of biology there has been an effort to make all classificatory terminology reflect evolutionary relationships based on DNA and other molecular analysis. Writers should therefore consider whether it is more appropriate in a given situation to use modern classifications when describing the organisms formerly referred to under the blanket term *alga*.

Modern schemes of classification, based on molecular and structural studies of these organisms, recognize many different groups, and these groups are often only distantly related to each other. The cyanobacteria (or blue-green algae) are simply bacteria that contain chlorophyll and other pigments that help them make their own food through photosynthesis. They belong to the "domain" of bacteria, not to the "domain" of eukaryotes (organisms whose cells have nuclei and a framework of proteins around which their cell membranes and complex internal structures are organized). The great variety of eukaryotic organisms called *algae* are now divided into a number of groups, including the phaeophytes (or brown algae), the rhodophytes (red algae), the chrysophytes (a small group of freshwater organisms with yellow pigments), and the chlorophytes (green algae). Blooms of some species of dinoflagellates, another algal group, have been known to kill fish and cause illness in swimmers.

A comparison between brown and green algae will highlight the great differences between the algal groups. Brown algae, like kelp, have the kinds of chlorophyll called chlorophyll a and chlorophyll c as well as large quantities of the pigment fucoxanthin, which gives the group their characteristic brownish colors. This pigment absorbs the range of blue light frequencies available to brown algae when they are submerged and allows them to live in deeper waters than green algae. The brown algae store and transport the food in their bodies in compounds called laminarin and mannitol. Green algae, on the other hand, are quite different organisms. They have chlorophyll a and chlorophyll b and pigments called carotenoids, and are adapted to living nearer the surface of the water. They store their food as starch. In fact, plants probably evolved from a subgroup of the green algae, and some green algae are more closely related to the plants than they are to other green algae.

Because of these major differences, the unqualified term *alga* is often too imprecise to be used in scientific writing. When referring to a toxic algal bloom, writers should consider whether it would be better to write of a *toxic bloom of cyanobacteria* or *dinoflagellates*. However, when the context makes it clear, *alga* can serve as a convenient shorthand, especially for green algae in freshwater environments.

confusion of singular *alga* and plural *algae* Probably because of the abundance of these organisms, the plural form *algae* (pronounced ăl′jē) is much more common than the singular (much as *bacteria* is more common than *bacterium*). But familiarity with *algae* often leads people to mistake it for a singular mass noun. This error occurs even in more technical writing, as in *They found that toxic algae was growing in the water.* Unfortunately, the correct singular (*a toxic alga was*) can sound somewhat stiff and ungainly, and phrases like *toxic algae were growing* can sound odd as well to some readers. When writing under more formal circumstances for a general audience, it is probably better to rewrite such sentences to remove *algae* from the subject position, as in *They observed the growth of toxic algae in the water,* and to avoid other phrases where plural agreement can be a problem, as in *this algae.* In technical scientific writing, however, *alga* should always be used as the singular form.

all

***all* in negative sentences**   Sentences that have an *all . . . not . . .* form are tricky and can easily give rise to ambiguity or unintended readings. The sentence *All of the departments did not file a report* may mean either that some departments did not file or that none did. The first meaning can be expressed unambiguously as *Not all of the departments filed a report.* Expressing the second meaning requires a paraphrase such as *None of the departments filed a report* or *All of the departments failed to file a report.* Note that the same problem can arise with other universal terms like *every* in negated sentences, as in the ambiguous *Every department did not file a report.*

***all* used to introduce quotations**   Among the newest ways of introducing direct speech in the United States is the construction consisting of a form of *be* with *all,* as in *I'm all, "I'm not gonna do that!" And she's all, "Yes you are!"* This construction is particularly common in the animated speech of young people in California and elsewhere on the West Coast, who use it more frequently than the informal East Coast alternatives, *be like* and *go,* as in *He's like* [or *He goes*], *"I'm not gonna do that!"* These indicators of direct speech tend to be used more often with pronoun subjects (*He's all, "I'm not . . . "*) than with nouns (*The man's all, "I'm not . . . "*), and with the historical present (*He's all . . .*) than with the past (*He was all . . .*). All of these locutions can introduce a gesture or facial expression rather than a quotation, as in *He's all . . .* followed by a shrug of the shoulders. *Be all* and *be like* can also preface a statement that sums up an attitude, as in *"I'm all 'No way!'"*

See more at **go** and **like.**

alleged

An *alleged* burglar is someone who has been accused of being a burglar but whose innocence or guilt has yet to be established. An *alleged* incident is an event that is said to have taken place but has not yet been verified. In their zeal to protect the rights of the accused, newspapers and law enforcement officials sometimes misuse *alleged.* A man arrested for murder may be only an *alleged* murderer, for example, but he is a real, not an *alleged,* suspect in that his status as a suspect is not in doubt. Similarly, if the money from a safe is known to have been stolen and not merely mislaid, then we can safely speak of a theft without having to qualify the description with *alleged.*

all right / alright

Despite the appearance of *alright* in the works of such well-known writers as Flannery O'Connor, Langston Hughes, and James Joyce, the merger of *all* and *right* has never been accepted as standard. This is peculiar, since similar fusions like *already* and *altogether* have never raised any objections. The difference may lie in the fact that *already* and *altogether* became single words back in the Middle Ages, whereas *alright* (at least in its current meaning) has only been around for a little over a century and was called out by language critics as a misspelling. *Alright* can be found nonetheless in magazine and newspaper articles, literature, correspondence, and informal writing, especially in Britain. It is used especially in dialogue and in first-person narration to convey the impression of speech. But its use in formal writing runs the risk that some readers will view it as an error and others as a deliberate break from convention.

Note that in certain instances, *all right* and *alright* are not synonymous. The sentence *The figures are all right* means that the figures are all accurate, that is, perfectly correct, while *The figures are alright* means that they are satisfactory or sufficiently accurate for a purpose at hand, even if not perfect.

all that

The phrase *all that* is used in negative sentences as an intensive, much like *very*. While this expression is somewhat informal, most of the Usage Panel accepts it. Seventy-three percent allowed as standard the sentence *The movie was not all that interesting* in our 1997 survey, with another 7 percent approving it in informal contexts. If it seems too casual a fit, you can drop the *all*, use *very* instead, or simply do without the modifier.

all told / all tolled

The expression *all told* is an absolute construction meaning "with everything considered, in all" as in sentences like *All told, the damage was much less than had been expected.* The phrase is sometimes misspelled *all tolled.* Undoubtedly such misspellings result from confusion with the verb *to toll*, "to announce by ringing a bell," and perhaps the noun *toll* meaning "fixed tax or charge" and also by extension "amount of damage." However, the *told* in *all told* is in origin the past participle of the verb *tell*, here used in its somewhat archaic meaning "to count." This meaning is preserved elsewhere in phrases such as *tell one's beads*, "pray (as by counting beads on a rosary)."

See more at **absolute constructions.**

alms

The older and more widely accepted pronunciation is (ämz), but the spelling pronunciation (älmz) is increasingly common.

See more at **L** and **spelling pronunciation.**

alongside / alongside of

Both of these forms are acceptable as prepositions; which one sounds best is mostly a matter of one's sense of the rhythm of the sentence: *The barge lay alongside* [or *alongside of*] *the pier.*

along with   See **together.**

a lot

Teachers of writing have seen the spelling *alot* in student papers more times than they care to remember, and they can expect to keep on seeing it. Even experienced writers find themselves writing *alot* for *a lot,* especially when working under pressure or dashing off a note. In our 1996 survey 13 percent of the Usage Panel confessed to having made this blunder. The fusion of an article and a noun into a single word is a normal linguistic phenomenon, having occurred in *another* and *awhile,* so it is possible that we all may write *alot* one day. For the time being, however, keep in mind that *alot* is still considered an error in print. Fully 93 percent of the Usage Panel stated that they always correct *alot* to two words and that they considered it to be an error in other people's writing. Don't be surprised if writing teachers and copyeditors keep prying it apart.

See more at **lot.**

alright   See **all right.**

also

***also* beginning a sentence**   Some people maintain that it is wrong to begin a sentence with *also.* They are probably in the minority, since there seems no reason to condemn *also* and not another conjunctive adverb like *nevertheless.* In our 1988 survey, 63 percent of the Usage Panel found the usage acceptable in this example: *The warranty covers all power train components. Also, participating dealers back their work with a free lifetime service guarantee.*

***also* used ambiguously**   *Also* shares with *only* the virtue of modifying the parts of the sentence to which it is closest, but this can sometimes lead to ambiguity. In the following examples, the sentence containing *also* is exactly the same, but in each example it modifies a different part and creates a different meaning:

> I read in the paper that their band was coming to town. I also heard that the band would play here.

> Mary heard that their band is coming to town. I also heard that the band would play here.

The band has been playing out on the West Coast for weeks. I also heard that the band would play here.

To avoid misunderstandings, it's a good policy to check that the context is sufficiently clear to limit the meaning of *also*. A good way to check is to move *also* to another position in the sentence and see if the meaning is less ambiguous: *I heard that the band would also play here.*

See more at **adverbs, conjunctive adverbs, only, plus,** and **too.**

alternative

two or more *alternatives*   A traditional view holds that *alternative* should be used only when the number of choices involved is exactly two. This reasoning is based on the word's historical relation to Latin *alter,* "the other of two." The Usage Panel has never favored this edict in large numbers, and it would appear that a willingness to accept constructions like *a number of alternatives* is growing. Even back in 1964, 58 percent felt that *alternative* should not be restricted to a choice involving only two. In 1988 49 percent accepted the sentence *Of the three alternatives, the first is the least distasteful.* This sentence was also accepted by 66 percent in our 1999 survey, in which the same percentage accepted *Doctors and patients often overlook many alternatives like exercise, weight loss, and measures to relieve the load on affected joints.*

The complexity of this situation arises from the multiplicity of senses that *alternative* has. It can mean "a choice or a situation that requires a choice between two things," as in *The only alternative to continuing down the river was to give up and hike out of the gorge.* From this it is a short leap in meaning to "one of a number of things from which only one can be chosen," and here is where we may be forced to choose *from several alternatives.*

***alternative* used as an adjective**   As an adjective, *alternative* can mean "allowing or requiring a choice between two or more things," as in *We wrote an alternative statement in case the first was rejected by the board.* It may also refer to a variant or substitute in cases where no choice is involved, as in *We will do our best to secure alternative employment for employees displaced by the closing of the factory.* Seventy-five percent of the Usage Panel accepted this sentence in our 1999 survey. *Alternative* is also used to indicate things that are outside established traditions or institutions, as in *the alternative press* or *alternative rock.*

confused with *alternate*   *Alternative* and *alternate* are synonyms when *alternate* means "serving in place of another, substitute," as in *We had an alternate plan for the outing in case it rained.* But when *alternate* means "happening in turns," correct usage requires *The class will meet on alternate* [not *alternative*] *Tuesdays.*

although / though

As conjunctions, *although* and *though* are generally interchangeable: *Although* [or *though*] *she smiled, she was angry. Although* usually occurs at the beginning of its clause (as in the preceding example), whereas *though* may occur elsewhere and is the more common term when used to link words or phrases, as in *wiser though poorer.*

In certain constructions, however, only *though* is acceptable. When *though* introduces only a part of a clause rather than a whole clause, *although* is not possible: *Most people in attendance applauded loudly after the performance, though* [not *although*] *not everyone.* Another construction that requires *though* is the following: *Fond though* [not *although*] *I am of sports, I'd rather not sit through another basketball game.*

altogether / all together

Altogether and *all together* are in fact quite different expressions. *All together* indicates that the members of a group perform or undergo an action collectively: *The nations stood all together. The prisoners were herded all together.* Sentences with these words can generally be rephrased so that *all* and *together* are separated by other words. Thus *The nations stood all together* can be rephrased as *The nations all stood together* or *All the nations stood together* with only a slight change in emphasis.

The adverb *altogether,* on the other hand, has several different meanings. It is clear that confusion might arise with the phrase *all together* when *altogether* is used to mean "all told, in all": *Altogether, there were fifty people at the wedding.* Most frequently, however, *altogether* is a synonym for *entirely* or *completely: The researchers tried an altogether different approach this time.* It can also be used as a sentence adverb meaning "with everything considered, on the whole": *Altogether, I can understand why she took offense.*

Thus, if the local scout troop goes *all together* on a hike, they may be *altogether* tired when they get back.

alumna / alumnus / alumnae / alumni

These words referring to the graduates of a school are derived from the Latin verb *alere,* "to nourish," also the source of *alma mater,* or "nourishing mother." *Alumna* is a feminine noun with the plural *alumnae,* and *alumnus* is a masculine noun whose plural is *alumni.* Coeducational institutions usually use *alumni* for graduates of both sexes, but those who object to masculine forms in such cases sometimes use *alumni and alumnae, alumnae/i,* or the more casual *alums.* The word *graduates* also presents a gender-neutral alternative.

pronunciation As an Anglicized Latin word, *alumni* is usually pronounced (ə-lŭm′nī). Likewise, *alumnae* is usually pronounced (ə-lŭm′nē). Confusion comes about in part because in English *i* has several possible pronunciations and *ae* is an unusual combination. Also, in Classical Latin pronunciation, which attempts to approximate the pronunciation of ancient Roman times, the opposite would be true, that is, the final vowel sound of *alumni* would be (ē), and the final vowel sound of *alumnae* would be (ī). Graduates who have studied Latin are naturally tempted to put their learning to good use, but the results can sometimes be confusing in Modern English.

a.m. / p.m.

By definition, *12 a.m.* denotes midnight, and *12 p.m.* denotes noon, but there is sufficient confusion over these uses to make it advisable to use *12 noon* and *12 midnight* where clarity is required.

Amerasian

Amerasian is not a synonym for *Asian American.* Broadly speaking, an *Amerasian* is a person of mixed Asian and American parentage, but in practice the term is used almost exclusively of the child of an Asian mother and an American father; in the great majority of cases, the father is a serviceman or other temporary resident abroad, and the child is born and often raised in its mother's country. The term, which dates to the Korean War in the early 1950s, came into wider use during the Vietnam War, when the prolonged presence of American servicemen in South Vietnam and other Southeast Asian countries resulted in an increased number of such children. Since American servicemen are of varying racial and ethnic backgrounds, there is no fixed racial connotation to *Amerasian* apart from the fact that one parent, virtually always the mother, is an ethnic Asian.

See more at **Asian American** and **Eurasian.**

American Indian

American Indian is fully acceptable in contemporary American English, used by many where *Native American* might sound too formal or bureaucratic or where *Indian* alone might seem too casual or might be mistaken as referring to the inhabitants of India. However, it is less acceptable and often offensive in Canadian English, where *First Nations* is generally preferred.

In principle, *American Indian* can apply to all native peoples throughout the Americas except the Eskimos, Aleuts, and Inuits, but in practice it is generally restricted to the Indian peoples of the United States and Canada. For native peoples in the rest of the hemisphere, usage generally favors *Indian* by itself or, less frequently, the contractions *Amerindian* or *Amerind.*

See more at **First Nation, Indian,** and **Native American.**

Amerindian

The contractions *Amerindian* and *Amerind* occur infrequently in modern American English, especially with reference to the Native American peoples of the United States and Canada. They are somewhat more common in anthropological contexts or when used of the native peoples of the Caribbean and Central and South America.

See more at **American Indian, Indian,** and **Native American.**

amid / amidst

There are several words in English that have alternative or related forms ending in
–st: amid, amidst; among, amongst; unbeknown, unbeknownst; while, whilst. The
forms with *–st* are still current in British English, but they often have an archaic or
poetic feel in American English. Some Americans avoid the forms with *–st* except
when an ironically formal or deliberately archaic effect is sought. Others may feel
that, from among this group of words, *amidst* and *amongst* have a different nuance of
meaning from *amid* and *among* and are especially appropriate in expressing the notion of scattered distribution in a larger group or occurrence in a surrounding mass
that is in motion.

The similar word *betwixt,* a distant relative of *between,* is archaic in both American and British English, however.

Most of the words with the extra *–st* developed in the 14th and 15th centuries
from earlier forms without *-t,* such as *amiddes* and *amonges.* In the minds of speakers
of Middle English, the final *-s* in these words was probably interpreted as a suffix appropriate to adverbs and prepositions. This final *-s* then acquired a *-t,* most likely by
analogy with the superlative suffix *–est* and other words like *next.* In the case of at
least one word, it is in fact the form in *–st* that has become standard: the Modern
English word *against* has replaced the Middle English form *agains,* without *-t.*

See more at **whilst.**

an   See **a.**

analogous

This word is properly pronounced (ə-năl′ə-gəs), with a hard *g* sound, never (ə-
năl′ə-jəs), with a (j) sound.

See more at **g.**

and

A traditional grammatical rule asserts that sentences beginning with *and* or *but* express incomplete thoughts and are therefore incorrect. Yet the line of esteemed writers who have started sentences with *and* and *but* runs from Shakespeare to Joyce
Carol Oates. Most of the Usage Panel sees some virtue in the practice. In our 1988
survey, members were asked whether they paid attention to the rule in their own
writing, and 24 percent answered "always or usually," 36 percent answered "sometimes," and 40 percent answered "rarely or never."

Certainly, starting a sentence—even a paragraph—with *and* can have a dramatic
effect, calling attention to the increased significance of the sentence. For this reason,
the practice appears to be more common in storytelling than in expository writing.
Here is an example from Doris Lessing's short story "To Room Nineteen":

> A high price has to be paid for the happy marriage with the four healthy children in the large white gardened fence.
> And they were paying it, willingly, knowing what they were doing. . . .

And here is an example from "Envy," a narrative essay by Kathryn Chetkovich. Note how the *and* starting the new paragraph intensifies the tension building through four *and*'s in the previous sentences.

> At home bad things might be happening, and no expert, no breezy young man with a stethoscope, was there to take charge. There was only my mother with her fraying nerves, and later a willing but underqualified aide and a nurse who visited a couple of times a week. In the hospital there had at least been the grim herd comfort of other ill people and other worn-out families.
> And of course the hospital was a place you could always leave. In the hospital my father was someone else's responsibility. At home, he was ours.

But even in nonnarrative discourse, starting a sentence with *and* or another conjunction can add to its rhetorical punch. A final example comes from the concluding paragraph of Elizabeth Loftus's essay *Memory Faults and Fixes,* in which she rounds out a list of deleterious effects stemming from myths about memory with a clincher:

> The mental health profession has also suffered from a proliferation of dubious beliefs about memory. The ridicule of a subgroup with questionable memory beliefs drags down the reputation of the entire profession. And finally there is one last group that is harmed by a system that accepts every single claim of victimization, no matter how dubious. That system dilutes and trivializes the experiences of the genuine victims and increases their suffering.

See more at **both, but,** and **try and.**

and/or

And/or is widely used in legal and business writing. Its use in general writing to mean "one or the other or both" is acceptable but can appear stilted.
See more at **or.**

anesthetist

The pronunciation (ə-nĕs′tĭ-tĭst) is an example of *assimilation,* a phonological process that involves one sound being influenced by another sound, usually a following sound, so that the sounds become more alike or identical. In the case of *anesthetist,* the (th) becomes (t) by assimilating to the following (t), with the result that the sound segment (tĭ) occurs twice. In careful speech the word should properly be pronounced (ə-nĕs′thĭ-tĭst).
See more at **assimilation.**

angina

The pronunciation (ăn′jə-nə), which more accurately reflects the word's Latin pronunciation, is more common in medicine. However, both pronunciations, the one with stress on the second syllable, (ăn-jī′nə), and the one with stress on the first syllable shown above, are acceptable in all circumstances.

Anglo

In contemporary American English, *Anglo* is used primarily in distinguishing a white English-speaking person from a person of Hispanic heritage. In this context it is not limited to persons of English descent but can be generally applied to any non-Hispanic white person. Thus in parts of the United States with large Hispanic populations, an American of Polish, Irish, or German heritage might be termed an Anglo just as readily as a person of English descent. However, in parts of the country where the Hispanic population is small, or in areas where ethnic distinctions among European groups remain strong, *Anglo* has little currency as a general term for non-Hispanic whites.

Anglo is also used in non-Hispanic contexts. In Canada, where its usage dates at least to 1800, the distinction is between persons of English and French descent. And in American historical contexts, *Anglo* is apt to be used more strictly to refer to Americans of English descent, as in this passage describing the politics of nation-building in pre-Revolutionary America:

> The "unity" of the American people derived . . . from the ability and willingness of an Anglo elite to stamp its image on other peoples coming to this country (Benjamin Schwartz, "The Diversity Myth," *Atlantic Monthly*)

Antarctic

The original spelling of the word *Antarctic* in English left out the first *c,* which was reintroduced into the spelling apparently at the beginning of the 17th century, most likely in a conscious effort to make the English word conform more closely to its Greek ancestor. The spelling with the *c* is now, of course, the only acceptable one, but the pronunciations (ănt-ärk′tĭk) and (ănt-är′tĭk) are equally acceptable.

See more at **arctic.**

ante–   See **anti–.**

antecedent

An antecedent is the word, phrase, or clause to which a pronoun refers. In the sequence *The dog needs to be fed. Would you feed her?* the antecedent of the pronoun *her* is the noun *dog*. In the sequence *The players and the coach reviewed tapes of their games*, the antecedent of *their* is the phrase *the players and the coach*. In the sentence *What he did was foolish, and it got him into trouble*, the antecedent of *it* is the clause *what he did*. Although *antecedent* comes from the Latin for "that which goes before," linguists sometimes use the word even when a pronoun precedes the noun it is linked to. Thus *John* can be described as the antecedent of *he* in the sentence *When he first moved here, John had a hard time making friends*.

See more at **pronouns, agreement of.**

anti– / ante–

The prefix *anti–* goes back to Greek *anti*, meaning "against." *Anti–* is so recognizable and its meaning is so clear that it is frequently used to make up new words. For example, the meanings of words such as *anticrime* and *antipollution* are easy to guess. Sometimes, when followed by a vowel, *anti–* becomes *ant–*: *antacid*.

Depending on the word in which the prefix occurs as well as the personal idiom of the speaker, *anti–* can be pronounced in a variety of ways: (ăn′tī), (ăn′tē), and (ăn′tĭ). For example, the word *antibody* is most often pronounced (ăn′tĭ-bŏd′ē), but in a word like *antihero*, *anti–* is perhaps most usually pronounced (ăn′tē) or (ăn′tī). The dictionary should be consulted when the pronunciation of *anti–* in a particular word is in doubt.

Writers should remember to distinguish *anti–* from another common prefix, *ante–*, meaning "in front of, before, earlier." This prefix can be pronounced either (ăn′tē) or (ăn′tĭ)—though never (ăn′tī). *Ante–* derives from the Latin word *ante*, "before." Remembering the separate etymological origins of *anti–*, "against," and *ante–*, "before," may help some writers recall the correct spelling of such words as *antebellum* ("before the war"), *antedate* ("to date from before, occur earlier than"), and *antediluvian* ("dating from before the biblical Flood, very old").

anticipate

Many usage commentators have insisted that the verb *anticipate* be restricted in its use to mean only "to feel or realize beforehand" (as in *We didn't anticipate the crowds at the zoo*) and "to deal with in advance, forestall" (as in *We anticipated the storm by boarding up the windows*).

Other uses of *anticipate*, especially when meaning "to look forward to, expect," where no preventive action is taken, have been criticized as unlicensed extensions of meaning. The Usage Panel would beg to differ. In our 2002 survey, 87 percent of the Panel approved of the sentence *He is anticipating a visit from his son*. This represents a substantial increase over the 62 percent in our 1964 survey. Even when the event being anticipated is expressly stated to be positive, the Panel overwhelmingly approves, with 81 percent accepting *We are anticipating a pleasant hike in the country.*

Oddly enough, the Panel has less enthusiasm for the traditional "forestall" use, though a clear majority (57 percent) still accepted it in 2002 in the *anticipated the storm* example given above. This suggests that the extended use of *anticipate* as a synonym of *expect* now is considered the primary one and is overshadowing the others.

antidote

The word *antidote* may be used with a variety of prepositions; all of the following constructions are acceptable: *The movies are a good antidote to boredom; The doctor gave me an antidote for my snakebite; There is no known antidote against folly.*

anxious

People have been using *anxious* as a synonym for *eager* for over 250 years, and for over 100 years language critics have been objecting to it. Objectors feel that *anxious* should be used only when the person it refers to is worried or uneasy about the upcoming event. By this thinking, it is acceptable to say *We are anxious to see the strike settled soon* but not *We are anxious to see the new show of contemporary sculpture at the museum.* The Usage Panel splits down the middle on this issue. In our 1999 survey, 52 percent rejected *anxious* in the second example, and the same percentage rejected it in our 1988 survey. Resistance to this usage therefore appears to remain strong.

Nevertheless, people who like using *anxious* to mean "eager" can justify the usage on the grounds that it adds emotional urgency to an assertion. It implies that the subject so strongly desires a certain outcome that frustration of that desire will lead to unhappiness. But they should bear in mind that the usage will not please everyone.

any

***any* as a pronoun**   When used as a pronoun, *any* can take either a singular or plural verb depending on how it is construed: *Any of these books is suitable* [that is, *any one*]. *But are any* [that is, *some*] *of them available?*

of any   The construction *of any* is often used in informal contexts to mean "of all," as in *He is the best known of any living playwright.* Although this construction has been in use for centuries, the phrase *of all* followed by a plural noun may be more suitable for formal writing: *He is the best known of all living playwrights.*

***any* as an adverb**   *Any* is also used as an adverb to mean "at all" before a comparative adjective or adverb in questions and negative sentences: *Is she any better? Is he doing any better? He is not any friendlier than before.* This usage is entirely acceptable. The related use of *any* to modify a verb is also acceptable but usually considered informal: *It didn't hurt any. If the child cries any, give her the bottle.*

See more at **every, he.**

anyone

***anyone* is always singular**   *Anyone* and *anybody* are singular terms and always take a singular verb: *Anyone who wants to can come along.*

anyone* or *any one   The one-word form *anyone* means "any person." The two-word form *any one* means "whatever one (person or thing) of a group." Thus, *Anyone may join* means that admission is open to everybody. *Any one may join* means that admission is open to one person only. When followed by *of*, only *any one* can be used: *Any one* [not *Anyone*] *of the boys could carry it by himself.*

anyone* instead of *everyone   *Anyone* is often used in place of *everyone* in sentences like *She is the most thrifty person of anyone I know.* While this construction has been used for centuries, it can provoke strong feelings. Back in 1964, 64 percent of the Usage Panel found the previously quoted sentence unacceptable in writing. It was still rejected by 60 percent of the Panel in 2001. Animosity to it may stem from the fact that *of anyone* is unnecessary and can be dropped without altering the sense.

anyone* with *he   For the acceptability of generic *he* used to refer to *anyone* (as in *Anyone worth his salt would have done a better job*), see **he.**

***anyone* with plural pronouns**   For a discussion of whether a plural pronoun can refer to *anyone*, as in *Anyone who wants to go must bring their canteens*, see **every.**

anyplace   See **everyplace.**

aplomb

Confusion arises with the pronunciation of this word probably because the sequence *omb* has several conspicuously different ways of being pronounced—(ŏm) as in *bomb*, (ōm) as in *comb*, (o͞om) as in *tomb*. You can pronounce *aplomb* (ə-plŏm′) or (ə-plŭm′).

apostrophe

omissions

1. An apostrophe indicates the omission of letters in contractions.

isn't	that's
couldn't	o'clock
you'll	won't

2. An apostrophe indicates the omission of figures in dates.

way back in '68	the class of '80

plurals

1. An apostrophe is used to indicate the plurals of letters or words when necessary for clarity. The plurals of most numerals do not require an apostrophe.

x's, *y*'s, and *z*'s	count by 3s
the paragraph with too many	the 1950s
also's	

2. If an abbreviation contains periods, the plural is formed by adding an apostrophe and *s*. If an abbreviation does not contain periods, the plural is formed just by adding *s*.

M.D.'s *or* MDs	v.p.'s
Ph.D.'s *or* PhDs	VCRs

3. To form the possessive of a singular noun, add an apostrophe and *s*.

someone's idea	Marx's theories
my aunt's house	Dickens's novels
the baby's bottle	

4. To form the possessive of a plural noun ending in *s*, just add an apostrophe.

their aunts' houses	the Smiths' cats
the babies' bottles	the Joneses' horses
the leaves' colors	

5. To form the possessive of a plural noun that does not end in *s*, add an apostrophe and *s*.

everyone's books	the people's voices
the children's toys	the sheep's heads

6. For certain classical and biblical names that end in *s* or an *eez* sound, the possessive is formed by just adding an apostrophe.

Moses' journey	Socrates' beliefs
Euripedes' plays	

7. To form the possessive of a company title, add an apostrophe and *s* unless the last word of the title is a plural, in which case the possessive is indicated by an apostrophe alone.

Capital Management's hiring practices	Broadway Systems' annual report

8. To form the possessive of an italicized noun, use a roman apostrophe and a roman *s*.

the space shuttle *Discovery*'s mission

9. In an expression indicating joint possession, only the name of the person last mentioned should be in the possessive case. In an expression indicating individual possession, each person's name is in the possessive case.

Have you seen Ann and Bob's new house?

Butch Cassidy and the Sundance Kid was Redford and Newman's first collaborative effort.

Chris's and Miguel's cars are both in the driveway.

Monette's and McNichol's performances as elves were stiff but sympathetic.

10. An apostrophe should be included in certain expressions of duration and amount.

> It's all in a day's work.   I bought ten dollars' worth of gas.
> We made it in four hours' time.

11. Don't forget to include an apostrophe when the thing possessed is implied but not stated.

> I'm going to my parents' for the weekend.
> He's at the doctor's.
> On Thanksgiving they'll go to Vijay's sister's.

See also **possessive constructions.**

apparent

Used before a noun, *apparent* means "seeming": *For all his apparent wealth, Pat always had trouble paying the rent.* However, when used after the verb *be* and similar verbs, *apparent* can mean either "seeming" (as in *His virtues are only apparent*) or "obvious" (as in *The effects of the drought are apparent to anyone who sees the parched fields*), so be careful that the intended meaning is clear from the context. After the verb *become, apparent* only means "obvious": *At first I thought they were just admiring my bicycle, but their intentions quickly became apparent when they pulled out their wallets.*

applicable

Although *applicable* can be pronounced with the stress on either the first or second syllable, in our 1995 survey an overwhelming majority—83 percent—reported using the pronunciation with stress on the first syllable.

appositive

An *appositive* is a noun or noun phrase that is placed next to another to help identify or explain it. *The composer* in *The composer Beethoven lived in Bonn* and *sailing his sloop* in *His main interest, sailing his sloop, has brought him many friends* are appositives.

See more at **comma** and **restrictive and nonrestrictive clauses.**

apt   See **liable.**

archetype

The *ch* in *archetype,* and in other English words of Greek origin such as *architect* and *chorus,* represents a transliteration of Greek X (chi), and is usually pronounced like (k). In our 1997 survey, 94 percent of the Usage Panel indicated that they pronounce *archetype* (är′kĭ-tīp′), with a (k) sound, while 6 percent preferred the pronunciation (är′chĭ-tīp′), with a (ch) sound. Of those who preferred the traditional (k) pronunciation, 10 percent noted that the (ch) pronunciation was also acceptable. Only the traditional pronunciation is widely accepted as standard, however.

arctic / Arctic

Arctic was originally spelled in English without the first *c,* which was later reintroduced after the original spelling of Latin *arcticus,* from Greek *arktikos.* Both (ärk′tĭk) and (är′tĭk) are acceptable pronunciations.

See more at **Antarctic.**

argot

Argot is a borrowing from French, where it means "slang." In English, however, it refers to a specialized vocabulary of a group or trade, and especially an obscure vocabulary whose primary purpose is to render outsiders incapable of understanding what is being talked about. *Argot* is often used to refer to the language of criminals, and so may carry associations with illegal or at least underground activities. The pronunciation (är′gō), a remnant of the word's French origin, still appears to be the most common one, although (är′gət) is also acceptable, especially in American English.

arguably   See **sentence adverbs.**

arrant   See **errant.**

articles

Articles are words that indicate that the word which follows is a noun and that specify the noun's application. Linguists categorize articles in the larger group known as *determiners.* The indefinite articles are *a* and *an.* The definite article is *the.*

See more at **definite article** and **indefinite article.**

as

as . . . as versus so . . . as   A traditional usage rule draws a distinction between comparisons using *as . . . as* and comparisons using *so . . . as*. The rule states that the *so . . . as* construction is required in negative sentences (as in Shakespeare's *"tis not so deep as a well"*), in questions (as in *Is it so bad as she says?*), and in certain *if* clauses (as in *If it is so bad as you say, you ought to leave*). But this *so . . . as* construction is becoming increasingly rare in American English, and the use of *as . . . as* is now acceptable in all contexts.

as . . . as and than   When making comparisons involving both *as . . . as* and *than*, remember to keep the second *as* when writing in formal style. Write *He is as smart as, or smarter than, his brother*, not *He is as smart or smarter than his brother*, which is considered unacceptable in formal style.

as instead of that   In many dialects, people use *as* in place of *that* in sentences like *We are not sure as we want to go* or *It's not certain as he left*. But this use of *as* is limited mostly to speaking, and it will likely seem inappropriate in formal writing.

as instead of that or who   Some nonstandard varieties of American English differ from the standard language in the form and usage of relative pronouns. Where Standard English has three relative pronouns—*who, which,* and *that*—regional dialects, particularly those of the South and Midlands, allow *as* and *what* as relative pronouns: *"They like nothing better than the job of leading off a young feller like you, as ain't never been away from home much"* (Stephen Crane, *The Red Badge of Courage*). *The car what hit him never stopped.*

as meaning "because" or "when"   When *as* expresses a causal relation, it should be preceded by a comma, as in *She won't be coming, as we didn't invite her*. When *as* expresses a time relation, it is not preceded by a comma: *She was finishing the painting as I walked into the room*. When an *as*-clause begins a sentence, it may be necessary to make clear whether *as* is used to mean "because" or "at the same time that." The sentence *As they were leaving, I walked to the door* may mean either "I walked to the door because they were leaving" or "I walked to the door at the same time that they were leaving."

as used redundantly   *As* is sometimes used superfluously with verbs like *consider* and *deem*, as in *The trial was considered as unnecessary*. For more on this, see **consider as.**

as in parallel constructions   Constructions of the *as . . . as . . .* form are sometimes difficult to keep parallel. For more on this, see **parallelism.**
    See more at **comparisons with *as* and *than;* like; pronouns, personal; so;** and **that.**

as discussed   See **discuss.**

as far as

The expression *as far as* introduces a clause and means "to the extent or degree that." It is sometimes used with *be concerned* or *go* to mean "with regard to," as in *As far as rush-hour traffic is concerned, the new tunnel should make a big difference.* Sometimes people are the subjects of the clause, which takes on the meaning "in the opinion of," as in *As far as my parents go, getting a new car is out of the question.*

But in recent years *as far as* has also been used as a preposition meaning "as for" or "regarding," especially in speech. That is, the verb *be concerned* or *go* drops out. A large majority of the Usage Panel frowns upon this usage. In our 1994 survey, 80 percent found the *as far as* construction unacceptable in this example: *As far as something to do on the weekend, we didn't even have miniature golf.* Another 84 percent rejected the sentence *The Yankees are still very much alive, as far as the divisional race.* And 89 percent objected to *as far as* when followed by a noun clause in *As far as how Koresh got shot, we don't know yet.*

as follows

The phrase *as follows* is correct regardless of whether the noun that precedes it is singular or plural: *The regulations are as follows.* When the noun is plural, it is sometimes written incorrectly as *as follow.*

Asian

People who are native to Asia or who are of Asian ancestry are of course termed *Asians;* when they are citizens or residents of the United States they can properly be called *Asian Americans.* Calling such persons *Orientals* is likely to cause offense today, even where none is intended. As always with such a broad label, it is generally preferable, where appropriate, to use a more specific ethnic, national, or geographic term, such as *Hmong, Japanese, Korean American,* or *South Asian.*

Asia is the largest of the continents with more than half the world's population. Though strictly speaking any of the peoples native to the continent are Asians, in American English this term is used most commonly of East, Central, and Southeast Asian peoples (such as Chinese, Japanese, Mongolians, Vietnamese, and Thais), a bit less commonly of South Asian peoples (such as Indians, Sri Lankans, and Pakistanis), and rarely, in most contexts, of West or Southwest Asian peoples (such as Arabs, Turks, Iranians, and Armenians), who are usually designated as *Middle* or *Near Eastern* rather than *Asian.* Indonesians and Filipinos are generally included under *Asian,* but not the Melanesians, Micronesians, and Polynesians of the central and southern Pacific Ocean, who are now known collectively as *Pacific Islanders.*

Asian American

An American of Asian descent is an *Asian American,* not an *Amerasian,* the latter term being largely restricted to children fathered by American servicemen stationed in Asia during the Korean and Vietnam wars. As with *Latin American* and *Euro-American*, the designation *Asian American* can apply to many different people with different national origins and widely varying cultural backgrounds. Wherever appropriate a more specific term, such as *Chinese American* or *Korean American*, should be used in place of the comprehensive one.

Both as a noun and an adjective, *Asian American* may be spelled with or without a hyphen.

See more at **Amerasian, Eurasian,** and **hyphenated Americans.**

Asiatic

The use of *Asiatic* in referring to the contemporary peoples and cultures of Asia sounds conspicuously dated in modern American English, and it would likely cause offense as well. The preferred ethnic term is now clearly *Asian.* In certain historical, academic, and geographical contexts, however, *Asiatic* may be entirely appropriate and need not automatically be replaced with *Asian.* For instance, the ancient Greeks who settled in Asia Minor (modern Turkey) on the coasts of the Aegean Sea are sometimes referred to as *Asiatic Greeks.*

ask

The pronunciations (ăks) and (ăst) for *ask* are both considered nonstandard, although they occur fairly frequently, especially in the southern or central sections of the United States. The variant (ăks), sometimes spelled *ax* or *aks,* is often identified as a feature of African American English. While it is true that the form is frequent in the speech of African Americans, it is also heard in the speech of white Americans as well, especially in the South and middle sections of the country. It was once common among New Englanders, but has largely died out there as a local feature. The widespread use of this pronunciation should not be surprising since *ax* is a very old pronunciation and spelling in English, having been used in England for over 1,000 years. In Old English we find both *āscian* and *ācsian,* and in Middle English both *asken* and *axen.* Moreover, the forms with *cs* or *x* had no stigma associated with them. Chaucer used *asken* and *axen* interchangeably in *The Canterbury Tales,* as in the lines *"I wol aske, if it hir will be / To be my wyf"* and *"Men axed hym, what sholde bifalle."* After 1600, *axe* and similar forms saw less use in writing but their pronunciations survived in certain dialects.

The forms in *x* arose from the forms in *sk* by a linguistic process called *metathesis,* in which two sounds are reversed. The *x* thus represents (ks), the flipped version of (sk). Metathesis is a common linguistic process around the world and does not arise from a defect in speaking. Nevertheless, (ăks) has become stigmatized as substandard—a fate that has befallen other words, like *ain't,* that were once perfectly acceptable in educated society. The pronunciation (ăst) for *asked,* on the other hand, is extremely common all over the US and can be considered standard.

aspect

Aspect is a property of verbs that designates the relation of the action to the passage of time, especially in reference to completion, duration, or repetition. In English, aspect is normally conveyed by tenses, especially progressive and perfect tenses, as in *Have you worked on the puzzle today? The professor was walking in the park yesterday,* and *The rookie has been scoring a lot of points lately.*

See more at **verbs, tenses of.**

as regards / in regard to / in regards to

The phrase *as regards* is less well accepted than the phrase *in regard to* when used to describe the topic or theme of a noun that it modifies. In the sentence *Please call between 9 a.m. and 5 p.m. Monday–Friday if you have any questions (as regards/in regard to/in regards to) the status of your application,* where the phrase modifies the noun *questions,* only 28 percent of the Usage Panel accepted *as regards,* while 84 percent accepted *in regard to* in our 2004 survey. When either phrase is used to specify a topic or theme more precisely, the results are less clear. In the sentence *These surveys show a high level of satisfaction with government policy among the elderly in the Scandinavian countries, especially (as regards/in regard to/in regards to) the medical services provided by the state,* 53 percent accepted *as regards,* while 67 percent accepted *in regard to.* A number of Panelists pointed out that in such cases the participial preposition *regarding* might be a more straightforward option; other options include *with regard to* and *with respect to.* The phrase *in respect of* is also possible, but is primarily a British usage and sounds somewhat stilted to American ears. The Panel had little enthusiasm for the phrase *in regards to* in the above sentences; only 6 percent found this phrase acceptable.

assimilation

Assimilation is a phonological process that occurs when the articulation of one sound is influenced by another adjacent or nearby sound, usually a following one, so that the two sounds become more alike or even identical. An example of a partial assimilation is the pronunciation (ĭng′kŭm′) for *income,* where (n), which is made near the front of the mouth, becomes (ng), made near the back of the mouth, before (k), also made near the back of the mouth. An example of a total assimilation is the pronunciation (hôrsh′sho͞o′) for *horseshoe,* where (s) before (sh) becomes (sh). The main result of assimilation, as with other types of historical sound change, is that articulation is made easier for a speaker, particularly when speech is rapid. Particular instances of assimilation, such as those above, or the pronunciations (lĕnth) and (strĕnth) for *length* and *strength,* or (pŭng′kĭn) for *pumpkin,* may draw adverse criticism despite the fact that such criticism is groundless from a historical or phonological point of view.

assure / ensure / insure

Assure, ensure, and *insure* all mean "to make secure or certain." Only *assure* is used with reference to a person in the sense of "to set the mind at rest": *The ambassador assured the prime minister of his loyalty.* Although *ensure* and *insure* are generally interchangeable, only *insure* is now widely used in American English in the commercial sense of "to guarantee persons or property against risk." Thus, it makes sense to keep these words distinct: *I assure you that we have insured the grounds to ensure that we will be protected in case of a lawsuit stemming from an accident.*

as well as   See **together.**

athlete

The pronunciation (ăth′ə-lēt′) is an example of *intrusion,* a phonological process that involves the addition or insertion of an extra sound within a word or between words in speech. Most people pronounce *athlete* (ăth′lēt′), with just two syllables.

See more at **intrusion.**

–ation

The very common noun suffix *–ation* has its origin in the Latin suffix *–ātiō,* which was used to make nouns from the many verbs ending in *–are* in that language. For example, *vocātiō,* "a calling, summons," the source of our word *vocation,* is formed from *vocāre,* "to call." Latin verbs ending in *–āre* tend to be borrowed into English as verbs in *–ate,* and so English nouns ending in *–ation* are often paired with verbs ending in *–ate.* For example, we have the noun *creation* beside the verb *create.*

In medieval times, both the English and French began using *–ation* as a convenient way to form nouns from verbs, even when the verb itself did not exist in Classical Latin (that is, the Latin used by the Romans before the end of the Roman Empire, as opposed to Medieval Latin, used as the scholarly and liturgical language of medieval Europe). In particular, *–ation* was used to make nouns corresponding to the many new verbs coined using the suffix *–ize,* such as *civilization* from the verb *civilize.* Later, in the 17th and 18th centuries, *–ation* began to be added to native English verbs to create nouns like *flirtation* from *flirt* or *starvation* from *starve.* At first, innovations like these received a great deal of criticism based on the notion that Latin and native English elements should not be mixed when forming new words. Nevertheless, *starvation* and other words like it have fully established themselves in the standard vocabulary of English.

ATM machine

There are a number of recent expressions that add to an acronym the noun that the last letter of the acronym stands for. Thus, an *ATM machine* is an Automated Teller

Machine machine, a *PIN number* is a Personal Identification Number number, and a *VAT tax* is a Value Added Tax tax. In our 1995 survey, 70 percent, or in some cases even more, of the Usage Panel accepted expressions like these, probably because they have become fixed from so much use, and their redundancy is not salient. They should be considered standard in all contexts.

See more at **redundancy.**

atomic / nuclear

Atomic weapons and *nuclear weapons* are the same thing, as are *atomic energy* and *nuclear energy.* But the meaning of *atomic* is not strictly identical to that of *nuclear,* and there are contexts where the distinction is important.

The term *atomic* refers to the structure and dynamics of the atom as a whole, including both its nucleus and the electrons that orbit it. The mass of an atom is mostly contained in its nucleus, while the way the atom interacts with the outside world depends mostly on the outermost layers of orbiting electrons. It is primarily the configuration of these electrons that determines the chemical properties of an atom (what other sorts of atoms the atom interacts with, how much energy is exchanged in the process, what shapes they take when put together, and so on). *Atomic physics* is thus the study of the structure of the atom as a whole; an electron in, say, a deuterium atom might have an *atomic binding energy* of 13.6 electron volts (the amount of energy needed to free the electron from the atom completely).

The term *nuclear* is more specific, referring only to the properties of the atom's core: its nucleons (the protons and neutrons bound together in the nucleus), their structure, and their dynamics. *Nuclear physics* is thus the study of these properties, and a *nuclear binding energy* is the energy binding nucleons together. This sort of energy, which is millions of times higher than the energy binding electrons to the nucleus (2.3 million electron volts for the deuterium atom mentioned above), is what is absorbed and given off in the *nuclear reactions* that produce *nuclear energy.* Thus, while nonscientists commonly use the less precise terms *atomic reactions* and *atomic energy* in these cases, the words *atomic* and *nuclear* cannot be considered synonymous.

attention-deficit disorder   See **ADHD.**

attention-deficit hyperactivity disorder   See **ADHD.**

attributive

An attributive is a word, such as an adjective or a noun, that is placed before the noun it modifies, as *small* in *the small garden* and *city* in *the city streets.*

See more at **adjectives.**

auger / augur

These identically pronounced (and often confused) words have entirely different meanings. An *auger* is a tool used for boring holes. An *augur* is a seer or soothsayer. The verb *augur* means "to foretell or betoken," as in *This development augurs change in the software business. Augur* is used most commonly as a verb without an object in phrases such as *augur well* or *augur ill,* as in *The rehearsal miscues did not augur well for opening night.*

aural / oral

For many speakers of English, these words sound the same. But for all, their meanings are distinct. *Aural* refers to the ear or to hearing: *aural disease, a memory that was predominantly aural. Oral* refers to the mouth or to speaking: *an oral vaccine, an oral report.*

In certain contexts, the difference can be more subtle than might be expected. An oral tradition is one that is conveyed primarily by speech (as opposed to writing, for example), whereas an aural tradition is one that is conveyed primarily by sounds (as opposed to images, for instance).

Australoid

The term *Australoid,* referring to the grouping of peoples indigenous to Australia and certain of the large islands to the north, belongs to the vocabulary of racial classification proposed by 19th-century European anthropologists. These terms are now considered inappropriate and potentially offensive outside the context of physical anthropology. When referring to the indigenous peoples of this region, it is usually best to use the relevant ethnic name, if known, or a term such as *native Australian* or *native Bornean.*

author

***author* as a verb**   As a verb, *author* first appeared in the late 16th century but fell out of use for 250 years. It was rejuvenated in the mid-20th century with the sense "to be the author of a written text." In most cases it refers to material that has been published—and not to unpublished texts such as love letters or diaries. Therefore it does not have quite as broad a meaning as the verb *write.* For this reason, it is unlikely that someone who has ghostwritten a book for a celebrity will be said to have "authored" the manuscript. Perhaps because of the relative newness of the verb, many usage critics have condemned it as illegitimate. The Usage Panel tends to sympathize with this view, but this sympathy has been slowly eroding over the decades. In 1964, 81 percent of the Panel found the verb unacceptable in writing. In our 1988 survey, 74 percent rejected it in the sentence *He has authored a dozen books on the subject.* In 2001, the proportion of Panelists who rejected this same sentence fell to 60 percent. This suggests that the verb will eventually be accepted by most people.

Journalists frequently use the verb *author* to apply to the creation or sponsoring of legislative acts, as in *The senator authored a bill limiting uses of desert lands in California.* In these cases the lawmaker may not have actually written the bill that bears his or her name but rather promoted its idea and passage. While the Panelists were a bit more tolerant of this legislative usage, the nays still have the slightest edge, with 51 percent rejecting the previously quoted sentence in 2001, down from 64 percent in 1988.

authors and writers in science   In February 1995, the discovery of the top quark spurred two four-page articles submitted to the journal *Physical Review Letters,* each including over four hundred *authors* or *coauthors.* Although an article with this number of authors submitted to a trade magazine might be an editor's worst nightmare, at a professional science journal four hundred authors would be expected for a result eighteen years in the making. Within scientific journals, the term *author* takes on a broader meaning than the term *writer.* An author is someone who has played a critical role in the outcome of an experiment or calculation. For example, an author might be the individual who maintains crucial laboratory equipment or develops a useful method of collecting data. In all cases, a writer is a person who has contributed to the actual writing of the article and is one of the authors.

coauthor   The verb *coauthor* is well established in reference to scientific and scholarly publications, where it serves a useful purpose since the people listed as authors of such works routinely include research collaborators who have played no part in the actual writing of the text but who are nonetheless entitled to credit for the published results.

auxiliary

The pronunciations (ôg-zĭl′yə-rē) and (ôg-zĭl′ə-rē) are probably the most common. Other acceptable pronunciations are (ôg-zĭl′ē-ēr′ē), (ôg-zĭl′ē-ə-rē), and (ôg-zĭl′rē).

auxiliary and primary verbs

Auxiliary verbs, sometimes called *helping verbs,* help complete the form and meaning of main verbs. The auxiliary verbs include the *modal verbs,* the *primary verbs,* and a few special verbs like *dare* and *need.* The modal verbs are *can, could, may, might, must, shall, should, will,* and *would.* They are called *modal* because they express the *mood* of verbs (for more on this, see **verbs, mood of** and **subjunctive**). The primary *verbs* are *be, do,* and *have.* The primary verbs have the distinction of being able to function either as main verbs or as auxiliaries.

The auxiliary verbs differ from main verbs in the following ways:

1. They do not take word endings to form participles or agree with their subject. Thus, we say *She may go to the store,* but never *She mays go to the store.*
2. They come before *not* in negative clauses, and they do not use *do* to form the negative: *You might not like that.* A main verb uses *do* to form the negative and follows *not: You do not like that.*

3. They come before the subject in a question: *Can I have another apple? Would you like to go to the movies?* Main verbs must use *do* and follow the subject to form questions: *Do you want to go to the movies?*

4. They take the infinitive without *to: I will call you tomorrow.* A main verb that takes an infinitive always uses *to: I promise to call you tomorrow.*

When functioning as auxiliary verbs, the primary verbs serve the following functions. *Be* shows continuing action (*We are working on a new plan*) and forms the passive voice (*The shed was destroyed in the storm*). *Have* is used to make perfect tenses—tenses that show completed action (*She has finally finished her book. Have you ever gone windsurfing? We had planned to go out tonight*). *Do* is used to form negatives (*I do not wish to offend you*), to ask questions (*Do you ever write to her?*), to show emphasis (*I do want you to come to the party*), and to stand for a full verb in certain other constructions (*She likes jazz more than he does*).

In their capacity as auxiliaries, the primary verbs retain some features of main verbs. All the primary verbs can change form to agree in number with their subject. We say *I am going, He has eaten,* and *She does not travel much. Have* and *be* can form participles and still play an auxiliary role in a verb phrase: *Having finished in the garage, he went home. They did not give up even when being badly outplayed. Have* and *be* are used with participles and cannot take an infinitive without *to.*

As main verbs, *have* and *be* present certain exceptions to the criteria stated in rules 2 and 3 above (distinguishing main verbs from auxiliaries). They can come before *not* in negative sentences (*We haven't any pickles. He is not there*). They can also appear before the subject in questions (*Is anybody home? Have you no shame?*).

See more at **can, dare, have, may, must, need, ought, shall, should,** and **used to.**

average / arithmetic mean / median / mode

The average number of people per family in the United States in 2000 was 3.037. *Average,* in this sense, is identical with *arithmetic mean,* or simply *mean.* The arithmetic mean of a group of values is the sum of those values (in this case, the total number of people in the United States) divided by the number of values in the group (in this case, the number of families). How one should define 0.37 people might seem mysterious, but it is not really an issue: the arithmetic mean is an abstract notion that doesn't correspond to any particular case.

The mean of a group of values must be distinguished from its *median.* The median effectively splits the group into two halves, such that the values in one half are greater than or equal to the median, and the values in the other half are less than or equal to it. The median can be found by listing the values in increasing order and picking the value halfway down the list. (Values that occur more than once must, incidentally, be listed more than once.) If there is an even number of quantities, then the median is defined as the arithmetic mean of the middle two numbers; so for the set of numbers {1, 3, 6, 8, 9, 12}, for example, the median is the mean of the two middle numbers 6 and 8, that is, 7. (The median family size in the United States in 2000 was three people.)

Another related concept is that of the *mode,* which is the most frequent value in a group of values. For example, if 50 percent of all families consist of three people, 30 percent consist of four people, and 20 percent consist of families of other sizes, then three people is the mode for family size. There can be more than one mode in a group of quantities, in case there are ties for first place, but if all values occur with the same frequency, no mode is considered to exist. Unlike the mean and the median, the mode, when it exists, always corresponds to a value that does apply to particular cases.

See more at **normal.**

aviator / aviatrix   See **feminine suffixes.**

awake / awaken   See **wake.**

aweigh / away

Anchors aweigh, my boys / Anchors aweigh / Farewell to college joys / We sail at break of day, day, day, day! Writers quoting the official song of the United States Navy often misspell the resounding phrase *Anchors aweigh!* as *Anchors away!* and thus rob the expression of much of its thrill. The word *aweigh* is a technical nautical term meaning "hanging clear of the bottom so that a vessel can move." It is related to the verb *weigh* in the sense "heave up, hoist up," most often heard in the phrase *weigh anchor.* Naturally, a ship must *weigh* anchor before it can sail *away,* and when anchors are *aweigh,* they could be considered to hang *away* from the sea floor or riverbed. These natural associations, as well as the much greater frequency of the adverb *away* (on land at least), have doubtless led to the common confusion of the two words. Nonetheless, *anchors away* is a sure sign of a landlubber.

awhile / a while

People often confuse the adverb *awhile* with the noun phrase *a while.* This is hardly surprising because they sound the same, and the noun phrase can function like an adverb. In fact, noun phrases denoting periods of time can often be used as adverbs, as *an hour* in *It took an hour to get down the hill.* The same is true for *a while.* Thus *It took a while to get down the hill* is correct, since *a while* functions here like other noun phrases such as *an hour* or *a long time.* Similarly, *It took awhile to get down the hill* is correct, where *awhile* functions like any other adverb phrase, such as *quite long* or the comparative adverb *longer.*

Care should be taken with prepositional phrases. Only *a while* can follow a preposition in a prepositional phrase, since only noun phrases can be the objects of prepositions. Thus *I'll stay for a while* is acceptable, but not *I'll stay for awhile.* (Note that if the preposition is dropped, both *I'll stay a while* and *I'll stay awhile* are acceptable, since the noun phrase *a while* can be used adverbially.)

See more at **someday.**

axiom / postulate / theorem / hypothesis / theory

The nouns *axiom* and *postulate* are synonymous in mathematics. They are statements that are accepted as true in order to study the consequences that can be deduced from them. A mathematical *theorem* is based on a set of axioms and can be deduced from them. For example, the system of natural numbers (whole numbers greater than or equal to zero) is based on axioms such as "there exists a number zero" and "every natural number n has a unique successor, $n+1$."

In nonmathematical usage, the word *postulate* is also used to refer to something assumed to be true without having been proven (for the sake of argument, for example), but the word is often used when the truth of the postulate could, in principle, be verified. This is not possible in mathematics; if a statement can be proven true given other statements, then it is not a postulate or an axiom, but a *theorem*. (Outside of mathematics, *postulate* may also mean "a requirement or prerequisite.")

Something proposed to be true but not yet proven to be true is called a *hypothesis* in mathematics. Mathematicians attempt to prove or disprove the validity of interesting hypotheses. In the natural sciences, a hypothesis similarly denotes something assumed to be true, though not yet entirely verified, as in *a working hypothesis*—a hypothesis that is reasonable, worth trying to verify, or worth assuming in order to proceed with research.

Everyday use of the word *theory* is actually close to the mathematical and scientific use of the word *hypothesis*. For example, the sentence *My theory is that he takes the train because he is afraid to fly* lends sense to a situation but remains to be shown true. In mathematics and science, however, the word *theory* generally refers to a set of axioms, hypotheses, proofs, experimental observations, and so on, that work together in a consistent way in order to explicate or explain something, as in *a theory of prime numbers* or *the theory of general relativity*. Certain kinds of work not a part of the empirical sciences, such as literary criticism, use the word theory somewhat more generally to refer to systems of analytical techniques, as in *critical theory*.

Sometimes the word *theory* is confused with the word *theorem* described above. A mathematical theorem may be a part of a larger theory, but it is not itself a theory: for example, it can be proven that two nonidentical straight lines intersect at either zero or one point, given the axioms of Euclidean geometry; this *theorem* is thus a part of an overall *theory* of geometry.

Thus, axioms and postulates form the roots of a particular deductive system; theorems are the logical consequences that fill out the deductive system; hypotheses drive theoretical development forward.

See more at **deduction** and **law.**

· B ·

bachelor   See **spinster**.

back-formation

Back-formation is a common linguistic process in which an existing word is treated as if it were derived (typically by affixation or compounding) from a previously non-existent word that is then put to use, thereby creating a neologism. Our word for the little green vegetable *pea,* for example, is a back-formation: the earlier form of this word was *pease* (a form still found in the Mother Goose rhyme "Pease porridge hot, pease porridge cold . . . "). *Pease* was analyzed by many speakers as being a plural form of the (previously nonexistent) word *pea,* possibly since peas are generally dealt with in large numbers. *Pea* was then adopted into the language generally as the singular form, with *peas* as its plural. Other examples are the verb *self-destruct* (from the noun *self-destruction;* note that there is no verb *to destruct*), *burger* (from *hamburger,* treated as a compound of *ham* with *burger,* even though ham is not an ingredient), and *diagnose* (from *diagnosis*).

Many back-formations have been criticized as unlicensed neologisms by usage writers, and a few of these, such as *commentate* (from *commentator*) and *kudo* (from *kudos*) are discussed in this book.

backward / backwards

As adverbs, *backward* and *backwards* are interchangeable: *stepped backward, a mirror facing backwards.* As an adjective modifying a following noun, the form without the *-s* predominates in standard usage: *a backward view.* This is especially true of the metaphorical uses of the adjective: *a region that was considered by urbanites to be culturally backward* [not *backwards*].

bacteria / bacterium

Bacteria is the plural of *bacterium,* a word that refers to any of a variety of unicellular microorganisms that lack a cell nucleus and are sometimes pathogenic in plants and animals. Since these organisms are normally present in abundant numbers, we encounter the plural far more often than the singular. It's hardly surprising, therefore, that the plural is often used incorrectly for the singular, as in *This bacteria produces dangerous toxins.* Correct usage can be phrased in several ways: *This bacterium produces . . . , This species of bacteria produces . . . , These bacteria produce . . . .*

bad / badly

***bad* as adverb**   *Bad* is often used as an adverb in sentences such as *The house was shaken up pretty bad* or *We need water bad*. This usage is common in informal speech but is widely regarded as unacceptable in formal writing. As far back as 1965, 92 percent of the Usage Panel rejected the sentence *His tooth ached so bad he could not sleep.*

want badly / need badly   The use of *badly* with *want* and *need* was once considered incorrect, since in these cases it means "very much" rather than "in an inferior manner or condition" or "immorally." But this use is widespread, even in formal contexts, and is now considered standard. Just a couple of examples will show how natural these constructions are:

> He wanted so badly to be the sort of father who spent time with his boy, walking and riding about—the father he never had (Brooks D. Simpson, *Ulysses S. Grant*)

> Those identifying themselves as Middle Easterners and Africans—controlling the world's gold, oil, diamonds, and rare earths—quickly made deals they said raised US $300 billion. They needed it badly, they felt, to protect themselves from a Russian named Boris (Joel Garreau, "Conspiracy of Heretics," *Wired*)

feel badly   For many speakers of English, the sentence *I feel bad* suggests that one feels physically unwell or emotionally sad. *I feel badly,* however, suggests only an emotional state, as in *I felt badly about the whole affair.* In fact, this usage bears analogy to the use of other adverbs with *feel,* such as *strongly* in *We feel strongly about this issue.* Some speakers would restrict *feel badly* to refer to emotional distress and let *feel bad* cover physical ailments, but not everyone maintains this distinction, so be sure that readers will understand *feel badly* from its context.

***badly* meaning "unwell"**   In some regions the word *badly* is used to mean "unwell," as in *He was looking badly after the accident. Poorly* is also used in this way. However, this usage has never been considered standard. Verbs like *look* are considered linking verbs in standard English, and so the word following *look* should properly be an adjective, since it modifies the subject, just as an adjective is required in sentences like *The pie tastes delicious.* An adverb used here (*The pie tastes deliciously*) would clearly be incorrect.

Note that *badly* is required following *look* when it modifies another word or phrase in the predicate, as in *The motorcycle looked badly in need of repair* and *The reporter looked badly put out by the sudden change in deadline.* The word *bad* cannot be used in such contexts.

baited   See **bated.**

baleful / baneful

Baleful and *baneful* both mean "harmful," but *baneful* most often describes something that is actually harmful or destructive, and it frequently modifies words such as *effects, consequences,* and *influence:*

America's zoning laws, intended to control the baneful effects of industry, have mutated, in the view of one architecture critic, into a system that corrodes civic life, outlaws the human scale, defeats tradition and authenticity, and confounds our yearning for an everyday environment worthy of our affection (James Howard Kunstler, "Home from Nowhere: Can the Momentum of Sprawl be Halted?" *Atlantic Monthly*)

Whether she is looking at the depredations of judicial activism, the efficacy of testing as a reform strategy, the baneful consequences of modern educators' obsession with student "self esteem," or a dozen other issues, she has generally shown herself to be well informed, clear eyed, and sensible (Chester E. Finn Jr., "Unwillingly to School—Pros and Cons of a National Curriculum," *National Review*)

In due course, the Committee found that Keynes was, indeed, exerting a baneful influence on the Harvard economic mind and that the Department of Economics was unbalanced in his favor (John Kenneth Galbraith, "How Keynes Came to America," *Economics, Peace and Laughter*)

Baleful is the more common word. Like *baneful*, it is used to characterize harmful effects and influences, but it is also applied to something that is menacing or that foreshadows evil, so the range of words it modifies is much broader:

Speak, Winchester; for boiling choler chokes
The hollow passage of my poison'd voice,
By sight of these our baleful enemies (Shakespeare, *1 Henry VI* 5.4.122)

. . . along the Banks
Of four infernal Rivers that disgorge
Into the burning Lake their baleful streams (John Milton, *Paradise Lost*, Book 2: 574–576)

Her temper was too sweet for her to show any anger, but she felt that her happiness had received a bruise, and for several days merely to look at Fred made her cry a little as if he were the subject of some baleful prophecy (George Eliot, *Middlemarch*)

It is time for breakfast, and a gnawed rind of papaya sags in his jaws like the baleful mouth of a clown (Jane Avrich, *The Winter Without Milk*)

The baleful presence of Babe Ruth also seemed to throw a scare into Gharrity, the Senator's catcher (Glenn Stout, *Top of the Heap*)

ball out   See **bawl out.**

banal

The pronunciation of *banal* is not settled among educated speakers of American English. Sixty years ago, H.W. Fowler recommended the pronunciation (băn′əl), rhyming with *panel*, but this pronunciation is now regarded as recondite by most Americans: no member of the Usage Panel prefers this pronunciation. In our 2001 survey, (bə-năl′) is preferred by 58 percent of the Usage Panel, (bā′nəl) by 28 percent, and (bə-näl′) by 13 percent (this pronunciation is more common in British English). Some Panelists admit to being so vexed by the problem that they tend to avoid the word in conversation. Speakers can perhaps take comfort in knowing that any one of the last three pronunciations will have the support of a substantial minority and that none of them is incorrect. When several pronunciations of a word are widely used by educated speakers, there is really no right or wrong one.

barbarism / barbarity

Although these words are often used interchangeably, some writers prefer to maintain a distinction between them. Both words denote some absence of civilization, but the word *civilization* itself has several different senses, one the opposite of *barbarism* in this scheme, and the other the opposite of *barbarity.* In one use, *civilization* refers to the scientific, artistic, and cultural attainments of developed societies, and it is this sense that figures in the meaning of *barbarism.* Originally, *barbarism* was limited in meaning to the incorrect or nonstandard use of language, but it came to refer to ignorance or crudity as well:

> He is to resist the vulgar prosperity that retrogrades ever to barbarism, by preserving and communicating heroic sentiments, noble biographies, melodious verse, and the conclusions of history (Ralph Waldo Emerson, "The American Scholar")

> I hated talk of books. It embarrassed me when Buddy, who boasted of his barbarism, mentioned books in his unconvincing voice (Paul Theroux, *Hotel Honolulu*)

Civilization can also refer to the basic social order that allows people to resolve their differences peaceably, and it is this sense—that is, civilization as opposed to savagery—that figures frequently in the meaning of *barbarity,* which refers to savage brutality or cruelty in actions:

> Already the defenceless citizens had suffered through the barbarity of the Janissaries; and, in time of storm, tumult and massacre, beauty, infancy and decrepitude, would have alike been sacrificed to the brutal ferocity of the soldiers (Mary Wollstonecraft Shelley, *The Last Man*)

> A malcontent and sometime scoundrel, Mugezi has learned to manipulate and dissemble in the course of surviving a Dickensian childhood of alarming violence and barbarity (Michiko Kakutani, "Growing Up Tough in a Lawless Land," *New York Times Book Review*)

While this distinction has its merits, it is not followed by many able writers, and one should not presume that the reader will appreciate these differences in meaning without the aid of clarifying context.

barbiturate

When this class of drugs was introduced in the early part of this century, *barbiturate* had its main stress on the second-to-last syllable, a pronunciation that is still used (though rather infrequently) in the medical profession. As the word passed into the general vocabulary, the stress shifted to the third-to-last syllable, bringing the stress pattern more in line with words like *acculturate, accurate,* and *saturate.* Either pronunciation is considered correct now. Since at least the 1960s the pronunciation (bär-bĭch′ə-wĭt), without the second *r*, has been considered nonstandard despite the fact that it is quite common. In our 1997 survey, 62 percent of the Usage Panel still disapproved of this pronunciation, while 38 percent approved of it, suggesting that the usage is becoming less stigmatized. One reason for this may be that the pronunciation without the second *r* is simply easier to say, since the combination (-ər-ĭt) occurs relatively infrequently in English. In addition, the presence of the first *r* may influence the dropping out of the second *r* by the phonological process of dissimilation.

barely

See **hardly** and **scarcely**.

bar mitzvah / bat mitzvah / bas mitzvah

These terms describe both the coming of age of a Jewish child (thirteen years for a boy and either twelve or thirteen years for a girl) and the religious ceremony accompanying it, which can occur at this or any later age. *Bar mitzvah* means "son of the commandments" in Hebrew and indicates that a boy is considered to be an adult in terms of his religious responsibilities in the Jewish community. Similarly, *bat mitzvah* means "daughter of the commandments." *Bas mitzvah* is a Hebrew variant of *bat mitzvah*.

base form

A base form of a word is the form to which affixes or other base forms can be added to make new words, as *mystify* in *mystifying*, *build* in *rebuild*, and *cat* in *catnip*.
See more at **compound words**.

bated / baited

The phrase *bated breath* comes from the verb *bate*, meaning "to lessen or restrain," as in *"To his dying day he bated his breath a little when he told the story"* (George Eliot, *Adam Bede*). Thus the phrase *bated breath* means "with the breath restrained," that is, restrained from excitement or suspense. The verb *bate* is related to the word *abate* but has fallen into disuse. As a result, some people use the spelling *baited breath*, which (despite its greater familiarity) is widely regarded as incorrect.

bat mitzvah

See **bar mitzvah**.

bawl out / ball out

Because the words *bawl* and *ball* sound alike, the informal expression *bawl out*, "to reprimand loudly or harshly," is sometimes misspelled *ball out* in such sentences as *I was balled out* [properly *bawled out*] *by my parents for getting home late.* Some speakers may even associate being *bawled out* with the mental image of being pelted with words like balls. Or perhaps the phrase *bawling one's eyes out* has been associated with the word *eyeball.* In any case, writers should be aware of this frequent error in order to avoid being *bawled out* themselves by readers with a sharp eye for spelling mistakes.

bayou

The last syllable of *bayou* is usually pronounced like the word *you.* There is a variant pronunciation with a long *o* (as in *toe*), a pronunciation that was acceptable to 40 percent of the Usage Panel in the 2002 survey.

BC   See **AD.**

BCE   See **AD.**

because

***because* beginning a sentence**   *"Because I could not stop for Death, / He kindly stopped for me;"* So begins one of Emily Dickinson's most well-known poems, and so falls another of the more arbitrary rules of usage, which states that a sentence should never begin with *because.* As Dickinson's poem attests, there are occasions when *because* is perfectly appropriate as the opening word of a sentence. In fact, sentences beginning with *because* are quite common in written English, as this sequence of recent citations attests:

> He shifts uncomfortably in his leather jacket. Because she is sitting close to him, and because it is a little too warm to be wearing leather, she can smell, in small gusts, a shadowy scent of the animal the garment was fashioned from (Carol Anshaw, *Seven Moves*)

> Because he was a prodigy, he was somewhat isolated within his own generation (Frank Conroy, *Dogs Bark, but the Caravan Rolls On*)

> Because *C. elegans* lives only nine days, it is also an ideal animal in which to study aging; researchers can find out fast whether something has altered its life span (Denise Grady, "A Worm's Life: Right Mutation Makes It Long But Very Dull," *New York Times*)

The ban against beginning sentences with *because* may have received some support because sentence fragments that answer explicit or implicit questions are often begun in this way, as in George Leigh Mallory's famous response *"Because it is there"* to the question *"Why climb Mt. Everest?"* This use of *because* violates the standard rule on complete sentences, but it can have a dramatic effect in some contexts.

***because* in clauses that are the subject**   A related rule states that a clause beginning with *because* should not be used as the subject of a sentence, as in *Just because he* *thinks it's a good idea doesn't mean it's a good idea.* This construction is perfectly acceptable, but it carries a colloquial flavor and may best be saved for informal situations.

***because* after negated verbs**   When *because* follows a negated verb phrase, it must be preceded by a comma when the *because* clause explains why the event did not occur. *They didn't want her on the committee, because she was so outspoken* means roughly "Her outspokenness was their reason for not wanting her on the committee." When there is no comma, the *because* clause is included in what is being negated. Thus *They didn't want her on the committee because she was so outspoken* implies that they may in fact have wanted her on the committee but for some reason other than her outspokenness.

See more at **reason is because.**

beg the question

The expression *beg the question* refers to a logical fallacy known in Latin as *petitio principii,* which translates roughly as "seeking the beginning." The term is applied to situations in which the writer assumes to be true the very thing that he or she has set out to prove. Many contentious political arguments succumb to this fallacy in their use of inflammatory words, which often betray an unstated assumption about what is being argued. But writing in neutral terms can also beg the question. If an editorial argues that same-sex marriage is wrong because marriage is a bond between a man and a woman, the editorial assumes that marriage can only be between a man and a woman—the very notion that same-sex marriage calls into question. The editorial thus begs the question.

Such is the traditional or strict use of the term. Trouble arises, however, because the "question" or assumption is usually left unstated in the statements it describes, and consequently *beg the question* often means "to evade or ignore the question." And since the point of claiming that something begs the question is to make explicit what has been assumed to be true, the expression is also used to mean simply "to raise the question." These looser meanings have long been condemned by usage commentators as incorrect or sloppy.

But sorting out exactly what is meant by *beg the question* is not always easy, especially in constructions such as *beg the question of whether* and *beg the question of how,* where the door is opened to more than one question. Consider the sentence *The proposal to increase funding for agricultural subsidies begs the question of whether these programs were successful in the first place.* If you interpret this to mean that the proposal assumes that the programs were successful, when that is precisely what needs to be established, then *beg the question* is used properly to refer to the logical fallacy. But we can easily substitute *evade the question* or even *raise the question,* and the sentence will be perfectly clear, even though it will violate the traditional usage rule.

Not surprisingly, the Usage Panel has responded differently to almost every example containing this construction, and approval has never been overwhelming for its use. The sentence given above, in which the proposal to increase funding clearly assumes the success of the programs, was acceptable to 71 percent of the Panel in our

1999 survey. A similar example in which what is assumed is not clear, and in which *evade the question* works well as a substitute, garnered approval of only 47 percent of the Panel: *The article begs the question of whether we should build a new school or reno-vate the old one.* A similar example in our 2001 survey was accepted by 45 percent. Yet in the same survey an example that would seem to refer clearly to the logical fallacy could muster only 60 percent acceptability: *I'm poised on the brink of turning fifty, and I refuse to let the occasion pass unnoticed—though that begs the question of whether turning fifty is an occasion.*

The moral of this story is that no matter how you use this expression, its ambi-guity will likely turn off a sizeable percentage of your audience. It is probably better to avoid the phrase entirely.

behalf   See **in behalf of.**

berry   See **fruit.**

besides   See **together.**

better / best

A traditional rule of grammar states that the comparative degree should only be used when comparing two things. Thus it is correct to say *She is the older* [not *the oldest*] *of the two cousins.* By the same token, *better* should be used in similar comparisons: *Which house of Congress has the better* [not *best*] *attendance record?* Native speakers will recognize the natural sound of *best* in this sentence (and of *oldest* in the previous example) and will conclude that this traditional rule is often ignored in practice. In fact, many celebrated writers have used *oldest, best,* and other superlatives to compare two things. But the traditional rule still dominates in publishing as the norm.

Keep in mind, however, that there are certain fixed expressions, such as *Put your best foot forward* and *May the best team win!,* where *best* is required.

See more at **had better.**

between

between* and *among   When exactly two entities are specified, the word *between* should be used, as in *The choice between* [not *among*] *good and evil* and *the rivalry between* [not *among*] *Great Britain and France.* But when more than two entities are involved or when the number of entities is unspecified, the word choice depends on the intended meaning. *Between* is used when the entities are considered as distinct individuals, while *among* is used when they are considered collectively or as a mass. Thus in the sentence *The balloon landed between the houses,* the houses are seen as points that define the boundaries of the area where the balloon touched down. We assume, therefore, that the balloon did not land on any of the individual houses. In *The balloon landed among the houses,* the area of landing is considered to be the general location of the houses, taken together. It leaves open the possibility that the balloon came down on one of the houses. By the same token, we may speak of *a series of wars between the Greek cities,* which suggests that each city was an independent participant in the hostilities, or of *a series of wars among the Greek cities,* which allows for the possibility that the participants were shifting alliances of cities. For this reason, *among* is used to indicate inclusion in a group: *She is among the best of our young sculptors. There is a spy among you.* Use *between* when the entities are seen as determining the limits or endpoints of a range: *They searched the area between the river, the farmhouse, and the woods. The truck driver had obviously been drinking between stops.*

between you and I   This oft-maligned phrase is discussed as one of the case problems of pronouns at **pronouns, personal.**

betwixt   See **amid.**

beyond the pale / beyond the pail

A good way to remember the proper spelling of an expression is to know its origin, and in the case of *beyond the pale,* pails and buckets are not part of the story. The word *pale,* related to the word *pole,* refers to a pointed stake or picket. Such stakes are commonly used to fence in or simply mark the boundaries of pieces of land. As early as the 1300s, the word *pale* came to be used for the boundary itself; by 1400 it was applied to the land inside the boundary. In the 1500s, it developed into a proper noun. People within *the English Pale* or *the Pale* were subject to English jurisdiction and protection; lands beyond the Pale were considered by the English to be hostile and dangerous. *Beyond the pale* eventually came to mean "outside of the limits of acceptability." Note that the word *pale* is not capitalized when the expression is used in this way.

biceps / triceps / quadriceps

The large muscle of the upper arm often flexed to show off its size is properly called the *biceps* in English. This term is short for the Latin medical names of the muscle, *biceps brachii,* literally "the two-headed (muscle) of the arm," and *biceps flexor cubiti,* "the two-headed bender of the elbow." The muscle is called the *biceps,* or "two-headed" in Latin, because at the end nearer the shoulder it divides into two strands, one of which runs along the humerus to attach to the scapula while the other attaches to the scapula directly at a different point. Similarly, the *triceps* of the arm is the three-headed muscle of the arm, and the *quadriceps* is the four-headed muscle of the leg.

The correct Latin plurals of these words are *bicipites, tricipites,* and *quadricipites,* but these seem to be used extremely rarely, if at all, in English—even in medical discussions. Instead, most speakers seem to prefer the plurals *biceps, triceps,* and *quad-*

riceps, whose forms are exactly the same as the singular. *Series* is an example of another noun ending in *-s* whose singular and plural are similarly identical. The alternative plurals *bicepses, tricepses,* and *quadricepses* are rare and should be avoided, though they are not, strictly speaking, mistakes.

Since the singular nouns *biceps, triceps,* and *quadriceps* sound similar to plural nouns with their ending *-s* and perhaps also because the plural forms like *biceps* were coming into use, at some time in the past English speakers began to form the singulars *bicep, tricep,* and *quadricep.* Such new singulars have been created many times in the history of English. In Middle English, the singular of the word for "pea" was *pease,* but speakers took this as a plural and made a new singular, *pea.* The old singular survives in the rhyme beginning *pease porridge hot . . . ,* where *pease porridge* just means "pea porridge."

If any conclusion can be drawn from history of other words in English, the singular nouns *bicep, tricep,* and *quadricep* will probably muscle out the competition and eventually become standard. For now, however, writers are advised to choose the singular forms *biceps, triceps,* and *quadriceps* in more formal and general writing and to reserve the forms without *-s* for informal writing or attempts to reproduce popular speech. In the plural, the forms *biceps, triceps,* and *quadriceps* are now standard.

bimonthly / biweekly / semimonthly / semiweekly

The prefix *bi–,* when modifying an adverb of time, means that the time interval should be doubled. Thus a *bimonthly* meeting takes place once every two months, and a *biweekly* meeting once every two weeks. The prefix *semi–,* in the same context, means that the interval of time should be halved. Thus, a *semimonthly* meeting is held twice a month (that is, every half month), and a *semiweekly* meeting twice a week. Words with the prefix *bi–* and *semi–*are often confused, so expressions such as *every two months* or *twice a month* are often preferable in order to avoid misinterpretation.

bio–

The word element *bio–* comes from Greek *bios,* meaning "life." *Biography,* for example, is a borrowing of Greek *biographia,* literally "life-writing, writing about the life (of a person)." When used to form words in English, *bio–* most often refers to living organisms in general or to *biology,* the science of living organisms. Many of the words that begin with *bio–* (such as *bioethics* and *biotechnology*) are relatively young, arising in the 20th century. When *bio–* is added to another element beginning with *o,* it often becomes *bi–.* For example, the word *biome,* "one of the major regional types of ecological communities, such as a grassland or a coral reef," is formed from *bio–* and the element *–ome,* meaning "a mass." In *biopsy,* "the examination of a sample of living tissue," *bio–* has been added to the element *–opsy,* also seen in *autopsy.*

See also **zoo–**.

bipolar / manic-depressive

The terms *bipolar* and *bipolar disorder* are relatively recent additions to the popular lexicon, which has more typically referred to this mood disorder as *manic-depressive illness* or *manic depression.* These terms all describe a psychiatric illness, of which there are several types, characterized by recurrent depression alternating with states of persistently elevated or irritable mood (mania).

The medical profession, however, no longer uses *manic-depressive,* which is completely absent from the *Diagnostic and Statistical Manual of Mental Disorders, Fourth Edition,* a comprehensive reference published by the American Psychiatric Association in 1994. Likewise, the National Depressive and Manic Depressive Association recently changed its name to the Depression and Bipolar Support Alliance. While the terms *manic-depressive* and *manic depression* still commonly appear in print, *bipolar* and *bipolar disorder* should be the preferred terms in formal writing and speaking.

bit See **lot.**

bit / byte

The word *bit* is short for *binary digit.* A bit consists of one of two values, usually 0 or 1. Computers use bits because their system of counting is based on two options: switches on a microchip that are either on or off. Thus, a computer counts to seven in bits as follows: 0, 1, 10 [2], 11 [3], 100 [4], 101 [5], 110 [6], 111 [7]. Notice that the higher the count, the more adjacent bits are needed to represent the number. For example, it requires two adjacent bits to count from zero to three, and it takes three adjacent bits to count from zero to seven. A sequence of bits can represent not just numbers but other kinds of data, such as the letters and symbols on a keyboard. The sequence of 0s and 1s that make up data are usually counted in groups of eight, and these groups of eight bits are called *bytes.* The word *byte* is short for *binary digit eight.* To transmit one keystroke on a typical keyboard requires one byte of information (or eight bits). To transmit a three-letter word requires three bytes of information (or twenty-four bits).

biweekly See **bimonthly.**

black

The Oxford English Dictionary contains evidence of the use of *black* with reference to African peoples as early as 1400. However, it was not until the late 1960s, with the advent of the Black Power movement, that *black* (or *Black*) gained its present status as a self-chosen ethnonym with strong connotations of racial pride, replacing *Negro* and *colored* among Blacks and non-Blacks alike with remarkable speed. Equally significant is the degree to which *Negro* and *colored*—the common terms used as late as the civil rights movement of the 1950s and 1960s—became dated and even discredited in the process, reflecting the profound changes taking place in the Black community during those decades.

The more recent success of *African American* offers an interesting contrast in this regard. Though by no means a modern coinage, *African American* achieved sudden prominence at the end of the 1980s when a number of Black leaders championed it as an alternative ethnonym for Americans of African descent. The appeal of this term is obvious, alluding as it does not to skin color but to an ethnicity constructed of geography, history, and culture, and again it won rapid acceptance in the media, joining similar forms such as *Asian American, Hispanic American,* and *Native American.* But unlike what happened a generation earlier, *African American* has shown little sign of displacing or discrediting *Black,* which remains both popular and positive. The difference may be that the campaign for *African American* came at a time of relative social and political stability rather than in the midst of a movement that sought to alter the political landscape both inside and outside the Black community. In these circumstances, there was little pressure to reject or stigmatize the familiar label even as the newer term gained favor.

capitalization of *black*   *Black* is sometimes capitalized in its racial or ethnic sense, especially in the African-American press, though the lowercase form is still widely used by authors of all backgrounds. The capitalization of *Black* does pose a problem for the treatment of *white.* Stylistic consistency would call for *White* wherever *Black* is used, and in fact that is often how it is styled in the African-American press. But there has been no concerted campaign among most white Americans for a wider use of this spelling; more importantly, uppercase *White* is often associated with the writings and ideology of white supremacists, a sufficient reason for many other whites to feel uncomfortable with it. Still, the use of *white* in the same context as *Black* will obviously raise questions as to how and why the writer has distinguished between the two groups. There is no entirely happy solution to this problem. In all likelihood, a reluctance to capitalize *white* has dissuaded many publications from adopting a capitalized *Black.*

Black English

In the United States, the term *Black English* usually refers to the everyday spoken varieties of English used by African Americans, especially of the working class in urban neighborhoods or rural communities. Linguists generally prefer the term *African American Vernacular English.* It is an error to suppose that Black English is spoken by all African Americans regardless of their background. In fact, the English spoken by African Americans is highly varied—as varied as the English spoken by any other racial or ethnic group.

Sometimes *Black English* is used to refer to other varieties of English spoken by Black people outside of the United States, as in the Caribbean and the United Kingdom.

blackguard

This rather old-fashioned and now chiefly literary word dates back to the 16th century when it was spelled and most likely pronounced as two distinct words and probably referred literally to a guard of soldiers or perhaps some kind of attendants. By the 18th century the two words had become a hyphenated or a solid compound with the meaning "scoundrel." As the two parts of the compound lost their separate meanings, so they eventually lost their separate pronunciations. *Blackguard* is pronounced (blăg′əd) in British English and (blăg′ərd) or (blăg′ärd′) in American English.

blatant / flagrant

Blatant and *flagrant* have overlapping meanings and are often confused. Both words attribute conspicuousness and offensiveness to certain acts, but the words differ in emphasis. *Blatant means* "offensively conspicuous," and thus emphasizes the actor's failure to conceal the act. *Flagrant,* on the other hand, means "conspicuously offensive," and emphasizes the serious wrongdoing inherent in the offense. Thus many actions, from an infraction of the rules in a football game to a violation of human rights, may be *blatant* or *flagrant,* depending on what is being emphasized. If the act is committed with contempt for public scrutiny, it is *blatant.* If the act seems extreme in its violation of norms, it is *flagrant.*

 Blatant and (to a much lesser extent) *flagrant* are sometimes used as synonyms of *obvious,* in contexts where there is no immediate connection to human behavior, as in *What surprised us was that they went ahead with the idea in spite of the blatant danger of the approach.* This usage has traditionally been considered an error, and it is not surprising, therefore, that a large percentage of the Usage Panel dislikes it. In our 2004 survey, only 42 percent accepted the sentence just listed.

 A collocation like *blatantly obvious* is thus open to criticism as a redundancy. This expression will in all likelihood convey exaggerated emphasis, indicating strong displeasure or in some cases derision.

 Blatant is still used occasionally in its older sense, "loud, noisy," but this meaning is being drowned out by the more visual meanings cited above and is likely to fade from the language altogether.

blind

There is no reason to avoid the word *blind* in referring to a person who cannot see at all or who has little or no functional vision. As with *deaf*—but unlike *crippled*—the substitution of a euphemistic expression for *blind* could itself be objectionable if perceived as implying that blindness is too unfortunate a condition to be stated in plain language. In particular, a person with no functional vision is preferably called *blind,* not *visually impaired,* the latter term being appropriate only in referring to persons with less severe visual limitations. When referring to persons with a range of vision problems that includes sightlessness as well as low vision, the appropriate term is *blind and visually impaired.*

Advocates for people with disabilities often advise "putting the person before the disability," which in the case of blindness would mandate saying *a person who is blind* instead of *a blind person,* and *people who are blind* instead of *blind people* or *the blind.* However, the awkwardness of phrases formed on this model may simply call attention to them, making them sound euphemistic rather than respectful; it should be noted that most organizations serving the interests of blind people, such as the American Council of the Blind, the American Foundation for the Blind, and the National Federation of the Blind, have neither changed their names nor come out in favor of this usage.

See more at **disabled** and **impaired.**

blond / blonde / brunet / brunette

Terms for hair color that have come into English from French, such as the word pairs *blond/blonde* and *brunet/brunette,* are often treated in English as they are in French: the gender-marked form of the adjective or noun, ending in *-e* or *-te,* is used when referring to a female, and the form without the ending is used when referring to a male.

But practice is mixed in English, and the words *blond* and *brunet* are also used to refer to members of either sex. The discrepancy in usage between forms like *blond/blonde* that have tended to be gender-marked in English and other French borrowings that have not (such as *entrepreneur* and *gourmand*) suggests to some people a sexist stereotype, namely that women should be defined by their physical characteristics, while men should be defined by their social roles. For this reason, some writers avoid the feminine forms of these hair-color words.

The use of *blonde* and *brunette* as nouns is also controversial, chiefly for two reasons. First, these words invariably refer to females and never to males. A sentence like *That blonde is getting up from her seat* is fairly common, but the counterpart usage applied to a man, as in *That blond is getting up from his seat,* is so rare as to sound comical. Second, the noun use reduces an individual to the attribute of hair color, as does the adjectival use applied to individuals (as in *the blonde woman*). Since men are not normally described in such terms, it is best to avoid these nouns and to restrict the adjective to modify the word *hair: The woman* [or *man*] *with blond hair got up and walked away.*

See more at **feminine suffixes.**

boast

Some have objected to the use of *boast* as a transitive verb meaning "to possess or own a desirable feature," as in *This network boasts an audience with a greater concentration of professionals and managers than any other network.* This usage is well established, however. In our 1988 survey, 62 percent of the Usage Panel found it acceptable.

boatswain

Usually pronounced (bō′sən), this word, like *blackguard*, has a pronunciation that is not easily predictable from the spelling. But whereas *blackguard* is never pronounced as two words, *boatswain* is often pronounced (bōt′swān′)—by landlubbers, of course—and that is not considered incorrect. The variant spellings *bosun, bo's'n*, and *bos'n*, reflecting the sailors' pronunciation, have been around for well over a hundred years. Other nautical words with tricky pronunciations include *bowline, forecastle, gunwale, mainsail,* and *topgallant,* to name just a few.

See more at **pronunciation spelling** and **spelling pronunciation**.

boogeyman

We are all frightened by this mysterious character, but we cannot seem to agree on what to call him. His aliases include *bogeyman, bogyman, boogeyman, boogyman, boogieman,* and also *boogerman, boogarman,* and *buggerman.* The original word was probably *bogey* or *bogy* with the other forms springing up as pronunciation spellings. Pronunciation options include (bō′gē), (bōō′gē), (bŏŏg′ē), or (bŏŏg′ər), (bōō′gər), or even (bŭg′ər). According to the *Dictionary of American Regional English,* the form *boogerman* prevails in the South, and *boogeyman* everywhere else in the United States.

bored with / bored of

The word *bored* is usually used with the preposition *with,* as in *I was bored with my life so I decided to make a fresh start elsewhere.* Occasionally, *bored* is accompanied by the preposition *of,* as in *I was bored of that game.* This use of the word *of,* rather than *with,* has become increasingly frequent in recent years, and some have objected to this development, insisting that only *bored with,* not *bored of,* is correct. Writers are therefore advised to use only *bored with* in order to avoid criticism. Of course, the preposition *by* is also correct, as in *The student, bored by the long explanations, wandered to another part of the museum.* The replacement of *with* by *of* in *bored of* is perhaps the result of influence from the similar expression *tired of.*

born / borne

These words are both past participles of the verb *bear.* By convention in Standard English they have separate uses. *Born* is used only in passive constructions referring to birth: *I was born in Chicago.* All other uses, including active constructions referring to birth, have the spelling *borne: She has borne both her children at home. I have borne his insolence with the patience of a saint.*

both

the meaning of *both*   *Both* indicates that the action or state denoted by the verb applies individually to each of two entities. *Both books weigh more than five pounds,* for example, means that each book weighs more than five pounds by itself, not that the two books weighed together come to more than five pounds. *Both* is inappropriate where the verb does not apply to each of the entities by itself.

Similarly, when used with *and, both* reinforces the conjunctive power of *and.* Thus, *Both Jack and Jill fell down the hill* emphasizes that it was the two of them that fell. But because of its application to each of two, *both* can cause a subtle distinction in meaning in these coordinate constructions. *Jack and Jill are getting divorced* suggests that they as a unit are getting divorced; that is, they are divorcing each other. *Both Jack and Jill are getting divorced* suggests that they are each individually getting divorced from their current spouses and that they could then get married.

possessive of *both*   In possessive constructions, *of both* is usually preferred in standard usage: *the mothers of both* (rather than *both their mothers*); *the fault of both* (rather than *both their fault* or *both's fault*). Nonetheless, constructions along the pattern of *both your,* as in "*A plague on both your houses*" (*Romeo and Juliet*) are idiomatic and should not be considered suspect.

redundancy of *both*   The use of *both* with other kinds of emphatic coordinators like *together with* and *as well as* tends to overemphasize the coordination and could be considered redundant: *Both Jack as well as Jill fell down the hill.* Note that *together with* and *as well as* function as prepositions, not conjunctions.

Strictly speaking, verbs such as *agree* and *resemble* also render *both* superfluous in its use as a pronoun and adjective: *Both researchers agree on this point. Kevin and Conor both resemble their mother.* The adjective *same* has the same effect. The sentence *They both have the same teacher* is no different in meaning from *They have the same teacher.* But sometimes the mysterious effect of rhythm and emphasis counts for more than frugality in the use of words. If *both* sounds better in such constructions, go ahead and use it.

See more at **both . . . and.**

both . . . and

When *both . . . and* link parallel elements, the words or phrases that follow them should correspond grammatically at the same level. That is, whatever grammatical construction follows *both,* the same construction should also follow *and.* Thus it should be *Sales have risen in both India and China* or *Sales have risen both in India and in China,* but not *Sales have risen both in India and China.*

See more at **parallelism.**

bouquet

When used to refer to a bunch of flowers, this 18th-century borrowing from French may be pronounced (bō-kā′) or (bōō-kā′) in American English. When used to refer to an aroma, as of wine, this word is usually pronounced (bōō-kā′).

bowline

This nautical word is traditionally pronounced (bō′lĭn), but the pronunciation (bō′līn′) is also correct.

See more at **spelling pronunciation.**

BP

Most writings dealing with the recent past employ the system of dating using the terms AD and BC or the system using CE and BCE. But another system is frequently encountered in archaeological or paleontological writings, especially those dealing with longer lengths of time, such as those over which the evolution of species or the development of agriculture occurred. The letters BP, standing for *before present,* are put after the number of years. This abbreviation is also sometimes written with periods, as B.P., especially in scholarly journals. The present is assumed to be the year 1950 CE by convention. In the science of paleontology, the abbreviation BP can be used as illustrated by the following sentence: *The Triassic Period began around 245 million years* BP.

Dates nearer the present, such as those reported in publications dealing with human prehistory, are often determined by the use of radiocarbon dating. This method can by applied to find the age of materials that were once alive, such as wood or bone, since living things incorporate small amounts of carbon 14 in their bodies while alive but cease doing so at death. Carbon 14 is radioactive and the amount present in a material will decrease regularly over time. By measuring the amount of carbon 14 in the dead material and comparing it with the amount normally present in living tissue, the length of time since death can be determined. However, the amount of carbon 14 that is available in the environment for absorption by living things has fluctuated over the centuries. In addition, after radiocarbon dating came into wide use, scientists discovered that carbon 14 took longer to decay·than was previously thought. The dating of materials must be adjusted, or *calibrated,* to account for these fluctuations and this new knowledge. Therefore archaeologists often indicate whether a date given in terms of BP is calibrated or not and how it was calibrated. Often, the abbreviation BP is reserved for uncalibrated dates and BCE is used to indicate calibrated dates. However, a variety of notations are used in the field of archaeology to indicate dates. Writers should make certain they understand how archaeologists have arrived at a date given in terms of BP or BCE before reporting the date in their own writing.

See more at **AD.**

brackets

1. Brackets enclose editorial clarifications or explanations by someone other than the original writer.

    On these two commandments hang [are based] all the Law and the Prophets.
    And summer's lease [allotted time] hath all too short a date [duration].
    Morgan then asserted that [Riley] had been mistaken.

2. Brackets indicate the correction of an error in quoted material.

    On the fourth [fifth] of January, Chuck Rogers took office.

3. The Latin word *sic* (meaning "thus" or "so") in brackets indicates a misspelling or a nonstandard usage in the original source.

    In a small-claims action, the defendent [*sic*] receives notice by certified mail.

4. Brackets enclose material inserted within text that is already in parentheses.

    (Washington [DC], January, 1983)

breeches

The noun meaning "trousers" rhymes with *itches,* and may be spelled *britches.*

brief respite

This expression is generally redundant, since *respites* are by definition brief. But the expression has become so common in everyday speech that it is tempting to use it in formal writing. Nonetheless, it is best to avoid this redundancy, unless respites of different lengths are being compared.

bring

bring* and *take   The difference between *bring* and *take* is one of perspective. *Bring* indicates motion toward the place from which the action is regarded—typically toward the speaker—while *take* indicates motion away from the place from which the action is regarded—typically away from the speaker. Thus from a customer's perspective, the customer *takes* checks to the bank and *brings* home cash, while from the banker's perspective the customer *brings* checks to the bank in order to *take* away cash.

When the point of reference is not the place of speaking itself, either verb is possible, but the correct choice still depends on the desired perspective. For example, *The labor leaders brought their requests to the mayor's office* suggests a point of view centered around the mayor's office, while *The labor leaders took their requests to the mayor's office* suggests a point of view centered around the labor leaders. Be aware that the choice of *bring* or *take* determines the point of view emphasized. For example, a parent sitting at home may say of a child, *She always takes a pile of books home with her from school,* describing the situation from the child's viewpoint leaving school. If the viewpoint shifts to the speaker, *bring* becomes appropriate, as in *Look, I see her coming right now, and she's bringing a whole armful of books!*

brung The form *brung* is common in colloquial use in many areas, even among educated speakers, but it is not standard in formal writing.

brooch

This word, also spelled *broach,* is pronounced (brōch), and less often (broōch).

brown

As a description of skin color, *brown* stands apart from *white, black, red,* and *yellow* in that it is not strongly associated with any specific racial group. In certain contexts it denotes a relatively light skin color in a person of mixed white and black ancestry. In other contexts it is simply used to mean *nonwhite* or *non-European.* While *brown* is often used with positive connotations, it can also sound condescending or offensive when used by whites. Where race or skin color is relevant to a discussion, the term *people of color* is generally preferable to either *nonwhite* or *brown-skinned peoples* in referring to peoples of other than European origin.
　　See more at **person of color.**

brunet / brunette   See **blond.**

bug / insect

The word *bug* is often used to refer to any *insect,* and sometimes to spiders and crustaceans (such as the pill bug), none of which are insects. But in strict biological usage, a *bug* (or *true bug*) is an insect that has mouthparts that are adapted for piercing and sucking and that are contained in a beak-shaped structure called a *rostrum.* Thus, aphids, leaf bugs, and stinkbugs are classified as true bugs.
　　Originally, a *bug* referred to a hobgoblin or scarecrow, but by the 1600s the word was used popularly to describe any of various insects or similar organisms, such as the centipede. The word *insect* derives from the Latin *insectum,* a translation of the Greek *entomon,* "segmented, cut up," which is the source of our word *entomology,* "the study of insects." All insects, including bugs, have six legs and a body divided into three sections—head, thorax, and abdomen. Spiders, on the other hand, belong to a group called arachnids and are characterized by having eight legs and two body sections—a cephalothorax consisting of a combined head and thorax and an abdomen.
　　See more at **pill bug.**

bulimia

The older pronunciations (bōō-lĭm′ē-ə) and (byōō-lĭm′ē-ə) are fading from use, though they are still sometimes used by medical professionals. The word is now more commonly pronounced (bōō-lē′mē-ə) or (byōō-lē′mē-ə).

buoy

Traditionally and in Britain this word is pronounced like *boy* (boi). In the United States the more common pronunciation seems to be (bōō′ē), except in the compound *life buoy*, where (boi) is entrenched. The pronunciation (bwoi), which is also traditional, is now rarely heard in either Britain or the US.

burgeon

Some usage critics in the 1960s denounced the figurative use of *burgeon* as a needless, fancy neologism, even though it was at least thirty years old at the time. The word, which originally meant and still means "to put forth buds," has seen widespread use in recent years in a remarkable variety of contexts, in which it means "to grow rapidly and become established." The word is used most frequently as the participial adjective *burgeoning*, though use of the verb is not uncommon. Interestingly, the figurative uses far outstrip the plant-bud use, and because the word is used in both positive and negative contexts, the associations with foliage and blossoms are sometimes quite remote. Here is a brief sampler of positive uses:

> Below the level of the family, the Cambrian explosion produced relatively few species, whereas in the post-Permian a tremendous species diversity burgeoned (Richard Dawkins, *A Devil's Chaplain*)

> Maggie saw the tenderness of this life, how it had burgeoned and made room for itself. All at once the canyon seemed to arrange itself around the baby's body, not exactly to protect it but to celebrate it (Kate Wheeler, *Not Where I Started From*)

> But a new study of parental leave laws in Europe and Canada, which burgeoned in the 1970s, suggests that they may actually boost employment and total economic output (Jonathan Marshall, "Leave Act May Benefit Everyone," *San Francisco Chronicle*)

And now some negative uses:

> Petulant pundit Bill Ballenger is fed up with people who won't pay attention to his miracle fix for Michigan's burgeoning budget crisis (Daniel Howes, "Pundit's Idea to Wipe Out State Deficit May Simply Go Up in Smoke," *Detroit News*)

> Generalists in Congress usually deferred to an individual committee's expertise, particularly as policy grew more complex. The proliferation of specialized subcommittees attested to the burgeoning workload and explosion of technical data (Paul C. Milazzo, "The Environment," in Julian Zelizer, ed., *The American Congress: The Building of Democracy*)

Her cold, which had been growing worse for weeks, burgeoned into full-scale flu
(Anita Desai, *Diamond Dust*)

The Usage Panel has seen the value of these uses. In our 1969 survey, only 51 percent accepted the phrase *the burgeoning population of Queens;* twenty years later 74 percent accepted the same phrase. The Panel was less reluctant to accept the figurative use of the verb in 1988, when only 29 percent accepted the sentence *News programs are less expensive to produce than entertainment series, and the public's appetite for them has burgeoned.* But this use is so widespread now that it must be considered standard.

burnt

Burnt is both a past tense (*I burnt my finger on the iron*) and a past participle (*I have burnt my finger on the iron*) of the verb *burn,* varying with the regular form *burned.* Both as a simple past tense and as a past participle used in perfect and passive constructions, *burnt* is more common in British English, but it is acceptable as a past tense in American English as well: *I burnt the tracks onto the CD.* When functioning as an adjective, however, the past participle *burnt* is common in American English: *the smell of burnt rubber.* In some phrases, such as *burnt toast* or *burnt-sugar cake,* the participle *burnt* is idiomatic, and the form *burned* is less frequent. As in all instances where two slightly different grammatical forms are in free variation, writers should take care to use only one form throughout a given piece of writing, unless a specific form is required by an idiomatic expression like *burnt toast.*

but

***but* beginning a sentence**   Traditional usage lore enjoins writers not to begin a sentence with a coordinating conjunction like *and* or *but.* The idea is that these sentences express "incomplete" thoughts. But a glance at any newspaper or magazine today will show that the practice of beginning a sentence with *but* has become common in the writing of most writers and must be considered standard. The practice is rhetorically effective, since starting a new sentence heightens the contrast already signaled by *but,* as Steven Weinberg shows in his essay "The Truth About Missile Defense":

If it were possible tomorrow to switch on a missile defense system that would make the United States invulnerable to any missile attack, then I and most other opponents of missile defense would be all for it. But that is not the choice we face.

This usefulness is evident in narrative writing too, as in E.M. Forster's short story "The Eternal Moment":

Now, with her scanty hair in curl-papers, and the snuff-coloured shawl spread over her, she entertained the distinguished authoress with accounts of other distinguished people who had stopped, and might again stop, at the *Biscione.* At first her tone was dignified. But before long she proceeded to village news, and a certain bitterness began to show itself.

but not followed by a comma   *But* is generally not followed by a comma. Correct written style requires *Kim wanted to go, but we stayed,* not *Kim wanted to go, but, we stayed.*

but ... _however_ ...   Too much contrast can ruin a photograph, and it can ruin a sentence as well. The contrastive conjunction *but* is redundant when used with *however.* It is hard to justify a sentence such as *But the management, however, went on with its plans.* Use one word or the other, but not both.

    See more at **and, cannot, however, pronouns, personal,** and **other.**

by virtue of   See **in virtue of.**

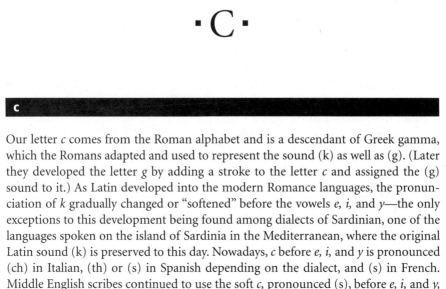

· C ·

c

Our letter *c* comes from the Roman alphabet and is a descendant of Greek gamma, which the Romans adapted and used to represent the sound (k) as well as (g). (Later they developed the letter *g* by adding a stroke to the letter *c* and assigned the (g) sound to it.) As Latin developed into the modern Romance languages, the pronunciation of *k* gradually changed or "softened" before the vowels *e, i,* and *y*—the only exceptions to this development being found among dialects of Sardinian, one of the languages spoken on the island of Sardinia in the Mediterranean, where the original Latin sound (k) is preserved to this day. Nowadays, *c* before *e, i,* and *y* is pronounced (ch) in Italian, (th) or (s) in Spanish depending on the dialect, and (s) in French. Middle English scribes continued to use the soft *c*, pronounced (s), before *e, i,* and *y*, when spelling words borrowed from French, and they also began to use *k* more frequently instead of the hard *c* before these vowels in native English words. In Modern English, *c* is, with very few exceptions, soft before *e, i,* and *y* and hard before *a, o, u,* and consonants.

cabal

Both (kə-băl**′**) and (kə-bäl**′**) are acceptable pronunciations.

cache / cachet

Both of these words come from French, and they sometimes are confused. *Cache,* meaning "a store of goods stashed in a hiding place," began to appear frequently in English in the early 19th century. Thus, the police might find *a cache of drugs* hidden at a crime scene. It is properly pronounced like the word *cash.* (Note that there is no accent mark over the *e.*) The word is sometimes pronounced with two syllables as (kă-shā**′**), but this pronunciation is not considered standard and may be viewed as a mistake by people who know French. *Cachet* means "a mark of distinction, prestige." It originally referred to a seal that closed letters and identified the writer, who was often an important person or aristocrat. Nowadays a prestigious university might attract students because it *has cachet,* or a certain brand of product might be popular because it *has a certain cachet. Cachet* is pronounced with two syllables: (kă-shā**′**).

cadre

This 19th-century borrowing from French has a variety of pronunciations in English. In our 1996 survey of the Usage Panel, (kä′drä) was the pronunciation of 67 percent; (kä′drə), 16 percent; (kăd′rē), 9 percent; and (kä′dər), 3 percent. While any of these pronunciations should be considered acceptable in American English, the pronunciations (kä′drə) and (kä′dər) are closest to the French pronunciation, as the French word has no accent on the final *e.* This means that the Panel's most favored pronunciation (which may well be the most common in the US) is an American invention and might be considered a mistake by speakers of French. This pronunciation probably came about by influence of the French borrowing *cachet,* whose last syllable is pronounced with an (ā) sound in both French and English, and similar borrowings like *forte,* whose last syllable is sometimes pronounced in this manner by influence of the Italian musical direction with the same spelling. In any case, the (ā) sound at the end of *cadre* may strike many American ears as more Frenchlike and hence more correct. The British, perhaps thanks to their greater exposure to the French language, predominantly say (kä′dər).

callous / callus

A *callus* is a patch of toughened skin, often on a hand or foot and caused by sustained friction. In British English, *callous* is an acceptable spelling variant for this word, but not so in Standard American English, where *callous* is used solely as an adjective that means "having calluses, toughened," and, metaphorically, "emotionally hardened, unfeeling," as in

> . . . in a world saturated, even hypersaturated, with images, those which should matter to us have a diminishing effect: we become callous (Susan Sontag, "Looking at War")

Both *callus* and *callous* are also verbs, used mainly as past participles and in passive constructions. *Callus* means "to cause to form calluses":

> Mama's fingers were so stiff and callused that I doubted she could thread a needle anymore (Katherine Shonk, *My Mother's Garden*)

While *callused* is sometimes used metaphorically to mean "toughened by hard experience," *calloused* is by far the more common term in such contexts:

> And although Philadelphia has been rocked by one police scandal after another in recent years, the new charges reveal a group of officers so corrupt, so calloused to the rights and welfare of residents, that the details have shaken this city to its roots (Don Terry, "Philadelphia Shaken by Criminal Police Officers," *New York Times*)

Calorie / calorie

Officially, the word *calorie* has different interpretations depending on whether it is capitalized. A *Calorie* with a capital *C* is defined as 4,184 joules, approximately the amount of energy required to raise the temperature of 1 kilogram of water 1 degree Celsius (1°C). *Calorie* with a capital *C* also goes by the names *large calorie, kilocalorie,* and *kilogram calorie,* and is abbreviated *kcal* in scientific contexts. This is the Calorie encountered on food packaging labels and in most dietary guidelines. However, it should be noted that in these contexts the word is usually not capitalized, in spite of scientific convention.

A *calorie* with a lowercase *c* is defined as 4.184 joules, approximately the amount of energy required to raise the temperature of 1 gram of water 1°C. *Calorie* with a lowercase *c* also goes by the names *small calorie* and *gram calorie,* and is abbreviated *cal.* Thus, 1,000 small calories equal 1 large calorie. The *calorie* is used as a unit in scientific contexts; however, other units such as joule, erg, and electron volt are often preferred over calorie, especially in physics and engineering.

Since the capitalization rule is often not followed, the ambiguity of *calorie* is rampant, and indeed any sentence beginning with the word *Calorie* is inherently ambiguous. While usual practice in nutritional and dietary texts may render the issue moot, it is often good policy to use one of the alternative expressions or to explain which unit is being referred to.

See more at **Centigrade.**

can

can and may   *Can I go to the bathroom?* Nearly every child has asked this question only to be corrected with *You mean, May I go to the bathroom?* Generations of teachers have insisted that *can* should be used only to express the capacity to do something and that *may* must be used to express permission. But children don't use *can* to ask permission out of a desire to be stubbornly perverse. They have learned it as an idiomatic expression from adults: *If you finish your spaghetti, you can have dessert. After you clean your room, you can go outside and play.* In these and similar spoken uses, *can* is perfectly acceptable. This is especially true for negative questions such as *Can't I have the car tonight?* probably because using *mayn't* instead of *can't* sounds unnatural. Nevertheless, in more formal usage the distinction between *can* and *may* still has many adherents. In our 1988 survey only 21 percent of the Usage Panel accepted *can* instead of *may* in the sentence *Can I take another week to submit the application? May* is common in official announcements: *Students may pick up the application forms tomorrow.* The increased formality of *may* sometimes highlights the role of the speaker in giving permission. *You may leave the room when you're finished* implies that permission is given by the speaker. *You can leave the room when you're finished* implies that permission is part of a rule or policy rather than a decision on the part of the speaker.

can showing possibility   Like *may, can* is also used to indicate what is possible: *It may rain this afternoon. Bone spurs can be very painful.* In this use, both *can* and *may* often have personal subjects: *You may be right. You may see him at the concert. From the mountaintop you can see the ocean on a clear day. Even an experienced driver can get lost in this town.*

See more at **auxiliary and primary verbs** and **may.**

cannot

cannot but   "*I cannot but be gratified by the assurance*," Thomas Jefferson once wrote. He might have said *I can but be gratified by the assurance* and meant the same thing! This is possible because *but* is used in these two sentences in different ways. The *but* of *cannot but* indicates an exception, as it does in sentences such as *No one but Jefferson could have written such a document*. But the *but* of *can but* means "only," as it does in the sentence *We had but a single bullet left*. So the two phrases *cannot but* and *can but* mean essentially the same thing: "cannot do otherwise than." Both *cannot but* and *can but* are standard expressions that have been in use for hundreds of years.

cannot help   The construction *cannot help* is used with a present participle to roughly the same effect as *cannot but* in a sentence such as *We cannot help admiring his courage*. This construction usually bears the implication that a person is unable to affect an outcome normally under his or her control. Thus saying *They could not help laughing at such a remark* implies that they could not suppress their laughter.

cannot help but   The construction *cannot help but* probably arose as a blend of *cannot help* and *cannot but*; it has the meaning of the first and the syntax of the second: *We cannot help but admire his courage*. The construction has sometimes been criticized as a redundancy, but it has been around for more than a century and appears in the writing of many distinguished authors. If it seems ungainly for formal prose, it is easily enough shortened.

cannot seem to   The expression *cannot* (or *can't*) *seem to* has occasionally been criticized as illogical, and so it is. *Brian can't seem to get angry* does not mean "Brian is incapable of appearing to get angry," as its syntax would seem to require; rather, it means "Brian appears to be unable to get angry." But the idiom serves a useful purpose, since the syntax of English does not allow *Brian seems to cannot get angry*. This phenomenon, in which a negative is transferred from a subordinate to a main clause, is called *raising* by linguists. Raising occurs in some other idiomatic constructions that pass with no notice given to their apparent illogic, notably in sentences like *I don't think it will rain* instead of *I think it will not rain*. In this case, being illogical is just speaking plain English.

cannot . . . too   See under **too**.

capital / capitol

Capital and *capitol* are terms that are often confused, mainly because they refer to things that are in some ways related. The term for a town or city that serves as a seat of government is spelled *capital*, while the term for the building in which a legislative assembly meets is spelled *capitol*. Note that *capital* has an additional sense, meaning "wealth in the form of money, property, or human resources, especially when considered in terms of their cumulative contributions to an economy."

capitalization

abbreviations

1. Acronyms, abbreviations formed from the initial letters of a name and pronounced as words (*OPEC, UNESCO*), are ordinarily capitalized. Because it can be distracting to see longer acronyms in "all caps" in running text, some publications opt for an upper- and lowercase styling (*NASDAQ/Nasdaq*). Some acronyms that have entered the language in a generic sense no longer require capitals (*awol, laser*). If in doubt about a specific word, consult a dictionary.

2. Initialisms, abbreviations pronounced letter by letter, tend to be uppercase if they represent nouns (*HIV, YMCA*) and lowercase if they function as adverbs (*rpm, mph*). As with acronyms, the styling of initialisms is largely a matter of convention, and it is best to consult a dictionary in doubtful cases.

3. Scientific abbreviations are rife with capitalization inconsistencies (*FM* for *frequency modulation, fp* for *freezing point,* and so forth), and it is best to refer to a dictionary to assure accuracy.

   See more at **abbreviations** under **period.**

beginnings

1. The first word of a sentence is capitalized.

   > Some diseases are acute; others are chronic.
   > Don't you live in my building?
   > Great! Let's go!

2. The first word of a direct quotation is capitalized. If the quotation is split into two parts within the sentence, the second part begins lowercase.

   > Helen asked, "Do you think Satie was a serious composer?"
   > "For me," I answered, "he was simply amusing."

3. If a quotation is grammatically connected to the sentence in which it appears, a capital is not necessary.

   > Van Zandt concludes that "the lawsuit is frivolous and vexatious."

   > Malls are proliferating, and as Furlong observed, "we are becoming an exit-ramp economy."

4. In traditional verse the first word of each line of a poem is capitalized. In contemporary verse lines often begin lowercase. The original capitalization of the poet should always be duplicated.

   > Poets that lasting marble seek
   > Must carve in Latin or in Greek.
   >   —Edmund Waller

   > but new as this our thousandth kiss,
   > no now is so
   >   —e.e. cummings

5. A sentence enclosed in parentheses or dashes within another sentence should not begin with a capital letter.

Devan didn't hear the phone (he was playing music in his room), so I answered it.

Simone was tired—it had taken twenty hours to get from Boston to Delhi—and she went straight to bed.

6. A direct question within another sentence does not need to be capitalized. If the question is long, however, a capital can add clarity.

Wearily he asked himself, why do I bother?

The council needs to consider the question, Is the proposed extension of Route 11 necessary to reduce traffic on Route 85, or is it merely a scheme to enable commercial development?

courts   Capitalize the names of specific judicial courts and the word *court* when it is used alone to refer to the US Supreme Court or to an international court.

the United States Supreme Court; the US Supreme Court; the Supreme Court; the Court

the Court of Justice of the European Communities; the Court

the Supreme Court of Virginia; the supreme court; the court

the United States Court of Appeals for the Fourth Circuit; the court of appeals; the court

cultural and philosophical terms   Terms denoting cultural movements, philosophical schools, and artistic styles are generally capitalized only when they are derived from proper nouns. When in doubt, consult a dictionary.

Hellenism	existentialism
Platonism	abstract expressionism
Aristotelian	surrealism
Gothic	impressionistic
Pre-Raphaelite	nihilistic

Some words of this kind are capitalized to distinguish them from the same words used in a general sense.

the Romantic poets
Stoic philosophy
the Gothic architecture of Italy
a romantic sojourn
a stoic outlook on life
gothic fiction as a phenomenon of popular culture

days, months, and holidays   Days of the week, months of the year, holidays, and holy days are capitalized. The seasons are lowercased.

Monday	Easter
January	the first day of spring
Labor Day	the summer solstice
Passover	the fall of 2005
Ramadan	the winter semester

geographical terms

1. Global divisions and distinct geographical regions are capitalized.

the Western Hemisphere	the Far East
the South Pole	Central America
the Tropics	the Gulf Coast
the Tropic of Capricorn	the South
the Torrid Zone	the Deep South
the Continental Divide	the Midwest
the Arctic Circle	the Southwest

2. Terms identifying well-defined topographic and cultural entities are capitalized.

the Bible Belt	the Lake District
the Lower East Side	Chinatown
Little Italy	the Back Bay
the South End	the Great Plains

3. The names of streets, highways, parks, famous buildings, and public areas are capitalized.

42nd Street	the Sears Tower
Route 66	Trinity Church
US Highway 1	the Boston Common
Roger Williams Park	Times Square

4. The names of rivers, lakes, mountains, and oceans are capitalized.

the Connecticut River	the Rocky Mountains
Lake Geneva	the Pacific Ocean

If a generic geographical term follows two or more proper names, it should be lowercased.

the Missouri and Mississippi rivers	the Allegheny and Blue Ridge mountains

5. If a generic geographical term precedes two or more proper names, it should be capitalized if the singular form in the same position is part of each name.

Lake Superior, Lake Huron; Lakes Superior and Huron
Mount Rainier, Mount Baker; Mounts Rainier and Baker

6. Points of the compass or words derived from them are lowercased when they indicate direction.

Turn south onto I-95.
Because of the snow, all eastbound flights are delayed.
The dromedary is native to northern Africa and western Asia.

When compass points or directional terms occur in the names of recognized geographical entities, they are properly capitalized. If in doubt, consult a dictionary.

Travelers to Southeast Asia should bring a passport.
Internet use is rapidly increasing in the Middle East and North Africa.
In January, the comet was only observable from the Southern Hemisphere.

historical terms

1. Terms in standard usage for historical periods, events, and eras are capitalized. Newer such terms are generally lowercased. When in doubt, consult a dictionary or an encyclopedia.

the Middle Ages	the New Deal
World War II	the March on Washington
the Battle of the Bulge	the Iran-Contra affair
the Great Depression	the Iran hostage crisis
the Cuban Missile Crisis	the baby boom
the Great Society	Space Age *or* space age

2. The names of treaties, pacts, acts, laws, amendments, and historic documents are capitalized. Abbreviated forms are usually lowercased.

the Panama Canal Treaty; the treaty
the Warsaw Pact; the pact
the Civil Wrights Act; the act
the Sherman Antitrust Law; the law
the Fifth Amendment to the Constitution; the amendment
the Constitution of the State of Connecticut; the constitution

3. The word *Constitution* is usually capitalized when it refers to the US Constitution.

the Constitution of the United States; the United States Constitution; the US Constitution; the Constitution

nicknames or epithets   Capitalize nicknames or epithets used as substitutes for the names of people, places, or things.

the Iron Chancellor	the Desert Fox
the Belle of Amherst	the Big Apple

personification   Capitalization may be used to signify personification, a figure of speech in which an object or a concept possesses human qualities.

Because I could not stop for Death,
He kindly stopped for me;
          —Emily Dickinson

In most modern writing, however, personification is expressed without the use of capital letters.

He moved toward the house, which now—high, gleaming roof, and spun-gold window—seemed to watch him and to listen . . . the water, like a million warning voices, lapped in the buckets he carried on each side; and his mother, beneath the startled earth on which he moved, lifted up, endlessly, her eyes.
          —James Baldwin, *Go Tell It on the Mountain*

proper names

1. The names of people, organizations and their members, sports teams, and councils and congresses are capitalized.

   Albert Einstein   the Republican Party
   Marie Curie   a Democrat
   the Free and Accepted Masons   the Nuclear Regulatory Commis-
   a Mason   sion
   Roman Catholic Church   the House of Representatives
   a Catholic   Parliament
   the New England Patriots   the Diet

2. The names of nationalities, peoples, ethnic groups, and languages are capitalized.

   Canadians   the Bantu languages
   the Maori   German
   Latinos   Old High German

3. The names of ships, airplanes, and spacecraft are capitalized.

   the USS *Kitty Hawk*   Lindbergh's *Spirit of St. Louis*
   the *Andrea Gail*   *Voyager II*

4. Words derived from proper names are capitalized unless the derivation is part of a compound that has taken on a nonliteral meaning. If in doubt consult a dictionary.

   Roman numeral   byzantine maneuvers
   roman type   Epicurean doctrines
   Byzantine coins   epicurean delights

religious terms   Names of deities and sacred works are capitalized.

   God   Krishna
   the Almighty   the Bible
   Allah   the Koran
   the Holy Spirit   the Talmud
   Jehovah   the Upanishads

Although pronouns that refer to a deity are sometimes capitalized in religious writings, in a general context they are lowercased.

   We pray to God and honor him.
   Jesus chose twelve men to be his disciples.

salutations and complimentary closes   The first word of the salutation and the first word of the complimentary close of a letter are capitalized.

   My dear Carlos,   Sincerely yours,
   Dear Ms. Restivo: Yours sincerely,

scientific terms

1. The names of geological eras, periods, epochs, and strata are capitalized.

the Paleozoic Era	the Pleistocene Epoch
the Precambrian Period	the Age of Reptiles

2. The names of stars, constellations, planets, and galaxies are capitalized.

the North Star	Jupiter
Vega	the Milky Way
the Southern Cross	the Andromeda Galaxy
the Summer Triangle	

3. The distinction between *(the) Earth* in the sense of our planet and *the earth* in the sense of our world is difficult to apply consistently across a variety of contexts. The following notes offer general guidelines. When in doubt, choose the style that seems most appropriate to the context at hand.

In scientific contexts, and especially when used with other astronomical terms, *Earth* is usually capitalized and *the* is left out.

> Quasars are billions of light-years from Earth.
> Venus is the brightest object in the night sky aside from Earth's moon.

In general contexts, *earth* is usually lowercased and preceded by *the*.

> Magellan led the first expedition to circumnavigate the earth.
> Mount Everest is the earth's highest mountain.

In many idioms, *earth* is lowercased.

> Vilma was the salt of the earth.
> I would move heaven and earth to make you happy.

4. In the scientific (Latin) names of plants and animals, the genus name is capitalized. The names of species and subspecies are lowercased. See more at **scientific names** under **italics**.

Chrysanthemum leucanthemum	*Rana pipiens*
Corvus corax	*Betula lenta*

Classes, orders, families, and all other groups higher than the genus level are capitalized. Adjectives and nouns derived from scientific names are lowercased.

Gastropoda, gastropod	Hominidae, hominid
Nematoda, nematode	Carnivora, carnivore

titles of people

1. Capitalize words indicating familial relationships when they precede a person's name and form a title. Lowercase such words when they are used descriptively.

Uncle Bud	my uncle, Bud Ellis
Grandmother Walker	her grandmother, Mrs. Walker

2. For the proper capitalization of names containing lowercase particles (*da, de, la, van, von,* and such), consult a biographical dictionary. If the surname appears alone, style may vary among names with similar particles in accordance with common usage.

Charles de Gaulle; de Gaulle
Miguel de Cervantes Saavedra;
    Cervantes
Vincent van Gogh; Van Gogh
Ludwig van Beethoven; Beethoven

Alexander von Humboldt; Hum-
    boldt
Wernher von Braun; von Braun
Daphne du Maurier; Du Maurier
Leonardo da Vinci; Leonardo

3. Capitalize titles—civil, military, royal and noble, religious, and honorary—when they precede a name.

Justice Ginsburg
Mayor White
General Marshall
Queen Elizabeth II

Lord Nelson
Pope John Paul II
Professor Malone

4. *President* and *Vice President* are capitalized when they refer to the incumbent officials of the United States.

Secretary of State Colin Powell will accompany President Bush.
The Vice President's family will hold a press conference at 9:00 p.m.

When used in a generic sense, they are lowercased.

According to the Twenty-Second Amendment, the president may not serve for more than two terms.

Andrew Johnson was elected vice president in 1864.

titles of works

1. In the titles and subtitles of literary, dramatic, artistic, and musical works, capitalize the first and last word and all nouns, pronouns, verbs, adjectives, and adverbs. Lowercase articles and coordinating conjunctions. Prepositions may be lowercased regardless of length with the exceptions noted in paragraph 2. Do not capitalize *to* when it precedes an infinitive.

Bad Bears in the Big City
The Man Who Came to Dinner
The Sparkling-Eyed Boy
A Human Being Died That Night
Words to Live By
Bringing Up Baby
Self-Portrait with Turtles
Leading Quietly: An Unorthodox Guide to Doing the Right Thing
Cat on a Hot Tin Roof
Wheat Field and Cypress Trees
Concerto for Orchestra

2. If a preposition is an important element of the title, it may be capitalized.

Winning Through Intimidation   *Across the River and Into the Trees*
Clock Without Hands

Note, however, that it is the alternative style of some publishers to capitalize all prepositions of four or more letters or of five or more letters.

3. The word *the* in the title of a newspaper or magazine is lowercased except for a few cases in which it is considered an integral part of the title.

the *Christian Science Monitor*   *The New Yorker*
the *Wall Street Journal*   *The Nation*

See more at **titles of works** under **italics** and **titles of works** under **quotation marks**.

trademarks and service marks   Registered trademarks are capitalized. Many trademarks are listed in dictionaries. Trademarked terms should be used with caution when they do not refer to a specific product or service, particularly in published writing. Where possible, writers may choose to use generic terms instead. When a trademark must be used, it is not necessary to append the symbol ® or ™ to the name.

Kleenex; tissue
Ping-Pong; table tennis
Xerox; photocopy
Seeing Eye dog; guide dog
Rollerblades; in-line skates
Walkman; portable cassette [*or* CD] player

cardiac / coronary

Although closely related and often used interchangeably, the words *cardiac* and *coronary* are not exactly the same. *Cardiac* means "of, near, or relating to an area of the heart," as in *cardiac disease* or *cardiac catheterization.* In clinical medicine, the term also refers to the esophageal opening of the stomach, called the *cardia.*

Coronary is also frequently used to refer generally to the heart, as in *coronary care unit.* But *coronary* also refers specifically to the arteries that surround and feed the heart. *Coronary* comes from the Latin word *corona,* which means "crown," or "that which encircles." *Coronary artery disease,* or occlusion of the coronary arteries, can cause a *heart attack,* the death of heart tissue, or *cardiac arrest,* the failure of the heart to function.

The popular use of *coronary* as a synonym for *heart attack,* as in a newspaper article that asks *"Is it safe for them to continue a normal sexual life after a coronary?"* is colloquial and is not usually encountered in scientific or medical writing.

caring

Some people object to the use of *caring* as an adjective, and the acceptability of the usage seems to vary according to the relation between the source and object of the caring. In our 1987 survey, 74 percent of the Usage Panel accepted the sentence *A child has a right to certain things: a secure home, a healthful environment, and caring parents.* A smaller majority, 58 percent, accepted *We are looking for a few caring people to help with this program,* where the nature of caring appears vague and the object is any number of concerns that might arise. When *caring* is applied to circumstances instead of people, acceptability fell even further. Only 29 percent of the Panel accepted *A child has the right to grow up in a healthful, caring environment.*

case

Case is the form of a noun, pronoun, or modifier that indicates its grammatical relationship to other words in a clause or sentence. In English, only pronouns are differentiated by case. English pronouns have three cases: nominative or subjective (*she*), objective (*him*), and possessive (*his*). See more at **possessive constructions** and **pronouns, personal.**

catacomb

The final syllable of this word usually rhymes with *comb* in American English and *comb* or *tomb* in British English.

catalyst / enzyme / vitamin

The word *catalyst,* ultimately from Greek *katalusis,* meaning "dissolution," refers to a substance that increases the rate of a chemical reaction without undergoing any permanent chemical change itself. *Enzymes* are a specific type of catalyst that are produced by living organisms and are active in biochemical reactions involving organic compounds. An enzyme is composed of a protein that combines with a nonproteinaceous substance called a *coenzyme.*

Vitamins are substances that function as coenzymes in the body. Like enzymes, these organic compounds are essential in small quantities for normal body functioning. Unlike enzymes, vitamins are not synthesized by the body and must be obtained through foods. Originally thought to be incidental nutrients, vitamins were dubbed "accessory factors." The term *vitamin* came into use in the early 1900s when an organic compound that prevented the disease beriberi was discovered. The new compound was called a *vitamine,* or "live amine." Later research showed that not all vitamins contain the organic group known as an amine.

Caucasian / Caucasoid

Caucasian and *Caucasoid* belong to the system of racial classification developed by European anthropologists at the end of the 18th century. In this sense they refer to a broad grouping of ethnically diverse peoples indigenous to Europe, northern Africa, western Asia, and parts of the Indian subcontinent. While *Caucasoid* is rarely found outside the context of physical anthropology, *Caucasian* has come into much wider use as another term for *white* or *European.* This may seem surprising, given that many of the peoples included in the Caucasian racial category—including Berbers, Arabs, and peoples of the Indian subcontinent—are non-European and have relatively dark pigmentation. Nevertheless, the usage is now common, especially in semiformal contexts such as police reports and public health studies, and cannot be considered either inaccurate or offensive. Even so, there is generally no reason to prefer this term over a more straightforward one such as *white, European American,* or *Euro-American.*

Caucasian, but not *Caucasoid,* is also a geographic term referring to the Caucasus (the mountainous region between the Black and Caspian seas for which the racial category was named) or to any of its indigenous peoples such as Azerbaijanis, Armenians, and Ossetians. In most contexts there is little risk of confusing the geographical and racial senses of *Caucasian,* but in some cases it might be advisable to use a phrase such as *a people inhabiting the Caucasus* instead of *Caucasians* or *a Caucasian people.*

See more at **Euro-American** and **white.**

CE   See **AD.**

celebrant

The word *celebrant* originally referred to an official participant in a religious ceremony or rite. Its meaning has extended greatly in American English, however, and as far back as 1982 a majority of the Usage Panel accepted the use of *celebrant* to mean "a participant in a celebration," as in *The New Year's Eve celebrants went wild at the stroke of midnight.* The uncontroversial alternative *celebrator* may be preferable for non-American readers, however.

celibate

Historically, *celibate* meant simply "unmarried"; its use to mean "abstaining from sexual intercourse" without regard to marital status is a 20th-century development. But the new sense of the word seems to have displaced the old, and the use of *celibate* to mean "unmarried" is now almost sure to invite misinterpretation in any but narrowly ecclesiastical contexts. In our 1988 survey, 68 percent of the Usage Panel rejected the older use in the sentence *He remained celibate* [unmarried], *although he engaged in sexual intercourse.*

Celt / Celtic

Although many people pronounce these words with an initial (s) sound, an initial (k) sound is standard in historical, linguistic, and sociological contexts. The *c* was probably pronounced (s), as is usual before *e,* when the words entered English from French in the 17th century. The later pronunciation with (k) imitates that of the original Latin word *Celtae,* a name for the Gauls, the ancient Celtic tribes of France. The (s) pronunciation has no doubt been reinforced by the prominence of Boston's professional basketball team, the Celtics, a name that is sometimes shortened to the Celts. Both are always pronounced with the (s) sound.

cement / concrete

The terms *cement* and *concrete* are often used interchangeably, but the substances to which they refer are not quite the same. *Cement,* from Latin *caementum,* "rough-cut stone," is made from limestone and clay that is crushed, heated, and ground into a powder. Cement mixed with water (wet cement) forms a paste that is used to bind other materials together as it hardens. (The term has also extended its meaning to include other substances used to bind things together, as in *rubber cement.*) *Cement* may be mixed with water and materials such as sand, gravel, and broken stone; when these materials harden together, *concrete* is formed. (The word *concrete* is a combination of the Latin prefix *com–,* "together," and the past participle of the verb *crēscere,* "to grow.") *Reinforced concrete* is made by pouring concrete around steel bars. *Prestressed concrete* is made by pouring concrete around steel cables stretched by jacks. When the jacks are released, the cables compress the concrete and strengthen it.

centenary

The pronunciation with the main stress on the first syllable is the correct historical pronunciation, but the pronunciation with stress on the second syllable, which probably came about through association with *centennial,* is now equally acceptable.

center

As a verb *center* can represent various relations involving having, finding, or turning about a center. The choice of a preposition to accompany *center* depends on the meaning you want to convey. For certain physical uses, the Usage Panel favors *in* more than *at.* In our 1996 ballot, 73 percent found *in* acceptable, but only 23 percent accepted *at* in the sentence *The company has been centered (in/at) Atlanta for the last five years.* (That 27 percent could not even tolerate *in* suggests that as a verb, *center* makes some people uneasy no matter how it is used.)

center around   In figurative contexts, there is ample evidence for *center in, on, upon,* and *around,* as in *Our hope centered in the young leader, His thoughts centered on the long journey before him,* and *The discussion centered around the need for curriculum reform.* Some language critics have denounced *center around* as illogical—if it's in the center, after all, it cannot be "around" anything else.

Nonetheless, 71 percent of the Usage Panel accepted *center around* in the 1996 ballot, suggesting that, logical or no, it is well on its way to becoming a standard idiom. Still, if the expression does not fit comfortably, use *revolve around* instead.

Centigrade / Celsius / Kelvin

The history of the names of temperature intervals revolves around the ambiguity introduced by the word *degree* and confusion over the prefix *centi–*. In 1742, Anders Celsius, a Swedish astronomer, proposed dividing up the temperature interval between the boiling point of water and the freezing point of water into one hundred steps. This is regarded as the origin of the *centigrade* temperature scale. The prefix *centi–*, meaning "one hundred" (as in *centipede),* is combined with the word *grade,* which is derived from the Latin word *gradus,* meaning "step." Thus, *centigrade* means "one hundred steps."

In 1795, fifty-three years after Anders Celsius proposed a centigrade temperature scale, the prefix *centi–* began to be used in the metric system to mean "one hundredth," as in *centimeter, centigram,* and *centiliter.* Later, in the 1850s, with the widespread introduction of the metric system, the correct use of the word *centigrade* became unclear in many contexts. This is because many European languages have a word similar to *grade* as their word for *degree.* For example, German has *Grad,* Swedish has *grad,* and Spanish and Italian have *grado.* Thus, scientific communications developed an ambiguity. Did *centigrade* refer to the temperature scale or to one hundredth of some degree measure? To eliminate this confusion, scientists agreed in 1948 that the temperature unit *degree centigrade* would henceforth be called *degree Celsius* and the symbol would be °C.

In 1954, the definition of the Celsius scale itself was changed. Rather than using the freezing and boiling points of water at one atmosphere of pressure, the degree interval *Kelvin* was set equal to 1/273.16 of the thermodynamic temperature of the triple point of water, which was defined to be 273.16 degrees Kelvin. (The triple point of any substance is the temperature at which, under pressure, the substance can take solid, liquid, or gaseous form.) At the same time, 0°C was defined to be equal to 273.16 degrees Kelvin. Thus, the Kelvin scale became the fundamental temperature scale. Its fundamental unit was the degree Kelvin, with the symbol K. Unfortunately, here also the word *degree* introduced complications as temperature measurements became finer. For example, the metric system dictates that 0.01 meter is equal to 1 centimeter. However, is 0.01 degree Kelvin equal to 1 centidegree Kelvin, or 1 degree Centikelvin? Using one word, *degree,* for the interval, and another, *Kelvin,* for the scale, was confusing, so in 1967 scientists decided that *degree Kelvin* would no longer be used to describe the fundamental temperature interval. Instead, the fundamental temperature interval would be called simply *kelvin* (with a lowercase *k*), and its symbol would be K without any degree symbol. The temperature interval in the Celsius scale, scientists decided, would retain the word *degree,* the capitalized *C* in Celsius, and the symbol °C.

Therefore, at the present time, the accepted ways of indicating the freezing point of water at one atmosphere of pressure in the metric system are 273.16 kelvins, 273.16 K, 0 degrees Celsius, or 0°C.

See more at **heat.**

centrifugal / centripetal / inertia

The word *centrifugal* is used to describe any feature that appears to flee the center of something, while *centripetal* is used to describe any feature that appears to seek the center of something. These terms have been used to describe the growth of flower petals and the transmission of nerve impulses. However, the most common use of *centrifugal* and *centripetal* is to describe the forces present in circular motion.

A *centrifugal* force is an illusory force that appears to push an object away from a center of rotation. Actually, this tendency is nothing more than the *inertia* of the object; the object simply tends to continue in a straight line, not accelerating or changing direction—unless it is acted upon by some external force, such as gravity, or is pulled by some other object, or otherwise forced out of a straight path. *Inertia* is the property of an object proportional to mass that opposes acceleration. A centripetal force is a force on an object that tends to move it toward a center of rotation and can be a result of gravitation, electricity, a mechanical connection, or any other force.

For example, if a bucket of water is held by the handle and spun in a circle, the bucket pulls on the arm in a direction away from the center of rotation. This is perceived as a centrifugal force, but it is simply the inertia of the bucket and the water; without being connected to the arm by the hand, the bucket would fly off, and any loose parts of the bucket that were not physically bound to it would fly off as well. The effort required to hold onto the bucket and keep it spinning is the *centripetal* force. The arm transmits the centripetal force, so the person holding the bucket feels the inertia of the bucket resisting acceleration. Each part of the bucket, transmitting the force to its neighboring parts, is subject to the force as well.

It is easy to see that centrifugal force is not a real force by looking at a body in orbit. Orbits result from a centripetal gravitational force, which affects all parts of an object equally, whether they are physically connected or not. When Apollo 8 orbited the moon in 1968, the centripetal force was provided by the gravitational attraction between the spacecraft and the moon, causing the spacecraft to move in a circle around the moon. But unlike the arm's pull on the spinning bucket, gravity affected each part of the spacecraft separately; no part of the spacecraft was transmitting the force to any other. Thus no part was tugging at any other, so the astronauts felt no apparent centrifugal force.

See more at **mass** and **revolve.**

cerebral

The pronunciation with stress on the first syllable is the older, Anglicized one, but the pronunciation with stress on the second syllable, which is especially common in American English, is equally acceptable.

certain

It is often claimed that *certain* is an absolute term like *unanimous* or *paramount* and cannot be modified; something is either certain or it is not. However, a majority of the Usage Panel accepted the construction *Nothing could be more certain* as early as 1965, and phrases such as *fairly certain, quite certain,* and so on are readily understood as expressing varying degrees of confidence. Their effectiveness can be seen in the following examples:

> The [taxidermic] piece was precise and lovely, almost haunting, since the more you looked at it the more certain you were that the birds would just stop building their nest, spread their wings, and fly away (Susan Orlean, "Lifelike," *The New Yorker*)

> Years from now, when USA-67 is decommissioned, having fought and won many a battle at sea, I'm fairly certain of one thing: they'll still find traces of my fingernails on that black nonslip deck (Ron C. Judd, "Race a Memorable First for Seventeenth Man," *Seattle Times*)

Note that since *certain* must always suggest overall confidence, its range is restricted to the upper range; one is unlikely to be *slightly, somewhat,* or *a little bit certain,* for example.

ch

In Old English, the sounds (k) and (ch) were both represented by the letter *c.* After the Norman conquest of England, however, Middle English scribes began to use *ch* to represent the (ch) sound as the result of French influence on spelling. In early Old French, the letters *ch* were used to write the sound (ch). (It was only later that the Old French sound (ch) developed into Modern French (sh), and the letters *ch* came to be pronounced as they are in French today.) French spelling habits were applied to native English vocabulary, and the word spelled *cild* in Old English, for instance, came to be spelled *child* in Middle and Modern English. Many English words beginning with *ch* are borrowings from Old French, and in these cases English preserves the original medieval French pronunciation of *ch* as (ch). The English word *chase,* for example, is equivalent to Modern French *chasser,* "to hunt," in which *ch* is pronounced (sh). However, more recent English borrowings from French have the Modern French value (sh) heard in *charlatan* and *cachet.* The sequence *tch* became the usual way to represent the (ch) sound following short vowels in English, as in *catch.*

In English words of Greek origin, the digraph *ch* represents a transliteration of Greek χ (chi), and so is usually pronounced (k), as in *chorus* and *architect.*

challenged

People who find the terms *handicapped* and *disabled* offensive or insensitive sometimes propose substituting them with *challenged,* as in describing a person who uses a wheelchair as *physically challenged* rather than *disabled* or *physically handicapped.* The purpose of such a phrase is to emphasize the positive aspect of the challenge that a particular condition presents over the negative aspect of hindrance or incapacity. While this usage has gained acceptance in some quarters, it has also been widely criticized, not just by those who view it as an example of the excesses of political correctness but also by some disabled people themselves, who may well see it as a condescending euphemism. In fact, this usage has become a favorite target of those who find politically correct labels more offensive than the terms they are meant to replace, and it has been widely parodied in such phrases as *vertically challenged* for "short" and *horizontally challenged* for "obese."

Given this situation, writers should consider their audience before using a term formed with *challenged*. Whereas *physically challenged* and *mentally challenged* in particular are now quite common in certain circles, especially in academic, government, and other official contexts, their use in other areas, or the extension of this usage to phrases such as *visually challenged* or *behaviorally challenged,* could actually provoke scorn or even offense.

Chicana

A Mexican-American woman who identifies herself with Chicano culture or heritage is properly called *a Chicana* in contemporary American English. Although calling her *a Chicano* cannot be considered ungrammatical in English, as it would be in Spanish, it might well be considered insensitive or uninformed. When the article is omitted, however, an interesting distinction between the masculine and feminine forms arises: saying *She is Chicano* may be taken as emphasizing an identity with Chicano culture in general, while *She is Chicana* may suggest a feminist perspective on that identity.

See more at **Latina.**

Chicano

Although the early usage of the word in both English and Spanish is debated, it is clear that *Chicano* was never used in referring to Mexican-Americans in general but only to the poorest laborers among them, and it was probably used derogatorily in both languages when it was first introduced. However, Mexican American students and activists in the 1960s and 1970s reclaimed *Chicano* as a term of ethnic pride, capitalizing it as an ethnonym and building a political and artistic movement around it that still endures.

Chicano is used only of Mexican Americans, not of Mexicans living in Mexico. Though popularized throughout the United States by Chicano writers and artists, the term has not found universal acceptance within the Mexican-American community as a whole. For some it signifies pride and ethnic identity, while others may see it as associated with a political or cultural stance that they don't share. For this reason it should be used by outsiders with care and only of people who wish to be so identified. When unsure of how *Chicano* will be received, the neutral term *Mexican American* or the more general terms *Latino* or *Hispanic* should be considered instead.

The word *Chicano* itself is a shortening of an old variant pronunciation of the Spanish word *mexicano,* "Mexican." The element *mexi–* in *Mexico* and other words derived from it ultimately comes from the name of an Aztec war god, Mexitli. By origin, Mexico means "the place of Mexitli," although the area originally referred to is not the entirety of the modern country of Mexico. The *x* of the name of the god represents the sound (sh) found in Nahuatl, the language of the Aztecs and other peoples of the area. At the beginning of the 1500s, at the time of the Spanish conquests in North, Central, and South America, the Spanish language as well had the sound (sh), spelled with the letter *x*, and the Spanish used *x* to represent the sound (sh) in words borrowed from the indigenous languages of the Americas, like the name *Mexico*. Later in the history of the Spanish language, however, the sound (sh) changed to (KH) or (h), although it remained (sh) in the indigenous languages of the area. In a few cases, such as in *mexicano*, the pronunciation with (sh) was kept, perhaps owing to the influence of the sounds in the original indigenous words. Since Modern Spanish does not have the sound (sh), however, some speakers replaced (sh) with (ch), as the Modern Spanish sound most similar to (sh). The (ch) in *chicano* is thus an attempt to render the sound (sh) found in the original Nahuatl word at the root of the name *Mexico*.

See more at **Hispanic.**

choleric

The older pronunciation (kŏl′ə-rĭk), which is the only one recognized by British dictionaries, has stress on the first syllable like *cholera*. The newer and chiefly American variant (kə-lĕr′ĭk) has stress on the second syllable.

chord / cord

These two words are often confused—and with good reason, for they are really three. There are two words spelled *chord*. One comes from the word *accord* and refers to a harmonious combination of three or more musical notes. The other is an alteration of *cord*, taking its spelling from Greek *chorda*, "string, gut," by way of Latin. A mathematical chord is a line segment that joins two points on a curve.

Cord means "a string or rope." It has many extensions, as in *an electrical cord* and *a cord of wood*. When referring to anatomical structures, it can be spelled in general usage either as *cord* or *chord* (again by influence of Greek and Latin). Strict medical usage requires *cord*, however. A doctor may examine a *spinal cord* or *vocal cords*, not *chords*.

The expression *to strike a chord* is metaphorical, suggesting a harmonious or significant mental resonance with something rather than actual musical notes.

cite   See **sight.**

clause

A clause is a group of words containing a subject and a predicate and forming part of a compound or complex sentence. A *main* or *independent clause* can stand alone as a complete sentence, as *the cat jumped off the table* in the sentence *When the book fell on the floor, the cat jumped off the table*. A *subordinate* or *dependent clause* cannot stand alone as a full sentence and functions as a noun, adjective, or adverb within a sentence. *When the book fell on the floor* in the previous example, and *who answered the phone* in *The woman who answered the phone was very helpful* are examples of dependent clauses.

clique

The pronunciation (klēk) was preferred by 84 percent of the Usage Panel in 1996, and the less common Anglicized variant (klĭk) was acceptable to about half of the Panelists.

close proximity

Strictly speaking, the phrase *close proximity* says nothing that is not said by *proximity* itself. But like a few other common redundancies such as *old adage* and *mental telepathy,* this usage is too widespread and too innocuous to be worth objecting to.

closure

The word *closure* goes back to the 1300s, when it referred to a fence or wall enclosing an area; about a century later, it also referred to the enclosed area itself. But these uses have fallen by the wayside and been replaced with several others that derive from the idea of closing something up (such as a wound), or shutting something down (such as a business), and bringing something to completion as well.

Closure is standard when it has the meaning of "a bringing to an end, a conclusion." Usually it bears with it the implication of a satisfactory or unambiguous result. In our 2001 survey, 78 percent of the Usage Panel accepted the sentence *Voters are becoming impatient with the lengthy recount and yearn for closure.*

This usage has been extended to refer to a feeling of finality or completion after a negative or traumatic experience, and in an era in which self-help and pop psychology are categories of bestsellers, the term has done yeoman's work. Many people dislike this usage, however, perhaps because of its trivializing assumption that there is a definable limit to dealing with life's most trying experiences. When one reaches closure, the implication is that one is emotionally "over" something and can now "move on." Not surprisingly, the Usage Panel is divided on this matter. In our 2001 survey, 49 percent of the Panel rejected the sentence *The book is the troubling story of a teenage girl's journey with her father to South Africa in search of closure after her older sister's murder there.* There is no easy substitute for the term, however, and avoiding it means rephrasing and perhaps rethinking what one wishes to say.

closure / cloture *Closure* is also used as a synonym for *cloture,* the parliamentary procedure in which debate is ended and a vote is taken on the matter under discussion. Either term is acceptable, but since these procedures are conducted under rules of order, be careful not to use these terms to refer to the ending of any legislative debate.

clothes

The pronunciation (klōz) has been recorded in various dictionaries since the 1700s including Samuel Johnson's (1755) and Noah Webster's (1828). The pronunciation (klōthz), while not incorrect, is sometimes considered pedantic. Either pronunciation is acceptable, but (klōz) is much more common.

co–

We can trace the prefix *co–* back to the Latin prefix *co–*, a form of *com–*, meaning "with." In English, the prefix *co–* means "together, joint, jointly." In words such as *co-heir* and *coedit*, *co–* has simply been affixed to words that already existed to create new words whose meanings are easy to guess.

See more at **com–**.

coauthor   See **author**.

coed

Although the word *coed* once referred to male or female university students, it now refers only to a young woman who attends a coeducational college or university. Because there is no separate word for male college students and it carries a connotation of frivolity, the term *coed* is often considered derogatory and is best avoided.

cohort

The English word *cohort* comes from the Latin word *cohors*, which meant "an enclosed area" or "a pen or courtyard enclosing a group cattle or poultry." By extension, the word could refer to any group in general and in particular to a company of soldiers or a troop of cavalry in the army of ancient Rome. The group of men forming the bodyguard of a Roman general or the retinue of a provincial governor was also called a *cohors*. In fact, the English word *court*, meaning both "an enclosed area" and "the retinue of a monarch or noble," also comes from Latin *cohors* by way of Old French *cort*.

Some people insist that the English word *cohort* should be used to refer only to a group of people and never to an individual person, in accordance with the original meaning of the word in Latin. But over the last thirty years or so, the use of *cohort* has become increasingly common, especially in the plural, in reference to individuals. In fact, this has become the predominant usage, overshadowing the use in the singular to refer to a group. Both in our 1988 and 1999 surveys, 71 percent of the Usage Panel accepted the sentence *The cashiered dictator and his cohorts have all written their memoirs.* These results stand in stark contrast to those of our 1965 survey, in which

69 percent rejected the usage. By contrast, only 43 percent in 1988 accepted *The gangster walked into the room surrounded by his cohort,* and 56 percent in 1999 accepted *Like many in her cohort, she was never interested in kids when she was young.*

colander

Traditionally, the first vowel was pronounced as a short *u,* as in *cull.* The pronunciation with a short *o,* as in the first syllable of *collie,* is now much more common. Interestingly, in our 2002 survey, two thirds of the Panelists found the traditional pronunciation to be unacceptable, whereas the acceptance of the newer pronunciation was almost unanimous.

collective nouns

Some nouns, like *committee, clergy, enemy, group, family,* and *team,* refer to a group but are singular in form. These nouns are called *collective nouns.* In American usage, a collective noun takes a singular verb when it refers to the collection considered as a whole, as in *The faculty was united on this question* or *The enemy is suing for peace.* It takes a plural verb when it refers to the members of the group considered as individuals, as in *The faculty are always fighting among themselves* or *The enemy were showing up in groups of three or four to turn in their weapons.* In British usage, collective nouns are more often treated as plurals: *The government have not announced a new policy. The team are playing in the test matches next week.*

In general, writers should try not to treat a collective noun as both singular and plural in the same construction. Consistency requires *The family is determined to press its* [not *their*] *claim.* Sometimes, though, sense requires mixing singulars and plurals. Consider the following passage, for instance:

> The family is never put to any of the tests of snobbery. They are never excluded, everywhere thought to be winning and always wanted; and, because so confident are they of their own quality, they have no thought of excluding anyone else (Joseph Epstein, "In a Snob-Free Zone," *Washington Monthly*)

Here the author looks at the family first as a unit, and then as a group of individuals, each with a separate attitude and outlook. Writing *it has no thought of excluding anyone else* as if the family was a single mind would be impossible.

Collective nouns always refer to living creatures. Similar inanimate nouns, such as *furniture* and *luggage,* differ in that they cannot be counted individually. That is why it is ungrammatical to say *a furniture* or *a luggage.* These nouns are usually called *mass nouns* or *noncount nouns.* They always take a singular verb: *The bedroom furniture was on sale.*

See more at **count nouns** and **subject and verb agreement.**

colon

with series and lists   A colon introduces a series or list when what precedes it is a complete sentence.

The lasting influence of Greece's dramatic tradition is indicated by words still in our vocabulary: *chorus, comedy,* and *drama.*

She has three sources of income: salary, stock dividends, and interest from savings accounts.

The catalog offers the following items: backpacks, tents, sleeping bags, and coolers.

Travelers to Cuzco should bring the following: sunscreen, sunglasses, a hat, a raincoat, and comfortable shoes.

with words, phrases, or clauses   A colon introduces words, phrases, or clauses that explain or amplify what has preceded.

Suddenly I knew where we were: Paris.

The army was cut to pieces: more than fifty thousand men had been captured or killed.

When a colon introduces a complete sentence, the sentence may begin with a capital letter, depending on the publication's style.

The senators had only one goal: They hoped to persuade the board to drop its accounting reforms.

More often, however, the sentence following the colon is not capitalized.

with quotations   A colon often introduces a long quotation.

In his Gettysburg Address, Lincoln said: "Four score and seven years ago our fathers brought forth on this continent, a new nation, conceived in Liberty, and dedicated to the proposition that all men are created equal. . . . "

other uses

1. A colon separates chapter and verse numbers in references to biblical quotations.

    Esther 2:17

2. A colon separates city from publisher in footnotes and bibliographies.

    Scott, *Wall Street Words* (Boston: Houghton Mifflin, 2003)

3. A colon separates hour and minute in time designations.

    11:30 a.m.   an 8:15 class

4. A colon follows the salutation in a business letter or other formal correspondence.

    Dear Sir or Madam: Members of the Board:
    Dear Mr. Quill:

inappropriate uses

1. In general, a colon should not be used after *that is, namely, for example, such as,* or *for instance.*

At supersonic velocities, drag is influenced by Mach number, that is, the velocity of the object as a multiple of the speed of sound.

We will discuss three of Robert Frost's best-known poems, namely, "The Road Not Taken," "Stopping by Woods on a Snowy Evening," and "Fire and Ice."

The team has a host of top defensive players such as Jeff Colt, John Madden, Ed Hardy, and Keith Crow.

2. A colon should not separate a verb and its direct object.

The five biological kingdoms are animals, plants, fungi, bacteria, and protists. Foods that give me hives include strawberries, tomatoes, and chocolate.

color See **person of color.**

colored

Colored, or *coloured,* is recorded in its racial sense as early as 1611, but it did not become widespread in American English until after the Civil War, when the newly freed Black population began to embrace it as a respectful alternative to *black* or *negro.* Well into the 20th century, *colored* remained a self-chosen term of pride, as evidenced by its use in the name of the NAACP (the National Association for the Advancement of Colored People) founded in 1909 and continuing under that name even today. By mid-century, however, the term *colored* had been largely supplanted among Black Americans, first by the recently capitalized *Negro* and later by *Black* and *African American.* As *colored* lost favor in the Black population, its use by outsiders became more clearly offensive; like *Negro,* it should be limited now mainly to historical contexts.

In the United States, *colored* has usually been spelled lowercase. Though it was originally used of persons with relatively light skin, it later became virtually synonymous with *Black* or *Negro* as those terms are used in American society, that is, with reference to any person of African ancestry regardless of mixture with European or other non-African peoples. In South Africa it is written uppercase—*Coloured*—and has long been applied specifically to persons of mixed-race parentage as opposed to racially unmixed Blacks, whites, and Asians. Although still a part of the informal racial vocabulary of South Africa, the use of *Coloured* as an official racial category ended when apartheid was dismantled in 1991.

colored* meaning *nonwhite Although its primary use in American English has been in referring to people of African descent, *colored* has also long been used in the broader sense of *nonwhite,* as when W.E.B. Du Bois spoke of "the inevitable relation of the colored folk of the United States to the colored peoples of America, Africa, Asia, and the world" in a 1953 article in *Monthly Review.* Once *colored* came to be viewed as offensive, however, its usage to mean *nonwhite* declined as well; this sense is now usually expressed in phrases formed with the words *of color.*

See more at **person of color.**

com–

Like the element *ad–*, *com–* does not create new words in English, but it appears in many familiar words under a variety of spellings. The basic meaning of the prefix *com–* is "together, with." It comes from the Latin prefix *com–*. Before the consonants *l* and *r*, Latin *com–* became *col–* and *cor–*, respectively, as we see in our words *collaborate* and *correspond*. Before all other consonants except *p, b,* or *m, com–* became *con–*, as in *confirm, constitution,* and *contribute.*

comedic / comic / comical

The word *comedy* has a broad range of meanings, but in general it indicates a dramatic or literary work that is light and often humorous or satirical in tone and that usually contains a happy resolution of the thematic conflict. The adjectives *comic* and *comedic* can relate to any work of this sort, whether the work is humorous or simply has a happy ending. *Comedic,* however, is normally used to mean "relating to comedy as a dramatic or artistic form," and not "humorous." Writers should avoid using *comedic* in such sentences as *No one was fooled by his comedic attempt to hide his blunder,* when the intended meaning is "laughable." *Comic* is also frequently used in the same sense as *comedic,* "characteristic of or having to do with comedy," as in the phrase *comic actor.*

　　In contrast to *comedic,* the adjectives *comic* and *comical* can both mean simply "amusing, humorous." *Comic,* however, is more often used of intentional efforts to be funny, as in *Her comic rendition of the song had everyone in stitches. Comical,* on the other hand, is often reserved for unintentional humor: *His comical misuse of the English language doomed his political career.*

comma

appositives

1. Commas set off a word or phrase that is in apposition to (equivalent to) a noun.

   > Plato, the famous Greek philosopher, was a pupil of Socrates.

   > The composer of *Tristan and Isolde,* Richard Wagner, was a leading exponent of German romanticism.

   > The Democratic candidate for state senate, Andy Maynard, spoke at the rally.

2. Restrictive appositives (words or phrases that further specify the noun) should not be set off with commas.

   > The Greek philosopher Plato was a pupil of Socrates.
   > The composer Richard Wagner was a leading exponent of German romanticism.
   > The Dostoevsky novel *Crime and Punishment* was required reading.

compound predicates　　The parts of a compound predicate are not normally separated by a comma except to prevent misreading.

The element was discovered in 1862 and was later used in explosives.
We worked hard on the project but could not finish in time.
I called the loan officer who left me the message, and asked for more information.

compound sentences   A comma often separates the clauses of a compound sentence connected by a coordinating conjunction, such as *and, but, or, nor, yet,* or *so.*

There is a difference between the works of Mozart and Haydn, and it is a difference worth discovering.

She didn't know where they got such an idea, but she didn't disagree.

Their car broke down, so they won't be arriving until tomorrow.

If the clauses are short and closely connected, the comma may be left out.

Tim cooked and I cleaned.   Use a small brush and paint
Should I stay or should I go?   quickly.

coordinate adjectives   A comma usually separates two or more adjectives that modify the same noun if *and* could be inserted between them without changing the meaning.

a solid, heavy gate   the hungry, impatient travelers
a large, high-ceilinged room   a simple, unadorned style
a grainy, old, black-and-white film

If the adjectives are short, the comma may be left out.

fresh green grass   large pointed ears

No comma should be used if the last adjective and the noun constitute a unit or denote a single idea.

elegant high-rise buildings   the complicated mathematical
common compound nouns   formula
a polished mahogany desk   favorite classical music
a silver metallic element

dates   Commas set off the year from the month in a full date.

Louis XVI of France was guillotined on January 21, 1793.
November 1, 2004, was the day I returned to work.

In an expression consisting of just the month and the year, a comma is not needed.

The book came out in September 2005.

direct address   Commas set off words used in direct address.

Ranjit, please submit your report as soon as possible.
Thank you, Sonja, for all your help.
Where is the cash, my friend?

interrogative phrases   A comma separates an interrogative phrase from the rest of the sentence.

You remembered the keys, didn't you?
Beethoven's Sixth Symphony is on the program, isn't it?

introductory elements

1. Words used to introduce a sentence are set off by a comma.

> No, I haven't seen her.
> Yes, the dress will be ready by Friday.
> Oh, I thought you had already left.
> Well, why don't you listen to me next time?

2. A long phrase or a subordinate clause that precedes the main clause is usually set off by a comma.

> Of all the illustrations in the book, the most striking are those of the tapestries.
>
> Because the weather has been so dry, thousands of trees are being destroyed by forest fires.

A comma is not needed after a short introductory phrase or even after a longer one if the sentence flows easily on its own.

> Last summer we camped in the Rockies.
> When peeling an orange you should take care to remove the pith.

locations   A comma separates the parts of a full address run into text.

> Payment should be mailed to the Lakeview Inn, 512 Peaks Street, Bedford, VA 01234, by June 15.

If the name of a place is followed by the state or country in which it is located, use commas around the state or country name.

> Boston, Massachusetts, is the most populous city in New England.
> While in Valparaiso, Chile, we visited Pablo Neruda's house.

nonrestrictive and restrictive modifiers

1. Use commas to set off a nonrestrictive phrase or clause—that is, one that merely provides additional information and could be eliminated without changing the meaning of the sentence.

> The thief, who had entered through the window, went straight to the safe.

2. Do not use commas to set off a restrictive phrase or clause—that is, one that limits the noun it modifies and is essential to the meaning of the sentence.

> The thief who had entered through the window went straight to the safe; the thief who had entered by the skylight searched the attic for silver.

numbers   Figures of four digits or more are generally written with commas, although an alternative style is to use commas only in figures of five digits or more. Page numbers, street addresses, years of four digits, and decimal fractions should not contain commas.

2,000 entries *or* 2000 entries	page 1100
$5,000 in debt *or* $5000 in debt	2866 Lawndale Avenue
10,000 miles	the year 1776
20,000 BC	3.14159
57,685,901 votes	

omissions   When two or more clauses in a sentence have the same verb, a comma may replace the verb in the second and later clauses.

> To err is human; to forgive, divine.
> Dad votes conservative, and Mom, liberal.
> Bud cooked the turkey; Eva, the goose; and Sina, the duck.

quotations

1. A comma sets off a direct quotation from the rest of the sentence.

> "Please join me for dinner," said Dexter.
> "I don't know if I can," replied Colin, "but maybe I will."

2. If a direct quotation within a sentence serves as a subject, direct object, object of a preposition, or other integral component of the sentence, do not set it off with commas.

> "I'll do it" was her defiant reply.
> Franklin Roosevelt promised "a new deal for the American people."
> The story is full of clichés, such as "live dangerously" and "dressed to the nines."

salutations   A comma follows the salutation in a personal letter and the complimentary close in a business or personal letter.

> Dear Akiko,   Very truly yours,
> Sincerely,

series   A comma separates items in a series.

> Lights of red, green, and blue wavelengths may be mixed to produce all colors.
> The radio, television set, and stereo were all arranged on one shelf.
> Shall we have ice cream, cake, or pie?

An alternative style is to omit the comma when a conjunction, such as *and* or *or*, joins the last two items.

> We visited the government palace, the national museum and the historic district.

However, the comma should always be included in cases where confusion could result without it.

> The book treats the traditional usage bugbears, such as *disinterested, lay* and *lie,* and *impact.*

titles, degrees, and names   Commas set off titles and degrees from the rest of the sentence.

> Cassandra Z. Warshowsky, Esq., specializes in civil litigation.

> Carmen Ruiz, MD, was an expert witness in the malpractice case.
> Methods for Elementary School Reading will be taught by Charley Kihn, EdD.

It is not necessary to place commas around *Jr.* and *Sr.*, but if commas are used they should appear on both sides of the abbreviation.

> Jared Foster Jr. married Eliza Cornwell in 1889.
> *or*
> Jared Foster, Jr., married Eliza Cornwell in 1889.
>
> Kelly McGowan Sr. is writing a book on venomous reptiles.
> *or*
> Kelly McGowan, Sr., is writing a book on venomous reptiles.

to prevent misreading   A comma separates sentence elements that might be confusing if the comma were not present.

> Some time after, the actual date was set.
> To Carl Thomas, Alfred Martin was just a nuisance.
> Add the sugar, and cream until light and fluffy.

transitional words   Short transitional expressions such as *however, therefore, consequently, unfortunately, of course, as a matter of fact, for example,* and *indeed* are set off by commas if they require a pause in reading or speaking.

> Queen Victoria, however, was not amused.
> Unfortunately, Tyler hadn't read many Russian novels.
> All of the passengers, of course, were transferred to another bus.
> Indeed, the sight of him gave me quite a jolt.
> Yes, as a matter of fact, I did overhear you.

Transitional words or expressions that do not require a pause do not require commas.

> Of course you may come!   Indeed I will.
> My argument is therefore com-
>   plete.

comma splice   See **run-on sentence.**

commentate

Commentate, a back-formation from *commentator,* is normally used to mean "to serve as a commentator": *The retired tennis pro commentated on the upcoming match.* This usage does not sit well with the Usage Panel, however. In our 2004 survey, some 85 percent of the Panel found this usage unacceptable, and 87 percent rejected the transitive usage of this word (that is, the same sentence quoted above without the word *on*).

See more at **back-formation.**

common era See **AD.**

common nouns

A common noun is a noun, such as *book, furniture,* or *dog,* that can be preceded by the definite article and that represents one or all of the members of a class. Note that common nouns can be abstractions like *decisiveness, singularity,* and *resolution,* as well as concrete objects. See also **proper nouns.**

compact disk / compact disc See **disk.**

comparable

Usually when the suffix *–able* is attached to a word, the stress pattern of the original word remains the same. For example, *manage* is stressed on the first syllable, and by adding *–able* to form *manageable,* the stress remains on the first syllable. One prominent exception occurs when *–able* is added to *compare,* which is stressed on the second syllable. *Comparable* is traditionally pronounced with stress on the first syllable, sometimes as a four-syllable word (kŏm′pər-ə-bəl) and sometimes as a three-syllable word (kŏm′prə-bəl). In our 2002 survey, 70 percent of the Usage Panel found the pronunciation in which the second syllable is stressed (kəm-pâr′ə-bəl) to be unacceptable. This pronunciation is very common, however, and would seem likely to become more acceptable because so many other words are stressed in this pattern.

comparative degree

The comparative degree is the intermediate degree of comparison of adjectives, as *better, sweeter,* or *more wonderful,* or adverbs, as *more softly.* Except for some irregular cases (such as *better* above), the comparative degree forms are formed by addition of the suffix *–er* (for adjectives) or by modification with *more* (for adjectives and adverbs, as in *I drive more aggressively than Frank does*).

See more at **adjectives** and **adverbs.**

compare to / compare with

Compare usually takes the preposition *to* when it refers to the activity of describing something in terms of its resemblance with something else: *He compared her to a summer day. Scientists sometimes compare the human brain to a computer.* It takes *with* when it refers to the act of examining two like things in order to discern their similarities or differences: *The police compared the forged signature with the original. The committee will have to compare the Senate's version of the bill with the version that was passed by the House.*

comparison

In grammar, the term *comparison* refers to the modification or inflection of an adjective or adverb to indicate the positive, comparative, and superlative degrees. Many adjectives and adverbs can undergo comparison, as in *fast, faster, fastest.* Many others, such as *biological* and *opposite,* cannot.

See more at **adjectives** and **adverbs.**

comparisons with *as* and *than*

In comparisons using *as* and *than,* it is the second element that can cause trouble, making it is easy to set up a faulty parallel, especially when prepositional phrases are involved. In the sentence *I want the photos in our brochure to look as impressive as their brochure,* the writer wants to compare photos in two different brochures, but the syntax compares the photos of one brochure with the entire brochure of the other organization. To be parallel, the sentence must read *I want the photos in our brochure to look as impressive as those in their brochure.* Note the addition of the pronoun *those* to counterbalance *photos* in the previous section of the sentence, and the repetition of the preposition *in.* In place of the pronoun, the noun *photos* could be repeated with similar effect.

Here is a second example: *They felt that the condition of the new buildings was not much better than the old ones.* In this sentence the condition of the new buildings is compared with the old buildings themselves, not with their condition. The pronoun *that* must be added to balance the noun *condition.* Again, the noun can be repeated instead, but in either case the prepositional phrase with *of* must follow: *They felt that the condition of the new buildings was not much better than that* [or *than the condition*] *of the old ones.*

Sometimes only the second preposition gets left out in these comparative constructions, as in *More cars are built in Canada than Mexico,* where perfect parallelism requires . . . *than in Mexico.*

As and *than* comparisons pose additional problems when the noun following *as* or *than* is the subject or object of an implied clause. Does the sentence *The employees are more suspicious of the arbitrator than the owner* mean that the employees distrust the arbitrator more than they distrust the owner or that the employees distrust the arbitrator more than the owner does? To clarify this, a verb must be added to the second element of the comparison: *The employees are more suspicious of the arbitrator than they are of the owner* or *The employees are more suspicious of the arbitrator than the owner is.*

Sentences containing *as* and *than* comparisons may be unambiguous but still be in need of balancing. Here are two other examples: *More than twice as many tons of corrugated cardboard are recycled each year than* [*are tons of*] *newspaper. The factory is producing as many transmissions as* [*it did*] *last year.* The material in brackets is often left out in sentences of this type, but parallelism requires it.

See more at **parallelism.**

compendious

The word *compendious* means "containing or stating briefly and concisely all the essentials," that is, "succinct." It is ultimately derived from the Latin noun *compendium,* "a saving, a shortcut." However, since compendious reference works that summarize a great deal of knowledge, like encyclopedias, are often quite hefty books, *compendious* is sometimes mistakenly given the meaning "voluminous, capacious," or "thorough, all-inclusive." Perhaps the phonetic similarity of the words *complete, compilation,* and *comprehensive* has contributed to the misunderstanding of *compendious.* In any case, writers should be wary of imitating such sentences as *The biographer spent ten years in the preparation of this compendious but often long-winded volume* or *The author displays his amazingly compendious knowledge of world mythology on every page.*

Similarly, the English noun *compendium* means "short, complete summary, an abstract" or "a list or collection of various items," but not "a comprehensive, in-depth compilation."

complacent / complaisant

Complacent means either "overly contented, self-satisfied" (as in *After making a string of successes, the film director grew complacent*), or "eager to please; agreeable." Be sure that the context makes it clear which sense is intended. If it does not, one way of guaranteeing the "eager to please" reading is to use the identically pronounced word *complaisant,* which shares this latter meaning. Thus the sentence *We were taken on a tour by a complaisant guide* is unambiguous. The ambiguity of a sentence such as *We were taken on a tour by a complacent guide* could be resolved with the use of another adjective: *We were taken on a tour by a complacent and unresponsive guide.*

complement

The *complements* of a verb are its direct and indirect objects. In *The prime minister gave the staff a puzzled look,* for example, the verb *gave* has two complements, *the staff* and *a puzzled look.* Similarly, the infinitival clause *to eat ice cream* in *We like to eat ice cream* is the verb's complement.

Nouns and adjectives also take complements. In these cases the word *of* often stands in front of the direct object and is generally considered a part of the complement. For example, in the phrases *pictures of John* and *jealous of John,* the entire prepositional phrase *of John* is the complement.

complement / compliment

Complement and *compliment,* though quite distinct in meaning, are sometimes confused because they are pronounced identically. As a noun, *complement* means "something that completes or brings to perfection" (*The antique silver was a complement to the beautifully set table*); used as a verb it means "to serve as a complement to." The noun *compliment* means "an expression or act of courtesy or praise" (*They gave us a compliment on our beautifully set table*), while the verb means "to pay a compliment to." The following sentence illustrates both words: *She* complimented *him on the way his necktie* complemented *his jacket.*

complete

Although *complete* is often held to be an absolute term like **perfect** or *chief,* and therefore not subject to comparison, it is actually often qualified as *more* or *less.* As far back as 1965, a majority of the Usage Panel accepted the example *His book is the most complete treatment of the subject.* It is not hard to see why, as the comparison of *complete* is very handy, as the following examples demonstrate:

> Astronomers said they expected further observations to give them a more complete picture of the planet's atmosphere, and to widen the study to other extrasolar worlds (John Noble Wilford, "In a Golden Age of Discovery, Faraway Worlds Beckon," *New York Times*)

> . . . Bannister was not the same man anymore. He had a mentor in Stampfl, training partners in Chataway and Brasher, and a more complete understanding of how important it was to have faith in himself (Neal Bascomb, *The Perfect Mile*)

> Traditional fuels are hydrocarbons (that is, their component molecules are made only of hydrogen and carbon). Biodiesel molecules contain oxygen, as well. The extra oxygen promotes more complete combustion to carbon dioxide and water (*The Economist*)

> As they removed piece after piece from the gully bank, Walker and the rest of the team slowly realized that they were uncovering the most complete early human remains that had ever been found, more complete than the vaunted Lucy discovery a decade earlier (Craig Stanford, *Upright*)

See more at **absolute terms, certain, equal, infinite, parallel, perfect,** and **unique.**

complex sentence

A complex sentence consists of at least one independent clause and one dependent clause, as in the following examples: *When I grow up, I want to be a doctor. The man that I most admire is my history teacher. We went for a walk, even though it was raining.*

compose   See **comprise.**

compound-complex sentence

A compound-complex sentence consists of at least two coordinate independent clauses and one or more dependent clauses, as *I wanted to go, but I decided not to when it started raining. I wish you would stay, but I can understand why you have to leave. I told him that the water was too cold for swimming, and once he put his foot in, he had to agree with me.*

compound sentence

A compound sentence consists of two or more coordinate independent clauses, often joined by a conjunction, as *The problem was difficult, but I finally found the answer; I have enjoyed talking to you, and I am glad to have finally met you; Either we should buy a new car, or we should move into the city.*

compound verbs and ambiguity

When the first part of a compound verb is followed by a subordinate clause, the second part of the verb may appear to belong to the subordinate clause. For instance, in the sentence *Jim knew that Candace had discovered the thief and felt it was OK to tell the reporters,* who felt it was OK to tell the reporters, Jim or Candace? The verbs are structured in parallel fashion—with two possibilities—and the end result is ambiguity.

In these cases, it is best to give the second verb its own subject: *Jim knew that Candace had discovered the thief, and he felt it was OK to tell the reporters.* As an alternative, the sentence can be recast to avoid the ambiguous parallelism in the verbs: *Once Jim knew that Candace had discovered the thief, he felt it was OK to tell the reporters.*

See more at **parallelism.**

compound words

A compound word, often simply called a *compound,* is made up of two or more words that together express a single idea. There are three types of compounds. An *open compound* consists of two or more words written separately, such as *salad dressing, Boston terrier,* or *April Fools' Day.* A *hyphenated compound* has words connected by a hyphen, such as *age-old, mother-in-law, force-feed.* A *solid compound* consists of two words that are written as one word, such as *keyboard* or *typewriter.* In addition, a compound may be classified as permanent or temporary. A *permanent compound* is fixed by common usage and can usually be found in the dictionary, whereas a *temporary compound* consists of two or more words joined by a hyphen as needed, usually to modify another word or to avoid ambiguity. In general, permanent compounds begin as temporary compounds that become used so frequently they become established as permanent compounds. Likewise many solid compounds begin as separate words, develop into hyphenated compounds, and later become solid compounds. Although the dictionary is the first place to look when trying to determine whether a particular compound should be hyphenated or not, reference works do not always agree on the current styling of a compound, nor do they include temporary compounds.

Many English words are borrowings of Greek and Latin compounds formed from independent words or the other specially modified combining forms used in these languages. For example, the English word *parasite* is a borrowing of the Greek *parasītos*, "one who eats at another's table," a compound made from *para–*, "beside," and the noun *sītos*, "grain, food."

See more at **hyphenation.**

comprise / compose

The traditional rule for these words states that the whole *comprises* the parts and that the parts *compose* the whole. Thus one would say *The Union comprises fifty states* and *Fifty states compose* [or *constitute* or *make up*] *the Union.* In usage books, the passive use of *comprise*, as in *The Union is comprised of fifty states*, is especially called out as a mistake.

Our surveys suggest that in at least some contexts, resistance to this usage is abating. When *comprise* has the physical meaning of "to make up the substance of something," the Usage Panel is split, with 53 percent in our 1996 survey disapproving of the sentence *New cells comprising the brain's blood vessels form only as a result of injury or disease.* The use of *comprise* as a synonym of "constitute" wrinkled even more brows, with 58 percent rejecting *They bantered back and forth about what comprised "restaurant food" as opposed to "home food."* But 65 percent approved of *comprise*, even in its passive use, in *The university disciplinary board is comprised of ten faculty members, three administrators, and two students.* This stands in stark contrast to the 53 percent who disapproved of the construction back in 1965. This may mean that *comprise* is less likely to grate on a reader's nerves when the context lists a number of components that make up the whole. But even if the traditional distinction may be destined to fall by the wayside, observing it in one's own writing is still justifiable since it is both logical and idiomatic.

See more at **include.**

comptroller / controller

Around 1500, the word *controller* developed the alternate spelling *comptroller* as a result of an association between the first part of the word, *cont–*, and the etymologically unrelated word *count* and its variant *compt.* Although the historical pronunciation of *comptroller* would be the same as for *controller*, evidence suggests that the spelling pronunciations (kŏmp-trō′lər) and (kŏmp′trō′lər) may now be used by a majority of speakers. In our 1995 survey, 43 percent of the Usage Panel indicated that they pronounce *comptroller* like *controller*, while 57 percent pronounce it with *mp*, as it is spelled, with stress on either the first or second syllable. And half of those Panelists who pronounce *comptroller* like *controller* indicated that they also consider the *mp* spelling pronunciations acceptable.

See more at **spelling pronunciation.**

conch

Among those who are familiar with *conchs* as seafood, the *ch* in the name of these mollusks is usually pronounced (k), as it is in *concha, conchoid,* and *conchology.* These words all ultimately derived from Greek *konkhē,* "mussel." The word *conch* was sometimes spelled *conk* or *congh* in Middle English, which indicates that the pronunciation with (k) has long been in use. (In Middle English, the word was also used with the meaning "bowl" or "basin," from the hollow shape of the conch's shell.) However, some people nowadays say (kŏnch). This pronunciation is perhaps based on the spelling with *ch,* but it is also possible that pronunciation with (ch) is just as old in English as the pronunciation with (k). The existence of the two pronunciations may indicate that the word *conch* entered the English language through two different routes, both beginning with the original Greek source of the word. On the one hand, Greek *konkhē* was first borrowed into Latin as *concha,* pronounced (kōn′ka) in Latin, and then it may have entered English directly as *conch* with a (k). On the other hand, as Latin developed into French, the word *concha* became *conche,* pronounced (kōn′chə) in Old French. The French word may then have been borrowed into English as *conch* with a (ch), or it may otherwise have exerted influence over the pronunciation of the English word *conch.* (The word *conche* is still used in dialectal French today in the sense "pond of a salt marsh," a development of the meaning "basin," although the word is now pronounced (kōɴsh). The Modern French form of the word for the bivalve mollusk is *conque,* a direct borrowing from Latin.) In English, the same variation in pronunciation between (k) and (ch) also occurs in the compound *conchfish,* a small fish which inhabits the cavity within the body of conchs.

According to the pronunciation used, the plural of *conch* is *conchs* (kŏngks) or *conches* (kŏn′chĭz).

See more at **ch** and **spelling pronunciation**.

concord   See **agreement**.

concupiscence

Concupiscence, meaning "a strong sexual desire, lust," is traditionally pronounced with the primary stress on the second syllable (kŏn-kyōō′pĭ-səns). An alternative pronunciation with primary stress on the third syllable (kŏn′kyōō-pĭs′əns) is a more recent innovation; however, in our 2002 survey, only 54 percent of the Usage Panel approved of this newer pronunciation.

condemn / contemn

Condemn can mean "to express strong disapproval of, declare unfit" as in *The inspector condemned the lack of safety precautions,* or "to pronounce judgment against; sentence," as in *The judge condemned the felons to prison.* In origin, *condemn* is related to *damnation.* Both derive from Latin *damnum,* meaning "injury, damage," and also "legal penalty."

Contemn, on the other hand, means "to despise, hold in contempt." In the sentence *He contemned the wasteful society in which he lived,* the verb *contemn* simply describes the subject's attitude of scorn, whereas in the sentence *He condemned the wasteful society in which he lived,* the verb *condemn* suggests that the subject voiced his disapproval openly or came to a mental realization of previously unformed objections. The verb *contemn* is also found in legal writing with the technical meaning "to display open disrespect or willful disobedience of (the authority of a court of law or legislative body)." *Contemner* or *contemnor,* the agent noun formed from *contemn,* is sometimes found in the meaning "person held in contempt of court." *Contemn* is the verb corresponding to the noun *contempt,* and both words are ultimately derived from the Latin verb *contemnere,* "despise, disdain."

Contemn can furnish a useful if rather literary synonym for "despise," and although the word can sound somewhat stiff and artificial today, it has an illustrious pedigree in English. Shakespeare used it on several occasions, and the translators of the Authorized Version (King James Version) of the Bible chose *contemn* almost a dozen times in rendering words meaning "scorn," as in *Because they rebelled against the words of God, and contemned the counsel of the most High: Therefore he brought down their heart with labour* (Psalms 107:11–12).

conditional clause / conditional sentence

A conditional clause expresses a condition, that is, a circumstance that is necessary for something else to happen. Conditional clauses usually begin with *if, unless, provided that,* or a similar conjunction. Conditional sentences are sentences that contain conditional clauses: *If it starts to rain, we will have to leave. We cannot go to the beach unless he lends us his car. Your friends can stay for dinner, provided that we have enough food.*

condole / console

The verb *condole* has an uneasy perch in English. It is normally an intransitive verb meaning "to express sorrow or sympathy" and is usually accompanied by a *with* phrase, as in *He condoled with the family on the death of their grandfather.* But this construction was acceptable to only 34 percent of the Usage Panel in our 1996 ballot. *Condole* is sometimes used transitively, probably by confusion with *console,* as in *The President condoled families whose sons died in the battle.* The Panel has even less enthusiasm for this usage, with 82 percent finding it unacceptable. A similar percentage rejected the transitive use meaning "to express sympathy about" in the sentence *Iroquois diplomats condoled the deaths of non-Iroquois allies.*

It is far better, then, to stick with *console* or to use the plural noun *condolences,* which has long been standard in expressions of sympathy. You *send, offer,* or *express* your condolences to the members of the family.

conduction   See **radiation.**

conflicted

The word *conflicted* is gaining currency as an adjective meaning "having conflicting feelings or opinions," but resistance to it has been high. In our 1988 survey, 92 percent of the Usage Panel rejected *Caught between loyalty to old employees and a recognition of the need to cut costs, many managers are conflicted about the reorganization plan.* To avoid this usage, the sentence might be reworded as *Caught between loyalty to old employees and a recognition of the need to cut costs, many managers have conflicting feelings about the reorganization plan.*

congenital / inherited

The words *congenital* and *inherited* both refer to diseases or conditions that exist at birth. Abnormal characteristics or conditions that are *inherited* are a result of genetic or chromosomal defects, as in hemophilia. Inherited diseases are also called *genetic* diseases. The signs of disease may be present at birth, as in Down Syndrome, or they may not appear until later in life, as in Huntington's disease. The word *congenital* is derived from the Latin *com–,* meaning "together," and *genitus,* meaning "born." Although all inherited diseases are technically congenital, not all congenital conditions are inherited.

The word *congenital* is most often used to describe what are called *congenital anomalies,* or structural defects present at birth. These conditions may be inherited, or they may result from toxic factors in the prenatal environment, such as drugs, chemicals, infections, radiation, poor nutrition, or traumatic injuries, as from oxygen deprivation. The defect may be apparent, as in congenital deafness or dwarfism, or microscopic. Sometimes it is not known whether a congenital defect is a result of an inherited mutation or environmental influences, as in many kinds of congenital heart disease. *Congenital* is also often used to describe conditions resulting from trauma during labor or delivery, such as cerebral palsy.

congeries

Congeries means "a collection, an aggregation," as in the following sentence from *Roger's Version* by John Updike: *Our city, it should be explained, is two cities, or more—an urban mass or congeries divided by the river.* Many writers use it with the further connotation of "a hodgepodge of items of disparate nature" or "a chaotic mixture," as in *The new empire was a mere congeries of disparate ethnic groups, and it fell to pieces after the death of its charismatic founder.*

Congeries is in origin a Latin word meaning "that which is brought together, a heap." The proper English (and Latin) plural of *congeries* is the same as the singular, like the plural of several other English words of Latin origin such as *series, species,* and the scientific word *facies.* The singular is in fact far more commonly used than the plural, as in the examples above.

Appropriately enough for its meaning, *congeries* has a variety of pronunciations. The most common current pronunciations in American English are (kŏn′jə-rēz′) and (kən-jîr′ēz′). The older British pronunciation (kŏn-jē′rĭ-ēz′), with four syllables and stress on the second syllable, reflects more closely the original pronunciation in Latin.

conjugal

Conjugal is traditionally pronounced (kŏn′jə-gəl), with the stress on the first syllable and roughly rhyming with *bondable*. This was the preferred pronunciation of 94 percent of the Usage Panel in our 2004 survey. The pronunciation with stress on the second syllable (kən-jōō′gəl), rhyming roughly with *a bugle* was the pronunciation of only 6 percent of the Panel and is often considered incorrect.

conjunctions   See **coordinating conjunctions, correlative conjunctions,** and **subordinating conjunctions.**

conjunctive adverbs

Conjunctive adverbs connect independent clauses or sentences. Accordingly, they must occur in a new sentence or in an independent clause following a semicolon. Using a comma to separate a clause that has a conjunctive adverb results in the grammatical fault known as a *comma splice.* Conjunctive adverbs are thus different from subordinating conjunctions, which introduce dependent clauses. Conjunctive adverbs include words like *accordingly, besides, furthermore, however, likewise, moreover, nevertheless, therefore.*

Note that, unlike conjunctions, conjunctive adverbs do not have to be placed at the beginning of a clause. Thus one can say *Megan sings in the choir; however, her brother plays in the band* or *Megan sings in the choir; her brother, however, plays in the band* or *Megan sings in the choir; her brother plays in the band, however.*

See more at **transition words.**

connive

As it has been used traditionally, *connive* has more than one widely accepted meaning. One is "to cooperate secretly in an illegal or wrongful action, collude," as in *The dealers connived with customs officials to bring in narcotics.* Another meaning is "to feign ignorance of or fail to take measures against a wrong, thus implying tacit encouragement or consent," as in *The guards were suspected of conniving at the prisoner's escape.* Thus, in standard usage, the complement of *connive* is usually an infinitive or a prepositional phrase beginning with *at,* as in the example sentences above. *Connive* is also used in the general sense "to scheme," frequently heard as a participial adjective in denunciations beginning *You conniving little rat . . .* and the like.

In colloquial English, the verb *connive* has acquired further, nontraditional usages in which the verb is transitive and takes a direct object that is usually a person or a noun like *way*. In this regard, *connive* is sometimes used in the sense "to dupe, con," as in *Their broker connived them into buying the worthless stock*. (The verb *con*, in the sense of "to swindle by winning the victim's confidence," is not directly related to *connive* but is in fact just a shortening of the word *confidence*.) *Connive* is also used popularly with the meaning "to manage (to do) or to obtain through underhanded means." Here the word seems to be influenced by *contrive*, a verb often found in sentences describing devious or criminal undertakings, such as *He somehow contrived* [not *connived*] *to hide his criminal record from everyone*. The development of these uses of *connive* probably arose from the similarity in sound of *con*, *connive*, and *contrive*. Writers should be aware that no major American dictionary accepts these transitive senses of *connive*, and so should avoid constructing sentences like *I connived him into letting me use his beach house* or *The politician connived his way into voters' hearts with promises that he never intended to keep*.

consensus

Many grammarians have condemned the expression *consensus of opinion* as redundant since a consensus itself entails a judgment about which there is general agreement. But many reputable writers have used *consensus of opinion*, and some have defended it on the grounds that a consensus may involve attitudes other than opinions; thus, there may be a *consensus of beliefs* or a *consensus of usage*. Nonetheless, the qualifying *of* phrase can usually be omitted with no loss of clarity. The sentence *It was the consensus of opinion among the sportswriters that the game should not have been played* says nothing that is not said by *It was the consensus of the sportswriters that the game should not have been played*.

Expressions such as *overall consensus* and *general consensus* are harder to defend against the charge of redundancy.

consider as / deem as

The use of *as* with verbs like *consider* is more likely to appear in print in passive constructions than in active ones. This may be because *as* intervenes and disrupts the naturalness of the double complement in sentences like *We consider him* [*as*] *a good hire*. It would seem, in any case, that copyeditors more readily delete *as* in these active sentences. It may be too that in passive constructions *as* serves the purpose of highlighting the contrast between what a thing is and what it is considered. In the examples *This document is still more striking when considered as political propaganda* and *This drug should not be considered as a way to lose weight*, the inclusion of *as* underscores the perception involved in making the judgment.

console   See **condole**.

contact

The verb *contact* is a classic example of a verb that was made from a noun and of a new usage that was initially frowned upon. The noun meaning "the state or condition of touching" was introduced in 1626 by Francis Bacon. Some two hundred years later it spawned a verb meaning "to bring or place in contact." This sense of the verb has lived an unremarkable life in technical contexts. It was only in the first quarter of the 20th century that *contact* came to be used to mean "to communicate with," and soon afterward the controversy began. *Contact* was declared to be properly a noun, not a verb—and besides, it was argued, as a verb it was vague.

Neither of these arguments holds water. Turning nouns into verbs is one of the most routine ways in which new verbs enter English. The examples are countless and familiar. *Curb, date, elbow, hand, interview, panic, park,* and *service* are but a few. The verb *contact* is but another instance of what linguists call *functional shift* from one part of speech to another. As for *contact*'s vagueness, this seems a virtue in an age in which forms of communication have proliferated. The sentence *We will contact you when your application has been processed* allows for a variety of possible ways to communicate: by mail, telephone, computer, or fax.

It appears that the usefulness and popularity of this verb has worn down resistance to it as a part of Standard English. In 1969, only 34 percent of the Usage Panel accepted the use of *contact* as a verb, but in 1988, 65 percent of the panel accepted it in the sentence *She immediately called an officer at the Naval Intelligence Service, who in turn contacted the FBI.* In 2004, fully 94 percent accepted *contact* in this same sentence.

See more at **impact.**

contagious / infectious

The adjective *contagious* refers technically to any disease that can be transmitted from one living being to another through direct contact (as with measles or AIDS) or indirect contact (as with cholera or typhus). In common usage, however, it is most frequently used to describe diseases or conditions that are easily communicable. *Infectious* diseases are those caused by an infectious pathogen, such as a bacterium, virus, fungus, or parasite. While all contagious diseases are infectious, not all infectious diseases are contagious. The word *infectious* refers to the cause of an illness, namely an infectious agent, while *contagious* refers to its transmissibility. Thus, genital warts are an infectious condition, caused by a virus, but are contagious only through sexual contact. While the notion of contagiousness goes back to ancient times, the concept of infectious diseases is rooted in the germ theory of disease, which was not proposed until the late 19th century.

contemn   See **condemn.**

contemptible / contemptuous

These two useful words can sometimes be confusing, but it is not difficult to keep them distinguished. *Contemptible* means "deserving of contempt, despicable." It leads a healthy existence in denunciations of all kinds but also has led a distinguished life in literature, as the following quotations will show:

> A moment's reflection will, I am sure, convince you, that a man with whom the secrets of a lady are not safe must be the most contemptible of wretches (Henry Fielding, *Tom Jones*)

> As a general principle and abstract proposition, Miggs held the male sex to be utterly contemptible and unworthy of notice; to be fickle, false, base, sottish, inclined to perjury, and wholly undeserving (Charles Dickens, *Barnaby Rudge*)

> Never mind, Harriet, I shall not be a poor old maid; and it is poverty only which makes celibacy contemptible to a generous public (Jane Austen, *Emma*)

Contemptuous means "manifesting or feeling contempt; scornful," as in

> Anyone who had looked at him as the red light shone upon his pale face, strange straining eyes, and meagre form, would perhaps have understood the mixture of contemptuous pity, dread, and suspicion with which he was regarded by his neighbours in Raveloe (George Eliot, *Silas Marner*)

The word is often followed by the preposition *of*, as in

> Contemptuous of all his own underlings, politicians, generals, and diplomats alike, Stalin showed himself impressed by his alliance partners; they were men of power and destiny, whom he considered to be of his own stature in history (Peter Grose, *Operation Rollback*)

continual / continuous

These adjectives are sometimes confused because their meanings overlap. Both words can be used to mean "continuing without interruption": *living in a continual state of fear, enjoying a continuous state of peace*. But *continual* usually refers to something that recurs or is interrupted periodically:

> Discerning the impracticable state of the poor culprit's mind, the elder clergyman, who had carefully prepared himself for the occasion, addressed to the multitude a discourse on sin, in all its branches, but with continual reference to the ignominious letter (Nathaniel Hawthorne, *The Scarlet Letter*)

> I like much the general idea of framing a government which should go on of itself, peaceably, without needing continual recurrence to the State Legislatures (Thomas Jefferson, Letter to James Madison, *The Jeffersonian Cyclopedia*)

Only *continuous* is used to refer to physical continuation:

> The walls are shelved waist-high for books, and the top thus forms a continuous table running round the wall (Robert Louis Stevenson, *Essays of Travel*)

continuance / continuation

Both of these words mean "the act or fact of continuing," but only *continuance* is used to refer to the duration of a state or condition:

> . . . I shall conclude, therefore, with telling you that after a life of 102 years' continuance, during all which I had never known any sickness or infirmity but that which old age necessarily induced, I at last, without the least pain, went out like the snuff of a candle (Henry Fielding, *A Journey from This World to the Next*)

Continuance also has a legal sense, referring to a postponement or adjournment to a future date.

Continuation applies especially to prolongation or resumption of a state, action, or narration (*a continuation of the meeting, the continuation of the story*) or to physical extension (*the continuation of the street*):

> To Marianne, indeed, the meeting between Edward and her sister was but a continuation of that unaccountable coldness which she had often observed at Norland in their mutual behaviour (Jane Austen, *Sense and Sensibility*)

contra– / counter–

The prefixes *contra–* and *counter–* both derive from the Latin word *contra,* meaning "against." *Contra–* is found in words borrowed directly from Latin or modeled on Latin. *Counter–,* on the other hand, came to English through Norman French and was originally found in English words of French origin. Both prefixes have become extremely productive in the formation of new English words. *Contra–* means primarily "against, opposite," while *counter–* has a slightly different shade of meaning, "contrary, opposite." Thus *contraposition* means "an opposite position," and *countercurrent* means "a current flowing in an opposite direction."

contractions

A contraction is a word formed by omitting or combining some of the sounds of a longer phrase, as in *won't* from *will not* or *o'clock* from *of the clock.* Although many writers avoid contractions in writing that requires some degree of formality, there is nothing inherently "wrong" or "sloppy" about contractions. Many auxiliary verbs and forms of the verb *to be,* as well as the negative word *not,* are almost always contracted in everyday speech, except when they are being stressed or emphasized, and contractions have been part of the English language since Old English times. In the 18th century, however, a tendency to avoid contracting words in writing began to gain strength, and *don't, haven't, won't, it's* and other forms were banished from the page, unless the writer was trying to represent actual speech.

Nonetheless, some have held a more favorable view of contractions. Since contractions are heard in all but the most formal levels of everyday speech, using them in writing can lend a graceful air of ease and sincerity to a writer's sentences and lend a sense of confident forward movement. The reaction of the intended readership should be the deciding factor in whether or not to use contractions. If it seems likely that most readers will welcome the confident and candid air that contractions add to prose, then the writer should feel free to use them. If not, the writer should probably avoid contractions as inappropriate to the circumstances.

See more at **ain't, have, it's,** and **whose.**

contrast

The noun *contrast* may be used with the prepositions *between, with,* and *to:*

> Mere yellow skeleton that he was now he felt the contrast between them, and thought his appearance distasteful to her (Thomas Hardy, *Tess of the d'Urbervilles*)

> Small shreds and patches of it must be very beautiful in the full flush of spring, however, and all the more beautiful by contrast with the far-reaching desolation that surrounds them on every side (Jane Austen, *Northanger Abbey*)

> With characteristic intellectual independence Bacon strikes out for himself an extremely terse and clear manner of expression, doubtless influenced by such Latin authors as Tacitus, which stands in marked contrast to the formless diffuseness or artificial elaborateness of most Elizabethan and Jacobean prose (Booker T. Washington, *Up from Slavery*)

Note that *with* and *to* are interchangeable in this case: *We took note of the work's contrast with* [or *to*] *pieces by earlier composers.*

When *contrast* is used as a verb, however, *between* cannot be used; furthermore, *with* is much more common than *to* in these sentences and is actually preferred by some editors: *He contrasts the naturalistic early plays with* [less commonly, *to*] *the brittle later comedies.* The use of *with* predominates in great literature and other fine writing, in both transitive and intransitive uses:

> She had been used before to feel that he could not be always quite sincere, but now she saw insincerity in everything. His attentive deference to her father, contrasted with his former language, was odious (Jane Austen, *Persuasion*)

> Her sisterly thoughts were much with Herbert; she was anxious for his future, and in imagination painfully contrasted his solitary prison with the seeming cheerfulness of his father's house (Catherine Maria Sedgwick, *The Linwoods*)

controller See **comptroller.**

convection See **radiation.**

convince / persuade

According to a traditional rule, one *persuades* someone to act but *convinces* someone of the truth of a statement or proposition: *By convincing me that no good could come of staying, he persuaded me to leave.* If the distinction is accepted, then *convince* should not be used with an infinitive: *He persuaded* [not *convinced*] *me to go*. In our 1981 survey, 61 percent of the Usage Panel rejected the use of *convince* with an infinitive. But the tide of sentiment against the construction appears to be turning. In our 1996 survey, 74 percent accepted it in the sentence *I tried to convince him to chip in a few dollars, but he refused*. Even in passive constructions, a majority of the Usage Panel accepted *convince* with an infinitive. Fifty-two percent accepted the sentence *After listening to the teacher's report, the committee was convinced to go ahead with the new reading program*. *Persuade*, on the other hand, is perfectly acceptable when used with an infinitive or a *that* clause in both active and passive constructions. An overwhelming majority of Panelists in the 1996 survey accepted the following sentences: *After a long discussion with her lawyer, she was persuaded to drop the lawsuit. The President persuaded his advisors that military action was necessary*. Some writers may wish to preserve the traditional distinction, but they should be forewarned that most readers will not be in a position to appreciate the effort.

coordinating conjunctions

Coordinating conjunctions include words like *and, but, or, so,* and *yet,* words that connect grammatical units that have the same function and status in a sentence: *We went to the grocery store and the dry cleaner. We looked for, but did not find, the ring. Laura or Linda will be playing in goal. We went down to the landing, yet we weren't sure when the boat was due to arrive*.
    See more at **and, but, or, nor,** and **so.**

coronary   See **cardiac.**

correlative conjunctions

A correlative conjunction is one of a pair of conjunctions, such as *either . . . or* or *both . . . and,* that connect two parts of a sentence and are not used adjacent to each other. The second of the pair is always a coordinating conjunction.
    A rule of traditional grammar limits the use of correlative conjunctions to two elements. Sentences using three or more correlative conjunctions are widely viewed as erroneous in their construction. Thus sentences like the following are widely viewed as mistakes: *Both her mother, her father, and her sister are great public speakers. The team has neither the talent, discipline, nor stamina to win the championship*.
    Traditional grammar holds that correlative conjunctions bear the burden of parallelism, in that the same grammatical construction following the first conjunction should also follow the second. Thus it should be *The witness either is lying or doesn't know what happened,* where each conjunction is followed by a full verb phrase, and not *The witness is either lying or doesn't know what happened*. Because the unbalanced use of correlative conjunctions is very common in spoken English, these violations of parallelism often show up in writing, where they are likely to be viewed as infelicitous, if not wrong.
    See more at **both . . . and, either, neither, not only . . . but also,** and **parallelism.**

could See **auxiliary and primary verbs** and **have.**

could care less / couldn't care less

Taken literally, the phrase *I could care less* means "I care more than I might." However, this locution has been used with the meaning "I don't care at all," originally as a form of sarcasm and later as a fixed idiomatic expression. This sarcastic use of *could care less* is informal and (as is the case with much sarcasm) may be open to misinterpretation when used in writing.

The phrases *cannot but* and *can but* present a similar case of a positive and a negative meaning the same thing. For more on this, see **cannot.**

council / counsel / consul

Although they sound similar, *council, counsel,* and *consul* are never interchangeable as such, though their meanings are related. *Council* and *councilor* refer principally to a deliberative assembly (such as a city council or student council), its work, and its membership. *Counsel* and *counselor* pertain chiefly to advice and guidance in general and to a person (such as a lawyer or camp counselor) who provides it. *Consul* denotes an officer in the foreign service of a country.

count nouns / mass nouns

Common nouns (nouns other than proper nouns) fall generally into two categories—those that can be counted (called *count nouns*) and those that cannot (called *noncount* or *mass nouns*). Count nouns can be used with the indefinite article (*a* or *an*) and can occur in the plural. Thus, one can have a book or ten books, a toy or many toys, an idea or several ideas.

Noncount nouns typically refer to a mass instead of an individual item. They do not occur with the indefinite article, never occur in the plural, and always take a singular verb. Typical examples include words such as *bread, clothing, furniture, laughter, luggage,* and *warmth.* Like count nouns, noncount nouns can be abstract as well as concrete: *advice, honesty, information, music.* Most noncount nouns can be modified by a partitive determiner such as *some* or *much* or by a partitive phrase such as *a piece of, a bit of, an item of: Give me some bread. That was a beautiful piece of music. I heard a bit of news.*

Many words can be count nouns in one use and noncount in another. Consider these examples:

> The house is made of brick.
> The supplier delivered another load of bricks.
> This child likes to eat cake for dessert.
> Let's bake a cake.

This applicant does not have enough relevant experience.
Her experiences traveling in Australia were eye-opening.

Some count nouns have related noncount words:

a machine, some machinery   a laugh, a lot of laughter
a poem, some poetry

See more at **collective noun.**

coup de grâce

The Western Roman Empire had been in decline long before the Germanic chieftain Odoacer delivered the coup de gras by deposing the last emperor and proclaiming himself king of Italy. The French phrase *coup de grâce,* "stroke of mercy," was originally used to describe a deathblow delivered to end the misery of a mortally wounded victim. From there it was extended to indicate any finishing stroke or decisive event. Miswriting and mispronouncing the phrase as *coup de gras*—literally, "stroke of fat"—will certainly put a decisive end to a reader's confidence in the author of a piece of writing. This common error among English speakers probably results from the influence of other well-known phrases of French origin found in English, such as *Mardi Gras* and the name of the delicacy *foie gras,* "fattened goose liver." In English, these are usually pronounced (mär′dē grä′) and (fwä grä′), respectively, as approximations of their original French pronunciations. The error *coup de gras* may also reflect a mispronunciation based on the widespread knowledge that many letters found in the written form of French words are silent in pronunciation, and in particular, final *s.* Among English speakers otherwise unfamiliar with the French language, the pronunciation of the *s* sound at the end of French *grâce* may then come to be perceived as an error, although it is in fact correct.

Coup de grâce is pronounced (ko͞o′ də gräs′) in English. The French noun *grâce,* "grace, clemency," found in this phrase is the source of English *grace* and is related to the well-known Spanish expression *gracias,* "thanks." These facts may help English speakers remember the correct pronunciation. The *a* in *grâce* should be written with a circumflex accent whenever possible.

couple

with singular or plural verb   When used to refer to two people who function socially as a unit, as in *a married couple,* the word *couple* may take either a singular or a plural verb, depending on whether the members are considered individually or collectively: *The couple were married last week. Only one couple was left on the dance floor.* When a pronoun follows, *they* and *their* are more common than *it* and *its: The couple decided to spend their* [less commonly, *its*] *vacation in Quebec.*

inexactitude of   Some people dislike the phrase *a couple of* for being inexact. After all, saying you had a couple of friends over could mean you entertained two, six, or even more. But this inexactitude of *a couple of* may actually serve a useful purpose, suggesting that the writer is indifferent to the precise number of items involved. Thus the sentence *She lives only a couple of miles away* implies not only that the distance is short but that its exact measure is unimportant. For more on this, see **collective noun.**

***a couple* as modifier**   In speech especially, *a couple of* is often reduced to *a couple,* as in *A couple friends came over to watch the game.* This usage has a decidedly informal flavor. In our 1997 survey, 79 percent of the Usage Panel disapproved of it in formal situations, while 20 percent accepted it in informal uses.

coupon

This word, which was borrowed from French in the 19th century, was originally pronounced (ko͞o′pŏn′). The variant pronunciation (kyo͞o′pŏn′) developed in American English perhaps through association with words such as *cube, cupid,* and *cute.* Both pronunciations are acceptable.

court-martial   See **marshal.**

covert

The traditional pronunciation of *covert,* which is related to *cover,* is (kŭv′ərt). In American English, however, a relatively new variant pronunciation with a long *o* in the first syllable has become the more common one. This is probably the result of the association of *covert* with its antonym *overt,* which is pronounced with a long *o.* Both pronunciations are acceptable.

craft

Craft has been used as a verb since the Old English period and was used in Middle English to refer specifically to the artful construction of a text or discourse. In recent years, *crafted,* the past participle of *craft,* has been in vogue as a participle referring to well-wrought writing. *Craft* is more acceptable when applied to literary works than to other sorts of writing and is more acceptable as a participle than as a verb. In our 1988 survey, 73 percent of the Usage Panel accepted the phrase *beautifully crafted prose.* By contrast, only 35 percent accepted the sentence *The planners crafted their proposal so as to anticipate the objections of local businesses.*

credentialed

The use of the participle *credentialed* to refer to certified teachers and other professions is standard (*She became credentialed through a graduate program at a local college*). Its use with the more general meaning "possessing professional or expert credentials," as in *The board heard testimony from a number of credentialed witnesses,* is less well established; it was unacceptable to 85 percent of the Usage Panel in our 1988 survey.

credible / credulous

Properly used, *credulous* refers to people and means "believing too readily" or "gullible":

> The wisest and most experienced are generally the least credulous (Adam Smith, *The Theory of Moral Sentiments*)

Credible can refer both to people and to forms of discourse and certain other things like evidence, statistics, memories, and so on. Referring to people, *credible* means "believable," as in *a credible witness,* but it often bears the implication that the person is worthy of confidence or reliable in some enterprise: *Having just entered the race, she now must prove herself a credible candidate for governor.*

When it refers to discourse, *credible* means "capable of being believed" or "plausible":

> My fable, credible enough at first, and so long as my clothes were in good order, must have seemed worse than doubtful after my coat became frayed about the edges, and my boots began to squelch and pipe along the restaurant floors (Robert Louis Stevenson, *The Wrecker*)

Credulous is often used incorrectly where *credible* would be appropriate. Thus describing terms like *story* and *account* as *credulous* will be viewed as erroneous by many readers.

crescendo

Crescendo is a music term referring to a gradual increase in the volume or intensity of a sound. It is sometimes used to refer to a climax or peak (rather than an increase) in noise level, though this usage is not well received. In our 1988 survey, 55 percent of the Usage Panel rejected it in the sentence *When the guard sank a three-pointer to tie the game, the noise of the crowd reached a crescendo.*

cripple / crippled

The adjective *crippled* and the corresponding noun *cripple* are now considered offensively blunt when used of a person with a hindering or incapacitating physical condition. The current preference in most cases is for *disabled,* as in *an accident that left her disabled* or *improved access for the disabled.* But when the emphasis shifts from the person to the impairment itself, there is generally no reason to avoid the stronger term. Thus while one might choose to say *He was increasingly disabled by multiple sclerosis,* the disease itself could be described as *crippling,* especially if the point is to stress the seriousness of its physical effects. There is a great difference between the insensitive labeling of a particular person as a *cripple* and the deliberate use of such a word for its vivid effect, as in this quote from the *Washington Post:* "*There is no more devastating blow to the human psyche than to be transformed in microseconds from a healthy robust human being into a cripple.*"

See more at **disabled.**

criterion

Like *phenomenon, criterion* comes directly from Greek and is singular. In standard usage, the plural is generally *criteria,* although *criterions* is sometimes used as well. Properly speaking, the form *criteria* should never be a singular noun, and phrases like *this criteria* and *single criteria* are widely viewed as erroneous. Similarly, the plural *criterias* is also viewed as a mistake and is usually edited out of published prose.

See more at **phenomenon.**

critique

as verb *Critique* has been used as a verb meaning "to review or discuss critically" since the 18th century, but lately this usage has gained much wider currency, in part because the verb *criticize,* which once had the neutral meaning of "evaluate," is now mainly used for negative evaluating. The verbal use of *critique* is still regarded by many as pretentious jargon, although resistance appears to be weakening. In our 1997 survey, 41 percent of the Usage Panel rejected the sentence *As mock inquisitors grill the President, top aides take notes and critique the answers afterward.* Ten years earlier, 69 percent disapproved of this same sentence. Resistance is still high when a person is *critiqued.* In 1997, 60 percent of the Usage Panel rejected the sentence *Students are taught how to do a business plan and then are critiqued on it.* Thus, it may be preferable to avoid this word as a verb. There is no exact synonym, but in most contexts one can usually substitute *go over, review,* or *analyze.*

as noun Note, however, that *critique* is widely accepted as a noun in a neutral context; 86 percent of the Panel approved of its use in the sentence *The committee gave the report a thorough critique and found it both informed and intelligent.*

cross section

In informal usage, a *cross section* of a population suggests a group of different types of people that need not be representative of the population as a whole. Thus the sentence *You meet a cross section of Americans when you travel by interstate bus* should seem unobjectionable, even though it is clear that some types of Americans are likely to be underrepresented among the people who ride interstate buses. When *cross section* is used in reference to the samples used in surveys and other investigations, the presumption is usually that the group has been chosen so as to be representative of the larger population, and this would render the phrase *representative cross section* redundant. In our 1987 survey, 84 percent of the Usage Panel rejected this phrase.

culinary

The pronunciation (kyŏŏ'lə-nĕr'ē) is older, but (kŭl'ə-nĕr'ē) appears to be more common now in both American and British English. Either pronunciation is acceptable.

culture

Ever since C.P. Snow wrote of the gap between "the two cultures" (the humanities and science) in the 1950s, the notion that *culture* can refer to smaller segments of society has seemed implicit. The application of the term *culture* to the collective attitudes and behavior of corporations, which arose in business jargon during the late 1980s and early 1990s, was perhaps more natural than it seemed. Its usage in the corporate world may also have been facilitated by increased awareness of the importance of genuine cultural differences in a global economy, as between Americans and the Japanese, that have a broad effect on business practices. Unlike many locutions that emerge in business jargon, though, it spread to popular use in newspapers and magazines. Few Usage Panelists object to it. In our 1997 survey, more than 80 percent of Panelists accepted the sentence *The new management style is a reversal of GE's traditional corporate culture, in which virtually everything the company does is measured in some form and filed away somewhere.*

The Panel is much less sanguine about extensions to other sorts of organizations. Only 55 percent approved the usage in *The new law is forcing state officials to change the culture of welfare agencies around the country.*

current / voltage / wattage / power

In everyday usage concerning electricity, these terms tend to blur together into one: an electrical cable can be dangerous because there's a lot of current in it, or it's at a high voltage or wattage, or has high power. This is all true, but in fact only the last two terms are synonymous, with wattage (measured in *watts*) being a measure of electrical power. (For more on power, see **force.**)

. *Current* refers to the amount of electric charge (typically carried by electrons) that flows through a cross section—of a wire, for example—per unit time. It is measured in *amperes* (more often called *amps*). The concept of electrical current is similar to that of water current.

Voltage is a different idea, being a relation between two points in space, such as two ends of a wire or two points in an electrical circuit. Its value, expressed in *volts,* is an indication of how much energy *would* be needed to move a unit of electric charge from one point to the other, whether or not any charges are actually moving. Hence voltage is also called *electrical potential.* There is a similarity to water flow here too: voltage is much like water pressure.

Thus, there is a real difference between current and voltage. Two points in space, such as the two poles of a car battery, might have some voltage (typically twelve volts, in this case), but there might be no current flowing at all, if the poles are not hooked up to any electrical conductor. The opposite case arises in superconductors, where the resistance to electrical current is practically zero, so there can be high current flow through a circuit with almost zero voltage between any two points. Most electrical circuits operate between these two extremes.

Wattage is a combination of voltage and current. Mathematically, it is simply the voltage between two points multiplied by the current flowing between them. It expresses how much power is dissipated by a circuit or a device. For example, a 60-watt light bulb hooked up to a 120-volt power supply (the standard voltage in household electrical plugs) has a current flow of one-half amp, and the 60 watts of power are dissipated in the form of light and heat.

cyclone   See **tornado.**

czar / tsar

The word *czar*, a borrowing from Russian originally referring to the emperor of Russia, is a cousin of the German word *Kaiser;* both words descend from the name of the Roman emperor Julius Caesar. The spelling *tsar* is preferred in most Slavic scholarship, as it follows the standard conventions of Russian transliteration and reflects the proper Russian pronunciation more intuitively. In general, however, the spelling *czar* is the more common form in American English and is the only one employed in the extended senses "tyrant" or, informally, "someone in authority," as in *drug czar,* "a person in charge of the design and execution of policies related to illicit drugs."

· D ·

dais

The one-syllable pronunciation (dās) is older, but the two-syllable pronunciations (dā′ĭs) or (dī′ĭs) are much more common now. In fact, in the 1997 survey, only 5 percent of the Panelists found the old single-syllable pronunciation acceptable. The (dā′ĭs) pronunciation was almost unanimously accepted, and 80 percent accepted the (dī′ĭs) pronunciation.

dame

There may have been "nothing like a dame" in 1949 when the musical *South Pacific* hit theaters, but in the 21st century the word *dame* is rarely used anymore. Some consider it to be glib and insensitive unless used by a woman or group of women in reference to themselves. An exception is its use as a royal title, analogous to that of a knight, conferred by a sovereign on a woman in Great Britain and a few other countries.

dangling modifiers

Dangling modifiers include participles, infinitive phrases, clauses, and prepositional phrases that are structurally associated with the noun or noun phrase that immediately follows them, but they are intended to modify or describe a noun or noun phrase that is elsewhere in the sentence or is absent altogether. These constructions are common in speech, where they often go without comment, and they can be found occasionally in edited prose. But they are distracting to the reader, and they can sometimes lead to unintended absurdities. Consider this example, penned by a well-respected writer and published by the *New York Times:*

> *After wading through a long, quasi-academic examination of the statistical links between intelligence, character, race and poverty,* the reader's reward is a hoary lecture on the evils of the welfare state.

This sentence begins with a prepositional phrase that has a gerund for its object. As a verb form, the gerund cries out for a subject, and we must supply it mentally. The sense requires *reader,* but the subject of the main clause is *reward.* Logic demands that the reader, not the reward, do the wading. This conflict can easily be resolved by keeping the modifying phrase as it stands and giving the main clause the proper subject:

125

> After wading through a long, quasi-academic examination of the statistical links between intelligence, character, race and poverty, the reader is rewarded with a hoary lecture on the evils of the welfare state.

Here is another example, also taken from a famous writer in the *New York Times*. Describing the perils of being a newspaper columnist, the writer imagines interviewing his spouse as the first in a series of increasingly desperate measures to come up with material:

> *Once hooked on interviewing his wife,* degradation proceeds swiftly.

Again the syntax requires the reader to connect the modifying portion of the sentence with the grammatical subject of the main clause. But the meaning of the modifier prevents this. The meaning demands that a person—in this case the husband—be hooked, not an abstraction like degradation. Here the solution is to turn the phrase into a full clause with the subject specified:

> Once the newspaper columnist is hooked on interviewing his wife, degradation proceeds swiftly.

A third example, also from the *New York Times,* puts the modifying element at the end of the sentence:

> Mr. Clinton acknowledged the role played by the men who subdued the gunman *when he spoke at a dinner on Saturday night.*

In this case, the modifier is a full clause that can't be made fuller. (The clause would be elliptical if it read *when speaking at a dinner on Saturday night.*) It is clearly Mr. Clinton who spoke, not the gunman (who missed dinner, as he was in jail at the time). The grammatical ambiguity caused by the misplaced modifier makes the sentence sound absurd. Here the answer is to reposition the clause so that it is closer to the noun it modifies:

> When he spoke at a dinner on Saturday night, Mr. Clinton acknowledged the role played by the men who subdued the gunman.

Modifiers often dangle because the agent of the action is not the subject of the verb in the main clause. The chief culprit here is the passive voice, which banishes the agent of the action from being the subject. Consider these examples, one using an infinitive phrase and another using a prepositional phrase with a gerund:

> *To improve company morale,* three things were recommended by the consultant.
>
> *In reviewing the company's policy,* three areas of improvement were identified by the committee.

These sentences can easily be fixed by making the consultant and the committee the subjects:

> To improve company morale, the consultant recommended . . .
> In reviewing the company's policy, the committee identified . . .

For more on the passive voice, see **verbs, voice of** and **passive voice.**

Sometimes, of course, what the opening phrase refers to is not an agent, as this sentence attests: *Baked, boiled, or fried, you can make potatoes a part of almost any meal.* Better to put the non-agents like potatoes where they belong: *Baked, boiled, or fried, potatoes make a welcome addition to almost any meal.*

Bear in mind as well that, while most danglers occur at the beginning of a sentence, a modifier can dangle just about anywhere. In fact, as was seen with Mr. Clinton, delayed danglers can be treacherously ambiguous. Remember too that when a sentence ends with a modifying phrase that follows a comma, the phrase always refers to the subject of the sentence, not the closest noun. Thus, the sentence *A few guests lingered near her, mumbling pleasantries* can only mean that the guests mumbled the pleasantries. She may have well been silent.

Some participles, such as *concerning, considering, failing,* and *granting,* function as prepositions and can be used to introduce a sentence without causing a dangling modifier. A few participial phrases, such as *speaking of* and *judging by,* also work this way:

> Concerning the proposal, there was little debate among the board members.
> Considering his reputation for honesty, his arrest came as a shock.
> Speaking of exceptional performances, did you see her latest movie?
> Judging by the applause, the play was a success.

See more at **having said that, participles,** and **prepositions.**

dare

Depending on its sense, the verb *dare* sometimes behaves like an auxiliary verb (such as *can* or *may*) and sometimes like a main verb (such as *want* or *try*). When used as an auxiliary verb, *dare* does not change to agree with its subject: *He dare not do that again.* It also does not combine with *do* in questions, negations, or certain other constructions: *Dare we tell her the truth? I dare not mention their names.* Finally, it does not take *to* before the verb that follows it: *If you dare breathe a word about it, I'll never speak to you again.* When used as a main verb, *dare* does agree with its subject (*If he dares to show up at her house I'll be surprised*), and it does combine with *do* (*Did anyone dare to admit it?*). It may optionally take *to* before the verb following it: *No one dares* [or *dares to*] *speak freely about the political situation.*

The auxiliary forms differ subtly in meaning from the main verb forms in that they emphasize the attitude or involvement of the speaker while the main verb forms present a more objective situation. Thus *How dare she take the exam without ever once coming to class?* expresses indignation at the student's action, whereas *How did she dare to take the exam without ever once coming to class?* is a genuine request for information. When *dare* is used as a transitive verb meaning "to challenge," only main verb forms are possible and *to* is required: *Anyone who dares* [not *dare*] *him to attempt* [not just *attempt*] *it will be sorry.*

See more at **auxiliary and primary verbs** and **need.**

dash

em dash

1. The em dash (so called because it is roughly the same width as a capital *M*) indicates interrupted or faltering speech.

   > We'll be late if—oh, here's Dorothy now.
   > Well, you see, I—I've—I'm just not sure.

2. An em dash indicates a break in the continuity of a thought.

   > He seemed very upset about—I never knew what.
   > The total amount needed—we have the statistics to support this—is $5 million.

3. An em dash sets off an explanatory or defining phrase.

   > The region's climate—cold, arid, and windy—is unsuitable for the cultivation of crops.

   > Dave Corrsin—the linebacker—was an intimidating presence.

4. Em dashes set off parenthetical material.

   > She stares soulfully heavenward—to the great delight of the audience—when she plays Chopin.

   > I paid the bill—what else could I do?—but I'll never go out with them again.

5. An em dash marks an unfinished sentence.

   > Well, then, I'll simply tell her that I—
   > "But if the plane is late—" he began.

6. An em dash sets off a summarizing phrase or clause.

   > Pablo Picasso, Joan Miró, Salvador Dalí—these are Spain's most famous 20th-century artists.

   > Heated bathroom floors, remote-controlled curtains, plasma TVs—the accoutrements of this hotel bring new meaning to the word *luxury*.

7. An em dash sets off the name of an author or a source, as at the end of a quotation.

   > There never was a good war, or a bad peace.
   >   —Benjamin Franklin

en dash

1. The en dash, which is half the length of the em dash but longer than the hyphen, is used between numbers and words when the meaning is *through*, *to*, or *from . . . to*.

   > The years 2000–2004 were politically divisive.
   > Eva Perón (1919–52) was born to a poor family in Buenos Aires.
   > For tomorrow, please complete exercises 4–10 on pages 232–233.
   > The New York–Madrid flight is full.

We are open Monday–Friday, 9:00 a.m.–5:00 p.m.

Do not use an en dash if the first number is preceded by the word *between* or *from*. Instead use *and, to,* or *through.*

Between 1953 and 1957 they lived in Jackson Heights.
The reception will be from 5:30 to 7:30.
From July 1 through August 30 we will be in Poland.

2. Use an en dash in a compound adjective when one of the elements consists of two words.

the pre–Civil War era   a Pulitzer Prize–winning novel

data

The word *data* is the plural of Latin *datum,* "something given." In English, this plural usage is still common, as these examples show:

Although few data are available regarding the extent of suggestive questioning of eyewitnesses, a British study using actual interviews indicates that approximately one of every six questions that police posed to eyewitnesses was in some way suggestive (Daniel Schacter, *The Seven Sins of Memory*)

Eventually, his data suggest, a tumor's hydroxyl-induced DNA alterations give rise to mutant cells that can invade and thrive where their parent cells could not (Janet Raloff, "How Anti-Oxidants Might Fight Cancer," *Science News*)

Most notably in scientific usage, *data* is often used in this way as a plural form. But *data* is also standard in denoting a singular mass entity (like *information*), especially in writing for a more general audience:

Before data is transmitted in bulk around the internet, it is routinely compressed to reduce redundancy (Richard Dawkins, *A Devil's Chaplain*)

Our senses bring us a great deal of information every moment about the reality outside our heads. This sensory data is the primary source of information for ego consciousness and the intellect (Andrew Weil, *The Natural Mind*)

Goodall's chimps began to travel in larger groups and sleep near her camp. In the beginning Goodall didn't mind: she wanted to get as much data as possible from her animals before she had to leave them (Elizabeth Royte, *Tapir's Morning Bath*)

In our 1988 survey, 60 percent of the Usage Panel accepted the use of *data* with a singular verb and pronoun in the sentence *Once the data is in, we can begin to analyze it.* A still larger number, 77 percent, accepted the sentence *We have very little data on the efficacy of such programs,* where the quantifier *very little* (like *much* in the last quotation given above), which is not used with similar plural nouns such as *facts* or *results,* implies that *data* here is indeed singular.

The singular *datum,* denoting an individual piece of information, is also in standard use today, though it is less common than *data* and usually imparts an air of technical precision:

Even a Congo walker as seasoned as Fay has to spend much of his time looking down, stepping carefully, minimizing the toll on his feet. Of course Fay would be looking down anyway, because that's where so much of the data are found—scat piles, footprints, territorial scrape marks . . . Each datum goes into the notebook, referenced to the minute of the day, which will be referenced in turn by his GPS to longitude and latitude at three decimal points of precision (David Quammen, "Megatransect," *National Geographic*)

Datum is nonetheless used in other contexts as well:

They [northern merchants] knew the most significant datum in this whole se-quence, one that is rarely mentioned in treatments of the Chesapeake incident, and one that came as a surprise to Jefferson when he had Gallatin look into the matter: fully half the able seamen on America's foreign-trade vessels were British subjects, mainly deserters from the British navy (Gary Wills, *The Negro President*)

Thus, it is acceptable to use *data* either as a singular mass noun or as a plural noun. The less common form *datum* is always a singular count noun.

See more at **count nouns.**

dates and times

full dates

1. Specific dates are expressed in numerals.

Francis was born on December 10, 1950.

Do not use the endings *-nd, -rd, -st,* and *-th* in dates unless the date is preceded by *the.*

May 2   the 2nd [*or* second] of May

2. If just the month and year are given, a comma is not needed.

Here are the sales figures for January 2004.

decades   Decades may be expressed in words or numerals.

the twenties   the '20s
the 1920s

centuries   Centuries may be expressed in words or numerals.

words for the twenty-first [*or* 21st] century
seventeenth-century [*or* 17th-century] English literature

eras   The era designations AD and BC may be set in small capitals with or without periods, or full capitals with or without periods. AD precedes the year; BC follows the year. Both AD and BC follow references to centuries.

AD 1101   975 BC
the twelfth [*or* 12th] century AD   the tenth [*or* 10th] century BC

time of day Time can be expressed in words or numerals. The abbreviations *a.m.* and *p.m.* are usually set lowercase with periods, but they may also be set in small capitals with or without periods.

9:30 a.m. *or* 9:30 A.M. *or* 9:30 AM	half past one
8:00 p.m. *or* 8:00 P.M. *or* 8:00 PM	quarter of two
8:15 in the evening	noon
nine-thirty in the morning	midnight
eight o'clock at night	

See more at **AD, a.m., comma,** and **numbers.**

de–

The prefix *de–* can be traced back in part through Middle English and Old French to Latin *dē* meaning "from, off, apart, away, down, out." In other cases, English *de–* descends from Latin *dis–,* "apart, away" by way of the Old French prefix *des–.* In English, *de–* is used in a very large number of words, and it usually indicates reversal, removal, or reduction. Thus *deactivate* means "to make inactive," *decontaminate* means "to remove the contamination from," and *decompress* means "to remove or reduce pressure."

deaf

A person who is unable to hear at all or who has little or no functional hearing is properly called *deaf*—a word that need not be avoided out of politeness or sensitivity. In fact, many deaf people, and even many people whose hearing loss is less than total, take offense at being called by a less direct term and especially by the term *hearing-impaired.* The term preferred by many people with partial hearing loss is now *hard of hearing,* and the acceptable term for a group that includes people with both total and partial loss is *deaf and hard of hearing.*

The rise of the Deaf Pride movement in the 1980s has introduced a distinction between the lowercase *deaf* and the capitalized form *Deaf.* Any person with complete or significant hearing loss may be termed *deaf.* A deaf person who belongs to the community that has formed around the use of American Sign Language as the preferred means of communication is now said to be *Deaf* or to be a member of *Deaf culture.* The issue of capitalization is different for *deaf* than it is for *black.* In the case of *black,* the decision whether to capitalize is essentially a matter of personal or political preference; use of the capitalized form, though, does not differentiate one black person from another. With *deaf,* on the other hand, the capitalized form has a different meaning than the lowercased form, and the two should be carefully distinguished so as to avoid misunderstanding. Only if a person is self-identified as belonging to Deaf culture should he or she be referred to as *Deaf.*

See more at **impaired.**

deaf and dumb

The phrase *deaf and dumb*, meaning "deaf and unable to speak," has a long history in English. In Old English, the two adjectives are usually found in reverse order, as for example in the Old English poem called *Soul and Body*, in which the soul addresses the dead body that it once inhabited in the following terms, *Eart thu nu dumb ond deaf*, "You are now dumb and deaf." The alliterative phrase has survived to this day in the opposite order. The *dumb* in *deaf and dumb* does not, of course, mean "lacking intelligence" but rather "incapable of speech," but even when this point is clear the expression is offensive in any but a historical or figurative context.

See more at **mute.**

deaf-mute

Though it may sound somewhat less offensive than *deaf and dumb*, the term *deaf-mute* is similarly objectionable for its implicit equation of deafness with an incapacity for speech or communication.

See more at **mute.**

deal   See **lot.**

debacle

Although this borrowing from French has shed its accent marks and shifted its meaning since entering English nearly two hundred years ago, it has managed for the most part to hang on to most of its original pronunciation. Many people continue to pronounce this word (dĭ-bä′kəl), or often (dā-bä′kəl), reflecting even more closely the French spelling *débâcle*. In American English the pronunciations (dĭ-băk′əl) and (dā-băk′əl) are also acceptable. The pronunciation (dĕb′ə-kəl), with stress on the first syllable, is becoming more common, but it is not yet widely accepted; in fact, in our 1999 survey, only 25 percent of the Usage Panel found this pronunciation acceptable.

deceptively

When *deceptively* is used to modify an adjective, the meaning is often unclear. Consider the sentence *The pool is deceptively shallow.* Is the pool shallower or deeper than it appears to be? In our 1982 ballot, 50 percent of the Usage Panel thought the pool is shallower than it appears, while 32 percent thought the pool is deeper than it appears, and 18 percent said it was impossible to decide. Thus, when using *deceptively* with an adjective, be sure the context leaves no room for doubt. An easy way to remedy the situation is to rewrite the sentence without *deceptively*: *The pool is shallower than it looks* or *The pool is shallow, despite its appearance.*

decimate

Decimate originally referred to the killing of every tenth person, a punishment used in the Roman army for mutinous legions. Today this meaning is commonly extended to include the killing of any large proportion of a group. In our 1988 survey, 66 percent of the Usage Panel accepted this extension in the sentence *The Jewish population of Germany was decimated by the war,* even though it is common knowledge that the number of Jews killed was much greater than a tenth of the original population. The word is now used of plants and animals as well as humans:

> Yet having decimated the brook trout population, Americans developed an incurable nostalgia for its return (George Black, *The Trout Pool Paradox*)

However, when the meaning is further extended to include large-scale destruction other than killing, as in *The supply of fresh produce was decimated by the nuclear accident at Chernobyl,* only 26 percent of the Panel accepted the usage.

deconstruct

The verb *deconstruct* emerged from the philosophy or critical method known as *deconstruction,* which attempts to show that the meanings and structures identified in documents and works of art are inherently unstable. Strictly speaking, when one deconstructs a work of literature, one uses this method. Typically, standard interpretations of a work of art are shown to undermine themselves or contain the "seeds of their own destruction," and structures based on binary oppositions (like nature as opposed to civilization, or children as opposed to adults) are shown to crumble under sustained analysis. By extension, the verb has been used somewhat more loosely for criticism that exposes the underlying (and usually unmentioned) assumptions, ideology, or even prejudices that inform a text or piece of art, whether or not the criticism adheres strictly to the tenets of deconstruction. Someone who wants to deconstruct the authority of science is likely to claim that its principles are social conventions produced by specific cultural moments in history, and are not the product of logical analyses that stand apart from historical contexts.

Thus *deconstruct* has a somewhat technical or refined air, and using the verb bears the risk of sounding pretentious. The Panel has mixed feelings about looser applications of the verb, when it means that something is adapted or interpreted in an ironic or subversive manner. In our 1996 ballot, 43 percent accepted the sentence *Dylan redefines his songs each night but has not been deconstructing them to the point that he did in the mid-70s.* The Panel was less fond of a sentence in which the word *explain* might serve as ably without the rarefication: only 34 percent accepted *The professor agreed to help deconstruct some of the more unusual credits used in current movies and began by defining 'gaffer' as a lighting technician.* Panel enthusiasm sagged to 27 percent when the word is used to mean "analyze" or "examine part by part": *The show deconstructed the rock king's life into fresh, evocative snippets of biodrama.*

deduction / induction

These words describe different forms of logical reasoning. *Deduction* refers to reasoning from general principles to specific cases, as in applying a mathematical theorem to a particular problem or in citing a law of physics to predict the outcome of an experiment. The word also refers to a conclusion reached by such reasoning:

> These two deductions from the theory have both been confirmed (Albert Einstein, *Relativity: The Special and General Theory,* translated by Robert W. Lawson, M.Sc.)

Valid deductive conclusions follow necessarily from their premises.

Induction refers to the process of forming a general principle or law on the basis of a number of individual observations:

> Principles such as the law of gravitation are proved, or rather are rendered highly probable, by a combination of experience with some wholly a priori principle, such as the principle of induction (Bertrand Russell, *The Problems of Philosophy*)

definite article

A definite article is a word that restricts or particularizes a noun. In English the definite article is *the.* It identifies a noun that has already been referred to (*I found the book under the chair*). It helps specify a particular thing (*I am reading about the development of the polio vaccine*). It also indicates a noun that stands as a typical example of its class (*The golden retriever is an ideal pet*).

See more at **the.**

definite / definitive

Definite and *definitive* both apply to what is precisely defined or explicitly set forth. A parent might leave definite instructions to a caregiver about what to do in case of an emergency, and the caregiver might ask the parent to be definite in what was expected under such circumstances. *Definite* can also mean "indisputable, certain," as in *We were at a definite disadvantage in the last game* or *There was a definite smell of antiseptic in the room.* In some cases, it can be hard to tell which sense is meant. A *definite account* is likely to be both explicitly set forth and certain or even indisputable. It is important therefore to make sure the context is clear when the intended meaning calls for one sense rather than the other.

Definitive has similar tendencies to ambiguity. When a detective pieces together a definitive reconstruction of an event or a definitive clarification from a witness, what is sought is a precise rendering of what happened. Quite often this precision leads to a definitive statement that amounts to a conclusion. Just as *definite* connotes certainty, *definitive* often means "authoritative and complete," and refers specifically to a judgment or description that serves as a standard or reference point for others, as in *the definitive decision of the court* (which sets forth a final resolution of a judicial matter) or *the definitive biography of Nelson* (i.e., the biography that sets the standard against which all other accounts of Nelson's life must be measured).

The ambiguities inherent in these words are harmless in many cases, and they may be desirable in others, but a good writer remains cognizant of them nonetheless.

degree

The term *degree* is applied to the forms used in the comparison of adjectives and adverbs. For example, *sweet* is the positive degree, *sweeter* the comparative degree, and *sweetest* the superlative degree of the adjective *sweet*.

See more at **adjectives** and **adverbs.**

deify / deity

Traditionally these are pronounced (dē′ə-fī′) and (dē′ĭ-tē), with a long *e* in the first syllable. Although the pronunciation with a long *a* (first syllable sounds like *day*) has become fairly common, some people still dislike it. In our 1996 survey, the traditional pronunciation was preferred by 85 percent of the Usage Panel.

delegate   See **relegate.**

delusion   See **illusion.**

demagogic / demagogy

Either (dĕm′ə-gŏg′ĭk) with a hard *g* or (dĕm′ə-gŏj′ĭk) with a soft *g* at the end is acceptable. Similarly, *demagogy* can be acceptably pronounced with a hard or soft *g* at the end.

demagogue

Even though *demagogue* has been used as a verb meaning "to speak about something in the manner of a demagogue" since the 1600s, the verb has kept a low profile in the language. Recently, however, it has become a favorite of newspaper columnists. The Usage Panel does not view the verb with much favor in either its transitive or intransitive use. In our 1997 survey, 94 percent rejected it in the sentence *Clinton will demagogue Medicare, unwilling to acknowledge that fundamental reforms need to be made in the system.* A similar percentage rejected an example in which a representative *can demagogue about price-fixing.* Perhaps this resistance should not be surprising, since the use of familiar nouns as verbs is often the subject of complaints.

demonstrative

In grammar, the term *demonstrative* means "specifying or singling out the person or thing referred to." The words *this, these, that,* and *those* function as demonstrative adjectives and pronouns: *These tomatoes are ripe, but those are not.*

denote / connote

The difference in meaning between these words is important to the very notion of meaning. *Denote* has three meanings: first, "to mark, indicate," as in *Her frown denoted her increasing impatience;* second, "to serve as a symbol or name for," as in *A yellow light denotes caution;* and third, "to signify directly," as in *The word* river *denotes a moving body of water. Connote* means "to signify indirectly" or "to suggest or convey what is not explicit."

The confusion lies in these signifying senses, for *denote* describes the relation between the expression and the thing it conventionally names, whereas *connote* describes the relation between the word and the images or associations it evokes:

> . . . the term "leisure," as here used, does not connote indolence or quiescence (Thorstein Veblen, *The Theory of the Leisure Class*)

depend

In writing, *depend* is followed by *on* or *upon* when indicating condition or contingency, as in *It depends on who is in charge.* Leaving out the preposition is typical of casual speech and dialogue:

> "But she and he still get on?"
> "That depends what you mean by getting on" (Louis Auchinloss, "Geraldine: A Spiritual Biography")

But this usage is not considered standard in formal writing.

dependent clause   See **clause.**

deprecate / depreciate

Like many words, the verb *deprecate* has seen some changes in meaning over its history. It originally meant "to pray in order to ward off something, ward off by prayer." Perhaps because the occasion of such prayers was invariably one of dread, the word developed the more general meaning of disapproval, as in this well-known quotation from Frederick Douglass, *"Those who profess to favor freedom, yet deprecate agitation, are men who want crops without plowing up the ground."* From here it was a small step to add the meaning "to make little of, disparage," what was once the proper meaning of *depreciate.* This meaning of *depreciate* appears to have been overwhelmed by the word's use in the world of finances, where it means "to diminish in price or value."

In similar fashion, the "disparage" sense of *deprecate* may be driving out the word's other uses. In our 2002 survey, only 50 percent of the Usage Panel accepted *deprecate* when it meant "to express disapproval of" in the sentence *He advocates a well-designed program of behavior modification and deprecates the early use of medication to address behavioral problems.* Moreover, a similar example in the same survey elicited the same split in opinions among Panelists: *He acknowledged that some students had been wronged by the board's handling of the matter and deprecated the board's decision to intervene.* It seems clear, then, that the Panel has very mixed feelings about the use of *deprecate* to mean "disapprove of."

But a majority of Panelists accept *deprecate* when used to mean "make little of, disparage." Fully 78 percent accepted *He deprecated his own contribution to the success of the project, claiming that others had done just as much.* Perhaps the popularity of the adjective *self-deprecating* has helped bolster this use of the verb.

descriptive clause

The term *descriptive clause* is sometimes used for a nonrestrictive clause. See more at **restrictive and nonrestrictive clauses.**

desert / dessert

There are three words spelled *desert* in English. The noun meaning "a wasteland" (the only one of the three to be pronounced with stress on its first syllable) and the verb meaning "to abandon" both ultimately derive from Latin *dēserere,* "to forsake, leave uninhabited." The Latin word is made up of *dē–,* expressing the notion of undoing, and the verb *serere,* "to link together." The third *desert* comes from the past participle of Old French *deservir,* "to deserve." The word thus means "something that is deserved or merited." It normally occurs in the plural in the phrase *just deserts.* The sweet food ending a meal and known as a *dessert* comes from Old French *desservir,* which meant "to clear the table," or etymologically, "to unserve."

Because these words are similar in appearance and three of them have identical pronunciations, *just deserts* is commonly misspelled as *just desserts,* as in this example from a London newspaper: *"Arthur Koestler's novel* Darkness at Noon *might make one pity the old Bolsheviks about to be shot at the Lubyanka prison, but they were frankly only getting their just desserts after years of massacring innocent Russians."*

despicable

Up until the mid-20th century most people pronounced this word with stress on the first syllable (dĕs′pĭ-kə-bəl), and many deplored the pronunciation with stress on the second syllable (dĭ-spĭk′ə-bəl). But now the pronunciation with stress on the second syllable is the usual one; in our 1996 survey, two thirds of the Usage Panel preferred it. Of the one third who reported a preference for the stress on the first syllable, a little more than half of them found (dĭ-spĭk′ə-bəl) acceptable as well.

dessert   See **desert.**

desultory

This rather fancy and rarely heard word is pronounced with stress on the first and third syllables (dĕs′əl-tôr′ē).

determiner

A determiner is a kind of noun modifier, such as an article, a demonstrative adjective, a possessive adjective, or a word such as *any, both, every,* or *whose.* Determiners are generally the first elements of the noun phrase, preceding other modifers such as adjectives. Determiners indicate which noun is, or how many instances of the noun are, being talked about, rather than simply describing the noun (as ordinary adjectives do, for example). This can be seen by comparing a few examples, such as *the book, this book, those books, a book, no books, all the books, some books, each book,* and *our book.* The words before *book* in these examples are determiners, specifying which book is under discussion, rather than describing some property of a book or books.

dialect

A dialect is a distinct variety of a language that is associated with a particular region or social group and that is typically distinguished from other varieties by features of pronunciation, grammar, or vocabulary. The difference between a language and a dialect is not clear-cut. Some languages (such as Danish and Norwegian) are mutually intelligible, while what some people regard as different dialects (such as Mandarin and Cantonese, often considered to be dialects of Chinese) are so different that communication across them is impossible.

The term *dialect* is sometimes used disparagingly outside of linguistics to refer to a variety of language that differs from the standard literary language or speech pattern of the culture in which it exists.

See more at **General American.**

dialogue

In recent years the verb sense of *dialogue* meaning "to engage in an informal exchange of views" has been revived, particularly with reference to communication between parties in institutional or political contexts. Although Shakespeare, Coleridge, and Carlyle used it, this usage today is widely regarded as jargon or bureaucratese. In our 1988 survey, 98 percent of the Usage Panel rejected the sentence *Critics have charged that the department was remiss in not trying to dialogue with representatives of the community before hiring the new officers.*

dicot / eudicot

Since the 17th century, botanists have traditionally classified all flowering plants, from the lowliest grasses to the loftiest oaks, in two large classes, the dicotyledons (dicots) and the monocotyledons (monocots). The basic characteristic defining each group was the form of the embryo within the seed: a dicot embryo has two cotyledons (embryonic leaves) while a monocot embryo has only one. The presence of two cotyledons in the embryo of dicots is often accompanied by other features in the plant, including flower parts in multiples of four or five, pollen grains with three pores or furrows, and leaf veins arranged in a netlike pattern. By contrast, monocots have flower parts in multiples of three, their pollen grains have a single pore or furrow, and their leaf veins are parallel.

However, many groups of flowering plants display some characteristics of monocots but other characteristics of dicots. The older classification scheme is thus too simplistic, placing undue emphasis on the distinctiveness of the monocots while ignoring important differences among the dicots. Modern botanists believe that the first flowering plants had dicot characteristics and the various groups with monocot characteristics have evolved from these primitive dicots, and they now employ much more finely divided classifications in order to reflect evolutionary relationships. In fact, some plants traditionally classified as dicots are now considered to be more closely related to monocots than to the other dicots. The typical monocots, such as members of the lily, orchid, grass, and palm families, are still grouped together as the Liliopsida. The former dicots have been broken up into a variety of groups, including the eudicots and many smaller groups. The eudicots include many of the traditional dicots, such as members of the large rose and aster families. (The Greek prefix *eu–,* "good, well," has the meaning "true" here—eudicot plants usually display all the dicot characteristics.) Writers should be aware that many botanists, ecologists, and other scientists now use the word *dicot* only as a convenient label for plants displaying the typical suite of dicot characteristics. The term *monocot* is still used to refer to members of the class Liliopsida. Because of recent advances in the study of plant genomes, newer classification schemes are in a state of flux, and writers drawing upon older sources should be aware that the schemes in older works may no longer be valid.

different from / different than

The phrases *different from* and *different than* are both common in British and American English. The British also use the construction *different to.* Since the 18th century, language critics have singled out *different than* as incorrect when used before nouns and noun phrases, though it is well attested in the works of reputable writers. Traditionally, *from* is used when the comparison is between two persons or things: *My book is different from* [not *than*] *yours.* Note that noun phrases, including ones that have clauses in them, also fall into this category: *The campus is different from the way it was the last time you were here.*

The Usage Panel is divided on the acceptability of *different than* with nouns and noun phrases, with a majority finding several of these constructions unacceptable. In our 2004 survey, 57 percent rejected the use of *different than* with a gerund in the sentence *Caring for children with disabilities in a regular child-care setting is not new and, in many cases, is not particularly different than caring for other children.* Some 55 percent disapproved of the construction with a noun phrase containing a clause in *The new kid felt that the coach's treatment of him was different than that of the other players who were on the team last year.* Some 60 percent rejected the sentence *New York seemed very different than Rome, where they'd been on good terms.*

There should be no complaint, however, when the object of comparison is expressed by a full clause: *The campus is different than it was twenty years ago.*

differently abled

The term *differently abled* is sometimes proposed as a substitute for *disabled* or *handicapped*. *Differently abled* emphasizes the fact that many people with disabilities are quite capable of accomplishing a particular task or performing a particular function, only in a manner that is different from or takes more time than that of people without the disability. It can also be taken to mean that a person who is incapable of one act may nevertheless be capable of many or even most others. On the other hand, *differently abled* is often criticized as an awkward euphemism and in some cases may be taken as offensively condescending by disabled people themselves. Like the similarly upbeat *challenged,* it is used most frequently in academic, government, and social service environments; its use outside those contexts may be problematic.

digital / analog / virtual

The word *digital* has general application in computer technology and can be used for almost any device or activity that makes use of or is based on such technology, such as a *digital camera* or a *digital network*. Technically, digital technology refers to electronic technology that processes signals encoded in the form of binary numbers—numbers represented using only the digits 0 and 1, corresponding electronically to "off" and "on" states of electrical components. These numbers, which are used to represent actual numbers, letters, images, or other data, are manipulated, sequenced, and sent to storage devices and displays by one or more central processors.

Analog devices process signals that are encoded as levels of voltage, current, or some other parameter that can vary continuously. Analog components are therefore not simply "off" and "on," but take on a range of values corresponding to the value of the signal. For example, the amplifier of a stereo is an analog device: it takes as an input a signal that represents (in the form of a fluctuating voltage) the sound wave to be reproduced, and uses electronic components to create a signal of high power that can drive a set of speakers. There is no central processor manipulating the signal in an analog device; the signal simply interacts with its various components.

The term *virtual* is an abstract term gaining great currency in the world of electronic information technology. It is used to refer to simulations of things using electronic technology, especially the digital technology of computers. For example, a *virtual library* would be a library that exists exclusively in electronic form; there are no books in such a library that one can hold in one's hands. A *digital library,* on the other hand, could be a library that involves information technology in some way, such as a brick-and-mortar library equipped with networked computers.

dilemma

In its traditional use, *dilemma* refers to a situation in which a choice must be made between courses of action or argument, as in *Many women today face the dilemma of how to juggle family, work, and other responsibilities.* The word is also used more loosely to mean simply "problem" or "predicament," without an implied choice to be made, as in *Herman Hollerith solved the dilemma of census-taking with the invention of the punch-card tabulating machine.* This looser usage has been criticized as a mistake by many usage commentators, and the Usage Panel tends to support this view, but somewhat less vigorously than it once did. In 1966, 79 percent rejected the sentence *Juvenile delinquency represents the dilemma of our time,* and in 1988, 74 percent rejected the similar sentence *Juvenile drug abuse is the great dilemma of the 1980s.* Resistance slipped a bit in the 1999 survey, in which 58 percent rejected the sentence *Historically, race has been the great dilemma of democracy.* This suggests that the usage may one day become standard.

It is sometimes claimed that because the *di–* in *dilemma* comes from the Greek prefix meaning "two," the word should be used only when exactly two choices are involved. While this dictum would appear to be given credence by some Panelists, 64 percent of the Usage Panel in our 1988 survey accepted the use of *dilemma* for choices among three or more options in the example *Ph.D. students who haven't completed their dissertations by the time their fellowships expire face a difficult dilemma: whether to take out loans to support themselves, to try to work part-time at both a job and their research, or to give up on the degree entirely.*

diminutive

A diminutive is a word or name that indicates smallness, youth, familiarity, affection, or contempt. In English and many other languages, diminutives are made by adding an affix to the base word. Such affixes are called *diminutive affixes* or simply *diminutives* as well. Some English suffixes that form diminutives include *–let* and *–kin,* as in *booklet* and *lambkin.* The suffix *-y* (also spelled *–ie*) usually suggests affection and familiarity, rather than mere small size, as in *doggy* or *sweetie.* English has borrowed many French words that contain the French diminutive suffix *–et,* whose feminine form in French is *–ette.* For example, the English word *floret,* "a small flower (especially one forming part of a larger group of flowers)," comes from Old French *florette,* a diminutive of Old French *flor,* "flower." In more recent borrowings from French, the difference in spelling between French *–et* and *–ette* is maintained in English spelling, and the specifically feminine *–ette* can sometimes have derogatory overtones.

See more at **feminine suffixes.**

diphtheria

This word is properly pronounced (dĭf-thîr′ē-ə), with the *ph* pronounced (f). Many people, however, say (dĭp-thîr′ē-ə), including medical professionals, and most dictionaries (of American English anyway) have included this variant pronunciation with the (p) sound for *ph* since the 1960s.

diphthong

As is the case with *diphtheria*, the *ph* should properly be pronounced (f), not (p). Because so many people say (dĭp-) as opposed to (dĭf-), though, this variant has gradually become acceptable.

direct object

A direct object is a noun, pronoun, or noun phrase that refers to the person or thing that receives the action of a transitive verb. In *Tom mailed the letter, Let's call him,* and *The snow covered all of the roses,* the direct objects are *the letter, him,* and *all of the roses.*

See also **indirect object.**

dis– / dys–

The prefix *dis–* has several senses, including "not, not any," "lacking," or "the opposite of, the reverse of, away from," and is used in the formation of nouns, adjectives, and verbs. Thus *discomfort* means "a lack of comfort" and *dissimilar* means "not similar." When prefixed to a verb, *dis–* often means "to do the opposite (of the action indicated by the verb prefixed)," or "to undo (the action indicated by the verb)," as in *disbelieve,* "to refuse to believe," and *disenfranchise,* "to deprive of a right." The prefix ultimately derives from Latin *dis–,* meaning "apart, asunder." As Latin developed into Old French, the prefix took the form *des–,* and it entered Middle English in this form through borrowings from French. In Middle English, words like *disturbed,* for example, are often spelled *desturbed.* Middle English also borrowed words containing *dis–* directly from Latin, and the spelling of both Middle English and Old French was deeply influenced by Latin norms, so that the original Latin form of the prefix *dis–* began to be used even in words borrowed from French. Nowadays, the Latin spelling has entirely replaced *des–* except in a few words where *des–* was no longer interpreted as a prefix, like *descant.*

Dis– should not be confused with the prefix *dys–* meaning "abnormal, difficult, bad." *Dys–* comes from Greek *dys–,* "bad," and it is often used in combination with other Greek word-building elements to form medical, scientific, or scholarly terms, like *dyslexia* or *dystopia.* The prefix *eu–* functions as the opposite of *dys–,* as can be seen in such pairs of words as *euphoria,* "a feeling of great happiness or well-being," and *dysphoria,* "a feeling of anxiety, depression, or unease." Because *dis–* and *dys–* are both pronounced (dĭs), the more common of the two prefixes, *dis–,* is sometimes miswritten for *dys–.* Take care to avoid such misspellings as *distrophy* for *dystrophy.*

disabled / disability

Disabled is the clear preference in contemporary American English in referring to people having either physical or mental impairments, while the impairments themselves are preferably termed *disabilities. Handicapped*—a somewhat euphemistic term derived from the world of sports gambling—is still in wide use but is sometimes taken to be offensive, while more recent coinages such as *differently abled* or *handicapable* are often perceived as condescending euphemisms and have gained little currency in the general population.

The often-repeated recommendation to "put the person before the disability" would favor *people with disabilities* over *disabled people* or *the disabled,* and *person with paraplegia* over *paraplegic.* Such expressions are intended to focus on the individual rather than on a particular functional limitation, and they are preferred by many people with disabilities as well as by organizations and agencies that serve them. Respect for the wishes of this community calls for observing this rule, despite the awkward phrasing that it can sometimes entail.

See more at **blind, deaf, handicap,** and **impaired.**

disastrous

This word is properly pronounced (dĭ-zăs′trəs) or (dĭ-săs′trəs). Mispronouncing the word (dĭ-zăs′tər-əs), as if the word had four syllables, has led to the common spelling error *disasterous.*

disc

See **disk.**

discomfit / discomfort

Discomfit originally meant "to defeat, frustrate," as in Shakespeare's *1 Henry IV* 3.2.114: *Thrice has this Hotspur, Mars in swathing clothes, / This infant warrior, in his enterprises / Discomfited great Douglas.* But the word also developed another meaning, "to embarrass, disconcert, disturb." This meaning probably arose through confusion with *discomfort,* but it is now by far the most common in all varieties of writing and has long been standard:

> His theories of special and general relativity overturned the notions of absolute space and time, and described the structure of the universe, but Einstein himself was discomfited by a second revolution in 20th-century physics that governed the atomic realm of that universe, known as quantum mechanics (Dennis Overbye, "The Cosmos according to Darwin," *New York Times Magazine*)

> As long as taxidermy served to preserve wild animals and make them available for study, it was viewed as an honorable trade, but most people were still discomfited by it. How could you not be? It was the business of dealing with dead things, coupled with the questionable enterprise of making dead things look like live things (Susan Orlean, "Lifelike," *The New Yorker*)

discreet / discrete

These words sound alike and are related to each other etymologically, but they have different meanings. *Discreet* means "prudent in speech and behavior": *He told me the news but asked me to be discreet about it.* *Discrete* means "separate, distinct": *The summer science program consists of four discrete units.*

discuss

The verb *discuss* is normally transitive. We can discuss ideas, plans, proposals, and so on, both in a group and individually, since the verb means both "to talk about something in a group" and "to talk or write about something for consideration by others." But in certain constructions using *as, discuss* can be used intransitively as well. In our 1996 ballot, 86 percent of the Usage Panel accepted the sentence *As we discussed last Tuesday, we will need a new plan for the reorganization.* This might be because the matter under discussion is mentioned immediately, and the implied object of the verb is clear. The Panel also accepted (though at 67 percent) the intransitive use meaning "to present information on a subject" in the sentence *As Bloch discusses in his book on medieval misogyny, women were a silent presence in the literature of the Middle Ages.*

as discussed   The compressed construction *as discussed* is also acceptable to the Panel, even though the *as* clause has neither a subject nor a complete verb. Fully 92 percent of the Panel accepted *As discussed in last week's meeting, the proposal to charge for parking at athletic events could offer a new means of raising revenue for sports teams.* This construction may not seem so jarring because of the longstanding use of similar *as* constructions such as *as seen in magazines* and *as used in desktop publishing.*

disenfranchise / disfranchise

Both of these synonymous words are acceptable and have been in use for hundreds of years. *Disfranchise* is a somewhat older form and was historically preferred, but *disenfranchise* is far more common and is more readily recognized now.

disfunction   See **dysfunction.**

disingenuous

The word *disingenuous* has been undergoing some shifts or extensions in meaning lately. The word usually means "insincere" and often seems to be a synonym of *cynical* or *calculating.* Not surprisingly, the word is used often in political contexts, as in *It is both insensitive and disingenuous for the White House to describe its aid package and the proposal to eliminate the federal payment as "tough love."* This usage was accepted by 94 percent of the Usage Panel in our 1997 survey. Fully 88 percent accepted the extended meaning of "playfully insincere, faux-naïf," in *"I don't have a clue about late Beethoven!" he said. The remark seemed disingenuous, coming from one of the world's foremost concert pianists.* Sometimes *disingenuous* is used as a synonym for *naive,* as if the *dis–* prefix functioned as an intensive (as it does in certain words like *disannul*) rather than as a negator. This usage did not find much admiration among Panelists, however. Seventy-five percent rejected it in the phrase *a disingenuous tourist who falls prey to stereotypical con artists.*

disinterested

In traditional usage, *disinterested* can only mean "having no stake in an outcome, unprejudiced," as in *Since the judge stands to profit from the sale of the company, she cannot be considered a disinterested party in the dispute.* This usage was acceptable to 97 percent of the Usage Panel in our 2001 survey.

Disinterested has also seen widespread use, even by well-educated writers, with the meaning "uninterested" or "having lost interest," as in *Since she discovered skiing, she is disinterested in her schoolwork.* This usage has come under fierce criticism by language critics. Oddly enough, "not interested" is the oldest sense of the word, going back to the 17th century. This sense became outmoded in the 18th century but underwent a revival in the first quarter of the early 20th. Despite this history, the "not interested" usage has never had many fans on the Usage Panel. In four surveys spanning thirty-five years (1966, 1980, 1988, 2001), the Panel has overwhelmingly disapproved of it. In our 2001 survey, for example, 88 percent of the Panel rejected the sentence *It is difficult to imagine an approach better designed to prevent disinterested students from developing any intellectual maturity.* In our 1988 survey, 89 percent of the Usage Panel rejected the similar sentence *His unwillingness to give five minutes of his time proves that he is disinterested in finding a solution to the problem.* This usage thus is likely to be viewed as a sign of ignorance of the traditional use of the word.

See also **uninterested.**

disk / disc

Both spellings, *disk* and *disc,* are acceptable, though for historical reasons the spelling *disc* is more common in contexts referring to audio-visual devices such as CDs ("compact discs") and DVDs ("digital video discs; digital versatile discs"), while *disk* is more common in computer contexts in reference to storage devices (*hard disks, compact disks*).

But in American English, *disk* is the more common spelling for most ordinary uses of the word:

> The flat little disk of autumn sun was retreating, high up over the neighbors' buildings (Deborah Eisenberg, "Some Other, Better Otto," *Yale Review*)

> The opposite team can intercept the Frisbee or, if it hits the ground, the other team takes possession. Each team scores by advancing the disk past its goal line (Steve Olson, *Count Down*)

The three sepals form the bulk of each flower. Though sometimes fused into a disk or boat shape, they retain a basically triangular orientation (William Cullina, *Orchids*)

disparate

The usual pronunciation is (dĭs′pər-ĭt), with stress on the first syllable. The pronunciation (dĭ-spăr′ĭt), with stress on the second syllable, is also acceptable, although less common.

dissect

There are people who still object to the pronunciation that has a long *i* in the first syllable, although most dictionaries have listed it as an acceptable variant pronunciation for decades. Those who dislike this pronunciation prefer the more established (dĭ-sĕkt′), which has a short *i* in the first syllable. In our 1997 survey, 55 percent of the Usage Panel preferred the traditional pronunciation, 35 percent preferred the newer one, and the remainder reported using both forms.

dissimilation

Dissimilation is a phonological process that involves one of two similar or identical sounds within a word becoming less like the other or even disappearing entirely. Because *r*'s in successive syllables are particularly difficult to pronounce, they frequently dissimilate. One historical example of dissimilation is *marble,* from French *marbre.* In this case the second *r* has dissimilated to *l* in order to prevent a repetition of the *r* and ease articulation. Other contemporary examples of dissimilation include *enterprise, governor, impropriety, prerogative, surprise,* and *thermometer,* in which there is a tendency for the first *r* to drop out of the pronunciation resulting in (ĕn′tə-prīz′), (gŭv′ə-nər), (ĭm′pə-prī′ə-tē), (pə-rŏg′ə-tĭv), (sə-prīz′), and (thə-mŏm′ĭ-tər). None of these examples really receives any adverse criticism, but some instances of dissimilation may, such as the pronunciation (lī′bĕr′ē) for *library.* Note that other consonants besides *r* may be altered or omitted as a result of dissimilation, such as *n* in *government* (gŭv′ər-mənt).

distinct / distinctive

A thing is *distinct* if it is sharply distinguished from other things; a property or attribute is *distinctive* if it enables us to distinguish one thing from another. *There are two distinct colors on the wings of the goshawk* means that the two colors are clearly different from each other, while *There are two distinctive colors on the wings of the goshawk* means that the two colors are different from colors found on the wings of other birds, and the goshawk may be identified by these two colors.

dived / dove

The verb *dive* has two past tenses, *dived* and *dove,* and both are acceptable. *Dived* is the form that was used in early Modern English, but a new past tense *dove* began to appear in the 19th century. The development of the past tense *dove* doubtless reflects the influence of verbs like *drive* with its past tense *drove.*
    See also **sneaked; verbs, principal parts of;** and **wake.**

divers / diverse

Cases in which similarly spelled words have related meanings lead easily to confusion. This pair of words is such a case, although *divers* has become somewhat antiquated, largely replaced by *various,* which has the same meaning, "miscellaneous, sundry, several" (as in *minor tasks assigned to divers employees*). *Diverse,* contrastingly, means "differing from one another, unlike" (as in *people with diverse interests*) and "made up of distinct elements, characteristics, or qualities" (as in *a magazine with a diverse readership*).
    Note that *divers* is pronounced (dī′vûrz) and *diverse* is pronounced (dĭ-vûrs′) or (dī′vûrs).

divisive

The word *divisive,* meaning "creating dissension or discord," is properly pronounced (dĭ-vī′sĭv), with the stressed syllable having a long *i.* This pronunciation was the preferred pronunciation of 82 percent of the Usage Panel in 2001. The pronunciation with a short *i* in the stressed syllable was acceptable to only 16 percent of the Panel and may be considered by many people to be a mistake.

divorcé / divorcée   See **feminine suffixes.**

doctrinal

The adjectival form of *doctrine* is *doctrinal,* which can be pronounced either with the stress on the first syllable (dŏk′trə-nəl) or on the second (dŏk-trī′nəl). In our 1996 survey, the pronunciation with the initial stress was the one that 69 percent of the Usage Panel reported using, and the pronunciation with the stress on the second syllable was the choice of 31 percent.

double genitive

This term is used for possessive constructions such as *that friend of Bob's* and is discussed under **possessive constructions.**

double negative

double negative equals a positive It is a truism of traditional grammar that double negatives combine to form an affirmative. Readers coming across a sentence like *He cannot do nothing* will therefore interpret it as an affirmative statement meaning "He must do something" unless they are prompted to view it as dialect or nonstandard speech. Readers will also assign an affirmative meaning to constructions that yoke *not* with an adjective or adverb that begins with a negative prefix such as *in–* or *un–*, as in *a not infrequent visitor* or *a not unjust decision*. In these expressions the double negative conveys a weaker affirmative than would be conveyed by the positive adjective or adverb by itself. Thus *a not infrequent visitor* seems likely to visit less frequently than *a frequent visitor*.

double negative equals a negative *"You ain't heard nothin' yet,"* said Al Jolson in 1927 in *The Jazz Singer,* the first talking motion picture. He meant, of course, "You haven't heard anything yet." Some sixty years later President Reagan taunted his political opponents by saying *"You ain't seen nothin' yet."* These famous examples of double negatives that reinforce (rather than nullify) a negative meaning show clearly that this construction is alive and well in spoken English. In fact, multiple negatives have been used to convey negative meaning in English since Old English times, and for most of this period, the double negative was wholly acceptable. Thus Chaucer in *The Canterbury Tales* could say of the Friar, *"Ther nas no man nowher so vertuous,"* meaning "There was no man anywhere so virtuous," and Shakespeare could allow Viola in *Twelfth Night* to say of her heart, *"Nor never none / Shall mistress of it be, save I alone,"* by which she meant that no one except herself would ever be mistress of her heart.

double negative equals trouble But in spite of this noble history, grammarians since the Renaissance have objected to this form of negative reinforcement employing the double negative. In their eagerness to make English conform to formal logic, they conceived and promulgated the notion that two negatives destroy each other and make a positive. This view was taken up by English teachers and has since become enshrined as a convention of Standard English. Nonetheless, the reinforcing double negative remains an effective construction in writing dialogue or striking a folksy note.

double negative with minimizing adverbs The ban on double and multiple negatives also applies to the combination of negatives with adverbs such as *barely, hardly,* and *scarcely.* In Standard English, it is therefore considered incorrect to say *I couldn't hardly do it* or *The car scarcely needs no oil.* These adverbs have a minimizing effect on the verb. They mean something like "almost not at all." They resemble negative adverbs such as *not* and *never* in that they are used with *any, anybody,* and similar words rather than *none, nobody,* and other negatives. Thus it is standard usage to say *You barely have any time left* and *You don't have any time left,* but it is not acceptable to say *You barely have no time left,* since this violates the double-negative rule.

exceptions to the rule The ban on using double negatives to convey emphasis does not apply when the second negative appears in a separate phrase or clause, as in *I will* *not surrender, not today, not ever* or *He does not seek money, no more than he seeks fame.* Note that commas must be used to separate the negative phrases in these examples. Thus the sentence *He does not seek money no more than he seeks fame* is unacceptable, whereas the equivalent sentence with *any* is perfectly acceptable and requires no comma: *He does not seek money any more than he seeks fame.*

See more at **hardly, rarely ever,** and **scarcely.**

double passive

It is sometimes necessary to conjoin a passive verb form with a passive infinitive, as in *The building is scheduled to be demolished next week* and *The piece was originally intended to be played on the harpsichord.* Sentences like these are perfectly acceptable, but these "double passive" constructions can often cause trouble. For instance, they sometimes end in ambiguity. In the sentence *An independent review of the proposal was required to be made by the committee,* is the committee making the demand or doing the review? What is worse, double passives often sound ungrammatical, as this example shows: *The fall in the value of the yen was attempted to be stopped by the Central Bank.*

Here's how to tell an acceptable double passive from an unacceptable one. If the first passive verb can be changed into an active one, making the original subject its object, while keeping the passive infinitive, the original sentence is acceptable. Thus it is acceptable (and more straightforward) to say *The city has scheduled the building to be demolished next week* and *The composer originally intended the piece to be played on the harpsichord.* If such changes cannot be made, then the original sentence is not acceptable. Note that these changes cannot be made in the Central Bank sentence, since they would produce an ungrammatical result: *The Central Bank attempted the fall in the value of the yen to be stopped.*

This is all very technical and involved, however, and it is much simpler just to judge the sound and flow of the sentence. If a double passive sounds awkward or tinny, rewrite the sentence.

See more at **passive voice** and **verbs, voice of.**

doubt / doubtful

doubt **and** ***doubtful*** **with** ***that, whether,*** **or** ***if***   *Doubt* and *doubtful* may be followed by clauses introduced by the conjunction *that, whether,* or *if.* The choice depends somewhat on the intended meaning. Since *whether* has long been the preferred word in more formal contexts to introduce indirect questions (*I asked whether he could come along*), *whether* is the traditional choice when the subject of *doubt* is in a state of genuine uncertainty about alternative possibilities: *Sue has studied so much philosophy this year that she's begun to doubt whether she exists.* Similarly, when *doubtful* indicates uncertainty, *whether* is probably the best choice: *At one time it was doubtful whether the company could recover from its financial difficulties, but the government loan seems to have helped.* *If* is sometimes used in place of *whether,* but *if* is more informal in tone.

When *that* is used, the emphasis is less one of a questioning, but of negative expectations: *I doubt that they'll be on time* suggests a strong expectation that they will be late. *That* is also used when *doubt* expresses disbelief in an understated way. Thus *I doubt that we've seen the last of* that *problem,* implies "I think we haven't seen the last of that problem." *That* is also the usual choice when the truth of the clause following *doubt* is assumed, as in negative sentences and questions. Thus *I never doubted for a minute that I would be rescued* implies "I was certain that I would be rescued." By the same token, *Do you doubt that you will be paid?* may be understood as a rhetorical question meaning "Surely you believe that you will be paid," whereas *Do you doubt whether you will be paid?* expresses a genuine request for information (and might be followed by *Because if you do, you should make the client post a bond*). Note that it is also acceptable to omit *that* in these sentences: *I doubt she will accept the nomination.*

In other cases, however, this distinction between *whether* and *that* is not always observed.

doubt but   When *doubt* is negated to indicate belief or certainty, the clause following *doubt* is sometimes introduced with *but that* or simply *but,* as in *I do not doubt but that they will be come.* This construction has been used by many fine writers, but some critics object to its use in formal writing. Dropping the *but* easily solves this problem.

doughty

Pronounce this (dou′tē), with the *ou* as in *doubt* or *pout.*

dour

This word, which is etymologically related to *duress* and *endure,* traditionally rhymes with *tour.* The variant pronunciation that rhymes with *sour* is, however, widely used and must be considered acceptable. In our 1996 survey, 65 percent of the Usage Panel preferred the traditional pronunciation, and 33 percent preferred the variant.

dove   See **dove.**

dowager

This term for an older woman of high station or a widow who owns property inherited from her late husband has no masculine counterpart. Historically, it refers to a woman with a royal title who has become widowed, as a dowager duchess or empress. When used outside of these contexts, however, *dowager* not only defines a woman by her advanced age but also implies that a woman who acquires significant financial assets after her spouse's death warrants being characterized as such. For these reasons, the word may be considered sexist and should therefore be used cautiously.

Down syndrome

The congenital disorder *Down syndrome,* caused by the presence of an extra 21st chromosome and characterized by mental retardation and other abnormalities, is also referred to as *Down's syndrome,* after the British physician who first described the disorder, John Langdon Down. The spelling *Down syndrome,* however, is the one used most frequently in medical and scientific literature and among organizations that deal with the condition.

See more at **Mongoloid.**

drunk / drunken

As an adjective meaning "intoxicated by or as if by alcohol," the form *drunk* is generally used after a verb such as *be* or *seem,* while the form *drunken* is used in front of a noun to modify it directly: *They were drunk last night,* but *A drunken waiter at the restaurant ruined our evening.* Using *drunk* in front of a noun is less formal, although the phrases *drunk driver* and *drunk driving,* which have become fixed expressions, are exceptions to this.

Drunken also has a more general use, with the meaning "characterized by or related to alcohol or intoxication," as in *a drunken sauce* (one that has something containing alcohol, such as beer or wine, as an ingredient), *a drunken laugh* (one that gives the impression that the person laughing is drunk), or *a drunken affair* (a celebration in which the participants become drunk). *Drunk* generally does not have this meaning, although the noun *drunk* comes close, being a disparaging term for someone characterized by frequent drunkenness or alcoholism.

A differentiation between *drunk* and *drunken* is sometimes made in legal language, wherein a *drunk driver* is a driver whose alcohol level exceeds the legal limit, and a *drunken driver* is a driver who is inebriated.

due   See **make do.**

due to

Due to has been widely used for many years as a compound preposition like *owing to,* but some critics have insisted that *due* should be used only as an adjective. According to this view, it is incorrect to say *The concert was canceled due to the rain* but acceptable to say *The cancellation of the concert was due to the rain,* where *due* functions as an adjective modifying *cancellation.*

Although there is still some support for this notion among members of the Usage Panel, the tide has turned toward accepting *due to* as a full-fledged preposition. Back in 1966, the "adverbial" use of *due to* (as in *was canceled due to the rain*) was rejected by 84 percent of the Panel. In our 2001 survey, however, 60 percent accepted this construction.

There is no linguistic reason to avoid using *due to* as a preposition, but English has a variety of ready substitutes, including *because of, on account of,* and *owing to.*

See more at **virtue.**

dumb

The sense of *dumb* meaning "stupid" is much more recent in English than the sense of "lacking the power of speech." However, the later sense has overwhelmed the earlier to such a degree that any reference to a person who cannot speak as *dumb* is clearly offensive. Indeed, *dumb* now has such strong connotations of dimwittedness that even using it of animals, as in *the dumb creatures of the forest,* is likely to cause either mirth or misunderstanding.

See more at **mute.**

Dutch

A number of English expressions formed with the word *Dutch* are considered objectionable because of the unflattering stereotypes they perpetuate. Some of these, such as *Dutch uncle* (a stern critic) and *Dutch courage* (courage gained by drinking liquor), are little used today. Others, however, such as *in Dutch* (in trouble) and *go Dutch* (to pay one's own expenses on a date), have retained their currency. Although many Americans are only vaguely aware of the stereotypes evoked by these phrases, it is often best to avoid them.

duty

When the sound (o͞o) follows (t), (d), or (n), in some varieties of English the glide sound (y) is often inserted before the (o͞o). Thus, the word *duty* is correctly pronounced either (do͞o′tē) or (dyo͞o′tē). Words with similar variants include *news* and *tune.* With other sounds, such as (b), (g), (k), (m), and (p), the presence or absence of the (y) sound differentiates words, as with *beauty* (byo͞o′tē) and *booty* (bo͞o′tē) or *cue* (kyo͞o) and *coo* (ko͞o).

dwarf / midget

In legends and fairy tales, a *dwarf* is a small creature resembling a human. In medicine, the term *dwarf* is used to refer to abnormally short individuals whose stature results from any of various conditions, most commonly achondroplasia, an inherited failure of cartilage to develop normally into bone, especially on the ends of long bones. This manifests itself in disproportionality of the limbs and the skull. *Midget* is not a medical term and is considered offensive when referring to people of very short stature. Some individuals find the term *dwarf* to have negative connotations and prefer *little person* or *person of short stature,* both of which are always acceptable.

plural of *dwarf***   The plural of *dwarf* is either *dwarfs* (dwôrfs) or *dwarves* (dwôrvz). Throughout most of the Modern English period, *dwarfs* has been the usual plural. The plural *dwarves* has recently become common, however, especially in literary works of fantasy. The creation of the more archaic-sounding form *dwarves* is usually attributed to the author and historian of the English language J.R.R. Tolkien, who formed it by analogy with words like *thief/thieves, leaf/leaves,* and *wife/wives,* in which *f* becomes *v* in the plural. Many writers object to the plural form *dwarves* as an unwarranted innovation that is inappropriate outside of fantasy.

See more at **roof.**

dys–   See **dis–.**

dysfunction

The noun *dysfunction,* "impaired functioning, especially of a bodily system or social group," was formed by adding the prefix *dys–,* "abnormal, difficult, bad," to the noun *function.* The term, along with its derivatives like *dysfunctional,* first appeared in English in the early 20th century. The spelling variant *disfunction* is also occasionally seen, and it has been accepted by several American dictionaries. However, many consider spellings like *disfunction* or *disfunctional* to show a careless confusion of the prefix *dys–,* "bad," with another prefix, *dis–,* which has various meanings including "lacking" or "opposite." Writers are therefore advised to use only the spelling *dysfunction* in order to avoid criticism. Variant spellings with *dis–* for *dys–* are also seen along with other medical terms that have entered common use, such as *distrophy* for *dystrophy.* None of these variants has become established as acceptable, however.

See more at **dis–.**

· E ·

each

***each* with singular or plural verb**   In standard usage the subject of a sentence beginning with *each* is grammatically singular, and so the verb and following pronouns must be singular. Thus proper usage requires *Each of the apartments has* [not *have*] *its* [not *their*] *own private entrance* [not *entrances*]. When *each* follows a plural subject, however, the verb and subsequent pronouns remain in the plural: *The apartments each have their own private entrances* [not *has its own private entrance*]. But when *each* follows a verb that has *we* as its subject, there is an exception. It is acceptable to say *We boys each have our own room, We boys have each our own room,* or *We boys have each his own room,* though the last of these may strike readers as stilted.

each and every   The expression *each and every* is likewise followed by a singular verb and singular pronoun: *Each and every driver knows* [not *know*] *what his or her* [not *their*] *job is to be.* This expression is sometimes criticized as a redundancy, and so it is, but it serves the purpose of emphasizing both the universality and individuality of the collection being discussed, much like *every single one.* A greater danger lies in the condescension that sometimes accompanies these constructions.

See more at **every, he,** and **subject and verb agreement.**

each other / one another

The pronouns *each other* and *one another* indicate a reciprocal relationship among the members of a group: *Dick and Maggie gave each other a knowing look. The team members hugged one another at the end of the game.* A traditional usage rule stipulates that *each other* should refer only to two, and *one another* should refer to more than two. In our 1987 survey, 64 percent of the Usage Panelists said that they follow this rule in their own writing. There is certainly no harm in observing the rule, but it is one often observed in the breach without causing confusion, as the following quotations show:

> At 9 Highland even the very psychotic are able to talk things over, pack a suitcase, then leave for the hospital quietly, usually in a counselor's car. Civil liberties are not an issue. Everyone knows each other too well (Michael Winerip, "A Home for Anthony," *New York Times Book Review*)

> Closer to home, geoseismologists routinely map Earth's inner structure, including its oil and mineral deposits, by analyzing patterns of sound waves that reverberate and interfere with each other (Malcolm W. Browne, "Deep Solar Rumblings May Offer Key to Sun's Inner Structure," *New York Times*)

154

Nonetheless, many people like to maintain a stylistic distinction between the two expressions. When an ordered series of events or stages is involved, *one another* is often preferred. Thus, in the 1987 survey, *one another* was preferred by 73 percent of the Usage Panel in the sentence *The waiters followed one another into the room.*

Note that *one another* is sometimes used to refer to two or to pairings of two, as in the phrase *the young / In one another's arms* from W. B. Yeats's poem *Sailing to Byzantium.*

With certain verbs that have a reciprocal meaning, like *kiss* and *meet,* these reciprocal pronouns are often redundant: The sentence *We met each other in Ann Arbor* means the same thing as *We met in Ann Arbor.* But in certain contexts, reciprocal pronouns can help dispel ambiguity: *Yes, Bob and Alice are finally getting married—to each other!*

the possessive of *each other* and *one another*   The possessive forms of *each other* and *one another* are written *each other's* and *one another's,* that is, with an apostrophe before the *s: The boys wore each other's* [not *each others'*] *coats. They had forgotten one another's* [not *one anothers'*] *names.*

ebullience / ebullient

Traditionally, these are pronounced (ĭ-bŭl′yəns) and (ĭ-bŭl′yənt), with a short *u* in the second syllable as in *gull.* This is apparently still the preferred pronunciation in British English. In American English, the variant pronunciations (ĭ-bo͞ol′yəns) and (ĭ-bo͞ol′yənt), with the second syllable like *bull,* are now equally common.

–ed

The suffix *–ed,* which is used to form the past tense and past participle of regular verbs, may be pronounced (t), (d), or (ĭd) depending on the phonological environment. That is, *–ed* is always pronounced (t) after the consonant sounds *p, f, s, ch, k;* (d) after vowels and the consonant sounds *b, m, n, v, l, z, j, r, g;* and (ĭd) after *t* and *d.* In a small group of adjectives including *aged, alleged, beloved, blessed, cursed, dogged,* and *learned, –ed* may also be pronounced (ĭd) following consonants other than *t* and *d.* This distinction between the pronunciation of the adjective form and the pronunciation of the past tense or past participle form is not always strictly preserved, though. We say *a learned* (lûr′nĭd) *professor* but *a beloved* (bĭ-lŭv′ĭd or bĭ-lŭvd′) *spouse.* There is some justification for retaining the pronunciation (ĭd) since it does signal a subtle shift in meaning. For example, (lûrnd) is not applied to people, but (lûr′nĭd) is.

–ee

The English suffix *–ee* originates in the French passive participle ending *–é* (feminine *–ée*), the French equivalent of the English passive participle suffix *–ed.* It entered

English as part of legal terminology and in military and political jargon, and nouns ending in –*ee* were used to refer to persons directly affected by an action, just as they were in French. This use is still seen today in words like *draftee, trainee,* or *nominee.* But the suffix also came to be used in English to form nouns denoting the person that benefited from an action or was otherwise indirectly affected by it—that is, the person who would be the indirect object of the verb from which the noun ending in –*ee* is formed, if that verb were to be used in the full sentence implied by the noun. For example, in the rather legalistic-sounding sentence *The owner leased the lessee the property,* the noun *lessee* refers to the person to whom the property is leased (the indirect object of the verb), and is not used to refer to the thing leased (the direct object of the verb). Other nouns like *lessee* are *donee,* "the recipient of a gift" (not "the thing given to someone") and *trustee,* "the person to whom one entrusts something" (not "the thing entrusted to someone's care"). From around the mid-19th century, primarily in American English, the use of the suffix was extended even further, and it began to be used to make nouns denoting the agent or subject of an intransitive verb, as in *standee, returnee,* or *attendee.* (A *returnee* is not "one who has been returned," but rather "one who has come back.")

The coining of new words ending in –*ee* continues to be common. A number of these coinages, such as *honoree, deportee,* and *escapee,* have become widely accepted. The suffix –*ee* has come to be used to create passive counterparts to agent nouns ending in –*or* or –*er,* giving us words like *benefactee* (from *benefactor*) and *biographee* (from *biographer*). Many new words ending in –*ee,* such as *firee, invitee, jokee,* and *roastee,* are created ad hoc and often have a comic effect.

The French masculine passive participle suffix –*é* and its feminine counterpart –*ée* can also be found in more recent English borrowings from French. In these cases, the difference in spelling between the masculine and feminine suffixes is often maintained in English spelling, leading to the development of an ending spelled –*ée* with specifically feminine meaning. Thus the feminine word *divorcée* exists alongside the masculine form *divorcé* ending in –*é.* The two English nouns are simply the feminine and masculine forms, respectively, of the French passive participle *divorcé,* used to mean "one who has been divorced."

See more at **feminine suffixes.**

effectual / efficacious / effective / efficient

This cluster of related words needs disentangling. *Effectual* and *efficacious* are synonymous, meaning "producing or capable of producing a desired effect," as in *an effectual business plan* and *an efficacious drug therapy. Effectual* also has the legal meaning "valid or binding." The term *effective* can also refer to desired effects (*an effective strategy to reduce unemployment*), but differs in having additional meanings and much broader applicability. It may also mean "operative, in effect" (*the law is effective immediately*), "actual, existing in fact" (*a decline in the effective demand*), or "prepared for use or action" (*an effective infantry unit*). The term *efficient* also has the "desired effect" meaning shared by the others, but in this case the meaning is restricted almost entirely to frozen phrases such as *efficient cause.* Its more common meaning, "acting or producing effectively with a minimum of waste, expense, or unnecessary effort" is not shared by the other words in this group.

effeminate   See **feminine.**

egomania / egotism / egoism / egocentrism

All of these words share a core meaning of being strongly oriented to the self, but each offers its own psychological or philosophical variations on this meaning. *Egomania* is an extreme or obsessive preoccupation with the self, as when someone lusts after fame or is unable to think about any topic other than himself. *Egotism* is milder, suggesting conceit, an inflated sense of one's importance, or a tendency to speak or write about oneself excessively or boastfully. *Egoism* has the meaning of egotism, but also has important philosophical and ethical senses, denoting doctrines or beliefs that morality is essentially rooted in or justified by self-interest. *Egocentrism* also has philosophical senses and may refer to the belief that the ego is the center and object of all experience or that one's own self may be taken as the center or starting point of a philosophical system. Egocentrism may also refer to simple conceit or selfishness.

either

either of more than two   A traditional rule holds that *either* should be used only to refer to one of two items and that *any* is required when more than two items are involved: *Any* [not *either*] *of the three opposition candidates still in the race would make a better president than the incumbent.* Note that the rule applies only to the use of *either* as a pronoun or an adjective (as in *Either computer will run the software*). When used as a conjunction, *either* can apply to more than two elements in a series: *She left her glove either at the convenience store, the library, or the playground. Either the union will make a counteroffer or the owners will close the factory or the mayor will intervene.*

either with singular or plural verb   When used as a pronoun, *either* is normally singular and takes a singular verb: *The two surgeons disagree with each other more than either does* [not *do*] *with the pathologist.* But when *either* is followed by *of* and a plural noun, it is often used with a plural verb: *Either of the parties have enough support to form a government.* As frequent as this usage may be, it is widely regarded as incorrect. Ninety-two percent of the Usage Panel rejected it in an earlier survey.

either . . . or and verb agreement   When all the elements in an *either . . . or* construction (or a *neither . . . nor* construction) used as the subject of a sentence are singular, the verb is singular: *Either Eve or Herb has been invited.* Analogously, when all the elements in the *either . . . or* construction are plural, the verb is plural too: *Either the Clarks or the Kays have been invited.* When the construction mixes singular and plural elements, however, there is some confusion as to which form the verb should take. Some people argue that the verb should agree with whichever noun phrase is closest to it. The Usage Panel has much sympathy for this view. Fifty-five percent prefer the plural verb for the sentence *Either the owner or the players is going/are going to have to give in.* Another 12 percent find either verb acceptable, meaning that, overall, 67 percent accept the plural verb in such situations, and only 33 percent would require the singular. If none of these solutions seems satisfactory, the only alternative is to revise the sentence to avoid the *either . . . or* construction.

***either . . . or* and parallelism** Both conjunctions in *either . . . or* (or *neither . . . nor*) constructions should be followed with parallel elements. Thus, if a verb and an object follow *either,* a verb and an object must follow *or* as well. Thus, a sentence like *She can either take the examination offered to all applicants or ask for a personal interview* is parallel, but *She can take either the examination offered to all applicants or ask for a personal interview* is not. Similarly, *You may have either the ring or the bracelet* is properly parallel, but *You may either have the ring or the bracelet* is not.

pronunciation of *either* The usual pronunciation in American English is (ē′thər), with a long *e* sound. According to the *Dictionary of American Regional English,* the pronunciation (ī′thər), with a long *i,* is used mostly by well-educated speakers in urban areas of the Northeast, and is often considered affected by others. Almost the opposite is true in British English, however, where (ī′thər) is more common. Both pronunciations have been recognized by English dictionaries since the 18th century. The same variation occurs in *neither.*

See more at **neither, or, parallelism,** and **subject and verb agreement.**

elder

***elder* as an adjective** In comparisons between two persons, *elder* is simply a more formal term for "older" and has no implication of advanced age: *My elder sibling is fourteen; my younger is nine.* In other contexts it does denote relatively old age, but with the added component of respect for a person's position or achievement: *an elder statesman, an elder member of the court.* If the simple fact of advanced or relatively advanced age is the point, *older* or *elderly* are usually more appropriate than *elder: a survey of older Americans, an elderly waiter.*

***elder* as a noun** As with the adjective, the noun *elder* can be used comparatively without implying old age: *He is my elder by three years.* It can also refer to an office in certain churches or, more broadly, to a position of authority or respect conferred by age and experience: *an elder in the Presbyterian Church, a tribal elder.* The use of *elder* in the sense of "an elderly person" is uncommon in contemporary English, though it is widely used as an attributive in such phrases as *elder care* (or *eldercare*) and *elder services.*

elderly

Elderly applies to the stage of life well past middle age. When used as a noun in referring to older persons in general, it is relatively neutral, denoting a group of people whose common characteristic is advanced age: *policy issues of special interest to the elderly.* However, when used as an adjective in describing a particular person, *elderly* has a range of connotations that go beyond the denotation of chronological age. On the one hand it can suggest dignity, and its somewhat formal tone may express respect: *sat next to an elderly gentleman at the concert.* On the other hand it can imply frailty or diminished capacity, in which case it may sound condescending: *was stuck in traffic behind an elderly driver.* Regardless of other connotations, a phrase such as *the elderly couple in the second row* suggests greater age than if the couple were described as *older.*

electric / electrical / electronic

The terms *electric* and *electrical* are basically synonymous. Both terms can refer to anything involving electricity, be it a thunderstorm, a generator, a motor, a heater, or a computer. All that is required for something to be electric or electrical is that it involve forces created by the presence of charged particles, such as electrons, protons, and the atoms and molecules made from them. Chemical bonds are ultimately electric in nature, and even the magnetic field of a bar magnet can be considered an electrical phenomenon, since it results from the motion of electrons in the atoms of the magnet. The word *electric* is somewhat more common in compounds naming devices such as *electric motor* and *electric oven.*

The term *electronic* is more specific. It is reserved for man-made electrical devices that process electrical signals using *amplification.* For example, a transistor radio is electronic because incoming radio waves are turned into a varying voltage signal that is amplified and processed by transistors (together with other components) before being sent to a speaker. Computers are electronic devices, since they process large numbers of electrical signals, amplifying them slightly at each stage of their processing to prevent them from fading out. So if your stove uses electricity to power its heating elements, it's electric, but if it uses a microprocessor to drive a timer and a temperature regulator, then it's electronic as well.

elicit / solicit / illicit

Elicit is a verb meaning "to bring or draw out something that is latent or potential," as in *Duke Ellington elicited some amazing sounds from his band.* By extension, a discussion or inquiry can elicit a finding, truth, or principle. *Elicit* can also mean "to call forth a reaction":

> Thus, oxytocin may elicit any number of responses or no response at all, depending on the body's general biochemical balance of the moment (Natalie Angier, *The Beauty of the Beastly*)

The word *solicit* has a related, but distinct and more specific set of meanings, most commonly "to seek to obtain by persuasion, entreaty, or formal application":

> It is believed that only the famous, the busy, the talented have the power to solicit funds from the rich, notice from the press, and envy from the opposition (Elizabeth Hardwick, "The Apotheosis of Martin Luther King," *The New York Review of Books*)

> Once again Puckering solicited expressions of Indian grievance and considered some of them well founded (Gary Wills, *The Negro President*)

Less frequently, the object of *solicit* (and not of *elicit*) may be a person, namely the person being asked or implored:

> Upon leaving him on the night of our adventure, he solicited me, in what I thought an urgent manner, to call upon him very early the next morning (Edgar Allan Poe, "The Assignation")

Solicit also has another related pair of meanings, "to entice or incite to evil or illegal action; to approach or accost with an offer of sexual services."

> Eighty-two men in Shenzhen had recently been stripped of their Party membership for being "prostitution patrons" (a half year of reeducation was also part of their punishment). Still, women quietly solicited in many bars (Paul Theroux, *Fresh Air Fiend*)

> Vice also flourished. In the red brick hotels along First Street, parallel to the railroad tracks, gamblers set up their rooms, and prostitutes solicited patrons by rapping on the windows (James Hirsch, *Riot and Remembrance*)

Neither of these words, of course, should be confused with the adjective *illicit*, meaning "unlawful," as in *money acquired by illicit means.*

ellipsis points

Ellipsis points, also known as *ellipsis dots* or *ellipses,* are indicated by three spaced periods preceded and followed by spaces.

1. Three ellipsis points indicate an omission of one or more words within quoted material. What remains should constitute a grammatically complete sentence.

> This ended, the council . . . and the former regents were put on trial.

If the omission occurs at the end of a sentence, four points are used: the first point represents the period of the sentence.

> Nor have we been wanting in Attentions to our British Brethren. . . . They too have been deaf to the Voice of Justice. . . .

2. To indicate the omission of one or more lines within a section of quoted poetry, use a line of spaced ellipsis points. The line of points should be about the same length as the omitted line or the line above it.

> Inebriate of air am I,
> . . . .
> Reeling, through endless summer days
> —Emily Dickinson

3. Three ellipsis points may be used to indicate a pause in speech or to show that a sentence is trailing off.

> "Hot!" said the conductor to familiar faces. "Some weather! . . . Hot! . . . Hot! . . . Hot! . . . Is it hot enough for you? Is it hot? Is it . . . ?"(F. Scott Fitzgerald, *The Great Gatsby*)

4. Ellipsis points are used as a device to catch and hold the reader's interest, especially in advertising copy.

> To help you Move and Grow
> with the Rigors of
> Business in the 21st century . . .
> and Beyond.
> —*The Journal of Business Strategy*

elliptical

In grammar, the term *elliptical* means "characterized by the omission of a word or phrase that is necessary for a complete grammatical construction but is not necessary for understanding." In the sentence *The mayor supported the fee increase, and the board of supervisors did too*, the clause *the board of supervisors did too* is elliptical for *the board of supervisors supported the fee increase too*.

else

redundancy of *else*   *Else* is often used redundantly in combination with prepositions such as *but, except,* and *besides*. The sentence *No one else but Sam saw the accident* would thus do better without the *else*.

possessive of *else*   When a pronoun is followed by *else,* the possessive form is generally written with an apostrophe and *s* following *else: That must be someone else's* [not *someone's else*] *book*. Both *who else's* and *whose else* are in use, but not *whose else's: Who else's book could it have been? Whose else could it have been?* Note that *who else's* is a phrase that modifies a noun, while *whose else* functions as a noun itself.

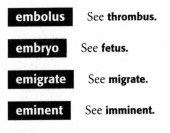

embolus   See **thrombus.**

embryo   See **fetus.**

emigrate   See **migrate.**

eminent   See **imminent.**

empower

The verb *empower* has become a buzzword in recent years, and its meaning has broadened. Today teachers are empowering students to think for themselves, computers empower us to become explorers on the information frontier, women are empowering each other as professionals by using the services of other women, and so on.

The word *empower* is not new, having arisen in the mid-17th century with the legalistic meaning "to invest with authority, authorize." Shortly thereafter it began to be used with an infinitive in a more general way meaning "to enable or permit." Both of these uses survive today.

Its modern use probably comes from the civil rights movement, which sought political *empowerment* for its followers. The word got taken up by the women's movement and its appeal has not flagged, as in this quotation from 1992:

> We need freedom from male domination and male-defined standards, so that we can create the fullness of our own lives, based on empowered choices (Karen Henry, *Ms. Magazine*)

But *empower* proved too irresistible to remain in the hands of just one group, and it is now ubiquitous, applied to people of all sorts, for example, the poor:

> But Robert Kennedy differed from those who now call themselves "new" Democrats, because he also insisted on national policy, national leadership, and national funding to help empower people at the bottom and address other pressing issues (Peter Edelman, *Searching for America's Heart*)

the rich:

> . . . the gradual turning away from the founding ideals of a Declaration of Independence, a Constitution, and a Bill of Rights toward governmental institutions and practices that empower the rich at the expense of the poor . . . (John Edgar Wideman, *Hoop Roots*)

medical patients:

> This book is our attempt to fight that stigma, raise awareness about the true nature of anxiety and depression, help people find optimal treatment, and empower them so they can better navigate often complicated health-care systems (Dennis S. Charney, M.D., and Charles B. Nemeroff, M.D., Ph.D., with Steven Braun, *The Peace of Mind Prescription*)

educators:

> We must empower our educators to create interactive learning environments rather than merely presenting information to passive students (George Leonard, "The End of School," *Atlantic*)

terrorists:

> We have a window now, while terrorists still have difficulty obtaining reliable recipes for [biological] weapons. If we continue to allow these cookbooks to improve, buttressed by helpful articles in professional journals, then over the next 10 years we may empower terrorists to kill us on an unimaginable scale (Nicholas Kristoff, "Recipes for Death," *New York Times*)

and everyone but the terrorists:

> This is not as grim as it may appear as we look on this situation presently and consider these things. The nature of God is to empower us as the pressure comes upon us (George W. Bush, Speech to Congress, September 20, 2001)

In social and political contexts, the Usage Panel gives a strong yes vote to *empower*. In our 1994 survey, 80 percent approved of the example *We want to empower ordinary citizens.* But in other contexts the Panel was markedly less enthusiastic. The sentence *Hunger and greed and then sexual zeal are felt by some to be stages of experience that empower the individual* garnered approval from only 33 percent of the Panelists. The Panel may frown on this kind of psychological empowering because it resonates of the self-help movement, which is notorious for trendy coinages.

empty rhetoric

In the ancient and medieval world, *rhetoric,* the study of persuasive argumentation, chiefly by public speaking, was an important branch of philosophy and a crucial skill to professional advancement. The word still refers to this ancient study, but has been extended to other meanings, such as the skill of using language effectively and persuasively itself (*your rhetoric is highly developed*), or a style of speaking or writing (especially the argumentative language in a particular subject, as in *fiery political rhetoric*). In recent years, however, people have also used the term in a pejorative sense to refer to pompous and devious language. This suspicion of rhetoric may result from a modern belief that language used in legitimate persuasion should be plain and free of artifice—which is itself an argument from ancient rhetoric. Given the newer sense of the term, the phrase *empty rhetoric,* as in *The politicians talk about solutions, but they usually offer empty rhetoric,* can be construed as a redundancy. However, *empty* here arguably serves the purpose of picking out this more modern meaning of *rhetoric* from among the others. In our 1987 survey, only 35 percent of the Usage Panel judged this example to be redundant. Rhetoric may or may not be empty.

en–

There are two prefixes spelled *en–*. One comes from the Latin prefix *in–*. As Latin developed into Old French, *in–* became *en–*, and it was in the form *en–* that the prefix entered English through borrowings from Old French. The basic meaning of *en–* is "into or onto," and it chiefly forms verbs. Thus *encapsulate* means "to put into a capsule," and *enplane* means "to get on an airplane." This same *en–* also has the meanings "to cause to be," as in *endear,* and "to cover or provide with," as in *enrobe.* It sometimes has intensive force, as in *entangle. En–* has a variant spelling *in–,* seen in such pairs like *enclose/inclose* and *enquire/inquire.* This variation results from the influence of the original Latin spelling of the prefix as *in–,* the spelling which is usual in the numerous direct borrowings from Latin found in modern English vocabulary today.

The second *en–* goes back to Greek and means "in, into, within." It occurs chiefly in scientific terms like *enzootic,* which is used of diseases and means "affecting animals within a particular area."

Both prefixes change from *en–* to *em–* before *b* and *p: embroil, empathy.* Some more recent coinages may not follow this rule, such as *enplane,* also sometimes spelled *emplane.*

See more at **in–**.

–en

There are a variety of suffixes spelled *–en* in English. One has the basic meaning "to cause to be" or "to become" and is added to nouns and adjectives to form verbs, like *lengthen* from *length* and *soften* from *soft*. This suffix descends from the Old English suffix *–nian*. Another suffix *–en*, meaning "made of, resembling," makes adjectives from nouns: *golden, wooden, woollen*. This adjectival suffix *–en* is from Old English *–en*. Another suffix *–en* is found in the past participles of some strong verbs, like *broken* from *break* or *ridden* from *ride*. When the base form of a strong verb ends in a vowel sound, the *–e–* is dropped, as in *flown* from *fly* or *grown* from *grow*.

There are also two plural nouns in Modern English that are formed by the addition of a suffix *–en* to the singular: *children* (after the irregular addition of an *–r–* to the base form *child*) and *oxen*. In the Middle English period, many more nouns made their plural in this way, but by the 18th century almost all plurals in *–en* had been replaced by plurals in *-s*. *Brethren*, an older plural of *brother*, is still sometimes used in the meaning "kinsmen, fellows."

See more at **strong verbs.**

endemic / epidemic / pandemic

These three words are closely related but have different scopes of reference. The word *endemic* is an adjective consisting of the prefix *en–*, "in or within," and the Greek *demos*, "people." It describes an outbreak of a disease or illness that is confined to a particular location, region, or people, such as cholera and plague in certain parts of Asia and malaria in many tropical regions. An endemic disease is often one that is characteristic of a particular locale but is not necessarily widespread within it. The word *epidemic* is both an adjective and a noun, consisting of the prefix *epi–*, "upon," and *demos*. It refers to a disease that spreads rapidly among individuals in an area or population at the same time. Occurrences of influenza have resulted in *epidemics*. The term *pandemic* is also used as both an adjective and a noun, and combines the prefix *pan–*, "all," with *demos*. It refers to an *epidemic* that spreads over a very wide geographic area, such as an entire country or continent.

energy   See **force.**

enervate / innervate

The word *enervate*, which properly means "to weaken, deplete of strength," is sometimes mistakenly used to mean the opposite, that is, "to invigorate or excite." The confusion has a number of possible causes. First, *enervate* resembles the similar-sounding word *innervate*, which has the meaning "to stimulate a nerve, muscle, or body part to action." Many speakers could also assume some connection with another word with a similar sound, *energy*. But *energy* is completely unrelated to *enervate*, which goes back ultimately to Latin *nervus*, "sinew" (from which our word *nerve,* and later *innervate,* also derive). From *nervus,* Latin created the verb *ēnervāre,* which meant "to remove the sinew (of an animal, for instance)" or more generally "to weaken." English ultimately created the verb *enervate* from the past participle form of this verb, *ēnervātus,* with the same meaning:

> But why do men degenerate ever? What makes families run out? What is the nature of the luxury which enervates and destroys nations? (Henry David Thoreau, *Walden*)

enormity / enormousness

Enormity is frequently used to refer simply to the property of being great in size or extent, but many people would prefer that *enormousness* (or a synonym such as *immensity* or *hugeness*) be used for this general sense and that *enormity* be limited to situations that demand a negative moral judgment, as in *Not until the war ended and journalists were able to enter Cambodia did the world really become aware of the enormity of Pol Pot's oppression.*

A majority of the Usage Panel has rejected the general use of *enormity* since the 1960s, and although resistance to this usage has lost some of its intensity, it remains strong. In our 1967 survey, 93 percent of the Panel rejected the word's use to refer to physical extent in the example *The enormity of Latin America is readily apparent from these maps.* In both our 1988 and 2002 surveys, 59 percent of the Usage Panel rejected the use of *enormity* as a synonym for *immensity* in the example *At that point the engineers sat down to design an entirely new viaduct, apparently undaunted by the enormity of their task.*

Even if you side with the dissenting 41 percent and allow for *enormity*'s largeness, you may want to avoid it in phrases like *the enormity of the President's election victory* and *the enormity of her inheritance,* where *enormity*'s sense of monstrousness may cause unintended smirks among your readers.

ensure   See **assure.**

enthuse

The verb *enthuse,* a back-formation from the noun *enthusiasm,* sees a lot of use in newspapers but is still viewed as an irritant by many. The sentence *The majority leader enthused over his party's gains* was rejected by 76 percent of the Usage Panel in our 1982 survey and by 65 percent in our 1997 survey. Back-formations often meet with disapproval on their first appearance and only gradually become accepted. For example, *diagnose,* which was first recorded in 1861, is a back-formation from *diagnosis* and is perfectly acceptable today.

Since *enthuse* dates from 1827, there may be something more at play here than a slower erosion of popular resistance. Unlike *enthusiasm,* which denotes an internal emotional state, *enthuse* denotes either the external expression of emotion (as in *She enthused over attending the Oscar ceremonies*) or the inducement of enthusiasm by an external source (as in *He was so enthused about the diet pills that he agreed to do a testimonial in a television ad*). It is possible that a distaste for this emphasis on external emotional display and emotional manipulation is sometimes the source of distaste for the word itself. In 1997, 68 percent of the Usage Panel disapproved of these other uses of the verb.

See more at **intuit**.

entire   See **throughout the entire**.

envelope

Some people dislike the pronunciation (ŏn′və-lōp′), arguing that it is pretentious for being pseudo-French and that it is unnecessary, since there exists a perfectly acceptable Anglicized pronunciation, (ĕn′və-lōp′). In our 1992 survey, however, the (ŏn′-) pronunciation was used exclusively by 30 percent of the Usage Panel; 61 percent used only (ĕn′-). Another 9 percent said they used both pronunciations, putting the (ŏn′-) pronunciation in active use by some 40 percent of the Panel. Still others claimed not to use this pronunciation but to find it unobjectionable. It must be considered standard.

environment

A careful pronunciation of this word is (ĕn-vī′rən-mənt), which closely reflects the spelling. In conversation, this word is more often pronounced (ĕn-vī′ərn-mənt) or (ĕn-vī′ər-mənt) or (ĕn-vīr′mənt). All of these pronunciations are acceptable.

enzyme   See **catalyst**.

epicenter

Epicenter is properly a geological term identifying the point of the earth's surface directly above the focus of an earthquake. No doubt this is why the Usage Panel approves of figurative extensions of its use in dangerous, destructive, or negative contexts. In our 1996 survey, 82 percent of the Panel accepted the sentence *If Rushdie were not at the terrifying epicenter of this furor, it is the sort of event he might write about.* The Panel was less fond but still accepting of *epicenter* when it is used to refer to the focal point of neutral or positive events. Sixty-two percent approved of the sentence *The indisputable epicenter of Cortina's social life is the Hotel de la Poste, located squarely in the village center.*

epicure   See **gourmet**.

epidemic   See **endemic.**

epithet

The word *epithet* was taken from Classical Greek and means a descriptive phrase, especially one that could serve as a second or auxiliary name for something. Epithets of the Greek gods abound in classical literature: *gray-eyed* Athena, *ox-eyed* Hera, *rosy-fingered* Dawn, and so on. The word retains this meaning in studies of ancient literature, and has related meanings in linguistics. But *epithet* has also developed a use as a synonym for a *term of abuse* or *slur,* as in the sentence *There is no place for racial epithets in a police officer's vocabulary.* In our 1988 survey, 80 percent of the Usage Panel accepted this usage.

epitome

The word *epitome* comes from a Greek word that meant "summary" or "abridgement," and ultimately derives from a verb meaning "to cut short." In English, *epitome* originally meant "summary" as well, but this usage has become rare and appears to be dying out. In our 2004 survey, only 33 percent of the Usage Panel accepted the sentence *The book begins with an epitome of the health-care crisis in California.*

Today, the predominant use of *epitome* is to mean "a representative or example of a class or type," as is evident in the examples listed below. The word is normally followed by an *of* prepositional phrase, which specifies the class or type. Note that both people and abstractions can be epitomes, that is, that the word is used of a variety of things, and that in most cases the word means "the finest or most typical example":

> And the process of natural selection, through painstaking trial and error, could result only in perfection, or something close to it. The Panglossian perspective was reinforced by the notion that the tropics were imperturbable, the epitome of evolutionary stability (David Campbell, *A Land of Ghosts*)

> Women could and should be brilliant and strong, but Brace never considered for a moment that they could achieve a "manly" force of intellect or independence of will, nor that marriage was anything but the epitome of feminine achievement (Stephan O'Connor, *The Orphan Trains*)

> [Marilyn Monroe's] celebrity was the female equivalent of his, as he saw it: just as he was the epitome of the macho man, so Monroe was some kind of supersymbol of womanhood (Mary V. Dearborn, *Mailer*)

> Prairie dogs have long been viewed, particularly by urban dwellers, as the epitome of cute (William K. Stevens, "Prairie Dog Colonies Bolster Life in the Plains," *New York Times*)

The Usage Panel overwhelmingly accepts this usage, with a number of Panelists preferring its use in positive contexts. Thus, in the 2004 survey, 70 percent accepted the sentence *The senator from our state is the epitome of a failed leader,* but 80 percent accepted *Their business model is the epitome of efficiency.*

Sometimes the word is also used to mean "the highest point, the pinnacle or cul-mination," as in *Kilkenny Castle reached an epitome of splendor in the 17th century.* Only 40 percent of the Panel found this sentence acceptable.

Note that *epitome* is pronounced with four syllables as (ĭ-pĭt′ə-mē).

equable

See **equitable.**

equal

It has been argued that *equal* is an absolute term—two quantities either are or are not equal—and hence cannot be qualified as to degree. Therefore one cannot logically speak of *a more equal allocation of resources among the departments.* But this usage is fairly common, and was acceptable to 71 percent of the Usage Panel as far back as 1967. Objections to the *more equal* construction rest on the assumption that the mathematical notion of equality is inherent in the description of a world where the equality of two quantities is often an approximate matter, and where statements of equality are always relative to an implicit standard of tolerance. When someone says *The two boards are of equal length,* we assume that the equality is reckoned to some order of approximation determined by the context; if we did not, we would be re-quired always to use *nearly equal* when speaking of the dimensions of physical ob-jects. What is more, we often speak of the equality of things that cannot be measured quantitatively, as when we say *The college draft was introduced in an effort to make the teams in the National Football League as equal as possible,* or *The candidates for the job should all be given equal consideration.* In all such cases equality is naturally a gradient notion and can be modified in degree. This much is evident from the existence of the word *unequal,* for the prefix *un–* attaches only to gradient adjectives. We say *unmanly* but not *unmale;* and the word *uneven* can be applied to a surface (whose evenness may be a matter of degree) but not to a number (whose evenness is an either/or af-fair).

See more at **absolute terms, center, complete, infinite, parallel, perfect,** and **unique.**

equally as

The adverb *equally* is often viewed as redundant when used in combination with *as,* as in *Experience is equally as valuable as theory* or *Equally as important is the desire to learn.* To get rid of the redundancy, *equally* must be deleted from the first example and *as* from the second.

equi–

The prefix *equi–* means "equal" or "equally." *Equi–* is from the Latin prefix *aequi* , which came from Latin *aequus,* meaning "even, flat, on the same level" and also "equal." Thus *equidistant* means "equally distant." *Equi–* often occurs in words with

Latin elements. For example, *equinox* means "having the night equal (to the day),"
from Latin *nox*, "night." *Equivalent* is from *valere*, "to be worth, amount to," and so is
literally "amounting to the same thing."

equitable / equable

Equitable is a fairly common term, meaning "characterized by equity, fair":

> It had formerly been my endeavour to study all sides of his character: to take the
> bad with the good; and from the just weighing of both, to form an equitable judg-
> ment (Charlotte Brontë, *Jane Eyre*)

The word should not be confused with the less common *equable*, which means
"steady, unvarying":

> She preserved an equable cheerfulness in the midst of her sympathy, which was not
> the least astonishing part of the change that had come over her (Charles Dickens,
> *David Copperfield*)

Equable is often extended to mean "unflappable, serene":

> Do you remember old Lord Brock? He was never troubled. He had a triple
> shield—a thick skin, an equable temper, and perfect self-confidence (Anthony Trol-
> lope, *Phineas Redux*)

-er   See **-or.**

err

The pronunciation (ûr) is the older, traditional one, but in recent years the pronunciation (ĕr) has gained currency, perhaps as a result of association with *errant* and
error. In our 1988 survey, 56 percent of the Usage Panel preferred (ûr), 34 percent
preferred (ĕr), and 10 percent accepted both pronunciations.

errant / arrant

The word *arrant* has strayed in spelling and meaning from its source in the word *errant*, though not in pronunciation, leading to occasional confusion. *Arrant* means
"completely such, thoroughgoing," and often suggests a degree of disapproval (*the arrant luxury of an ocean liner; the arrant incompetence of the speaker*). *Errant* has retained a core set of meanings related to wandering, such as "roving for adventure"
(*errant knights on a quest*), "straying from the proper course or standards" (*errant
schoolchildren*), "wandering outside established limits" (*lambs errant from the pas-
tures*), and "aimless or irregular in motion" (*an errant afternoon breeze*).

escape

Traditionally, *escape* is used with *from* when it means "to break loose" and with a direct object (and no intervening preposition) when it means "to avoid." Thus we might say *The forger escaped from prison by hiding in a laundry truck* but *The forger escaped prison when he turned in his accomplices and received a suspended sentence.* However, *escape* may also be used with a direct object in the sense "to break free of":

> I filled the Belgian's pouch with river gravel before I escaped the camp of the Abyssinians whose prisoners we were (Edgar Rice Burroughs, *Tarzan and the Jewels of Opar*)

This usage is well established and should be regarded as standard.

The pronunciation (ĭk-skāp′) is often viewed by many as incorrect and is probably a result of confusion with words beginning with the prefix *ex–*. The word is properly pronounced without the (k) sound between the short *i* and the (sk) sound: (ĭ-skāp′).

Eskimo

Eskimo has come under strong attack in recent years for its supposed offensiveness, and many Americans today either avoid this term or feel uneasy using it. It is widely known that *Inuit,* a term of ethnic pride, is the preferred alternative, but it is less well understood that *Inuit* cannot substitute for *Eskimo* in all cases, being restricted in usage to the Inuit-speaking peoples of Arctic Canada and Greenland (and often including the closely related Inupiaq of northern Alaska). In western Alaska and Arctic Siberia, where Inuit is not spoken, the comparable terms are *Yupik* and *Alutiiq,* neither of which has gained as wide a currency in English as *Inuit.* While use of these terms is generally preferable when speaking of a specific linguistic group, none of them can be used of the Eskimoan peoples as a whole; the only inclusive term for the peoples of the circumpolar Arctic remains *Eskimo.*

The claim that *Eskimo* is offensive is based primarily on a popular but disputed etymology tracing its origin to an Abenaki word meaning "eaters of raw meat." Modern linguists speculate that the term may actually derive from a Montagnais word referring to the manner of lacing a snowshoe, but evidence is scarce, and the matter remains undecided. The point to keep in mind is that while *Eskimo* will likely cause offense when used of Inuit-speaking peoples, *Inuit* may itself be taken as offensive when used of most Alaskan and Siberian Eskimos.

–ess   See **feminine suffixes.**

et cetera

This Latin phrase meaning "and the rest" is usually pronounced (ĕt sĕt′ər-ə) or (ĕt sĕt′rə). The pronunciation (ĕk sĕt′ər-ə), with a (k) substituted for the first *t*, is considered nonstandard.

ethnic / ethnicity

The English word *ethnic* can be traced ultimately to the Greek word for "people" in the sense of "foreign nation." ("People" meaning "the general populace" was expressed in Greek by *demos*.) Thus the idea of otherness, as measured by such attributes as nationality, religion, language, or race, is central to ethnicity. But the question is, other than what? When the adjective *ethnic* is applied to such cultural items as food and dress, the presumption is generally of a difference from a surrounding norm; Thai food is considered ethnic fare in the United States and Mexico but not in Bangkok. When it comes to people, the same assumption of departure from a perceived norm is sometimes made. Specifically, in American English since the 1960s, *ethnic* has been used as both an adjective and a noun to denote Americans of southern European and eastern European background:

> His 1969 book "The Emerging Republican Majority" which came out of his work on the Nixon campaign and explained how to effect a realignment of the parties, coined the term "Sun Belt" and described a new kind of American who would replace the core Democratic voters, the older northern urban ethnics (George Packer, "The Decade Nobody Knows," *New York Times Book Review*)

This usage can be offensive in many contexts because of its implication that those who are so labeled fall outside the mainstream culture.

***ethnic* plus a noun of nationality** *Ethnic* is sometimes used before a noun of nationality, as in *ethnic Chinese* or *ethnic Albanian,* in reference to people belonging to the stated nation by culture and heritage but living permanently outside that nation's borders. This construction is typically used of long-established communities whose members, though usually citizens of the country they now live in, have retained their traditional national culture and have generally resisted or been denied assimilation into their country of residence. Thus members of the large, long-standing Chinese communities found in many countries of Southeast Asia are often called *ethnic Chinese,* whereas Chinese living in most Western countries, where assimilation typically takes place within a couple of generations, are not.

Ethnic populations in this sense of the word are sometimes created when borders shift around them, as after a war or treaty, or when an empire comprised of widely distributed ethnic groups collapses and is carved into separate nation-states whose borders don't correspond exactly to preexisting settlement patterns. In a country such as the United States, whose diverse population is generally held to constitute a single society, this sense of *ethnic* doesn't apply. An *ethnic American* is usually understood to be a US citizen living at home, not abroad, and self-identified as belonging to an ethnic minority.

–ette   See **feminine suffixes.**

eudicot   See **dicot.**

Eurasian

Eurasian has been in use since the mid-19th century to refer to a person of mixed European and Asian birth. It was coined during the British rule over India (then including modern Pakistan and Bangladesh) and was long used primarily in designating a person born to a British father and an Indian mother. In a contemporary context *Eurasian* has a much wider application, denoting only that one parent is Asian and the other white—that is, either European or of European descent.

The geographic sense of *Eurasian* is quite distinct, referring to the land mass comprising the European and Asian continents and especially to the large indeterminate region where they join. Peoples indigenous to this region can also be termed *Eurasians,* creating a potential ambiguity when used of an individual as opposed to a group or culture. If the ambiguity is not resolved by context, a descriptive phrase such as *a member of a Eurasian people* or *a person of European and Asian parentage* can be added for clarity.

Euro-American / European American

Euro-American and *European American* have gained a certain currency in recent years as designations for white Americans, that is, Americans of European descent. *Euro-American* is first recorded as a noun in a passage by the anthropologist Margaret Meade written in 1949, but its growing use outside of anthropology is probably a response to the popularity in American English of compound ethnic designations such as *Hispanic American, Asian American, Native American,* and more recently *African American.* The addition of *Euro-American* and *European American* to this list offers a useful alternative to *white* or *Caucasian,* which emphasize skin color or race over cultural heritage. However, while these terms are relatively common in academic and sociological discourse, the general public has so far been slow to adopt them.

ever   See **rarely ever.**

every

Every is representative of a large class of English words and expressions that are singular in form but felt to be plural in sense. The class includes, for example, noun phrases introduced by *every, any,* and certain uses of *some.* These expressions invariably take a singular verb: *Every car has* [not *have*] *been tested. Anyone is* [not *are*] *liable to fall ill.* But when a sentence contains a pronoun that refers to a previous noun phrase introduced by *every,* grammar and sense pull in different directions. The grammar of these expressions requires a singular pronoun, as in *Every car must have its brakes tested,* but the meaning often leads people to use the plural pronoun, as in *Every car must have their brakes tested.* The use of plural pronouns in such cases is common in speech, but it is still widely regarded as incorrect in writing.

The effort to adhere to the rule causes complications, however. The first is grammatical. When a pronoun refers to a phrase containing *every* or *any* that falls within a different independent clause, the pronoun cannot be singular. Thus it is simply not English to say *Every man left; he took his raincoat with him.* Nor is it grammatical to say *No one could be seen, could he?* If the plural forms seem wrong in these examples (*Every man took their raincoat with them*), one way around the problem is to rephrase the sentence so as to get the pronoun into the same clause (as in *Every man left, taking his raincoat with him*). Another is to substitute another word for *every* or *any,* usually by casting the entire sentence as plural, as in *All the men left; they took their raincoats with them.*

The second complication is political. When a phrase introduced by *every* or *any* refers to a group containing both men and women, the choice of pronoun bespeaks an approach to sexism in language and hence to sexual politics in general. Consider the example *Every person in this office must keep track of his* [*her? his or her? their?*] *own expenses.* This matter is discussed in greater detail at the entry for the pronoun **he.**

See more at **all, any, each, either, neither, none,** and **subject and verb agreement.**

everyplace / anyplace / someplace / no place

The adverbial forms *everyplace* (or *every place*), *anyplace* (or *any place*), *someplace* (or *some place*), and *no place* are widely used in speech and informal writing as equivalents for *everywhere, anywhere, somewhere,* and *nowhere,* as in *I didn't see them anyplace.* These usages may be well established, but they are not normally used in formal writing.

The two-word expressions *every place, any place, some place,* and *no place,* when used as nouns, are a different matter. They have the meanings "every (any, some, no) spot or location," as in the phrase *at every place and time.* Such phrases are entirely appropriate at all levels of style.

evoke / invoke

To *evoke* something is to draw out or call to mind a mental image, state of mind, or memory of something: actions can evoke mistrust, songs can evoke memories, a novel can evoke a bygone era. The result of evoking something is always a new psychological state; to describe something that can bring on such a state we can use the related adjective *evocative.*

To *invoke* something is to call on it and bring it to bear on the situation at hand: a lawyer may invoke a courtroom procedure, a conjurer might invoke the power of a spirit, a computer program can invoke a subroutine. Thus *invoke* results not in a psychological change but the activation of something outside the mind, usually by means of words.

evolution / natural selection

These two terms are commonly but improperly used as synonyms, and their meanings in the field of evolutionary biology are distinct. *Evolution* refers to inheritable changes in the structure and physiology of organisms, changes that develop over the course of generations. There are in fact multiple theories of evolution, but all current theories assume that changes in genetic makeup are largely responsible for changes within species and for the creation of new species over time.

There are many interesting questions regarding what conditions these changes, and the theory of *natural selection* is one very significant piece of the puzzle. It posits that whatever the source of genetic change, only certain changes are likely to be passed down to the next generation: those changes that enhance or at least do not impair the ability of the organism to survive and reproduce. Genetic changes that lower the organism's chance of survival are less likely to be passed on to the next generation and are thereby eliminated from the species' genetic makeup.

Natural selection is thus an important part of most theories of evolution, but is not itself a complete theory of evolution, and most evolutionary biologists agree that many other factors are at work influencing the evolution of life.

ex–

The prefix *ex–* comes from Latin *ex–, e–,* meaning "out of, from." It usually occurs with base forms that come from Latin verbs. Thus combining *ex–* with the Latin verb *tendere,* "to stretch," gives us *extend,* "to stretch out." Similarly, in *express, ex–* combines with the base form *press,* which comes from the verb *premere,* "to squeeze." So when we express ourselves, we "squeeze out" our thoughts. When followed by *f, ex–* becomes *ef–,* as in *efface.* Sometimes *ex–* takes the form of *e–,* as in *emit* (from Latin *mittere,* "to send"). Today *ex–* only forms new words when it means "former," and it is always followed by a hyphen: *ex-President.*

except   See **nothing** and **pronouns, personal.**

exceptionable / exceptional

Exceptionable and *exceptional* are not interchangeable. Only *exceptionable* means "objectionable" or "causing disappoval":

We can't have perfection; and if I keep him, I must sustain his administration as a whole, even if there are, now and then, things that are exceptionable (Harriet Beecher Stowe, *Uncle Tom's Cabin*)

Exceptional means "uncommon" or "extraordinary":

Nobody was jealous of the weaver, for he was regarded as an exceptional person, whose claims on neighborly help were not to be matched in Raveloe (George Eliot, *Silas Marner*)

exclamation point

1. The exclamation point terminates an emphatic word, phrase, or sentence.

She gasped out his name— "Eddie! Oh, Eddie!"—and it was a war cry, an accusation, a spear thrust right through him and pulled out again (T.C. Boyle, *Riven Rock*)

"Mr. Holmes, they were the footprints of a gigantic hound!" (Arthur Conan Doyle, *The Hound of the Baskervilles*)

2. An exclamation point may substitute for a question mark to convey emotion.

Who would have known!   How do you figure that!
Wasn't that amazing!   Can you believe it!

expedient / expeditious

Something that is *expedient* is appropriate to a specific purpose, but may not be ethically or morally appropriate. For instance, one might take an expedient course of action to get a job done, but if one is friendly only when friendliness is expedient to getting that job done, one is being dishonest. The similar-looking word *expeditious* is more straightforward: an action that is expeditious is an action done with speed and efficiency.

explicable

This word can be pronounced either with stress on the second syllable (ĭk-splĭk′ə-bəl) or on the first syllable (ĕk′splĭ-kə-bəl). In our 1997 survey, 52 percent preferred stressing the second syllable, 44 percent preferred stressing the first syllable, and the remainder showed no preference between the two.

exponential

In nontechnical use, the term *exponential* suggests a sudden or very rapid increase, and is often used where the term *explosive* might fit just as easily, as in *The company is poised for exponential growth in sales.* But technically speaking, the exponential growth of a quantity does not necessarily entail that the growth is rapid. In mathematics, an exponent is the power to which a number is raised; exponential growth is generally described by a number raised to some power, where the power is multiplied by the duration of time over which the growth proceeds. But that power can still be very small. For example, the amount of money in a bank account earning interest grows exponentially, yet for most of us it certainly does not seem to be growing at a very fast rate.

The most important quality of exponential growth is not just that the amount of some quantity increases over time, but that the rate of growth itself increases over time—in fact, the rate itself grows exponentially. A simple example of exponential growth is a population explosion, starting small, but ending catastrophically. For example, consider a population of bacteria that doubles in size every twelve hours on average. Starting out with one bacterium, there would be only four bacteria twenty-four hours later, and only sixteen after two days; a fairly low rate of growth. Five weeks later, however, there would be 3,459,738,368 bacteria, with the population increasing at a rate of 795,364 new bacteria per second (and rising).

It should also be noted that a quantity can decrease exponentially. This does not mean that the rate of decrease grows, but that it decreases with time. When a quantity is reduced by some constant fraction over some unit of time, it is decreasing exponentially. For example, the amount of a radioactive element in some substance decreases exponentially (the half-life of that element being the unit of time over which its quantity is halved).

exquisite

The older pronunciation (and the one defended staunchly by usage writers for decades) has stress on the first syllable, rhyming with *requisite.* A newer pronunciation with stress on the second syllable, rhyming roughly with *exhibit,* is now fairly common, however. In our 1995 ballot, 55 percent of the Usage Panel indicated they prefer the first pronunciation, 35 percent indicated they prefer the second pronunciation, and a small percentage accepted both.

extra–   See **inter–**.

· F ·

fact

Since the word *fact* means "a real occurrence, something demonstrated to exist or known to have existed," the phrases *true facts* and *real facts*, as in *The true facts of the case may never be known,* would seem to be redundant. But *fact* has a long history of use in the sense of "an allegation of fact" or "something that is believed to be true," as in *"This tract was distributed to thousands of American teachers, but the facts and the reasoning are wrong"*(Albert Shanker). This usage has led to the notion of "incorrect facts," which causes qualms among critics who insist that facts must be true. The usages, however, are often helpful in making distinctions or adding emphasis.

factious / fractious

These words are very close in spelling, pronunciation, and meaning, though they have slightly different emphases. *Factious* means "characterized by, inclined to form, or promoting factions." Thus a political party might be ineffective because it is factious. A member of that party or a remark made by a member can be factious too, causing internal dissent. The word *fractious* derives from an obsolete sense of *fraction* meaning "rupture, discord." Traditionally, it has applied to individuals. A fractious person is thus inclined to make trouble or is unruly or cranky, and does not necessarily belong to an organized group. Either by confusion with *factious* or by a natural semantic extension, *fractious* has also been applied to groups and their actions: *the fractious state legislature, fractious domestic politics.*

The difference in emphasis can be summed up neatly in this way: A fractious child is a disobedient one; a factious child is one who causes dissension in a group.

factitious / fictitious

These words share one meaning, "lacking authenticity, not believed to be true" but each word has differing related senses. Something that is *factitious* can also be something that was produced artificially (or is related to the artificial production of something), as when a troublemaker stirs up a factitious conflict, or a biologist creates a factitious environment in which to grow and study plant cells. Something that is *fictitious* can be fictional, or it can be something that is accepted out of convention (a fictitious belief) or something that is assumed in order to deceive (a fictitious name).

See more at **fictional.**

factoid

The suffix *–oid* normally imparts the meaning "resembling, having the appearance of." Thus, *factoid* originally referred to a piece of information that has the appearance of being reliable or accurate, often because it has been repeated so often that people assume it is true. The word still has this meaning in standard usage. In our 1995 survey, 73 percent of the Usage Panel accepted it in the sentence *It would be easy to condemn the book as a concession to the television age, as a McLuhanish melange of pictures and factoids, which give the illusion of learning without the substance.*

Factoid has since developed a second meaning, that of a brief, somewhat interesting fact. The Usage Panel had less enthusiasm for this usage, however, as only 43 percent accepted it in *Each issue of the magazine begins with a list of factoids, like how many pounds of hamburger were consumed in Texas last month.* Many Panelists preferred terms such as *statistics, trivia, useless facts,* and just plain *facts* in this sentence.

See more at **hominoid.**

fall through the cracks / fall between the cracks

The literal sense of the idiom *fall through the cracks* is straightforward: something that has fallen through the cracks has somehow escaped notice or attention as if it fell through a crack in an otherwise solid surface. The cracks thus represent imperfections in a system of action or categorization and often entail gaps between assigned duties of personnel. One occasionally also sees *fall in* or *into the cracks,* with the slightly different sense of something having found its way into a place where it is difficult to retrieve or deal with. But the surprisingly common phrase *fall between the cracks* makes no literal sense at all, so while its use as an idiom might be nonetheless easy to understand, it remains an awkward turn of phrase.

farther / further

Many writers since the Middle English period have used *farther* and *further* interchangeably. A relatively recent rule, however, states that *farther* should be reserved for physical distance and *further* for nonphysical, metaphorical advancement. Accordingly, in our 1987 survey, 74 percent of the Usage Panel preferred *farther* in the sentence *If you are planning to drive any farther than Ukiah, you'd better carry chains,* while 64 percent preferred *further* in the sentence *We won't be able to answer these questions until we are further along in our research.* In many cases, however, it is hard to see the difference. If we speak of *a statement that is far from the truth,* for example, it seems that we should allow the use of *farther* in a sentence such as *Nothing could be farther from the truth.* But *Nothing could be further from the truth* is so common that it has become a fixed expression.

father

The verb *father* traditionally means "to sire offspring," but it has developed the additional sense of "to perform the child-rearing functions of a father." In this it is analogous to the verb *parent* and to the sense of the verb *mother* that refers to parenting a child. Unlike those words, however, the use of *father* is much more common as a gerund (that is, as the verbal noun *fathering*) than as an ordinary verb. It is possible that people shy away from using *father* as a verb in this way to avoid potential confusion with or at least overtones of the word's meaning "to beget."

The current "parenting" usage is evident in the following examples:

> The middle-income fathers, therefore, perceive themselves as falling short, not only with respect to traditional visions, but of attaining the new cultural ideals of fathering as well (Beth Skilken and Patrick McKenry, "Class-Based Masculinities: Divorce, Fatherhood, and the Hegemonic Ideal," *Fathering*)

> Probably in the past much of fathering involved hands-on teaching of tasks like plowing, hunting, or carpentry, and the setting of behavior and values. The current public notion is vague. Is it like mothering, or different? (Janna Malamud Smith, *A Potent Spell: Mother Love and the Power of Fear*)

See more at **parent.**

fay / fey

These words are pronounced the same and have similar meanings, but should be kept distinct. The word *fay* is rare in contemporary English, so it should be used with caution. It is a noun and is an old word meaning "fairy" or "elf":

> Most of all, he brought back the yesterday's long excitement and delight of seeing the Irish coast hills—his first foreign land—whose faint sky fresco had seemed magical with the elfin lore of Ireland, a country that had ever been to him the haunt not of potatoes and politicians, but of fays (Sinclair Lewis, *Our Mr. Wrenn: The Romantic Adventures of a Gentle Man*)

The adjective *fey* is more widely used today. It describes things or people having otherworldly, magical, or fairylike qualities:

> The guide stepped closer to me and raised his hands in a proprietary way, trying to hold my attention. The cuffs of his baggy black sleeves were torn, and one was encrusted with something pink, like a splash of Pepto-Bismol. His face was dirty, and the area around his right eye looked as though it had been roughly besmirched with a lump of coal. He was delicate and fey (Rosemary Mahoney, *The Singular Pilgrim*)

> The pursuit of dolphins is like the pursuit of beauty: you never quite attain it. They are as fey as rain. You have no choice but to wait for them to come to you on their own terms (David Campbell, *A Land of Ghosts*)

In other contexts, *fey* suggests overrefinement, affectation, or effeminacy:

> Like a concert pianist or a conductor he would toss back his blond forelocks in a fey, haughty manner that made arts types want to earn his respect and jocks want to shove that cigarette holder and fancy lighter down his throat (Steven Heighton, *The Shadow Boxer*)

> Once you're familiar with the mash-up, though, the old XTC track is pretty hard to sit through: plodding, relentlessly asexual, with a mincing vocal, painfully fey melody, and dated dopey political lyrics (Dale Lawrence, "Two Boots," *Village Voice*)

Fey originally meant "doomed or fated to die" and "about to die, at the point of death." The word also developed the meaning (in the definition of *The Oxford English Dictionary*) "disordered in mind like one about to die," and this survives in English in certain uses:

> He stood a moment as a man who is pierced in the midst of a cry by an arrow through the heart; and then his face went deathly white, and a cold fury rose in him, so that all speech failed him for a while. A fey mood took him. "Éowyn, Éowyn!" he cried at last. "Éowyn, how come you here? What madness or devilry is this? Death, death, death! Death take us all!" (J.R.R. Tolkien, *The Return of the King*)

faze / phase

The verb *faze* comes from Old English and means "to disrupt the composure of, disconcert." It is usually used in negative contexts, as in *She was not fazed by the setback but carried on as determined as ever. Faze* is sometimes mistakenly spelled *phase*, which is both a noun and a verb that is derived from Greek. The noun means "a stage of development." The verb usually occurs in the phrases *phase in* and *phase out*, which mean introducing or ending something one stage at a time.

February

The preferred pronunciation among usage writers is (fĕb′rōō-ĕr′ē), but in actual usage the pronunciation (fĕb′yōō-ĕr′ē) is far more common and so cannot be considered incorrect. The loss of the first *r* in this pronunciation can be accounted for by the phonological process known as *dissimilation,* whereby one of two similar or identical sounds in a word is changed or dropped so that a repetition of that sound is avoided. In the case of *February,* the loss of the first *r* was also helped along by the influence of *January,* which has only one *r*.

See more at **dissimilation.**

feeble-minded   See **idiot.**

female / male

As adjectives, the words *female* and *male* should be used in parallel and only when gender is relevant, as in this example from a Canadian newswire: *"She produced the report after a confrontation in Kingston's infamous prison for women in which male guards forcibly subdued female inmates.*" Descriptions such as *a female police officer* and *a male nurse* are offensive if the gender marking is gratuitous because they convey inappropriate assumptions about gender roles in a given profession or social context.

As nouns, *male* and *female* are usually used in technical, medical, or scientific writing, often to refer to groups of human or animal subjects in an experiment: *The control group consisted of twelve females and eleven males.* It is sometimes convenient to use the word *female* when speaking collectively about both women and girls or *male* when referring to both boys and men. If that is not the case, *women and men* or *girls and boys* is preferable to *females and males.*

See more at **lady.**

feminine / masculine / effeminate

A *feminine* trait is one that is characteristically considered to be female, while a *masculine* trait is associated with males. These words become problematic because notions of femininity and masculinity are strongly influenced by cultural stereotypes that are offensive to many people. Qualities often considered to be feminine include complacency, amiability, soft-spokenness, submissiveness, flirtatiousness, and a lack of competitiveness. This quotation from *The Greenville News* demonstrates the insidiousness of the stereotype: "'*Some girls don't want to exceed the boys in math and science for social reasons,*' he said. '*They don't want to seem unfeminine.*'"

Stereotypic masculine qualities are often defined as aggressiveness, strength, confidence, stoicism or emotional insensitivity, and resoluteness or ambition. The following quotation from an article in the *New York Post* typifies these preconceptions: "*I think getting plastic surgery is not very masculine. Your appearance can be dealt with in other ways, by working out or eating well.*" Men who exhibit qualities traditionally associated with women are sometimes labeled *effeminate,* a term that is invariably derogatory.

Because these stereotypes about gender roles are created by cultural expectations that vary from one culture to another, it is prudent to be cautious in using the words *feminine* and *masculine* as objective descriptors.

feminine suffixes

The common suffixes *–ess, –ette,* and *–enne* are used by some people to feminize nouns in English. While this practice is acceptable to some, others find the use of these suffixes to be gratuitous and, therefore, sexist. According to this view, the addition of suffixes such as *–er* and *–or* to a word, as in *adventurer* and *aviator,* represents a generic standard rather than a specifically masculine form, and using a different form (such as one ending in *–ess*) suggests that a man is performing an expected role and that a woman's participation is somehow unexpected or different. (Historically, this was likely the case and often the reason that traditional forms came to be regarded as masculine and separate feminine suffixes came into use.) The implication may be not only that the woman's assumption of the role is unconventional, but that it is in some way auxiliary or less important. In addition, while the traditional forms usually are indicative of power or respectability, as in *sorcerer* or *master*, the feminine forms tend to emphasize sexuality, as in *sorceress* or *mistress*.

Nonetheless, some words with feminine suffixes have become more acceptable than others, perhaps because they refer to occupations or positions that have long been available to women, such as *actress, heiress,* and *hostess. Actor* is used increasingly for females, however, and is often preferred by women in theater and film. In some cases, newly created gender-neutral terms have become the only acceptable usage, as in *flight attendant* for *steward* or *stewardess*. Use of the gender-marked terms in such instances will likely be seen as willful resistance to nonsexist language or as simple insensitivity.

Frequently, the feminine suffixes are derived from French, which distinguishes grammatically between males and females in many words. The suffix *–ess* has traditionally been used for positions of rank and nobility, as in *princess* or *duchess,* as well as in many other words. Some of these, such as *poetess, sculptress,* and *adventuress,* are widely considered to be demeaning and have fallen out of favor.

Sometimes a final *-e* is added to a word to designate a feminine form. This is widely accepted for the words *divorcée* and *fiancée,* but less so for *protégée*. The masculine form of *divorcée* is rarely used, however, and so again, the imbalance renders the feminine form offensive to some people.

Masculine nouns ending in *–eur* often have feminine forms ending in *–euse* as in *chanteur/chanteuse,* but *masseuse* stands as the only commonly used word among them. A variety of *–eur* words, like *entrepreneur* and *raconteur,* have no feminine counterpart, and so should be acceptable to all.

Historically, the suffix *–ette* is the feminine form of the French diminutive suffix *–et* that occurs in inanimate borrowings such as *banquet, clarinet,* and *tablet*. The feminine form occurs in words such as *cigarette* and *lorgnette*. These words began to come into English in the 1600s, and the suffix was very productive in the 20th century for inanimate diminutives, as in *kitchenette, launderette, luncheonette,* and *novelette.*

The use of *–ette* to form nouns referring to women is a separate and much later development that probably comes from the French convention of forming feminine versions from masculine names, as in *Antoinette* and *Paulette*. The suffix was first applied in this sense to an English common noun in *suffragette,* which became the recognized term for women involved in the suffrage movement in England. However, *suffragette* was always considered insulting by the suffragists in the United States, who were often mocked. Nonetheless, *suffragette* served as the model for many words that referred to women who occupied positions once reserved for men, such as *chaufferette* and *sailorette,* but of these only *usherette* and *majorette* have survived. Unlike the other feminine suffixes, *–ette* is historically a diminutive, and worse, it is sometimes used to indicate an imitation or lesser version of something, as in *leatherette*. As such, it may be viewed as even more patronizing and belittling than the other feminizing suffixes.

Other feminine suffixes include *–enne,* which is seen in *comedienne* and *equestrienne,* and *–trix,* as in *executrix, aviatrix,* and *dominatrix*. They are sometimes seen in specialized contexts such as legal documents (*executrix*) or historical writing (*aviatrix*). Like other feminine suffixes, they are considered offensive by some people and should be used with caution.

See more at **blond, hero, master, mistress, sexist language,** and **suffragist.**

fetus / embryo

Even science writers have trouble distinguishing an embryo from a fetus. For example, an Internet article on stem-cell research states that certain researchers "*were using a mixed population of cells . . . they were taking them from the mid-brain of a . . . ten-week embryo.*" But an embryo can't really be ten weeks old, because when it reaches the age of eight weeks it is correctly described as a *fetus.* In humans, an *embryo* is the product of conception from implantation of the zygote in the uterine wall through the eighth week of development. At this point, the unborn offspring is properly called a fetus until the time of birth or the termination of pregnancy.

fever / temperature

When a child is sick, a parent usually checks to see if the child has a *temperature.* Literally, this makes no sense, since all individuals have a measurable body temperature. What the parent really means—and what a physician would be interested in—is whether the child has an abnormally elevated body temperature, or a *fever.* In medical usage, the article is often dropped, so that doctors commonly say that a patient *has fever.*

fewer / less

Usage critics have long decried the confusion of mass and count distinctions in English, notably in the use of *less* where *fewer* should appear, as in *There are less players on this year's team than last year's.* This sentence violates the traditional rule requiring that *fewer* be used for items that can be counted, what are called *count nouns* (*fewer than four players*), and *less* for items of measurable extent, what are called *mass nouns* (*less paper, less paint*). However, there are a number of exceptions to this rule, especially in less formal writing. *Less* is often used with count nouns in the expressions *no less than* and *or less,* as in *No less than thirty of his colleagues signed the letter* and *Give your reasons in twenty-five words or less. Less than* can be used before a plural noun that denotes a measure of time, amount, or distance: *less than three weeks, less than four hundred dollars, less than fifty miles. Less* is also used with singular count nouns in the expression *one less,* as in *There is one less boat at the landing now.*

See more at **count nouns.**

 fey   See **fay.**

fiancé/ fiancée   See **feminine suffixes.**

fictional / fictive / fictitious / fictionalized

All of these words have the idea of "fiction" at their core. *Fictional* sticks closely to this idea, meaning "being or relating to fiction; untrue or imaginary," as in *a fictional account* of an event (i.e., one that is completely imaginary). *Fictive* is essentially synonymous with *fictional,* but is used especially to denote conventions in which something is treated as having certain characteristics not inherent to it. For example, the months of the year are sometimes described as fictive, insofar as the days of the year are not organized into particular months by nature, but by human convention (indeed, various cultures have grouped the days of the year into months quite differently). In anthropology, certain kinship relations such as "godparent" are considered fictive.

Fictitious is also used to describe something accepted or believed out of convention (as in *a fictitious belief*), but it is also applied to things assumed or put on in order to fool someone (as in *a fictitious name*), or things thought to be a sham (as with *a fictitious smile*).

If an account of an event has been *fictionalized,* it is not simply fictional; it is an account in which certain aspects of the events are deliberately altered or invented in order to create a more effective or evocative story, or simply because certain details of what actually happened are not known. A fictionalized account of a story may thus be not entirely fictional.

See more at **factitious.**

finalize

Even though the verb *finalize* has been around since the early 1920s, the word is still criticized because of its associations with the language of bureaucracy. In our 1997 survey, 72 percent of the Usage Panel found this sentence unacceptable: *We will send you more information once we finalize plans for the reunion.* A similar percentage rejected the passive use in *Their divorce has not yet been finalized.* But perhaps the word's bureaucratic past lends it to use in institutional contexts, since it occurs frequently with words like *deal* and *agreement.* It is hard to see how the following examples could be improved:

> The park was established by executive decree in 1975, but its boundaries weren't finalized for nearly a decade, until after its hundreds of unofficial residents could be relocated (Barbara Kingsolver and Steven Hopp, "Seeing Scarlet," *Audubon*)

> Even in 1991, when it finalized its agreement with INBio, the company's $8.6 billion in sales considerably exceeded Costa Rica's entire $5.2 billion gross national product (Seth Shulman, *Owning the Future*)

The trouble with avoiding *finalize* is that it has no exact synonym, though rough substitutes include *complete, conclude, make final,* and *put into final form.*

See more at **–ize.**

finite

In grammar, the term *finite* refers both to verbs and clauses, and means "showing features that indicate person, number, tense, and mood." A finite clause is a clause with a verb in finite form. A finite verb can serve as the predicate of a sentence (as *loves* in *Conor loves to go to the mall*) or as the initial verb in a verb phrase that is the predicate (as *has* in *Conor has just gone to the mall*). Finite verb forms are thus "limited" to a specific use; in English, the person and number of the finite verb must be the same as the person and number of the subject of the sentence. Such verbs are usually contrasted with the infinitive, which is not limited by person, number, or any of the ways mentioned above.

See more at **subject and verb agreement** and **verbs, tenses of.**

firstly

Both *first* and *firstly* are well established to begin an enumeration: *Our objectives are, first* [or *firstly*], *to recover from last year's slump.* It is important however, to be consistent and to use parallel forms in the series, as in *first . . . second . . . third* or *firstly . . . secondly . . . thirdly.*

See more at **transition words.**

First Nation

First Nation has gained wide acceptance in Canada since the 1970s in referring to that country's aboriginal peoples. Like *Native American* (which has little currency in Canada), it provides a respectful alternative to *Indian,* a term that, when used by itself, is more likely to be taken as offensive in Canada than it is in the United States. However, there are several important differences between the Canadian and American expressions. Unlike *Native American, First Nation* is not a comprehensive term for all indigenous peoples of the Americas or even of Canada, since it specifically does not include non-Indian peoples such as Inuit or Métis. (The comprehensive Canadian terms are *First Peoples* or *Aboriginals.*) Also, as a singular noun, *First Nation* cannot refer to an individual, only to an organized group, usually to one of the bands or tribes formally recognized by the Canadian government under the Indian Act of 1876. (An individual of such a group can be called *a member of a First Nation,* or more commonly a *status Indian* or *non-status Indian,* depending on whether or not the group to which the person belongs is recognized under the 1876 provisions.) As a result, *First Nation* is more frequently used as a plural noun or as a modifier, as in *a history of the First Nations in eastern Canada* or *a program designed for First Nation youth.*

See more at **Indian** and **Native American.**

flaccid

The older pronunciation is (flăk′sĭd), but the variant (flăs′ĭd) has been recorded in dictionaries since about the middle of the 20th century, and has become increasingly common. In our 1997 ballot, 66 percent of the Usage Panel preferred the pronunciation with the (s) sound.

flammable   See **inflammatory.**

flaunt / flout

Flaunt means "to exhibit ostentatiously" and often has as its object a material thing or an abstraction that is manifested in a striking visual way. Thus, sentences like *She flaunted her diamonds at the reception, Veblen criticized the rich for flaunting their wealth,* and *The students dressed in peculiar outfits to flaunt their individuality* are all correct. The word is sometimes confused with *flout,* which means "to show contempt for." Properly used, *flout* usually has a word like *rules, norms, laws, convention,* or *tradition* for its object. The confusion can be seen in this passage from a newspaper article: *"Medoff flavors his piece with Sarah's mother, a bitter woman rejected by her daughter despite attempts to aid her . . . and a student who flaunts the rules and flirts with Leeds."* The following sentence uses both words correctly:

> Circuses flouted convention as part of their pitch—flaunted and cashed in on the romance of outlawry, like Old World Gypsies (Edward Hoagland, "Circus Music" *Harper's Magazine*)

floe / flow

An *ice floe,* or simply a *floe,* is an expanse of flat, floating ice smaller than an ice field, commonly found near the North Pole and Antarctica. Some ice floes do indeed drift about significantly, but they certainly do not *flow.* Nor are the words themselves etymologically related (*floe* comes from Old Norse *flō,* "layer"). The noun *flow* is made from the verb *flow,* which goes back to Old English *flōwan.*

flotsam / jetsam

Flotsam in maritime law applies to wreckage or cargo left floating on the sea after a shipwreck. *Jetsam* applies to cargo or equipment thrown overboard (jettisoned) from a ship in distress that is either sunk or washed ashore. The common phrase *flotsam and jetsam* is now used loosely to describe any objects found floating or washed ashore.

flounder　See **founder.**

flout　See **flaunt.**

fluid / liquid / gas

In science, the word *fluid* refers to both *liquids* and *gases*. A *fluid* is a substance that does not have a fixed shape. The molecular constituents that make up a fluid move freely past one another. Thus, fluids take on the shape of their containers. The distinguishing feature between a liquid and a gas is that a *liquid* is a fluid that has a relatively fixed volume, and a *gas* is a fluid that does not have a fixed volume. Gases can be compressed and can expand to fill a container entirely; liquids generally cannot.

One exception to this scientific use of *fluid* is *bodily fluids*. Here the word *fluid* applies to liquids only.

follow　See **as follows.**

for

The word *for* has been used as a conjunction meaning "because, since" for more than one thousand years. It is familiar in many famous quotations, from the beatitudes (*Blessed are the meek: for they shall inherit the earth,* Matthew 5:05) to Shakespeare's sonnets (*For thy sweet love rememb'red such wealth brings / That then I scorn to change my state with kings*). Today this use of *for* is rare in speech and informal writing, and it often lends a literary tone or note of formality to what is being said.

Like the word *so, for* can be viewed as either a subordinating or a coordinating conjunction, and it has been treated variously as such. It has the meaning of a subordinating conjunction, since it clearly subordinates the clause that follows it to the previous clause or sentence. But like a coordinating conjunction, *for* has a fixed position in the sentence, and its clause cannot be transposed to precede the superordinate clause containing the main idea. Note that it is ungrammatical to say *For they shall inherit the earth: blessed are the meek.*

Perhaps because of this ambiguity in function, *for* is treated variously with regard to punctuation. Sometimes it begins a dependent clause and follows a comma, and sometimes it begins an independent clause (as if it were a conjunctive adverb like *moreover*) and follows a semicolon or period (when it is capitalized as the first word of a new sentence). All treatments are acceptable in standard usage. The difference is really one of emphasis: starting a new sentence with *for* tends to call more attention to the thought that it introduces. Here are some examples of the use as a subordinating conjunction by contemporary writers:

> Let our recent mistakes bring a resurgent commitment to the basic principles of our Nation, for we know that if we despise our own government we have no future (Jimmy Carter, Inaugural Address)

These players are not spoiled miscreants, for they make on average $46,000 a year (as opposed to $4.5 million for their NBA counterparts), travel on commercial air-lines, and submit to twenty-two unpaid personal appearances a year on behalf of the league's sponsors (Robert Draper, "Beauty in the Beast," *GQ*)

The apples that the Seneca had grown would have been from French varieties, for they received the seeds from Jesuit missionaries (Sue Hubbell, *Shrinking the Cat*)

These are the deepest aspirations of human beings, aspirations for immortality—that is, for an experience beyond time and space, for we are the only beings who are aware that we shall die (Sayyed Hossein Nasr, "In the Beginning Was Consciousness," *Harvard Divinity Bulletin*)

Here are some contemporary examples of conjunctive *for* starting an independent clause or sentence:

I didn't even pay much attention to my parents' accented and ungrammatical speech—at least not at home. Only when I was with them in public would I become alert to their accents. But even then their sounds caused me less and less concern. For I was growing increasingly confident of my own public identity (Richard Rod-riguez, "Aria—A Memoir of a Bilingual Childhood," *The American Scholar*)

On her way through the kitchen she walks through the pool of grape juice. She knows that she will have to mop it up, but not yet, and she walks upstairs leaving purple footprints and smelling her escaping blood and the sweat of her body that has sat all day in the closed hot room.
 No need for alarm.
 For she hasn't thought that crocheted roses could float away or that tombstones could hurry down the street. She doesn't mistake that for reality, and neither does she mistake anything else for reality, and that is how she knows that she is sane (Al-ice Munro, "Meneseteung," *The New Yorker*)

I believed then that I would die, and perhaps because I no longer had a future I be-gan to want one very much. But what such a thing could be then for me, I did not know; for I was standing in a black hole, and the other alternative was another black hole, and this other black hole was one I did not know (Jamaica Kincaid, "In Ro-seau," *The New Yorker*)

Gabor asserted, in essence, that no observation can be made with less than one photon—the basic particle, or quantum, of light—striking the observed object. In the past several years, however, physicists in the increasingly bizarre field of quan-tum optics have learned that not only is this claim far from obvious, it is, in fact, incorrect. For we now know how to determine the presence of an object with essen-tially no photons having touched it (Paul Kwiat, Harald Weinfurter, and Anton Zeilinger, "Quantum Seeing in the Dark," *Scientific American*)

for-   See **fore-**.

force / momentum / work / energy / power

These terms all have scientific meanings, some of which are distinct from their ev-eryday meanings. How they differ in scientific use is also important.

Force is a kind of action on an object. For example, the earth's gravity exerts a force (*weight*); jet engines exert a force (*thrust*). Forces can change the internal structure or shape of objects (bending, crushing, or stretching them, for example). They also cause things to move. A force applied to an object, such as jet engine thrust causing an airplane to accelerate over some distance, can cause the object's *momentum* to change. Even if the engines are turned off, and no more force is applied, the airplane will tend to keep moving forward due to its acquired momentum. In fact, the change in momentum of a rigid object exactly equals the force applied to it.

In physics, *work* is distinct from force. Work is the result of force applied to an object as it moves over some distance and is calculated as force times distance. When work has been done, *energy* has been expended. Generally speaking, something is said to have energy if it has the capacity to do work on some other thing, and energy and work are in fact measured using the same units.

Energy and power are distinct concepts in physics as well. *Power* is the rate at which energy is expended, that is, energy per unit time. Imagine an airplane equipped with a small jet engine. After accelerating for five minutes, the plane reaches a speed of five hundred miles per hour. For its next flight, the engine is replaced with a larger, more powerful one. This time the airplane reaches the same speed in one minute. The larger engine can be said to have five times the power of the smaller one, since it provided the same amount of energy five times as quickly.

A common confusion of power and energy concerns electricity: a kilowatt is a common unit of electrical power, but on an electric bill, the customer is not charged for power in the scientific sense (the rate at which the energy was used), but for the total amount of energy used (measured in kilowatt-hours).

See more at **current.**

forceful / forcible / forced

The adjectives *forceful, forcible,* and *forced* have related but distinct meanings. *Forceful* describes someone or something that possesses or is filled with strength or force: *a forceful speaker, a forceful personality. Forceful measures* may or may not involve the use of actual physical force. *Forcible,* however, is used for actions carried out by physical force: *There had been a forcible entry into the apartment. The police had to use forcible restraint in order to arrest the suspect. Forced* is used for an act or a condition brought about by control or an outside influence: *a forced smile, a forced landing, forced labor.*

fore– / for–

The prefix *fore–* means "before, in front." A *forerunner* is "one that goes before" and a *foreleg* is "a front leg of an animal." The prefix descends from an Old English prefix of the form *fore–,* closely related to the element *–fore,* seen in the Modern English word *before.*

English has another prefix *for–* that is pronounced exactly like *fore–.* It is added to verbs to express a variety of notions relating to exclusion, rejection, abstention, or neglect. This *for–* descends from the Old English prefix *for–*. It appears in a large number of common English words like *forbear, forbid, forget, forgive,* and *forswear,* but it can no longer be used to form new words.

Some words beginning with *for–* have spelling variants with *fore–* that are accepted by major American dictionaries, such as *forswear,* also sometimes written *foreswear.* Conversely, some words usually spelled with *fore–* also have accepted spelling variants in *for–* like the noun *forebear,* "ancestor," also sometimes written *forbear.* Only the spelling *forbear,* however, is acceptable for the homophonous verb meaning "to refrain from, resist." The noun *forebear* is in fact unrelated to the verb *forbear.* A *forebear* is literally a "fore-be-er, one who has been before," and derives from the prefix *fore–* added to the verb *be,* while the verb *forebear* comes from an Old English verb *forberan,* "endure," and derives from the prefix *for–,* conveying the notion of abstention, and the verb *beran,* "bear." When in doubt about the spelling of words beginning *fore–* or *for–,* writers should consult their dictionary to ascertain the preferred form. In many cases, the difference in spelling between the two prefixes helps distinguish two different words that sound alike.

See more at **forego.**

forecastle

Pronounced (fōk′səl) by sailors, this word, like *boatswain,* has a pronunciation that is not easily predictable from the spelling. The variant spelling *fo'c'sle,* reflecting this pronunciation, has been around since at least the 1870s. Note that it is also acceptable to pronounce *forecastle* (fôr′kăs′əl) or (fōr′kăs′əl). Other nautical words with tricky pronunciations include *bowline, gunwale, mainsail,* and *topgallant,* to name just a few.

See more at **pronunciation spelling** and **spelling pronunciation.**

forego / forgo

The verb *forgo,* meaning "to abstain from, do without," has as an acceptable variant the spelling *forego.* Thus, one can *forgo* or *forego* dessert, though the spelling without the *e* is far more common and is preferred in most dictionaries. *Forego* also exists as a separate word meaning "to go before, either in place or time," as in *A bad reputation often foregoes you.*

See more at **foregone.**

foregone

Foregone, the past participle of *forego,* is sometimes used to mean "assured, certain," as in *It is by no means foregone that the team will relocate next season.* This construction, which is probably an abridgement of *a foregone conclusion,* was unacceptable to 84 percent of the Usage Panel in our 1997 survey.

forehead

Forehead is a word that has a long history in English, and over the course of the centuries, the vowel sounds in its pronunciation were reduced to (fôr′ĭd), rhyming with *horrid*. However, the word is now commonly pronounced with two stressed syllables (fôr′hĕd′), rhyming with *bore head*. In our 1997 survey, three quarters of the Panel preferred the fully stressed form (fôr′hĕd′).

foreign nouns, plurals of   See **plural nouns.**

former / latter

Traditionally, the words *former* and *latter* are viewed as comparatives, and hence *the former* should refer to the first of two things, and *the latter* to the second:

> Born in Kentucky and reared in Indiana and Illinois, Lincoln pursued the twin professions of law and politics. As the former prospered, the latter languished, and Lincoln had to be content with several terms in the Illinois state legislature and a single term in the lower house of Congress (Robert W. Johannsen, "Lincoln," in Robert Cowley and Geoffrey Parker, eds., *The Reader's Companion to Military History*)

The word *latter* is often used without *former* to refer to the second of two things, as in

> Some of his fellow diners were content to ignore him and carry on their own conversations, while others listened to Auden in fascination. Among the latter was Jane Bowles, now utterly under Auden's spell and avidly incorporating his ideas and opinions into her novel (Sherill Tippins, *February House*)

> Modern people, therefore, would not share an ancestry with Neandertals—the latter would be mere twigs on the human family tree, driven into extinction by our ancestors without leaving a genetic trace (Craig Stanford, *Upright*)

Some authors see nothing amiss in using *former* and *latter* with enumerations of more than two things, even though this violates the traditional rule. In some cases, the meaning is clear enough. Presumably, *stubborn opposition* is what is referred to as *the latter* in the following passage:

> Her face had closed again. She never disagreed with him, but he was perfectly well aware that her lapses into silence might conceal anything, consent, indifference, even stubborn opposition. He suspected the latter, in the present instance (Jane Stevenson, *The Shadow King*)

But the question of ambiguity does arise with compound entities in these constructions. What exactly does Peggy agree to in the quotation below—the car rental business *and* the auto mechanic's shop? or just the auto mechanic's shop?

Raoul wanted Peggy to buy him a sports car; he also asked her to set him up with his own car rental business and then an auto mechanic's shop, both of them on the mainland outside Venice. The latter she agreed to, but the sports car was a sticking point (Mary V. Dearborn, *Mistress of Modernism*)

One sensible solution to these problems is to use *first* and *last* in place of *former* and *latter* when referring to the beginning and end of a series containing more than two items. But when some items in a series are compounds connected by a conjunction like *and* or *or,* care should be taken to specify what exactly is being referred to.

formidable

Traditionally this word has been pronounced with stress on the first syllable, as (fôr′mĭ-də-bəl), but recently the pronunciation with stress on the second syllable, (fôr-mĭd′ə-bəl), which is a common variant in British English, has seen considerable use in American English. The pronunciation with stress on the first syllable is apparently still preferred by a large majority of educated speakers, however. In our 1992 survey, 80 percent of the Usage Panel said they pronounced the word with stress on the first syllable, 14 percent said they stressed the second syllable, and a small percentage said they used both pronunciations.

forte

This word, meaning "strong point," from French *fort,* meaning "strong point," can be pronounced with one syllable, like the English word *fort,* or with two syllables. The two-syllable pronunciation, (fôr′tā′), is probably the most common in American English and was the choice of 74 percent of the Usage Panel in our 1996 survey, but some people dislike it, arguing that it properly belongs to the music term *forte,* which comes from Italian, where it is pronounced with two syllables.

fortuitous

The basic meaning of *fortuitous* is "happening by chance, accidental." Many chance events are favorable, and perhaps because of contexts such as *The company's profits improved after a fortuitous drop in oil prices,* or because of similarity to *fortunate* and *felicitous,* the word *fortuitous* has acquired the meaning "characterized by good fortune, lucky." (The word *fortunate* underwent a similar shift in meaning centuries ago.) Thus, a reader may not be certain which meaning is intended in sentences such as *Their project was the result of a fortuitous meeting between acquaintances* and *A series of fortuitous events led the explorers to change their course,* where the meeting and the events could be fortunate, unfortunate, neither, or both. Many people would prefer to keep *fortuitous* semantically distinct from *fortunate,* but given the prevalence of its usage with the meaning "fortunate," doing so requires that the context make clear which meaning is intended. When modified by an adverb such as *very* or *somewhat,* *fortuitous* can only mean "lucky." Constructions like these will strike some readers as objectionable.

founder / flounder

The verb *founder* ultimately comes from the Latin word *fundus,* meaning "bottom" (also seen in *foundation*), and originally referred to knocking enemies down. In nautical use, it means "to sink to the bottom," as in *After striking the reef, the ship foundered.* The word has been extended figuratively to mean "to fail utterly, collapse": *The business had a promising start but foundered. Founder* is sometimes confused with the verb *flounder,* meaning "to move clumsily, thrash about" and hence "to proceed in confusion." Thus, if a student is *foundering* in Chemistry 101, he had better drop the course; if he is *floundering,* he may yet pull through.

fragment   See **sentence fragment.**

free gift

Though this phrase often occurs in advertising, it is literally redundant. If an object is given to someone as *free,* then it is given without any obligation on the part of the recipient. But in normal parlance, a *gift* is itself, by definition, an object given to someone without any obligation on the part of the recipient. The word *gift* is sometimes used deceptively to suggest that something is being given away with no strings attached when in fact the strings are simply hard to see, but this attempt at deception does not absolve the expression *free gift* of its redundancy.

It should be noted that in anthropology, the word *gift* is used in contexts referring to certain cultural practices of *exchanging gifts.* These practices can involve complex systems of expectation and obligation on the parts of givers and receivers. In this context, the notion of a *free gift* is not redundant, but an oxymoron.

free rein / full rein / free reign / full reign

To grant someone *free rein* or *full rein* was originally a metaphorical extension of giving or letting slack both reins on a horse, allowing the horse to go at its own pace and in the direction it found suitable. Since giving free rein or full rein is thus granting control and power to another, it is not surprising that these expressions have been reanalyzed as *free reign or full reign,* when the metaphor evokes the power that a monarch has over his or her dominion. But the expressions remain properly *free rein* or *full rein.*

frequency / pitch / pitch class

In the vernacular of music, the *pitch* of a sound is completely determined by its *frequency* of vibration. Typical pitch standards in Western music assign a given frequency to one of the twelve notes in an octave: C, C♯, D, D♯, E, F, F♯, G, G♯, A, A♯, B, and another symbol to indicate the relative position of the octave. For example, American

Standard Pitch uses a subscript to indicate the octave and assigns to C_4 (middle C) a frequency of 261.63 vibrations per second. Thus, a sound with the frequency 261.63 has the pitch C_4 in American Standard Pitch. The *pitch class* of a sound is determined only by its note assignment and not by the octave in which the note occurs. Therefore, there are twelve pitch classes in Western music. C_3 and C_4 are in the same pitch class, but they have different pitches.

In acoustics, a sound is also quantified by its frequency of vibration. However, scientists refer to another quality of sound called *pitch* that is a subjective measure of the combination of the frequency and intensity of a sound. This is related to but distinctly different from the vernacular use of *pitch* in music. In acoustics, a unit of pitch called the *mel* (from *mel*ody) has a dependence on the frequency and the intensity at which a note is heard. For example, in acoustics, the note C_4 heard with an intensity of 10^{-4} watts per meter^2 has a different pitch than the note C_4 heard with an intensity of 10^{-2} watts per meter^2. In music, however, both of these sounds are considered to have the same pitch.

frigid

When the word *frigid* is used to describe a woman, it means that she is considered to be persistently averse to sexual activity or is chronically unresponsive sexually, as in this film review in a London newspaper: "*an American investment banker, married to this increasingly distant and frigid woman, succumbs to the charms of a beautiful, dark and brilliant colleague.*" The word is often considered sexist because it applies only to females and has no counterpart that is used to refer to males. In fact, men are rarely described in this way. *Frigid* in a sexual context is also considered offensive because it carries a negative judgment of a woman who does not meet male sexual needs and implies that sexual activity or responsiveness is the only desirable norm.

Note that *frigid* is not a medical term and is not used in reference to the physiological or psychological aspects of sexual arousal or activity. By contrast, the term *impotent,* which is used exclusively of men, is a medical term that refers to a condition that can be diagnosed and treated. Sexual dysfunction, whether stemming from physiological or psychological causes, is a medical condition and should be described as such in women or men.

from hence / from thence / from whence   See **hence.**

fruit / seed / vegetable / berry

To most people, a *fruit* is the fleshy part of a plant that contains seeds, tastes sweet, and is usually eaten as a dessert or snack. To a botanist, however, a fruit is the mature ovary of a flowering plant. The ovary is the female part of the flower that contains the ovules, and the ovules in turn are the structures that contain egg cells. When an egg cell within an ovule has been fertilized after pollination, the egg cell becomes an embryo, the tiny plant within a *seed* that grows into a seedling when the seed germinates. The ovule around it then develops into the remaining portion of the seed, which contains a supply of food for the embryo. At the same time, the ovary surrounding the ovule develops into the rest of the *fruit*. During this process, the ovary may join with other ovaries or other parts of the plant to develop into a fruit of complex structure. In an apple, for instance, the base of the flower to which the ovary is attached grows around the ovary and swells to become the edible flesh of the fruit. Fruits help plants disperse their seeds, as when birds eat berries and transport the seeds away from the parent plant in their digestive tract to be deposited elsewhere.

In this technical botanical sense, the fruit of a plant need not be juicy or fleshy. Thus many structures described as *seeds* in everyday usage are *fruits* in the botanical sense. For example, the winged "helicopter" seeds of the maple tree and the fluffy seeds of a dandelion are fruits from the botanical perspective, since their structures develop from the entire ovary. Dry fruits like these are dispersed from the parent plant by the wind. The many forms taken by fruits, besides the fleshy, sweet ones favored by humans as food, reflect the different strategies that plants have evolved to help their seeds reach new places to grow, but all of these varied structures are developments of the structures called ovaries, sometimes fused with other parts of the plant.

In everyday, nonscientific speech we make the distinction between nonsweet plant parts, called *vegetables,* and sweet plant parts, called *fruits.* The leaves of spinach, the roots of carrots, the flowers and stems of broccoli, and the stalks of celery are all vegetables, while apples, peaches, plums, and bananas are considered to be fruits. When trying to understand how plants have evolved and how they interact with their environment, however, botanists have found it more helpful to classify plant structures by their origin and development than by their sugar or juice content. Many edible plant parts called *vegetables* in everyday usage should thus be termed *fruits* when considered from the botanical point of view. Green peppers, tomatoes, eggplants, pea pods, cucumbers, and squash are therefore fruits in the eyes of a botanist, since they develop from a maturing ovary just like an apple or a peach.

Botanists use the term *berry* to describe any fleshy fruit that develops from a single ovary of a single flower and contains more than one seed. Thus a tomato, a cucumber, and a banana are all berries to a botanist. Conversely, some fruits called berries in everyday usage would not be classified as such by a botanist. In a strawberry, for example, the red juicy edible flesh develops from the base of the flower where it connects to the stem, rather than from the ovaries of the flower. The actual fruits of the strawberry are the small dry "seeds" embedded in the surface. A mulberry too is not a berry in the botanical sense, since it develops from the fusion of the ovaries of many small separate flowers.

–ful

The suffix *–ful* comes from the Old English adjective *full,* meaning "full." *Full* was commonly added to a noun in order to form adjectives meaning "full of, characterized by" whatever quality was denoted by the noun: *playful, careful.*

The use of –*ful* to form nouns meaning "a quantity that would fill" a particular receptacle (*cupful, mouthful*) also goes back to Old English. In modern usage the correct way to form the plural of these nouns is to add an -*s* to the end of the suffix: *cupfuls, handfuls, spoonfuls.*

full rein / full reign

See **free rein.**

fulminant / fulminate

Traditionally, these are pronounced (fŭl′mə-nənt) and (fŭl′mə-nāt′), with a short *u* in the first syllable as in *gull.* This is apparently still the preferred pronunciation in British English. In American English, the variant pronunciations (fŏŏl′mə-nənt) and (fŏŏl′mə-nāt′), with the first syllable like *full,* are more common.

fulsome

The word *fulsome* had as its original meaning "copious, abundant," and this usage survives today, especially in constructions like *He was fulsome in his praise of his rival, calling him the best goal-scorer in the league.* The word is also used with positive meanings, such as "full, strong," as in *a fulsome sound,* and "full-bodied, hearty," as in *a wine with a fulsome flavor.*

But *fulsome* usually is used of complimentary remarks and connotes excessive praising or offensive flattery. Thus the word may invite misunderstandings in contexts in which someone could infer a deprecatory interpretation. Sentences like *The editor-in-chief was given a fulsome tribute in the writer's memoir, The prime minister offered his fulsome apologies for the intelligence failure,* and *She was fulsome in her praise of her superiors* could easily be misunderstood if the context does not make clear which sense is meant. If an implication of excessiveness or insincerity is not intended, use an adjective like *full* or *abundant* instead.

Perhaps because of this potential confusion, much of the Usage Panel is unhappy with this word when it is used in neutral or positive contexts. *Fulsome* found few fans when used as a synonym of *full.* In our 2002 survey, only 14 percent accepted the example *You can adjust the TV's audio settings for a more fulsome bass in movie soundtracks.* Use of the word as a synonym of *copious* or *expansive* found but slightly more takers, as 16 percent accepted *The final report will furnish a more detailed and fulsome discussion of the issues involved.*

The use as a synonym of *praising* without a clear indication of inordinacy or insincerity split the Panel down the middle, with 51 percent accepting the example *The research director claimed that the product was a major advance that would improve Web access for everyone, and the marketing VP was equally fulsome in her remarks.*

Thus it may be best to avoid this word unless the context is unambiguous in conveying the notion of excessiveness or offensiveness. A similar problem exists with the word *enormity.*

Note that the older pronunciation is (fŭl′səm), with the first syllable rhyming with *dull*. This pronunciation was recorded in dictionaries (increasingly as a less common variant) until the middle of the 20th century. *Fulsome* is now always pronounced (fŏŏl′səm), with the first syllable like *full,* in both British and American English.

fun

The use of *fun* as an adjective developed from the use of the noun in compounds such as *fun fair* (a fair consisting mostly of amusements) and *fun-fest.* The adjective has become widespread now and must be considered standard, as in these newspaper examples:

> The roles of stepsisters Tisbe and Clorinda virtually demand some scenery-chewing, and Rossini supplies great tunes and vocal fireworks. It makes for a genuinely fun evening at the opera, even for the youngster (Scott Cantrell, "Dallas Opera's 'Cinderella' at Fair Park Music Hall," *Dallas Morning News*)

> It's the worst season Johnson has endured since his freshman year at Yale, when he barely played and football was supposedly a fun activity (Alan Greenberg, "High Degree of Success for Ex-Yale Receiver," *Hartford Courant*)

The inflection of the adjective (as *funner, funnest*) is another matter, however. Although this practice goes back to the 1950s and 1960s, the inflected forms are almost never used in edited prose aside from direct quotations, usually of children.

function word

A function word is a word such as a preposition, conjunction, or article that has little meaning on its own and chiefly indicates a grammatical relationship between other words.

fungi

Although this word, the Latin plural of *fungus,* can be pronounced with a soft or hard g, as (fŭn′jī) or (fŭng′gī), the former is the most common pronunciation in medicine, as well as in American English in general. Note that g may also be soft or hard in *fungicide, fungiform, fungivorous,* and in other similar compounds.
See more at **g.**

further   See **farther.**

fused participle   See **gerunds.**

fused sentence   See **run-on sentence.**

futile

The pronunciation of the word *futile* as fyōo t′l was preferred by 69 percent of the Usage Panel in our 1997 survey, with 22 percent preferring the long *i* variant (fyōo′tīl′); the remainder responded having no preference for one or the other. Even though the long *i* pronunciation was less popular, it was still considered an acceptable variant by half of the people who preferred (fyōot′l).

future perfect tense

The future perfect tense expresses action that is completed by a specified time in the future. It is formed by combining *will have* or *shall have* with a past participle, as in *will have improved.*

See more at **verbs, tenses of.**

future tense

The future tense expresses action that has not yet occurred or a state that does not yet exist. In English, it is formed by combining the auxiliary verb *will* or *shall* with an infinitive, as in *will go* and *will arrive.* The future tense is not the only way English indicates future action. The present tense is often used with an adverbial of time to do this (as in *We are going to the beach tomorrow*), and certain verb phrases like *be about to* can express futurity as well.

See more at **verbs, tenses of.**

–fy

The verb suffix *–fy*, which means "to make or cause to become," derives from the Latin suffix *–ficāre* or *–ficārī*, from *facere*, meaning "to do or make." Thus *purify* means "to make pure, cleanse" (coming from Latin *pūrificāre*, from *pūrus*, "clean," plus *–ficāre*). In English the suffix *–fy* now normally takes the form *–ify: acidify, humidify, speechify.* Verbs ending in *–fy* often have related nouns that end in *–fication* or *–faction: magnify, magnification; satisfy, satisfaction.*

· G ·

g

The earliest form of the Roman alphabet had no letter *g*. Instead, *c* could represent both the sound (g) and the sound (k). The Roman letter *c* was in fact a development of the Greek letter gamma, written Γ. This is why *c*, not *g*, still occupies the place in the Roman alphabet corresponding to gamma in the Greek alphabet, even though the sounds of gamma and *g* might seem to correspond better than gamma and *c* from a modern point of view. In order to make the distinction between (g) and (k) clear in writing, the Romans developed the letter *g* by the addition of a small stroke to *c*. The Greek historian Plutarch ascribes the invention of *g* to a Roman named Spurius Carvilius Ruga, who lived in the 3rd century BC. The new letter *g* was given the place corresponding to the letter *z* (zeta) in the Greek alphabet, since zeta was not used to write native Latin words. (When the Romans later began to use the letter *z* again, it was added to the very end of the alphabet, the place it still holds today.)

As Latin developed into the Romance languages, the pronunciation of (g) before *e, i,* and *y* gradually changed, resulting in the soft *g* pronounced like (j). After the Norman Invasion of Britain in the 11th century, Middle English scribes continued the use of soft *g* before *e, i,* and *y* in words borrowed from French. (In Modern French, *g* before *e, i,* and *y* is now pronounced (zh).) Also through the influence of French the symbol *g* began to replace the symbol ȝ, called *yogh*, which was the Irish form of Roman *g*. Yogh had been used to represent several sounds in Old English, including the hard *g*. In Modern English, words beginning with soft *g* before *e, i,* and *y* are generally of French or Latin origin, such as *gelid* and *giblet,* and words beginning with hard *g* before *e, i,* and *y* are generally of native English or Germanic origin, such as *gear* and *give*. Like *c, g* is generally hard before *a, o, u,* and consonants.

gaff / gaffe

Gaff and *gaffe* are doublets, words borrowed at different times from the same source word in another language and now treated as different words in English. *Gaff* goes back to the 1300s, when it was borrowed from Old French with the meaning "iron hook." It can now refer to various hook- or pole-shaped instruments used in fishing, sailboat rigging, climbing telephone poles, and other activities. Its extended meanings include "a trick or gimmick," and "an instance of harsh treatment or abuse," especially verbal abuse, as in *He gave me quite a gaff for my sloppy work.* By contrast, *gaffe* is a relative newcomer to our language, dating from the early 20th century. It is a borrowing from Modern French, though it ultimately goes back to the same Old French word for "hook." *Gaffe* means "a clumsy social error; a blatant mistake or misjudgment."

While the spelling *gaff* has historically been a spelling variant of *gaffe,* the latter spelling is the one predominantly used for the meaning of "blunder."

gal   See **guy.**

gamut / gambit

A *gamut* is the complete extent or range of something (in music, for example, where the word originated, it expresses the entire range of notes). Thus, to *run the gamut* is to traverse an entire range. This expression is idiomatic and standard, as in this sentence from *Phantom Illness* by Carla Cantnor: "*The biological markers for depression can run the gamut from insomnia and weight change to memory loss and sexual dysfunction.*"

As is often the case with idioms, the original meanings of the words composing them can be lost, obscured, or confused. In this case, the uncommon word *gamut* is sometimes confused with the word *gambit.* Serious chess players know that a gambit is an opening move in which a minor piece like a pawn is risked or even sacrificed to gain a favorable position. Some people familiar with chess maintain that *gambit* should not be used in an extended sense except to refer to maneuvers that involve a tactical sacrifice or loss for some advantage. But *gambit* is well established in the general sense of "maneuver," and it does much service in the field of foreign affairs, as in this sentence from an article in the *New York Times:* "*So when the Chinese Government declared on Wednesday that it had found the new Panchen Lama—Tibetan Buddhism's second-highest religious authority—by a drawing of lots, it was more than the latest slippery gambit in China's 45-year occupation.*" *Gambit* is also used correctly in the related sense of "a remark intended to open a conversation," in which there is no implication of risk, except for the risk of being rebuffed. This sense can be illustrated by the following quotation from William Least Heat-Moon's *River Horse:* "*That Monday in Townsend, population 1,600, an elderly fellow wearing a cap imprinted who? me? asked where I was from—the standard opening gambit in rural cafés—and I told him.*"

In any case, the phrase *run the gambit* is a mistake.

gas   See **fluid.**

gauntlet / gantlet

There are two words in English that are spelled *gauntlet.* One comes from the Old French word *gantelet,* a diminutive of *gant,* "glove." It originally referred to a glove worn as part of medieval armor. Since its introduction in the 15th century, the word has also been spelled *gantlet*. *To throw down the gauntlet* means to offer a challenge, which in medieval times was done by throwing down a glove or gauntlet.

The other *gauntlet*, which also has the spelling variant *gantlet*, refers to a form of punishment in which the offender runs between two lines of men who beat him with sticks or other weapons, such as knotted cords. This word is an alteration of the obsolete word *gantlope*, which comes from the Swedish word *gatlopp*, a compound of *gata*, "lane," and *lopp*, "course." Shortly after *gantlope* appeared in English in the mid-17th century, the spelling *gauntlet* began to compete with it.

To *run the gauntlet* means to undergo this form of punishment. The expression is also used idiomatically to mean "to be exposed to danger, criticism, or other adversity," as in this quotation from a Massachusetts newspaper:

> But what about putting a disabled person's life at risk every day by normal and disabled drivers alike parking on pavements . . . preventing wheelchair users from travelling safely as other pedestrians do? Both of these force wheelchair users to ride in the road and run the gauntlet of traffic they really don't wish to encounter . . . (*Plymouth Evening Herald*)

The railroad term *gantlet* arose from the spelling variant of this second meaning of *gauntlet*. It refers to a section of track designed so that one rail of each track is inside the rails of the other to allow trains on separate tracks to pass through a very narrow space.

gay

The word *gay* is now standard in its use to refer to people whose sexual orientation is to the same sex, in large part because it is the term that most gay people prefer when referring to themselves. *Gay* is distinguished from *homosexual* primarily by the emphasis it places on the cultural and social aspects of homosexuality as opposed to sexual practice. Many writers reserve *gay* for males, but the word is also used to refer to both sexes; when the intended meaning is not clear in the context, the phrase *gay and lesbian* may be used.

Gay is often considered objectionable when used as a noun to refer to particular individuals, as in *There were two gays on the panel*; here phrasing such as *Two members of the panel were gay* should be used instead. But there is no objection to the use of the noun in the plural to refer collectively either to gay men or to gay men and lesbians, so long as it is clear whether men alone or both men and women are being discussed.

See more at **lesbian.**

gender

In grammar, gender is a category used in the selection or agreement of nouns, pronouns, and adjectives with modifiers, words being referred to, or grammatical forms. Grammatical gender may be arbitrary, or it may be based on characteristics such as sex or the quality of being animate. In English, grammatical gender applies only to pronouns, which normally coincide with the sexual identity of their antecedents. In other languages, abstractions and inanimate objects may be grammatically masculine or feminine. In German, for example, the word for *fork* is feminine, the word for *spoon* is masculine, and the word for *knife* is neuter.

The word *gender* also refers to sexual identity. For more on this word, see **gender / sex.**

gender-neutral

The term *gender-neutral* means "free of explicit or implicit reference to biological gender or sexual identity." Thus the term *police officer* is gender-neutral, where *policeman* and *policewoman* are not. A longstanding problem in English usage is the absence of a singular, gender-neutral pronoun referring to a person.

See more at **he.**

gender / sex

Traditionally, writers have used the word *gender* to refer to the grammatical categories of masculine, feminine, and neuter, as in languages such as French or Spanish whose nouns and adjectives carry such distinctions. While its use to refer also to sociological and cultural distinctions between males and females was evident as early as the 1300s, this use fell out of favor at the beginning of the 20th century and reemerged in the past few decades in both noun and adjectival forms, as in *gender gap, politics of gender,* and *gender bias.* Some people maintain that the word *sex* should be reserved for reference to the biological aspects of being male or female or to sexual activity and that the word *gender* should be used only to refer to sociocultural roles. Accordingly, one would say *The effectiveness of the treatment appears to depend on the sex of the patient* and *In society, gender roles are clearly defined.*

In some situations this distinction averts ambiguity, as in *gender research,* which is clear in a way that *sex research* is not. The distinction can be problematic, however. Linguistically, there isn't any real difference between *gender bias* and *sex bias,* and it may seem contrived to insist that *sex* is incorrect in this instance. In addition, because perceptions about sexual identity are quite personalized and may not coincide with an individual's physiology, the distinction may be offensive. Hence, a preoperative transsexual who identifies herself as a female but who is still biologically male might identify both her sex and gender as female.

The words *sex* and *gender,* therefore, are increasingly used interchangeably in contexts that are not purely biological, as illustrated in the following examples:

> So what we've got here is two high-status women in a love relationship trying to negotiate issues of economic and cultural power without the help—or hindrance—of traditional gender roles (Cary Tennis, *Salon.com*)

> The report says 11 of 13 abstinence-only curricula "contain errors and distortions" about contraceptives, sexually transmitted diseases (STDs), abortion, sex roles and sexual activity (Cheryl Wetzstein, "Democrat's Report Calls Abstinence Plans 'Misleading'" *Washington Times*)

A careful writer should be aware that the word *sex* in isolation, as in a chapter heading or on a census form, is usually interpreted to refer to physical acts or differences.

See more at **transvestite.**

genealogy

The effect of the influence of words ending in *–ology* is such that people now almost always say (jē′nē-ŏl′ə-jē), with a short *o,* and much less frequently (jē′nē-ăl′ə-jē), with a short *a.* Both pronunciations are acceptable, however.

General American

The label *General American* is often used to describe speech used by Americans that lacks any of the stereotypical markers of regional speech or of the speech of particular social groups. These markers include accents and the omission of certain sounds, as the (r) sound in words like *car* and *card.* General American has traditionally been associated with northern, inland varieties of speech. It should be noted, however, that the label still allows for a great deal of regional and social variation, especially in pronunciation.

See more at **dialect.**

genetic   See **congenital.**

genitive

The genitive is the case that expresses possession, measurement, or source. For nouns, English normally indicates these relationships by adding an apostrophe and an *s* at the end of the word: *the car's motor, the movie's final scene.* Pronouns indicate these relationships by the genitive case, that is, by changing form. Thus *his* is the genitive of the pronoun *he, her* is the genitive of *she,* and *our* is the genitive of *we.*

See more at **possessive constructions** and **pronouns, personal.**

genotype / phenotype

The word *genotype* refers to the inherited genetic makeup of an organism. In contrast, *phenotype,* from the Greek *phainein,* "to show," denotes the observable physical or biochemical characteristics of an organism, which depend on both genetic and environmental influences. For example, a person's natural color of hair and eyes, blood type, and fingerprints are phenotypic expressions of genetically determined traits. An individual's hairstyle, altered hair or eye color, and style of eyeglasses are examples of phenotypic expressions of environmental influences.

genuine

There is some evidence that the pronunciation (jĕn′yōō-īn′), with long *i* in the last syllable, is becoming more prevalent, but the most widely accepted pronunciation is still (jĕn′yōō-ĭn). In our 1996 survey, 97 percent of the Usage Panel reported using the pronunciation with the short *i*. And of those 97 percent, only 17 percent found the pronunciation with the long *i* to be acceptable.

genus

Genus comes from Latin, where it was pronounced with a hard *g*, at least until the end of the Roman empire. Its plural was *genera*. Both forms came into English with a soft *g*, as in *gentle*. *Genus* is pronounced with a long *e* in the first syllable (jē′nəs), and *genera* with a short *e* in the first syllable (jĕn′ər-ə).

geo–

The basic meaning of the prefix *geo–* is "earth" or "land." It comes from the Greek prefix *geo–*, from the Greek word *gē*, meaning "earth, land, ground." Thus *geography* (from Greek *geo–* plus *graphia*, "writing") is "the study of the earth and its surface features." (*Gaia*, familiar as the name of the Greek goddess of the earth, is in fact a variant form of the Greek word *gē*.) When used to form words in English, *geo–* can have the meaning "relating to the planet Earth as a whole" or "relating to geography." For example, *geomagnetism* refers to the magnetism of the earth, and *geopolitics* refers to the relationship between politics and geography.

germ / microbe / microorganism / pathogen

The *germ* theory of disease, popularized by Louis Pasteur and others in the 19th century, recognized that infectious organisms could cause and transmit disease even though they were invisible to the naked eye. Today, the word *germ,* from the Latin *germen,* "bud," is sometimes used popularly to refer to a *microorganism* that is capable of causing disease. A *microorganism,* built from the prefix *micro–,* "small" and the noun *organism,* is simply a one-celled microscopic organism, especially a bacterium or protozoan. *Microorganisms* may be disease-causing or benign in the human body. The word *microbe,* derived from the Greek prefix *mikro–,* "small," and *bios,* "life," is a synonym for *microorganism.* It is used popularly and is generally not seen in scientific or medical literature. The scientific and medical term, *pathogen* (derived from Greek *pathos,* "suffering" and the suffix *–gen,* "producer"), describes any agent that causes disease, including microorganisms, viruses, prions, or parasites.

gerrymander

In 1812, when he was governor of Massachusetts, Elbridge Gerry signed into law a bill that created an oddly shaped electoral district, which included his hometown of

Marblehead and was said to resemble a salamander. Thus was born the gerrymander. Gerry pronounced his name (gĕr'ē), with a hard *g*, but as Gerry faded from political memory, people pronounced the word on the basis of its spelling, with a soft *g* as in *geranium*. Today both pronunciations are still acceptable, though the one with the soft *g* (jĕr'ē-măn'dər) predominates.

See more at **spelling pronunciation.**

gerunds

Gerunds are verb forms ending in *–ing* that act as nouns. They can be the subject of a sentence (*Skiing is her favorite sport*), the object of a verb (*She enjoys skiing*), or the object of a preposition (*She devoted her free time to skiing*). Gerunds can be modified like nouns (*That book makes for difficult reading*). But they can also act like verbs in that they can take an object (*Convincing him was never easy*) and be modified by an adverb (*Walking daily can improve your health*).

gerunds and possessives (fused participle)   Some people insist that when a gerund is preceded by a noun or pronoun, the noun or pronoun must be in the possessive case. Accordingly, it would be correct to say *I can understand his wanting to go,* but incorrect to say *I can understand him wanting to go*. But the construction without the possessive (in this case, *him wanting*), which is sometimes called the *fused participle,* has been used by respected writers for at least three hundred years and is perfectly idiomatic. Moreover, there is often no way to "fix" the construction by inserting the possessive. This is often the case with common nouns. Thus one can say *We have had very few instances of luggage being lost,* but not . . . *of luggage's being lost.*

Sometimes syntax makes using the possessive impossible. Consider the sentence *What she objects to is men making more money than women for the same work.* Changing *men making* to *men's making* not only sounds awkward, but it requires *women's* at the other end to keep the sentence parallel, and *women's* simply does not work. Perhaps for these reasons 53 percent of the Usage Panel found the phrase *men making* acceptable in this sentence in our 1995 survey, and an additional 36 percent found *men making* acceptable in informal contexts. Only 11 percent rejected it outright.

However, when the construction is more complicated so that a word or phrase intervenes between the noun and the gerund, the Panel was less sanguine. Only 25 percent accepted the sentence *I can understand him not wanting to go,* where the negative *not* intervenes between the pronoun and the gerund. Thirty-one percent said this sentence was acceptable in informal contexts, leaving 44 percent as naysayers. Panel acceptance dropped even further for a sentence in which the syntax is more complicated. Only 16 percent accepted the sentence *Imagine a child with an ear infection who cannot get penicillin losing his hearing,* where both a phrase and a clause intervene between the noun *child* and the gerund *losing*. And only 17 percent found this sentence acceptable in informal contexts, so that 66 percent rejected it under any circumstances.

Be aware that sometimes nouns ending in *-s* can be confused with a singular noun in the possessive. Thus, *I don't approve of your friend's going there* indicates one friend is going, and *I don't approve of your friends going there* indicates that more than one friend is going.

See more at **participles** and **possessive constructions.**

get

***get* in passive constructions**   The use of the word *get* instead of *be* in passive constructions gives a different tone and emphasis. Compare these two sentences: *The demonstrators were arrested by the state police* and *The demonstrators got arrested by the state police.* The first example suggests that the responsibility for the arrests lies primarily with the police. As usual with a passive, the subject of the sentence is the passive recipient of the action. The second example, which uses *get,* suggests a more active role played by the demonstrators, implying that they were arrested as a consequence of their actions (presumably having something to do with the act of demonstrating).

If the subject of a *get* passive is not something that could influence the activity described by the verb, then the construction tends to suggest that the subject was in some way affected and changed by the activity. For example, in response to the question *Why are you so attached to that old bed?* one might answer, *It was slept in by all my little cousins,* thereby simply describing a fact about the bed. But if the mattress is sagging and the frame twisted, the question *What in the world happened to that bed?* might be better answered with the *get* passive: *It got slept in by all my little cousins.*

See more at **got** and **verbs, voice of.**

gibberish

The overwhelming majority of people pronounce this word with a soft *g* as (jĭb′ər-ĭsh). A very small minority of people pronounce it with a hard *g,* as in *goat.*

gibe / jibe / gybe / jive

These words sound alike (or nearly alike) and are easily confused. The word *gibe,* as a verb, means "to make taunting, heckling, or jeering remarks," as in *Quit gibing at me!* It may also be used as a noun meaning "a derisive remark." *Gibe* is sometimes spelled as *jibe,* and this inevitably leads to confusion with the verb *jibe* in the sense "to be in accord with or be consistent with" (as in *These figures don't jibe with what he lead us to expect*). There is also a sailing term *jibe,* which means "to swing the sail from one tack to the other while running with the wind," and it is sometimes spelled *gybe.* Both variant spellings for these words are acceptable.

The one outlier in this group, spelled with a *v,* is *jive,* which has origins in African American Vernacular English, and is first attested in 1928 as the title of a song by

Louis Armstrong. As a noun, *jive* has several meanings: it refers to loose, misleading talk or conversation and was a kind of dance associated with jazz in the 1930s. As a verb, it may mean "to mislead, kid, or taunt" or "to dance the jive."

Jive is occasionally used for *jibe* in American English, but is not considered acceptable. Two versions of a story should jibe (not jive) with the facts. In our 2004 survey, 93 percent of the Usage Panel rejected this use of *jive*.

girl / woman

The word *girl* should almost always be reserved for female children and teenagers under the age of eighteen in formal speaking and writing. The use of *girl* to describe an adult is offensive to many people and is always unacceptable as a reference to a female servant or employee, such as a secretary. In contrast, the word *woman* is an acceptable way to refer to any adult female.

An exception is when women are referring to themselves, as in this Minneapolis newspaper: . . . *there are times when some of us moms don't need a night out with the girls, or an afternoon in the shops, or even the luxury of taking a long, hot bath without any interruptions. Girl* is also generally considered to be an acceptable description of a daughter of any age, as in "our eldest girl." Some people condone its use in describing a very young woman, or in certain conventionalized or informal uses, as in *country girl,* indicating how a woman's place of childhood affects her outlook, and *my girl,* describing a female romantic interest. These expressions may be offensive to other people, however, and should therefore be used with caution.

glamour

The spelling of *glamour* makes it an exception to the usual American pattern of ending words in *–or* instead of *–our,* as is customary in British English. Witness *honor, vapor,* and *labor.* The related adjective is usually spelled *glamorous* in both American and British English.

go

Go has long been used to describe the production of nonlinguistic noises, notably in conversation with children, as in *The train went "toot," The cow goes "moo."* In recent years, however, many speakers have begun to use *go* in informal conversation to report speech, as in *Then he goes, "You think you're real smart, don't you?"* This usage parallels the quotation introducers *be all* and *be like* (as in *He's all* [or *He's like*], *'There's no way I'm paying for your parking ticket'*). But unlike these other expressions, which can also indicate thoughts or attitudes, the quotational use of *go* is largely restricted to dialogue related in the narrative present, especially when the narrator wishes to mimic the accent or intonation of the original speaker.

See more at **all** and **like.**

good   See **well.**

got / gotten

The notion that *gotten* is an illegitimate "nonword" has been around for over two hundred years and refuses to die. The word itself is much older than the criticism against it. As past participles of *get,* both *got* and *gotten* go back to the Middle Ages. In American English, *have got* is chiefly an intensive form of *have* in its senses of possession and obligation and can only be used in the present tense: *I have got three tickets to the game. We have got to improve our teamwork if we want to succeed. Gotten* sees regular use as a variant past participle of *get* and can occur in a variety of past and perfect tenses: *Had she gotten the car when you saw her? I would not have gotten sick if I had stayed home.* In Britain, *gotten* has mostly fallen out of use.

There are subtle distinctions in meaning between the two forms. *Got* often implies current possession, where *gotten* usually suggests the process of obtaining. Accordingly, *I haven't got any money* suggests that one is broke, while *I haven't gotten any money* suggests that one hasn't been paid. This sense of process or progression applies to many other uses of *gotten,* and in some of these cases *got* just doesn't sound as natural to the American ear: *The bridge has gotten weaker since the storm. We have finally gotten used to the new software. Mice have gotten into the basement.*

Remember that only *got* can be used to express obligation, as in *I've got to go to Chicago.* The sentence *I have gotten to go to Chicago* implies that the person has had the opportunity or been given permission to go.

See more at **get** and **have.**

gourmet / gourmand / epicure

A *gourmet* is a person with discriminating taste in food and wine, as is a *gourmand.* But a *gourmand* can also be someone who enjoys food in great quantities. An *epicure* is pretty much the same as a *gourmet,* but the word may carry overtones of excessive refinement. (This use of *epicure* is a deliberate misrepresentation of Epicurean philosophy, which, while it professed that pleasure was the highest good, was hardly given to excessive concern with food and drink. It was concerned rather with personal happiness and freedom from pain. But rival schools of philosophy were offended by Epicurus's doctrine of pleasure and distorted the ideas of his school.)

government

In American usage, *government* always takes a singular verb. In British usage, *government,* in the sense of a governing group of officials, takes a plural verb: *The government are determined to follow this course.*

See more at **collective noun.**

governor

Standard pronunciations for this word include (gŭv′ər-nər), (gŭv′ə-nər), and (gŭv′nər). The second of these has lost an r through *dissimilation,* a phonological process that involves the change or loss of one of two similar or identical sounds in a word in order to avoid a repetition of that sound.

See more at **dissimilation.**

graduate

The verb *graduate* has denoted the action of conferring an academic degree or diploma since at least 1421. Accordingly, the action of receiving a degree should be expressed in the passive, as in *They were graduated from Yale in 2004.* This usage is still current, if slightly old-fashioned. In our 1988 survey, 78 percent of the Usage Panel accepted it. In general usage, however, the older transitive sense has largely yielded to the more recent intransitive sense "to receive a degree" (first attested in 1807): *They graduated from Yale in 2004.* In 1988, 89 percent of the Panel accepted this use, which ascribes the accomplishment to a student or group of students rather than to the institution. When the institution's accomplishment is emphasized, however, the older sense is preferable, as in *The university graduated more computer science majors in 2000 than in the entire previous decade.*

The Usage Panel feels quite differently about the use of *graduate* to mean "to receive a degree from," as in *She graduated Yale in 1980.* Fully 77 percent objected to this usage.

graffiti / graffito

The word *graffiti* is a plural noun in Italian, and in English it is far more common than the singular form *graffito.* The plural form *graffiti* is often used as a singular, too. When the reference is to a particular inscription (as in *There was a bold graffiti on the wall*), the *graffito* is technically correct but might strike some readers as peculiar or pedantic outside an archaeological context, much as the singular *biscotto* (for an individual cookie) strikes English speakers as odd, even though it is the singular of Italian *biscotti.*

There is no substitute for the singular use of *graffiti* when the word is used as a mass noun to refer to inscriptions in general or to related social phenomena. Thus, the sentence *Graffiti is a major problem for the Transit Authority Police* cannot be reworded *Graffito is . . .* since *graffito* can refer only to a particular inscription. Similarly, one cannot say *Graffiti are . . .* , which suggests that the police problem involves only the physical marks and not the larger issue of vandalism. In such contexts, the use of *graffiti* as a singular is justified by its usefulness. When the context calls for referring to an individual inscription, and the writer wishes to avoid the rare form *graffito,* the phrase *a piece of graffiti* is sometimes used.

grammar

The term *grammar* has a number of meanings. In linguistics, grammar is the system of rules that allows the speakers of a language to create meaningful and comprehensible sentences. A grammar has rules that govern how sounds can be combined, how words can be formed, what order the words can follow, and how they can be inflected (that is, altered in structure, especially in their endings) to indicate different functions in a sentence. If a language was a random collection of sounds without rules, no speaker could understand another. In this regard, all languages and dialects have grammars—systems of rules that make communication possible—and the notion of "good" and "bad" grammar is meaningless.

Grammar also refers to a set of rules and prescriptions that set forth the current standards or norms of usage in a language. Thus a person learning English as a second language is taught that correct English grammar requires *are* in the sentence *They are working,* and that sentences such as *They is working* and *They working* are incorrect, even though these sentences may occur regularly in some varieties of English. Sometimes the word *grammar* is used to refer to words in relation to this norm of usage. In this sense, a speaker may be said to have or use "good" or "poor" grammar.

grieve

Traditionally, when used as a transitive verb meaning "to cause to be sorrowful; distress," *grieve* has taken as its direct object the person who is sorrowful or distressed, as in *It grieves me to see so many homeless in the city.* More recently, an additional usage has developed, in which the direct object refers to that which causes sorrow or distress, as in *She took a week off to attend her father's funeral and grieve his loss.* In our 1996 survey, 62 percent of the Usage Panel approved of this usage in this sentence.

grievous

The pronunciation (grē′vē-əs), with three syllables, is considered nonstandard. It is an example of *intrusion,* a phonological process that involves the addition or insertion of an extra sound. The standard pronunciation of *grievous* has only two syllables, (grē′vəs).

See more at **intrusion.**

grisly / grizzly

It could be the image of a certain North American mammal that results in the confusion of these two words. *Grisly* means "horrible, gruesome, inspiring repugnance," while *grizzly* means "grayish or flecked with gray." *Grizzly* may also be a noun referring to a subspecies of bear, the *grizzly bear* or *silvertip,* named for the coloration of its fur. Perhaps the bear's reputation for ferociousness has led us to associate the word *grizzly* with its sound-alike *grisly,* though it should be noted that grizzly bears normally avoid human beings and rarely attack them.

grow

The word *grow* has been used since medieval times as an intransitive verb meaning "to increase in size, quantity, or degree," as in *Our business has been growing steadily for three years.* It has been used with an object since the 18th century, meaning "to produce or cultivate," as in *We grow beans and corn in our garden.* But the transitive use applied to nonliving things, often in reference to politics or business, is relatively recent, as in this newspaper quotation: *"'Brewing here is an option, but first we will need to grow our business so that our volume can sustain our minimum brewing requirements,' he said" (St. Louis Post-Dispatch).* Although 80 percent of the Usage Panel in our 1994 survey rejected the phrase *grow our business* and only 48 percent accepted *We will need to grow our way out of this recession,* these usages are becoming increasingly common and are likely to see continued use in business contexts.

gunwale

Like *boatswain* and *forecastle,* this nautical word has a pronunciation, (gŭn′əl), that is not easily predictable from the spelling. Note that although *gunwale* is the usual spelling, the word is always pronounced (gŭn′əl). The variant spelling *gunnel,* which reflects the pronunciation, has been used for several hundred years and is also acceptable, but it may suggest that the writer is a landlubber. Other nautical words with tricky pronunciations include *bowline, mainsail,* and *topgallant,* to name just a few.
     See more at **pronunciation spelling** and **spelling pronunciation.**

guy / gal

Used in the singular, *guy* is an informal noun that refers to a man or boy. A comparable word for a female is the equally informal word *gal,* though this word is less common. But while *gals* refers only to a group of females, *guys* is used to refer to a group of males, to a mixed group of males and females, or to a group of females.
     The collocation *you guys* arose in the northern United States in part as a way of differentiating the singular pronoun *you* from its identical plural form, serving much the same function as *you-all* or *y'all* in the American South. *You guys* has spread broadly throughout the country.

gybe   See **gibe.**

Gypsy   See **Roma.**

· H ·

h

The letter *h* comes from the Roman alphabet. In Old English *h* represented the sound (h) at the beginning of words and before vowels, although in Middle English *h* "weakened" somewhat and was often silent before vowels in unstressed syllables. In Modern English, *h* is usually pronounced in native English words such as *happy* and *hot*. During the development of Latin in classical times, the (h) sound originally heard in Latin disappeared, although the letter continued to be used in the Latin spelling system. Thus, in many of the Romance languages, which are the descendants of Latin, *h* is silent in words of Latin origin even though the letter is retained in the spelling. When English borrowed words from French, a Romance language, it also borrowed the spellings with silent *h*. In a few of these words borrowed from French, the *h* has remained silent, as in *honor, honest, hour,* and *heir*. But in other words borrowed from French, an (h) sound has been reintroduced into the pronunciation because of the influence of writing, as in the word *hotel*. In British English, (h) has also been reintroduced in the pronunciation of the word *herb*, and in this case the American pronunciation without (h) is actually the original form. To further complicate matters, words that begin with the sounds (hyo͞o) in many English dialects (such as *huge, human,* and *humor*) often begin simply (yo͞o) in other English dialects.

had better

Had better is an idiomatic verb phrase meaning "ought to, must." It resembles an auxiliary verb in that its form never changes to show person or tense and that it can't follow another verb in a phrase (that is, sentences like *He will had better leave* are impossible in English).

When speaking, people have a tendency to leave out *had: You better clean up your room!* But in writing, *had* should be kept either in full or as a contraction: *We had better revise the proposal* or *We'd better revise the proposal.*

See more at **rather** and **subjunctive**.

had have / 'd have / had've / had of   See under **subjunctive**.

had rather   See **rather**.

Haitian

In English, the (t) sound of *Haiti* becomes a (sh) sound in the word *Haitian* (hā′shən). *Haitian* is sometimes pronounced with three syllables as (hā′tē-ən). In our 2002 survey, 82 percent of the Usage Panel disapproved of this pronunciation.

half

The phrases *a half, half of,* and *half a* or *half an* are all correct, though they may differ slightly in meaning. For example, *a half day* is used when *day* has the special sense "a working day," and the phrase then means "four hours." *Half of a day* and *half a day* are not restricted in this way and can mean either four or twelve hours.

handicap / handicapped

In recent years *handicap* and *handicapped* have lost ground to *disability* and *disabled* in referring to physical or mental impairments. To many, *handicap* sounds outdated now, reminiscent of a time before people with disabilities had begun to assert their civil rights and increase their visibility in society. It is also sometimes held to imply a helplessness that is not suggested by the more forthright *disability,* a stigma that may have developed from a mistaken belief that the original phrase *hand in cap* referred to a beggar holding out a cap to collect coins (though that would more logically come from *cap in hand*). In fact, *hand in cap* (or *hand i' cap*) was a 17th-century game of chance in which participants drew items from a cap. A later sense, still in use today, refers to an advantage or compensation given to different contestants to equalize the chances of winning. By its nature, a sports handicap implies competitiveness, not helplessness, and a contestant who loses with a handicap has the satisfaction of knowing that under other circumstances the outcome might well have been different. In contrast a *disability,* strictly speaking, is a condition that makes performance not just more difficult but impossible. But logic is one thing, and respect for a group's preferences is another; the clear choices today are *disability* and *disabled.*

While *handicapped* is now likely to cause offense when used as a noun, as in *programs designed for the handicapped,* or as an adjective referring directly to a person, it is still quite common as a modifier in phrases such as *handicapped parking* or *handicapped accessible.* These phrases, which are frequently formed with *handicap* as well, may have retained their currency out of familiarity, or it may be that people construe them loosely as acknowledging that an inaccessible building or website represents a handicap, not a disability, to those trying to use it. Whatever the reason, *disabled accessible* is far less common in electronic searches than either *handicap accessible* or *handicapped accessible.*

See more at **disabled.**

hanged / hung

In edited prose, *hanged* is used as the past tense and past participle of *hang* in the sense of "to execute by suspending by the neck," as in *Frontier courts hanged many a prisoner after a summary trial.* In all other senses of the word, *hung* is the preferred form as past tense and past participle, as in *I hung my children's picture above my desk.* This applies to the various phrasal verbs and idioms that are made with *hang: hang around, hang on, hang out,* and so on. They all form their past tense as *hung.* The idiom *hang someone out to dry* meaning "to leave someone in a difficult position," is included in this pattern because it is a laundry metaphor.

harass

The pronunciation with stress on the first syllable is the older, traditional pronunciation, and is the one still recommended by some, notably British, usage guides. The pronunciation with stress on the second syllable is a newer pronunciation that first occurred in American English. Its use has steadily increased since the middle of the 20th century. In our 1987 survey, 50 percent of the Usage Panel preferred the pronunciation with stress on the first syllable, and 50 percent preferred stress on the second syllable. Only fourteen years later in our 2001 survey, 70 percent preferred the pronunciation with the stress on the second syllable, and 30 percent preferred stress on the first syllable.

Note that *harass* and *harassment* each have only one *r.* These words are frequently misspelled with two *r*'s.

hardly

Adverbs like *hardly, scarcely, barely,* and *rarely* carry both a negative and positive meaning. They can be said to be negatives in that they minimize the state or event they describe, and in Standard English, they cannot be used with another negative. It is not acceptable to say *I couldn't hardly see him* and *We barely never went there.*

Nonetheless *hardly* and its companion adverbs are different from thoroughgoing negatives like *not* and *never.* Thus *hardly* means "almost not at all"; *rarely* means "practically never"; and so forth. The minimized activity or condition that these words delineate still exists in some form or other. The sentence *Mary hardly laughed at all* means that Mary did laugh a little, unlike *Mary didn't laugh at all.*

Even though adverbs like *hardly* and *scarcely* may not have a purely negative meaning, they share some important features of negative adverbs. They combine with *any* and *at all,* which are characteristically associated with negative contexts. Thus we say *I hardly saw him at all* or *I never saw him at all* but not *I occasionally saw him at all.* Similarly, we say *I hardly had any time* or *I didn't have any time* but not *I had any time,* and so on.

Like *not* and other purely negative adverbs, *hardly, scarcely,* and their companions cause inversion of the subject and auxiliary verb when they begin a sentence. Thus we can say *Hardly had I arrived when she left* on the pattern of *Never have I read such a book* or *At no time has he condemned the policy.* Other adverbs do not cause this kind of inversion. English grammar does not permit sentences like *Occasionally has he addressed this question* and *To a slight degree have they changed their position.*

hardly . . . than   Some usage commentators ban the use of *hardly* and other minimizers with *than,* as in *Hardly had we sat down to eat than he got up and left.* While this can hardly be cited as a serious blunder, it is easily avoided by using *when* or *before* instead of *than.*

See more at **double negative, rarely ever,** and **scarcely.**

harebrained / hairbrained

Harebrained means "having or showing no more sense than a hare." It is a well-established word that dates to 1548. The spelling *hairbrained* also goes back to the 1500s, when *hair* was a variant spelling of *hare,* and was preserved in Scotland into the 18th century. Although it is considered incorrect today in Standard English, *hairbrained* continues to make frequent appearances in print, as in this movie review from a Canadian newspaper: *"I thought that some scenes were overdone and a bit unrealistic. For instance, along the way they pick up a travelling Gypsy girl, who begins to scare them, so the kids all pile into the front seat. The movie gets a bit hairbrained after that and dips and dives all over the place."*

harelip

The term *harelip* refers to the congenital condition of having a cleft upper lip; this word is no longer in medical use and is often considered offensive. The word was derived from resemblance between the shape of such a lip and that of the upper lip of a hare. The spelling *hairlip* is incorrect.

hark back / hearken back / harken back / harp back

The phrases *hark back* and *hearken back* (along with its variant *harken back*) mean the same thing: "to return to or remind one of a previous point in time, as in a narrative." These phrases are used correctly in the following examples: *The show harks back to the days when expectations were lower, and people were less cynical. Some modern symphonies hark back to the works of the last century. The design of the new car hearkens back to the sleek muscle cars of the 1960s.* The phrase *harp back* is an error. The confusion may arise because people who harp on something may be given to telling anecdotes about, and so harking back to, their past.

harpy   See **shrew.**

harridan   See **shrew.**

have

have / of   The auxiliary verb *have* is commonly miswritten as *of* in many verbal phrases like *could have, would have, should have,* and *might have: could of, would of, should of,* and *might of.* It is easy to see why. *Have* is usually pronounced (əv) or (ə) in everyday speech, and this phonetic reduction is often spelled *'ve* in standard contractions like *would've.* The preposition *of* is also pronounced both as (əv) and (ə), so these two words are often sound-alikes. *Of* is sometimes rendered as *o'* or just *a* in representations of colloquial speech, as in *a whole lotta shakin' goin' on.* Consequently, writers should be on guard against making this careless mistake, especially since the spelling of *'ve* as *of* is sometimes used in fiction to represent everyday speech: *I could of made somethin' of myself.*

have to / have got to   The verb phrases *have to* and *have got to* express necessity and obligation. They differ subtly in meaning from the auxiliary verb *must.* While all of these verbs can be used to express a command or warning (*You have got to leave now, You must not shout*), *have to* and *have got to* are somewhat more forceful than *must* in expressing necessity. *There has* [or *has got*] *to be some mistake* conveys a bit more emphasis than *There must be some mistake.* Only *have to* can form verb phrases with *may, be,* and *have.* Standard English permits *I may have to go* but not *I may have got to go.* Similarly, we can say *You are having to do a lot more work these days* but not *You are having got to . . .* And we can say *The town has had to repave its main road* but not *The town has had got to . . .* In spoken English people often drop the *have* from *have got to,* as in *We got to get up early.* But in formal writing *got to* without *have* is not ordinarily considered acceptable.

See more at **auxiliary and primary verbs** and **subjunctive.**

having said that / having said this

Like the adverbs *however* and *nonetheless, having said that* and similar phrases are often used to provide a transition from one set of remarks that are conceded to be true to another set of remarks that tend to qualify the first. These "having said" phrases share the same function as absolute constructions like *that having been said* and *that said.*

But *having said that* and *having said this* are not absolute constructions, at least by the traditional grammatical definition, and so they should properly be followed by the word they modify, a personal subject responsible for what is being said, as in *Having said that, I think it's only wise to be cautious* or *Having said that, he then conceded that the situation was more serious than he had thought.* In this regard a phrase like *having said that* might be interpreted as being just another part of a narrative, and is not making a concession about the following statement, as in *Having said that, he then walked out of the room,* where the meaning is more like "after saying that" or "once that was said." To avoid the implication of narrative, highlight the concession more clearly by using a phrase like *in spite of that.*

When the subject of the sentence is not a person, constructions like *having said that* may be viewed as dangling modifiers and may therefore be considered mistakes.

Consider this example from a website on teaching English as a foreign language, where using an adverb like *still* or *nonetheless* would be unassailably grammatical:

> Indeed, if you are teaching a class of students who have ten different mother tongues, as is not impossible, even your fluency in say three foreign languages would have little relevance. The ability, therefore, to speak a foreign language is not a requirement for teaching English. Having said that, some experience of learning and speaking a foreign language will help you understand language in general and how we learn it, as well as help you learn more about English—especially English grammar—itself.

The Usage Panel takes a dim view of these constructions. In our 2002 survey, only 18 percent accepted *having said this* in a similar example.

See more at **absolute constructions, dangling modifiers,** and **that having been said.**

he / she

he as generic pronoun   English has traditionally used the pronouns *he, him,* and *his* as generic or gender-neutral singular pronouns to refer to both males and females, as in *A novelist should write about what he knows best* and *No one seems to take any pride in his work anymore.* While some consider this generic use of masculine pronouns to be simply an efficient grammatical convention that is not inherently offensive, many others consider this usage to be sexist, comparable to using *man* to refer to both men and women.

ways of avoiding generic *he*   There are several ways that writers avoid generic *he* if they are concerned about offending readers. Some simply use the feminine pronoun *she* as the standard usage. This is often the case in academic writing:

> Just as a lawmaking body is entitled to declare how certain of its words are to be taken, a speaker of English can sometimes assert a degree of authority over her own language use, at least for limited purposes. Thus someone who writes a book or makes a scholarly presentation could declare that when she uses the term *convention,* she is doing so in a very specific sense (Peter Tiersma, *Legal Language*)

Using *she* in this way still carries an air of unconventionality, at least in mainstream publications, but it clearly illuminates the difficulty of passing off gender-specific pronouns as gender-neutral. Other writers switch between *he* and *she* in alternating sentences, paragraphs, or chapters. Although it can become cumbersome, this approach offers a balanced way of proceeding.

Compound and coordinate forms such as *he/she, she/he, he or she, her or him* are sometimes used in place of *he,* and these work well in isolated sentences but are unwieldy when used in a sustained fashion. The neutral articles *a, an,* and *the* can also work well when context allows: *Every student handed in an assignment. A child who develops this sort of rash on the hands should probably be kept at home for a couple of days.* Sometimes the pronoun can simply be eliminated with no loss in meaning or accuracy, as in the sentence *A writer who draws on personal experience for (his) material should not be surprised if the reviewers seize on that fact.*

Perhaps the easiest and most effective alternative to generic *he* is to rewrite the sentence in the plural form, using *they*. Thus, *Each student handed in his assignment* becomes *All of the students handed in their assignments*. Some writers use the third-person plural pronouns *they, them, themselves,* and *their* to refer to singular antecedents such as *one, a person, an individual,* and *each*. Distinguished writers have used this construction since the 1300s, as Thackeray does in *Vanity Fair: A person can't help their birth*. Other writers avoid it, however, giving more weight to conventional grammatical rules of subject-verb agreement. The Usage Panel values these rules, at least in formal writing. In our 1996 survey, while 60 percent said that they had used sentences such as *Someone has lost their gloves* and *A person at that level should not have to keep track of the hours they put in,* 80 percent considered such usages to be errors, and only 16 percent said they would use them in formal contexts such as news reports or scholarly articles. Fully 70 percent, however, thought that these sentences were permissible in informal contexts.

Another way to avoid *he* is to replace it with a noun or an indefinite pronoun, such as *one, someone,* or *anyone*. Thus, *He who is late won't be able to ski* can be written as *Anyone who is late won't be able to ski* or *The people who are late won't be able to ski*. Some sentences can also be rewritten in the second person, although this usage usually imparts an informal tone: *If you are late, you won't be able to ski*.

she referring to inanimate objects The feminine pronoun forms *she* and *her* have been used since the Middle Ages to refer to such inanimate objects as the earth, the sea, and ships. The use in reference to ships still occurs in nautical contexts:

> The biggest rogue [wave] on record was during a Pacific gale in 1933, when the 478-foot Navy tanker *Ramapo* was on her way from Manila to San Diego. She encountered a massive low-pressure system that blew up to sixty-eight knots for a week straight and resulted in a fully developed sea that the *Ramapo* had no choice but to take on her stern (Sebastian Junger, *The Perfect Storm*)

She and *her* have also been used to refer to female personifications of nations and cities, where they once evoked loyalty, but today they tend to have an archaic feel or to hark back to an earlier era, as in

> . . . the efforts of others to win British passports for the majority of Hong Kong residents failed. Britain was happy to include them within her Empire but not her nation (Nisid Hajari, "A Most Dignified Retreat," *Time*)

The practice is sometimes extended to other kinds of groups or organizations, as in

> If NASA and her sister space agencies eventually send a manned mission to Mars, they will need to know more about the physics of the magnetosphere in order to protect astronauts who might fly through a deadly maelstrom of high radiation, principally alpha particles and x-rays (Bruce Dorminey, "In the Forecast: A Space-Weather Service," *Boston Globe*)

Referring to objects or abstractions as feminine may have originated in, and was certainly encouraged by, reference to words that were grammatically feminine in the language from which they had been translated. Thus, the soul was sometimes conceived as female, at least in part because it is a feminine noun in Latin (*anima*). A further influence was the personification of certain objects, such as the moon, and certain ideas, such as fortune or philosophy, as goddesses by ancient writers.

Whatever the full story of its origin, some writers still observe this usage today, especially informally to express a sense of intimacy in reference to close or important personal possessions such as cars and musical instruments. But many people object to this practice because it seems to ascribe stereotypically feminine characteristics to these entities and because the absence of masculine personification seems sexist. These objections contributed to the decision by the National Weather Service to discontinue its practice of identifying hurricanes solely by women's names.

See more at **pronouns, personal.**

head

A head is the word in a construction that has the same grammatical function as the construction as a whole and that determines relationships of agreement to other parts of the construction or sentence. Thus the word *variety* is the head of the phrase *a wide variety of gardening tools* in the sentence *You can buy a wide variety of gardening tools at that store.*

headquarters

The noun *headquarters* can be used as either a singular or a plural verb. The plural is more common: *The corporation's headquarters are in Boston.* But when referring to authority rather than physical location, many people prefer the singular: *Division headquarters has approved the new benefits package.*

healthful / healthy

Some people maintain a distinction between these words. In this view, *healthful* means "conducive to good health" and is applied to things that promote health, while *healthy* means "possessing good health," and is applied solely to people and other organisms. Accordingly, healthy people have healthful habits. However, *healthy* has been used to mean "healthful" since the 16th century, as in this example from John Locke's *Some Thoughts Concerning Education*: "*Gardening . . . and working in wood, are fit and healthy recreations for a man of study or business.*" In fact, the word *healthy* is far more common than *healthful* when modifying words like *diet, exercise,* and *foods,* and *healthy* may strike many readers as more natural in many contexts. Certainly, both *healthy* and *healthful* must be considered standard in describing that which promotes health.

heat / temperature

Heat and *temperature* represent two different but related properties of matter. *Heat* is related to the entire energy transferred to or from a quantity of matter, adding up the kinetic and potential energies of the particles (atoms or molecules) of which the matter is composed. Kinetic energy is the energy associated with the motion of each particle of matter, while potential energy is the energy stored in a particle as a result of its position or condition, as opposed to its motion. Note that there are no restrictions on the kinds of energy that can be heat. Chemical reactions may generate or absorb heat, as energy is lost to or freed from bonds between atoms. Nuclear reactions also generate or absorb heat, as energy is lost to or freed from the bonds between protons and neutrons in the nuclei of atoms.

Temperature, on the other hand, is related to the average kinetic energy per molecular or atomic constituent. Note that two qualifiers are included in this statement: temperature is related to the kinetic energy only; and temperature describes an average property per constituent particle. Consider a large kettle of boiling water. If you measure the temperature of the water, you will find that it is 100°C. Suppose that you capture the steam that is rising off the surface of the kettle and measure its temperature. You will find that the temperature of the steam is also 100°C. Even though the temperature of the steam and that of the water are identical, the average energy content per molecule of each is different. The molecules of water in the steam are at a higher potential energy than the molecules of water in the liquid water, since additional energy is needed to overcome the molecular attraction that binds water molecules together in liquid form. For this reason, being burned by steam at 100°C is more damaging than being burned by water at the same temperature. The kinetic energy of the molecules is the same, but the potential energy of the steam is higher. Temperature is related to the kinetic energy only.

Now consider a large kettle of water and a small teapot of water. Suppose that the small teapot has one fourth the volume of the large kettle. Starting from the same temperature, it takes more energy to boil the large kettle of water than it takes to boil the small teapot of water. For every molecule of water in the small teapot that has an increase in kinetic energy, there are four molecules in the large kettle that require the same average increase in kinetic energy. It requires four times as much energy, and therefore four times as much heat, to raise the water in the large kettle to the same temperature as that of the water in the small teapot. Thus, *heat* is a measure of total energy transfer, while *temperature* is an average property per molecule or atom.

See more at **energy, kinetic energy.**

hegemony

Although this word may be pronounced (hĭ-jĕm′ə-nē), with stress on the second syllable, or (hĕj′ə-mō′nē), with stress on the first syllable, in our 1988 survey, a clear majority of the Usage Panel, 72 percent, preferred the first pronunciation.

height

Although many people pronounce this word with a final *th* as in the word *eighth,* the pronunciation (hīt) is still considered the only standard pronunciation by most dictionaries. In fact, in our 1997 survey, 90 percent of the Usage Panel disapproved of the *th* pronunciation.

heinous

The first syllable of this word normally rhymes with *mane,* and this pronunciation was preferred by 87 percent of the Usage Panel in our 1999 survey. *Heinous* is sometimes pronounced so that the first syllable rhymes with *me.* One third of the Panel found this pronunciation acceptable.

help

can help   The verb *help* is sometimes used in the sense conveyed in the sentence *Don't change it any more than you can help* (that is, "any more than you have to"). The expression is a well-established idiom.

cannot help / cannot help but   For a discussion of these expressions, see **cannot.**

helping verbs   See **auxiliary and primary verbs.**

helpmeet / helpmate

These two words are synonyms meaning "a helper and companion, especially a spouse." Although both are correct in Standard English, their existence is the result of an error compounded. God's promise to Adam in Genesis 2:18, as rendered in the King James Version of the Bible (1611), was to give him *an help* [helper] *meet* [fit or suitable] *for him.* The poet John Dryden's 1673 use of the phrase *help-meet for man,* with a hyphen between *help* and *meet,* was the first step toward the establishment of the phrase *help meet* as an independent word. *Help meet,* without *for man,* then came to mean "a suitable helper," who was usually a spouse, as Eve had been to Adam. Despite such usages, *helpmeet* was not usually used as a word in its own right until the 19th century. The phrase *help meet* probably played a role in the creation of *helpmate,* from *help* and *mate,* first recorded in 1715.

hence / thence / whence

These adverbs are rare in spoken English but used somewhat more frequently in writing, to which they impart a decidedly formal tone. The basic meaning of *hence* is "from here," though the spatial sense is almost never used nowadays. A temporal meaning, "from now" or "from a certain point in time," is common enough in published works:

> And perhaps, who could say how many ages hence, there would be in their descendants not even this gesture of remembrance for the sea (Rachel Carson, "The Marginal World," *The Edge of the Sea*)

By far the most common use of *hence* is to mean "for that reason, therefore," and this use makes it the most common of all three words in contemporary English:

There is great survival value, for the individual and hence for the species, in avoiding the predictable, in scrambling the patterns to which predators could become too precisely attuned (David M. Carroll, *Swampwalker's Journal*)

Thence means "from there" and "from then." Unlike *hence*, it is used predominantly with a spatial meaning:

George Freeth's real legacy, though, is his vigorous, silent life: the introducing, by glamorous example, of surfing into Southern California, and thence to the world . . . (Ian Whitcomb, "Beach Boy," *American Heritage*)

Whence means "from where," and it is also used in spatial contexts:

In the early seventeenth century Cossack explorers first reached the banks of the Lena and established the *ostrog*, or stockade town, of Ust' Kut, whence they made a trip downstream into eastern Siberia, on log rafts, and built another *ostrog* at Yakutsk (Jeffrey Tayler, "White Nights in Siberia," *Atlantic Monthly*)

It is also common in figurative contexts indicating a source or origin:

Not many of more than minimal education and pretense get through life without adverting at some time or other to "conspicuous consumption," "pecuniary emulation" or "conspicuous waste," even though they may not know whence these phrases came (John Kenneth Galbraith, "Who Was Thorstein Veblen?" *Annals of an Abiding Liberal*)

These words are sometimes used in the phrases *from hence, from thence,* and *from whence,* and strictly speaking, these are redundant, since the preposition *from* is implicit in the meanings of the adverbs. Yet these phrases have a long history of distinguished use, notably in earlier times when people did not make a fuss about redundancy, as the following sampler will demonstrate. First, *from hence:*

But if you fail, without more speech, my lord,
You must be gone from hence immediately (Shakespeare, *The Merchant of Venice* 2.9.8–9)

But granting that the conqueror, in a just war, has a right to the estates, as well as power over the persons of the conquered, which, it is plain, he hath not, nothing of absolute power will follow from hence in the continuance of the government (John Locke, *Of Civil Government*)

Sollicitations, which cannot be directly refused, oblige me to trouble you often with letters recommending and introducing to you persons who go from hence [Paris] to America (Thomas Jefferson, Letter to James Madison, *The Jeffersonian Cyclopedia*)

The schoolhouse stood in a rather lonely but pleasant situation, just at the foot of a woody hill, with a brook running close by . . . From hence the low murmur of his pupils' voices, conning over their lessons, might be heard in a drowsy summer's day, like the hum of a beehive . . . (Washington Irving, *The Legend of Sleepy Hollow*)

Next, *from thence:*

Then crush this herb into Lysander's eye;
Whose liquor hath this virtuous property,
To take from thence all error with his might,
And make his eyeballs roll with wonted sight (Shakespeare, *A Midsummer Night's Dream* 3.2.366–369)

. . . but taking my leave of them, I went from thence into Macedonia (*King James Bible,* 2 Corinthians 2:13)

Without saying a word, Queequeg, in his wild sort of way, jumped upon the bulwarks, from thence into the bows of one of the whale-boats hanging to the side (Herman Melville, *Moby Dick*)

What was Oliver's horror and alarm as he stood a few paces off, looking on with his eyelids as wide open as they would possibly go, to see the Dodger plunge his hand into the old gentleman's pocket, and draw from thence a handkerchief! (Charles Dickens, *Oliver Twist*)

Finally, *from whence:*

I will lift up mine eyes unto the hills, from whence cometh my help (*King James Bible,* Psalms 121:1)

I know from whence this same device proceeds (Shakespeare, *Titus Andronicus* 4.4.52)

. . . first, Hell,
Your dungeon, stretching far and wide beneath;
Now lately Heaven and Earth, another world
Hung o'er my Realm, linked in a golden chain
To that side Heaven from whence your legions fell (John Milton, *Paradise Lost* 2.1002–1006)

Elizabeth was at no loss to understand from whence this deference for her authority proceeded (Jane Austen, *Pride and Prejudice*)

The same strong susceptibilities which make the personal impulses vivid and powerful, are also the source from whence are generated the most passionate love of virtue, and the sternest self-control (John Stuart Mill, *Essay on Liberty*)

Of those who knew him intimately, not one in twenty were aware from whence he came, what was his parentage, or what his means of living (Anthony Trollope, *Phineas Finn*)

Of these, only *from whence* sees some use today, notably in the construction *from whence . . . came:*

By now, the Western Hemisphere was supposed to be well on its way to energy independence. Oil from Mexico, Venezuela and Colombia was supposed to be pouring into U.S. refineries, sating our demand while boosting the emerging economies from whence it came (*Houston Chronicle*)

Until the end, when he recedes from us completely, locked away, speechless, returned to the distant state of idiocy from whence he came, his is the sensibility through which we perceive everything that happens (Wendy Lesser, *Nothing Remains the Same*)

her See **he / she** and **pronouns, personal.**

herb

In British English this word and its derivatives, such as *herbaceous, herbal, herbicide,* and *herbivore,* are pronounced with *h.* In American English the situation is not as simple. *Herb* and *herbal* are more often pronounced (ûrb) and (ûr′bəl) than (hûrb) and (hûr′bəl), and the opposite is true of *herbaceous, herbicide,* and *herbivore,* which are all more often pronounced with the *h.*

See more at **h.**

hermaphrodite See **intersex.**

hero / heroine

The word *hero,* previously restricted to males, is now widely considered to be a gender-neutral term. It is used to refer to admired women as well as men, as in this quotation from the *Washington Post:* "*Already a national hero in her economically troubled South Korea, . . . [Se Ri] Pak is packing galleries at [golf] tournaments stateside.*" The word *heroine* is still acceptable, however, and is used routinely in accordance with literary convention to refer to the principal female character of a fictional work such as a novel or a dramatic production, as in *Jane Eyre is a well-known literary heroine.*

hew / hue

The verb *hew,* meaning "to make, shape, or cut down with or as if with an axe," is occasionally used mistakenly in the phrase *hew and cry,* which is properly *hue and cry,* an expression used mostly to describe a public outcry. The mistake is understandable, since the word *hue* as used in this expression means "an uproar or shout," and this word has dropped out of use in Standard English except in this phrase. The word *hue* we know today, meaning "gradations, or a particular gradation, of color," is an unrelated word.

hijack / carjack

The object of the verb *hijack* is properly something stolen, seized, or taken control of: *The plane was hijacked and flown across the border.* The use of *hijack* to refer to any seizure of control of a vehicle from someone, as in *Someone hijacked me in my own car last night,* in which the object of *hijack* is the human victim rather than the thing seized, is considered by some to be incorrect. But this usage is becoming increasingly common. More generally, *hijack* is now used to describe any situation in which control is suddenly usurped or undermined.

Perhaps owing to this extended usage, the word *carjack* has also come into existence, meaning "to steal a car from someone who is driving it." The presence of a victim in the car is essential to this meaning, since otherwise the car would simply be considered stolen. The object of *carjack* is usually the driver (and possibly the passengers) of the car: *Someone in a ski mask carjacked my uncle on this street yesterday.*

The variant *highjack* for *hijack*, perhaps influenced by the common use of the word to describe the takeover of airplanes flying high in the sky, is becoming increasingly common, though occasional usage critics reject it.

Hispanic

Hispanic and *Latino* are both widely used in American English in referring to a person of Spanish-language heritage living in the United States. Though often used interchangeably, they are not identical, and in certain contexts their differences can be significant. *Hispanic,* from the Latin word for "Spain," is the broader term, potentially encompassing all Spanish-speaking peoples in both hemispheres and emphasizing the common denominator of language among communities that sometimes may seem to have little else in common. *Latino*—a shortening of the Spanish word *latinoamericano*—refers more exclusively to persons or communities of Latin American origin. Of the two, only *Hispanic* can be used in referring to Spain and its history and culture; a native of Spain residing in the United States is a *Hispanic*, not a *Latino*, and one cannot substitute *Latino* in the phrase *the Hispanic influence on native Mexican cultures* without garbling the meaning. In practice, however, these distinctions are of little significance when referring to residents of the United States, since the great majority of people in this group are of Latin American origin and can be denoted by either word.

A more important difference concerns the sociopolitical divide that has opened between *Latino* and *Hispanic* in American usage. For a certain segment of the Spanish-speaking population, *Latino* is a term of ethnic pride while *Hispanic,* with its perceived echo of Spanish imperialism, is an offensive label imposed from outside the community. According to this view, *Hispanic* lacks the authenticity and cultural resonance of *Latino*, which is derived directly from Spanish and can change to *Latina* to indicate female gender. From the other point of view, *Latino* is sometimes viewed as a divisive term associated with the politics of culture, class, and race. For this segment, *Hispanic* is the traditional term that needs no replacement.

While these views are strongly held by some, they are by no means universal, and the division in usage is as much related to geography as it is to politics. *Latino* is widely preferred on the West Coast, especially California, whereas *Hispanic* is the more usual term in Florida as well as in Texas and much of the Southwest (though in these regions *Chicano* is also widely used). Even in these regions, however, usage is often mixed, and it is not uncommon to find both terms used by the same writer or speaker.

Note that *Hispanic* and *Latino* refer only to language and culture; neither term should be thought of as specifying racial makeup. It is worth remembering, too, that the growing Hispanic population of the United States is made up of people from many different national and ethnic backgrounds who do not necessarily compose a unified community. Depending on circumstances, using such terms as *Mexican American, Cuban American,* or *Puerto Rican* is often preferable to lumping people together as *Hispanic* or *Latino*.

See more at **Chicano** and **Latino**.

historic / historical

Historic and *historical* have similar, though usually distinct, meanings. *Historic* refers to that which is associated with significant events in history: *the historic first voyage to the moon.* Thus, *a historic house* is likely to be of interest not just because it is relatively old, but because an important person lived in it or was otherwise associated with it. In contrast, *historical* refers more generally to that which happened in the past, regardless of significance: *a minor historical character in the novel, the historical architecture in the center of town.* These distinctions are not always observed, however, and a *historic* tour of a city might include the same sights as a *historical* tour. Therefore, it is important to make sure that the context explicates the intended meaning.

hoard / horde

These two words sound alike and can be confused. A *hoard* is a cache, a hidden fund or supply stored for future use; to *hoard* something is to gather or accumulate a hoard of it. *Hoard* is an old Germanic word derived from an Indo-European root. The noun *horde,* which looks like a close cousin, is actually of Turkic origin, and originally referred to a collection of families forming a tribe or group. In English, it is used to refer to any large group, especially a crowd or swarm. There is no verb *horde*.

Thus *hoard* is used primarily of things, while *horde* applies to people and other living things (such as insects). Only a horde of reporters should follow a movie star around, never a hoard. When large numbers of people are turning up in different places, the plural *hordes* is common: *hordes of students returning to campus, hordes of volunteers helping to get out the vote.*

Hobson's choice / Hobbesian choice

Hobson's choice, meaning no choice at all or a choice between two bad alternatives, is named after Thomas Hobson, an English keeper of a livery stable, who required his customers to take either the horse nearest the stable door or no horse at all. The name of philosopher Thomas Hobbes, a contemporary of Hobson, is sometimes used in this expression instead as *Hobbesian choice* (possibly due to Hobbes's deterministic account of human volition and his authoritarian politics), but this is widely considered an error.

hoi polloi

The peculiar rhyming word *hoi polloi* is used sometimes to refer to the upper crust of society, and sometimes to refer to the common people. But which is correct?

Hoi polloi is a Greek phrase that means "the masses," and so etymologically speaking it is used correctly in a sentence such as *Stars who had arrived in stretch limos were elbow-to-elbow with the hoi polloi who had come on the subway.* In our 2002 survey, 95 percent of the Usage Panel approved of this example.

The confusion in meaning may have arisen because of the similarity in sound of *hoity toity,* which means "pretentiously self-important, haughty." A small but significant portion of the Usage Panel found this usage acceptable, with 28 percent accepting the example *The luxurious sets in the movie evoke the lifestyle of the hoi polloi in the early 20th century.* This suggests that some people will allow either meaning of the word, perhaps out of sympathy for fellow speakers of English who did not study Greek.

A second problem is related to the word *hoi,* which is the Greek definite article. Thus, for those who take their Greek seriously, the expression *the hoi polloi* is a redundancy meaning "the the masses." In the examples we presented to the Panel, we put *the* in parentheses to allow for its use or disuse, but we also asked if the Panelists used *the* with *hoi polloi,* and 78 percent said they did.

The main lesson then is a familiar one: To avoid raising eyebrows, make sure that the context makes the meaning of the term *hoi polloi* unambiguous in referring to the common people. The minor lesson is that the use of *the* with this word is standard, and omitting *the* may strike some readers as peculiar.

holocaust

Holocaust has a secure place in the language when it refers to the massive destruction of humans by other humans. In our 1987 survey 99 percent of the Usage Panel accepted the use of *holocaust* in the phrase *nuclear holocaust.* Sixty percent accepted the sentence *As many as two million people may have died in the holocaust that followed the Khmer Rouge takeover in Cambodia.*

But because of its associations with genocide, people may object to extended applications of *holocaust.* The percentage of the Panel's acceptance drops sharply when people use the word to refer to death brought about by natural causes. In our 1999 survey 47 percent approved the sentence *In East Africa five years of drought have brought about a holocaust in which millions have died.* Just 16 percent approved *The press gives little coverage to the holocaust of malaria that goes on, year after year in tropical countries,* where there is no mention of widespread mortality. The Panel has little enthusiasm for more figurative usages of *holocaust.* In 1999, only 7 percent accepted *Numerous small investors lost their stakes in the holocaust that followed the precipitous drop in stocks.* This suggests that these extended uses of the word may be viewed as overblown or in poor taste.

home in / hone in

The verb *home* has been used to mean "to move toward" since the 1920s, but the introduction of radar in World War II gave this expression an added boost. Originally, pilots and aircraft *homed on* a target. In the 1950s this construction was extended to figurative uses meaning "to focus attention on," and *in* was added, so the expression became *home in on.* A decade later *hone in on* arose as a synonym. Perhaps the similarity in sound led to this development, or the notion that sharpening (honing) one's focus seemed as appropriate as directing it homeward. Whatever its origin, *hone in,* despite being well established, is often viewed as a mistake. In our 1999 survey, 41 percent of the Usage Panel disapproved of the example *Direct mail allows you to hone in on your target audience,* and 54 percent would not accept *The purpose of the meeting was to hone in on strategies for improving the company's performance.* A safer bet is to stick with *home in* or to use *zero in* instead.

homemaker   See **housewife.**

hominoid / hominid / hominin / humanoid

These words are confusing not only because they look and sound alike, but because some of their meanings are in flux within the scientific community. *Hominoid, hominid,* and *hominin* refer to taxonomic classifications of mammals within the order called Primates, consisting of ape and human species. Hominoids are considered either a suborder or a superfamily (a subdivision of the order), and the term *hominoid* has been used consistently in this way by scientists. As recently as the 1980s, the hominoids were divided into three families, one of which was the hominids (from the taxonomic name Hominidae). The hominids consisted only of human lineages, while the other two families included chimpanzees, gorillas, and other apes.

Recent anthropologic research has shown that because of close evolutionary ties between human beings and certain apes, this classification is not correct. The family of hominids now includes several types of apes, including chimpanzees, gorillas, and orangutans. The new term *hominin* (from the family Hominini) now refers to a branch (known as a *tribe*) within the hominid family that includes only the human lineages. The older use of *hominid* to refer to humans is still current in the scientific literature, however.

Humanoid refers to something that is not human but possesses human characteristics or form, as in this article from London's *Daily Telegraph:* "*The statues have humanoid shapes, but their dappled, ridged surfaces bear little resemblance to skin.*" The term is often applied to robots and is used extensively in science fiction. It is also used at times in anthropology, usually when the taxonomic grouping has not yet been determined, as in *the discovery of humanoid fossils.*

homosexual   See **gay.**

hoof

The plural of this word is either *hoofs,* (ho͞ofs) or (ho͝ofs), or *hooves,* (ho͞ovz) or (ho͝ovz). The latter spelling is the older of the two, the change from *f* to *v* being the result of a sound change in Old English. Other words that follow this pattern are *thief/thieves, leaf/leaves,* and *wife/wives.* While many of the words that are in this category still have their traditional plurals, some have also adopted modern plurals ending in just *s,* as *hoof* has. And some words of this type have lost the older plural almost completely, as is the case with *roof,* whose only plural spelling in standard usage is now *roofs.*

See more at **roof.**

hopefully

When used as a sentence adverb (as in *Hopefully the measures will be adopted*), *hopefully* has been roundly criticized since the 1960s, when it saw a sudden increase in use, for being potentially ambiguous and for lacking a clear point of view. It is not easy to explain why people selected this word for disparagement. Its use can be justified by the similar use of many other adverbs, such as *mercifully* and *frankly: Mercifully, the play was brief. Frankly, my dear, I don't give a damn.* And though this use of *hopefully* may have been a vogue word back in the 1960s, it has long since lost any hint of jargon or pretentiousness for the general reader. In fact, its widespread use reflects popular recognition of its usefulness; there is no precise substitute. Someone who says *Hopefully, the treaty will be ratified* makes a hopeful prediction about the fate of the treaty, whereas someone who says *I hope* (or *We hope* or *It is hoped that*) *the treaty will be ratified* expresses a bald statement about what is desired. Only the latter could be continued with a clause such as *but it isn't likely.*

continued objections against *hopefully* People often warm to a usage once its novelty fades and it becomes well established. But not so with *hopefully.* Opposition continues to run high or even higher to this usage than it did in the 1960s. In our 1968 survey, 44 percent of the Usage Panel approved the usage. This dropped to 27 percent in our 1986 survey. We asked the question again in 1999, and 34 percent accepted the sentence *Hopefully, the treaty will be ratified,* while only 22 percent accepted the adverb when placed at the end of a sentence in the example *The new product will be shipped by Christmas, hopefully.*

By way of comparison, we also included the sentence adverb *mercifully* in our 1986 and 1999 surveys. In 1986, 60 percent of the Panel approved of the sentence *Mercifully, the game ended before the Giants could add another touchdown to the lopsided score.* This percentage increased to 82 in 1999.

It would seem, then, that it is not the use of *hopefully* as a sentence adverb per se that bothers the Panel, since the comparable use of *mercifully* is acceptable to a large majority. Rather, *hopefully* seems to have taken on a life of its own as a sign that the writer is unaware of the canons of usage.

See more at **sentence adverbs.**

horde See **hoard.**

housewife / homemaker / househusband

The word *housewife*, meaning "a woman who manages her own household as her main occupation," is still commonly used and acceptable to many people. In the past several decades, however, *homemaker* has become increasingly popular and frequently appears in occupational surveys. Because *homemaker* has the virtues of eliminating reference to both gender and marital status and defines the role solely in terms of function, it is considered by many people to be a more respectful and dignified term. Although most homemakers are women, more and more men stay home with their children. The word *househusband* has become an acceptable reference to stay-at-home fathers, as in an article from the Scripps-Howard news service: "*[John] Lennon was particularly proud of staying home and being a father in the late '70s. His role as househusband caused an uproar at the time.*" Perhaps because the word is relatively new and it defines a role reversal for men, the word *househusband* does not have the offensive connotations that some attribute to *housewife.* As language changes to reflect changing social norms, it is possible that *homemaker* may eventually apply to both men and women.

hovel

In American English *hovel* is most commonly pronounced with a short *u* sound in the first syllable (hŭv′əl) and less commonly with a short *o* (hŏv′əl).

hover

In American English *hover* is most commonly pronounced with a short *u* sound in the first syllable (hŭv′ər) and less commonly with a short *o* (hŏv′ər).

however

Unlike similar words such as *nevertheless,* the word *however* can be either a conjunctive adverb used in an independent clause or a subordinate conjunction introducing a dependent clause. When *however* is used as a conjunctive adverb, its clause must either follow a semicolon or be a new sentence. In these uses *however* is usually set off by one or more commas:

> The older students had little trouble organizing themselves into a team; the younger students, however, needed help.

> Peebles insisted that his version of the story was accurate. However, no other witness could corroborate it.

When used as a subordinating conjunction, *however* itself is not set off by commas:

Dress however you like.
However you get into Mystic, be sure you end up on Route 1.

As an adverb, *however* can modify an adjective or adverb: *The two friends walked, however slowly, to the principal's office.* The word is also used in this way with the force of a subordinating conjunction to introduce a dependent clause:

> However witty the remark was, it made us cringe with embarrassment. However loudly he spoke, no one in the back of the room could hear him.

Sometimes the verb *be* is omitted in these dependent clauses: *However weak my resolve at the outset, I found the strength to see the project through to the end.*

When positioned at the beginning or end of the sentence, the conjunctive adverb *however* suggests that the sentence it modifies is contrastive with what has been written previously: *These are the facts as we knew them. There was more to be discovered, however.* When positioned elsewhere in the sentence, it emphasizes the preceding word or phrase as a particular point of contrast: *Most of the girls were awake by six. Evelyn, however, stayed in bed much later.*

however beginning a sentence   *Sailing in rough weather can be very unpleasant. However, we found it exciting.* An old usage rule states that *however* should never begin a sentence when it means "nevertheless" or "on the other hand." The Usage Panel was asked in our 1994 survey if they observed this rule, and 36 percent said "usually or always," 19 percent said "sometimes," and 42 percent said "rarely or never." Since *however* functions in these cases as a conjunctive adverb, the situation is little different from that of a conjunction like *but,* and in fact placing *however* at the start of a sentence can emphasize the starkness of a contrast. Because of its relative formality, though, *however* does not see much use in modern fiction, but it does yeoman's work in academic and scientific writing, as these examples should indicate:

> Most astronomers believed the answer lay in the sky, but Harrison, a clockmaker, imagined a mechanical solution—a clock that would keep precise time at sea. By knowing the exact times at the Greenwich meridian and at a ship's position, one could find longitude by calculating the time difference. However, most scientists, including Isaac Newton, discounted a clock because there were too many variables at sea. Changes in temperature, air pressure, humidity and gravity would surely render a watch inaccurate (John Ellsworth, reviewing *Longitude* by Dava Sobel in *The New York Times Book Review*)

> Another disease that annually afflicts more than 200 million people worldwide is schistosomiasis. The disease is caused by a flatworm, or fluke, that develops inside the blood vascular system of the human body. However, it is not the adult worms themselves that cause the most common manifestations of the disease but rather the body's response to eggs laid by the worms (Chris Murphy and Leona Fitzmaurice, "Medical Biotechnology and Developing Countries: Global Challenges and Limited Resources," *Wisconsin BioIssues*)

but . . . however   When used following *but, however* is redundant, as in *But the Orioles, however, are poised for a strong finish to the season.* One or the other word should be used, not both.

See more at **and, but,** and **whatever.**

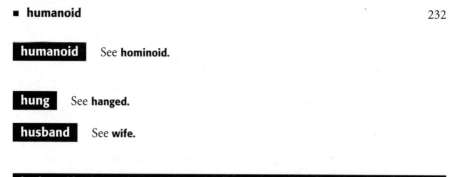

humanoid See **hominoid**.

hung See **hanged**.

husband See **wife**.

hydro– / hygro–

The prefix *hydro–* is from the Greek prefix *hudro–* or *hudr–*, derived from the Greek noun *hudōr* meaning "water." In fact, the words *hudōr* and *water* are close cousins, both descended from the word for "water" in the prehistoric language (called Proto-Indo-European) that is the ancestor of Greek and English as well as many other languages of Europe and Asia. The prefix *hydro–* is used in many new scientific and technical words, such as *hydroelectric, hydroplane,* and *hydrosphere.* Before a vowel, *hydro–* sometimes becomes *hydr–*: *hydrate, hydrous.* In the word *hydrophobia, hudro–* combines with the suffix *–phobia,* "fear." Although the word *hydrophobia* is nowadays sometimes used in the sense "an irrational fear of water," in the past the word was more often used to mean "rabies," since characteristics of this disease include throat spasms and the inability to swallow despite extreme thirst. *Hydrophobia* was in fact coined in Greek itself and later borrowed into Latin and then into English.

Writers should take care not to confuse *hydro–* with the similar-sounding prefix *hygro–* used to form words relating to moisture and humidity, such as *hygrometer* and *hygroscopic.* This prefix comes from the Greek adjective *hugros,* "wet, liquid," which is unrelated to Greek *hudōr,* "water," despite the similarity in sound and meaning between the two words.

hygienic

This word is most commonly pronounced (hī-jĕn′ĭk), with three syllables and a short *e* in the stressed syllable. In our 2004 survey, this pronunciation was preferred by 82 percent of the Usage Panel. It has clearly replaced the traditional pronunciation, which is pronounced with four syllables as (hī′jē-ĕn′ĭk) and was considered acceptable only to 13 percent of the Panel. Another pronunciation is (hī-jē′nĭk), spoken with three syllables and a long *e.* Although the preference of only 10 percent of the Panel, it was nonetheless considered acceptable by 42 percent. All three pronunciations should be considered standard.

hyper–

The basic meanings of the English prefix *hyper–* are "over or above" and "excessive or excessively." For example, *hyperactive* means "highly or excessively active." The anthropological term *hypergamy* means "marrying into an equal or superior social caste or group." *Hyper–* comes from the Greek prefix *huper–*, which in turn comes from the preposition *huper*, meaning "over, beyond." Since the 17th century, *hyper–* has become very productive in the formation of new words such as *hypercritical* and *hypersensitive*. In fact, relatively few English words beginning with *hyper–* are borrowings of words already created in the Greek language itself, like *hyperbole*. Most English words beginning with the prefix are recent creations and belong to the vocabulary of medicine and the sciences, such as *hyperventilate* and *hyperspace*.

See more at **hypertension** and **hypo–**.

hypercorrection

A hypercorrection is a construction or pronunciation that is produced by mistaken analogy with standard usage out of a desire to be correct, as in the substitution of *I* for *me* in *on behalf of John and I.* For standard usage students are taught to say *John and I* instead of the informal *John and me*; however, what often goes unmentioned is that the pronoun form *I* should be used only as the subject or as a predicate nominative (that is, following *to be*), as in *John and I are going to sing in the concert* and *The soloists in the concert are John and I.* The objective form of the pronoun, *me,* is required as a direct object or the object of a preposition. The sentences *She told John and me the news* and *My roommate came with John and me* use the correct form, but because of a misapplication of the rule, one often hears *I* instead of *me* in these contexts. Another example of hypercorrection is the use of *whom* as a subject, probably on the mistaken assumption that the word seems prestigious or learned, as in *They didn't tell us whom she believes is coming to the reception.* These uses of *I* and *whom* are hypercorrections and are incorrect.

hypertension / hypotension

Although many people think the word *hypertension* implies a problem with tension or stress, the condition is simply one of high blood pressure in the arteries. The disease has many possible causes, and even infants and animals can be hypertensive. The prefix *hyper–*, used commonly in medicine, means "excessive or elevated," as in *hyperthyroidism* (overactive thyroid) or *hypercalcemia* (too much calcium in the blood). Since the prefix *hypo–* means "less than," *hypotension* is blood pressure that is lower than normal.

hyphenated Americans

Naturalized immigrants to the United States and their descendants are sometimes referred to as *hyphenated Americans,* a term that dates to the end of the 19th century and that reflects the tendency in American English, particularly in earlier times, to hyphenate such forms as *Irish-American, German-American,* and *Mexican-American* both as nouns and as adjectives. In contemporary usage, such compounds often appear without hyphens, especially as nouns.

The term *hyphenated American* has itself come under strong criticism as suggesting that those so labeled are somehow different from, and perhaps not as fully American as, citizens whose immigrant past is less a part of their identity in American society. While this term might be appropriate in discussing the history of immigration to the United States or the immigrant experience in America, it is best to avoid it in other contexts.

hyphenation

compound nouns

1. Compounds nouns may be open (written as two words), hyphenated, or solid (written as one word), and often more than one style is acceptable.

byproduct *or* by-product	goodwill *or* good will
grownup *or* grown-up	lifestyle *or* life-style *or* life style
fundraiser *or* fund-raiser	

If the compound in question cannot be found in a dictionary, the general principle is to write it as two words unless a hyphen is needed for clarity. When a noun that is an open compound is preceded by an adjective, a hyphen is often added to prevent confusion.

costume designer; best costume-designer	broom closet; tiny broom-closet desk lamp; large desk-lamp

2. Compound nouns consisting of a noun and a gerund are generally open. However, many such compounds have become solid, and when in doubt it is best to consult a dictionary.

crime solving	faultfinding
house hunting	housekeeping
trout fishing	

3. A compound consisting of two nouns of equal importance should be hyphenated.

priest-king	city-state
secretary-treasurer	singer-songwriter

compound modifiers

1. Compound nouns used attributively should be hyphenated if there is any possibility of misreading. Adjectives beginning with *high–* or *low–* are generally hyphenated.

fine-wine tasting	hot-spot volcano
hot-water bottle	high-school teacher
minimum-wage worker	high-quality programming
rare-book store	low-budget films
real-life experiences	low-res scan

If there is no possibility of misreading, or if the hyphen would look clumsy, it may be omitted.

organic chemistry class	mechanical engineering degree
hedge fund manager	bubonic plague outbreak
small claims court	temp agency employee

Names of chemical substances used as adjectives should not be hyphenated.

carbon monoxide poisoning	dichromic acid solution

2. A compound modifier consisting of an adverb ending in *–ly* plus a participle or an adjective should not be hyphenated.

a finely tuned mechanism	a highly motivated student
a carefully worked canvas	unusually mild weather
a skillfully written screenplay	an especially pleasant evening
the slowly moving train	a completely hopeless case

3. A compound modifier consisting of an adverb that does not end in *–ly* plus a participle or an adjective is hyphenated when it precedes a noun.

a well-known actor	a much-improved situation
an ill-advised move	a so-called cure
best-loved poems	less-expensive options

Such a compound is not hyphenated when it follows a noun unless it is appears as a hyphenated compound in the dictionary.

Nicole's essay was the best organized.
His art was less appreciated back then.
The house was well designed.
They are well-known in Paris.

4. A compound modifier consisting of a noun or adjective plus a participle is hyphenated when it precedes the noun it modifies.

helium-filled balloons	good-looking sons
thirst-quenching drink	long-lasting friendship
bone-chilling tale	

Compounds of this type may be left open when they follow a noun unless they appear hyphenated or solid in the dictionary.

The drink was thirst quenching.	The consequences are
That job will be time-consuming.	far-reaching.
She remained tongue-tied.	The noise was earsplitting.

5. A compound modifier consisting of an adjective plus a noun to which *-d* or *-ed* has been added is hyphenated when it precedes a noun. It is best to consult a dictionary if in doubt as some of these compounds have become solid.

yellow-eyed cat	fine-grained wood

many-tiered cake   kindhearted person
stout-limbed toddler

Leave such compounds open when they follow a noun unless they are hyphenated or solid in the dictionary.

The child is rosy cheeked.   That hat is old-fashioned.
Our boss is even-tempered.   I was feeling lightheaded.

color

1. Compound color adjectives are hyphenated.

a red-gold sunset   blue-green eyes
a cherry-red sweater

2. Color compounds whose first element ends in *–ish* are hyphenated when they precede the noun but open when they follow the noun.

a darkish-blue color   The sky is reddish gold.
a reddish-gold sunset   My car is a darkish blue.

phrases

1. Phrases used as modifiers are normally hyphenated.

a happy-go-lucky person
a here-today-gone-tomorrow
    attitude

2. A foreign phrase used as a modifier is not hyphenated.

a bona fide offer   a per diem allowance

proper names

1. Compound modifiers formed of capitalized words should not be hyphenated.

Korean War veterans   Iron Age manufacture
New Jersey shore   New World plants
Old English poetry

2. Usage is divided with regard to compounds designating a nationality or ethnic group. It is generally unnecessary to hyphenate such terms whether used as nouns or adjectives. However, with some exceptions, compounds of this type frequently appear with hyphens.

Native Americans; Native American nations
Latin Americans; Latin American countries
Italian Americans; Italian American neighborhood
French Canadians; French-Canadian ancestry
Mexican Americans; Mexican-American community
African Americans *or* African-Americans
African American literature *or* African-American literature
Asian Americans *or* Asian-Americans
Asian American studies *or* Asian-American studies

numbers and measurements

1. A hyphen punctuates the compound numbers from 21 through 99 when they are written out.

thirty-five students   four hundred eighty-six dollars
at age ninety-two

2. Compound modifiers with a numerical first element are generally hyphenated.

second-rate movie   100-yard dash
seven-minute miles   13-piece band
three-hour tour   19th-century novel
third-story window   four-odd years
ten-thousand-year-old bones   60-odd chairs

If, however, the second element is an abbreviated unit of measurement, the hyphen is omitted.

500 mL beaker   10 g mass

3. Spelled-out numbers used with *–fold* are not hyphenated; figures and *–fold* are hyphenated.

tenfold   20-fold

4. Spelled-out fractions used as nouns may be open or hyphenated.

He ate seven eighths [*or* seven-eighths] of the pizza.
Three quarters [*or* Three-quarters] of the students are English majors.
Two thirds [*or* Two-thirds] is plenty.

When used as adjectives or adverbs, however, fractions are generally hyphenated.

She owns a three-fourths interest.
The refrigerator is four-fifths empty.
I am two-thirds finished with this assignment.

prefixes

1. Normally, prefixes are joined to a second element without a hyphen unless doing so would double the same vowel.

antianxiety   anti-intellectual
anticrime   anti-inflammatory
antiwar   anti-infective

However, many common prefixes, such as *co–*, *de–*, *pre–*, *pro–*, and *re–*, are added without a hyphen even though a double vowel is the result.

coordinate   preeminent
cooperate   reenter

2. A hyphen is used if the element following a prefix is capitalized or is a numeral.

anti-Semitism   non-Germanic
pro-French   pre-1900
un-American

3. The hyphen is usually retained in words that begin with *all–*, *ex–* (meaning "former"), *half–*, and *self–*.

all-around
ex-governor
half-baked, half-life *but* halfhearted, halfcocked, halftone, halfway, half dollar
self-defense *but* selfhood, selfish, selfless, selfsame

4. Terms that begin with *quasi–* are hyphenated if used as adjectives and open if used as nouns.

quasi-scientific research   a quasi success
quasi-stellar object   a quasi corporation
quasi-judicial proceedings

5. Some prefixes are followed by a hyphen to prevent a misunderstanding of meaning.

re-form [compare *reform*]   re-create [compare *recreate*]
re-cover [compare *recover*]   re-lease [compare *release*]

other uses

1. A hyphen indicates that two or more compounds share a single base.

six- and seven-year-olds   pre- and postseason practice
three- and four-volume sets   first-, second-, and third-class
low- and high-range models   mail
lower- and uppercase letters

2. Nouns or adjectives consisting of a short verb combined with a preposition are either hyphenated or written solid depending on current usage. The same words used as a verb are written separately.

a bang-up job *but* bang up the car   a breakup *but* break up a fight

3. A hyphen indicates that a word has been divided at the end of a line of text.

Anatole France's actual name was Jacque Anatole Thibault.

hypo–

The prefix *hypo–* means "beneath, below, or under." It can be traced back to the Greek prefix *hupo–*, from the word *hupo*, meaning "beneath, under." A few English words, such as *hypocrite, hypocrisy,* and *hypochondria,* come from Greek words using *hupo–*. But most English words beginning with *hypo–* have been made up by scientists and physicians. *Hypo–* either means "below or under," as in *hypodermic,* or "less than normal," as in *hypoglycemia.*

See also **hyper–** and **hypertension.**

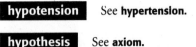

hypotension   See **hypertension.**

hypothesis   See **axiom.**

I See **pronouns, personal.**

–ible See **–able.**

identical

Both *to* and *with* are acceptable following *identical*. Though the use of *to* is a more recent development, it has become the more common expression: *On this issue, the position of the Democrats is nearly identical to* [or *with*] *that of the Republicans.*

identify

When used in the sense "to associate or affiliate (oneself) closely with a person or group," *identify* suggests a psychological empathy with the feelings or experiences of another person, as in *Most young readers readily identify* [or *identify themselves*] *with Holden Caulfield, the main character in* Catcher in the Rye. This usage derives originally from psychoanalytic writing, where it has a specific technical meaning, but like other terms from that field, it was widely regarded as jargon when introduced into wider use. In particular, some critics seized on the fact that in this sense the verb was often used intransitively, with no reflexive pronoun. In recent years, however, this use of *identify with* without the reflexive has become standard. In our 1988 survey, 82 percent of the Usage Panel accepted the sentence *I find it hard to identify with any of his characters.* Note, however, that only 63 percent accepted *identify* when used with the reflexive pronoun in the same context: *I find it hard to identify myself with any of his characters.*
See more at **self-identify.**

idiot / imbecile / moron / feeble-minded

The noun *idiot* first appeared in English in the 14th century, when it was used both for uneducated persons or laypersons and for people who were severely intellectually impaired, in contrast to those suffering from mental illness. (The meaning "uneducated person" disappeared around 1700.) The term *imbecile* was originally an adjective referring to physical weakness, but by the 18th century it was applied to mental weakness or intellectual disability as well. In the 19th century it developed its noun use, eventually referring to a person with impaired mental capacity above the level of an idiot. The use of *imbecile* in the emerging field of psychology rendered the word's associations with physical weakness obsolete. *Feeble-minded* has been in use since the 1500s. In the late 19th and early 20th century, the term was applied to people who lacked the mental capacity to live independently but were able to support themselves with proper guidance. The term *moron* was coined in 1910 for those with the highest level of functionality among people classified as feeble-minded.

These terms were used in psychology and medicine until the late 1950s, but they have been discarded and are now considered to be offensive when used in reference to the mentally impaired, as are the terms *slow, mentally defective,* and *mentally deficient.* The word *idiot* is still used acceptably in the term *idiot savant,* which refers to an intellectually disabled person who has extraordinary ability in a particular area, such as music. Individuals who are born with intellectual impairment are now described as having mild, moderate, severe, or profound mental retardation. Older individuals who have lost mental function may have dementia, as in Alzheimer's disease. Psychiatric illnesses should be accurately identified when they are known and appropriate to the context.

See also **insane** and **Mongoloid.**

if

if or whether   In informal writing, both *if* and *whether* are standard for introducing a clause indicating uncertainty after a verb such as *ask, doubt, know, learn,* or *see: We shall soon learn whether* [or *if*] *it is true.* In such contexts, however, the use of *if* can sometimes create ambiguities. Depending on the intended meaning, the sentence *Let her know if she is invited* might be better paraphrased as *Let her know whether she is invited* or *If she is invited, let her know.*

In more formal writing, *whether* is often preferred to introduce such clauses.

if and the subjunctive   See under **subjunctive.**

if not

When used as a coordinator, the phrase *if not* always signals a contrast, but it can have almost contradictory meanings, depending on the context. Sometimes it can mean "but not," as in *Greene won her team's admiration, if not its award, for her performance in the playoffs* and *The board was encouraged, if not convinced, by the budgetary projections.* At other times, especially when there is a comparison of two adjectives or noun phrases in which the second represents a significant increase in degree above the first, *if not* usually means "and even," as in *This job will be difficult, if not impossible* and *The law practice includes clients from all over the state, if not the country.* Since many sentences of this kind can be interpreted one way or the other, it is important that the context make clear what sort of contrast is being indicated by *if not,* as in *The law practice is so big that it includes clients from all over the state, if not the country.* Using *but not* instead of *if not* avoids this problem for sentences with this kind of contrast: *The law practice includes clients from all over the state, but not the country.*

illegitimate child

Using the term *illegitimate child* to describe a child born to an unmarried mother is considered offensive and should be done only in historical contexts, as when indicating a prevailing attitude. If the context requires the designation of such a child, the phrases *born to a single mother, born to an unmarried mother, born to unmarried parents,* and *born out of wedlock* can be used, although this last phrase has become somewhat outdated.

illusion / delusion

The words *illusion* and *delusion* both refer to false perception or belief. However, there are distinctions in how they are used. An illusion is an unsubstantiated belief that ordinarily is not associated with either mental illness or with willful deception. It may represent wishful thinking on the part of an individual that can be dissolved with the presence of realistic evidence, as in *The quarterly report destroyed his illusions of success.* An illusion can also be a visual distortion of reality, such as a mirage.

Delusion is a medical term used to describe a symptom of psychiatric illness consisting of a false but fiercely held belief, as in *delusions of persecution* or *delusions of grandeur.* In popular usage *delusion* is also used to refer to a persistent misinterpretation of reality that the holder clings to even in the face of strong invalidating evidence, hence the phrase *to labor under a delusion. Delusion* sometimes connotes intentional deception or manipulation in a way that the word *illusion* does not, as in this example from a British newspaper: *"It was experience that taught them to ignore the ill-informed prognostications of those . . . Englishmen who somehow embraced the delusion that victory . . . was a formality."*

imbecile   See **idiot.**

immigrate   See **migrate.**

imminent / immanent / eminent

These sound-alikes have very different meanings but are frequently confused. *Imminent* means "impending," as in *an imminent storm,* while *immanent,* which is used mainly in theological contexts, means "inherent, indwelling," as in *the belief that God is immanent in humans.* The word *eminent* means "prominent, noteworthy," as in *an eminent businessman.*

immune

When the word *immune* is followed by a preposition, either *to* or *from* is acceptable. In situations where the immunity is related to criminal prosecution, *from* is much more common, as in this quotation from the *Los Angeles Times: "Elected officials in Mexico are immune from prosecution, but the federal attorney general is backing an effort in Congress . . . to lift the mayor's immunity in the case."* When *immune* is used in biology or medicine, *to* is the most common usage, as in this comment from a physician quoted in the *Seattle Times: " . . . most hospitals . . . require new employees to be immune to certain diseases . . . either through vaccinations or by having had the illness."*

impact

Impact came under criticism in the 1960s for its use both as a noun and verb, at least in the figurative use describing a dramatic influence or effect. The noun was criticized as a pointless hyperbole and as a vogue word. But complaints about the noun were not long-lived, and this usage has firmly established itself as standard. In our 2001 survey, 93 percent of the Usage Panel accepted the noun in the sentence *The program might have a positive moral impact on inner-city youth.*

But the verb is a different matter and ranks among the most detested of English usages. In the 1990s, National Public Radio conducted an informal poll of listeners, asking for pet peeves in usage, and the verbal use of *impact* won, hands down. Many people assume that popular distaste for the verb results from its conversion from the noun, in the manner of voguish and bureaucratic words like *leverage* and *interface*. But in fact *impact* was a verb long before it was a noun (the verb dates from the early 1600s; the noun from the late 1700s). Nor can the animosity to the figurative use of the verb stem from its novelty in the 1960s, since this use dates from the 1930s, allowing plenty of time for people to grow accustomed to it.

Whatever the reason, a large majority of the Usage Panel has disapproved of the use of the verb meaning "to have an effect" since the early 1980s. (The issue is a relatively recent one in the history of usage commentary and was not included in the earlier surveys.) Even in our 2001 survey, 85 percent of the Panel rejected the intransitive use in the sentence *These policies are impacting on our ability to achieve success,* and 80 percent rejected the transitive use in the sentence *The court ruling will impact the education of minority students.*

It may be that the verb's frequent appearance in jargon-riddled remarks by politicians, military officials, and financial analysts has given it an odor of pretentiousness or prevarication. Even the literal use of the verb was found unacceptable by a majority of the Panel (66 percent) in 2001 in the sentence *Thousands of meteors have impacted the lunar surface.*

Since the verb continues to see abundant use in corporations and institutions, it may be that younger speakers will come to see it as standard, much as the public has accepted another once-detested verb, *contact.* On the other hand, because it continues to be so widely disliked, *impact* might have become indelibly tainted as a hallmark of bad writing.

See more at **contact.**

impaired / impairment

Impaired and *impairment* are relatively recent additions to the vocabulary of disability. Although they are generally considered neutral terms and rarely cause offense when used appropriately, they do present certain usage problems. In many contexts, they mean the same as *disabled* and *disability*—for example, a *speech impairment* is the same thing as a *speech disability,* and a person who is *learning disabled* could also be called *learning impaired* without implying any difference in the degree of diminished capacity. But in the context of sensory deficits—sight and hearing—*impaired* and *impairment* are used to distinguish a partial loss of function from a total or near total loss. Thus a person who is *visually impaired* may be presumed to have some degree of useful sight, as distinct from a person who is *blind.* The distinction is meaningful, and a person with total loss of sight or hearing may take offense at being referred to as *impaired,* a term that may sound in such circumstances like a condescending euphemism. When referring to a group of people with varying degrees of sensory loss, including total, it is usually best to combine the two terms, as in *deaf and hearing impaired.* (Note, however, that many deaf people now take offense at the term *hearing impaired* even when used appropriately; the preferred term among this group is *hard of hearing.*)

Some people make a distinction between an *impairment* (a functional limitation of the body or mind) and a *disability* (a loss of ability or opportunity associated with a person's impairment, especially as a result of physical or societal barriers). In this scheme, a person who is *physically* or *mentally impaired* may or may not be *disabled* in a particular circumstance, depending on the environment. For example, a person in a wheelchair is disabled by stairs but not by an elevator or ramp. This distinction, however useful, is not widely observed outside certain academic and advocacy groups.

See more at **deaf, disabled,** and **handicap.**

impeach

When an irate citizen demands that a disfavored public official be impeached, the citizen clearly intends for the official to be removed from office. This popular use of *impeach* as a synonym of "throw out" (even if by due process) does not accord with the legal meaning of the word. When a public official is impeached, that is, formally accused of wrongdoing, this is only the start of what can be a lengthy process that may or may not lead to the official's removal from office. In strict usage, an official is impeached (accused), tried, and then convicted or acquitted. The vaguer use of *impeach* reflects disgruntled citizens' indifference to whether the official is forced from office by legal means or chooses to resign to avoid further disgrace.

imperative

The imperative is the verbal mood that expresses a command or request. Verb forms in this mood are also called *imperatives.* Second-person imperatives are identical to the base form of the verb, and they have no stated subject. The verbs *stop* in *Stop running, open* in *Open the door,* and *do* in *Don't be fooled by that remark* are in the imperative mood. First-person and third-person imperatives are formed by the verb *let* followed by a pronoun in the objective case: *Let's not argue anymore. Let no one call that man a liar. Let them ask for help if they need it.*

See more at **verbs, mood of.**

impinge / infringe

The verb *impinge* sounds a little like and has the same basic meaning as *infringe,* so it's not surprising that these words are often used interchangeably. *Impinge* comes from Latin *impingere,* "to drive into, strike against." The word still has this meaning, especially in science where one reads of waves or particle streams impinging on a surface. *Infringe* ultimately derives from Latin *frangere,* "to break," and was most often used in English to express the idea of violating a law or right. Both words have had the meaning "to encroach" since the 18th century, and *infringe* can be both transitive and intransitive, while *impinge* is only used intransitively. Thus, in standard usage, a person might infringe, infringe on, or impinge on someone else's constitutional rights.

Looser uses of these words in nonlegal contexts may raise some eyebrows, however. In our 2002 survey, only 47 percent of the Usage Panel accepted the sentence *What the recovered diary revealed about the villagers directly impinged on the lives of people living there many years later.* In such cases, the verbs *affect* and *have an effect on* are ready substitutes. Another synonym, *impact,* is among the most frequently condemned expressions in English, and using it may create a worse usage problem.

See also **affect** and **impact.**

impious

The traditional pronunciation is (ĭm′pē-əs), with stress on the first syllable. The pronunciation (ĭm-pī′əs), with stress on the second syllable and a long *i,* has been included in dictionaries since the middle of the 20th century and is now the most common pronunciation.

implement

People have been using *implement* as a verb meaning "to put into practice, carry out" since the 19th century. Some have objected to the verb as jargon, but its usefulness is obvious. In our 1988 survey, 89 percent of the Usage Panel accepted the usage in the sentence *The mayor's office announced the creation of a special task force that will be responsible for implementing the new policy.*

See also **utilize.**

importantly

Some people object to the use of the phrase *more importantly* in place of *more important* as a means of introducing an assertion, as in *More importantly, there is no one ready to step into the vacuum left by the retiring senator.* But both forms are widely used, and there is no obvious reason for preferring one or the other.

impracticable / impractical

The adjective *impracticable* applies to a course of action that is impossible to carry out or put into practice: *Refloating the sunken ship proved to be impracticable because of its fragility.* *Impractical* can also be used in this way, but it also has a weaker sense, suggesting that the course of action would yield an insufficient return, have little practical value, or be difficult to carry out. A plan for a new baseball stadium might be rejected as *impracticable* if the site was too marshy to permit safe construction, but if the objection were merely that the site was too remote for patrons to attend games easily, the plan would better be described as *impractical.*

See more at **practicable.**

impunity

The word *impunity* means "exemption from punishment, penalty, or harm." It is commonly preceded incorrectly by the word *without* when *with* is required, as in this newspaper column: "*If we can, without impunity, ignore truth, deny it, or act against it, then we will no longer be truly free . . . and none of our votes will ultimately matter.*"

in–

There are two prefixes spelled *in–*. Both come from Latin, but they are not related to each other. The basic meaning of one prefix is "not." Thus *inactive* means "not active." This *in–* is related to and sometimes confused with the prefix *un–* that means "not" (unfortunately, there are also two *un–*'s). In fact, sometimes *in–* is used interchangeably with *un–*, as when *incommunicative* is used instead of *uncommunicative.* However, as a general tendency, *in–* is more commonly used to negate words of obvious Latin origin, while *un–* is more often used to negate words of native English origin or that otherwise do not seem to be of immediate Latin origin, such as in the pair *indefatigable* and *untiring.* The dictionary should be consulted when a writer is uncertain whether a distinction of meaning exists between two similar words, one formed with *in–* and the other with *un–*.

Before the consonants *l* and *r*, *in–* becomes *il–* and *ir–*, respectively: *illogical, irregular.* Before the consonants *b*, *m*, and *p*, *in–* becomes *im–*: *imbalanced, immeasurable, impossible.*

The second *in–* has for its basic meaning "in, within, or into." For example, *inlay* means "to set something in something else." As with the other prefix *in–*, before the consonants *l* and *r*, *in–* becomes *il–* and *ir–*: *illuminate, irrigate.* Before the consonants *b*, *m*, and *p*, *in–* becomes *im–*: *imbibe, immigrate, implant.*

Some words in English, such as *enquire* and *inquire,* can be spelled with either *en–* or *in–*. In fact, from a historical point of view, these two prefixes are the same. As the Latin language developed into French, Latin *in–* became *en–*. For example, Latin *inflammāre* developed into French *enflammer,* borrowed into English as *enflame.* Later the word came to be written as *inflame* in imitation of the original Latin form. During the Middle English period, a great number of French words beginning with *en–* came into the English language, and in many instances the spelling of these words was similarly remodeled to begin with *in–*. In some pairs of words, however, the difference in spelling between *en–* or *in–* has been used to distinguish a difference in meaning, such as in the pair *ensure* and *insure.* Because of the difference in spelling, most English speakers today probably consider *ensure* and *insure* to be two entirely different verbs, but in origin *insure* is just a specialized financial use of the word *ensure,* "make secure."

See also **en–** and **un–**.

in addition to   See **together.**

inalienable / unalienable

The *unalienable rights* that are mentioned in the Declaration of Independence could just as well have been *inalienable,* which means the same thing. *Inalienable* or *unalienable* refers to that which cannot be given away or taken away.

in behalf of / on behalf of

A traditional rule holds that *in behalf of* and *on behalf of* have distinct meanings. According to this rule, *in behalf of* means "for the benefit of," as in *We raised money in behalf of the earthquake victims,* while its counterpart *on behalf of* means "as the agent of, on the part of," as in *The guardian signed the contract on behalf of the child.* But as the two meanings are quite close, the phrases are often used interchangeably, even by reputable writers. Statistically, *on behalf of* is used far more frequently than *in behalf of,* and in fact the Usage Panel prefers *on behalf of* for both meanings. In our 2004 survey, 87 percent of the Panel preferred *on behalf of* in the sentence *The lawyer spoke to the media (in behalf of/on behalf of) his client,* conforming to the traditional rule for using *on behalf of.* But some 75 percent also preferred *on behalf of* in the sentence *After sitting silently as one complaint after another was raised, he finally spoke up (in behalf of/on behalf of) his kid's coach,* where the speaker is less of a spokesperson than an ad-hoc defender, and so the meaning "in defense of, for the benefit of" is a better fit, and the traditional rule therefore would require *in behalf of.* All this suggests that *on behalf of* may be supplanting *in behalf of* in many contexts.

incentivize / incent

Corporate executives, car dealers, and politicians often cite the need to *incentivize* people to act in certain ways. They may want salespeople to work harder, customers to be more eager to spend, or businesses to take more risks. *Incentivize* has been motivating people since the mid-1970s—the more informal *incent* came along about ten years later. Both words mean the same thing, "to give an incentive to" or "to provide a motivation for." Usually the incentive is in the form of a material reward—a bonus, rebate, or tax break. But although these two verbs are popular with business leaders, they curry little favor with the Usage Panel, which sees them as trendy jargon. In our 1995 survey, some 94 percent of the Panel rejected *incentivize* in the sentence *He's the leader of this organization, and he's got to have the whole team of people incentivized to improve shareholder value.* Similarly, 96 percent rejected *incent* in *The management incented the employees to improve the shareholder value of the company.* Panelists suggested *motivate, encourage,* and *give incentives to* as alternatives.

See more at **–ize.**

incidence / incidents

The singular noun *incidence* and the plural noun *incidents* sound alike and are sometimes confused. *Incidence* refers to the rate at which something happens, as in *The city has taken measures to reduce the incidence of vandalism.* An incident is an event, so proper use in the plural would be *There were fewer incidents of vandalism in schools last year.* In many contexts, the difference between these two things can be subtle. The incidence of vandalism might be figured at fifty incidents over the course of a year.

The word *incidence* can be plural too, and here the confusion gets worse. In a sentence like *In adult animals, the incidences of leukemia and of mammary, lung, and thyroid tumors were increased with both types of radiation,* incidences (which properly means "rates" here) might be interpreted as a mistake for *incidents.* It is important that the context make clear which meaning is intended in such cases.

The plural *incidences* is sometimes used where *incidents* is properly required, as in *There were several incidences of unruly behavior after the game, leading to arrests.*

include

The word *include* generally suggests that what follows is a partial list, not an exhaustive list, of the contents of what the subject refers to. Therefore a sentence like *New England includes Connecticut and Rhode Island* is acceptable, since it implies that there are states that are also a part of New England but are not mentioned in the list, and in fact this is correct. When a full enumeration is given, a different construction, such as one using *comprise* or *consist of,* must be used: *New England comprises/consists of* [not *includes*] *Connecticut, Rhode Island, Massachusetts, Vermont, New Hampshire, and Maine.*

There are cases, however, in which *include* does not rule out the possibility of a complete listing. One such case is when the exact makeup of the subject is unknown or yet to be determined. Thus the sentence *The bibliography should include all the journal articles you have used* does not entail that the bibliography must contain something other than journal articles, though it does leave that possibility open. Another case in which the list following *include* may be exhaustive is when the list explicitly or implicitly describes what is not included: *We decided to include only those artists who had written works within the last five years* is acceptable, since the set of artists not included is implicitly defined as those who have not written works within the last five years. The same goes for cases of explicit exclusion from the list: *My shopping list includes everything you told me to buy, and nothing else.*

See more at **comprise.**

incredible / incredulous

Incredible means "hard to believe, unbelievable": *His explanation of the cause of the accident was simply incredible.* It is often used more loosely to mean "astonishing, extraordinary" as in *The new pitcher has an incredible fastball. Incredulous* usually means "skeptical, disbelieving," as in *The incredulous reporters laughed at the manager's explanation of how the funds disappeared.* It is sometimes extended to mean "showing disbelief," as in *an incredulous stare.* Less commonly, *incredulous* is used where one might expect to see *incredible,* as in *an incredulous story* and *an incredulous display of rudeness.* This usage had some frequency in the 1600s but fell out of favor around two hundred years ago. It is now considered an error.

inculcate

The verb *inculcate* is a transitive verb and traditionally has had the meaning "to impress something upon the mind of another by frequent instruction or repetition." The object of the verb is what is being inculcated, especially values or principles, as in *The school hopes to inculcate civic values in all the students.* More recently, *inculcate* has acquired for its object the individuals in whom the values or ideas are being instilled. The verb is often used in the passive voice followed by the preposition *with,* as in this quotation from media critic Tom Shales in the *Washington Post:* "*Impressionable kids and perhaps equally impressionable adults are watching this trash and being inculcated with wrong-headed concepts about life, liberty and the pursuit of pleasure.*"

This usage has come under criticism for being an unjustified extension of the verb and may have become popular because its synonym *indoctrinate* has overtones of ideological or political "education" and even brainwashing. It is likely that writers have sought out *inculcate* as a nonpolitical alternative to *indoctrinate.* The usage is listed in most dictionaries and should be considered standard. Writers who want to avoid it can use constructions such as *children need to be educated about values* (or *taught values*), although these expressions may not convey as strongly the notion of values being internalized or instilled.

indefinite article

An indefinite article is an article that does not fix the identity of the noun it modifies. In English the indefinite articles are *a* and *an*. They are typically used when the noun has not been mentioned before and so is unfamiliar: *A waiter appeared and asked to take our order.*

See more at **a.**

indefinite pronouns

An indefinite pronoun is a pronoun such as *any, each, everyone, everything, no one, nothing,* or *some,* that does not specify the identity of its object: *Everyone in the class can try out for the play. Has anyone got an answer to the last question? Some of the racers were disqualified.* The indefinite pronouns stand in contrast to the personal, reflexive, possessive, and demonstrative pronouns.

independent clause   See under **clause.**

Indian

Assuming that he had reached the Indies, Columbus called the people on the islands his ships visited "indios," or "Indians," and the misnomer has stuck ever since. It is natural that people would propose alternatives to this term, whether to avoid confusion between the inhabitants of America and India or to indicate respect for the original occupants of the American continents. Thus *Native American* has become widely established in American English, being acceptable in most contemporary contexts and preferred in many, especially in formal or official communication.

However, the acceptance of *Native American* has not brought about the demise of *Indian.* Unlike *Negro,* which was quickly stigmatized once *Black* became preferred, *Indian* never fell out of favor with a large segment of the American population, including most Indians themselves. In fact, Indian authors and those sympathetic to Indian causes often prefer it for its unpretentious familiarity as well as its emotional impact, as in this passage from the Kiowa writer N. Scott Momaday's memoir *The Names* (1976): "*It was about this time that* [my mother] *began to see herself as an Indian. That dim native heritage became a fascination and a cause for her.*"

See more at **First Nation, Native American,** and **red.**

indicative

The indicative mood is the verbal mood used to make statements.

See more at **verbs, mood of.**

indirect object

An indirect object is a noun, pronoun, or noun phrase that is indirectly affected by the action of the verb, as *me* in *Sing me a song; the turtle* in *He feeds the turtle lettuce;* and *most of the children* in *I gave most of the children their presents.*

See also **direct object.**

indiscrete   See **discrete.**

indisputably / undisputably / indisputedly

While both *indisputably* and *undisputably* mean "undeniably," *indisputedly* is not listed as a word in most dictionaries and is widely considered a mistake.

individual

The word *individual,* when used as a noun, refers to an individual person as opposed to a larger social group or as distinguished from others by some special quality:

> History is the long and tragic story of the fact that privileged groups seldom give up their privileges voluntarily. Individuals may see the moral light and voluntarily give up their unjust posture; but as Reinhold Niebuhr has reminded us, groups are more immoral than individuals (Martin Luther King, Jr., "Letter from Birmingham Jail")

> The modern business organization, or that part which has to do with guidance and direction, consists of numerous individuals who are engaged, at any given time, in obtaining, digesting or exchanging and testing information (John Kenneth Galbraith, *The Essential Galbraith*)

While the word can impart an inappropriate formal tone to such contexts, this formality can be a virtue in certain fields, supported by the fact that *individual* is a gender-neutral term. In evolutionary biology and genetics, for instance, *individual* can refer to the organisms in a given population and to organisms across a range of different species, sometimes including humans:

> The composition of MHC genes, it turns out, does affect body odor. Because related individuals tend to have similar MHC genes, they also have similar body smells. So mice can literally smell their family. Virtually every vertebrate from wood frog to wolf carries the MHC set of genes, though it varies widely in size and shape from species to species. A chicken has a set of only nineteen such genes; humans, a set of four hundred or so, all on Chromosome 6 (Jennifer Ackerman, *Chance in the House of Fate*)

Individual is also a favorite term of medical writers, where humans are regarded as the objects of study, and an air of scientific impartiality may be desirable:

> . . . neurology and neuroscience have stayed close to the idea of brain fixity and localization—the notion, in particular, that the highest part of the brain, the cere-

bral cortex, is effectively programmed from birth: this part to vision and visual processing, that part to hearing, that to touch, and so on. This would seem to allow individuals little power of choice, of self-determination, let alone of adaptation, in the event of a neurological or perceptual mishap (Oliver Sacks, "The Mind's Eye," *The New Yorker*)

Although increasing choline in the brain does have beneficial effects as far as certain kinds of memory function is concerned, these effects are only seen in normal individuals (Vernon H. Mark, *Reversing Memory Loss*)

The term is also favored in the social sciences, when the emphasis is on discrete decision-making and behavior:

Individualism is a word to which economics has lent a very special meaning. Economists take the individual as a given, rather than as a work in process, as the ever-changing synthesis of myriad social interactions. In particular, economics sees individuals as unique bundles of preferences, a term that includes everything from taste in dessert to ethical principle (Stephen A. Marglin, "John Kenneth Galbraith and the Myths of Economics," in Helen Sasson, ed., *Between Friends*)

And sometimes the term is used primarily out of a desire for stylistic variation:

America is supposed to be the land of opportunity, where people are free to make their own futures. Yet the idea that individuals are stuck with an inborn set of talents seems to weigh heavily on many U.S. schoolchildren (Steve Olson, *Count Down*)

indoctrinate   See **inculcate.**

inexpense

A magazine article about CDs states: *"The relative inexpense and ease of their production is offset by their current lack of proven durability."* *Inexpense*, a noun that would be a back-formation from the adjective *inexpensive*, is not a word that appears in any dictionary, and it is almost always considered an error. Usually a short phrase such as "lack of expense" can be substituted.

infect / infest

Each of the words *infect* and *infest* refers to the presence of a contaminating agent, but the similarity ends there. *Infest* means "to inhabit or overrun in numbers or quantities large enough to be harmful" or "to live as a parasite in or on," as in *The livestock were infested with tapeworms.* Agents of infestation are usually large enough to be seen with the unaided eye. *Infect* refers to contamination with a microscopic organism or agent, such as a virus or bacterium, that causes disease, as in *The patient's respiratory tract was infected with a virus.*

Both words are also used metaphorically:

It seemed that he had bent, and for a long time, too, all of his energies toward dying. Now death was ready for him but my father held back. All of Harlem, indeed, seemed to be infected by waiting (James Baldwin, "Notes of a Native Son," *Harper's Magazine*)

. . . Ronny was at first determined not to be sheltered in a "prep-school crowd"; he dreaded the aridity of social snobbery which he knew infected the Ivy League colleges (Louis Auchincloss, *East Side Story*)

Corsican protection rackets infested the neighborhood, demanding and usually getting money from club owners who wanted to stay open (Tyler Stovall, *Paris Noir*)

All but the hardiest of its people deserted Ithilien and removed west over Anduin, for the land was infested by Mordor-orcs (J.R.R. Tolkien, *The Return of the King*)

infectious   See **contagious**.

infer / imply

The words *infer* and *imply* should not be confused. When a speaker or sentence implies something, information is conveyed or suggested without being stated outright: *When the mayor said that she would not rule out a tax increase, she implied* [not *inferred*] *that some taxes might be raised.* To infer something, on the other hand, is to draw conclusions that are not explicit in what is said. It is the activity of a reader or listener: *When the mayor said that she would not rule out a tax increase, we inferred that she had been consulting new financial advisers, since her old advisers were in favor of tax reductions.*

infest   See **infect** and **invest**.

infinite

Infinite is sometimes grouped with absolute terms such as *unique, absolute,* and *omnipotent,* since it would seem that quantities or sets that are by definition limitless cannot be compared, measured, or measured against something else. Thus the idea of a set that is *more infinite* than another, or a set that is *somewhat infinite,* seems illogical.

As far as mathematics goes, the analogy with other absolute terms is not precise, for two reasons. First, there are in fact different kinds of infinities, and some are considered to be "larger" (in a certain mathematical sense) than others. For example, the set of real numbers is taken to be *uncountably infinite* and is considered larger than the number of integers, which is *countably infinite.* Thus the phrase *more infinite* is mathematically definable (though *somewhat infinite* is not). Also, *infinite* is different from other absolute terms in that it cannot be modified by *nearly* and *almost:* a list of numbers increasing in the direction of infinity, for example, never actually gets any closer to infinity and never reaches it; there is therefore no number that is "almost" infinity.

In nontechnical usage, of course, *infinite* is often used to refer to an unimaginably large degree or amount, and in these cases it is acceptable to modify or compare the word: *We thought of retracing our steps to see where George might have lost his keys, but we soon realized that the possibilities were almost infinite.*

See more at **absolute terms, center, complete, equal, parallel, perfect,** and **unique.**

infinitive

The infinitive is a verb form that can function as a noun while retaining certain verbal characteristics, such as modification by adverbs or taking an object. It is called the *infinitive* because the verb is not limited or "made finite" to indicate person, number, tense, or mood. In English the infinitive may be preceded by *to,* as in *We want him to work harder, To cooperate means to be willing to compromise,* and *I decided to bake a cake,* or it may appear without *to,* usually following an auxiliary verb, as in *We may leave tomorrow* and *She had them read the letter.* The infinitive without *to* is called the bare infinitive.

See more at **auxiliary and primary verbs** and **finite.**

inflammatory / inflammable / flammable

Contrary to what one might expect, the word *inflammatory* has never referred literally to fire or materials that can start a fire. In medicine, it means "characterized or caused by inflammation," as in *an inflammatory response caused by an infection.* Otherwise it refers to something that arouses passion or strong emotion, especially anger, belligerence, or desire. It frequently modifies words and terms for verbal material such as rhetoric and editorial:

> Though still in want of a Democratic candidate willing to wed a fledgling congressional campaign to his inflammatory rhetoric, Winchell went ahead to set up his soapbox outside the gates to the factories of Bridgeport and at the entrance to the shipyards in New London . . . (Philip Roth, *The Plot Against America*)

The word *inflammable* is sometimes confused with *inflammatory* in contexts like these, but it properly refers to that which is excitable or easily aroused to strong emotion:

> There was nothing in the tale to kindle the most inflammable imagination . . . (Edith Wharton, *The Pelican*)

Literally, *inflammable* means "combustible," and, interestingly, has the same meaning as the word *flammable.* The prefix *in–* is not the Latin negative prefix *in–,* which is related to the English *un–* and appears in words such as *indecent* and *inglorious,* but is derived from the Latin preposition *in,* "in." (This prefix also appears in the word *enflame.*) However, some people mistakenly think that *inflammable* means "not flammable." Therefore, for clarity's sake, it is best to use only the word *flammable* to give warnings.

inflection

An inflection is a change in a word that expresses a grammatical relationship, such as case, gender, number, person, tense, or mood. The term *inflection* can also refer to a word form or element that is involved in this change. In English most inflections are indicated by suffixes, such as *-s,* which indicates the plural of many nouns (*dogs*) and the third-person singular present tense form of main verbs (*thinks*), and *-ed,* which indicates the past tense and past participle in many verbs (*relaxed*). Some English inflections involve a change in the base form of the word to indicate the past tense or the past participle, as *spoke* and *spoken* from *speak.*

See more at **plural nouns** and **verbs, principal parts of.**

infringe   See **impinge.**

ingenuous   See **disingenuous.**

inherence / inherent

Traditionally, these are pronounced (ĭn-hîr′əns) and (ĭn-hîr′ənt), where the middle syllable sounds like the word *here.* However, the pronunciations with short *e,* (ĭn-hĕr′əns) and (ĭn-hĕr′ənt), where the middle syllable rhymes with the first syllable of *cherry,* are equally common now. The change is perhaps a result of association with *inherit.*

inherited   See **congenital.**

injustice / unjust

Usually the prefixes in the negatives of adjectives correspond to those in their noun forms, as in *indiscreet* and *indiscretion.* The word *just* is an exception. The opposite of *just,* meaning "fair, equitable," is *unjust,* but the corresponding noun form is *injustice.* The forms *injust* and *unjustice* are usually not listed in dictionaries and are considered to be misspellings. The corresponding noun for *unjust* is *unjustness.*

See more at **discreet** and **un–.**

in memoriam

This phrase is commonly misspelled as *in memorium.*

in regard to / in regards to   See **as regards.**

insane

The word *insane* is commonly used to describe people who are severely mentally ill. But *insane* actually has no medical meaning at all and is not used to describe mental illness or deficiency in psychiatric or scientific literature.

Insane is a legal term that refers to unsoundness of mind that is sufficient in the judgment of a civil court to render a person unfit to maintain a contractual relationship or to warrant commitment to a mental health facility. Its definition is based on a precedent established in a famous English case in 1843, known as *M'Naghten's* (or *McNaghten's*) *rule*. According to this standard, a person found to be criminally insane is judged to be too mentally impaired to understand either the true nature of the crime or whether the act was right or wrong. The person is therefore considered not legally responsible for the act.

Any number of psychiatric or mental disorders can result in the impaired judgment that constitutes criminal insanity, including mental retardation, schizophrenia, or multiple personality disorder. When discussing an actual mental condition, the label of *insane* should be avoided, and specific diagnostic information should be given when possible.

See more at **nervous breakdown.**

insect   See **bug.**

inside of

The construction *inside of* has been criticized for being both redundant and colloquial. However, its use in formal writing is not unprecedented:

> Seeing all these colonnades of bone so methodically ranged about, would you not think you were inside of the great Haarlem organ, and gazing upon its thousand pipes? (Herman Melville, *Moby Dick*)

> He actually lived in a small two-story Vietnamese house deeper inside of Cholon, as far from the papers and the regulations as he could get (Michael Herr, "Illumination Rounds," *The New American Review*)

In less formal contexts and in speech rendered in dialogue, both *inside* and *inside of* are often used to denote an interval of time, as in *I'll get this job done inside (of) a week.* In formal writing, *within* predominates in these contexts.

insignia

Insignia in Latin is the plural form of *insigne,* "mark, sign," but it has long been used in English as both a singular and a plural form: *The insignia was visible on the wingtip. There are five insignia on various parts of the plane.* From the singular use of *insignia* English speakers derived the plural *insignias,* which is also acceptable. The Latin singular *insigne,* is largely restricted to military contexts; in other contexts, it may strike some readers as pedantic.

in situ

The phrase *in situ,* which comes from Latin, is used in English to mean "in the original position." The primary pronunciation in English is the one that most closely approximates the Latin pronunciation: (ĭn sē′tŏŏ) or (ĭn sē′tyŏŏ). In our 1999 survey, 47 percent of Usage Panelists said they used one or the other of these pronunciations. Another 32 percent claimed (ĭn sĭ′chŏŏ), and a further 12 percent used (ĭn sī′tŏŏ) or (ĭn sī′tyŏŏ). All of these pronunciations are acceptable.

insure   See **assure.**

integral

The word *integral* can be pronounced with stress on the first or second syllable, as (ĭn′tĭ-grəl) or (ĭn-tĕg′rəl). In mathematics, the noun *integral* is usually pronounced with the stress on the first syllable.

There is a tendency among some speakers to insert an *r* in the second syllable, either as (ĭn′tər-grəl) or (ĭn′trə-gəl). These pronunciations are not considered standard.

See more at **intrusion.**

intense / intensive

The meanings of *intense* and *intensive* overlap considerably, but the two adjectives often have distinct meanings. *Intense* often suggests a strength or concentration that arises from an inner disposition and is particularly appropriate for describing emotional states:

> He wondered vaguely why all this intense feeling went running because of a few burnt potatoes (D.H. Lawrence, *Sons and Lovers*)

Intensive is more appropriate when the strength or concentration of an activity is imposed from without:

> . . . they worked out a system of intensive agriculture surpassing anything I ever heard of, with the very forests all reset with fruit- or nut-bearing trees (Charlotte Perkins Gilman, *Herland*)

Thus a reference to *Mark's intense study of German* suggests that Mark engaged in concentrated activity, while *Mark's intensive study of German* suggests that the program in which Mark was studying was designed to cover a great deal of material in a brief period.

intensives and intensifiers

Intensive words, sometimes called *intensives* or *intensifiers,* tend to emphasize or intensify the meaning of the words they modify. Thus the adjectives *absolute, complete, simple, definite,* and *utter* act as intensifiers in the following examples: *Their garden is an absolute marvel, O'Reilly's boss is a complete fool, The simple truth is that he doesn't care, We have a definite problem in the shipping department, What he says is utter nonsense.* The adverbs made from such adjectives can also function as intensives, as in *Their home is absolutely beautiful, That statement is simply ridiculous, You are entirely correct,* and so on. A variety of other adverbs can be used in the same way, words such as *fully, thoroughly, really, highly* (as in *highly intelligent*), *extremely, totally,* and *perfectly.* Adverbs such as *so, very,* and *quite* function as intensives as well, as in *The music was so beautiful, We found the climb to be very demanding, The exhibit is quite interesting.* In addition, the reflexive pronouns ending in *–self* can be used to intensify the meaning of a sentence, as *yourself* in *How can you ask me to help when you haven't done anything yourself?*

See more at **pronouns, reflexive and intensive** and **so.**

inter–

The prefix *inter–* comes from the Latin prefix *inter–,* from the preposition *inter,* meaning "between, among." Thus the word *intercede,* in which *inter–* combines with the Latin verb *cedere,* "to go," means "to go between." Similarly, *interject,* which comes from Latin *iacere,* "to throw," means literally "to throw something between or among others." And *intervene,* coming from Latin *venire,* "to come," means "to come between people or things." In English, *inter–* is still producing new words, such as *interfaith, intertwine,* and *Internet.*

The prefix *inter–* should not be confused in either writing or pronunciation with *intra–,* meaning "inside, within," from Latin *intrā,* "on the inside, within." Thus *intercellular* means "occurring or located among or between cells," while *intracellular* means "occurring or located within a cell or cells." The prefix *extra–,* "outside, beyond," is also used to form words opposite in meaning to those formed with *intra–.* Thus *intramural* activities are those carried out by students from only one school or university, while *extramural* activities involve the participation of students from more than one institution.

interest

This word is usually pronounced as if it were spelled *intrist* or *intrest,* with only two syllables, although the three-syllable pronunciation (ĭn'tər-ĭst) is also acceptable. The pronunciation without the first *t* sound, as though it were spelled *innerest,* is considered nonstandard.

interface

The noun *interface* has been in use since the 1880s, meaning "a surface forming a common boundary, as between bodies or regions." In the 1960s it began to be used in the computer industry to designate the point of interaction between a computer and another system, such as a printer. The word was applied to other interactions as well—between departments in an organization, for example, or between fields of study. Since it referred to a point of interaction in these contexts, *interface* soon developed a verbal usage, but it didn't catch on well outside its niche in the computer world, where it still thrives. The Usage Panel has been unable to muster much enthusiasm for the verb. In our 1995 survey, 37 percent accepted it when used to designate the interaction between people in the sentence *The managing editor must interface with a variety of freelance editors and proofreaders.* But the percentage dropped to 22 for examples in which the interaction is between a corporation and the public or between various communities in a city. Many Panelists complained that *interface* is pretentious and jargony. Certainly, there is no shortage of synonyms: *cooperate, deal, exchange information, interact,* and *work* present themselves as ready substitutes.

interment / internment

Interment refers to the act or ritual of interring, or burying: *The interment will take place immediately after the memorial service.* It is sometimes confused with the word *internment,* which is the state of being interned, or confined, usually without due process or trial. *Internment* generally refers to the confinement of civilians, especially people sharing the same nationality or political beliefs as the enemy, during wartime.

intersex / intersexual / hermaphrodite

In biology, the term *hermaphrodite* refers to a plant or animal that has both male and female reproductive organs. This is a normal condition in certain organisms, such as the earthworm, but in others it is a physiological abnormality. In medical as well as popular literature, the term *hermaphrodite* has traditionally been used to describe humans in which both male and female reproductive organs or tissues are present. However, most people who have these conditions prefer the terms *intersex* and *intersexual* (used both as nouns and adjectives). *Intersex* sometimes occurs in scientific literature to refer to hermaphroditic plants or animals, but *hermaphrodite* is more common.

See more at **transvestite.**

in the throes of

A *throe* is a severe pang or spasm of pain. The word is used mainly in the plural, as in *the throes of labor,* and it occurs commonly in the collocation *death throes,* literally referring to the final spasms before death but often used figuratively to refer to the violent or chaotic final stages of something, as in *the death throes of a star* or *the death throes of an aging industry*. The word may occur most frequently in the phrase *in the throes of,* which is used to describe being in grave difficulty or a desperate struggle, as in *a country in the throes of economic collapse.* This expression is sometimes miscast as *in the throws of,* as in this newswire report: *"Venerable parties, such as Germany's Social Democrats, are currently in the throws of similar internal upheavals."* This is an understandable error, since being *in the throes of* implies turmoil, that is, being "thrown about."

intra–   See **inter–**.

intransitive verb   See **verbs, transitive and intransitive.**

intrigue

The verb *intrigue* has long been used in English in the meaning "to plot or scheme." In the 1890s, however, the verb *intrigue* began to take on a new meaning, "to arouse the interest or curiosity of," through the influence of the meaning of the related French verb *intriguer.* In this new sense, *intrigue* was soon condemned as a gallicism and an unnecessary substitute for established English words such as *interest, fascinate,* and *puzzle.* Nonetheless, it quickly became widespread and continues to be used by all sorts of writers to this day. Its success suggests that it is not in fact an exact synonym of any earlier English word. Rather, *intrigue* connotes a greater engagement with the intellect than *interest,* but a less overwhelming effect than *fascinate.* It may thus be well suited to some contexts where other words would be less precise. The Usage Panel has long considered the word standard. In our 1988 survey, 78 percent accepted it in the sentence *The special-quota idea intrigues some legislators, who have asked a Washington think tank to evaluate it.* This constituted a dramatic increase over the results of the 1968 survey, in which only a slim majority (52 percent) accepted this same sentence.

intrusion

Intrusion is a type of phonological variation that involves the addition or insertion of a sound where there is no historical basis for it. The pronunciation (ə-krôst′) for *across,* (fĭl′əm), with two syllables, for *film,* (grē′vē-əs), with three syllables, for *grievous,* (pûr′kyə-lāt′) for *percolate,* and (wôrsh) for *wash* are all examples of intrusion. Although these pronunciations may be pervasive or even standard within a particular region, they are often stigmatized as regionalisms or viewed as a sign of ignorance, since people sometimes conclude that the speaker does not know how to spell the word.

intuit

The use of *intuit* as a verb is well established, but some object to it. In our 1988 survey, only 34 percent of the Usage Panel accepted it in the sentence *Dermot often intuits my feelings about things long before I am really aware of them myself.* People often attribute this lack of acceptance to the verb's status as a back-formation from *intuition,* but in fact the verb has existed as long as other back-formations, such as *diagnose* from *diagnosis,* that are now wholly acceptable. The source of the objections most likely lies in the fact that the verb is often used in reference to more trivial sorts of insight than would be permitted by a full appreciation of the traditional meaning of *intuition.* In this connection, a greater percentage of the Panel, 46 percent, accepted *intuit* in the sentence *Mathematicians sometimes intuit the truth of a theorem long before they are able to prove it.*

See more at **enthuse.**

Inuit

The preferred term for the native peoples of the Canadian Arctic and Greenland is now *Inuit,* and the use of *Eskimo* in referring to these peoples is often considered offensive, especially in Canada. *Inuit,* the plural of the Inuit word *inuk,* "human being," is less exact in referring to the peoples of northern Alaska, who speak dialects of the closely related Inupiaq language, and it is inappropriate when used in reference to speakers of Yupik, the Eskimoan language branch of western Alaska and the Siberian Arctic.

See more at **Eskimo.**

inveigle

The pronunciation that rhymes with *beagle* is older, but the pronunciation that rhymes with *bagel* is predominant now in American English.

invest / infest

Infest means "to inhabit in quantities large enough to be harmful," or "to live as a parasite in or on another organism." One of the less common meanings of *invest* is "to cover completely or envelop." Because these words sound so much alike and these meanings are similar, *invest* is sometimes used when *infest* is intended, especially in the adjectival form, as in this newspaper movie review: *"This low-budget Sundance hit about a pair of scuba-divers who are mistakenly abandoned in shark-invested waters will have you checking the swimming pool for trouble."*

In certain cases, it is hard to determine if *invest* is an error for *infest* or if *invest* is used properly but metaphorically to mean "to direct one's resources or energy toward something, make an investment of one's time in something," as in this quotation from Mark Twain's *Roughing It:* *"There was only one cruet left, and that was a stopperless, fly-specked, broken-necked thing, with two inches of vinegar in it, and a dozen preserved flies with their heels up and looking sorry they had invested there."*

in virtue of

The phrase *in virtue of* is sometimes used to mean "on the basis of, by reason of," where one might expect to see *by virtue of* instead. To be sure, *by virtue of* is by far the more common usage, and the Usage Panel approves of this situation. In our 2004 survey, only 8 percent of the Panel preferred *in virtue of* in the sentence *The accountant had access to the records (in virtue of/by virtue of) his position,* while 90 percent preferred *by virtue of.* A similar percentage (83) preferred *by virtue of* in the sentence *(In virtue of/By virtue of) your hard work, you have been invited to the patron's dinner.* Writers who would like to avoid these constructions altogether can say *because of, by reason of,* or *on account of* instead.

invoke   See **evoke.**

Iran

The degree to which the pronunciation of the names of foreign countries and cities is Anglicized varies from place to place. As foreign locales become more familiar to English speakers, the pronunciation of these foreign names often becomes less Anglicized. *Prague* was once pronounced (prāg) in English but is now pronounced much as it is in Europe (präg), rhyming with *bog;* and English speakers say both (chĭl′ē) and (chē′lĕ) for *Chile.* In other cases the Anglicized pronunciation remains predominant, as is the case with *Brazil* (brə-zĭl′) instead of (brä-sēl′).

The former empire of Persia was officially renamed *Iran* in 1935. There are many acceptable variant pronunciations in English: (ĭ-rän′), with a short *i* and an *a* as in *father* (the preferred choice of 64 percent of the Usage Panelists in our 2001 survey); (ĭ-răn′), with a short *i* and a second syllable like the word *ran* (the preference of 31 percent); and (ī-răn′), with a long *i* and a second syllable like the word *ran* (the preference of 5 percent).

The country known as *Iraq* was so named after World War I and the dissolution of the Ottoman Empire, and it also has three variants, corresponding to the ones for *Iran* except with a (k) sound for the (n) sound.

ironic

In its nonliterary uses, *irony* often refers to a perceived incongruity between what is expected and what actually occurs, especially if what actually occurs thwarts human wishes or designs. People sometimes misuse the words *ironic, irony,* and *ironically,* applying them to events and circumstances that might better be described as simply *coincidental* or *improbable,* in that the events suggest no particular lessons about human vanity or folly. In our 1987 survey, 78 percent of the Usage Panel rejected the use of *ironically* in the sentence *In 1969 Susan moved from Ithaca to California where she met her husband-to-be, who, ironically, also came from upstate New York.* Some Panelists noted that this particular usage might be acceptable if Susan had in fact moved to California in order to find a husband, in which case the story could be taken as exemplifying the folly of supposing that we can know what fate has in store for us. By contrast, 73 percent accepted the sentence *Ironically, even as the government was fulminating against American policy, American jeans and videocassettes were the hottest items in the stalls of the market,* where the incongruity can be seen as an example of human inconsistency.

irregardless

Irregardless is a word that many people mistakenly believe to be correct in formal style, when in fact it is used chiefly in nonstandard speech or casual writing. The word was coined in the United States in the early 20th century, probably from a blend of *irrespective* and *regardless.* Many critics have complained that it is a redundancy, the negative prefix *ir–* duplicating the negativity of the *–less* suffix. Perhaps its reputation as a blend of ill-fitting parts has caused some to insist that it is a "nonword," a charge they would not think of leveling at a nonstandard word with a longer history, such as *ain't.* Since people use *irregardless,* it is undoubtedly a word in the broader sense of the language, but it has never been accepted in Standard English and is almost always changed by copyeditors to *regardless.* As a result, it rarely occurs in print.

irregular

In grammar, the term *irregular* means "departing from the usual pattern of inflection, derivation, or word formation." The plural noun *children* and the present tense forms of the verb *be* are irregular.

See more at **plural nouns** and **verbs, principal parts of.**

Islam / Islamism

Islam is the religion founded in 7th-century Arabia by the Prophet Muhammad and embraced today in various forms by people in all parts of the world. The adjective used in referring to the religion is *Islamic,* and all believers in Islam, regardless of what branch they belong to or what doctrine they follow, are called *Muslims.* *Islamism,* in contrast, is a modern-day movement among certain Muslims aimed at institutionalizing Islamic beliefs and practices throughout the public and private life of a society. The adjective referring to this movement is *Islamist,* and Muslims who favor this kind of social and political reform can be called *Islamists.* Thus an *Islamic* or *Muslim* country is one in which the majority of inhabitants practice Islam, regardless of what form of government it has, whereas an *Islamist* country is an Islamic country in which the political, legal, and social institutions are under the control of religious rather than secular authorities.

Islamists generally hold strongly conservative religious beliefs, and to the extent that they seek to revive a version of the theocratic rule of earlier Islamic societies, they are also typically antimodern (and by extension anti-Western) in their outlook. It should not be assumed, however, that Islamism is an inherently violent movement or that its opposition to the West is necessarily militant. While some Islamists may tolerate or even espouse violence against Western nations as well as against secular Islamic regimes, many Islamists seek similar political and social reforms by popular, nonviolent means.

–ism

The suffix *–ism* forms nouns and has a great variety of meanings, including "action, practice," as in *terrorism;* "characteristic behavior or quality," as in *heroism;* "state of being," as in *pauperism;* "condition resulting from an excess of something," as in *strychninism;* and "doctrine, system of principles," as in *animism* and *pacifism.* Recently the suffix has become especially productive in the formation of nouns meaning "discrimination against a group based on a given trait," as in *sexism, ageism,* and *speciesism.* The suffix *–ism* comes from the Greek noun suffix *–ismos.* Nouns that end in *–ism* often have related verbs that end in *–ize* (*criticism/criticize*), related agent nouns that end in *–ist* (*optimism/optimist*), and related adjectives that end in *–istic* (*optimism/optimistic*).

issue

The word *issue* is often used to refer to a problem, difficulty, or condition, especially an embarrassing or discrediting one. The word sees much use in the plural. Thus, an athlete might have legal issues (what might otherwise be called "trouble with the law"), a business might be saddled with financial issues (be deeply in debt), and a person might have to confront sexual issues stemming from child abuse.

Many people find this usage objectionable as an unwarranted semantic extension and as a vogue word. Despite its popularity, the Usage Panel tends to frown on it. In our 2002 survey, 61 percent rejected it in these examples: *We've got a couple of kids who've got issues and will need to see the guidance counselor. She's got issues with sexuality that don't fit comfortably in the Republican big tent.*

Any number of phrases, including *financial problem, emotional condition,* and *psychological difficulty,* can be used as substitutes for *issue* in such contexts, if the word seems unappealing.

The Panel is considerably more unhappy when *issue* is used for a technical problem. Only 18 percent accepted the example *There were a number of issues installing the printer driver in the new release of the software.*

In these cases, words like *glitch* and *complication* can be used in addition to *problem.* It should be noted, however, that *issue* is widely used in this sense by writers of technical manuals, mostly likely out of reluctance to admit that a product has a *problem.*

–ist

The suffix *–ist*, which comes from the Greek suffix *–istēs*, forms agent nouns, that is, nouns that denote someone who does something. Although *–ist* frequently forms agent nouns from verbs ending in *–ize* or nouns ending in *–ism*, it has also come to be combined with words that do not end in *–ize* or *–ism*. In fact in some cases *–ist* can be used much like the suffix *–er*. In pairs such as *conformer/conformist*, *copier/copyist*, and *cycler/cyclist*, *–ist* and *–er* may sometimes be used almost interchangeably. Nouns ending in *–ist*, however, often connote habitual engagement in an activity or the practice of a profession: a *copier* is simply one who copies, while a professional scribe copying manuscripts in medieval times is more often designated a *copyist*.

italics

foreign words   Foreign words and phrases not yet assimilated into the English language are italicized.

> editors, machinists, *pâtissiers*, barbers, and hoboes
> his *Sturm und Drang* period

for emphasis   Italics may be used to emphasize a word or phrase in a sentence.

> "Yes, you are my fate, young man. Only you can tell me what it really is. Do you understand?"
>
> "I *think* I do, sir." (Ralph Ellison, *Invisible Man*)

A similar effect may likewise be conveyed by casting the sentence so that the stressed element falls at the end.

> The diaphanous veil that Sophocles' Antigone wears at the beginning of the play comes in quite handy at the end—as a noose. (Michael Roberts, "Grecian Formula," *The New Yorker*)

legal citations   The names of plaintiff and defendant in legal citations are italicized.

> *Madison* v. *Kingsley*
> *Estate of Katharine Briggs* v. *Town of Old Saybrook*

letters of the alphabet   Letters of the alphabet referred to as such are generally italicized. Plurals of lowercase letters are formed by adding a roman apostrophe and a roman *s*. Plurals of uppercase letters do not require an apostrophe. Letters that designate shapes or represent scholastic grades are roman.

> The vowels *e* and *a* occur most frequently in English.
> There are four *s*'s in *Mississippi*.
> The living room is L-shaped.
> Students in the debate class got mostly As and Bs.

punctuation   In the traditional style, periods, commas, colons, and semicolons following an italicized word are also italicized. A simpler, alternative system is to put these punctuation marks in the same typeface as the main or surrounding text, as in the following examples:

> Richard Wright's autobiography, *Black Boy*, was published in 1945.

> We won't be reading *War and Peace*: it is too difficult for this age group.

> Wright won popular acclaim for *Native Son*; the novel was an instant best-seller and became a Book-of-the-Month Club selection.

The choice of typeface for question marks and exclamation points depends on the context. Parentheses and brackets should be in the same typeface as the main text even if they contain italicized material.

> Albee wrote *Who's Afraid of Virginia Woolf?* in 1962.
> Who wrote *The Crucible*?
> Irish moss (*Chondrus crispus*) collects along the beach at low tide.

scientific names   The Latin names of genera, species, subspecies, and varieties in botanical and zoological nomenclature are italicized. Higher levels—kingdoms, phyla, classes, orders, and families—are set in roman.

> *Brassica oleracea* var. *botrytis*

> the house mouse (*Mus muscularis*) in the family Muridae, order Rodentia, class Mammalia, and phylum Chordata

titles of works

1. The titles of books, plays, short stories published separately, and very long poems are italicized.

   > *For Whom the Bell Tolls*
   > *A Streetcar Named Desire*
   > *Leo the Late Bloomer Bakes a Cake*
   > *Paradise Lost*

2. The titles of newspapers and magazines are italicized. Even if the word *the* appears at the beginning of the name on the masthead or cover, it is neither capitalized nor italicized except in a few cases where it is considered integral to the title.

   > the *New York Times*   *The New Yorker*
   > the *Patriot Ledger*   *The Nation*
   > *GQ*

3. The names of holy books are not italicized.

   > Bible
   > Talmud
   > Koran *or* Qur'an

4. Unless they are part of the periodical's official name, the word *magazine* and other words used descriptively are lowercased and set in roman type.

> *American Heritage* magazine   the *New York Times Magazine*
> *People* magazine   the New York *Daily News*

5. The titles of movies and radio and television series are italicized.

> *Dial M for Murder*   *A Prairie Home Companion*
> *Gone with the Wind*   *Masterpiece Theater*
> *All Things Considered*   *The Simpsons*

6. The names of operas and long musical compositions are italicized. Compositions referred to by their musical form (symphony, sonata, concerto, and so forth) are capitalized and set in roman. The names of songs and short musical pieces are roman and enclosed in quotation marks.

> *Madame Butterfly*
> Handel's *Messiah*
> Symphony no. 3 in E-flat Major; the Third Symphony; the *Eroica* Symphony
> Piano Sonata in C-sharp Minor; the *Moonlight* Sonata
> Schubert's "Death and the Maiden"
> "The Star-Spangled Banner"

7. The names of paintings and sculptures are italicized.

> *Mona Lisa*   *The Gates of Hell*
> *Guernica*   *Discus Thrower*

See more at **titles of works** under **quotation marks.**

transportation   The names of ships, submarines, planes, and spacecraft are italicized. The designations *SS*, *USS*, and *HMS* are not italicized when they precede ships' names. The names of space programs are set in roman.

> the SS *Titanic*   *Air Force One*
> the USS *Tennessee*   *Apollo 11*
> the HMS *Racoon*   the Apollo missions

words as words   Words used as words are italicized.

> The word *buzz* is onomatopoeic.
> *Can't* has the same meaning as *won't* in his lexicon.

its / it's

Its is the possessive form of the pronoun *it* and is never written with an apostrophe: *The cat licked its paws.* The contraction *it's* (for *it is* or *it has*) always has an apostrophe: *It's the funniest show I've seen in years. It's been three years since our last trip to the islands.*

See more at **contractions.**

–ize

The suffix *–ize* has been and continues to be a productive means of turning nouns and adjectives into verbs, as in such well-established forms as *formalize, criticize, jeopardize,* and *hospitalize.* In many cases, *–ize* creates verbs with more than one meaning. Thus *computerize* may mean "to furnish with computers" (as in *The entire office has been computerized*) or "to enter or store on a computer" (as in *The records are not yet computerized*). In some cases this can cause ambiguity. For example, the sentence *Earthquake relief requirements must be prioritized* may mean that all relief requirements must be assigned a high priority or that the relative priority among requirements must be determined. It is important therefore that the context make clear which sense is intended.

Many words formed with *–ize* come from bureaucratic and corporate jargon, and for this reason they often meet with resistance when the general public first sees them. The verbs *Americanize, nationalize,* and *jeopardize* were all objected to when they were introduced, but they have since become standard. Although some recent words of this type have been quickly accepted—for example, *computerize, institutionalize,* and *radicalize*—many others have not shaken their association with bureaucratese. Among these are *incentivize, prioritize, privatize,* and *finalize.* You should be careful with coinages of this sort, especially when writing for a general audience.

See more at **finalize, incentivize,** and **prioritize.**

· J ·

jetsam See **flotsam.**

Jew

It is widely recognized that the attributive use of the noun *Jew,* in phrases such as *Jew lawyer* or *Jew ethics,* is highly offensive. In such contexts *Jewish* is the only acceptable possibility. Some people, however, have become so wary of this construction that they have extended the stigma to any use of *Jew* as a noun, a practice that carries risks of its own. In a sentence such as *There are now several Jews on the council,* which is unobjectionable, the substitution of a circumlocution like *Jewish people* or *persons of Jewish background* may in itself cause offense for seeming to imply that *Jew* has a negative connotation when used as a noun.

However, when the speaker's intention is merely to distinguish someone, an expression such as *Jewish comedian* may be appropriate, particularly in speech. *Is the Jewish singer still performing?* suggests that *Jewish* is mentioned only for the purpose of indicating that a specific person previously referred to is being talked about. In the same context, the use of *Jew* (instead of *Jewish singer*) might suggest that the speaker had questionable reasons for focusing on the person's religion or ethnic status. In this regard, *Jewish* is parallel to other social indicators such as *Irish.*

jewelry

The standard pronunciation for this word has three syllables (jōō′əl-rē), which is somewhat difficult to say, and is why the word is often pronounced with only two syllables (jōōl′rē). The pronunciation (jōō′lə-rē) is considered nonstandard and may lead to the misspelling of this word as *jewelery.*

jibe See **gibe.**

jive See **gibe.**

Judaism

The standard pronunciations for this word are (jōō′dē-ĭz′əm) and (jōō′dā-ĭz′əm). The first was the preferred choice of 37 percent of the Usage Panel, and the second

269

was favored by 40 percent, respectively, in our 2001 survey. The less common variants (jōō'də-ĭz'əm) and (jōō-dā'ĭz'əm) were the choice of 19 percent and 7 percent of the Panel, respectively. Interestingly, each of these four variants was considered unacceptable by roughly one fifth of the Panelists. This may reflect a desire on the part of some Panelists to simplify a situation in which there are numerous competing pronunciations for the same word.

junta

For a long time this 18th-century borrowing from Spanish was pronounced (jŭn'tə) by English speakers on both sides of the Atlantic. By the middle of the 20th century, however, the pronunciation (hōōn'tə), an approximation of the Spanish pronunciation, had gained currency in the US. This word is now usually pronounced (hōōn'tə) in American English and (jŭn'tə) in British English.

just deserts   See **desert.**

juvenilia

This uncommon word, which is related to *juvenile,* is a plural noun meaning "works produced by an author or artist when young." It takes a plural verb: *The author's juvenilia are part of the library's collection.* The word is properly pronounced (jōō'və-nĭl'ē-ə) or (jōō'və-nĭl'yə), with a short *i* in the third syllable. The misspelling *juvenalia* reflects the commonly heard pronunciation (jōō'və-nāl'yə), with a long *a* in the third syllable. This pronunciation arose probably by association with words such as *bacchanalia* and *paraphernalia,* or by confusion with *Juvenalian* (referring to the Roman satirist Juvenal), all of which are pronounced with a long *a.* Neither the spelling *juvenalia* nor the pronunciation with a long *a* has yet to be included in any dictionary, however, and so cannot be considered standard.

· K ·

Kanaka

The word *Kanaka* simply means "human being" in the Hawaiian language. When borrowed into English, however, it was naturally used in referring not to people in general but rather to Hawaiians of Polynesian descent, or more broadly, to any Polynesian person. Since this usage has often been perceived, and has sometimes been intended, as derogatory, *Kanaka* is best avoided by outsiders. Among Native Hawaiians, however, it is often used today as a term of ethnic pride, especially in the form *Kanaka Maoli,* a traditional Hawaiian ethnonym which can be translated as "true human being" or "real person."

kerchief

The plural of this word is either *kerchiefs,* pronounced (kûr′chĭfs) or (kûr′chĕfs′), or *kerchieves* pronounced (kûr′chĭvz) or (kûr′chēvz′). The word comes from Old French *couvrechief,* which is itself derived from the verb *covrir,* "to cover," and the noun *chief,* "head." Since its adoption into English during the 14th century or perhaps even earlier, the word has had both the regular plural *kerchiefs,* as well as the plural *kerchieves,* the latter fitting the pattern displayed by words descended from Old English like *thief/thieves, leaf/leaves,* and *wife/wives.*

See more at **roof.**

kilometer

Many people insist that this word should have its primary stress on the first syllable so that it will conform to the same stress pattern in *millimeter* and *centimeter.* Language, however, does not always operate as regularly or logically as we might wish. Despite objections to the pronunciation with stress on the second syllable, which originally came about by analogy with *barometer* and *thermometer,* it continues to thrive in American English. In our 1988 survey, 69 percent of the Usage Panel preferred the pronunciation with stress on the second syllable, 29 percent preferred the pronunciation with stress on the first syllable, and 10 percent said they use both. Most dictionaries have given both pronunciations since the middle of the 19th century.

kind / sort

singular or plural The use of the plural *these* and *those* with singular *kind* and *sort*, as in *these kind* (or *sort*) *of films*, has been a traditional bugbear of American grammarians. By and large, British grammarians have been more tolerant. After all, the construction appears in the works of honored British writers from Pope to Churchill and beyond. Grammatically, the question boils down to whether *kind* and *sort* should be treated as head nouns (like *species* or *variety*) or whether they function more like adjectives, much like *bunch of* in *A bunch of kids are at the front door* and *number of* in *A number of rings were found in the drawer.* If *kind* and *sort* are nouns, you would expect to see only *this* or *that* and a singular verb accompanying them, as in *This kind of films is popular,* in the same pattern as *This variety of spices makes the dish interesting.* If *kind* and *sort* function as adjectives, however, you would expect *these* or *those* and a plural verb, as in *These kind of films are popular.* In fact, the *kind of* construction can be legitimately viewed in either way, which is doubtless one reason why writers don't follow a uniform pattern in usage.

Whatever the interpretation, the plural *kinds* requires the plural *these* or *those,* and the verb must also be plural: *These* [not *this*] *kinds of films are* [not *is*] *popular.* By the same token, when both *kind* and the noun following it are singular, you must use a singular verb: *This kind of film is* [not *are*] *popular.*

***kind of / sort of* as adverbs** *Kind of* and *sort of* are used colloquially as adverbs to mean "somewhat," "in some way," and "to some extent." They are sometimes referred to as idioms and are most frequently encountered in informal speech and writing, as in this quotation from the *Boston Herald:* "*In the most shocking moment in 'The Forgotten,' Alfre Woodard's decent police detective is sucked up into the skies in a kind of frightening cosmic explosion, never to be seen again.*"

See more at **subject and verb agreement.**

kindergarten

This word is frequently misspelled as *kindergarden,* which corresponds to one of its pronunciations.

kinetic energy / potential energy

Energy can take many different forms. One distinction made by physicists and engineers concerns whether or not the energy ascribed to an object or a physical system involves movement.

The *kinetic energy* of an object corresponds to the energy the object has by virtue of its motion. For example, the kinetic energy of a body moving in a straight line is equal to half its mass times the square of its speed. (The spin of rigid bodies, or the vibration of less rigid ones, is also considered kinetic energy, since movement is involved.)

When energy is ascribed to objects by virtue of their arrangement alone, we speak of *potential energy.* A ball held in the hand a few feet above the ground has potential energy; releasing the ball allows gravity to accelerate it, and by the time it hits the ground, its potential energy has been transformed into kinetic energy. The attractive and repulsive forces between arrangements of atoms in molecules also give rise to potential energy; like dropping a ball, the process of burning fuel in an engine is a means of transforming some of that potential energy into kinetic energy (the motion of a vehicle, for instance).

See more at **energy** and **heat.**

knot

In nautical usage, the word *knot* is a unit of speed, not of distance. It means "nautical miles per hour." Therefore, a ship travels at ten knots, not ten knots per hour.

Koran / Qur'an

The name of the sacred text of Islam, considered by Muslims to contain the revelations of God delivered to Muhammad, can be written either *Koran* or *Qur'an.* The spelling *Koran* is perhaps more familiar to the general public, and it is even used by many scholars of the Arabic language and Islamic civilization when writing in English.

The spelling *Qur'an* is an attempt to transcribe the Arabic name for the sacred text as well as possible within the constraints imposed by the Roman alphabet. In Arabic itself, the Koran is referred to as *al-qur'ān,* "the Koran." (The word *qur'ān* literally means "recitation" and is derived from the Arabic word *qara'a,* "read, recite.") The *q* in *Qur'an* represents a sound, called a voiceless uvular stop, that is not found in English. Arabic has two sounds, transcribed as *k* and *q,* that remind speakers of English of the sound (k). The sound transcribed *k* is quite similar to the English sound (k), while the voiceless uvular stop *q* strikes English speakers as a special kind of (k) made very deep in the throat. The difference between the two is very important in Arabic and helps distinguish words, such as *kalb,* "dog," and *qalb,* "heart." The sound written as an apostrophe (') in *Qur'an* is a glottal stop, the same sound heard in the middle of the English exclamation *Uh-oh!* and in the Cockney pronunciation of *t* heard in such words as *bottle* and *little.* (Writers should take care to use an apostrophe (') rather than a single quotation mark facing the opposite direction (') when writing *Qur'an,* since the latter symbol (') is sometimes used to represent another Arabic sound made deep in the throat, called *'ayn.*) The Arabic name for the sacred text of Islam, *al-qur'ān,* contains both the sound of *q* and the glottal stop, so that the English spelling *Qur'an* can be considered a closer rendering of the Arabic pronunciation and the way it is spelled in the Arabic alphabet. Yet another spelling occasionally encountered in English texts, *Qur'aan,* attempts to represent the long *ā,* of Arabic *al-qur'ān* by means of double *aa.*

The adjective derived from the name of the sacred text can also be spelled either *Koranic* or *Qur'anic.* Within a single piece of writing, the spelling of the adjective should match the spelling of the name of the text, *Koran* or *Qur'an,* for the sake of consistency.

The obsolete name for the Koran in English, *Alcoran,* should be avoided. The *al–* in this obsolete term is simply the Arabic definite article *al.* After Arabic became the main language of a large part of the Near East, North Africa, and the Iberian Peninsula, the languages of Europe began to borrow a great number of Arabic words, especially in the sphere of science and technology. During the process of transmission, the definite article and the noun were often borrowed together as a whole. For instance, Arabic *al-qubba,* "the vault," enters Spanish as *alcoba,* which was then borrowed into French as *alcôve,* from which we then get the English word *alcove.* The Arabic definite article *al–* can thus be seen at the beginning of many English words of Arabic origin, such as *alcohol, alembic, alfalfa,* and *algebra.*

kudos

Kudos is one of those words like *congeries* that look like plurals but are etymologically singular. Acknowledging the Greek history of the term requires *Kudos is* [not *are*] *due her for her brilliant work on the score.* But *kudos* has often been treated as a plural, especially in the popular press, as in *She received many kudos for her work.* This plural use has given rise to the singular form *kudo,* as in *The latest award added yet another kudo to her prize-laden career.* These innovations follow the pattern whereby the English words *pea* and *cherry* were shortened from nouns ending in an (s) sound (English *pease* and French *cerise*) that were mistakenly thought to be plural. The singular *kudo* remains far less common than the plural use; both are often viewed as incorrect in more formal contexts.

It is worth noting that even people who are careful to treat *kudos* only as a singular often pronounce it as if it were a plural. Etymology would require that the final consonant be pronounced as a voiceless (s), as in *pathos,* another word derived from Greek, so that the word rhymes with *loss.* More often than not, however, *kudos* is pronounced with a voiced (z) to rhyme with *doze.* Both pronunciations are acceptable.

· L ·

L

The letter *l* comes from the Roman alphabet, where it represented sounds similar to those represented by the letter in Modern English today. In Early Modern English, *l* was lost in the pronunciation of many words such as *should, would, calf, half, salmon, talk, walk, folk, yolk, balm, calm,* and *palm*. But in recent years, this silent *l* has made something of a comeback in a number of spelling pronunciations, as those for *almond, alms, balm, calm,* and *palm*, in which the *l* is now often pronounced.

See more at **spelling pronunciation.**

lack

When the verb *lack* is used in the sense of "to be wanting or deficient," it is typically followed by *in: You will not be lacking in support from me.* When *lack* is used in the sense of "to be in need of something," *for* is often used: *"In the terrible, beautiful age of my prime, / I lacked for sweet linen but never for time"* (E.B. White).

lady / ladylike

The word *lady* is used to refer to a female who behaves in a way that is considered to be refined or to be characterized by social courtesies. It is often used in conjunction with the word *gentlemen*, as in *Ladies and gentlemen, your attention, please*. Historically, a *lady* was the wife or widow of a knight, and *lady* is still used as a designation of noble rank among royalty. In general usage, when specific behaviors are not being considered, an adult female should be referred to as a *woman*. The substitution of *lady* for *woman* is considered condescending or trivializing by some people, perhaps because the word *lady* evokes a stereotype of a woman whose world is defined largely by manners and societally prescribed decorum. The adjective *ladylike* implies refined, courteous behavior befitting a *lady*. This word, too, can conjure up stereotypes of traditionally appropriate female behavior, including qualities such as docility or contrived politeness, and should also be used with caution.

The attributive use of *lady*, as in *lady doctor*, is offensive and outdated. When the gender of an individual is relevant, the preferred modifier is *woman* or *female*. *Lady* is also used sometimes as a sarcastic epithet for a stranger, as in *Hey, lady, I was in line before you!* This usage will likely be seen as hostile.

See more at **female.**

Latina

The use of the feminine forms *Latina* and *Chicana* as nouns referring to a woman or girl is proper in American English, but the use of forms ending in *-o* in such contexts (as in *She is a Latino*) may be resented on grounds of sexism. Moreover, when *Latina* and *Chicana* occur as modifiers, problems can arise that English does not usually have to solve. Is it wrong to use a masculine form such as *Chicano* to modify *woman*? Is the phrase *Chicana woman* redundant? Should one say *She is a Latino novelist*, or is *Latina novelist* required? And is the novel that such a person writes a *Latino* or a *Latina* novel?

There is no single answer to these questions, though a few guidelines can be offered. First, the rules of adjective-noun agreement required by Spanish grammar do not normally affect English usage; thus the choice between *She is the city's first Latino mayor* and *She is the city's first Latina mayor* does not depend on the gender of the Spanish word for mayor. Second, the use of the masculine form as a modifier with reference to a woman is common and unremarkable in English, as the following examples attest: *Bush Appoints Latino Woman to U.S. Court* (headline in the *Sacramento Bee*) and *"Juror 1427, a Latino woman who works for the Los Angeles County assessor"* (*Los Angeles Times*). Third, the use of the feminine form to modify words like *woman* or *girl* is often, though not always, associated with a liberal feminist viewpoint, as in *"I came to know Chicana women living in a barrio who were organizing women's health-care programs"* (*Ms. Magazine*). Finally, there are many cases in which the feminine modifier provides information that would be lost by using the masculine, as in *"Goldie Hawn plays a bleeding-heart liberal lawyer who rehabilitates the waifs and strays crossing her path [including] a pair of docile Chicana illegals"* (*Village Voice*).

See more at **Chicana.**

Latino   See **Hispanic.**

latter   See **former.**

laudable / laudatory / laudative

These words derived from the Latin root *laud–*, meaning "praise," are sometimes used interchangeably. Both *laudatory* and the less common *laudative* mean "expressing or conferring praise." *Laudable*, however, means "deserving commendation, worthy of praise." Thus, an artist's work might be laudable, while the review of that work might be laudatory.

lavish

The transitive verb *lavish*, meaning "to give or bestow in abundance," normally takes for its object what is being given, as in *The queen lavished gifts on her favorite courtier* and *The boy lavished affection on his dog*. Perhaps by the influence of the figurative use of the verb *shower,* however, *lavish* now sometimes occurs with a person as a direct object, as in *The queen lavished her favorite courtier with gifts* and *The boy lavished his dog with affection.* These usages are not included in contemporary dictionaries and should be considered suspect, particularly in formal contexts.

law / theory

In the natural sciences, the word *law* refers to firmly established principles within a scientific *theory,* especially principles that always hold true. Scientific theories are subject to change, of course, but the word *law* may still be used to refer to such principles within the context of the theory. For example, in the 17th century, when Newton devised his laws of motion and gravitation, the predictive success of this work was unprecedented. Since then, Einstein's *Theory of General Relativity,* developed in the early 20th century to explain gravitation, has supplanted Newton's principles, and it has had greater predictive success. Newton's principles are still referred to as *laws* in the context of his theory, even though that theory has been supplanted by Einstein's theory.

See more at **axiom.**

lay / lie

People have confused *lay* ("to put, place; prepare") and *lie* ("to recline; be situated") for centuries. They will probably continue to do so. *Lay* has been used to mean "lie" since the 1300s for several reasons. First, there are two *lay*'s. One is the base form of the verb *lay,* and the other is the past tense of *lie.* Second, *lay* was once used with a reflexive pronoun to mean "lie" and survives in the familiar line from the child's prayer *Now I lay me down to sleep.* It is not a long leap from *lay me down* to *lay down.* Third, *lay down,* as in *She lay down on the sofa* sounds the same as *laid down,* as in *She laid down the law to the kids.*

By traditional usage prescription, these words should be kept distinct according to the following rules. *Lay* is a transitive verb—it takes an object. *Lay* and its principal parts (*laid, laid, laying*) are correctly used in the following examples: *She lays* [not *lies*] *down her pen and stands up. He laid* [not *lay*] *the newspaper on the table. The table was laid for four. I am laying the baby in the crib. Lie* is an intransitive verb and cannot take an object. *Lie* and its principal parts (*lay, lain, lying*) are correctly used in the following examples: *She often lies* [not *lays*] *down after lunch. When I lay* [not *laid*] *down, I fell asleep. The rubbish had lain* [not *laid*] *there a week. I was lying* [not *laying*] *in bed when he called.*

There are a few exceptions to these rules. The phrasal verb *lay for* and the nautical use of *lay,* as in *lay at anchor,* though intransitive, are standard.

The two words are most commonly mixed up in speech, where *lay* is an especially common substitution for *lie.* Dog owners commonly command their pets to *lay down* instead of *lie down.* Golfers often play the ball as it *lays,* even though the rules stipulate what to do according to where the ball *lies.* On a lazy day, people are as given to *laying around* the house as they are to *lying around* it. *Lay* is also used for *lie* in a variety of song lyrics (where colloquial and nonstandard forms are common), especially in imperatives like *lay down beside me* and in set phrases like *lay down and die*. For many of these expressions, nonstandard *lay* is actually more common than standard *lie*, and in many contexts *lay* sounds more natural. Interestingly, in all of these cases, there is no ambiguity about what is meant. The substitution of one word for the other does not result in misunderstanding.

In writing, however, expectations are different, and copyediting tradition demands that the two verbs be kept distinct and used according to the prescribed rules. Unless the situation calls for writing dialogue, it is best to follow the rules, since not doing so may be viewed as a mark of ignorance.

leapt

The word *leapt*, the past participle and a past tense form of *leap*, is sometimes misspelled as *lept*, a form not found in dictionaries and considered to be a mistake. *Leap* also has *leaped* as an acceptable past tense. Thus, each of the following examples is correct: *He leaped over the fence. He leapt over the fence. He had leapt over the fence before the farmer saw him.*

leave / let

Some usage critics have insisted that the phrase *leave alone* should be restricted to mean "to depart from someone who remains in solitude" (as in *They were left alone in the wilderness*) and that *leave alone* should not be used to mean "to refrain from disturbing or interfering with someone." (For this meaning, they would use *let alone* instead.) The virtue of maintaining this distinction has never been clearly articulated, and in many cases it is hard to tell the difference: a person who is not to be interfered with is often left in solitude. The Usage Panel has never put much credence in the distinction. As far back as 1968, 68 percent of the Usage Panel accepted the sentence *Leave him alone, and he will produce.*

Note that in standard American usage the verb *leave* is not used as a substitute for *let* in the sense "to allow or permit." Thus in the following examples only *let* should be used: *Let me be. Let them go. Let us not quarrel. Let it lie.*

leeward

This nautical word is usually pronounced (lōo′ərd), rhyming with *steward,* but the spelling pronunciation (lē′wərd) is also acceptable.

leisure

In our 1987 survey, 71 percent of the Usage Panel said they use the pronunciation that rhymes with *seizure*, and 29 percent said they use the pronunciation that rhymes with *pleasure*. The tendency in British English is the reverse, with the pronunciation that rhymes with *pleasure* being the most common one.

lend   See **loan.**

length

Judging from its spelling, this word should be pronounced (lĕngth), but, in fact, it is probably more often pronounced (lĕngkth), with a (k) inserted between the (ng) and the (th). The (k) acts as a sort of anchor for the (ng), keeping it at the back of the mouth and preventing it from moving forward and becoming (n) before the (th), which is made at the front of the mouth. Another pronunciation, (lĕnth), which is made with (n) before (th), is often criticized by usage writers and is not generally listed as a variant pronunciation in dictionaries despite the fact that many people pronounce the word this way. The same situation exists for the word *strength.*

See more at **assimilation.**

lesbian

Since the word *gay* is well established in reference to either sex, as in *gay marriage,* common expressions that refer to both sexes, such as *gay and lesbian* and *lesbians and gay men,* might appear to be unnecessary. While *gay* can be used as an inclusive term for both men and women, it many contexts it is more closely associated with men only, making the phrase *gay and lesbian* not only respectful, but in many cases necessary for clarity.

See more at **gay.**

less   See **fewer.**

–less

The suffix *–less* comes from the Old English suffix *–lēas,* from the word *lēas,* meaning "without, free from." Old English *–lēas,* and its descendant in Middle English, *–less,* were often used to convey the negative or opposite of words ending in *–ful,* as in *careful/careless* and *fearful/fearless.* But *–less* was also used to coin words that had no counterpart ending in *–ful: headless, loveless, motherless.* Although *–less* normally forms adjectives by attaching to nouns, in Modern English it can also form adjectives by attaching to verbs, as in *tireless.*

lest

Lest is a rather formal word that generally means "for fear that" (a phrase that can often serve as a substitute): *She tiptoed lest the guard should hear her. Lest* is always followed by an auxiliary verb like *should* in the previous example or by a present subjunctive verb form, as in the following sentence from Bill Clinton's second inaugural address: *"Together with our friends and allies, we will work together to shape change, lest it engulf us."* In this case, *lest* introduces a negative result clause and means "so that . . . not." In certain instances, *because* or *or else* can also be substituted for *lest*, as in *Don't forget an umbrella, lest you (should) be caught in the rain.*

The word has a long pedigree in English, going back to the Middle English period, and is perhaps most familiar from its extensive use in the translations of the Bible. In the 16th century, for example, William Tyndale rendered Matthew 7:1 as *"Judge not, lest ye be judged."* While it is now rare in speech, the word occurs with some frequency in set phrases like *lest we forget* and is more common than one might think in edited prose, as in this example from Joseph Conrad's *Heart of Darkness*:

> The matter looked dreary reading enough, with illustrative diagrams and repulsive tables of figures, and the copy was sixty years old. I handled this amazing antiquity with the greatest possible tenderness, lest it should dissolve in my hands.

It also occurs regularly in newspaper articles, even in columns with a somewhat breezy tone, as in a column by Al Kamen in the *Washington Post*:

> On the foreign policy front . . . the British government, by tradition, goes into deep hibernation here in the months before a U.S. presidential election, with no officials even coming here, lest they make waves.

The word's association with memorial speeches and somber dignity can be used to comic effect too, as in the way Jon Pareles concludes a *New York Times* article on a music video TV channel: *"Lest anyone forget, adolescence is purgatory."*

 let See **leave.**

liable / apt / likely

The words *liable, apt,* and *likely* are used interchangeably in constructions with infinitives, as in *They are liable to lose, They are apt to lose,* and *They are likely to lose.* But the three words have subtle distinctions in meaning. A traditional rule holds that *liable* should be used only if the subject (often a person) would be adversely affected by the outcome expressed by the infinitive. Thus, the sentence *Zach is liable to fall out of his chair if he doesn't sit up straight* would be permissible but *The chair is liable to be slippery* would not be. Nevertheless, the latter construction is commonly seen in formal writing, as in this example:

> After Great-Aunt Nannie, no such announcement was liable to surprise my grandmother (Donald Hall, "A Hundred Thousand Straightened Nails," *The American Scholar*)

Apt usually suggests that the subject (whether a person or not) has a natural tendency to enhance the probability of an outcome and that the speaker is somewhat apprehensive about the outcome. Thus, *apt* is used appropriately in the sentence *The fuel pump is apt to give out at any day* but not in *Even the clearest instructions are apt to be misinterpreted by those idiots* (since "those idiots," not the instructions, are at fault). Similarly, one would not use *apt* in *The fuel pump is apt to give you no problems for the life of the car,* since there is no reason that the speaker should regard such an outcome as unfortunate.

   Likely is more general than either *liable* or *apt.* It ascribes no particular properties to the subject or to the outcome. Thus, *John is apt to lose the election* suggests that the loss will result from John's actions while *John is likely to lose the election* does not.

library

The most widely accepted pronunciation for this word is (lī′brĕr′ē), but the pronunciation (lī′brə-rē), which is probably more common in British English, is also considered acceptable. On the other hand, many people from usage writers to schoolteachers deplore the pronunciation (lī′bĕr′ē), which is generally considered nonstandard. In this pronunciation the first *r* is lost by dissimilation.

   See more at **dissimilation.**

lie   See **lay.**

lighted / lit

Either *lighted* or *lit* is acceptable as the past tense and past participle of *light.* Both forms are also well established as adjectives: *a lit* [or *lighted*] *pipe.*

like

like as a conjunction   *Tell it like it is. It's like I said. I remember it like it was yesterday. They don't make them like they used to.* As these familiar examples show, *like* is often used as a conjunction meaning "as" or "as if," particularly in speech. While writers since Chaucer's time have used *like* as a conjunction, the usage today has a decidedly informal or conversational flavor, as is illustrated by the following quotation from *The Heart Is a Lonely Hunter* by Carson McCullers:

> The radio was on as usual. For a second she stood by the window and watched the people inside. . . . Mick sat on the ground. This was a very fine and secret place. Close around were thick cedars so that she was completely hidden by herself. The radio was no good tonight—somebody sang popular songs that all ended in the same way. It was like she was empty.

Language critics and writing handbooks have condemned the conjunctive use of *like* for more than a century, and in accordance with this tradition, *like* is usually edited out of more formal prose. This is easy enough to do, since *as* and *as if* stand as synonyms: *Sales of new models rose as* [not *like*] *we expected them to. He ran as if* [not *like*] *his life depended on it.*

Like is acceptable at all levels as a conjunction when used with verbs such as *feel, look, seem, sound,* and *taste: It looks like we are in for a rough winter.* Constructions in which the verb is not expressed, such as *He took to politics like a duck to water,* are also acceptable, especially since in these cases, *like* can be viewed as a preposition.

intrusive *like* In informal speech *like* is used frequently as a particle, as in *The waves were, like, really big* or *He wrote two bestsellers and then he, like, stopped writing.* Linguists call this "intrusive" or "focus" *like.* It can appear anywhere in a sentence and is used to set off the most significant new information—the focus—of the sentence. A similar use of intrusive *like* is as an approximator to indicate that what follows may not be expressed clearly or accurately, as in *He's like a lab technician or something.* Intrusive *like* is also used to soften a request, as in *Could I, like, borrow your jacket? Like* also serves as a linguistic filler such as *um* or *uh,* allowing the speaker a pause for reflection about how to continue. These uses of *like* are typical of informal spoken language, especially of younger people, and their occurrence in writing is limited chiefly to dialogue.

***like* indicating direct speech or an attitude** *So I'm like, "Let's get out of here." Like* is also used in informal speech following a form of the verb *be* to introduce a quotation, much as *go* does in *And then he goes, "Where's the party?"* This construction can be used to signal a brief performance or imitation of someone's behavior, often elaborated with gestures and facial expressions. So, for instance, if a woman says *So I'm like "Get lost, buddy,"* she may or may not have used those actual words to tell the offending person to leave. In fact, she may not have said anything, but is merely summarizing her attitude at the time by stating what she would have said if she had chosen to speak.

See more at **all, as,** and **go.**

likely

See **liable.**

linking verbs

Linking verbs (sometimes called *copular verbs*) identify the predicate of a sentence with the subject and include *be, become,* and *seem: Jim is my brother. The country is becoming more conservative. The line seems crooked.*

See more at **auxiliary and primary verbs.**

liquefy / liquify

Traditionally, the word *liquefy* and its derivatives like *liquefaction* have been spelled with an *e* in the second syllable, rather than an *i,* although most dictionaries accept the common variant spelling *liquify,* so it should be considered standard. However, the spelling variant of the related noun, *liquifaction,* remains relatively rare. Thus, for the sake of consistency between the noun *liquefaction* and the verb *liquefy,* writers should use *liquefy.* The noun *liquification* should be avoided as an error.

See also **stupefy.**

liquid   See **fluid.**

lit   See **lighted.**

literally

For more than a hundred years, critics have remarked on the incoherence of using *literally* in a way that suggests the exact opposite of its primary sense of "in a manner that accords with the literal sense of the words." In 1926, for example, H.W. Fowler deplored the example "*The 300,000 Unionists . . . will be literally thrown to the wolves.*" The practice does not stem from a change in the meaning of *literally* itself—if it did, the word would long since have come to mean "virtually" or "figuratively"—but from a tendency to use the word as a general intensifier, as in *They had literally no help from the government on the project.* In this sense, it is similar to the adverb *really,* whose intensive use often has nothing to do with what is "real," as in *They really dropped the ball in marketing that product.*

With regard to *literally,* the Usage Panel supports the traditional view. In our 2004 survey, only 23 percent of the Panel accepted the following sentence, in which *literally* undercuts the sentence's central metaphor: *The situation was especially grim in England where industrialism was literally swallowing the country's youth.* The Panel mustered more enthusiasm for the use of *literally* with a dead metaphor, which functions as a set phrase and evokes no image for most people. Some 37 percent accepted *He was literally out of his mind with worry.* But when there is no metaphor at all, a substantial majority of the Panel was willing to allow *literally* to be used as an intensifier; 66 percent accepted the *literally no help* sentence cited above.

literate

For most of its long history in English, *literate* has meant only "familiar with literature," or more generally, "well-educated, learned." Only since the late 19th century has it also come to refer to the basic ability to read and write. Its antonym *illiterate* has an equally broad range of meanings: an *illiterate* person may be incapable of reading a shopping list or uneducated in a particular field. The term *functional illiterate* is often used to describe a person who can read or write to some degree but below a minimum level required to function in even a limited social situation or job setting. An *aliterate* person, by contrast, is one who is capable of reading and writing but who has little interest in doing so, whether out of indifference to learning in general or from a preference for seeking information and entertainment by other means. The meanings of the words *literacy* and *illiteracy* have been extended from their original connection with reading and literature to any body of knowledge, such as geography or computer science, as in

"I'm computer illiterate, and he knows everything about them," [she] said while her son surfed the Web for potential jobs for his mother (Lori Higgins, "Dearborn Heights Residents Give Library Rave Reviews," *Detroit Free Press*)

He needed nothing. He had everything. But he knew he had neglected the cultural side of his life. He had little formal education, no time for books. He was musically illiterate (Paul Theroux, *Hotel Honolulu*)

lived

The pronunciation with a long *i* (līvd) in compounds such as *long-lived* and *short-lived* is historically correct since the compound is derived from the noun *life*, not from the verb *live*. The pronunciation (lĭvd), however, is so common now that it cannot be considered an error. In the 1988 survey, 43 percent of the Usage Panel preferred the pronunciation with the short vowel, 39 percent preferred the one with the long vowel, and 18 percent accepted either pronunciation.

load   See **lode** and **lot**.

loan / lend

The verb *loan* has been criticized by usage writers since the 19th century as an illegitimate form. The verb had fallen out of use in Britain, and the British criticism of the word got picked up by writers in the United States, where the verb had survived. In fact, the use of *loan* goes back to the 16th century and possibly earlier. It has seen vigorous use in American English right up to today and must be considered standard. Here are a couple of contemporary examples:

First, we agreed to sell arms to Europe; next, we agreed to loan arms to Europe; then we agreed to patrol the ocean for Europe; then we occupied a European island in the war zone. Now we have reached the verge of war (Philip Roth, *The Plot Against America*)

Lenny was delighted and even loaned his friend the capital needed for a stake in the firm (Louis Auchincloss, *The Atonement*)

Note that *loan* is used to describe only physical transactions, as of money or goods, while *lend* is correct not just for physical transactions, but for figurative ones as well:

Experience with death does not lend wisdom to physicians any more than to undertakers (Bernard Lown, *The Lost Art of Healing*)

The moist odors in the barn—hay and manure and milk—lend a calmness to Virginia's morning (Allen Morris Jones, *Last Year's River*)

lode / load

These homonyms are sometimes confused because they both refer to large quantities. The word *lode* means "a rich source or supply" and is usually used in reference to an ore deposit. A *mother lode* is the main vein of ore in a region. Metaphorically, it can be used for a particularly abundant source of something, as in a street that has the mother lode of ethnic restaurants in a city or a newsletter that claims to be a mother lode of investment ideas. The word *load* refers generally to a large amount of something and has a somewhat informal feel. Not surprisingly, *mother load* is a common misspelling.

See more at **lot.**

look to

The phrasal verb *look to* has recently developed the meanings "expect to" and "hope to," as in *The executives look to increase sales once the economy improves* or *I'm looking to sell my car in July.* In our 1997 survey, the Usage Panel was divided almost evenly on this usage, with 52 percent of the Panelists finding it acceptable and 48 percent rejecting it. Of those rejecting this usage, a small number volunteered that they would find it acceptable in informal speech, and in fact the divided response of the Panel may be due in part to the informal flavor of this phrase.

lot

The common expression *a lot of* is a whole lot more complicated than you might think. It belongs to a class of words that include *deal* (in *a great deal of*), *plenty*, and *load*. In phrases such as *a lot of strawberries*, the word *lot* is not really a head noun analogous to the word *bowl* in *a bowl of strawberries*. Rather, expressions like *a lot of*, *a whole lot of*, and *a great deal of* are best thought of as complex modifiers analogous to words like *many*, *much*, or *several*. *Lot* and *plenty* can occur with noncount nouns like *furniture* and with plural count nouns like *chairs*. The verb agrees in number with the noun in the *of* phrase. Thus, when followed by a singular noun, *a lot of* takes a singular verb: *A lot of pizza was left on the table*. But when followed by a plural noun, it takes a plural verb: *A lot of the strawberries were ripe.*

Like *load*, *lot* has the further distinction of being used in the plural with similarly peculiar agreement rules. When followed by a singular noun, *lots of* takes a singular verb: *Lots of pizza was left on the table*. When followed by a plural noun, *lots of* is plural: *Lots of people were at the bookstore*.

A lot and some of its cousin phrases are also used as adverbs meaning "much" or "very much": *I'm feeling a whole lot* [or *lots* or *a great deal*] *better*. The phrase *a bit* or *a little bit* works in the other direction, meaning "somewhat."

Virtually all of the expressions discussed here have an informal tone, with the plural phrases like *lots of* having a decidedly more informal tone than the others.

See more at **a lot.**

lower / lour

The verb *lower*, also spelled *lour* and meaning "to frown," is properly pronounced (lou′ər) or (lour), to rhyme with *flower* or *flour*. The pronunciation (lō′ər) goes with *lower*, the comparative form of the adjective *low*.

lunatic

In medieval England, mentally ill individuals were called *lunatics* (from Latin *luna*, or "moon"), as mental instability was thought to be influenced by lunar phases. Eventually, the word applied broadly to people with mental illness that required state intervention or custody, as in confinement to a lunatic asylum. This usage persisted into the early 20th century. Today, the term is considered to be offensive when referring to mentally ill individuals, although it is used colloquially to refer to persons displaying odd or irrational behavior.

luxurious / luxuriant

The word *luxurious* means "of a sumptuous, costly, or rich variety." *Luxuriant* can mean the same thing, but it more commonly refers to that which is characterized by rich or profuse growth. Sometimes *luxurious* is used when *luxuriant* is meant, as in this example from a national newswire service: "[He] *had shaved the luxurious growth of beard* [she] *had known.*"

· M ·

machinate

The older pronunciation of this word is (măk′ə-nāt′), with the *ch* pronounced like (k), as it is in other English words derived from Greek such as *archetype, bronchus,* and *echo.* The pronunciation (măsh′ə-nāt′), with the *ch* pronounced like (sh), is a relatively new variant and has been given alongside the other pronunciation in most dictionaries since about the middle of the 20th century. Perhaps one reason for the change is the association of *machinate* with its etymological cousin *machine,* which derives from the same Greek ancestor but came into English through the intermediary of French. In our 1996 survey, 61 percent of the Usage Panel reported using the (k) pronunciation, and 36 percent reported using the (sh) pronunciation. Only a third of the respondents using the (k) pronunciation thought the (sh) pronunciation was acceptable.
    See more at **ch.**

macro–

See **micro–.**

main clause

See **clause.**

mainsail

This nautical word is usually pronounced (mān′səl), but the spelling pronunciation (mān′sāl′) is also acceptable.
    See more at **spelling pronunciation.**

main verb

A main verb expresses an action or a state and can be inflected (it can take word endings or different forms) to show tense, number, person, and mood. Main verbs are distinguished from auxiliary verbs, which cannot be inflected. *Swim* is the main verb in the sentence *I could have swum a mile today.*
    See more at **auxiliary and primary verbs.**

majority / plurality

majority and ***plurality*** The word *majority* refers to a number greater than 50 percent of the total of a group, also called an *absolute majority.* When there are more than two choices in question, as in many elections or surveys, the winner may receive more votes than any other in the group but less than 50 percent of the total. This is called a *plurality,* as in this newspaper article from the *Dallas Morning News:* "*Hispanic students in the Garland district have nearly overtaken white students' plurality, district records show.*" Sometimes, the word *majority* is used loosely to refer to the largest number in a group, but this can create ambiguity. For example, in the sentence *A majority of people surveyed didn't care where the new school was built so long as it was built within the next two years,* it is not entirely clear whether the group being referred to is a true majority or a plurality.

Both *majority* and *plurality* can also refer to the margin by which a contest has been won. Thus when a candidate wins an election by a majority of five votes, she wins five more votes than the votes for all of the other candidates combined. Similarly, when she wins by a plurality of five votes, she receives five more votes than that of the closest opponent.

singular or plural *majority*   When *majority* refers to a particular number of votes, it takes a singular verb: *Her majority was five votes. His majority has been growing by 5 percent every year.* When it refers to a group of persons or things that are in the majority, it may take either a singular or plural verb, depending on whether the group is considered as a whole or as a set of separate individuals. So it is correct to say *The majority elects* [not *elect*] *the candidate it wants* [not *they want*], since the election is accomplished by the group as a whole, but it is also correct to say *The majority of the voters live* [not *lives*] *in the city,* since living in the city is something that each voter does individually.

Majority is often preceded by *great* (but not by *greater*) in expressing emphatically the sense of "most of a group": *The great majority approved.* The phrase *greater majority* is appropriate only when considering two majorities: *He won by a greater majority in this election than in the last.*

See more at **subject and verb agreement.**

make do

This commonly used expression means "to manage to get along with the means available," as in *They had to make do on less income.* Occasionally it is misspelled as *make due,* as in this rendering of the words of a city council president in a New Jersey newspaper: "*For too long, people with disabilities throughout the world have had to make due, when it came to equal access.*"

man / woman

Traditionally, many writers have used *man* and certain compounds derived from it (like *mankind*) to designate any or all members of the human race regardless of sex. In Old English *man* only meant "a human being"; the words *wer* and *wīf* were used to refer to "a male human being" and "a female human being," respectively. But in Middle English *man* displaced *wer* as the term for a male human being, while *wifman* (which evolved into *woman*) was used for a female human being. *Man* also continued to carry its sense of "a human being," however, so the result is an asymmetry of language that many criticize as sexist: *man* can stand for all people, but *woman* cannot. Another concern about the use of generic *man* is that it can be ambiguous, at least in the plural, since *men* can refer exclusively to adult human males as well as to humanity in general.

Despite the objections to the generic use of *man,* a solid majority of Usage Panel members still approve of it. For example, the sentence *If early man suffered from a lack of information, modern man is tyrannized by an excess of it* was acceptable to 79 percent of the Panel in our 2004 survey, and the sentence *The site shows that man learned to use tools much earlier than scientists believed possible* was acceptable to 75 percent. However, only 48 percent approved of the generic plural form of *man,* as in *Men learned to use tools more than ten thousand years ago,* probably because the plural, unlike the singular *man,* suggests that one is referring to actual men of ten thousand years ago, taking them as representative of the species.

A substantial majority of the Panel also accepts compound words derived from generic *man,* and resistance to these compounds does not appear to be increasing. In the 2004 survey, 87 percent accepted the sentence *The Great Wall is the only manmade structure visible from space*—essentially the same percentage that accepted this sentence in 1988 (86 percent). In the 2004 survey, 86 percent also accepted *The first manmade fiber to be commercially manufactured in the US was rayon, in 1910,* suggesting that context makes no difference on this issue.

Acceptable substitutes for *man* as a generic term include *humans, humanity, humankind,* and *the human race.* In sentences such as *Man has* [or *men have*] *long yearned to unlock the secrets of the atom, people* can replace *man* or *men.*

As a verb, *man* was originally used in military and nautical contexts, when the group performing the action consisted entirely of men. In the days when only men manned the decks, there was no need for a different word to include women. Today, the verb form of *man* can be considered sexist when the subject includes or is limited to women, as in the sentence *Members of the League of Women Voters will be manning the registration desk.* But in our 2004 survey only 26 percent of the Usage Panel considered this sentence to be unacceptable. This is noticeably fewer Panelists than the 56 percent who rejected this same sentence in 1988. This suggests that for many people the issue of the generic use of *man* is not as salient as it once was.

See more at **he; *—man, —woman,* and *—person* compounds;** and **sexist language.**

—man, —woman, and *—person* compounds

Words that end with the element *—man* include those that describe occupations (*alderman, councilman, deliveryman, fireman, postman*), societal rank (*nobleman, workingman*), and evidence of skill (*craftsmanship, horsemanship, sportsmanship, marksmanship, showmanship*). These compounds sometimes generate controversy because they are considered sexist by some people who believe that *—man* necessarily excludes females. Others believe that *—man,* like the word *man* itself, is an accepted and efficient convention that is not meant to be gender-specific. This ongoing controversy is evident from our usage surveys. In the 2004 survey, 66 percent of the Usage Panel accepted the sentence *The chairman will be appointed by the faculty senate,* roughly the same percentage as in 1988, and 57 percent accepted *Emily Owen, chairman of the mayor's task force, issued a statement assuring residents that their views would be solicited,* a percentage that was actually higher than the 48 percent in the 1988 survey. Interestingly, *–man* words that denote types of behavior or skills are overwhelmingly acceptable to the Panel, suggesting that these words are much less likely to be seen as sexist. In our 2004 survey, the sentence *The umpire ejected Rosie Falcon from the game for her unsportsmanlike conduct after her outburst in the second inning* was acceptable to 95 percent of the Panelists. The acceptability of terms like *unsportsmanlike* and *showmanship* may stem from the fact that there are no exact synonyms for these words.

For writers interested in avoiding *–man* compounds that have synonyms, alternatives include compounds employing *–woman* and *–person,* as in *chairwoman* and *spokesperson,* and more inclusive terms that avoid the gender-marked element entirely, such as *chair* for *chairman, letter carrier* for *mailman,* and *workers' compensation* for *workmen's compensation.* Other gender-neutral terms available to replace the *–man* construction include *cleric* and *member of the clergy* for *clergyman* and *first-year student* for *freshman.*

See more at **he, man,** and **sexist language.**

manic-depressive   See **bipolar.**

manmade   See under **man.**

mantle / mantel

The word *mantle* has many different meanings, most commonly "a cloak or something that covers, envelops, or conceals." But *mantle* is also an acceptable spelling variant of the word *mantel,* which has just one meaning: "a structure, such as a facing or shelf, around or over a fireplace." *Mantel* remains the most common spelling of this word, however, and most dictionaries list it as the preferred spelling.

many a

The phrase *many a* is used before a singular noun and always takes a singular verb. This is true whether the verb comes before the phrase, as in *There is many a student who waits until the last minute to cram for exams* or after the phrase, as in *Many a speaker feels nervous before going on stage.*

Sometimes the plural verb is used mistakenly, as in this quotation from a syndicated columnist: *"But there are many a wall such as this in a home that are not bearing any weight whatsoever."*

marshal / martial

The adjective *martial* means "relating to war or the armed forces" and is derived from the name of the Roman war god Mars.

The noun *marshal,* homophonous with *martial,* has been used to designate a wide variety of officials since medieval times, when it denoted a high official in royal service. Nowadays in the United States, the title is given to persons such as the head of a police or fire department, the official in charge of a parade or ceremony, and the law-enforcement officer who carries out court orders. The word *marshal* is also used as a verb meaning "to arrange or place (troops, for example) in line." The marshal who fulfills court orders can be distinguished from other marshals, such as *fire marshals,* by the term *court marshal. Marshal* is spelled with one *l* (although an old spelling variant is preserved in the family and personal name *Marshall*).

The coexistence of the homonyms *marshal* and *martial* in the related fields of law enforcement, administration, and military organization has led to the frequent confusion between the two. *Court-martial* and *martial law* are often incorrectly spelled *court-marshal* and *marshal law,* as in *The commanding officer was court-marshalled and given a dishonorable discharge* and *We fled the country after the declaration of marshal law.* Sometimes *martial arts* is also miswritten *marshal arts.*

The term *court-martial* simply means "military or naval court," and it is also used as a verb meaning "to try by military tribunal." It is not directly connected with the term *marshal. Court-martial* displays an odd inversion of noun and adjective found in other administrative and legal terms like *attorney general, notary public,* and *president-elect,* which imitate the natural order of noun and adjective in French, the language of the courts in medieval England. The form *martial court,* without inversion, was used in the past, but it has disappeared. The exceptional word order in *court-martial* may have contributed to its reinterpretation as *court-marshal,* and this confusion begins to occur as early as the 17th century.

Court-martial should be hyphenated, and its correct plural is *courts-martial.*
See more at **plurals.**

masculine   See **feminine.**

mass nouns   See **count nouns.**

mass / weight

The difference in meaning between these two words is actually quite significant. The *mass* of an object is an intrinsic property of that object: electrons have a unique mass, protons have a unique mass, larger objects composed of these particles have mass, and so on. Thus, one's mass on the moon is identical to one's mass on Earth. *Weight,* on the other hand, is a force due to the gravitational attraction between two bodies. For example, one's weight on the moon is one sixth of one's weight on Earth. When we weigh an object to determine its mass, we are measuring the force that gravity exerts on it. A pound is technically a unit of force, not mass, while a kilogram is a true unit of mass, so it is technically correct to use pounds as a measure of weight, but not of mass. In nontechnical settings, however, we may use *weight* to refer to the mass of an object (as in *The weight of this box is one kilogram*), assuming that we are measuring its weight on the surface of the Earth.

master

Historically, a *master* is a man who is the head of a household. The word is still used in this way, although in contemporary contexts it can seem ironic:

> With gables, some of them real, cathedral ceilings, a two-story foyer and a big family room (pay no attention to the small living room), *McMansions* create the illusion of a rural estate— until the master and mistress look out their Palladian windows and find no rolling greensward but an undersized lot and a close view of their neighbors through *their* Palladian windows (Gerald Parshall, "Buzzwords," *US News & World Report*)

As a noun, *master* retains several senses relating only to males, including its use as a title for any of various male officers having specified duties in a British royal household, as a courtesy title for a young boy, and as a title for a male tutor. For some people, these meanings imbue the word indelibly with masculine connotations. When considered alongside the word's association with the management of servants and the institution of slavery, certain uses of this word will strike many as insensitive, if not offensive.

Traditionally, most uses of *master* to mean "teacher" or "expert" have referred to men:

> Without exception, these defeats were suffered by people who acknowledged Clausewitz as their master—even if they never read a word he wrote (Martin van Creveld, "War," in Robert Cowley and Geoffrey Parker, eds., *The Reader's Companion to Military History*)

> Even Nabokov, that master of language, found the subtle perfume of butterfly wings difficult to describe (Jennifer Ackerman, *Chance in the House of Fate*)

However, the noun sense of *master* meaning "an expert" and the verb sense meaning "to make oneself an expert at" are commonly used today in many contexts and are generally thought of as gender-neutral:

> Tiny and ethereal with long, fluid arms, she nonetheless possesses a tensile strength and immaculate control. She is a master of expressive gesture, conveying pain with the downward curve of her long neck and rapture with a mere lift of her radiant face (Karen Campbell, "Boston Ballet," *Dance Magazine*)

Master is also commonly used to refer to both men and women as an attributive modifying a noun, as in *master storyteller* or *master teacher*:

> Catt . . . was a master showwoman. On Independence Day she had suffragists position themselves on the courthouse steps of every county seat in New York and read a Woman's Declaration of Independence (Lillian Faderman, *To Believe in Women*)

See more at **mistress.**

masterful / masterly

It was H.W. Fowler who first recommended (in 1926) that the word *masterful* be restricted to mean "imperious, domineering" (as in *a masterful tone of voice*), even though it had long been used to mean "having or showing the knowledge or skill of a master" as well. He wanted to restrict this latter meaning to the word *masterly,* as in *a masterly performance of the sonata.* Many usage critics have since taken up his call.

But in practice, writers have been less heedful, and today *masterful* is well attested with the meaning "finely skilled":

> . . . pretentious critics have expended an enormous amount of ink trying to portray Warhol as a masterful satirist, social commentator and visionary . . . (Michiko Kakutani, "Andy Warhol," *New York Times Magazine*)

> Boxing, historically, has inspired masterful sports writing, fiction and nonfiction, from the Lardners to Hemingway to Mailer and . . . Joyce Carol Oates (Dick Schaap, Introduction, *Best American Sports Writing 2000*)

In fact, the word *masterful* is far more likely to occur before words like *performance* and *ability* than *masterly* is.

This is not to say that *masterly* has gone by the board. It is still in frequent use by respected writers:

> Together the two books present the strongest case for Koch as a masterly innovator, not merely a comedian of the spirit . . . (David Lehman, "Dr. Fun," *American Poetry Review*)

> . . . Powell adjusted his aim and concluded with one of the more masterly ad hominem indictments in American newspaper history (David Rains Wallace, *The Bonehunters' Revenge*)

And the "domineering" sense of *masterful* is also in contemporary use, though our citations suggest that its adherents tend to be—perhaps not surprisingly—traditionalists:

> Pop stood short but masterful in the sweaters, and his belly sticking out, not soft but hard. He was a man of the hard-bellied type. Nobody intimidated Pop (Saul Bellow, "A Silver Dish," *The New Yorker*)

> . . . there was no gainsaying four such masterful travellers, all armed, and two of them uncommonly large and strong-looking (J.R.R. Tolkien, *The Return of the King*)

See more at **master.**

materialize

In its original senses *materialize* is used without an object to mean "to assume material form" (as in *Marley's ghost materialized before Scrooge's eyes*) or with an object to mean "to cause to assume material form" (as in *Disney materialized his dream in a plot of orchard land in Orange County*). However, these uses are less common today than two extended senses of the verb. In the first, the meaning is roughly "to appear suddenly": *No sooner had we set the menu down than a waiter materialized at our table.* Some critics have labeled this use as pretentious or incorrect, but it has been around for more than a century, appears in the writing of highly respected writers, and seems a natural extension of the original sense. The second meaning is "to take effective shape, come into existence." In this use, *materialize* tends to be applied to things or events that have been foreseen or anticipated and usually occurs in negative constructions: *The promised subsidies never materialized. It was thought the community would oppose the measure, but no new objections materialized.* This usage, too, is well established in reputable writing and follows a familiar pattern of metaphoric extension.

matter / substance / material

In chemistry, a distinction is often made between the use of the terms *matter* and *substance.* The term *matter* has the broadest application in that it entails simply that an object possesses mass. If an object has mass, then it is part of the matter of the universe. An example of matter is the electron—a charged particle with mass—or a rock, or a cloud of gas. (Objects without mass are sometimes considered *energy,* though somewhat loosely, as the meaning of the word *energy* in physics is quite distinct. An example of energy in this loose sense is the photon, the carrier of electromagnetic radiation. The photon has no mass.)

Now consider the myriad of chemical properties that any large amount of matter can possess. The term *substance* is used as a label for a collection of matter with specific chemical properties. The smallest unit of a substance is an atom or molecule. *Pure substances* are made of only one kind of atom or molecule, while substances in general are often made of mixtures of pure substances.

Consider the sentence *Matter can exist in one of three states: a solid, a liquid, or a gas.* This statement is meant to indicate that *all* of the matter in the universe exists in one of three states. The focus is not on specific chemical properties unique to some molecules or atoms. In contrast, the sentence *Air is composed of the substances nitrogen, oxygen, argon, carbon dioxide, neon, and helium* lists the pure substances, chemical elements, and compounds of which air consists.

When we speak of metals, paper, and ink, we are referring to substances not in terms of their chemical properties per se but of their overall properties or structure. A term that is sometimes used to classify the characteristics of an object at this level is *material.* A material need not have consistent chemical properties and may even vary in chemical composition in various places. Wood, for example, is a *material* with (nonchemical) properties such as being hard but somewhat flexible and being able to float on water. A close look at the structure of wood shows a fine arrangement of different *substances* that make up fibers and fluids in the wood. So in a chemistry laboratory, a flask is made of the material glass, the safety goggles are made of various plastic materials, and the workbench is made of the material wood.

mauve

The pronunciation (mōv) is older and reflects the word's pronunciation in French. Also common now is the pronunciation (môv).

may

may* and *might   *It may rain. It might rain.* What's the difference? Just as *could* is the past tense of *can, might* is the past tense of *may: We thought we might win the tournament.* But *might* can also be used as a substitute for *may* to show diminished possibility. Thus, saying *We might go to the movies* means that the likelihood of going is somewhat less than that expressed by the sentence *We may go to the movies.* When used to express permission, *might* has a higher degree of politeness than *may.* Thus, *Might I express my opinion?* conveys less insistence than *May I express my opinion?*

may can / might could   In many Southern varieties of American English, *might* is used in the "double modal" construction with *could,* as in *We might could park over there.* Less frequently, one hears *may can* and *might should.* These constructions are not familiar to the majority of American speakers and are best avoided in formal writing.
    See more at **auxiliary and primary verbs** and **can.**

mayoral

In our 1992 survey, approximately 70 percent of the Usage Panel said they pronounce this word with stress on the first syllable (mā′ər-əl), and approximately 30 percent pronounce it with stress on the second syllable (mā-ôr′əl). Either pronunciation is acceptable.

me   See **pronouns, personal.**

means

In the sense of "financial resources," *means* takes a plural verb: *His means are more than adequate.* In the sense of "a way to an end," *means* may be treated as either a singular or plural noun. It is singular when referring to a particular strategy or method: *The best means of securing the cooperation of the builders is to appeal to their self-interest.* It is plural when referring to a group of strategies or methods: *The most effective means for dealing with the drug problem have generally been those suggested by the affected communities.*
    Means is most often followed by *of: a means of noise reduction.* But *for, to,* and *toward* are also used: *a means for transmitting signals, a means to an end, a means toward achieving social equality.*

meantime / meanwhile

The words *meantime* and *meanwhile* can be used as both nouns and adverbs in Standard English. However, *meantime* is more common than *meanwhile* as a noun: *In the meantime we waited. Meanwhile* is more commonly used as an adverb: *Meanwhile we waited.*

medal   See **mettle.**

meddle   See **mettle.**

media

The word *medium* comes from Latin. It has two plural forms—a Latin plural, *media*, and a normal English *-s* plural, *mediums*. Trouble arises when the Latin plural is used as a singular noun in the fields of mass communication and journalism, as in *The Internet is the most exciting new media since television.* This usage is widely considered an error. Fully 91 percent of the Usage Panel found this sentence unacceptable. Correct usage in these cases requires the singular *medium.*

Media also occurs with the definite article as a collective term that refers to the communities and institutions behind the various forms of communication. In this sense, *the media* means something like "the press." Like other collective nouns, it may take a singular or plural verb depending on the intended meaning. If the point is to emphasize the multifaceted nature of the press, a plural verb may be more appropriate: *The media have covered the trial in a variety of formats.* Quite frequently, however, *media* stands as a singular noun for the aggregate of journalists and broadcasters: *The media has not shown much interest in covering the trial.* All things being equal, the Usage Panel has a decided preference for the plural use in these sentences, with 91 percent accepting the *variety of formats* sentence and only 38 accepting the *covering the trial* sentence. This suggests that many people still think of *media* predominantly as a plural form, and that it will be some time before the singular use of *media* begins to crowd out the plural use in the manner of similar Latin plurals, such as *agenda* and *data.*

Inconveniently, the singular *medium* cannot be used as a collective noun for the press. Sentences like *No medium has shown much interest in covering the trial* are not standard and may be viewed as nonsensical.

medieval

There are several acceptable pronunciations for *medieval:* (mē′dē-ē′vəl), (měd′ē-ē′vəl), and (mĭ-dē′vəl). These pronunciations are all common, and none is favored over the others by the Usage Panel.

mega–

The basic meaning of the prefix *mega–* is "large." It comes from the Greek prefix *mega–*, from Greek *megas*, "great, large." In some of its grammatical forms, the base form of the Greek adjective was *megalo–*, and this is why English now has the two similar-sounding prefixes meaning "large," *mega–*, as in *megafauna*, and *megalo–*, as in *megalopolis*. *Mega–*, but not *megalo–*, has recently gained popularity in the formation of slang words like *megabucks* and *megahit*. When added to the name of a basic unit in the metric system of measurement, the prefix *mega–* means "one million (of the unit in question)," as in *megavolt*, "one million volts."

See more at **megabyte** and **micro–**.

megabyte

Depending on the context, the term *megabyte*, along with other numerical terms used in computer science, can be interpreted in different ways. In the context of describing the memory or storage capacity of an electronic device, the prefix *mega–* has a specific and unusual meaning. The calculation of data storage capacity (usually measured in bytes) is based on powers of 2 because of the binary nature of bits. (A byte is made of eight bits.) Each bit has the value 0 or 1, so a binary number made up of n bits can represent 2^n different numbers. One byte, for example, can represent 2^8, or 256, different numbers. Since each storage location in computer memory is addressed by a different number, and those numbers are represented in computers as binary numbers, storage devices are often designed with a number of storage locations that is a power of 2. In such contexts, the prefix *mega–* refers to the power of 2 closest to 1,000,000, which is 2^{20}, or 1,048,576. Thus, a megabyte is 1,048,576 bytes.

By contrast, in the context of data transmission rates, powers of 2 aren't involved, so prefixes such as *mega–* are used in more familiar ways. Thus, a rate of one megabit per second is equal to one million bits per second. Other prefixes show a similar split in meaning: for instance, the prefix *kilo–* refers to either 1,000 or 2^{10} (1,024); *giga–* to either 1,000,000,000 (one billion) or 2^{30} (1,073,741,824); and *tera–* to either 1,000,000,000,000 (one trillion) or 2^{40} (1,099,511,627,776).

meiosis   See **mitosis**.

–ment

The suffix *–ment* forms nouns, chiefly by attaching to verbs but occasionally to adjectives as well. It can have several meanings, the most common being "an act or an instance of doing something" or "the state of being acted upon." Thus an *entertainment* can be "an act of entertaining" and *amazement* is "the state of being amazed." Sometimes *–ment* can mean "result of an action," as in *advancement*. The suffix *–ment* can be traced back to the Latin noun suffix *–mentum*. Although its use in English dates back to the 1300s, it wasn't until the 1500s and 1600s that a great number of words were coined with *−ment*. When *−ment* is added to a verb or adjective ending in *y*, the *y* is changed to an *i*, as in *accompaniment* and *merriment*.

mercifully   See **hopefully** and **sentence adverbs.**

metal   See **mettle.**

metathesis

Metathesis is a term used in linguistics to refer to the transposition of elements in a word or sentence. There are many different kinds of metathesis, but one common case in the history of English involves two adjacent sounds in a word, especially the sounds represented by the letters *r* and *l* switching order with a vowel. Two historical examples of metathesis are Modern English *bird* and *third* from Old English *brid* and *thridda*. Over time the metathesized pronunciations became standard, and the spellings were changed to conform to the new pronunciations. An example of this from contemporary speech is the pronunciation (jōō′lə-rē) instead of (jōō′əl-rē) or (jōōl′rē) for *jewelry*. Although the kinds of pronunciations that arise from metathesis occur frequently, most dictionaries do not enter them as standard variants.

meteor / meteorite / meteoroid

The word *meteor,* which derives from Greek *meteōron,* originally indicated any type of atmospheric phenomenon. People spoke of rain, hail, and snow as *aqueous meteors;* of wind as *airy meteors;* of the aurora borealis as *luminous meteors;* and of shooting stars as *fiery meteors.* Nowadays, this sense of *meteor* lingers on in *meteorology,* which is the study of the atmosphere and weather conditions. The word *meteor* itself, however, has narrowed in meaning to indicate fiery meteors only. As the name suggests, meteors were considered to be of atmospheric origin. Prior to the 19th century, the possibility that they came from interplanetary space was considered unbelievable among the general public. Thomas Jefferson claimed in 1809 that people would rather *"believe that Yankee professors would lie, than that stones would fall from heaven."*

The term for a stone found on the earth and associated with the meteor phenomenon is *meteorite.* It has the suffix *−ite,* familiar from the names of many rocks and minerals such as *pegmatite* and *malachite.* The term *meteorite* is the second oldest term of the three in this group, and the first citations for it in *The Oxford English Dictionary* place it in the 1820s. It was at this time that scientific opinion about the source of meteorites began to change. An American scientist instrumental in this change was Huburt Anson Newton, a Yale astronomy professor. He predicted an 1866 meteor shower by associating the meteor phenomenon with a comet that was due to be observed that year. Newton is attributed with the first citation for *meteoroid* in *The Oxford English Dictionary: "The term meteoroid will be used to designate such a* *body before it enters the earth's atmosphere.*" Thus, the terminology for Earth-bound stones from interplanetary space is partitioned according to the stones' stages of descent: a *meteoroid* is a stone in interplanetary space ranging in size from a speck of dust to a chunk about one hundred meters in diameter—just shy of being an asteroid; a *meteor* is the bright flash of light produced by a meteoroid as it heats up while passing through Earth's atmosphere; the term *meteor* also refers to the stone itself while it is in Earth's atmosphere; finally, a *meteorite* is what remains of a meteoroid that has survived the fiery fall through Earth's atmosphere to land on Earth's surface.

meteoric rise / meteoric fall

The idiom *meteoric rise* is commonly used to describe a swift improvement in condition or status, as in this example from the magazine *Sports Illustrated: "This old school approach has fallen from favor since the meteoric rise of Tiger Woods, after which golf became obsessed with finding the next young phenom. . . ."* It might seem contradictory to describe an ascent of any kind as meteoric, since the path of a meteor is virtually always downward, but the definition of the word *meteoric,* namely "similar to a meteor in speed, brilliance, or brevity," is consistent with its usage in either *meteoric rise* or its less commonly used counterpart, *meteoric fall.* This quotation from the periodical *Reason* demonstrates the latter: *"It's hard to tell whether the meteoric fall of [Howard] Dean's candidacy had anything to do with his perceived secularism—or, for that matter, with his clumsy attempt to reinvent himself as a man of faith."*

mete out

The phrase *mete out* means "to distribute by or as if by measure" or "to allot." It is sometimes misspelled as *meat out* or *meet out,* as in this article from a Pennsylvania newspaper: *"After all, it was the only sports facility in the nation with a judge in residence to meet out justice to obstreperous fans."*

methodology

The noun *methodology* refers to the body of methods used by those who work in a discipline or engage in an inquiry, as in *objections to the methodology of an opinion survey* (objections dealing with the appropriateness of the methods used) or *the methodology of modern cognitive psychology* (the principles and practices that underlie research in the field). But in recent years, *methodology* has been used as a pretentious substitute for *method* in scientific and technical contexts, as in *The oil company has not yet decided on a methodology for restoring the beaches.* This extended use of *methodology* may owe something to the tendency to use *methodological* to refer to questions of method, as in *We want to restore the beaches but we haven't solved the methodological problem,* since *methodical* itself has been co-opted to mean "painstaking." But these extended uses of *methodology* and *methodological* obscure an important conceptual distinction between the tools of scientific investigation (*methods*) and the principles that determine how such tools are deployed and interpreted (*methodology*).

mettle / metal / medal / meddle

These sound-alikes are sometimes confused with one other, but they have very different meanings. The noun *mettle* means "courage and fortitude" or "quality of character," as in *The team's mettle was tested when it fell behind early in the game. Mettle* actually comes from the word *metal,* and the two words were once competing spelling variants, but *mettle* broke away with its own meaning around 1700. The two words come from Greek *metallon,* "mine ore, metal." *Metal* itself refers to any of various elements that can donate electrons in a chemical reaction and form alloys. *Metal* is also a verb, meaning "to cover or surface (a roadbed, for example) with metal, that is, with broken stones."

A *medal* is normally made of stamped metal, but the word *medal* comes from Late Latin *mediālia,* "little halves," a word that was eventually adopted into Italian to refer to coins worth half a denarius. (The denarius was the Roman equivalent of a penny, and the Latin word was later used to describe various coins in circulation in medieval Europe.) *Medal* can also be a verb meaning "to award a medal to" and "to win a medal," as in *They were the first Americans to medal in the Olympics.* The verb *meddle* is unrelated to any of these words, deriving ultimately from Latin *miscēre,* and means "to intrude or interfere."

micro–

The basic meaning of the prefix *micro–* is "small." It comes from the Greek prefix *mīkro–,* from *mīkros,* meaning "small." In English *micro–* has been chiefly used since the 19th century to form science words. It is the counterpart for the prefix *macro–,* "large," in pairs such as *microcosm/macrocosm* and *micronucleus/macronucleus.* (The prefix *macro–* comes from the Greek word *makros,* "long, large.") When added to the name of a basic unit in the metric system of measurement, the prefix *micro–* means "one millionth (of the unit in question)," as in *micrometer,* "one millionth of a meter." This unit of measurement used to be called a *micron,* but this particular name for the unit is no longer in scientific use.

See more at **mega–**.

microbe   See **germ**.

microorganism   See **germ**.

mid–

The prefix *mid–*, which means "middle," combines primarily with nouns to form compounds, most of which represent a time (*midmorning, midsummer, midyear*) or place (*midbrain, midstream, midtown*). When the prefix *mid–* is affixed to a word beginning with a capital letter, the compound should be hyphenated: *mid-November, Mid-Atlantic States.* It is always acceptable, however, to separate the two elements with a hyphen to prevent possible confusion with another form, as to distinguish *mid-den,* "the middle of a den," from the word *midden.*

In addition to the prefix *mid–*, there is also an adjective *mid*, meaning "middle" and "central" and written separately from the noun it modifies. As is the case with any adjective, *mid* may be joined to another word with a hyphen when used to modify a following noun. Writers should note the contrast between *in the mid Pacific,* "in the middle of the Pacific Ocean," and *a mid-Pacific island,* "an island in the middle of the Pacific." Both the adjective and the prefix can be traced back to the Old English adjective *midd,* meaning "middle." Writers should consult their dictionaries when uncertain whether a specific expression requires the prefix *mid–* or the separate adjective *mid,* or when they are in doubt whether the prefix *mid–* should be followed by a hyphen or not. For example, the name of the region in southwest Asia and northeast Africa should be written *the Mideast,* rather than *the mid-East* or *the mid East.*

midget   See **dwarf.**

might   See **may.**

migrate / emigrate / immigrate

The verb *migrate* usually indicates a permanent change of settlement when referring to people and implies historical demographic shifts of great magnitude, as in *In the 5th century AD the Angles, Saxons, and Jutes began migrating to England.* When referring to birds or other animals, *migrate* usually indicates a seasonal or other temporary change in habitat. The verbs *emigrate* and *immigrate* are used only of people and also imply a permanent move, generally across a political boundary. *Emigrate* describes the move relative to the point of departure: *After the Nazis came to power in Germany, many scientists emigrated. Immigrate* describes the move relative to the destination: *The promise of prosperity here in the United States encouraged many people to immigrate.*

militate   See **mitigate.**

millenary

The pronunciation with the main stress on the first syllable, (mĭl′ə-nĕr′ē), is the correct historical pronunciation, but the pronunciation with stress on the second syllable, (mə-lĕn′ə-rē), which probably came about through association with *millennium,* is now equally common.

millennium

The word *millennium* is very frequently misspelled, often as *millenium.* Keeping its derivation in mind makes it easier; the word comes from Latin *mille,* "thousand," and *annus,* "year." Both *millennia* and *millenniums* are acceptable plural forms.

mineralogy

Although this word has an *a* in the third syllable, it is usually pronounced (mĭn′ə-rŏl′ə-jē), which no doubt has led to the common spelling mistake *minerology.* This is undoubtedly due to the influence of the abundance of *–ology* words in English, such as *biology, geology,* and *paleontology.* Note that a similar situation exists with the word *genealogy.*

minimal / minimize

Minimal and *minimize* come from the Latin adjective *minimus,* "least, smallest," and *minimal* is therefore used to refer to the smallest possible amount, as in *The amplifier reduces distortion to the minimal level that can be obtained. Minimal* has also come to refer more loosely to any small amount, as in *If you would just put in a minimal amount of time on your homework, your grades would improve.* In our 1987 survey, the Usage Panel was asked what *minimal* meant in the sentence *Alcohol has a particularly unpleasant effect on me when I have a minimal amount of food in my stomach.* Under the strict interpretation of *minimal,* the sentence should mean "Alcohol has an unpleasant effect when I have eaten nothing," but with a looser interpretation the sentence can also mean " . . . when I have eaten a bit." Twenty-nine percent of the Panel held to the strict interpretation, 34 percent said that it could have only the looser meaning, and 37 percent said that it could have either meaning. Thus, 71 percent considered this sense acceptable, at least in nontechnical use.

The verb *minimize* has undergone a similar extension of meaning. In its strict sense it means "to reduce to the smallest possible level," but quite often the context requires interpretation as to what the smallest possible level might be. Thus when a manager announces that *The company wants to minimize the risk of accidents to assembly line workers,* this usually means that the company plans to reduce the risk to the smallest level after factors such as efficiency and cost have been considered, not that risks will be reduced to the lowest level regardless of disruptions and cost. *Mini-*

mize is also used more loosely to mean "to cause to appear to be of little importance; play down," as in *The President tried to minimize the problems posed by the nation's trade imbalance.* This sense is well established.

minority

Socially speaking, a *minority* is an ethnic, racial, religious, or other group having a distinctive presence within a larger society. Some people object to this term as negative or dismissive, and it should probably be avoided in contexts where a group's status with regard to the majority population is irrelevant. Thus we would normally say *a tour of the city's ethnic* [not *minority*] *restaurants* or *a poem celebrating the diversity of cultures* [not *minorities*] *in America,* where in both cases the emphasis is cultural as opposed to statistical or political. But in the appropriate context, as when discussing a group from a social or demographic point of view, *minority* is a useful term that need not be avoided as offensive.

A different problem arises when *minority* is used to refer to an individual rather than a group, as in the sentence *As a minority, I am particularly sensitive to the need for fair hiring practices.* Seventy-seven percent of the Usage Panel found this example unacceptable in our 2001 survey (roughly the same response as in 1995), possibly because it was felt that an individual could not have the same relationship to society as a group. However, when the word was used in the plural without a numeral or a quantifier like *many* or *some*—as in *The firm announced plans to hire more minorities and women*—the Panelists were more approving, with only 29 percent in the 1995 survey judging an example such as this one unacceptable. The discrepancy in these opinions can be explained by the fact that in this type of plural usage, the word is understood as referring to the members of a group taken collectively rather than as individuals.

mis– / miso–

The basic meaning of the prefix *mis–* is "bad, badly, wrong, wrongly." Thus *misfortune* means "bad fortune" and *misbehave* means "to behave badly." Likewise, a *misdeed* is "a wrong deed" and *misdate* means "to date wrongly or inaccurately." Most compounds of *mis–* are formed by attaching the prefix to verbs, as in *mishear, misremember,* or to nouns that come from verbs, such as *miscalculation, mismanagement, mispronunciation.* The prefix *mis–* has two sources. In many words, it can be traced directly back to Old English prefix *mis–,* as in *misdeed,* from Old English *misdǣd.* In a number of other words, however, it descends from the Old French prefix *mes–,* as in *misadventure* from Old French *mesaventure.* The Old French prefix *mes–* itself was borrowed from a Germanic language and is thus a close cousin of Old English *mis–.* During the Middle English period, the spelling *mis–* replaced *mes–* in English words of French origin.

The word *misanthropy,* "hatred or mistrust of humanity," might at first glance seem to contain *mis–,* "bad," as well. In this word, however, *mis–* is a variant of the prefix *miso–,* meaning "hatred, hating." *Miso–* and *mis–,* the variant used when adding the prefix to words beginning with vowels, come from the Greek prefix *mīso–* or *mīs–*. The Greek prefix in turn is derived from the Greek word *mīsos,* "hatred," which is not in fact related to the Germanic prefix *mis–* meaning "bad" discussed above. Thus, *misanthropy* comes from Greek *mīsanthrōpia,* derived from *mīs–* plus *anthrōpos,* "man, human being," while *misogyny,* "hatred or mistrust of women," comes from Greek *mīsogunia,* derived from *mīso–* plus *gunē,* "woman." In more recent times, *miso–* has been used to coin new words in the modern European languages, such as *misoneism,* "hatred of the new," first created in Italian as *misoneismo* and then borrowed into English.

mischievous

The pronunciation (mĭs-chē′vē-əs), which is considered nonstandard, is an example of *intrusion,* a phonological process that involves the addition or insertion of an extra sound. *Mischievous* is properly pronounced (mĭs′chə-vəs) with three syllables, with the stress on the first syllable. The word is often misspelled with the suffix *-ious,* which matches the mispronunciation.

    See more at **intrusion.**

miso– See **mis–.**

Miss See **Ms.**

mistress

The word *mistress* historically served simply as a neutral counterpart to *master* or *mister,* referring specifically to a woman in a position of authority or ownership, as the head of a household: *"Thirteen years had seen her mistress of Kellynch Hall"* (Jane Austen, *Persuasion*). Its use as a courtesy title is now archaic, and *mistress* is used most commonly to describe a woman who is involved in a sexual relationship with a married man. The use of the word in this context is considered sexist by some people because there is no masculine counterpart, implying that certain standards of sexual conduct for women are not applicable to men.

    See more at **master.**

mitigate / militate

The words *mitigate* and *militate* have entirely different meanings but are frequently confused. *Mitigate* means "to moderate the force or intensity of something, alleviate." It should not be followed by a preposition such as *against* or *for.* Thus a judge might mitigate the sentence of a person convicted of a crime, technology can be designed to mitigate the effects of burning fossil fuels, and measures can be taken to mitigate the risks associated with overcrowding in school buildings.

Properly used, *militate* means "to have force or influence," and is often followed by a prepositional phrase starting with *in favor of, for,* or *against*. Thus, a judge might find that the evidence militates in favor of dismissing an indictment, a large student population might militate for keeping older and younger students in separate wings of a building, and the proximity of a power plant to a neighborhood might militate against burning certain fuels.

Using *mitigate* instead of *militate* is a very common mistake, as seen in this article from the *New York Times*: "*One Kerry strategist argued that the stunningly high rates of early voting in some places could mitigate against sending the principals back, because it arguably reduces the additional gain from a candidate's visit.*"

See more at **vitiate.**

mitosis / meiosis

The words *mitosis* and *meiosis* both refer to ways in which the nucleus of a cell divides. During the process of *mitosis* (from the Greek *mitos,* "thread of a warp," and the suffix *–osis,* "action" or "process"), the nucleus of a cell divides to produce two new nuclei, each having two sets of chromosomes, the same number (called the *diploid* number) as in the original cell. *Mitosis* occurs in four stages and results in the duplication of somatic cells, cells that are used for body growth and metabolism.

The process of *meiosis* (from the Greek word meaning "less") occurs in sexually reproducing organisms and involves two consecutive divisions of the nucleus that result in the production of reproductive cells (called *gametes*) in animals or spores in plants, fungi, and most algae. Each gamete or spore contains only a single set of chromosomes, half the number of chromosomes (the *haploid* number) seen in somatic cells.

While both *mitosis* and *meiosis* refer properly to types of nuclear division, they are often used as shorthand to refer to the entire processes of cell division themselves. When *mitosis* and *meiosis* are used to refer specifically to nuclear division, they are often contrasted with *cytokinesis,* the division of the cytoplasm.

modifier

A modifier is a word, phrase, or clause that describes or restricts the sense of another word or word group. The adjective *smart* in the sentence *A smart dog would know that trick,* the adverb *suddenly* in the sentence *The cat suddenly jumped onto the bed,* the phrase *with a torch* in the sentence *He thawed the pipes with a torch,* and the clause *when I retire,* in the sentence *I plan on moving to Laredo when I retire,* all function as modifiers.

Mohammed   See **Muhammad.**

momentarily

The adverb *momentarily* is widely used in speech to mean "in a moment, shortly," as in *The manager is on another line, but she'll be with you momentarily.* Many critics dislike this use, insisting that the adverb should only be used to mean "for a moment," as in *He hesitated momentarily before entering the room.* The Usage Panel shows some dissatisfaction with the untraditional use, but resistance to it appears to be on the wane. In our 1988 survey, 59 percent of the Usage Panel accepted the example above containing *she'll be with you momentarily.* In 1999 this same example was acceptable to 68 percent of the Panel. An example in the 1999 survey, in which *momentarily* is used more vaguely to mean "for the time being, temporarily" and the length of time is open-ended, garnered approval from only 58 percent of the Panel: *The file server is momentarily out of order.*

momentum   See **force.**

Mongoloid

In its anthropological sense, *Mongoloid* refers to a large grouping of peoples indigenous to central and eastern Asia, including the peoples of China, Siberia, Korea, Japan, and Southeast Asia as well as the Mongols themselves and various other central Asian groups. It is often held to include Native American peoples as well. Like the other *–oid* terms used by 19th-century European anthropologists to divide humankind into racial categories, *Mongoloid* is potentially offensive today outside the narrow context of physical anthropology. In particular, it should not be confused with *Mongolian,* which is occasionally used in anthropological contexts but which ordinarily refers simply to the region or country of Mongolia and its peoples.

The use of *Mongoloid* or *Mongolism*—capitalized or not—in a medical sense is now clearly offensive. The acceptable terms for the congenital disorder are *Down syndrome* or *Down's syndrome.*

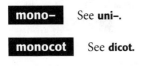

mono–   See **uni–.**

monocot   See **dicot.**

month

The singular noun *month,* preceded by a number and a hyphen, is used as a compound adjective: *a three-month vacation.* The plural possessive form without a hyphen is also standard: *a three months' vacation.*

See more at **dates and times.**

mood

Mood is a property of verbs that indicates the speaker's attitude toward the factuality or likelihood of the action or condition expressed. Mood determines whether a sentence is a statement, a command, or a conditional or hypothetical remark. English has three moods: indicative, imperative, and subjunctive.

See more at **subjunctive** and **verbs, mood of.**

moot

The adjective *moot* is originally a legal term going back to the 1500s. It derives from the noun *moot* in its sense of a hypothetical case argued as an exercise by law students. The noun *moot* in turn goes back to an Old English word meaning "a meeting, especially one convened for legislative or judicial purposes." Consequently, a *moot question* is one that is arguable or open to debate. But in the mid-19th century people also began to look at the hypothetical side of *moot* as its essential meaning, and they started to use the word to mean "of no significance or relevance." Thus *a moot point,* however debatable, is one that has no practical value. A number of critics have objected to this usage, but in our 1988 survey 59 percent of the Usage Panel accepted it in the sentence *The nominee himself chastised the White House for failing to do more to support him, but his concerns became moot when a number of Republicans announced that they, too, would oppose the nomination.* Writers who use this word should be sure that the context makes clear which sense of *moot* is meant. It is often easier to use another word, such as *debatable* or *irrelevant.*

The verb *moot* means "to bring forward a point, topic, or question for consideration or discussion," as in *an idea that was mooted before the committee. Moot* is also used in law, where it means "to render a question moot." It can also refer to arguing a case in a *moot court,* the mock court where hypothetical cases are tried for the training of law students.

Note that this word is properly pronounced (mo͞ot), never (myo͞ot), which goes with *mute.*

mores

This word, which comes from Latin and means "customs" or "ways," has two syllables and may be pronounced with either a long *a* or a long *e* sound in the second syllable. The pronunciation with a long *a* sound, which is probably the more common one in contemporary English, is closer to a Classical Latin pronunciation, while the pronunciation with a long *e* is an Anglicized Latin pronunciation.

more than   See **over.**

more than one

When a noun phrase contains *more than one* and a singular noun, the verb is normally singular: *There is more than one way to skin a cat. More than one editor is working on that project. More than one field has been planted with oats.*

When *more than one* is followed by *of* and a plural noun, the verb is plural: *More than one of the paintings were stolen. More than one of the cottages are for sale.*

When *more than one* stands alone, it usually takes a singular verb, but it may take a plural verb if the notion of multiplicity predominates: *The operating rooms are all in good order. More than one is* [or *are*] *equipped with the latest imaging technology.*

See more at **one** and **subject and verb agreement.**

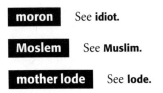

moron   See **idiot.**

Moslem   See **Muslim.**

mother lode   See **lode.**

Ms. / Mrs. / Miss

The term *Ms.* is now considered the standard way to address a woman unless she indicates that she wishes to be addressed differently. As a courtesy title, *Ms.* serves exactly the same function as *Mr.* does for men, and like *Mr.* it may be used with a last name alone or with a full name: *Ms. Pemberton; Ms. Miriam E. Pemberton. Ms.* has gained such widespread acceptance over the past few decades because it allows a woman to be addressed without reference to her marital status, a courtesy that has always been extended to men. The terms *Miss* and *Mrs.* are still used when preferred by an individual or when a woman is addressed using her husband's name, as in *Mrs. John Smith.*

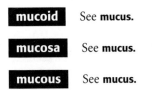

mucoid   See **mucus.**

mucosa   See **mucus.**

mucous   See **mucus.**

mucus / mucous / mucoid / mucosa

The words *mucus* and *mucous* are often confused because they sound the same and have similar but distinct meanings. *Mucus* is a noun referring to a viscous, sticky secretion that acts as a protective lubricant in the body. Mucus consists of the glycoprotein mucin, water, cells, and inorganic salts. *Mucous* is an adjective used to describe tissues that secrete mucus or secretions with the qualities of mucus. Mucous membranes, for example, line body passages that communicate with the exterior, such as the respiratory, genitourinary, and digestive tracts, and have cells and associated glands that secrete mucus. Mucous membranes are also referred to collectively as *mucosa.*

Mucoid is a less frequently used alternative to mucous. It is also used as a noun to refer to any of various glycoproteins similar to mucin.

Muhammad / Mohammed

Although *Mohammed* is still a common spelling of the name of the founder of Islam, *Muhammad* is preferred by the Muslim community.

multiple personality disorder / schizophrenia / split personality

The term *split personality* is frequently used to describe certain kinds of mental illness, especially *multiple personality disorder* and *schizophrenia.* Multiple personality disorder is a psychiatric illness in which an individual manifests at least two separate personalities, each of which is unaware of any other. In contrast, schizophrenia is a psychotic disorder characterized by withdrawal from reality and bizarre thoughts and behavior, including delusions and hallucinations. Although it is derived from Greek *schizo–,* "split," and *phrēn,* "mind," the etymology reflects antiquated ideas about the disease rather than current knowledge. This meaning is still retained in the nonpsychiatric use of the word for a situation resulting from the coexistence of disparate or antagonistic qualities, identities, or activities, as in this quotation from the *San Francisco Chronicle*: "*Their comments highlighted a national schizophrenia on immigration and the ensuing policy contradictions. . . .*" Since *split personality* is not a medical or scientific term, it is best avoided in reference to mental illness.

Muslim / Moslem

Muslim has become the preferred spelling in American usage for adherents of Islam. The Arabic word *muslim* means "one who surrenders." It is a participle of *'aslama,* "to surrender," the source of the word *Islam.* The older spelling *Moslem* is still widely used.

must

The auxiliary verb *must* is used to express necessity, obligation, and probability: *Plants must have water in order to live. Swimmers must take a shower before entering the pool. You must be joking.* Unlike other auxiliaries like *can* and *may, must* has no past form like *could* or *might: They insisted we must wait until tomorrow.* In this regard *must* resembles *need* and *ought.*

See more at **auxiliary and primary verbs, have, may, need, ought,** and **should.**

mute

In reference to deaf people who are unable to use oral language, *mute, deaf-mute,* and *deaf and dumb* are all considered objectionable today. *Deaf and dumb* is of course offensive in itself due to the confusion between the original sense of *dumb* meaning "incapable of speech" and its now far more common sense of "stupid." But even apart from such considerations, these terms give offense by implying that oral language (whether spoken or written) is the only kind of language that counts. In fact, many deaf people today communicate naturally and fully through the use of a signed language such as ASL, and advances in computer and telephonic technology have made communication with hearing people easier as well, making any expression such as *deaf-mute* or *deaf and dumb* not only offensive but in most cases simply inaccurate.

Mute is pronounced (myo͞ot), not (mo͞ot), which goes with *moot.*

mutual

The word *mutual* is used to describe a reciprocal relationship between two or more things. Thus, *their mutual animosity* means "their animosity for each other" or "the animosity between them," and *a mutual defense treaty* is one in which each party agrees to come to the defense of the other. But many people also use *mutual* to mean "shared in common," as in *The bill serves the mutual interests of management and labor.* This usage is perhaps most familiar in the expression *our mutual friend,* which was widespread even before Charles Dickens used it as the title of a novel.

myriad

Throughout most of its history in English, *myriad* was used as a noun to mean "a vast number," as in *a myriad of reasons.* In the early 19th century it had come to be used in poetry as an adjective, as in *myriad dreams.* The adjectival use became so well entrenched that many people considered it the only correct one. But both uses are acceptable today and are used in a wide variety of contexts, as the following quotations attest. First the noun use:

> Here she has provoked the reader to explore with twelve-year-old Joel a myriad of emotions, including fear, guilt, and blame, and reconciliation with his father, as Joel struggles with the drowning of his friend, Tony, and with his own decision on whether to tell the truth about his part in it (Anita Silvey, *The Essential Guide to Children's Books and Their Creators*)

> . . . water was limited, including that stored in the pond at the top of the vineyard, crucial for irrigation and for the survival of the bass, frogs, turtles, and a myriad of unseen aquatic life in the long dry season soon to follow (James Conway, *Napa*)

> In biomedicine, basic research findings often fail to translate into clinical practice for a myriad of illogical reasons (Jon Cohen, *Coming to Term*)

The adjectival use:

Art should certainly aspire to beauty, but there are myriad sorts of beauty: the presentation of a subject in the most economical way, for instance; a precise choice of language, of detail (Joyce Carol Oates, Introduction, *The Best American Essays of the Century*)

Nothing is fixed [in hyperfiction]; the same plot elements can be arranged and rearranged in myriad ways, the way children's lego blocks can be used to build a log cabin, skyscraper or train (Michiko Kakutani, "Never-Ending Saga," *New York Times Magazine*)

The Deschutes River tumbles down from the high lava fields of central Oregon, through ranches and pine forests and over myriad whitewater rapids on its way to the city of Bend (Bill Donahue, "End of the Run," *Outside*)

. . . panzanella constants are bread, tomatoes, onions, oil and vinegar, and basil or parsley, with celery and cucumber as near-constants—and best understood before a cook explores the myriad variations (Corby Kummer, "Tuscan Tomatoes," *Atlantic Monthly*)

· N ·

naphtha / naphthalene

As is the case with *diphtheria* and *diphthong,* the *ph* should properly be pronounced (f), not (p). Because so many people say (năp-), as opposed to (năf-), though, this variant has become acceptable. Because the (fth) sequence is difficult for English speakers to articulate, it was probably inevitable that the pronunciation of such words would shift over time to make them easier to say.

native

When used in reference to a member of an indigenous people, the noun *native,* like its synonym *aborigine,* can evoke stereotypes of primitiveness or cultural backwardness that many people now seek to avoid. As is often the case with words that categorize people, the use of the noun is more problematic than the use of the corresponding adjective. Thus a phrase such as *the peoples native to northern India* or *the aboriginal inhabitants of the Amazon* is generally much preferable to *the natives of northern India* or *the Amazonian aborigines.*

Despite any potentially negative connotations, *native* has become increasingly popular in ethnonyms such as *native Australian* and *Alaska Native,* perhaps due to the wide acceptance of *Native American* as a term of ethnic pride and respect. These compounds have the further benefit of being equally acceptable when used alone as nouns (a *native Australian*) or in an adjectival construction (a *member of a native Australian people*). Of terms formed on this model, those referring to peoples indigenous to the United States generally capitalize *native,* as in *Alaska Native* (or the less common *Native Alaskan*) and *Native Hawaiian,* while others usually style it lowercase.

Native American

Many Americans have come to prefer *Native American* over *Indian* both as a term of respect and as a corrective to the misnomer bestowed on the peoples of the Americas by Columbus. There are solid arguments for this preference. *Native American* eliminates any confusion between indigenous American peoples and the inhabitants of India. And despite some criticism, it is also historically accurate—one definition of *native* is "being one of the original inhabitants of a place," and that is true of all peoples living in this hemisphere when Europeans first arrived. (In Canada, native peoples are now known officially as *First Nations* or, if Inuit and Métis are included, *First Peoples*).

312

These arguments aside, however, the choice between these two terms is often made as a matter of principle or emotion. For some, *Native American* expresses respect toward America's indigenous peoples; *Indian* is seen as disrespectful, tainted by Hollywood stereotypes and chauvinistic history texts. For others, *Native American* smacks of official bureaucracy and the manipulation of language for political purposes, while *Indian* is the natural English word—a familiar, straightforward term that expresses pride in tribal history and culture. Although hotly debated during the 1970s and 1980s, this controversy has subsided in recent years, and it is now common to find the two terms used interchangeably in the same piece of writing. Furthermore, the issue has never been particularly divisive between Indians and non-Indians. While generally welcoming the respectful tone of *Native American,* many Indians have continued to prefer the older term (or the fuller form *American Indian*) in their own writings.

Native American and *Indian* are not exact equivalents when referring to the indigenous peoples of Canada and Alaska. *Native American,* the broader term, is properly used of all such peoples, whereas *Indian* is customarily used of the northern Athabaskan and Algonquian peoples in contrast to the Inuit, Alaskan Eskimos, and Aleuts. (*Alaska Native,* or less commonly *Native Alaskan,* is also properly used of all indigenous peoples residing in Alaska.) In certain official or government contexts, *Native American* is also sometimes defined to include Native Hawaiians, although this is rarely the case in ordinary discourse.

Note that *Native American* is not usually hyphenated as either a noun or an adjective.

See more at **American Indian, Eskimo, First Nation, Indian,** and **red.**

nauseous / nauseated / nauseating

Traditional usage lore has insisted that *nauseous* should be used only to mean "causing nausea" and that it is incorrect to use it to mean "feeling sick to one's stomach." Back in 1965, the Usage Panel was in step with this thinking, with 88 percent rejecting the "feeling sick" meaning of *nauseous.*

This attitude persisted for decades but has since begun to give way. In our 1988 survey, 72 percent of the Panel thought that a roller coaster should be said to make its riders *nauseated* rather than *nauseous.* A decade later, however, the Panel's attitude had changed dramatically. In our 1999 survey, 61 percent of the Panel approved of the sentence *Roller coasters make me nauseous.*

This change might have been inevitable once people began to think that *nauseous* did not properly mean "causing nausea," as traditional lore would have it. Even in our 1988 survey, this was the case, as 88 percent preferred *nauseating* in the sentence *The children looked a little green from too many candy apples and nauseating* [not *nauseous*] *rides.* The 1999 results for this same example were not significantly different.

Since there is abundant evidence for the "feeling sick" use of *nauseous,* the word presents a classic example of a word whose traditional, "correct" usage is being supplanted by a newer, "incorrect" one. In other words, what was now considered an error is becoming standard practice. *Nauseous* is now the far more common word to describe the sick feeling. While *nauseated* is still used in this sense and remains for some the only "correct" form, it is more apt to be interpreted metaphorically. *We were left nauseous by the movie* suggests that it made us ill. *We were left nauseated by the movie* implies that we were repulsed by the images.

need

Depending on the meaning, the verb *need* behaves sometimes like an auxiliary verb (such as *can* or *may*) and sometimes like a main verb (such as *want* or *try*). When used as a main verb, *need* agrees with its subject, takes *to* before the verb following it, and combines with *do* in questions, negations, and certain other constructions: *He needs to go. Does he need to go so soon? He doesn't need to go.* When used as an auxiliary verb, *need* does not agree with its subject, does not take *to* before the verb following it, and does not combine with *do: He needn't go. Need he go so soon?* Unlike *can* and *may,* however, auxiliary *need* has no other form like *could* and *might* for the past tense: *He said we need not worry about that.*

See more at **auxiliary and primary verbs, dare, have, must,** and **ought.**

Negro

Negro was borrowed into English from the Spanish and Portuguese words for *black* long before the first Africans were sold to settlers in Virginia in 1619, and it has undergone a series of ups and downs, at least in American English, ever since. Throughout the 17th and 18th centuries *negro,* generally spelled lowercase, was the most common label for referring to Africans or persons of African descent. After emancipation, however, Black Americans tended to reject both *negro* and *black* as part of the vocabulary of slavery, with *colored* becoming the preferred name instead. But neither of the earlier terms disappeared, and many Black writers, such as Booker T. Washington and W.E.B. Du Bois, used *negro* and *black* as readily as *colored.*

The 20th century saw a dramatic rise in the use of *negro.* Du Bois and the NAACP led a protracted and ultimately successful nationwide campaign for its capitalization, and by the 1930s *Negro* was established in most of the mainstream American press as the preferred racial label for Black Americans. During the civil rights movement of the 1950s and 1960s, it was *Negro* that speakers and writers most often chose, whether they were expressing racial pride or demanding social justice. But the ensuing Black Power movement swept *Negro* aside in a remarkably short time, establishing *Black* as the new term of pride. Today *Negro* is considered offensive by many Black Americans, although it is still used by some older speakers, especially in the South. For this reason it was retained on the 2000 US census in the racial category listed as "Black, African Am., or Negro."

Negroid

Negroid, one of the terms proposed by 19th-century European anthropologists as part of a system of human racial classification, refers primarily to African peoples living south of the Sahara Desert; it is often held to include certain peoples native to Indonesia, New Guinea, Melanesia, and the Philippines as well. *Negroid* is now rarely used, and is potentially offensive, outside the field of physical anthropology.

neither

neither or none   According to a traditional usage rule, *neither* is used only to mean "not one or the other of two." To refer to "none of several," *none* is preferred: *None* [not *neither*] *of the three opposition candidates would make a better president than the incumbent.*

neither with singular or plural verb   Like the pronoun *either, neither* normally takes a singular verb: *Neither candidate is having an easy time with the press.* But *neither* can also be used acceptably with a plural verb, especially when followed by *of* and a plural noun: *Neither of the candidates are really expressing their own views.* When *neither . . . nor* is used in a conjoined subject, the verb is singular if both nouns are singular (*Neither Jim nor Bernie wants to play golf today*), and the verb is plural if both nouns are plural (*Neither the students nor the teachers were much interested in the idea*). When the construction mixes singular and plural elements, practice is mixed. For more on this see **either.**

neither . . . (n)or   As a conjunction *neither* is properly followed by *nor,* not *or: Neither the ship nor its cargo* [not *or its cargo*] *received any damage in the storm.* The elements that follow *neither . . . nor* should be treated in parallel fashion. Thus, *She is to perform neither in the play nor in the concert* is parallel but *She is neither to perform in the play nor in the concert* is not.

pronunciation of *neither*   Most people pronounce this word (nē′thər), with a long *e* sound, in American English, but the pronunciation (nī′thər), with a long *i,* is also acceptable.
       See more at **either, every, none, nor, or,** and **subject and verb agreement.**

neo-

The prefix *neo–* means "new," "recent," or "young" and comes from Greek prefix *neo–,* from *neos,* "new, young." The Greek word *neos* is in fact a close cousin of the native English word *new.* Thus our word *neophyte,* which means "a recent convert" or "a beginner," comes from Greek *neophutos,* which meant literally "newly planted" and later by extension "a new convert (to a religion)." However, many English words beginning with *neo–* are not direct borrowings from Greek but recent coinages, or *neologisms,* made in English itself over the last 150 years. Often these words refer to a new or a modern form of a movement or doctrine, such as *neoconservatism* or *neoexpressionism.* Many other relatively recent formations are scientific words, such as *neolithic,* "relating to the New Stone Age in the development of human culture," and *neoteny,* "retention of juvenile characteristics in the adults of a species." The name of the noble gas *neon* means "the new one" in Greek and was bestowed on the element by its discoverers in 1898.

nervous breakdown

The term *nervous breakdown* is used frequently in popular writing to describe a sudden and severe deterioration of emotional or psychological functioning, usually necessitating hospitalization, as in this newspaper article: *"There are, however, gaps in the record, starting at the time of* [his] *nervous breakdown in 1961 and recurring over his final two decades as he struggled with mental illness."*

Nervous breakdown, however, has no specific medical meaning and is not used to diagnose illness. A decline in mental functioning or emotional collapse can have many possible causes. In medicine, such events are described using any one of many possible psychiatric terms, including the worsening of a mood disorder (such as depression), the manifestation of psychotic symptoms (as in schizophrenia), or an individual's response to severe psychological stress.

While *nervous breakdown* should not imply a medical diagnosis, its vagueness can be useful when a condition is not known. The term is also an acceptable colloquialism for a period of emotional stress or turmoil.

–ness

The suffix *–ness,* which goes back to Old English *–nes,* continues to have a productive life. It commonly attaches to adjectives in order to form abstract nouns, such as *artfulness* and *destructiveness.* The suffix *–ness* also forms nouns from adjectives made of participles, such as *contentedness* and *willingness.* It can also form nouns from compound adjectives, such as *kindheartedness* and *straightforwardness.* The suffix *–ness* can even be used with phrases: *matter-of-factness.* The word *forgiveness* seems at first glance to be a bit different, since it appears to be formed from the verb *forgive.* But in fact, *forgiveness* descends from Old English *forgifennes,* literally *forgiven-ness,* formed from the past participle of the verb *forgifan,* "forgive."

neurosis

The word *neurosis* has been used since the 18th century, when it referred broadly to a *"nervous disease."* With the advent of Freud's theory of psychoanalysis in the late 19th century, *neurosis* evolved to mean a chronic psychological disorder characterized by excessive anxiety or insecurity, often compensated for by various defense mechanisms. Unlike psychosis, there was no distortion of reality in a neurosis, nor was there evidence of neurologic or other organic disease.

Today, the words *neurosis* and *neurotic* and are no longer used in formal psychiatric diagnosis. In fact, they are not even indexed in recent editions of the *Diagnostic and Statistical Manual of Mental Disorders.* The conditions formerly referred to as *neurotic* are now described with many other terms, such as *anxiety disorder, adjustment reaction,* and *post-traumatic stress disorder. Neurosis* and *neurotic* are still frequently used in informal conversation and writing to denote recurrent worry, anxiety, or obsession, as in this quotation from a book review in *Newsday:* "[she] seems to *have gotten over the usual case of new-mother perfectionist-neurosis quicker than most.*"

niche

This 17th-century borrowing from French has traditionally been pronounced (nĭch), rhyming with *itch*. The pronunciation (nēsh), rhyming with *quiche*, is a 20th-century revival of the French pronunciation, which some people dislike because they think it seems affected. However, this pronunciation is now given by most dictionaries as a standard variant.

no holds barred

The commonly used phrase *no holds barred* implies that there will be no restrictions or limitations on a given activity, as in this article from the *St. Louis Post-Dispatch*: *"After a no-holds-barred campaign, Democrat Claire McCaskill and Republican Matt Blunt are scrambling for the right to succeed Gov. Bob Holden, whom McCaskill defeated in the August primary election."* The expression comes from the sport of wrestling, where a hold is "a manner of grasping an opponent," and *no holds barred* refers to a match in which any kind of hold is legal. The expression is sometimes misspelled as *no holes barred,* as in this Irish newspaper article: *"During the no-holes-barred interview Higgens said that during his heyday he had charisma, something which no one else had."*

nominative case

In English, the nominative case is the case of a pronoun used as the subject of a finite verb (as *I* in *I wrote the letter*) or as a predicate nominative (as *we* in *It is we who have made the mistake*). The nominative case stands in contrast to the objective case.

See more at **pronouns, personal.**

non–

The prefix *non–,* which means "not," ultimately comes from the Latin word *nōn,* "not." In Old French, Latin *nōn* came to be used as a negative prefix in the formation of such words as *nonchalant,* "unconcerned, indifferent," derived from *non–* plus the present participle of the French verb *chaloir,* "to cause concern to," and later borrowed into English along with the noun *nonchalance.* From Old French the prefix passed into Middle English, and by the 16th century, many compounds with *non–,* mostly legal terms, were in use in English. But in the 17th century the prefix began to be used with many different kinds of words. Today *non–* can be added to almost any adjective. Some examples include *nonessential, nonmetallic,* and *nonproductive. Non–* also combines with many nouns, as in *nonentity, nonresident,* and *nonviolence.* Most recently *non–* is used in combination with some verbs to form adjectives, as in *nonskid, nonstop,* and *nonstick.*

See more at **un–.**

noncount nouns   See under **count nouns.**

none

"... *and then there were none*." The closing words of this well-known nursery rhyme should dispel the notion that *none* can only take a singular verb. One rationale for opposing the plural use cites the fact that *none* comes from the Old English word *nān*, which is related to the Old English word *ān*, ancestor of our modern word *one*. But the citational evidence against restricting *none* is overwhelming. *None* has been used as both a singular and plural pronoun since the 9th century. The plural usage appears in the King James Bible (for example, "*And all the drinking vessels of king Solomon were of gold, and all the vessels of the house of the forest of Lebanon were of pure gold: none were of silver. . . .*" 2 Chronicles 9:20), in Shakespeare ("*I will converse with iron-witted fools / And unrespective boys; none are for me / That look into me with considerate eyes*" *Richard III 4.2.29*), as well as other paragons of elegant phrasing, such as John Dryden and Edmund Burke. This use of *none* is widespread in the works of respected writers today, as these quotations show:

> The Governor, B.K. Nehru, and his wife, Fori, among others, were on hand to see her off. But none of the usual civilities were observed (Katherine Frank, *Indira*)

> He looked at her tragically, to remind her (she supposed) that he was a tragic man, a failure in business, and unfaithful; none of his passions were perfectly requited, and Giddy would never understand him (Carolyn Cooke, *The Bostons*)

The usage with a singular verb is probably more common in edited prose, and continues to be both idiomatic and effective:

> However great his troubles, he never asked help or made any complaint, as if, like a philosopher, he had learned that without hard work and suffering there could be no pleasure worth having. Yet none of us was able to make out what Stickeen was really good for (John Muir, "Stickeen")

> Everywhere he looked—from cartilage to fungi to the notorious sedative thalidomide—Folkman found one compound after another that exhibited anti-angiogenic properties. But none of them was as effective as he wanted it to be (Christine Gorman, "The Hope and the Hype," *Time*)

Choosing between a singular or plural verb is thus more of a stylistic matter than a grammatical one. Note, however, that *none* can only be plural when used in sentences whose subject begins with constructions like *none but*, as in *None but his most loyal supporters believe* [not *believes*] *his story*. In this case the subject clearly is plural in meaning, and *none but* functions essentially as an adverb meaning "only."
See more at **every, neither, nothing,** and **subject and verb agreement.**

nonplus

The verb *nonplus*, from the Latin phrase *nōn plūs*, "not more," is well established with the meaning "to surprise and bewilder." The verb often implies that the affected person is at a loss for words. *Nonplus* is used predominantly in the passive voice, as in *The scientists were completely nonplussed—the apparatus had not acted at all as they had expected.* This use of the verb was acceptable to 84 percent of the Usage Panel in our 2001 survey.

However, the word is frequently used to mean "to make indifferent, bore," as if the *plus* part of the word meant "to overcome with excitement." This usage is still controversial and should probably be avoided since it may well be viewed as a mistake. In our 2001 survey, 61 percent of the Panel rejected the sentence *The nine panelists showed little emotion during the broadcast and were generally nonplussed by the outcome.* Here the implication is not that the people were stunned or bewildered, but rather the opposite—that they were unimpressed. Thus this usage bears with it the connotation of predictability rather than unexpectedness.

nonrestrictive clause   See **restrictive and nonrestrictive clauses.**

nonsexist language   See **sexist language.**

nonstandard / substandard

The term *nonstandard* was introduced by linguists and lexicographers to describe usages and language varieties that had previously been labeled with terms such as *vulgar* and *illiterate. Nonstandard* is not a euphemism but reflects the empirical discovery that the varieties of language used by low-prestige groups have rich and systematic grammatical structures and that their stigmatization more often reflects a judgment about the speakers rather than any inherent deficiencies in their logic or expressive power. Note that the use of nonstandard forms is not necessarily restricted to the communities with which they are associated in the public mind. Many educated speakers freely use forms such as *can't hardly* or *ain't I* to set a popular or informal tone. Some dictionaries use the term *substandard* to describe forms, such as *ain't,* associated with uneducated speech, while reserving *nonstandard* for forms such as *irregardless,* which are common in writing but are still regarded by many as uneducated. But *substandard* itself is sometimes disparaged, and most linguists and lexicographers now use only *nonstandard.*

nonwhite

Many people object to the term *nonwhite* for referring to people by what they are not rather than what they are. Of course there are occasions, as when discussing an exclusionary policy such as the former system of apartheid in South Africa, when this emphasis is entirely appropriate. In many other cases, if it is relevant to mention race or skin color at all, a term such as *person of color* is often preferable to *nonwhite.*

See more at **person of color.**

no other   See **other.**

no place   See **everyplace.**

nor

The rules for using *nor* are neither simple nor easy to spell out. When *neither* begins a balanced construction that negates two parts of a sentence, *nor,* not *or,* must introduce the second part. Thus standard usage requires *He is neither able nor* [not *or*] *willing to go.* Similarly, *nor* [not *or*] must be used to start the second of two negative independent clauses: *He cannot find anyone now, nor does he expect to find anyone in the future. Jane will never compromise with Bill, nor will Bill compromise with Jane.*

Note that in these constructions *nor* causes an inversion of the auxiliary verb and the subject (*does he . . . will Bill*). However, when a verb is negated by *not* or *never,* and is followed by a negative verb phrase (but not an entire clause), either *or* or *nor* is acceptable: *He will not permit the change or* [or *nor*] *even consider it.*

In noun phrases of the type *no this or that, or* is actually more common than *nor: He has no experience or interest* [less frequently *nor interest*] *in chemistry. Or* is also more common than *nor* when such a noun phrase, adjective phrase, or adverb phrase is introduced by *not: He is not a philosopher or a statesman. They were not rich or happy. The senator did not speak persuasively or movingly on the issue.*

Like other coordinating conjunctions, *nor* is sometimes used to begin a new sentence when the thought it introduces seems worthy of independent status, as in this concluding paragraph from an essay by Bruce Bartlett in the *National Review:*

> Finally, Bush should not underestimate how rapidly his power will dissipate as he approaches the end of his presidency. Nor should he underestimate the extent to which unexpected events—such as several Supreme Court vacancies or deterioration of the Iraq situation—can push everything else off the table. This also argues for a narrowing of his agenda to those things that are most needed and that have the highest chance of success.

While such sentences must be considered standard, their effectiveness depends on their rarity.

See more at **neither** and **or.**

normal / average

These words have broad connotations and are commonly confused when used to describe numbers. It is important therefore to keep them distinguished. *Normal* is a very inexact term, meaning only that something falls within the range of typical or expected cases or variation. So if one says, for example, that the temperature on some given day is "five degrees below normal," one is forgetting that a certain amount of variation in temperature might also be quite typical. In scientific usage, no single temperature can be normal; only a range of temperatures can be.

What one means in such a case is not a normal temperature but an *average* temperature: a precisely defined numerical figure, in this case calculated using figures gathered by a meteorologist, with which the temperature of the day in question can be compared. Average figures in themselves are abstractions and correspond to no actual individual case. The average family in the United States may have 1.7 children, but it is quite inconceivable that a normal family has 1.7 children!

Care should be taken especially when using the word *normal*, since deviations from what is considered normal suggest abnormality and hence a potentially negative judgment. A child who is an inch shorter than average might in fact be quite typical—in fact, it is possible for the majority of children in a fourth grade class to be an inch or so shorter than the average height of the class. Contrastingly, to say that a child is an inch shorter than normal suggests that the child is failing to grow quickly enough and that there is a problem.

See more at **average.**

no sooner than / no sooner when

In the phrase *no sooner,* the word *sooner* is a comparative adverb, just as the word *better* is in the phrase *no better.* As such, the expression should be followed by *than,* not *when: No sooner had she opened her book than the doorbell rang. I had no sooner left than she called.*

not

The positioning of *not* and other negatives in a sentence is important to avoid ambiguity. The sentence *All classes are not open to enrollment* could be taken to mean either "All classes are closed to enrollment" or "Not all classes are open to enrollment." Similarly, the sentence *Kim didn't sleep until noon* could mean either "Kim went to sleep at noon" or "Kim got up before noon."

See more at **adverbs, also, double negative,** and **only.**

nothing / nothing but

According to the traditional rule, *nothing* should always be treated as a singular noun, even when followed by an exception phrase containing a plural noun: *Nothing except your fears stands* [not *stand*] *in your way. Nothing but roses meets* [not *meet*] *the eye.*

But there are certain contexts in which *nothing but* sounds quite natural with a plural verb and should not be considered inappropriate. In these sentences, constructions like *nothing but* function much like an adverb meaning "only," in a pattern similar to one seen in *none but:*

> Sometimes, for a couple of hours together, there were almost no houses; there were nothing but woods and rivers and lakes and horizons adorned with bright-looking mountains (Henry James, *The Europeans*)

Note that the construction is sometimes used in the predicate following a form of the verb *be* to emphasize equivalence with the subject, even when plural:

> Years of selective breeding have produced turkeys that are nothing but cooking pouches with legs (Garrison Keillor, "With All the Trimmings," *Time*)

> Angels on horseback were nothing but oysters wrapped in thin rashers of bacon, fried and served hot on buttered toast (Gail Anderson-Dargatz, *Cure for Death*)

Nonetheless, the prevailing pattern is for *nothing but* and similar constructions to get singular verbs, even when emphasizing plural entities:

> As the launch floats farther and farther away from the noisy town docks, the houses and shops on the banks of the river change from brick and tin to mud and thatch, and then disappear entirely. In their place is nothing but trees and mud, water and sky (Sy Montgomery, *Spell of the Tiger*)

> I am used to the haphazard cemetery-keeping that is traditional in most Southern black communities, but this neglect is staggering. As far as I can see there is nothing but bushes and weeds, some as tall as my waist (Alice Walker, "Looking for Zora," *Ms. Magazine*).

not only . . . but also

not only . . . but also *Not only* and *but also* are usually classified as correlative conjunctions. They add emphasis to each part of the construction and suggest that the second part is particularly unexpected or surprising. As with *both . . . and* and other correlatives, parallelism requires that each conjunction be followed by a construction of the same grammatical type. Thus, *She not only bought a new car but also a new lawnmower* displays faulty parallelism, where *She bought not only a new car but also a new lawnmower* does not, because both *not only* and *but also* are followed by noun phrases.

not only . . . but Leaving out the *also* from this construction tends to heighten the intensification of the second part even further:

> Objects on a beach, whether men or inanimate things, look not only exceedingly grotesque, but much larger and more wonderful than they really are (Henry David Thoreau, *Cape Cod*)

> His clothes were deliberately cheap, not only because he was poor but because he wanted to be able to forget them (Walker Evans, Foreword, "James Agee in 1936," *Let Us Now Praise Famous Men*)

Sometimes even the *but* is left out, with a similar intensifying effect:

> He [Edward J. O'Brien] not only gave Hemingway his first publication, he dedicated that year's volume to Hemingway, then a twenty-four-year-old reporter for the *Tor-*

onto Star, thereby launching one of the most celebrated literary careers of our century (Katrina Kenison, Foreword, *The Best American Short Stories of the Century*)

Stanley gave himself not only a new name; he tried for the rest of his life to give himself a new biography (Adam Hochschild, *King Leopold's Ghost*)

See more at **correlative conjunctions** and **parallelism.**

not too   See **too.**

nouns

Nouns are words that are used to name a person, place, thing, quality, or action and that can function as the subject or object of a verb, as the object of a preposition, or as an appositive. The word *boat* in *The boat is crossing the bay,* and the word *happiness* in *Happiness is very important to them,* are nouns. Most nouns are classified as common nouns or proper nouns.

See more at **common nouns; pronouns, personal;** and **plural nouns.**

nubile

A city newspaper recently referred to *"the seemingly endless number of nubile corps de ballet members arranging themselves like artful flower beds in a ballet troupe."* A girl or woman who is *nubile* (from Latin *nūbere,* "to take a husband") is one who is considered marriageable. The word is also used more generally to describe a female who is young and sexually mature. *Nubile* is offensive to many people for several reasons. There is no masculine counterpart for the word, which describes a woman solely in relation to her attractiveness to men or her desirability as a marriage partner for a man. It objectifies a female, portraying her as "ripe on the vine." Because of these sexist connotations, the word should be used with caution.

nuclear

The pronunciation (no͞o′kyə-lər), which is generally considered incorrect, is an example of how a familiar phonological pattern can influence an unfamiliar one. The usual pronunciation of the final two syllables of this word is (-klē-ər), but this sequence of sounds is rare in English. Much more common is the similar sequence (-kyə-lər), which occurs in words like *particular, circular, spectacular,* and in many scientific words like *molecular, ocular,* and *vascular.* Adjusted to fit into this familiar pattern, the (-kyə-lər) pronunciation is often heard in high places. It is not uncommon in the military, even among commanders, in association with nuclear weaponry, and it has been observed in the speech of US presidents including Dwight D. Eisenhower and George W. Bush. The prominence of these speakers, however, has done little to brighten the appeal of (no͞o′kyə-lər), which was the preferred pronunciation of only 1 percent of the Usage Panel in our 2004 survey; furthermore, only 10 percent of the Panel considered it to be acceptable.

number

the word *number* and verb agreement   As a collective noun, the word *number* may take either a singular or a plural verb. It takes a singular verb when preceded by the definite article *the: The number of skilled workers is increasing.* It takes a plural verb when preceded by the indefinite article *a: A number of the workers have learned new skills.*

grammatical number   In grammar, the term *number* refers to the indication of whether a word is singular or plural. Number in English nouns is usually indicated by an inflection, that is, by the presence or absence of the suffix *-s* or *-es.*

See more at **collective noun; lot; pronouns, agreement of; plurals;** and **subject and verb agreement.**

numbers

basic guidelines

1. In general contexts, spell out whole numbers from one through one hundred, hundreds, and thousands. Express other numbers in figures. See throughout this section for exceptions.

    > Only ten tickets are left for tonight's performance.
    > He was forty-three by the time he entered graduate school.
    > The Falcons defeated the Bears before five hundred fans.
    > The original ballpark had a seating capacity of nine thousand.
    > There were 120 empty seats.
    > The capacity of the new park is 33,871.

2. An alternative system, common in journalism and scientific and technical writing, is to spell out only whole numbers from one through nine (or from one through ten) and to use figures for the rest.

    > There are some 9,000 species of marine-dwelling creatures in the phylum Cnidaria.
    > The Stauromedusae order of jellyfish includes about 50 described species.
    > Their goblet-shaped bodies generally have eight clusters of tentacles.

3. When two or more numbers referring to similar things occur in the same sentence or passage, all the numbers should be expressed in the same way. If one such number would ordinarily be expressed as a figure, use figures throughout.

    > Of the 200 students who signed up for the course, 102 are men and 98 are women.

    Numbers referring to different categories of things need not be made consistent in this way.

    > Of the 120 people who attended the play, 90 were children under age ten.

large numbers   Numbers in the millions or more may be spelled out but are often expressed as a combination of figures and words.

2.9 million people
93 million miles

4 billion years ago
$2 trillion in debt

numbers beginning a sentence   A number beginning a sentence is always spelled out. If the number is long and awkwardness results, it may help to rephrase the sentence.

Seven hundred fifty-five orders were shipped from the Centerbrook warehouse today.

The Centerbrook warehouse shipped 755 orders today.

adjacent numbers   When two numbers occur next to each other, one of them should be spelled out.

fifteen 12-inch rulers
twenty 15-year-olds

100 fifty-story buildings

ordinal numbers   The style chosen for cardinal numbers should likewise be used for ordinal numbers.

Martinez had thrown 101 pitches when he began the eighth inning.
My parents celebrated their fiftieth wedding anniversary in March.
There is a spectacular view of the city from the tower on the 102nd floor.

percentages   Use numerals for percentages. The word *percent* is more frequently used in general contexts and the symbol % in technical contexts, but often either style is acceptable.

We agree 100 percent with the board's assessment.
When tested, the mixture was found to be 15% sodium.

scores and votes   Use numerals to express scores and tabulations of votes.

The Patriots defeated the Rams by a score of 40–22.
The Supreme Court struck down the Texas law in a 5–4 vote.

money

1. In general contexts, isolated references to money may be correctly expressed according to the basic guidelines for cardinal numbers. The word *dollar(s)* should be used if the number is spelled out. With figures, the symbol $ should be used.

   The bidding started at seventy-five dollars.
   The hammer price was four thousand dollars.
   She made an offer of $350 for a watercolor by Waldo Midgley.
   Someone behind me paid $5 million for a painting.

Figures are often used when multiple sums of money are referenced in close proximity and spelling them out would be cumbersome.

The watch is $95, the bracelet is $68, and the earrings are $39.

The cost of the merchandise is $90.00, tax is $5.00, and shipping and handling is $10.75.

2. Isolated references to amounts of less than a dollar should be spelled out. Figures and the symbol ¢ are used when several such amounts are mentioned at once.

> The marzipan hearts cost ninety-five cents apiece.

> Tomomi bought a praline for 50¢, two peppermints for 60¢, and a caramel cluster for 89¢.

commas in numerals   Use commas in numerals of four or more digits unless it is the established style to leave four-digit numerals unpunctuated. Years of four digits, page numbers, street addresses, and decimal fractions do not contain commas.

3,000 people	the year 2006
1,400 years ago	page 1769
$2,500	1420 Central Street
10,000 BC	3.3333

fractions

1. In running text, fractions with small denominators should be spelled out. Noun forms may either be hyphenated or left open in accordance with the preference of the writer. Adjective forms should always be hyphenated.

> He drank two-thirds [*or* two thirds] of the punch.
> Ordinances may be passed only upon a four-fifths vote of the commission.

2. Mixed fractions, or quantities made up of a whole number and a fraction, are sometimes spelled out but more frequently expressed in figures.

> He's 5 feet 11½ inches tall.
> The recipe calls for 2⅔ cups of
>   milk.

See more at **hyphenation.**

· O ·

object

An object is a noun or word acting like a noun that receives or is affected by the action of a verb or that follows and is governed by a preposition.

See also **direct object** and **indirect object.**

objective case

The objective case is the case of a pronoun used as the object of a verb or preposition. The pronouns *me, you, him, her, it, us,* and *them* are in the objective case.

See more at **pronouns, personal.**

oblivious

The adjective *oblivious* can be followed by either *to* or *of: The party appeared oblivious to* [or *of*] the mounting pressures for political reform. The use with *to* is more than three times as common in contemporary English, however.

ocularist   See **ophthalmologist.**

of

The soldiers did not receive as warm of a welcome as expected from the local inhabitants, who considered them to be invaders rather than liberators. This sentence illustrates a common construction found in informal American English, in which the word *of* follows a phrase consisting of *as* and an adjective. Similar uses of *of* can be found with other words such as *so, that, too,* and *how.* In these constructions, *of* appears between an adjective and the noun phrase it qualifies as part of phrases that specify degrees of difference or equality, as in *How big of a job was it?* or *The band is still writing as good of songs as it has in the past.* These constructions with *of* are often too colloquial to be used in formal expository prose. In our 1997 survey 68 percent of the Usage Panel disapproved of the sentence *That's too long of a movie to sit through* in formal contexts, while 27 percent accepted it in informal speech and writing. Only 4 percent accepted it outright in formal contexts. However, it is usually quite easy to alter a sentence to remove this colloquial use of the word *of.* The construction *as X of a Y* can be fixed simply by omitting the word *of* (for instance, *as warm of a welcome* becomes *as warm a welcome*). Light rewriting is enough to remove the other instances of the constructions. The sentence *Although he spent many years in research, he did not produce all that useful or enjoyable of a book in the end* can be rephrased to read . . . *he did not produce a very useful or enjoyable book in the end.* The sentence *If he just made an effort, he would have realized how simple of a problem it was to solve* should be changed to . . . *how simple the problem was to solve.*

See more at **as, have,** and **possessive constructions.**

<h1>off</h1>

***off* meaning "from"** When *off* is used to indicate a source, it has an informal ring and should be avoided in formal contexts: *I borrowed the sander from* [not *off*] *my brother.* In less formal contexts, however, *off* may imply a conniving approach to obtaining something: *The fundraisers got a thousand dollars from the conventioneers* sounds entirely innocent, while *The fundraisers got a thousand dollars off the conventioneers* makes the fundraisers sound unappreciative or dishonest.

off of The compound preposition *off of* has traditionally been considered to have an informal tone and is often avoided in formal speech and writing: *He stepped off* [not *off of*] *the platform.* Note, however, that a very subtle distinction in meaning exists between *off* and *off of.* Used alone, the word *off* may focus either on the position of something or on the motion or path away from it. But the compound *off of* focuses attention exclusively on the motion or path. (In this regard, *off* and *off of* parallel *on* and *onto.*) Thus, a sentence such as *He jumped off a bridge* often suggests a deliberate act of suicide, since in that case the location of jumping is of primary interest; the implied consequence is that he was killed. But *He jumped off of a bridge* does not imply suicide so strongly, as it focuses on the bridge as a part of a path that was being followed; the implied consequence is that he ended up somewhere else (thus one might expect a follow-up phrase, such as . . . *and into a pond*). Similarly, one might claim *He needs to get off* [or *off of*] *those drugs,* suggesting a path to recovery, but *He is off those drugs* [not *He is off of those drugs*] focuses attention on his state of being.

A similar but more salient difference in meaning is found between *out* and *out of.* There is a difference between *Frank took the garbage out the kitchen door,* where *out* is a preposition and *the kitchen door* is the path Frank took, and *Frank took the garbage out of the kitchen door,* where *out* is an adverbial particle and *the kitchen door* is the place from which the garbage was removed.

<h1>officiate</h1>

Officiate has long seen use as an intransitive verb, but it has recently developed a transitive use. A vast majority of the Usage Panel (91 percent) approves of the intransitive use of *officiate,* as in the sentence *The wedding was held in the garden, a minister and priest officiating.* The Panel views transitive uses much less favorably. The use of *officiate* in sporting contexts, as in the sentence *He officiated National Hockey League games for fifteen years* is approved by only 38 percent of the Panel. This usage may be unremarkable when appearing on the sports page, but it should be avoided in general writing. Support for this usage in more traditional contexts, such as weddings, plummets further. Only 22 percent of the Panel approves of the sentence *A minister officiated the wedding, which was held in a garden.*

often

Simplification of consonant clusters has been an ongoing process in the history of English, but during the 16th and 17th centuries, English experienced an especially widespread loss of consonants, among them the *d* in *handsome* and *handkerchief,* the *p* in *raspberry,* and the *t* in *chestnut* and *often.* Because of the influence of spelling, however, there is sometimes a tendency to restore sounds that have become silent. This is the case with *often,* which is now commonly pronounced with the *t.* Curiously, in other words such as *soften* and *listen,* the *t* generally remains silent.
      See more at **spelling pronunciation.**

–oid

The basic meaning of the suffix *–oid* is "like, resembling" or "having the form or shape of." Words ending in *–oid* are generally adjectives but can also be nouns. Thus *humanoid* means "having human characteristics or form" (adjective sense) or "a being having human form" (noun sense). Nouns ending in *–oid* form adjectives by adding the suffix *–al: spheroid, spheroidal; trapezoid, trapezoidal.* The suffix *–oid* comes from the Greek suffix *–oeidēs,* from *eidos,* meaning "shape, form."
      See more at **factoid, hominoid.**

old adage   See **adage.**

old / older

Old, when applied to people, is a blunt term that usually suggests at least a degree of physical infirmity and age-related restrictions. It should be used advisedly, especially in referring to people advanced in years but leading active lives.
      As a comparative form, *older* might logically seem to indicate greater age than *old,* but in most cases the opposite is true. A phrase such as *the older woman in the wool jacket* suggests a somewhat younger person than if *old* is substituted. Where *old* expresses an absolute, an arrival at old age, *older* takes a more relative view of aging as a continuum—older, but not yet old. As such, *older* is not just a euphemism for the blunter *old* but rather a more precise term for someone between middle and advanced age. And unlike *elderly, older* does not particularly suggest frailness or infirmity, making it the natural choice in many situations.

omni– / pan–

The prefix *omni–* means "all." It comes from the Latin word *omnis,* also meaning "all." The prefix has long been used in English to make new words. For example, the meanings of words such as *omnipurpose* ("all-purpose") and *omnitolerant* ("tolerant of all things") are easy to guess, even without a definition. Another prefix with the same meaning as *omni–* is *pan–,* which comes from Greek rather than Latin. In English, *pan–* is commonly used in compounds with names of nationalities: *Pan–American.* The word *pandemonium* was invented by the 17th-century English poet John Milton using the elements *pan–,* "all," and Latin *daemōnium,* "demon," ultimately from Greek *daimōn,* "lesser god, spirit." *Pandemonium* (meaning something like "Place of All Demons") was the name Milton gave to the capital of Hell depicted in his epic poem *Paradise Lost.* The name has since become a common noun meaning "a wild uproar or noise."

on / onto / on to

Both *on* and *onto* can be used to indicate motion toward a position: *The cat jumped on the table* or *The cat jumped onto the table.* However, *onto* is more specific, indicating that the motion was initiated from an outside point. *They wandered onto the battlefield* means that they began their wandering at some point off the battlefield, while *They wandered on the battlefield* implies that the wandering began on the battlefield.

Onto is sometimes confused with the adverb *on* when used in conjunction with the preposition *to; onto* is correctly used in these examples: *Let's move on to* [not *onto*] *another subject* and *We want to hold on to* [not *onto*] *our gains.*

on behalf of   See **in behalf of.**

one

***one* as generic pronoun**   In formal usage, the pronoun *one* is sometimes used as a generic pronoun meaning "anyone": *One would hope that train service could be improved.* The informal counterpart of *one* is *you: You never know what to expect from her.* Trouble arises when *one* is used in a series of sentences, and there is a need for a relative pronoun to refer back to *one.* One option is to use *one* and *one's* repeatedly, as in *One tries to be careful about where one invests one's money.* But in a sequence of sentences this inevitably becomes tedious. A traditional alternative has been to use *he, him,* and *his: One tries to be careful about his investments.* This has the drawback of raising the specter of gender bias. For a more detailed discussion of pronouns and gender, see the entry for **he / she.** Because of these problems, the temptation may arise to switch to *you,* but this will undoubtedly be distracting to the reader. It is better to use the same generic pronoun throughout.

As a generic pronoun, *one* should be avoided as the direct object of a verb or a preposition, especially if it comes at the end of the sentence. Thus the sentence *Bad dreams can make one restless* may sound stilted, but *One must not tease the bears or they will attack one* sounds almost ungrammatical. As a subject or in the possessive form, *one* fares much better. *One should be cordial with one's colleagues* sounds somewhat formal, but is acceptable.

one of a greater number   When constructions headed by *one* appear as the subject of a sentence or relative clause, there may be a question as to whether the verb should be singular or plural. The sentence *One of every ten rotors was found defective* is perfectly grammatical, but sometimes people use plural verbs in such situations, as in *One of every ten rotors have defects.* The Usage Panel has a long tradition of preferring singular verbs in such constructions. In our 1964 survey, 92 percent of the Panel preferred the singular verb in such sentences; in 2001, 99 percent preferred *was found defective* in the example quoted above.

one of those who   Constructions such as *one of those people who* pose a different problem. Some critics argue that *who* should be followed by a plural verb in these sentences, as in *He is one of those people who just don't take "no" for an answer.* Their thinking is that the relative pronoun *who* refers to the plural noun *people,* not to *one.* They would extend the rule to constructions with inanimate nouns, as in *The sports car turned out to be one of the most successful products that were ever manufactured in this country.*

But the use of the singular verb in these constructions is common, even among the best writers, and the Usage Panel has a long history of division on this matter. In our 1965 survey, 42 percent of the Usage Panel accepted the use of the singular verb in such constructions. Nearly forty years later the Panel's opinion was almost unchanged: in 2001, 40 percent rejected *were* in the sports car example quoted above. Perhaps the only workable solution to this problem lies in which word sounds most appropriate as the antecedent of the relative pronoun—*one* or the plural noun in the *of* phrase that follows it. Note also that when the phrase containing *one* is introduced by the definite article, the verb in the relative clause must be singular: *He is the only one of the students who has* [not *have*] *already taken Latin.*

one or more   Constructions using *one or more* or *one or two* always take a plural verb: *One or more cars were parked in front of the house each day this week. One or two students from our department have won prizes.* Note that when followed by a fraction, *one* ordinarily gets a plural verb: *One and a half years have passed since I last saw her.* The fraction rule has an exception in that amounts are sometimes treated as singular entities: *One and a half cups is enough sugar.* Note also that the plural rule does not apply to these one-plus-a-fraction constructions that are introduced by the indefinite article. These constructions are always singular: *A year and a half has passed since I last saw her.*

See more at **each other, he, more than one,** and **subject and verb agreement.**

one another   See **each other.**

on the up and up   See **up and up**.

only

The adverb *only* is notorious for its ability to change the meaning of a sentence when placed in a different position in the sequence of words. Consider how the placement of *only* affects the meaning of the following examples:

> Dictators respect only force; they are not moved by words.
> Dictators only respect force; they do not worship it.
> She picked up the receiver only when he entered, not before.
> She only picked up the receiver when he entered; she didn't dial the number.

The surest way to prevent readers from misinterpreting *only* is to place it next to the word or words it modifies. Many usage sticklers view this policy as a rule that should always be followed, but in many cases it sounds more natural for *only* to come earlier in the sentence, and if the preceding context is sufficiently clear, there is scant likelihood of being misunderstood. Thus, the rule requires *We can come to an agreement only if everyone is willing to compromise.* But it may sound more natural, with slightly different emphasis and with no risk of misunderstanding, to say *We can only come to an agreement if everyone is willing to compromise.*

See more at **adverbs, also, not,** and **split infinitive.**

onto   See **on.**

ophthalmia

As is the case with *diphtheria, diphthong,* and *naphtha,* the *ph* should properly be pronounced (f), not (p). Because so many people say (ŏp-), as opposed to (ŏf-), though, this variant has gradually become acceptable.

ophthalmologist / optometrist / optician / ocularist

Each of these professionals deals with the eyes, but they all have different job descriptions. An *ophthalmologist,* with the *ph* properly pronounced as (f), not (p), is a physician who specializes in the diagnosis and treatment of eye diseases. Ophthalmologists perform surgery and prescribe drugs and glasses or contact lenses. An *optometrist* also attends four years of graduate school after college but has an OD (doctor of optometry) degree rather than an MD or a DO (doctor of osteopathic medicine). Optometrists diagnose and treat many eye conditions and provide preoperative and postoperative care. They can prescribe drugs in most states, but they don't do surgical procedures. An *optician* fills prescriptions for contact lenses and eyeglasses and sometimes manufactures the lenses. An *ocularist* makes and fits prosthetic eyes.

optician   See **ophthalmologist.**

optometrist   See **ophthalmologist.**

or

verb agreement with subjects using *or*   When the coordinating conjunction *or* connects singular elements in the subject of a clause, the verb is singular: *Tom or Jack is coming. Beer, ale, or wine is included in the charge.* When all the elements are plural, the verb is plural: *The raccoons or the squirrels are getting into the garbage.* When the elements do not agree in number, some usage commentators say that the verb should agree in number with the nearest element: *Tom or his sisters are coming. The girls or their brother is coming. Cold symptoms or a headache is the usual first sign.* But others object that these constructions are inherently illogical and that the only solution is to revise the sentence to avoid the problem of agreement: *Either Tom is coming, or his sisters are. The first sign is usually cold symptoms or a headache.*

***or* used to begin sentences**   Like other coordinating conjunctions, *or* can be used with good rhetorical effect to start a sentence or even a paragraph that is connected conceptually to the previous one but for some reason warrants separate attention:

> If my uncle was seen turning the corner we hid in the shadow until we had seen him safely housed. Or if Mangan's sister came out on the doorstep to call her brother in to his tea we watched her from our shadow peer up and down the street (James Joyce, "Araby," *Dubliners*)

Sentences beginning with *or* often present a second look at or reconsideration of the subject at hand:

> When the sand coating was wiped off, a green tint appeared. It was a lump of glass. . . . Perhaps after all it was really a gem; something worn by a dark Princess trailing her finger in the water as she sat in the stern of the boat and listened to the slaves singing as they rowed her across the Bay. Or the oak sides of a sunk Elizabethan treasure-chest had split apart, and, rolled over and over, over and over, its emeralds had come at last to shore (Virginia Woolf, "Solid Objects")

> Of course there were other possible explanations. For instance: perhaps Orpheus had found it impossible not to give in to a certain self-destructive impulse; that inability, upon being told "Don't cross that line," not to cross it. Only God has the power to turn back time. Or perhaps Orpheus, at the last minute, had changed his mind; decided he didn't want Eurydice back after all (David Leavitt, *The Marble Quilt*)

With its force of reconsideration, *or* often introduces thoughts that undercut or reverse what has just been established. The sentences it introduces are often fragments:

She didn't know me, the day she and Franklin Klemenhagen met at the motel, but he must have told her afterward that he recognized me. Or thought he did (Deirdre McNamer, *My Russian*)

To an uncanny degree, the story of the recent welfare revolution is a story of David Ellwood's ideas. Or, as he views it, a corruption of his ideas (Jason de Parle, "Mugged by Reality," *New York Times Magazine*)

Sentences and fragments beginning with *or* are thus not limited to narrative discourse, but are fairly common in expository prose in newspapers and magazines, where they sometimes introduce a number of questions probing an issue from different angles or a series of emphatic additions:

In 14 games, the teams pounded 48 home runs; the previous record was 29. Some homers sailed over the bleachers, 30 feet high, into a parking lot 450 feet from home plate. . . . So was it the strong tail wind? Or an exceptional crop of hitters? Or was it the state-of-the-art aluminum bats, which have revolutionized amateur baseball and sparked controversies over everything from the integrity of the game to the safety of its young players? (Stefan Fatsis, "Sporting-Good Firms Battle a Crackdown on Aluminum Bats," *Wall Street Journal*)

But 20 years ago, hardly anyone had personal computers. Or cell phones. Or laptops. Or any of the other "vampire" devices that draw electricity from the wall socket even when nobody is using them (Guy Gugliotta, "The Energy Drain," *Washington Post*)

But the effectiveness of this rhetorical technique stands in inverse proportion to its frequency.

See more at **either, neither, nor,** and **subject and verb agreement.**

−or / −er

The suffixes −*or* and −*er* often indicate a person or thing that performs a particular action determined by the base form to which the suffixes are added, as in *actor, governor, navigator, spectator, player, ruler, trailblazer,* and *onlooker*. Both suffixes are usually pronounced (ər), just like the suffix −*er*, although −*or* may be pronounced (ôr) in cases where an emphasis is being placed on contrasting roles, as in *lessor/lessee*. As a general rule, the suffix −*or* is more often added to base forms that come from Latin, like *inventor* and *possessor* from *invent* and *possess*, while −*er* is used with verbs of native English origin, like *finder* or *keeper* from *find* and *keep*. However, these are only tendencies, and writers should consult the dictionary whenever in doubt about the correct suffix to be used. Note that *eraser*, for instance, is made from the verb *erase*, which is of Latin origin, while *sailor* is built from the native English verb *sail*. In some instances, both −*or* and −*er* are found: *advisor, adviser*.

orbit / orbital / shell

These terms are closely related in physics, but there are important differences between them, and being aware of them helps keep the picture of atomic structure clear. Atoms consist of a tiny but heavy nucleus with a positive charge, surrounded by very light electrons with a negative charge. Since opposite charges attract each other, the electrons are set in motion around the nucleus, much as the earth revolves around the sun, guided by the attractive force of gravity. By analogy with the motion of planets, the motion of an electron is called an *orbit* or, especially when referring to a specific region of an atom in which the electron moves, an *orbital*.

Because atoms are extremely small, they can only be described by means of quantum mechanics. Quantum mechanics tells us that at small scales, all matter has wavelike properties, and the position of a particle can only be defined probabilistically in terms of these waves. It turns out that possible electron orbits are strongly delimited by their wavelike character: the number of wavelengths in the region of the orbit must be an integer, otherwise the electron would literally cancel itself out! This means that electron orbitals come in groups corresponding to such allowed orbits. Each of these groups is called a *shell*. Different shells correspond to different energy levels, with the outer shells corresponding to a higher energy than inner shells. Within each shell, there are multiple orbitals—two in the innermost shell, and increasingly more in outer shells, as the number of possibilities for different configurations of orbits increases. The shells have traditional labels K through Q, while differently shaped orbitals within each shell (also known as *subshells*) have labels s, p, d, f, and g.

ordinance / ordnance

These two words are etymologically related (both derive from Latin *ōrdināre*, "to ordain") and are pronounced almost identically. They are thus easy to confuse. An *ordinance* is, most frequently, a statute or regulation, especially one enacted by a town, city, or county government. For instance, a town might have an ordinance against the public consumption of alcohol. *Ordinance* can also refer to an authoritative command or order or to a custom or practice established by long usage, such as a religious rite.

The term *ordnance* is less familiar to most people. It is a military term, referring either to military material, especially weapons, ammunition, and vehicles, or to the branch of an armed force that procures, maintains, and issues such equipment. Thus, the mission of the Ordnance Corps of the US Army is *"to support the development, production, acquisition and sustainment of weapons systems and munitions, and to provide Explosive Ordnance Disposal, during peace and war, [in order] to provide superior combat power to current and future forces of the United States Army."*

Ordance is often used more restrictively to refer to munitions, including explosive weapons such as bombs, as in this quotation from Thomas Friedman writing in the *New York Times*: *"One arms cache alone found here [in Fallujah, Iraq] had 49,000 pieces of ordnance, ranging from mortars to ammo rounds."* Not surprisingly, *ordnance* is sometimes misspelled as *ordinance*, as in this quotation from ABC News online: *"The attackers were part-way through launching a cache of about nine home-made projectiles, however, when the remaining ordinance exploded in the vehicle."*

Oriental

Oriental is now considered outdated and often offensive in American English when referring to a person of Asian birth or descent. While this term is rarely intended as an outright slur, and may even be thought polite by some speakers, it is so associated with stereotypical images of Asians as portrayed in the West during an earlier era that its use in ethnic contexts should be routinely avoided. However, *Oriental* retains a certain currency in referring to Asian arts, foods, and practices, such as traditional medical procedures and remedies, where it is unlikely to give offense.

other

The sentence *Frank had no other choice but to give them what they asked for* is colloquially understood as meaning that there was no other option, hence no real choice, and Frank had to give them what they wanted. In informal speech, sentences like these have become idiomatic and unambiguous. But taken logically, this sentence does not mean that Frank had only one alternative. Compare it with the following: *There is no other chair but this one.* This sentence suggests that there was some chair under discussion, and the only *other* chair is "this one." Thus there must be two chairs. By the same logic, it becomes clear that in *Frank had no other choice but to give them what they asked for,* some other option must have been mentioned, and the only other option was to give them what they wanted. Thus there are two options, hence genuine choices.

To avoid this subtle difficulty of logic, consider phrasings that avoid the sequence *no other,* such as *Frank had no choice but to give them what they asked for* or *Frank had no choice other than to give them what they asked for,* each of which entails that Frank had no other options.

The word *other* in such sentences can be kept as long as all of the options are explicitly mentioned: *He had no choice other than to leave her or alienate his parents.*

See more at **cannot, each other,** and **comparisons with *as* and *than*.**

otherwise

When used to connect two related clauses, *otherwise* is usually classified as a conjunctive adverb, which by grammatical tradition should be preceded either by a semicolon or by a period. Since it introduces a new clause, *otherwise* is sometimes followed by a comma:

> His best self—the one that was fearless, resourceful, and generous, and that told the truth—was what he saved for the public, which included us; otherwise, as every relative of a star knows, the family had to make do with what was left over (John Lahr, "The Lion and Me," *The New Yorker*)

> From Leviticus it follows directly that, in Judaism, self-love is required; otherwise you are failing in a religious duty (David Gelernter, "Judaism Beyond Words: Conclusion," *Commentary*)

The British and the Boers controlled Southern Africa, and an enfeebled Portugal claimed most of what used to be the Kingdom of the Kongo, as well as Mozambique on the east coast. Along Africa's great western bulge, Portugal, Spain, Britain, and France owned a few islands and small pockets of territory. Otherwise, about 80 percent of the entire land area of Africa was still under indigenous rulers (Adam Hochschild, *King Leopold's Ghost*)

As in poker, bluffing is part of Scrabble, playing a word you know to be unacceptable and seeing if your opponent bites. But you have to know when and against whom to bluff. Otherwise you will be exposed as a fraud (Stephen Fatsis, *Word Freak*)

But because *otherwise* means "or else" in these contexts, and *or else* behaves as a subordinating conjunction, *otherwise* is often treated as a conjunction and is preceded by a comma, sometimes even in publications that predominantly treat it as a conjunctive adverb. Although standard, this usage is more common in first-person narration and dialogue:

Trousers that look like he's been sleeping in them. Ugly old lace-up shoes. Mr. Radish is flabby, slope-shouldered, otherwise he'd be tall as Ira Early (Joyce Carol Oates, "Doll: A Romance of the Mississippi," *The Gettysburg Review*)

"I know this Lana's sister," he said. "Always wearing those cocktail dresses in to work. Her boss is afraid to say anything, otherwise he might get a pink slip, too" (Walter Mosley, "Pet Fly," *The New Yorker*)

Though there is some disagreement on which grammatical classification is correct, copyeditors tend to prefer the more traditional punctuation using the semicolon, and it makes sense to follow this practice.

Note that when *otherwise* is used to introduce a contrasting phrase, where it means "in another manner," the comma is required: *The student has symptoms of pertussis, otherwise known as whooping cough.*

ought

** *ought* as auxiliary verb**   *Ought* is an auxiliary verb that usually takes *to* with its accompanying verb: *We ought to go.* Sometimes the accompanying verb is dropped if the meaning is clear: *Should we begin soon? Yes, we ought to.* In questions and negative sentences, especially those with contractions, *to* is also sometimes omitted: *We ought not be afraid of the risks involved. Oughtn't we be going soon?* This omission of *to*, however, is not common in written English. Like *must* and auxiliary *need*, *ought to* does not change to show past tense: *He said we ought to get moving along.*

** *ought* in regional expressions**   Usages such as *He hadn't ought to come* and *She shouldn't ought to say that* are common in many varieties of American English. They should be avoided in written English, however, in favor of the more standard variant *ought not to.*

See more at **auxiliary and primary verbs, have, must, need,** and **should.**

ourself / ourselves   See **pronouns, reflexive and intensive.**

–ous

The suffix *–ous,* which forms adjectives, has the basic meaning "having, full of, or characterized by." *Blusterous,* for example, means "full of or characterized by bluster." The suffix *–ous* can be traced back through Old French to the Latin adjective suffix *–ōsus.* Some English words ending in *–ous* that come from Latin adjectives ending in *–ōsus* are *copious, dolorous, famous, generous,* and *glorious.* Others, like *blusterous* above, are later creations built upon native English base forms. Adjectives ending in *–ous* often have related nouns ending in *–ousness* or *–osity: copiousness, generosity.*

out–

There are many words in English beginning with *out–.* In words such as *outbuilding, outcast, outpour,* and *outstanding, out–* has the same meaning as the adverb *out.* So an *outcast* is "one who is cast out," and one who is *outstanding* "stands out." But in other cases *out–* takes on the sense of doing better, being greater, or going beyond, as in *outdo, outnumber,* and *outrun.* Although *out–* can attach to nouns, adjectives, or verbs to form other nouns, adjectives, or verbs, it most frequently attaches to verbs: *outbowl, outcook, outride, outsing.*

over–   See **under–.**

over / more than

While working as a newspaper editor in the late 19th century, William Cullen Bryant forbade the use of *over* in the sense of "more than," as in *These rocks are over 5 million years old.* Bryant provided no rationale for this injunction, but such was his stature that the stipulation was championed by other American editors, who also felt no reason to offer an explanation. Later usage critics allowed the usage in some contexts, but their reasons are dubious at best. In point of fact, *over* has been used as a synonym of *more than* since the 1300s. Since no reasonable justification for its ban has ever been expounded, it may be safely ignored.

overlay / overlie

The confusion between these two words stems from the common confusion between *lay* and *lie,* from which they are derived. *Overlay,* like *lay,* is a transitive verb, and means "to cause the surface of something to be covered by laying or spreading something else over it": *We can overlay this photograph with the other to create a composite image.* Its meaning is causative: one thing is caused to be situated over the other.

Overlie, unlike *lie,* is a transitive verb, but it is not causative, meaning simply "to be situated over the surface of something": *The sandy sediment of the riverbed overlies the granite rocks beneath.*

Here is a sampling of how these words can be confused:

> The autographs overlaid [Read: *overlay*] the entire page (*Sacramento Bee*)

> Drive around the grid of gravel roads overlaying [Read: *overlying*] the prairie, and you'll also encounter deer, cranes, egrets, herons, pheasants and sharp-tailed grouse (*Duluth News Tribune*)

> Watching this movie is like watching an excellent story about passion and betrayal overlain [Read: *overlaid*] with a veneer of nonsensical supernatural violence (*Wichita Eagle*)

An explanation for these confusions is provided at the entry **lay.**

oxymoron

An oxymoron is a rhetorical figure in which contradictory or sharply contrasting terms are yoked together, often in a compound noun. Classic examples include Shakespeare's *sweet sorrow* in *Parting is such sweet sorrow* (from *Romeo and Juliet*) and *I must be cruel to be kind* (from *Hamlet*). In popular usage oxymorons are often set phrases and can see so much use that they can pass unnoticed. Some examples include *same difference, open secret, deafening silence,* and *original copy.*

People have made ample use of the oxymoron as a means of making ironic or sardonic commentary. Thus current management practices come in for a grilling when *business ethics* and *knowledge management* are identified as oxymorons. This practice has led to the looser use of the term to indicate an impossibility, even to the point where there are no contrasting terms that can be identified, as in *A soap opera without daily helpings of sex is an oxymoron.* In our 1999 survey, 67 percent of the Usage Panel disapproved of this example.

· P ·

pace

Pace, usually pronounced (pä′chā), is a form of the Latin word *pāx,* meaning "peace." It is used in English to mean "with deference to; with the permission of," and it expresses polite (or ironically polite) disagreement: "I have not, *pace* my detractors, entered into any secret negotiations." The word should be italicized.

pair

The noun *pair* can be followed by a singular or plural verb. The singular is always used when *pair* refers to a set considered as a single entity: *This pair of shoes is on sale.* A plural verb may be used when the members are considered as individuals: *The pair are working more harmoniously now.* After a number other than one, *pair* itself can be either singular or plural, but the plural is now more common: *She bought six pairs* [or *pair*] *of stockings.*

See more at **subject and verb agreement.**

pair of twins

The word *twins,* which might be expected to refer just to a pair of offspring born at the end of a single pregnancy, can invite criticism in a number of phrases. For some, the expression *a pair of twins* is redundant, since *twins* come by definition in pairs. For others, logic requires that *pair of twins* should refer only to two sets of twins, that is, to four people. But expecting all readers to interpret the expression in this way is unrealistic. *Two twins* may be less likely to be interpreted as referring to four people but is still open to the accusation of redundancy. The more neutral *set of twins* eliminates redundancy but does not unambiguously refer to one pair of people who are twins; it can be read as meaning "a set of pairs of twin siblings," which could be any even number of people, unless a specific number or further explanation is given. Certainly, the desire for clarity should trump the desire to eliminate redundancy, and the sentence *A pair of twins walked into the room* might be better rewritten as *Two twins entered the room,* or *Two sets of twins entered the room,* depending on what is intended.

Sometimes the writer just has to credit the reader with a certain amount of common sense. Standing alone, the phrase *the twins* can refer to a single pair or to multiple pairs, but in contexts such as *I was four when my mother gave birth to the twins,* seeing more than a single pair defies common experience.

340

pale   See **beyond the pale.**

pan–   See **omni–.**

pandemic   See **endemic.**

panegyric

Traditionally this word has a soft *g* and rhymes with *lyric*, but the pronunciation of *gyr* with a long *i* sound, as in *gyre* and *gyrus*, is now also acceptable.

papier-mâché / papier-mache / paper-mache

The word *papier-mâché*, pronounced (pā′pər mə-shā′) in English and (pä-pyā′ mä-shā′) in French, is a borrowing from that language, and may be spelled without the accents. Since *papier* is so close in spelling to the English word *paper* (which derives from it) and has the same meaning, it is most commonly pronounced like *paper*. As a result, the variant *paper-mache* has become so widespread that its incorporation into the standard lexicon seems inevitable. However, this variant is not listed in dictionaries as standard, so for now, write *papier-mache* or *papier-mâché*. Note that the use of the French pronunciation may be considered pretentious.

paradigm

Paradigm comes from a Greek word meaning "an example or pattern." It first appeared in English with this meaning in the 15th century, and it still bears this meaning today: *Their company is a paradigm of the small high-tech firms that have recently sprung up in this area.* For nearly four hundred years *paradigm* has also been applied to the patterns of inflections that are used to sort the verbs, nouns, and other parts of speech of a language into groups. Those who have studied a foreign language such as Latin will recall memorizing paradigms of word endings that distinguish verbs belonging to different conjugations or nouns of various declensions.

Since the 1960s *paradigm* has been used in science to refer to a theoretical framework, as when Nobel laureate David Baltimore cited the work of two colleagues that *"really established a new paradigm for our understanding of the causation of cancer."* Researchers in many different fields, including sociology and literary criticism, began referring to the paradigms within which they were working or from which they were trying to break free. People have since used the term in an even wider range of contexts so that it often seems to mean "the prevailing view of things." The Usage Panel splits down the middle on these nonscientific uses of *paradigm*. In 1994, 52 percent disapproved of the sentence *The paradigm governing international competition and competitiveness has shifted dramatically in the last three decades.*

parallel

Some grammarians see *parallel* as an absolute term: two straight lines, they might say, are either parallel or they are not, so no two lines can be considered "more" or "less" parallel. Thus *parallel* should not be modified by adverbs of degree. However, the world is not generally thought of as being made of straight lines, and the word *parallel* is usefully applied to all sorts of objects that are not straight at all. Indeed, there are many mathematical definitions of *parallel,* many of which can be quantified; curves, for example, can be more or less parallel depending on the degree to which their slopes deviate from each other at different points. Furthermore, the gradation of *parallel* when used metaphorically is often sensible and rhetorically effective, as in *The difficulties faced by the Republicans are quite parallel to those that confronted the Democrats four years ago.* Here what is being described is the structural correspondence between two distinct situations, which may be more or less consistent. In this sense, parallelism is clearly a matter of degree, and *parallel* may be modified accordingly.

See more at **absolute terms, complete, equal, infinite, perfect,** and **unique.**

parallelism

Most memorable writing has as one of its recognizable features the ample use of parallel grammatical structures. Consider these selections from famous political documents:

> We hold these truths to be self-evident, that all men are created equal, that they are endowed by their Creator with certain inalienable Rights, that among these are Life, Liberty, and the pursuit of Happiness (Declaration of Independence)

> It is rather for us to be here dedicated to the great task remaining before us—that from these honored dead we take increased devotion to that cause for which they gave the last full measure of devotion; that we here highly resolve that these dead shall not have died in vain; that this nation, under God, shall have a new birth of freedom; and that government of the people, by the people, for the people shall not perish from the earth (Abraham Lincoln, Gettysburg Address)

> Never in the field of human conflict was so much owed by so many to so few (Winston Churchill's tribute to the Royal Air Force after the Battle of Britain)

These celebrated passages are moving in no small measure because of their elegant cadences and parallel structures. Both the Declaration of Independence and the Gettysburg Address contain a series of *that* clauses whose rhythm reinforces the gravity of what is being said and puts great stress on the final elements in the sentence. In both passages the final elements themselves are constructed in parallel fashion. *Life, Liberty, and the pursuit of Happiness* is a series of nouns, with the last modified by a prepositional phrase. *Government of the people, by the people, for the people* presents a noun modified by a series of prepositional phrases, each with the same object so that the prepositions—commonplace words that usually have little meaning aside from connecting words together—have enormous significance and the word *people* is reinforced, thus emphasizing its underlying importance to the idea of government. Similarly, Churchill's famous line ends with a series of pronouns modified by the intensive *so,* which is repeated three times with prepositions indicating the relationship between the many (the British people) and the few (the heroic pilots).

Strictly speaking, parallel constructions have all the same elements treated at the same level so that the result is a balanced pair or series. Thus, if the series starts with a *that* clause, the other elements should be *that* clauses; if it starts with an infinitive, the other elements should be infinitives; if it starts with a participle, the other elements be participles; and so on. Mixing different grammatical forms in a series can produce inelegant or jarring sentences, such as *She had a strong desire to pursue medicine and for studying literature* or *The scientist asked for volunteers with allergies but who had not given blood recently.*

The grammatical forms in a parallel construction must be structured symmetrically. Remember that an initial article, preposition, auxiliary verb, or modifier will tend to govern all elements in the series unless it is repeated for each element. For example, if a series consists of nouns in which the first is modified by an adjective, the reader will expect the adjective to modify the other nouns in the series as well. Thus the sentence *The building has new lighting, plumbing, and carpeting* has a parallel series, implying that the lighting, plumbing, and carpeting are all new, but *The building has new lighting, plumbing, and different carpeting* does not have a parallel series, and the status of the plumbing is not clear. The same pattern holds true for articles: *He brought the rod, reel, and bait.* If the intended meaning requires that a modifier be restricted to only one noun, the article should be repeated for each noun: *He brought the light rod, the reel, and the bait.*

Similarly, a series of nouns introduced by a single preposition will set up the expectation that the preposition governs all the nouns: *He sent the letter to the provost, the dean, and the student who won the scholarship.* With contrastive conjunctions, it is often clearer or more balanced to repeat the preposition: *He sent the letter to the provost and the dean but not to the student or his parents.* Likewise, an auxiliary verb will govern all the verbs in the series unless each verb phrase is constructed separately with its own auxiliary: *We will always value her contributions, admire her fortitude, and wish her the best.*

Faulty parallels should be recast to give all the elements equivalent treatment, but sometimes the results do not brighten the penny. If the new parallel construction does not seem much of an improvement, rewrite the sentence completely to avoid the parallel construction. It is better to have no parallel structures than to have parallel structures that sound overblown or stilted.

parallelism is sometimes in the eye of the beholder   Sometimes making sure that all the elements in a parallel construction are equivalent is not as clear-cut as it would seem, and parallelism itself can be a matter of aesthetic judgment subject to debate. Is a series of nouns that has some gerunds in it parallel? On this problem the Usage Panel is divided. In our 1995 survey, 51 percent approved, while 49 percent rejected, the sentence *The committee has the power of investigation, negotiation, arranging contracts, and hiring new employees.*

The Panel is similarly divided when the first part of a compound verb has a series of objects, so that the second verb and its objects seem tacked on as the last element in the series. Thus, in the same survey 54 percent found the following example unacceptable: *These services will use satellite, copper cable, fiber optics, cellular communications and be accessible via suitably equipped computers.*

In other cases the Panelists are more unified, with 86 percent accepting the following example in which three nouns in the series are governed by the possessive *his,* while the fourth and final noun is modified by *the: In the hotel room the suspect had left his keys, briefcase, spare clothes, and the receipts for the cars he had rented.* This construction in fact has the virtue of adding emphasis to the final element. The receipts seem to be the most important piece of evidence that the suspect left behind.

When the situation is more clear-cut, however, and something in the construction is clearly out of balance, the Panel is more insistent on restoring parallelism. This is the case with the coordinate conjunction *not only . . . but also . . .* where it is easy to spot when one element is out of place. Some 73 percent rejected the sentence *The filmmakers not only concentrate on Edward VIII's abdication over his love for divorcée Wallis Simpson but also his leaning toward Nazi Germany.*

Sentences with elegant parallelism do not come naturally to most people, and writing of this kind takes effort and practice. Even if an anticipated audience won't notice or object to faults in parallelism, balance and symmetry are worth striving for in writing. Certain specific constructions often require grammatical parallelism in some form, and these potential sources of trouble are discussed as separate entries in this book.

See more at **both, both . . . and, comparisons with *as* and *than,* compound verbs and ambiguity, either, not only . . . but also,** and **rather than.**

parameter

In mathematics, a *parameter* is a term in an equation or expression that can be varied to produce other equations or expressions of the same form. The value of a parameter in the equation of a curve, for instance, can be varied to represent a family of curves. The parameters of the equation therefore determine the range of possible shapes of the curve. Applied more broadly to science, a parameter is one of a set of measurable factors, such as temperature and pressure, that define a system and determine its behavior. Here, the parameters of an experiment can be varied to produce different results, and again, the parameters determine a *range.*

Perhaps because of its ring of technical authority, people have applied *parameter* more generally in recent years to refer to any factor that determines a range of variations and especially to a factor that restricts what results from a process or policy. In this use, the word *parameter* is used to mean "the particular value of a parameter," and comes close to meaning "a set limit or boundary." For example, a budget can be thought of as a set of parameters that determine a range of activity, much like a set of mathematical parameters that establish the range of effects, or limits, of other variables. The sentence *A budget is a framework that defines the financial parameters within which an organization operates* was considered acceptable by 81 percent of the Usage Panel in our 2004 survey. *Parameter* is sometimes used incorrectly when it does not denote a range of variation, as if it were a technical-sounding synonym for *characteristic.* In 1988, 88 percent of the Usage Panel rejected the sentence *The Judeo-*

Christian ethic is one of the important parameters of Western culture. In 2004, 77 percent rejected this same sentence, suggesting that familiarity has not bred tolerance of this usage.

Some of the difficulties with the nontechnical use of *parameter* appear to arise from its resemblance to the word *perimeter,* with which it shares the sense "limit," though the two words differ in their precise meaning. This confusion probably explains the use of *parameter* in a sentence such as *US forces report that the parameters of the mine area in the Gulf are fairly well established,* where the word *perimeter* would have expressed the intended sense more exactly. In 1988, 61 percent of the Usage Panel found this example unacceptable. Resistance to this usage appears to be slipping, however, because 58 percent accepted the same sentence in 2004.

paramount   See **tantamount.**

parent / parenting / parented

The word *parent* was formerly used only as a noun but is now widely accepted both as a verb and as a gerund (*parenting*). Unlike *mother,* which can refer to general nurturing outside of parenthood, and *father,* which can refer simply to being the biological father of a child, *parent* is relatively unambiguous in reference to raising a child.

The uses of the verb are proliferating. It is now used both intransitively (*The participants in the study are asked how well they parent*) and transitively (*. . . how well they parent their children*), and transitively in the passive voice (*how they were parented*). The participle *parented* is used to mean "participated in or overseen by parents," as in *a parented program for young children.* It sometimes occurs in compound adjectives characterizing the nature of the family situation, as in *single-parented, lesbian-parented,* and *deaf-parented children.* While these usages are fairly recent, they are likely to survive because of their usefulness.

See more at **father.**

parentheses

asides   Parentheses enclose digressive sentences or asides on the part of the writer or character.

> Hunted out of existence, maimed, frozen, the victims of cruelty and injustice (she had heard Richard say so over and over again)—no, she could feel nothing for the Albanians, or was it the Armenians? but she loved her roses (didn't that help the Armenians?)—the only flowers that she could bear to see cut (Virginia Woolf, *Mrs. Dalloway*)

explanations

1. Like em dashes, parentheses may be used within a sentence to set off material that is explanatory or supplemental. Information enclosed in parentheses is often more extraneous than information enclosed in em dashes.

> Her mooring in the world seemed so tenuous that every spring when she went away (to Carmel for the month of April, abroad for the month of May), there were those who said that she had in truth been committed (Joan Didion, *Run River*)

> His ever-vigilant mother, Lydia, grand dame of *la escoba y los trapos*—the broom and rags—was nearly impossible to satisfy. Working hard and having to overcome numerous deficits (namely in terms of self-confidence, for he did not feel yet like an "inheritor of this earth") he had managed to maintain a high enough, if not perfect average (Oscar Hijuelos, *Empress of the Splendid Season*)

2. A sentence containing material in parentheses is grammatical only if it remains grammatical when the parenthetical element is removed. For example, it is incorrect to write *The draft bill was reviewed by the secretary of the interior (not to mention by the President's chief of staff) and they approved it,* since the plural pronoun *they* would require that *the President's chief of staff* serve as part of the antecedent. Similarly, one cannot write *He gave her a Bible (and later a rosary), which were found by her bedside when she died,* where part of the subject of the plural verb *were* would have to be drawn from the material in parentheses.

other uses

1. Parentheses often enclose letters or figures to indicate subdivisions of a series:

> A movement in sonata form consists of the following sections: (a) the exposition, (b) the development, and (c) the recapitulation, which is often followed by a coda.

2. Parentheses enclose figures following and confirming written-out numbers, especially in legal and business documents.

> Delivery will be made in sixty (60) days.

3. Parentheses enclose abbreviations of written-out words when the abbreviations are used for the first time in a text and may be unfamiliar to the reader.

> The study regarding antiballistic missiles (ABMs) is classified.

participles

uses of participles   A participle is a verb form that can be used as an adjective and is used with an auxiliary verb to form tenses and, in the case of the past participle, the passive voice. The present participle ends in *–ing* (*going, running*). The past participle for many verbs ends in *–ed* (*created, walked*); other past participles have a different form, and often a different vowel, from their base form (*made* from *make, ridden* from *ride, swum* from *swim*). The present participle is used with *be* to indicate a continuing action or state (*I am going, They were laughing, We have been talking*). The past participle is used with *have* to form past tenses (*We have climbed, She had ridden, They have sung*) and with *be* to form the passive voice (*The floor is being scrubbed, The ball was kicked, The car has been driven*).

dangling participles   Participial phrases are used chiefly to modify nouns, as in *Sitting at his desk, he read the letter carefully* where the *sitting* phrase modifies *he*. Readers will ordinarily associate a participle with the noun or noun phrase that is adjacent to it. Thus readers will consider a sentence such as *Turning the corner, the view was quite different* to be an error, for the view did not do the turning. A sentence like this needlessly distracts the reader and would be better recast as *When we turned the corner, the view was quite different* or *Turning the corner, we had a different view.* For more on this, see **dangling modifiers.**

participles and absolute constructions   Be careful not to confuse a participial phrase that modifies a noun with an absolute construction that employs a participle. The difference is between sentences such as *Taking down the poster, he went inside* and *The poster having been taken down, he went inside.* Absolute constructions can dangle where they please since by their "absolute" nature they do not modify a specific element in the rest of the sentence. For more on this, see **absolute constructions, having said that,** and **that having been said.**

participles as prepositions   A number of expressions originally derived from participles have become prepositions, and these can be used to introduce phrases that are not associated with the immediately adjacent noun phrase. Such expressions include *concerning, considering, failing, granting, judging by,* and *speaking of.* Thus there are no grounds for criticizing sentences like *Speaking of politics, the elections have been postponed* and *Considering the hour, it is surprising that he arrived at all.*

participles as adjectives   Many participles can also function as adjectives: *an interesting experience, an interested customer, the surprising results, the surprised researchers.* But it is often hard to tell when a participle is an adjective, especially with past participles. Linguists have a number of tests for confirming an adjective. Here are four of them:

1. Can the word be used attributively (i.e., before the noun it modifies), as in *an intriguing offer*?
2. Can it be used in the predicate, especially after the verb *seem,* as in *She thought the party boring* and *He seems concerned about you*?
3. Can it be compared, as in *We are even more encouraged now* and *The results are most encouraging*?
4. Can it be modified by *very,* as in *They are very worried about this*?

Some adjectives pass more of these tests than others and are thus more purely adjectival. *Disastrous,* for instance, passes tests 1, 2, and 3, but not 4. When used as adjectives, most participles pass all four tests, but modification by *very* is tricky. For more on this, see ***very* and past participles.**

A past participle is really part of a passive verb—and not an adjective—when it is followed by a *by* prepositional phrase that has a personal agent as its object. Thus, the participle *married* would be part of the verb in the sentence *Chuck and Wendy were married by a bishop* but an adjective in the sentence *Chuck and Wendy were happily married for about six months.* To confirm the adjectival status of a participle, try transforming the sentence to see if the participle can come before the noun: *For about six months Chuck and Wendy were a happily married couple.*

particle

A particle is a word that does not change form by inflections and does not fit easily into one of the major parts of speech. Phrasal verbs usually consist of a verb and a particle. Thus *up* is a particle in *He looked up the word* and *I hope my wallet will turn up soon.* When used in infinitives, *to* is also considered a particle.

party

Party is unexceptionable when used to refer to a participant in a social arrangement, as in *She was not named as a party in the conspiracy.* It is this sense that underlies the legal use of the term, as when one speaks of the *parties to a contract.* The legal use has in turn led to the presence of the word in many fixed expressions, such as *injured party* and *third party.* But *party* is also widely used as a general substitute for *person,* as in *Would all parties who left packages at the desk please reclaim their property?* This usage has been established for many centuries, but in the Victorian era it came to be associated with the language of the semieducated, and it has been the subject of many later criticisms. This use of *party* may have been reinforced in the 20th century owing to its adoption by telephone operators. In other contexts, when used in earnest, it may be perceived as a superfluous variant for *person.* But the jocular use of the term is well established, particularly in references such as *a wise old party.*

passed / past

These sound-alikes are easily confused. *Passed* is the past tense and past participle of the verb *pass: They passed several gas stations but forgot to fill up. The summer had passed slowly.* *Past* is the corresponding adjective (*in centuries past*), adverb (*The car drove past*), preposition (*We finally got past the crisis*), and noun (*living in the past*).

Use of the correct form is not just a matter of spelling; the wrong sense can be conveyed by using the wrong word. For example, *The years passed in Canada were lonely* refers to a specific set of years spent by a particular person who was lonely during those years, while *The years past in Canada were lonely* refers to some unspecified set of years in the past, which were lonely in general.

passive voice

The term *passive voice* refers to verb forms that allow the subject to be the receiver (rather than the performer) of the verb's action. Passive verbs consist of a form of the verb *be* and a past participle: *is needed, was bought, has been delivered.* Writing handbooks usually include warnings about the passive voice—it is wordy and clumsy and leads to static rather than dynamic writing. There is truth to this, certainly, but the passive voice also has legitimate uses, and in many instances it is preferable to the active voice.

uses of the passive voice   The passive voice is a very versatile construction. It is particularly useful when the performer of the action is unknown or irrelevant to the matter at hand. Thus a police report might say *A car was broken into last night on Laurel Road* when the perpetrator is unknown. As another example, an office memo might read *Office mail is now delivered twice a day* where what is important is the frequency of mail delivery, not the identity of the people working in the mailroom.

The passive voice can also conceal the performer of an action or the identity of a person responsible for a mistake: *We had hoped to report on this problem, but the data was inadvertently deleted from our files.* Who deleted the data? By using the passive voice the writer is able to avoid identifying the guilty party. This virtue of obscuring responsibility is in part what makes the passive voice so tempting to anyone working in an organization where something has gone wrong. Since the occasions for avoiding responsibility are multitudinous, passive verbs are bound to thrive for at least the foreseeable future.

Surprisingly enough, the passive voice can also be used to emphasize the performer of the action by putting the performer in a prepositional phrase using *by* at the end of the sentence: *The breakthrough was achieved by Burlingame and Evans, two researchers in the university's genetic engineering lab.* In this way the passive voice functions like a well-run awards ceremony. It creates suspense by delaying the announcement of the names.

Another virtue of passive constructions is that they allow a modifying adverb to be emphasized by placing it at the end of the sentence, as many politicians know well: *My remarks have been grossly distorted* rather than *The press has grossly distorted my remarks.*

Scientists ordinarily use the passive voice to describe natural processes or phenomena under study. In the following quotations, for instance, the author, a psychiatrist, uses the passive voice to emphasize real psychological processes in refuting the notion that children ordinarily suppress memories of trauma:

> . . . severe traumas are not blocked out by children but remembered all too well. They are amplified in consciousness, remaining like grief to be reborn and reemphasized on anniversaries and in settings that can simulate the environments where they occurred (Paul R. McHigh, "Psychiatric Misadventures," *The American Scholar*)

In technical and scientific articles, especially in the presentation of experimental methods, researchers use the passive voice as a conventional means of impersonal reporting. The passive voice allows them to avoid calling attention to themselves and to omit reference to any subjective thoughts or biases they might have brought to their work. The effect is to lend the article the air of objectivity. Here is a typical example from a paper in molecular biology:

> The protein concentration required to saturate the solid phase was determined and the amount of bound protein was quantified by the micro-bicinchoninic acid protein assay.

Thanks to the passive voice, the experiment seems to run itself.

On some occasions the passive voice helps preserve the coherence of a piece of writing. In the following quotation, economist John Kenneth Galbraith discusses the common European policy of using immigrant workers who are not citizens to make up for labor shortages:

> In the last forty years, in Germany, France, and Switzerland, and in lesser measure, Austria and Scandinavia, the provision of outside workers for the task for which indigenous laborers are no longer available has been both accepted and highly organized. The factories of the erstwhile German Federal Republic are manned, and a broad range of other work is performed, by Turks and Yugoslavs. Those in France are similarly supplied by what amounts to a new invasion of the Moors—the vast influx from the former North African colonies (John Kenneth Galbraith, *The Culture of Contentment*)

In this passage there are almost no active verbs. Galbraith thus violates one of the most common commandments of writing handbooks: "use active verbs." But would the passage be clearer or easier to read if Galbraith had made the workers the subject of the sentences?

> . . . Turks and Yugoslavs man the factories of the erstwhile German Federal Republic and perform a broad range of other work. What amounts to a new invasion of the Moors—the vast influx from the former North African colonies—supplies those in France.

For Galbraith's purpose—describing the economy rather than the social groups in European society—the passive voice works fine. In fact, using the active voice might seem oddly inappropriate and, hence, distracting to the reader.

abuses of the passive voice   Trouble can arise, however, when the passive voice is used in sentence after sentence without an overriding reason to do so. And it is easy for writers to fall into this habit, since written material full of passive verbs often sounds impressive. Perhaps because of the use of the passive voice in technical writing, a sequence of passive verb forms can have the air of authority, but what it often has is air. Passive constructions are by their nature more wordy than active ones, forcing the writer to rely on abstract nouns and strings of prepositional phrases to convey the bulk of the information. As a result, the meaning intended by the writer can get diffused in bloated sentences that are tedious to read and hard to understand. In the following example, the importance of supervisors is under discussion:

> Recognition and assessment of errors in quality control by the supervisors is required so that manufacturing procedures can be adjusted and the problems can be thereby eliminated.

The complicated syntax required to accommodate the passive verbs causes confusion. Are the errors recognized by the supervisors or committed by them? The prepositional phrases leave us unsure. Here is the same material rewritten with active verbs. Notice how much shorter it is:

> Supervisors must recognize and assess errors in quality control so that we can adjust manufacturing procedures to eliminate the problems.

When writers are concentrating on the content and overall organization of their writing, rather than on the style of their sentences and how well one sentence leads into another, it may be difficult for them to perceive whether they have used the passive too often. A good test is to look down the page and highlight every form of the verb *be* (*is, are, was, were,* etc.) and any other weak-sounding verbs like *seem, appear,* and *exist.* If the page is covered with highlights, writers should consider recasting the page using more vivid verbs and the active voice.

See more at **double passive; verbs, voice of;** and **wordiness.**

past participle

A past participle is a verb form that indicates past or completed action or time and may be used with auxiliary verbs to form the passive voice or the perfect and pluperfect tenses. Past participles may sometimes be used as adjectives as well. The verb *accept,* for example, has a past participle *accepted,* which is used to form perfect and pluperfect constructions (*The college has accepted/had accepted the student*), the passive construction (*My proposal has been accepted by the committee*), and adjectival constructions (*an accepted method*). In English, the past participle is formed by the addition of the suffix *–ed* as above, or by altering the base form of the verb, as *spoken* from *speak.*

Though their forms are often the same or similar, the passive participle of a verb should not be confused with its past form. The past form does not combine with auxiliaries, and cannot be used as an adjective. The past form thus functions only as a verb (as in *The university accepted my proposal*).

See more at **participles; verbs, principal parts of;** and **verbs, tenses of.**

past perfect tense   See **pluperfect tense.**

past tense

The past tense is the verb tense used to express an action or a condition prior to the present. For example, the sentences *I walked to the store yesterday* and *She took in the beautiful scenery* are in the past tense. The past tense is a simple (as opposed to compound) tense, since only one verbal element, the second principal part of the verb, is used to form it.

The term *past tense* is sometimes used to cover both the case of completed action described above and compound tenses that can denote past events or states, such as the *perfect tense* and the *pluperfect tense.* In such contexts, the past tense as described above is distinguished from the others by being called the *simple past.*

See more at **perfect tense** and **verbs, principal parts of.**

pathogen   See **germ.**

pejorative / perjorative

The fact that English has many words beginning with *per–,* such as *perfunctory, perform,* and *perfect,* leads some to misspell the word *pejorative* as *perjorative.* But *pejo-*

rative, which means "tending to make or become worse" and "disparaging; belittling," has only one *r,* since it does not contain the Latin prefix *per–*. Instead, *pejorative* comes from Latin *pēiōrātus,* the past participle of the verb *pēiōrāre,* "to make worse" (from which our word *impair* also derives).

penalize

The older pronunciation is (pē′nə-līz′), with a long *e* in the first syllable as in *penal.* A variant pronunciation with a short *e* in the first syllable is now common in American English, however, probably because of association with *penalty.*

penultimate / ultimate

Properly used, *penultimate* means "next to last," as in *the penultimate game of the season* and *the penultimate syllable in a word.* It is sometimes used incorrectly where the word *ultimate* is called for, especially when meaning "representing or exhibiting the greatest possible development or sophistication," as in *This car is the penultimate in engineering and design.* This mistake may reflect the misconception that *pen–* is a prefix that acts as an intensifier of the word *ultimate.* But *pen–* actually derives from the Latin word *paene,* meaning "almost." (*Pen–* is also found in the word *peninsula,* which means, etymologically at least, "almost an island.") People who know the correct meaning of *penultimate* reject its use as a synonym of *ultimate* and may be disposed to view the speaker or writer as ignorant or even pretentious.

people / persons

As a term meaning "a body of persons sharing a culture," *people* is a singular noun, as in *The Aztecs, a Nahuatl-speaking people, settled in Mexico during the 13th century* or *The process by which a distinct people finds its identity is very complex.* Its plural is *peoples,* as in *the many and varied peoples of West Africa.* But when used to mean "human beings," *people* is plural; its singular form is *person.* Interestingly, many languages, such as Spanish, Italian, Russian, and German, treat their words for *person* and *people* in a similar way, using two completely different or unrelated words to express the singular and plural.

Nonetheless, some grammarians have insisted that *people* should be used exclusively as a collective singular noun, and that *persons* should be used when referring to a specific number of individuals. By this thinking, *six persons* [not *people*] *were arrested during the protest* would be correct. But *people* has always been used in such contexts, and this usage should be considered standard. *Persons* is preferred in legal contexts, however, as in *Vehicles containing fewer than three persons may not use the left lane during rush hours;* for this reason, use of the word *persons* instead of *people* is considered to have legal or (oddly enough) impersonal connotations. Another distinction between *people* and *persons* is found in compounds: only the singular *person* is used in compounds involving a specific numeral, as in *a six-person car, a two-person show.* But *people* is used in other compounds: *people mover, people power.*

percent

A quantity may increase by any percentage, but cannot decrease by more than 100 percent unless the quantity can have a negative value. For example, once pollution has been reduced by 100 percent, it ceases to exist, and no further reduction is possible. In apparent defiance of this logic, however, one finds cases such as *a 150 percent decrease in lost luggage* or *a new dental rinse that reduces plaque on teeth by over 300 percent,* even though there can be no "negative" amount of lost luggage or plaque. Such constructions, common in advertising, make sense only if they are construed to refer indirectly to some previous quantity of decrease, especially one that has been "improved" in some way. For example, if the old dental rinse reduced plaque by X amount, the new one reduces it by 300 percent of X, or three times as much. This sort of phrasing allows one to use higher and more impressive-looking figures, but it takes unacceptable liberties with the way percentages are generally interpreted, and it should therefore be avoided.

Percent can take a singular or a plural verb, depending on the intended focus. Thus both *Eighty percent of the legislators are going to vote against the bill* or *Eighty percent of the legislature is set to vote the bill down* are possible, but in the second sentence, the group of legislators is considered as a singular body, not as a number of individuals. The word *percent* without a following prepositional phrase may take either a singular or plural verb; both are acceptable.

See more at **number** and **subject and verb agreement.**

percentage

When preceded by *the, percentage* takes a singular verb: *The percentage of unskilled workers is small.* When preceded by *a,* it takes either a singular or plural verb, depending on the number of the noun in the prepositional phrase that follows: *A small percentage of the workers are unskilled. A large percentage of the crop has spoiled.*

See more at **number** and **subject and verb agreement.**

peremptory   See **preemptive.**

perfect

The adjective **perfect** is often considered an absolute term like *chief* and *prime;* some maintain that it therefore cannot be modified by *more, quite, relatively,* and other qualifiers of degree. But the qualification of *perfect* has many reputable precedents (most notably in the preamble to the US Constitution in the phrase *"in order to form a more perfect Union"*). When *perfect* means "ideal for a purpose," as in *There could be no more perfect spot for the picnic,* modification by degree is considered acceptable; in fact 74 percent of the Usage Panel approved this example in our 2004 survey.

See more at **absolute terms, complete, equal, infinite, parallel,** and **unique.**

perfect tense

The perfect tenses are verb tenses that express action completed prior to a fixed point of reference in time. English has two perfect tenses: the present perfect (as in *I have cleaned my room*) and the past perfect, or pluperfect (as in *I had cleaned my room*).
See more at **verbs, tenses of** and **verbs, principal parts of.**

perfidious

The adjective *perfidious* has a long record of reference to treacherous persons and other agents:

> When our own nation is at war with any other, we detest them under the character of cruel, perfidious, unjust and violent: But always esteem ourselves and allies equitable, moderate, and merciful (David Hume, *A Treatise of Human Nature*)

It has less frequently been applied to human actions, as in

> . . . O spirit accurst, / Forsak'n of all good; I see thy fall / Determind, and thy hapless crew involv'd / In this perfidious fraud (John Milton, *Paradise Lost* 5.877–880)

But recently *perfidious* has also been applied to words like *effects* and *consequences*. While these usages may follow a similar pattern with a word like *treacherous*, a more common word with a broader range of reference (*treacherous roads, treacherous waters*), it may be viewed by many as a misapplication of the word. In our 2004 survey, only 20 percent of the Usage Panel accepted the sentence *She claims that the tax cuts have had a perfidious effect on the economy,* and only 30 percent accepted *His is a case of the perfidious consequences of alcohol abuse.*

period

sentences

1. A period terminates a declarative sentence, a sentence fragment, or an imperative sentence that is not emphatic enough to require an exclamation point.

   > The carved ornamentation of the façade dates back to the 14th century.
   > No, not now.
   > Come home when you can.

2. A request that is politely phrased as a question usually takes a period instead of a question mark.

   > Would you please sign here.

3. Do not place a period after a sentence that is enclosed in parentheses, em dashes, or quotation marks within another sentence.

   > The play (I have no doubt of it) is going to be awful.

   > I saw someone—I'm not sure if it was a man or a woman—leaving the house around midnight.

   > The remark "That solution won't work" was typical of Julius.

abbreviations

1. Most acronyms and other abbreviations consisting of capital letters do not contain periods.

NASA	DVD
NBC	URL
NEA	US *or* U.S.

2. Periods are retained in abbreviations consisting of lowercase or upper- and lowercase letters when there is a strong tradition for their use. In most scientific and technical abbreviations, the periods are omitted. When in doubt, consult a dictionary.

etc.	Rev.
op. cit.	PhD *or* Ph.D.
et al.	ppm
pp.	km
a.m.	Hz
Jan.	

periodic

In technical use, *periodic* means "occurring at regular or predictable intervals," as in the *Periodic Table of the Elements* that always appears in chemistry textbooks. But people often use *periodic* more loosely to mean "occasional, intermittent." This looser usage may be confusing to readers who are fond of the narrower sense of the word. The sentence *His periodic bad moods are a distraction* is ambiguous in this way; it is not clear whether these bad moods occur on a regular basis or only occasionally. In most cases, the context will make the correct interpretation clear, but if not, the ambiguity can be avoided by using *occasional* where this is the sense intended.

perjorative   See **pejorative**.

permit

In the sense "to allow for, be consistent with," *permit* is often followed by the preposition *of: The wording of the note permits of several interpretations.* But *of* should not be used when the meaning of *permit* is "to give permission": *The law permits* [not *permits of*] *camping on the beach.*

As a verb, *permit* is pronounced (pər-mĭt′), with the stress on the second syllable. As a noun, *permit* is generally pronounced with the stress on the first syllable (pŭr′mĭt), the choice of 80 percent of the Usage Panel in our 1992 survey; however, the pronunciation (pər-mĭt′) for the noun is also correct.

person

Person is a property of noun forms or verb inflections that indicates the speaker of the utterance (first person), the individual addressed (second person), or the individual or thing spoken about (third person). The pronouns *I, me, we, us* are first-person pronouns, while *you, thou,* and *thee* are second-person pronouns. The pronouns *he, him, she, her, they, them* are third-person pronouns, and most other nouns are usually third person as well. The verb form *indicates* is a third-person form.

See more at **pronouns, agreement of; pronouns, personal; pronouns, reflexive and intensive;** and **subject and verb agreement.**

personal pronouns   See **pronouns, personal.**

person of color

Dissatisfaction with *nonwhite* as a racial label may have contributed to the recent popularity of terms formed with the phrase *of color,* as in *person of color, women of color, communities of color,* and even such ad hoc groupings as *journalists of color* or *educators of color.* The two terms are synonymous, but where *nonwhite* identifies by means of a negative and implies exclusion from a European commonality, *of color* substitutes a positive and emphasizes inclusion in a diverse group of peoples from the rest of the world. There are those who find these phrases awkward or who dismiss them as politically correct jargon. But *of color* labels rarely give true offense, and in instances where reference to race or skin color is relevant, many people now prefer them to *nonwhite* or other loosely equivalent labels such as *minority* or *Third World.*

person of color / colored   The term *people of colour* is first cited in *The Oxford English Dictionary* in 1796, and, like *colored,* it was originally used in reference to light-skinned people of mixed African and European heritage as distinct from full-blooded Africans. But after the Civil War *colored* was increasingly adopted as a label for Black Americans in general, regardless of skin shade or ancestry, and was long used with pride in the Black community before eventually losing favor in the mid-20th century. In current American English, *colored* is viewed as dated and often offensive in referring to Black Americans. But no such stigma is attached to *person of color* and its variants, which are almost never used today in referring exclusively to African Americans. Instead, they are used inclusively of all non-European peoples—often with the assumption that there is a political and even cultural solidarity among them—and are virtually always considered terms of pride and respect.

See more at **colored.**

perspicuous / perspicacious

Although both these words involve the concept of "clarity," they are commonly confused, as they attribute this quality differently. Something that is *perspicuous* is clearly expressed and easy to understand, as in *perspicuous lesson plans for teaching children tough math concepts.* Similarly, a *perspicuous person* is a person who is easy to understand. But one might also attribute clarity of mind to the person doing the seeing or understanding, rather than to what is expressed and understood. Someone or something that shows such clear-sightedness is *perspicacious,* that is, having or showing acute mental discernment, as in *The students' perspicacious remarks suggested that they had been paying attention to the lecture.* One can even be perspicacious without being perspicuous: *Several perspicacious reviewers discovered some subtle flaws in the textbook but were not perspicuous enough to make these flaws clear to teachers.*

persuade   See **convince.**

peruse

Peruse has long meant "to read thoroughly," as in *She perused the pages, carefully looking for errors.* This example was acceptable to 78 percent of the Usage Panel in our 1999 survey. But the word is often used more loosely, when one could use the word *read* instead, as in *The librarians checked to see which titles had been perused in the last month and which ones had been left untouched.* Seventy percent of the Panel rejected this example.

Further extensions of the word to mean "to glance over, skim,"—what would seem almost opposite to its established meaning—tend to be frowned on by the Panel. In our 1988 survey, 66 percent rejected the sentence *I had only a moment to peruse the manual quickly,* and in 1999, 58 percent still disapproved of it.

Use of the word outside of reading contexts is likely to be considered a mistake. In 1999, 81 percent of the Panel disapproved of it in *We perused the shops in the downtown area.*

phase   See **faze.**

phenomenon / phenomena / phenomenons

The plural of *phenomenon,* which derives from Greek, is *phenomena* in scientific and most other contexts. But like the plurals *criteria* and *bacteria, phenomena* is sometimes misused as a singular form, as in *This phenomena has never been observed in nature.* This mistake may arise from the fact that *-a* is not a typical English plural ending, leading to the misunderstanding of *phenomena* as a singular noun. In fact, the mistaken plural *phenomenas,* which occurs sometimes in the scientific writing of nonnative English speakers and elsewhere, provides further evidence of this erroneous analysis. Second, *phenomena* might be taken to be a "noncount" use referring to a collection or range rather than a single countable item, much like *data, flour,* and *advice,* none of which have plural forms. Third, the tricky pronunciation of *phenomenon,* with its four nasal consonants, might encourage the reduction or dropping of the final (n) sound, leading to a pronunciation of the singular that is nearly identical with the plural and adding to the confusion. Despite all of this, the distinction between the singular *–non* and plural *–ena* forms is important and should be maintained.

The plural *phenomenons* is properly used in nonscientific writing when the meaning is "extraordinary things, occurrences, or persons," as in *The Beatles were phenomenons in the history of rock 'n' roll.* Thus, a phrase like *phenomenons of nature* would properly be interpreted as referring to natural wonders, not as a neutral expression describing natural processes or events.

phenotype See **genotype.**

phloem See **xylem.**

phrase

A phrase is a sequence of two or more words that form a grammatical unit that is less than a complete sentence. English can have noun phrases (*the great white whale, a little bit of rain, the best singer that we have ever heard*), verb phrases (*has slept, will remember, is escalating, may have been delayed*), prepositional phrases (*in the next room, along the river, after the party*), and various other kinds as well.

Phrases used as modifiers are normally hyphenated: *a happy-go-lucky person, a here-today-gone-tomorrow attitude.* But note that a foreign phrase used as a modifier is not hyphenated: *a bona fide offer, a per diem allowance.*

pill bug / sow bug

Many people, especially science teachers, like to make a distinction between pill bugs and sow bugs. According to this usage, a *pill bug*, also known as a *roly-poly*, is a terrestrial crustacean with seven pairs of legs and a segmented, flexible body that gives it the ability to curl up into a ball when disturbed. A *sow bug* is any of several similar looking crustaceans that lack this ability. In popular usage, however, *pill bug* and *sow bug* are both used to refer to these creatures that are often mistaken for insects. The names *slater, wood louse,* and *doodlebug* are also used for both kinds of creatures.

See more at **bug.**

PIN number See **ATM machine.**

plead

In a court of law, there are only two basic pleas: guilty and not guilty. In strict legal usage, then, it is possible to *plead guilty* or *plead not guilty* but it is not possible to *plead innocent*. In nonlegal contexts—that is, outside of the technical language of the law—people are often said to *plead innocent*. This is a widely used expression and should be considered acceptable.

plenty　See **lot**.

pluperfect tense

The pluperfect tense is the verb tense that is used to express action completed before a stated or implied past time. In English the pluperfect tense is formed with the auxiliary verb *had* and the past participle of a verb, as *had learned* in *He had learned to skate before his fourth birthday*.

See more at **verbs, tenses of; perfect tense; participles;** and **verbs, principal parts of.**

plurality　See **majority.**

plural nouns

general rules of plural formation

1. For most nouns, the plural is formed by adding *-s* to the singular: *apple, apples; bell, bells; epoch, epochs; grief, griefs; law, laws; month, months; pear, pears; shade, shades; George, Georges; the Walkers; the Romanos.*

2. Common nouns ending in *ch* (soft), *sh, s, ss, x, z,* or *zz* usually form their plurals by adding *-es: church, churches; slash, slashes; gas, gases* or *gasses; class, classes; fox, foxes; quiz, quizzes; buzz, buzzes.* (As can be seen from the foregoing examples, nouns that end in a single *s* or *z* preceded by a vowel sometimes double the consonant before adding *-es.*)
   Proper nouns of this type always add *-es: Charles, Charleses; the Keaches; the Joneses; the Coxes.*

3. Common nouns ending in *y* preceded by a vowel usually form their plurals by adding *-s: bay, bays; guy, guys; key, keys; toy, toys.*

4. Common nouns ending in *y* preceded by a consonant or by *qu* change the *y* to *i* and add *-es: baby, babies; city, cities; faculty, faculties; soliloquy, soliloquies.*

5. Proper nouns ending in *y* form their plurals regularly, and do not change the *y* to *i* as common nouns do: *the two Kathys, the Connallys, the two Kansas Citys.* There are a few well-known exceptions to this rule: *the Alleghenies, the Ptolemies, the Rockies, the Two Sicilies.*

6. Most nouns ending in *f, ff,* or *fe* form their plurals regularly by adding *-s* to the singular: *chief, chiefs; proof, proofs; roof, roofs; sheriff, sheriffs; fife, fifes.* However, some nouns ending in *f* or *fe* change the *f* or *fe* to *v* and add *-es: calf, calves; elf, elves; half, halves; knife, knives; life, lives; loaf, loaves; self, selves; shelf, shelves; thief, thieves; wife, wives; wolf, wolves.* A few nouns ending in *f* or *ff*, including *beef,*

dwarf, hoof, scarf, wharf, and *staff* have two plural forms: *beefs* or *beeves; dwarfs* or *dwarves; hoofs* or *hooves; scarfs* or *scarves; wharfs* or *wharves; staffs* or *staves.* In this case, sometimes different forms have different meanings, as *beefs* (complaints) and *beeves* (bovine animals) or *staffs* (people) and *staves* (long poles or sets of horizontal lines used in musical notation).

7. Nouns ending in *o* preceded by a vowel form their plurals by adding *-s* to the singular: *cameo, cameos; duo, duos; studio, studios; zoo, zoos.*

8. Most nouns ending in *o* preceded by a consonant also usually add *-s* to form the plural: *alto, altos; casino, casinos; ego, egos; Latino, Latinos; memo, memos; neutrino, neutrinos; poncho, ponchos; silo, silos.* However, some nouns ending in *o* preceded by a consonant add *-es: echo, echoes; hero, heroes; jingo, jingoes; no, noes; potato, potatoes; tomato, tomatoes.* Some nouns ending in *o* preceded by a consonant have two plural forms (the preferred form is given first): *buffaloes* or *buffalos; cargoes* or *cargos; desperadoes* or *desperados; halos* or *haloes; mosquitoes* or *mosquitos; zeros* or *zeroes.*

9. Most nouns ending in *i* form their plurals by adding *-s: alibi, alibis; khaki, khakis; rabbi, rabbis; ski, skis.* Three notable exceptions to this rule are *alkali, taxi,* and *chili: alkalis* or *alkalies; taxis* or *taxies; chilies* or *chiles* or *chillies.*

irregular plurals and other special formations

1. A few nouns undergo a vowel change in the stem in order to make their plural: *foot, feet; goose, geese; louse, lice; man, men; mouse, mice; tooth, teeth; woman, women.* Usually compounds in which one of these nouns is the final element form their plurals in the same way: *webfoot, webfeet; gentleman, gentlemen; dormouse, dormice; Englishwoman, Englishwomen.* Note, however, that *mongoose* and many words ending in *man,* such as *German, human,* and *shaman,* are not compounds. These words form their plurals by adding *-s: mongooses, Germans, humans, shamans.*

2. Three nouns have plurals ending in *en: ox, oxen; child, children; brother, brothers* (of the same parent) or *brethren* (fellow members).

3. Compounds written as a single word form their plurals the same way that the final element of the compound does: *dishcloth, dishcloths; hairbrush, hairbrushes; midwife, midwives; anchorman, anchormen; businesswoman, businesswomen.*

4. In rare cases both parts of the compound are made plural: *manservant, menservants.*

5. Compounds ending in *–ful* normally form their plurals by adding *-s* at the end: *cupful, cupfuls; handful, handfuls; tablespoonful, tablespoonfuls.*

6. Compound words, written with or without a hyphen, that consist of a noun followed by an adjective or other qualifying expression form their plurals by making the same change in the noun that is made when the noun stands alone: *attorney general, attorneys general; daughter-in-law, daughters-in-law; man-of-war, men-of-war; heir apparent, heirs apparent; notary public, notaries public.*

7. Some nouns, mainly names of birds, fishes, and mammals, have the same form in the plural as in the singular: *bison, deer, moose, sheep, swine.* Some words that follow this pattern, such as *antelope, cod, elk, fish, flounder, grouse, herring, quail, reindeer, salmon, shrimp,* and *trout,* also have regular plurals ending in *-s: antelope, antelopes; cod, cods; elk, elks;* and so forth. Normally in such cases the unchanged plural indicates that the animal in question is being considered collectively, while the plural ending in -s is used specifically to indicate different varieties or species or kinds: *We caught six fish* but *Half a dozen fishes inhabit the lake.* By far, however, most animal names take a regular plural: *dogs, cats, lions, monkeys, whales.*

8. Many words indicating nationality, place of origin, or ethnic affiliation have the same form in the plural as in the singular: *Iroquois, Japanese, Milanese, Swiss.* Many other such names have both an unchanged plural form and a regular plural form ending in -s: *Apache* or *Apaches; Cherokee* or *Cherokees; Zulu* or *Zulus.*

plurals of foreign words

1. Many nouns derived from a foreign language retain their foreign plurals: (from Latin) *alumna, alumnae; alumnus, alumni; bacillus, bacilli; index, indices* or *indexes; memorandum, memoranda* or *memorandums; series, series; species, species;* (from Greek) *analysis, analyses; basis, bases; crisis, crises; criterion, criteria* or *criterions; phenomenon, phenomena* or *phenomenons;* (from French) *adieu, adieux* or *adieus; beau, beaux* or *beaus; madame, mesdames;* (from Italian) *paparazzo, paparazzi;* (from Hebrew) *cherub, cherubim* or *cherubs; kibbutz, kibbutzim.* As you can see, many words of this type also have a regular plural ending in -s or -es, in which case the English plural is usually the one used in everyday speech, and the foreign plural is reserved for a technical sense or for use by a specialist: *antennas* (TV or radio part) or *antennae* (physiological structure).

2. English nouns from Latin that end in –*us* can pose special problems of plural formation. In Latin itself, several distinct types of nouns shared the common ending –*us* in the subject case of the singular. (Almost every Latin noun usually had a variety of forms, each expressing a different grammatical role of the noun in the sentence, that were made by attaching different endings to the base form of the noun. In much the same way, English pronouns have a variety of forms depending on their grammatical case, such as *I, me,* and *my.* English nouns borrowed directly from Latin are often based on the form that the Latin noun had in the subject case.) Latin nouns ending in –*us,* however, could make their plural in a variety of different ways, depending on the various types to which they belonged, and for this reason it is not possible to predict the English plural of a noun of Latin origin simply based on the ending –*us.* One Latin plural type is represented in English by nouns like *nucleus, nuclei* or *cactus, cacti.* Another type made its plural in –*era,* and is represented in English by pairs like *genus, genera.* Yet another type of noun in –*us* made its plural in –*ora,* and can be seen in English pairs like *corpus, corpora.* And a further type of Latin noun in –*us* made its plural by lengthening the *u* of the ending to *ū,* as in the Latin word *prōspectus,* "distant view, prospect," whose plural is *prōspectūs.* Since it is not possible to indicate the difference between –*us* and –*ūs* in normal English orthography, these nouns can only make their English plural by adding -es: *prospectuses.* Plurals in -*i* for such words, as for example *prospecti,* are not justified by the origin of the word and will draw criticism from those who know Latin grammar. Writers should therefore consult the dictionary whenever in doubt about the proper way of forming the plural of a noun of Latin origin.

plurals of letters and words used as words

1. Usage with regard to forming the plurals of letters, numbers, and abbreviations varies somewhat. In some cases there is a choice between adding *-s* or *-'s,* although the trend is increasingly to add *-s* alone: *three As* or *three A's; the ABCs* or *the ABC's; the 1900s* or *the 1900's; PhDs* or *PhD's; several IOUs* or *several IOU's.* With lowercase letters, symbols, abbreviations with periods, and in cases where confusion might arise without an apostrophe, use *-'s* to form the plural: *p's and q's; +'s; -'s; M.A.'s; A's and I's; 2's.* Mainly the goal is to be as clear as possible and avoid confusion.

2. The plural of a word being used as a word is indicated by *-'s: underline all the but's.* Note that in typed or typeset copy, only the word *but* would appear in italics (the apostrophe and the *s* would be in regular type).

plurals

The plural is the grammatical form that designates that more than one thing is being specified. In English most plurals of nouns are formed by adding *-s* or *-es* to nouns. Some words, like *sheep* and *deer,* have the same form in both plural and singular meanings. A few words form their plurals by the addition of *-en: children; oxen,* while others follow different patterns adopted from other languages, or have irregular plural forms: *strata, men, women.*

Verbs also have plural forms, though in English they are not indicated by a suffix. Thus the plural of *decide* is *decide* in the present tense, and *decided* in the past, whereas the third-person singular present tense is indicated by *-s* in *decides.*

See more at **plural nouns** and **verbs, principal parts of.**

plus

***plus* connecting clauses or sentences** *You get the knife, the bowl, and the book. Plus you get the free knife sharpener.* The use of *plus* as a conjunction connecting clauses or starting a sentence that emphasizes an additional thought occurs frequently in sales pitches, but it is not well established in formal writing. The usage tends to be limited to quoted speech and first-person accounts, as in the following examples:

> I wasn't particularly interested in competing with White No More. I knew who'd win. They were a tight funk band fronted by a spastic lead singer in skinny ties and porkpie hats who called himself Johnny Unforgettable. He wrote paranoid lyrics and lived up to his name. The band's horn section was formidable. Plus, they were from New York, a fact that in itself commanded some kind of grudging respect (Jessica Hagedorn, *Gangster of Love*)

> "Man, oh man, this is just so tough," he says. "It hasn't been like this since I was 13 playing for a Babe Ruth team. We were horrible. Awful. Plus, we had bad uniforms. Ugly green things. It was terrible." (Glenn Stout, *Top of the Heap*)

verb agreement when *plus* connects nouns in the subject The use of *plus* to connect nouns presents a more complicated issue. When equations involving addition are written out in words, the verb is usually singular: *Three plus two is five.* Similarly, when *plus* connects nouns or noun phrases, the verb is usually singular: *Their strength plus their intelligence makes them formidable opponents.* Some people would argue that in these sentences *plus* functions as a preposition meaning "in addition to," but if this were true, it would be possible to move the *plus* phrase to the beginning of the sentence, which is clearly ungrammatical. No one would say *Plus their intelligence, their strength makes them formidable.* It makes more sense to view *plus* in these uses as a conjunction that joins two subjects into a single entity requiring a singular verb by notional agreement, just as *and* does in the sentence *Chips and beans is her favorite appetizer.*

See more at **also, subject and verb agreement,** and **too.**

p.m.   See **a.m.**

poetess   See **feminine suffixes.**

poinsettia

Although the pronunciation (poin-sēt′ə) overlooks the fact that there is an *i* before the final *a,* so many people pronounce the word this way that it is now listed as a standard variant in most dictionaries. By the process of *intrusion,* some people even add a (t) sound at the end of the first syllable, saying (point) instead of (poin), but this variant is not considered correct.

politics

Politics takes a singular verb when used to refer to the art or science of governing or to political science:

> . . . to effect political change it is necessary to put one's ego aside, for politics is a collective, not a solitary, endeavor (Mary V. Dearborn, *Mailer*)

Sometimes when used as a singular noun, *politics* is modified by the indefinite article:

> Edmund Burke, the founder of modern conservatism, believed that the French Revolution had gone too far, that a healthy politics was built upon tradition—the successful inheritance of those who had gone before, and that we must be prudent in statesmanship (Neal Riemer, Douglas W. Simon, and Joseph Romance, *The Challenge of Politics*)

In its other senses, as when it refers to the activities or methods of politicians or a government, *politics* can take either a singular or plural verb:

> Our politics has been corrupted by money and suffused with meanness. Trust in government and public institutions has eroded (Peter Edelman, *Searching for America's Heart*)

By any objective comparative standard, however, Western condemnations of the country's institutions in the last ten years have been grossly overblown. Russia's politics have been among the most democratic in the region (Andrei Shleifer and Daniel Treisman, "A Normal Country," *Foreign Affairs*)

When *politics* means "political attitudes and positions," it is taken to be plural:

The selection process for the Miss America contest has always been political. Back in the days when only white college women, whose main interest in most instances was a degree in MRS, could win, the contest was indeed just as political as it is now, a clear ideological bow to both patriarchal ideals and racism. It is simply a matter of which politics you prefer, and while no politics are perfect, some are clearly better than others (Gerald Early, "Life with Daughters: Watching the Miss America Pageant," *Kenyon Review*)

She feels a strong affinity to other young men and women of means, even people she doesn't like, whose politics are anathema to her. . . . (Paul Kafka-Gibbons, *Dupont Circle*)

poor

In informal speech *poor* is sometimes used as an adverb, as in *They never played poorer.* In formal usage *more poorly* would be required in this example.

pore / pour

Although *pore* and *pour* are pronounced identically, as (pōr), by many people, these two words should be distinguished in spelling. Unaware that the verb *pore* exists, many writers use *pour* instead. *Pore* means "to read or study something intently." It is mainly used in the phrase *pore over:*

At the local library, I pored over documents and microfilm I requisitioned from the Library of Congress (Laura Hillenbrand, "A Sudden Illness," *The New Yorker*)

Naturally, the idea of *pouring* a liquid over something so as to cover it is easily evoked by the sound of the words *pore over,* and people may interpret the verb as a metaphor—pouring one's vision over a document.

Whatever the reasons for the confusion, these words should be kept distinct since they have different meanings and etymologies. Note that the object of *pore* can be things other than written texts:

On these cool September mornings, I've been poring over two sets of photographs, those from deep space and those from Eva's wedding. . . . (Scott Russell Sanders, "Beauty," *Orion*)

Recently I spent two hours poring over the time-lapse film of Silber's face—backward, fast-forward, in slow-mo, in freeze-frame—watching attitudes blossom and wilt like flowers in a nature film (Christopher Miller, *Simon Silber*)

portentous

The usual pronunciation of this word is (pôr-tĕn′tǝs). However, under the influence of words like *contentious, pretentious,* and *sententious, portentous* is sometimes pronounced (pôr-tĕn′shǝs), as if it were spelled *portentious.* Neither the pronunciation ending in (shǝs) nor the spelling ending in *–tious* (which crops up occasionally in print) is considered standard.

positive degree

The positive degree is the simple, uncompared form of an adjective or adverb. The adjective *fine,* for example, is a positive-degree adjective, while its comparative form (*finer*) and superlative form (*finest*) are not. Note that the word *positive* here has nothing to do with affirmation or acceptance, the root sense of the adjective. The form *bad,* for example, is the positive degree, contrasting with *worse* and *worst.*

See more at **adjectives** and **adverbs.**

possessed

Possessed is often followed by the prepositions *of, by,* or *with.* When it is used as the past participle of *possess* in its various senses, *by* may be used: *This house was possessed by the city government. No such weapon was ever possessed by any member of the family. He thought he was possessed by the devil.* When *possessed* indicates an obsession or lack of self-control, *with* may also be used: *The prosecutor described him as a man possessed with* [or *by*] *an urge to kill.*

Curiously, although the form *possessed* is that of a past participle or adjective, it can have the meaning of an *active* participle as well, becoming synonymous with "possessing" in the sense of owning something or having some property. In this case, however, the preposition *of* must be used: *She was possessed of a large estate. That child is possessed of a sharp tongue.* Furthermore, the prepositional phrase beginning with *of* cannot be omitted in this context without an alteration of meaning. Thus the sentence *She was possessed* can only mean that she was possessed *with* or *by* something, not that she possessed something herself.

possessive antecedents

Since the 1960s, some usage manuals and English teachers have condemned what is known as the *possessive antecedent* construction, in which a pronoun refers to a noun or proper noun that occurs earlier in the sentence as a possessive, as in *Susan Maxwell's readers adore her.* Why this construction, which is very common, even in the writing of people who condemn it, should be considered ungrammatical is something of a mystery. It is certainly very handy, and while it can occasionally lead to ambiguities, as in sentences like *Susan Maxwell's friend thinks she is working hard to promote her new novel* (where *she* could be Susan or her friend), this problem is not restricted to sentences of this type. It is present as well when the sentence begins, *A friend of Susan Maxwell . . .* and can be resolved by judicious rewriting.

The nature of the possessive construction, however, may have some bearing on the way readers react to it, and in general the more subordinated the possessive construction is to other parts of the sentence, the less likely readers are to view it favorably. Thus, in our 2004 survey, fully 91 percent of the Usage Panel accepted the uncomplicated sentence quoted above, *Susan Maxwell's readers adore her.* But when the possessive construction was subordinated in a prepositional phrase, in the sentence *In Susan Maxwell's new book, she castigates reporters who rehash articles they have seen elsewhere,* the acceptability fell to 76 percent—the Panel was still strongly in favor, but less so. And when the possessive was subordinated even further in a prepositional phrase modifying the object of another prepositional phrase, the Panel was even less enthusiastic. Some 63 percent accepted the sentence *In a new book by Susan Maxwell, she makes a case for living in the suburbs.* Thus a guideline for good writing emerges: When using a possessive noun that is referred to by a following pronoun, subordinate the possessive noun as little as possible.

See more at **possessive constructions.**

possessive case

In English, the possessive case is the form of a pronoun that indicates possession. The pronoun *my* is in the possessive case. Pronouns in the possessive case are often considered adjectives.

See more at **pronouns, personal.**

possessive constructions

English makes possessive forms of nouns by adding an apostrophe and an *s*, or sometimes just an apostrophe, at the end. Pronouns have their own possessive forms (*my, your, his, her, its, our, their*). Possession can also be indicated by a prepositional phrase using *of: the property of the town.*

Although these constructions are all called "possessives," they often do not indicate simple possession but a number of other relations. These include source or origin (*the ambassador's letter, Hardy's novels*), description or classification (*the car's speed, the stadium's design, a month's salary*), and purpose (*a women's college, boys' clothing*). Possessives can also indicate the subject or object of an implied verbal action: *her leaving Montana* (that is, she is leaving or has left Montana); *the building's destruction* (someone or something is destroying or has destroyed the building). The rules for forming possessives are listed below.

rules for forming possessives

singulars The possessive case of a singular noun is formed by adding *'s: one's home, by day's end, our family's pet, the witness's testimony, a fox's habitat, the knife's edge.* Note that although some people use just the apostrophe after singular nouns ending in *s* (*the witness' testimony, Burns' poetry*), the *'s* is generally preferred because it more accurately reflects the modern pronunciation of these forms. However, in a few cases where the *'s* is not pronounced, it is usual to add just the apostrophe: *for righteousness' sake.*

plurals The possessive case of a plural noun ending in *s* is formed by adding just an apostrophe: *the doctors' recommendations, the glasses' rims, the flies' buzzing noises.* However, when the plural noun does not end in *s*, form the possessive by adding *'s: children's clothes.*

proper nouns The possessive case of most proper nouns is formed according to the rules for common nouns: (singular) *Eliot's novels, Yeats's poetry, Dostoyevsky's biography, Velázquez's paintings;* (plural) *the McCarthys' and the Williamses' parties, the Schwartzes' trip.* By convention, however, certain proper nouns ending in *s* form the possessive by adding just the apostrophe since adding *'s* would make the pronunciation difficult or awkward: *Moses' children, Hercules' strength, Ramses' reign.*

compound names For compound names or titles that form short phrases the *'s* or apostrophe is added to the final element: *the King of Belgium's birthday, Saint Francis of Assisi's life, the governor of New York's speech.*

phrases using *and* When two or more people or things possess something jointly, the *'s* or apostrophe is added to the last element only: *Martha and Dan's house.* However, when two or more people or things possess something separately, the *'s* or apostrophe is added to each element: *The Smiths' and the Joneses' houses are for sale.*

other noun phrases The possessive for noun phrases is formed by adding *'s* or an apostrophe at the end of the phrase: *the Department of Chemistry's new requirements, a three months' journey.* This construction gets cumbersome when the noun phrase is long, in which case a prepositional phrase should probably be used instead. Thus instead of *the house that overlooks the bay's property line,* it is better to say *the property line of the house that overlooks the bay.*

***of mine, of yours* (double genitive)** The "double genitive" construction, in which a possessive form appears as the object of the preposition *of,* as in *a friend of my father's* or *a book of mine,* is looked down on by some grammarians and usage critics. But this construction has been used in English since the 14th century and serves a useful purpose. It can help sort out ambiguous phrases like *Bob's photograph,* which could mean either "a photograph of Bob" (i.e., revealing Bob's image) or "a photograph that is in Bob's possession." *A photograph of Bob's,* on the other hand, can only be a photo that Bob has in his possession and may or may not show Bob's image. There are also cases in which the double genitive may be more elegant; for example, many speakers find such sentences as *That's your only friend that I've ever met* or *That's your only friend I've ever met* to be awkward or impossible, but rephrasing using the double genitive provides an acceptable alternative, as in *That's the only friend of yours that I've ever met.*

See also **apostrophe, both, each, else, gerunds,** and **possessive antecedent.**

---

post–

The meaning of the prefix *post–* is "after" (in time) and "behind" (in spatial relation to something). The prefix ultimately comes from Latin *post,* meaning "after, behind."

Post– is often used in opposition to the prefixes *ante–* and *pre–: antedate/postdate; prewar/postwar.* And *post–* occurs frequently in medical terminology. *Postnasal* ("posterior to the nose") and *postnatal* ("after birth") are two common examples, but there are many others, such as *postcranial* ("behind the cranium") and *posttraumatic* ("following an injury or a psychological trauma or resulting from it").

posthumous

In American English, this word is most commonly pronounced (pŏs′chə-məs), with the stress on the first syllable and the *h* silent, which allows the *t* before *u* to assimilate to (ch), as it does in *culture* and *picture.*

See more at **assimilation.**

postulate   See **axiom.**

potpourri

The only pronunciation considered standard now in American English is (pō′po͞o-rē′), an approximation of the original pronunciation for this 17th-century borrowing from French. The pronunciation (pŏt-po͞or′ē) is an Anglicized variant that is sometimes heard in British English.

power   See **force, current.**

practicable / practical

It is easy to confuse these adjectives since they look so much alike and overlap in meaning. *Practicable* has only two meanings: "feasible" (as in *Sharon came up with a practicable plan*) and "usable for a specified purpose" (as in *A new, more practicable entrance was added to the house*). Note that *practicable* cannot be applied to persons. *Practical* has at least eight meanings, all related. These range from "acquired through practice rather than theory" (*I have practical experience using a lathe*) to "level-headed" (*He has always been a practical guy*) to "virtual" (*The party was a practical disaster*). It also has the sense "capable of being put into effect, useful," wherein the confusion with *practicable* arises. But a distinction between these words remains nonetheless: For the purpose of ordering coffee in a Parisian café, it would be *practical,* i.e., useful, to learn some French, but it still might not be *practicable* for someone with a busy schedule and little time to learn.

practically

Practically has as its primary sense "in a way that is practical": *We planned the room practically so we can use it as a study as well as a den.* The word has the extended meaning of "for all practical purposes," as in *After the accident the car was practically undrivable.* Here the idea is that the car can still be driven, but it is no longer practical to do so. In this context, the word comes close to meaning "for all intents and purposes," but language critics sometimes object when the notion of practicality is completely stripped from this word and it is used to mean "all but, nearly," as in *He had practically finished his meal when I arrived.* But this usage is widely used by reputable writers and must be considered acceptable:

> "Unless I go to bed early I get practically no sleep at all," Mrs. Paley was heard to explain, as if to justify her seizure of Susan, who got up and proceeded to wheel the chair to the door (Virginia Woolf, *The Voyage Out*)

> Having moved to Washington in 1877 . . . Adams quickly became an "insider," forming acquaintances with practically every president until his death at age eighty (Saul Bellow, "Graven Images," *News from the Republic of Letters*)

pre–

The basic meaning of the prefix *pre–* is "before." It ultimately comes from Latin *prae,* which means "before, in front." In fact, the word *prefix* comes from *prae* plus *fixus,* a form of the Latin verb *figere* ("to fasten"). *Pre–* often appears in combination with verbs of Latin origin. For example, *preconceive, preexist,* and *premeditate* are recorded in documents as early as the 16th century. *Predispose* and *prepossess* came into use in the 17th century, and *prepay* came into use in the 19th century.

precedence

Although *precedence* is related to the word *precede,* it has a distinct pronunciation. In our 1997 survey, the Usage Panel nearly unanimously reported that they used the pronunciation with the stress on the first syllable with a short *e* (prĕs′ĭ-dəns). Only 20 percent of the Panel found the pronunciation (prĭ-sē′dns), which sounds like the word *precede,* to be acceptable.

precipitate / precipitous

The adjective *precipitate* and the adverb *precipitately* were once applied to physical steepness but are now used primarily of rash, headlong actions: *Their precipitate entry into the foreign markets led to disaster. He withdrew precipitately from the race. Precipitous* currently means "steep" in both literal and figurative senses: *the precipitous rapids of the upper river, a precipitous drop in commodity prices.* But *precipitous* and *precipitously* are also frequently used to mean "abrupt, hasty," which takes them into territory that has traditionally belonged to *precipitate* and *precipitately: their precipitous decision to leave.* Many people object to this usage out of a desire to keep *precipitate* and *precipitous* distinct, but the extension of meaning from "steep" to "abrupt" is perfectly natural. After all, *a precipitous increase in reports of measles* is also an abrupt or sudden event. In fact, a majority of the Usage Panel now accepts this usage. In our 2004 survey, 65 percent accepted the sentence *Pressure to marry may cause precipitous decision-making that is not grounded in the reality of who you are and what you want from life.*

preconscious   See **unconscious.**

predicate

In traditional grammar, the predicate is one of two main parts of a sentence, the other being the subject. Thus, *opened the door* is the predicate of *Jane opened the door,* and *is very sleepy* is the predicate of *The child is very sleepy.*

But predicates can also be found in clauses and phrases containing a verb in some form. Gerunds, and sometimes other words derived from verbs, can also be the locus of predicates when they modify a preceding noun. For example, in the sentence *Harry, opening the door, was surprised to see his friend Jane,* both the phrase *opening the door* and the phrase *was surprised to see his friend Jane* are predicates.

predicate adjective

A predicate adjective is an adjective that follows the noun it modifies, generally through an intervening linking verb. The adjective *unhappy* is a predicate adjective in *John never seems unhappy.* In the sentence *John, unhappy with his poem, threw it into the wastebasket, unhappy* is also a predicate adjective—note that this construction can be thought of as a reduced form of *John, who is unhappy with his poem,* in which the linking verb *is* can be seen.

predicate nominative

A predicate nominative is a noun that serves to describe or determine a preceding noun phrase that is the subject of a clause. The predicate nominative and the noun it describes are usually associated through a linking verb. For example, in the sentence *Jim was a firefighter, firefighter* is a predicate nominative.

Nouns, like adjectives, can act as predicates in other constructions as well. In *Sandra, a bookseller, loves to read,* the phrase *a bookseller* describes the preceding noun *Sandra.* The phrase *Sandra, a bookseller* can be thought of as a reduced form of *Sandra, who is a bookseller,* in which the linking verb *is* can be seen directly.

See more at **predicate adjective.**

preemptive / peremptory

The original meaning of *preemptive* was "having the quality or the power of preemption," where *preemption* is a previously established right to purchase something before others do: *The preemptive purchase of the land by the settlers resulted in very few newcomers to the area.* Its sense has extended to describe any activity that is undertaken before an adversary can act, and is used now especially to describe military engagements designed to destroy enemy forces before they have attacked, as in *a preemptive air strike.*

Perhaps due to the latter usage, along with the similar sounds and spellings of these two words, *preemptive* is sometimes confused with *peremptory. Peremptory* has a range of meanings, including "putting an end to all debate or action" (*The court issued a peremptory decree*); "not allowing contradiction or refusal; imperative" (*The lawyers for each side are entitled to some peremptory challenges dismissing potential jurors*); "having the nature of or expressing a command; urgent" (*The teacher spoke in a peremptory tone*); and "offensively self-assured; dictatorial" (*a swaggering, peremptory manner*). Since a *preemptive* military action can be thought of as *peremptory,* the two words are sometimes confused. They should be kept distinct.

To sum up: a preemptive action is one that is undertaken to prevent an adversary from acting first; a preemptory action is one undertaken from arbitrary power or a belief in an unquestionable right.

prefixes

A prefix is an affix that is put before a word to alter its meaning. The element *dis–* in *disbelieve* is a prefix. Many individual prefixes and suffixes from Greek and Latin are discussed as separate entries in this book. The addition of a prefix to a word sometimes requires a hyphen.

See more at **hyphenation.**

premiere

In entertainment contexts, the verb *premiere* has by now become the standard way of saying "to introduce to the public" or "to be introduced to the public." Because it emphasizes the very first time something is presented to the public, *premiere* gets a lot of use. Thus a movie can premiere in selected theaters, and a year later it can premiere again to a different audience on television. The verb made its premiere in the 1930s and acceptance of it in general usage was slow at first but has recently accelerated, so that it must now be considered standard. In 1969, only 14 percent of the Usage Panel accepted it. Twenty years later, however, when asked to judge the example *The Philharmonic will premiere works by two young Americans,* 51 percent accepted this usage, and ten years later, in our 1999 survey, 77 percent of the Panel accepted this same sentence.

But extensions of the verb to contexts other than the entertainment industry may strike readers as inappropriate. Only 10 percent of the Panelists in the 1988 survey accepted the sentence *Last fall the school premiered new degree programs in science and technology.* The 1999 survey showed some increase in acceptability, to 25 percent, for the same sentence. Since this is still a decided minority, it's probably best to limit the verb's use to the world of show business.

prepositions

A preposition is a word, such as *in* or *to,* or a group of words, such as *in regard to,* that is placed before a noun or pronoun and indicates a grammatical relation to a verb, adjective, or another noun or pronoun. Prepositional phrases function as adjectives and adverbs in a sentence.

preposition ending a sentence   It was John Dryden, the 17th-century poet and dramatist, who first promulgated the doctrine that a preposition may not be used at the end a sentence. Grammarians in the 18th century refined the doctrine, and the rule became a venerated maxim of schoolroom grammar. There has been some retreat from this position in recent years, however—what amounts to a recognition of the frequency with which prepositions end sentences in English.

Sentences ending with prepositions can be found in the works of most canonical writers since the Renaissance. In fact, English syntax not only allows but sometimes even requires final placement of the preposition, as in *We have much to be thankful for* or *That depends on what you believe in.* Efforts to rewrite such sentences to place the preposition elsewhere can have awkward if not comical results, as Winston Churchill demonstrated when he objected to the doctrine by saying *"This is the sort of English up with which I cannot put."*

Even sticklers for the traditional rule can have no grounds for criticizing sentences such as *I don't know where she will end up* or *It's the most curious book I've ever run across;* in these examples, *up* and *across* are adverbs, not prepositions. One sure sign that this is so is that these examples cannot be transformed into sentences with prepositional phrases. It is simply not grammatical English to say *I don't know up where she will end* and *It's the most curious book across which I have ever run.*

participles as prepositions   Some participles, such as *concerning* and *considering,* are used as prepositions. For more on this, see **participles.**

prescient

Prescient, meaning "having knowledge of actions or events before they occur; foresight" can be pronounced as a two-syllable or three-syllable word—(prĕsh′shənt) versus (prĕsh′shē-ənt), and the first *e* can be pronounced either long or short. In our 1999 survey, the two-syllable pronunciation (prĕsh′ənt) was the preference of half of the Usage Panel. Each of the four combinations, however, had its proponents, and each should be considered acceptable.

prescribe / proscribe

These words have similar sounds but in meaning they are near opposites. The general meaning of *proscribe* is "to forbid or prohibit":

> . . . it is chiefly in its indirect effects, through the canons of decorous living, that the institution [of the leisure class] has its influence on the prevalent sentiment with

respect to the sporting life. This indirect effect goes almost unequivocally in the
direction of furthering a survival of the predatory temperament and habits; and this
is true even with respect to those variants of the sporting life which the higher
leisure-class code of proprieties proscribes; as, e.g., prize-fighting, cock-fighting, and
other like vulgar expressions of the sporting temper (Thorstein Veblen, *The Theory
of the Leisure Class*)

Sometimes this prohibiting takes the form of a public denunciation or condemnation, since what is officially proscribed must be formally announced, and quite often
the proscribing is written into the law:

There might be a tomorrow, but they don't bank on it, because what they are doing
now was illegal yesterday, and might be proscribed once again (Paul Theroux, *Fresh
Air Fiend*)

When applied to people, *proscribe* usually means "condemn by law, outlaw":

The country gentleman, therefore, the officer by sea and land, the man of liberal
views and habits, attached to no profession, will be as completely excluded from the
government of his country as if he were legislatively proscribed (Edmund Burke,
Reflections on the Revolution in France)

" . . . he had quitted his haven of rest and repentance, and had come back to the
country where he was proscribed. Being here presently denounced, he had for a
time succeeded in evading the officers of Justice" (Charles Dickens, *Great Expectations*)

Prescribe, on the other hand, means "to set down as a rule or guide":

And there seems to be an absurdity of the same kind in ornamenting a house after a
quite different manner from that which custom and fashion have prescribed (Adam
Smith, *The Theory of Moral Sentiments*)

After World War I, the Germans, unreconciled to defeat, turned to a leader who
prescribed a restructuring of German society along dictatorial and racial lines (Ger-
hard L. Weinberg, "World War II," in Robert Cowley and Geoffrey Parker, eds., *The
Reader's Companion to Military History*)

By far the most frequent use of *prescribe* is in medical contexts, where it means "to
order the use of a medicine or treatment."

Thus it makes sense to keep these words distinct: medicine that the doctor proscribes is quite likely dangerous.

presently

The original use of *presently* to mean "at the present time, currently" goes back to the
late 14th century. This usage seems to have disappeared from the written record in
the 17th century, but it probably survived in speech, as it is widely found nowadays in
both speech and writing. Perhaps because this sense was not treated in dictionaries
until relatively recently, some language critics have argued that this usage is an error
and that *presently* should only be used in the sense of "in a short time, soon," as in the
shopkeeper's *I will be with you presently*. Apparently, many people are still persuaded

by this criticism. In four surveys from 1965 to 1999, only 47–50 percent of the Usage Panel accepted the "currently" usage in sentences like *Madeleine Albright is presently the secretary of state.*

present participle

A present participle is a participle expressing present action. It is formed by adding the suffix *–ing* to a verb. The present participle is used with the auxiliary verb *be* to form the progressive tenses, as in *The cattle are feeding on the lush grass,* and *The musicians have been waiting for an hour to audition.* The present participle also functions more generally as an adjective, as *feeding* in the noun phrase *the feeding cattle.*

See more at **participles** and **verbs, tenses of.**

present perfect tense

The present perfect tense is a verb tense that expresses action that has been completed. It is formed by combining the present tense of *have* with a past participle, as in *He has spoken.*

See more at **verbs, tenses of.**

present tense

The present tense is the verb tense that generally expresses action at the present time, as in *She teaches at the university* and *She is teaching right now.* When consisting of just the simple form of the main verb, as *teaches* above, the present tense is sometimes called the *simple present.* The compound form, consisting of the linking verb *be* and the present participle of the verb (*is teaching*) is called the *progressive present* or the *present continuous.* The simple present may also be used to express generic actions that are typical of the type denoted by the subject, as in *A wise man wastes little time.*

See more at **verbs, tenses of.**

presumptive / presumptuous

These two words are related in meaning, but the careful writer should be attuned to their differences. A person who is *presumptuous* presumes too much about someone or a situation and so is overly confident or forward. Thus a remark like *It was highly presumptuous of you to talk like that* is normally intended to accuse someone of being arrogant or inappropriately bold.

Sometimes the word *presumptive* is used in such sentences instead of *presumptuous.* In fact, in its oldest use (going back to the early 1600s) *presumptive* actually meant "arrogant, impertinent"; thus the two words overlapped in meaning for a time, but went separate ways around 1900.

Presumptive is now a more abstract word. It often describes something that provides a reasonable basis for belief or acceptance, as in this quotation from a college handbook: *"The unlawful presence of a controlled substance in an automobile is presumptive evidence of knowing possession of each passenger, unless the substance is concealed on the person of one of these occupants."* In another use, *presumptive* means "based on presumption or probability, presumed," as in *The incumbent governor is her party's presumptive nominee for governor in the upcoming election,* which suggests that it is not yet known whether the incumbent governor will receive (or has received) the nomination. Thus, *presumptive* refers to the basis for believing something, and not to forward behavior. Care should be taken to avoid the implication that *presumptuous* was really intended instead of *presumptive* in sentences like *Her presumptive taking over as committee chair has been the occasion of many critical remarks.*

If some doubt lingers, use *presumed* instead of *presumptive.*

primary verbs   See **auxiliary and primary verbs.**

principal / principle

It is easy to confuse these sound-alikes. *Principle* is only a noun and usually refers to a rule or standard: *moral principles. Principal* is both a noun and an adjective. As a noun, it has specialized meanings in law and finance, but in general usage it refers to a person who holds a high position or plays an important role: *a meeting among all the principals in the transaction.* As an adjective it has the sense of "chief" or "leading": *The coach's principal concern is the quarterback's health.*

principal parts   See **verbs, principal parts of.**

prioritize

Prioritize serves a useful function in providing a single word to mean "arrange according to priority," but like many other recent formations with *–ize,* it is tainted by association with corporate or bureaucratic jargon. The verb has been in use since the mid-1960s, but even in 1997 nearly half of the Usage Panel found it unacceptable in the sentence *Overwhelmed with work, the lawyer was forced to prioritize his caseload.*

See more at **–ize.**

pro–

There are two separate but related prefixes having the form *pro–*. The first comes from Latin *prō,* meaning both "before, in front of, forward" and "for, in support of." In English, this *pro–* usually means "favoring" or "supporting," as when it is prefixed to names of nationalities: *pro-American.* In this sense, the opposite of *pro–* would be *anti: proslavery/antislavery.* The meaning "forward" can be found in such words as *proceed,* from Latin *prō,* plus *cēdere,* "go."

The other *pro–* comes from Greek *pro,* meaning "before, in front." The word *prologue* comes from Greek *prologos,* from *pro–,* plus *logos,* meaning "speech." In English, *pro–* often means "before" or "earlier" and is often used in science terms: *prophase,* "the first phase of mitosis or meiosis."

process

In recent years there has been a tendency to pronounce the plural ending *–es* of *processes* as (-ēz), perhaps by analogy with certain words of Greek origin, such as *analysis* and *neurosis*. But *process* does not come from Greek, and there is no etymological justification for this pronunciation of its plural. However, because this pronunciation is not uncommon even in educated speech, it is generally considered an acceptable variant, although it still strikes some listeners as a bungled affectation. In our 1997 survey, 79 percent of the Usage Panel preferred the standard pronunciation (-ĭz) for the plural ending *–es,* and 15 percent preferred the pronunciation (-ēz).

While the pronunciation for *process* with a long *o,* (prō′sĕs′), is widely used in British and Canadian English, it is not very common in American English. Nevertheless, it is not stigmatized and should be viewed as standard.

progressive

The term *progressive* refers to verb forms that express an action or condition in progress. In English progressive verb forms employ a form of the verb *be* and a present participle of the main verb, as in *He is walking, She has been walking, They will be walking.* The progressive forms are found in various combination of the basic verb tenses.

See more at **present tense** and **verbs, tenses of.**

prone

The adjective *prone* is traditionally used in contrast to *supine. Prone* means "lying on one's front," and *supine* means "lying on one's back." This useful contrast has been muddied lately by the broader use of *prone* to mean simply "lying flat," as in *People on the beach lay prone, reading books or staring into the sky.* The Usage Panel is evenly divided on this matter. In our 1997 survey, 49 percent accepted the sentence quoted above, and in 1999, 48 percent accepted the following sentence, which strongly implies that prone can mean "lying on one's back": *The bodies were found prone in the beds, their faces covered with purple cloths.*

The Panel is far more disapproving of the more general use of *prone* referring to things other than humans to mean "on the ground, flat," as in *Many acres of trees were laid prone by the earthquake.* In our 1999 survey, 75 percent of the Panel rejected this sentence.

pronouns

A pronoun is a word that functions as a substitute for some noun phrase or part of a noun phrase. For example, in *The president thinks she will win the race,* the noun *she* is a pronoun that substitutes either for *the president* or for some other phrase in context (for instance, *she* may refer to a woman running for the Senate). In the sentence *This plastic water bottle is lighter than the glass one,* the pronoun *one* substitutes for *water bottle,* a part of the preceding noun phrase. The most common pronouns are the personal pronouns, but English also has demonstrative, indefinite, possessive, and reflexive pronouns.

pronouns, agreement of

A pronoun—a word that functions as a substitute for a noun, noun phrase, or clause functioning as a noun—must agree with its antecedent in person, number, and gender. Most people have heard this grammatical rule, or one much like it, at some time in their lives. An *antecedent,* of course, is a noun or pronoun referred to by a pronoun. Usually an antecedent comes before its pronoun (as in *Dave played his guitar this morning*) but sometimes the pronoun anticipates the antecedent (as in *Although he knew he would be late, Mr. Stanton did not rush to get ready*).

The problems involving agreement of person are less inherent to the pronouns themselves than created by shifts in point of view. Sometimes it is difficult to stick to the same person when using generic pronouns, such as *one* and *you.* For more on this problem, see **one.**

Problems in number agreement are often initiated by indefinite pronouns such as *anyone, everybody,* and *somebody.* These problems often involve the related issue of gender. Which pronoun is best used in a sentence such as *Everyone thinks (he is/she is/they are) entitled to a raise this year*? Using the plural pronoun in such constructions avoids the problem of gender bias but violates the rule of number agreement since indefinite pronouns like *everyone* are grammatically singular. Similar problems arise in sentences with singular antecedents of undetermined gender, such as *A good judge should never indulge (his/her/their) personal prejudices.* Perhaps the easiest solution here is to write in the plural: *Good judges should never indulge their personal prejudices.* For a more detailed discussion of these problems, see **he.**

See more at **any, anyone, each, every,** and **none.**

pronouns, personal

This entry treats personal pronouns only; usage issues involving interrogative, relative, and indefinite pronouns are addressed at entries for specific words (*that, who,* etc.).

A number of usage problems involving personal pronouns are questions of which case to use in a given situation. The cases of personal pronouns are listed in the following table as an aid in understanding the case problems discussed here.

Nominative Case	Singular	Plural
First Person	I	we
Second Person	you	you
Third Person	he, she, it	they

Objective Case	Singular	Plural
First Person	me	us
Second Person	you	you
Third Person	him, her, it	them

Possessive Case	Singular	Plural
First Person	my	our
Second Person	your	your
Third Person	his, hers, its	their

personal pronouns after *as* *Your mother is just as proud as me,* said the father to the child with good grades. But should he have said, *Your mother is just as proud as I?* As with similar constructions using *than,* a traditional rule states that the pronoun following *as . . . as . . .* constructions must be in the nominative case because *She is just as proud as I* is really a truncated version of the sentence *She is just as proud as I am.* Another way to view this situation is to say that the second *as* functions as a conjunction, not as a preposition, in these sentences. Whatever the merits of this logic, the *as me* construction is very common in speech and appears regularly in the writing of highly respected writers. Moreover, it can be argued that the second *as* is really a preposition in these constructions and so requires the objective case. There is the further objection that *as I* constructions are overly formal, and even pretentious. In short, both constructions are defensible, and both are subject to attack. The safe bet is to include the final verb to make it a clause: *She is just as proud as I am.*

personal pronouns after forms of *be* Traditional grammar requires the nominative form of the pronoun following the verb *be: It is I* [not *me*]; *That must be they* [not *them*], and so forth. Nearly everyone finds this rule difficult to follow. Even if everyone could follow it, in informal contexts the nominative pronoun often sounds pompous and even ridiculous, especially when the verb is contracted. Would anyone ever say *It's we?* But constructions like *It is me* have been condemned in the classroom and in writing handbooks for so long that there seems little likelihood that they will ever be entirely acceptable in formal writing.

The traditional rule creates additional problems when the pronoun following *be* also functions as the object of a verb or preposition in a relative clause, as in *It is not (them/they) that we have in mind when we talk about "crime in the streets" nowadays,* where the plural pronoun serves as both the predicate of *is* and the object of *have.* In our 1988 survey, 67 percent of the Usage Panel preferred the nominative *they* in this example, 33 percent preferred the objective *them,* and 10 percent accepted both versions. Perhaps the best strategy is to revise such sentences to avoid the problem entirely: *They are not the ones we have in mind, We have someone else in mind,* and so on.

personal pronouns after *but* Which is correct: *No one but I read the book* or *No one but me read the book*? If *but* is a conjunction in these sentences, the nominative form *I* is correct. If *but* is a preposition, the objective form *me* is correct. Although some grammarians have insisted that *but* is a conjunction in such cases, they have had to admit that the objective form *me* is appropriate when the *but* phrase occurs at the end of a sentence, as in *No one has read it but me.* And in fact there is a strong case for viewing *but* as a preposition in all of these constructions. For one thing, if *but* were truly a conjunction, the verb should agree in person and number with the noun or pronoun following *but,* and so the verb should always be plural when the noun or pronoun following *but* is plural. It would thus be correct to say *No one but the students have read it,* even though *no one* is normally treated as a singular: *No one . . . has read it.* What is more, a conjunction cannot be moved to the end of a clause, as a prepositional phrase can be, as in *No one has read it but the students.* By comparison, the conjunction *and* cannot be repositioned in this way. That is, it is not grammatical to say things like *John left and everyone else in the class.*

For these reasons it seems best to consider *but* as a preposition in these constructions and to use the objective forms of pronouns such as *me* and *them* in all positions: *No one but me has read it. No one has read it but me.*

personal pronouns after *except* Just like *but, except* in the sense of "with the exclusion of" or "other than" is generally viewed as a preposition, not a conjunction. Therefore, a personal pronoun that follows *except* should be in the objective case: *No one except me knew it. Every member of the original cast was signed except her.*

personal pronouns after *than* Grammarians have insisted since the 18th century that *than* should be regarded as a conjunction in all its uses. By this thinking, a sentence such as *Bill is taller than Tom* is really a truncated version of the sentence *Bill is taller than Tom is.* Accordingly, when a pronoun follows *than* in sentences like this, it should be in the nominative case since it is the subject of the verb that is "understood." Thus the rule requires *Bill is taller than he* [not *him*]. But when applied to sentences in which the pronoun following *than* is the object of an understood verb, the rule requires that the pronoun be in the objective case, as in *The news surprised Pat more than me,* since this sentence is considered a truncated version of *The news surprised Pat more than it surprised me.*

The traditional rule is logical and neat, and no harm can come from following it in formal writing, but it often goes unobserved, especially in speech. The historical record shows that *than* has been used as a preposition since the 1500s in sentences like *John is taller than me.* Recall that in these cases the pronoun is in the objective case where the rule would require the nominative. This construction appears in the writing of many canonical writers, among them Shakespeare, Johnson, Swift, Scott, and Faulkner. Today, it occurs most commonly in first-person narration and dialogue; it is relatively infrequent in formal expository and argumentative prose, where the tendency (or perhaps, copyediting tradition) is to follow *than* with a clause (as in *taller than he is*). Writers who would ignore the grammarian's rule should bear this in mind. Constructions like *taller than him* have a colloquial or informal flavor.

between you and I *"All debts are cleared between you and I,"* writes Antonio to Bassanio in Shakespeare's *The Merchant of Venice.* Did Shakespeare commit a blunder, writing *I* where the objective form *me* is required?

When pronouns joined by a conjunction occur as the object of a preposition such as *between, according to,* or *like,* many people use the nominative form where the traditional grammatical rule would require the objective. They say *between you and I* rather than *between you and me,* and so forth.

Shakespeare can hardly have violated a rule of formal English grammar, since he and his contemporaries studied Latin grammar, not English. In fact, the rule outlawing *between you and I* did not get written until the 1860s. It has since become part of standard schoolroom grammar. Writing *between you and I* is now widely regarded as a sign of ignorance, even though the phrase occurs quite often in speech, where it may have become a set phrase. Formal writing requires *between you and me.*

personal pronouns in compound subjects   When pronouns are joined with other nouns or pronouns by *and* or *or,* there is a widespread tendency in speech to use the objective form even when the phrase is the subject of the sentence: *Robert and her are not speaking to each other. Me and Kate are going to the store.* In formal writing, the nominative forms should be used. Note that all the pronouns except *I* normally precede the noun in these compound subjects: *She and John* [not *John and she*] *will be giving the talk.* When the form *I* is used, it is almost invariably the last element in the phrase: *Mr. McCarty and I have formed a partnership.*

me **for *I did*—the objective case as acceptable subject**   *Who cut down the cherry tree?* When responding to questions seeking out a responsible party, English speakers normally say *Me!* In such cases the traditional rule requires the nominative form of the pronoun (*I!*) as a truncated version of the clause *I did!* But the nominative in these cases sounds overly formal, if not pompous, and is best avoided.

us **for *we* in subjects**   In speech, when a pronoun is used as a subject together with a noun, people tend to use the objective form, as in *Us forwards were left without any defensive support.* In formal speech or writing the nominative *we* is preferable in such sentences. If it seems awkward, rewrite the sentence to avoid the difficulty.

pronouns, reflexive and intensive

The reflexive and intensive pronouns end in *–self* (singular) or *–selves* (plural):

> First person: *myself, ourselves*
> Second person: *yourself, yourselves*
> Third person: *himself, herself, itself, oneself, themselves*

A reflexive pronoun is a pronoun that refers to a noun phrase or another pronoun in the same clause, usually the subject of the clause, as in *The cat washed itself carefully* or *I took a picture of myself in my Halloween costume.* Certain forms of reflexive pronouns, such as *themself,* in which the singular form of the suffix *–self* does not agree with the plural meaning of the pronominal element to which it is attached (*them*), are considered nonstandard. Similarly, the reflexive pronoun *ourself* is usually considered incorrect when it refers to a plural *we*. But *ourself* also has a long tradition of use when *we* is being used instead of *I* by a singular speaker or author, as in an editorial or a royal proclamation. Shakespeare's kings, for example, often speak in this way. Here is Lear speaking to his daughters after he has divided his kingdom among them:

> Ourself, by monthly course,
> With reservation of an hundred knights,
> By you to be sustain'd, shall our abode
> Make with you by due turns (*King Lear*, 1.01.132–135)

Ourself has also been used at times to refer to "us" generally, that is, people in general:

> . . . it may be pardonable to imagine that a friend, a kind and apprehensive, though not the closest friend, is listening to our talk; and then, a native reserve being thawed by this genial consciousness, we may prate of the circumstances that lie around us, and even of ourself, but still keep the inmost Me behind its veil (Nathaniel Hawthorne, "The Custom House: Introductory to *The Scarlet Letter*")

This usage survives in contemporary discourse in psychology, where the individual self is the focus of attention even when the author is generalizing about all people:

> One of his [Robert Johnson's] main points is that falling in love is based on projection. We project onto the other person some part of ourself, an idealized image of the perfect love object that we carry around in our psyche (Andrew Weil, *Natural Health, Natural Medicine*)

Both *yourself* and *yourselves* are correct, however, depending on whether the pronominal element *your–* refers to one person or more than one person. Here are some examples of the correct use of other reflexive pronouns:

> She freed herself from a difficult situation.
> They allowed themselves another break from work.
> He is not himself today.
> Their new business can't possibly pay for itself.

When the *–self* pronouns are used for emphasis, they are called *intensive* or *emphatic* pronouns:

> We ourselves would never have agreed to such a thing.
> She couldn't come herself.
> Myself, I wouldn't worry about it.

Sometimes the intensive pronoun does not refer to the subject of the sentence but is used as an emphatic substitute for a personal pronoun. This practice is particularly common in compound phrases, as in *Mrs. Evans or yourself will have to pick them up at the airport.* Although these usages have been common in the writing of reputable authors for several centuries, they may not sit well with many readers today. In our 1994 survey, a large majority of the Usage Panel disapproved of the use of *–self* pronouns when they do not refer to the subject of the sentence. Some 73 percent rejected the sentence *He was an enthusiastic fisherman like myself,* while 67 percent objected to *The letters were written entirely by myself.* The Panel was even less tolerant of compound usages, with 88 percent finding this sentence unacceptable: *The boss asked John and myself to give a brief presentation.*

pronunciation spelling

A *pronunciation spelling* is a spelling that more closely reflects the pronunciation of a given word than the word's traditional spelling does. Over time the new spelling may become as acceptable as the original spelling, as is the case with the pronunciation spelling *bosun* for *boatswain.* Many writers use pronunciation spellings, as *wanna* for *want to* or *talkin'* for *talking,* to convey speech.

See more at **spelling pronunciation.**

proper nouns

A proper noun is a noun that is used as a name for a specific individual, event, or place. Most proper nouns are capitalized: *Manny Ramirez, the World Series, Fenway Park.* Only in some cases can proper nouns be modified: *This tournament is the World Series of badminton. That golfer from Dayton could be the next Anika Sorenstam.*

See also **common nouns.**

prophesy / prophecy / prophesize

A *prophet* is the same thing as a *prophesier,* that is, someone who *prophesies,* who predicts or reveals something by or as if by divine inspiration, as in *Themis prophesied that the son born of Thetis would be mightier than his father.* The prediction itself—in this case, that the son of Thetis would be mightier than his father—is the *prophecy.*

Though the noun *prophecy* and the verb *prophesy* differ in spelling by a single consonant, it is in their final vowel that they differ in pronunciation: (ē) for *prophecy* and (ī) for *prophesy.*

The noun and verb are sometimes jumbled into miscast forms such as the past tense *prophecied* and the plural noun *prophesies.* This can hardly be surprising, given that the spellings with *c* and *s* were variants of each other when the noun first appeared in English in the 13th century, and as *The Oxford English Dictionary* states, the modern differentiation in spelling of the noun and verb "was not established till after 1700 and has no etymological basis." Nonetheless, the differentiation in forms has long been standard and should be adhered to.

Partly owing to the longstanding confusion of noun and verb forms, there is a tendency to differentiate the verb by making it fit the pattern of verbs ending in –*ize,* such as *criticize, formalize,* and *proselytize,* which also have a long *i* sound, as *prophesize: The oracle prophesized that the son of Thetis would be mightier than his father.* But *prophesize* has not gained broad currency in edited prose and is generally considered an error.

See more at **–ize.**

proscribe   See **prescribe.**

prosody

This word, which is etymologically unrelated to the more common word *prose,* is normally pronounced (prŏs′ə-dē), with the first syllable rhyming with *cross.*

prostate / prostrate

Medical patients sometimes talk about their "prostrate" problems, but it is the *prostate* that they are usually complaining about. The prostate is a chestnut-shaped gland of the male reproductive system that surrounds the urethra at the base of the bladder. *Prostrate* is a verb meaning "to lie face down" or "to cause to lie flat," and an adjective referring to the prone (face-down) position.

See more at **prone.**

protagonist

***protagonist* in drama**   The word *protagonist* comes from the Greek word *prōtagōnistēs* which referred to the first, or leading, actor in a Greek drama. By definition, there could be only one *protagonist* in a play. Ancient Greek also had words for the second actor and third actor. These were borrowed into English as *deuteragonist* and *tritagonist,* respectively, but the two terms are generally used only in technical discussions of drama.

But as early as 1671 John Dryden used *protagonists* to mean simply "important actors" or "principal characters": *"Tis charg'd upon me that I make debauch'd persons . . . my protagonists, or the chief persons of the drama."* Some writers may still prefer to confine *protagonist* to its original singular sense, but it is useless by now to insist that the looser use is wrong, since it is so well established and since so many literary works have no single main character. The Usage Panel accepts the looser use. In our 2004 survey, 86 percent of the Panel approved of the sentence *Joyce's* Ulysses *has two protagonists: Leopold Bloom and Stephen Daedalus.* Similarly, 84 percent accepted *The novel, written from multiple points of view, has several protagonists.*

protagonist* or *proponent   Some people use *protagonist* to refer to a *proponent,* a usage that became common only in the 20th century and may have been influenced by a misunderstanding that the first syllable of the word is the prefix *pro–,* "favoring." Many readers will therefore find erroneous a sentence like *He was an early protagonist of nuclear power.* Certainly, most of the Usage Panel does. In 2004, 83 percent rejected this same sentence. Fortunately, words like *advocate* and *proponent* can also be used in these contexts.

protest

A *protest* has traditionally been staged in opposition to something, such as a government policy. But lately the word has been used more loosely, both as a noun and a verb, in a more general or neutral manner that is reflected in the words *demonstration* and *demonstrate*. A solid majority of the Usage Panel rejects this usage. In our 2004 survey, 68 percent rejected the noun in the sentence *Supporters of the Administration's Iraq policy organized pro-war protests in several cities.* Similarly, 64 percent rejected the verb in *A number of students gathered to protest in favor of the new rules.*

prove

The verb *prove* has two past participles: *proved* and *proven*. *Proved* is the older form, while *proven* is a variant. Middle English spellings of *prove* included *preven*, a form which died out in England but survived in Scotland, and the past participle *proven* probably arose by analogy with verbs like *weave, woven* and *cleave, cloven*. *Proven* was used originally in Scottish legal contexts, such as *The jury ruled that the charges were not proven*. In the 20th century *proven* has made inroads into the territory once dominated by *proved,* so that now the two forms compete on equal footing as participles. However, when used as an adjective before a noun, *proven* is now the more common word: *a proven talent.*

provided / providing

In the past some critics have maintained that *provided* is preferable to *providing* as a conjunction meaning "on condition that." The logic is that the clause that follows describes what must "be provided," i.e., what conditions must be met, for the clause that precedes it to hold true. *Provided* is indeed the more commonly used word in such constructions, but both forms have been in use for centuries, with and without the additional word *that: You will receive a bonus provided* [or *provided that* or *providing* or *providing that*] *you finish the work on time.* Each of these variants is acceptable.

prurient

The adjective *prurient* is one of those words that is used infrequently enough for people to be unsure of its exact meaning. Most people know it has to do with sexual desire but can't get more specific. In fact, the word is usually applied to thoughts or mental activity. In 2001, almost half of the newspaper citations for the word were for the collocation "prurient interest." This no doubt results from the use of this phrase in the legal definition of obscenity—obscene material must appeal to the prurient interest.

People often use the word more loosely as a sophisticated synonym for *lewd* or even *sexual,* and these uses may rub readers the wrong way. In our 2002 survey, only 29 percent of the Usage Panel accepted the collocation *prurient acts* in the sentence

We need to protect children from perverted persons who would coerce them into committing prurient acts. The word was more acceptable when applied to people, with 57 percent accepting the sentence *I simply got tired of listening to him and his prurient teenage friends talk about sex all the time.* Note, however, the high percentage of Panelists who rejected this usage.

The Panel overwhelmingly (76 percent) accepted the phrase *prurient interest* in *Her neighbor struck her as having a prurient interest in gossip.* Acceptance was even higher for an example in which the word is applied to publications; 80 percent accepted *the publication's reliance on sexist and prurient advertisements.*

It is best, therefore, to restrict this word's use to mental activity or publications or films that are meant to arouse sexual interest.

psychiatrist / psychologist / psychotherapist

Individuals who provide mental-health services are frequently confused with each other. A *psychiatrist* is a physician who has completed a specialized four-year residency that deals with the diagnosis and treatment of mental disorders in the office and in the hospital. Psychiatrists can prescribe drugs and administer other treatments such as biofeedback, depending on the extent of their training. A *psychologist* has an advanced academic degree (usually a master's or a doctorate) in psychology, a science that deals with behavior and the mind. Psychologists usually conduct psychotherapy (counseling) sessions and may also be trained in other diagnostic and therapeutic techniques, such as psychological testing or hypnosis. They cannot prescribe medications, order laboratory tests, or attend psychiatric patients in the hospital.

Psychotherapist is a general term that does not imply any particular credential or license. A psychotherapist (sometimes called simply *a therapist*) can be a psychiatrist, psychologist, social worker, or other licensed professional with specific training, but anyone who offers psychotherapy can use the term. Consequently, listing a psychotherapist's credentials is helpful if not necessary.

psychologist   See **psychiatrist.**

psychotherapist   See **psychiatrist.**

puma

In English, the ($\overline{oo}$) sound is often preceded by a glide, or a (y) sound. In some cases, as with (b), the presence of the (y) sound distinguishes two different words, as *beauty* (by$\overline{oo}$'tē) and *booty* (b$\overline{oo}$'tē). In other cases, as with (d) and (t), the difference represents a simple variation: some people say (dy$\overline{oo}$'tē) and (ty$\overline{oo}$n) for *duty* and *tune*; others say (d$\overline{oo}$'tē) and (t$\overline{oo}$n). The English word *puma* comes from a Spanish word spelled the same way, and in English it was traditionally pronounced (py$\overline{oo}$'mə); however, the (y) is an Anglicization. Although 90 percent of the Usage Panel in our

2002 survey found that pronunciation acceptable, 70 percent also found the (y)-less pronunciation, which is closer to the Spanish pronunciation, (po͞o′mə), to be acceptable as well.

pumpkin

The pronunciations (pŭmp′kĭn), (pŭm′kĭn), and (pŭng′kĭn) are all widespread and are all considered standard in American English. In the pronunciation (pŭm′kĭn), the (p) drops out so that the consonant cluster *mpk* becomes simplified. This also occurs in the words *assumption, bumpkin,* and *symptom.* In (pŭng′kĭn) the (p) has been lost and the (m) has assimilated to the (k), becoming (ng).

See more at **assimilation.**

punctuation

Guidelines for using punctuation marks are given at separate entries for various marks and conventions. See **apostrophe, brackets, colon, comma, dash, ellipsis points, exclamation point, hyphenation, italics, parentheses, period, question mark, quotation marks, semicolon,** and **slash.**

· Q ·

quadriceps   See **biceps.**

quark

"Three quarks for Muster Mark! / Sure he hasn't got much of a bark / And sure any he has it's all beside the mark." This passage from James Joyce's *Finnegans Wake,* part of a scurrilous thirteen-line poem directed against King Mark, the cuckolded husband in the Tristan legend, inspired physicist Murray Gell-Mann to propose the name *quark* for a type of subatomic particle. Gell-Mann wanted to pronounce the word with (ô) not (ä), as Joyce seemed to indicate by rhyming words in the vicinity such as *Mark.* But the pronunciation rhyming with *pork* is the more common one today. Gell-Mann allowed this, noting that it's possible to interpret *"Three quarks for Muster Mark"* as a cry of "Three quarts for Mister . . . " heard in the pub of Joyce's character H.C. Earwicker.

quarter

When referring to the time of day, the article *a* is optional in phrases such as (*a*) *quarter to* (or *of, before,* or *till*) *nine* and (*a*) *quarter after* (or *past*) *ten.*

quasi

The pronunciation (kwä′sē) is Classical Latin and the pronunciation (kwā′sī) is Anglicized Latin. Note that in both of these the *s* is pronounced like *s.* In American English, speakers are more likely to pronounce the *s* like *z,* which is now also considered standard.

quay

This word is an etymological cousin of the words *key* and *cay,* which both mean "a low offshore island or reef." *Quay* is traditionally pronounced like *key,* although the pronunciation (kā) is now also considered standard in American English.

queer

The word *queer* is a reclaimed epithet—a word that was formerly used solely as a slur but that has been semantically overturned by members of the maligned group, who use it as a term of defiant pride. For decades *queer* was used solely as a derogatory adjective for gays and lesbians, but in the 1980s the term began to be used by gay and lesbian activists as a term of self-identification. Eventually, it came to be used as an umbrella term that included gay men, lesbians, bisexuals, and transgendered people. Nevertheless, a sizable percentage of people to whom this term might apply still hold *queer* to be a hateful insult, and its use by heterosexuals is often considered offensive. Other reclaimed words are usually offensive to the in-group when used by outsiders, so caution must be taken concerning their use when one is not a member of the group.

question mark

direct questions   A question mark terminates a direct question.

> What are your editorial skills?   Who's there?

A sentence phrased as a question but intended as a request is often followed by a period instead of a question mark.

> Will the audience please turn off all cell phones now.
> Would you please follow me.

indirect questions   An indirect question should not end with a question mark.

> We asked them what time it was.
> How the cat had eaten the entire turkey was the main question on her mind.

interrogative words   Do not use question marks after single interrogative words within sentences.

> Your article should answer the questions *who, what, when, where, why,* and *how.*

to indicate uncertainty   A question mark indicates editorial uncertainty.

> Ferdinand Magellan (1480?–1521)

quick / quickly

The adjective *quick* is sometimes used as an adverb, as in the usually spoken phrase *Come quick.* In formal writing, however, the adverb *quickly* is the correct usage.

quixotic

This word, pronounced (kwĭk-sŏt′ĭk), derives from a common British pronunciation of *Quixote,* the name of the hero of Cervantes' novel, *Don Quixote.* In British English *Quixote* is often pronounced (kwĭk′sət). The more common pronunciation in the US is (kē-hō′tē), which is closer to the Spanish pronunciation.

quotation marks

direct discourse

1. Quotation marks enclose direct discourse or dialogue.

> "Ladies and gentlemen," said the store manager, "all shoes are on sale today."

> "Are we lost?" Lucky asked the tour guide.

> "Of course not," replied the guide as he frantically thumbed through a sheaf of maps.

2. It is not necessary to enclose thoughts or other unspoken discourse in quotation marks.

> Manager Ren replied helplessly, "What else can I say? Even if you beat me to death, I can't come up with any cash. . . . all of our savings have gone to the medical bills."

> Go bankrupt! Guhan said mentally. (Ha Jin, "Alive")

quoted material

1. Quotation marks set off quoted material run into the text.

> Emerson wrote, "In every work of genius we recognize our own rejected thoughts."

> Will Rogers said, "Things in our country run in spite of government. Not by aid of it."

> Arnold Toynbee wrote that "though not lovable," Caesar was "fascinating."

2. Quotation marks may be placed around a word or phrase to indicate irony or sarcasm.

> She was always talking about her "condition." Her "condition" was in no way apparent, and no one would have known a thing about it but for her persistence in making it the subject of conversation. (Kate Chopin, *The Awakening*)

See more at **so-called.**

titles of works   Quotation marks enclose the titles of series of books, of articles or chapters in publications, of essays, of short stories not separately published, of short poems, and of songs and short musical pieces.

> "The Horizon Concise History" series
> "Some Notes on Case Grammar in English"
> Chapter 9, "Four in Freedom"

> Lamb's "Dissertation on a Roast Pig"
> Gogol's "The Nose"
> Tennyson's "Crossing the Bar"
> "God Save the Queen"
> Elgar's "Land of Hope and Glory"

See more at **titles of works** under **italics.**

translations and definitions

1. The translation of a foreign word or phrase is often enclosed in quotation marks.

> Don't confuse *hombre,* "man," with *hambre,* "hunger."
> The expression *déjà vu* means "already seen."

No quotation marks are needed if the explanatory word is not presented as a translation but denotes the thing the foreign word refers to.

> *Leche* is the Spanish word for milk.   *Sopa de verduras* is vegetable soup.

2. Quotation marks usually enclose definitions.

> The word *oblique* means "having a slanting direction."
> A more traditional meaning of *bodacious* is "remarkable, prodigious."

single quotation marks   Single quotation marks enclose quotations within quotations.

> "And then," Dennis said, "Ken started laughing and crowed, 'I can't believe you fell for that excuse!'"

with other punctuation   Put commas and periods inside closing quotations marks; put colons and semicolons outside. Other punctuation, such as exclamation points and question marks, should be inside the closing quotation marks only if it is part of the matter being quoted.

> Alleging "tortious interference with advantageous business relationships," the company filed suit in July.

> Hammurabi's punishment code was an example of "an eye for an eye": it ruled that the punishment must fit the crime.

> The *Courant* said the movie was "deeply moving"; the *Day* called it "a maudlin waste of time."

> Suddenly a voice cried, "Help us!"

> I love Priscilla's poem "Drifting"!

> Have you read "The Chambered Nautilus"?

> Shyly he asked, "Is your name Violet?"

quote

People have been using the noun *quote* as a truncation of *quotation* for over one hundred years, and its use in less formal contexts is widespread today. Language critics have objected to this usage, however, as unduly journalistic or breezy. It may therefore be best to avoid it in more formal situations. The Usage Panel, at least, shows more tolerance for the word as the informality of the situation increases. In our 1999 survey, only 29 percent accepted the example *He began the chapter with a quote from the Bible* in formal situations, but 50 percent of the Panel said that *quote* was acceptable in informal speech and writing, leaving only 21 percent that disapproved of it outright. The acceptability rose to 36 percent, even in formal settings, when the source of the quotation was less serious: *He lightened up his talk by throwing in quotes from Marx Brothers movies.*

People sometimes use *quote* as a synonym for "dictum, saying," as in *His career is just one more validation of Andy Warhol's quote that "In the future, everybody will be famous for fifteen minutes."* In our 1988 survey, the Usage Panel had little liking for this usage, with 76 percent finding it unacceptable.

Qur'an   See **Koran.**

· R ·

rack / wrack

A *rack* is a frame for holding or displaying things, as a *hat rack,* or an implement of torture, consisting of a frame on which the body is stretched. The latter sense is the source of the figurative meaning "pain or torment." *Rack* can also function as a verb, meaning "to torture on a rack" and, more commonly, "to cause physical or mental suffering to," as in *For weeks after the accident he was racked with pain.* This sense of *rack* also appears in the compound *nerve-racking* (variant spelling *nerve-wracking*) and in the idiom *rack one's brains.*

Most dictionaries list two nouns spelled *wrack.* One means "destruction," as in the phrase *wrack and ruin,* and the other means "wreckage, especially of a ship cast ashore." This *wrack* also can be a verb meaning "to wreck, cause the ruin of." Each of these *wrack*s has *rack* as an acceptable spelling variant, so a business that is *racked* by stiff competition is either ruined or in a state of metaphorical torment—or both. The context should elucidate the meaning, but this does not always occur. For example, in this quotation from a London newspaper, *wrack* could mean "ruin," but it is more likely that the intended meaning was "torment": *"Violence continues to wrack Iraq, a crisis over a vast nuclear programme simmers in Iran and religious fanatics challenge Saudi Arabia's regime."*

radiation / conduction / convection

The physical processes that are described by the words *radiation, conduction,* and *convection* all involve the transportation of energy, typically heat energy. The difference between these processes is that each is associated with a particular type of medium.

Radiation involves the transportation of electromagnetic energy, such as light and radio waves. The light that warms us from the sun is a form of electromagnetic radiation that has traveled through 93 million miles of empty space. Household radiators (both steam and electric) transmit most of their heat by infrared radiation, and microwave ovens heat substances using microwaves.

Conduction involves the transportation of heat through gases, liquids, and especially solids. The atoms of which any given substance is made are constantly vibrating, and the energy of their vibration corresponds with the temperature in a given region of the substance. When a portion of the substance is heated, the atoms increase their rate of vibration in that region. This vibrating motion propagates to neighboring atoms—ones that are not vibrating as much—and thus propagates away from the source of the heat. When a metal spoon is placed in a cup of hot water, for example, the vibrational energy propagates up the length of the spoon to its handle outside the water; this is a case of conduction.

Convection is an additional mode of transporting heat available to fluids (i.e. liquids and gases). Heating a region of a fluid can cause it to begin to flow, for a number of reasons. Most commonly, the heated region becomes less dense, and tends to float upwards, causing currents that carry the warmer parts to colder ones, and turbulence that mixes the warmer regions with colder ones, transferring their heat to them by conduction. Also, a heated region of gas tends to expand, pushing away colder regions and setting up currents that mix the warm and cold regions, carrying the heat energy away from its source. Convection ovens, for example, augment the natural convection currents of air in an oven with fans, keeping heat evenly distributed in the oven.

See more at **fluid** and **heat.**

raise / rear

A traditional usage rule holds that people *raise* crops and farm animals but *rear* children. Nonetheless, people have been raising children in English since the 1740s, when this sense of *raise* is first recorded, and the usage has been standard for many generations, at least in American English.

The Usage Panel finds the use of *raise* acceptable both for children and for livestock, but makes a distinction regarding the verb *rear,* which it approves for children but has reservations about for animals. Thus in our 2002 survey, 95 percent of the Panel approved of raising children in the example *They moved to a small town, which they felt was a better place to raise kids,* and 93 percent approved of raising animals in *They bought a farm and began raising sheep.* Similarly, rearing children was approved by 83 percent in this example: *The brothers were reared in a musical family.* But a majority of the Panel does not like the use of *rear* with animals. Only 40 percent accepted the sentence *The settlers reared cattle in the Valley before it was flooded.*

The lesson is clear: standard usage allows writers to *raise* both children and livestock, but writers should probably *rear* children only.

See more at **rise.**

rarely ever / seldom ever / scarcely ever / hardly ever

The use of *ever* after adverbs such as *rarely* and *seldom* has often been criticized as redundant. Thus the sentence *She rarely ever watches television* expresses nothing that is not conveyed by *She rarely watches television.*

While these constructions occur frequently in speech today, in print they are not used at similar rates. For some reason, both historically and in contemporary published prose, *rarely ever* and *seldom ever* are not very common, perhaps because *rarely* and *seldom* are more immediately associated with time than *scarcely* and other minimizing adverbs are, and so the overlap with *ever* is more obvious. In any case, *scarcely ever* has a long and distinguished track record of use by admired writers, and appears more frequently in contemporary prose:

As Bacon attained to degrees of knowledge scarcely ever reached by any other man, the directions which he gives for study have certainly a just claim to our regard (Samuel Johnson, *The Rambler,* No. 85)

They were scarcely ever without some friends staying with them in the house, and they kept more company of every kind than any other family in the neighbourhood (Jane Austen, *Sense and Sensibility*)

The tradesman scarcely ever gives an ideal worth to his work, but is ridden by the routine of his craft, and the soul is subject to dollars (Ralph Waldo Emerson, "Nature")

Several of Paul's teachers had a theory that his imagination had been perverted by garish fiction; but the truth was, he scarcely ever read at all (Willa Cather, *Youth and the Bright Medusa*)

The cold air of the fall morning had blown in through the rusted seams of the sort of vehicle that nobody in her family ever rode in, that scarcely ever appeared on the streets where she lived (Alice Munro, "Runaway," *The New Yorker*)

Similarly, the construction *hardly ever* also has a long history of use by distinguished writers, right up to today:

The quantity of metal contained in the coins, I believe of all nations, has, accordingly, been almost continually diminishing, and hardly ever augmenting (Adam Smith, *The Wealth of Nations*)

This baby was one of twins; and I may remark here that I hardly ever, in all my experience of the family, saw both the twins detached from Mrs. Micawber at the same time (Charles Dickens, *David Copperfield*)

From the looming roof of the great library, into which he hardly ever had time to enter, his gaze travelled on to the varied spires, halls, gables, streets, chapels, gardens, quadrangles, which composed the ensemble of this unrivalled panorama (Thomas Hardy, *Jude the Obscure*)

Since the fanciful vision of the future that had flitted through her imagination at their first meeting she had hardly ever thought of his marrying her (Edith Wharton, *Summer*)

They had a Swedish girl named Anna to do the housework and Mother and Daddy were hardly ever home when she came back from school (John Dos Passos, *The Big Money*)

When he was dead I realized that I had hardly ever spoken to him (James Baldwin, "Notes of a Native Son," *Harper's Magazine*)

Even though I've hardly ever been here in my life, and not at all since I was twelve years old, I feel that I'm home (Salman Rushdie, "A Dream of Glorious Return," *The New Yorker*)

Thus *scarcely ever* and *hardly ever,* though technically redundant, would appear to be valued for their emphatic expressiveness, while *rarely ever* and *seldom ever* have not won such favor. They are therefore best avoided.

See more at **hardly** and **scarcely.**

rather

would rather / should rather In expressions of preference *rather* is commonly preceded by *would: We would rather go to the lake than stay in town for the weekend.* In formal style, *should* is sometimes used instead of *would,* though this resonates of the upper class in American English and might appear snobbish: *I should rather see my daughter attend a private school.* In some cases, this *should* could be confused with the *should* expressing obligation. Thus the sentence *Susan should rather see her daughter attend a school closer to home* might be a judgment on the part of the speaker on what Susan should do instead of a factual statement of Susan's preference.

had rather Sometimes *had* appears with *rather* indicating preference, though this use of *had* has become less common when *had* is spelled out or fully pronounced: *I had rather work with Williams than work for him.* Language critics once condemned this use of *had* as a mistake. In truth the mistake was their own. They thought that people were incorrectly expanding the contraction as *had rather* instead of *would rather* in sentences like *I'd rather stay.* But this *had* is actually a survival of the subjunctive form *had* that also appears in constructions like *had better* and *had best,* as in *We had better leave now.* This use of *had* goes back to Middle English and is perfectly acceptable, though *had rather* has a decidedly highbrow feel. In American English, the similarly time-honored construction *would rather* has largely displaced *had rather* to indicate preference: *She would rather finish her book than go out.*

rather a Like *quite a,* the modifying construction *rather a* functions as an intensifier: *That was quite a party! Our date was rather a disaster.* When used in this way —by itself before an unmodified noun— *rather a* is more typical of British English than American English. When the noun is preceded by an adjective, however, both *rather a* and *a rather* are found with some frequency in American English, though the latter is more common: *It was rather a boring party. It was a rather boring party.* Note that, when *a rather* is used in this construction, *rather* qualifies only the adjective, whereas with *rather a* it qualifies either the adjective or the entire noun phrase. Thus *a rather long ordeal* can mean only "an ordeal that is rather long," whereas *rather a long ordeal* can also mean "a long process that is something of an ordeal." *Rather a* should be the only choice when the adjective itself does not permit modification. Thus it is preferable to say *The horse was rather a long shot* (where *long shot* is a compound noun), but not *The horse was a rather long shot.*

See more at **had better, rather than,** and **should.**

rather than

The phrase *rather than* consists of an adverb and a conjunction and often means "and not," as in *I decided to skip lunch rather than eat in the cafeteria again.* It is grammatically similar to *sooner than* in that it can be used with a "bare" infinitive—an infinitive minus *to: I would stay here and eat flies sooner than go with them. Rather than* is also used with inflected verb forms:

Over the lip of the little dell, on the side away from the hill, they felt, rather than saw, a shadow rise, one shadow or more than one (J.R.R. Tolkien, *The Fellowship of the Ring*)

Now we are once more enacting the changeless scene, curtain rising on two speechless characters in a furnished apartment, I in a straightback chair, Oskar in the velour armchair that smothered rather than supported him, his flesh gray, the big gray face, unfocused, sagging (Bernard Malamud, "The German Refugee," *Saturday Evening Post*)

Rather than is also used with nouns as a compound preposition meaning "instead of": *I bought a mountain bike rather than a ten-speed.* Some people object to this use, however, insisting that *than* should be used only as a conjunction. They therefore object to constructions in which *rather than* is followed by a gerund, as in *I kept my old car rather than buying a new one.*

But its versatility makes *rather than* a remarkably useful construction, and this is readily apparent from its varied use in the writing of many fine contemporary authors. The phrase can connect any of a wide variety of grammatical elements from nouns to prepositional phrases to adjectives and adverbs, and even full clauses, as this brief sampler will show:

The harbor is still crammed with sails, but now they belong to pleasure boats rather than ships of the line (Geoffrey Wheatcroft, "Oh to Be in Antigua," *Atlantic Monthly*)

Like human health research, animal health research concentrates on sickness and disease rather than on how or why certain individuals remain healthy in their natural surroundings (Cindy Engel, *Wild Health*)

Note the variable positioning of *rather than* with verbs, even at the beginning of a sentence, where ordinarily a conjunction like *or* or *and* followed immediately by a verb would be unacceptable:

Camp taste is a kind of love, love for human nature. It relishes, rather than judges, the little triumphs and awkward intensities of character (Susan Sontag, "Notes on Camp," *Partisan Review*)

Rather than wait, Edward nodded to her abruptly and walked out of the office. He desperately needed to think (Jane Stevenson, *London Bridges*)

Having never been one for timidity, in philosophy or in life, I decided, rather than return defeated to my sticky trailer, to explore a clear, deep channel closer to the river I had traveled along the previous day (Val Plumwood, "Being Prey," *Utne Reader*)

Here are some examples of *rather than* used with gerunds, also with variable positioning:

Parasites are part of the reason that we and most species have sex, rather than merely cloning ourselves in twain: we must stir our genes together in ever-changing combinations to develop resistance to parasites (Natalie Angier, *The Beauty of the Beastly*)

Rather than attempting to explain how he became the artist he was, he preferred to leave the question open to speculation (Belinda Rathbone, *Walker Evans*)

Thus, rather than following any consistent set of principles, Bush's record on race reflected a struggle between the forces of enlightenment and expediency (Jane Meyer and Jill Abramson, *Strange Justice*)

Clearly, it is grammatically defensible—one could say, stylistically commendable—to follow *rather than* with a gerund. Still, writers who want to reserve *than* for use as a conjunction can substitute *instead of* for *rather than* with gerunds.

ration

The older pronunciation of *ration* rhymes with *nation.* The pronunciation that rhymes with *fashion* gained ground in the 20th century and is now predominant in both American and British English.

rationale / rationalization

The word *rationale* is a simple noun, referring to the fundamental reasons or the basis for something: *The rationale behind the college's introductory writing course is that every student should be able to write well-constructed essays as soon as possible.* The word *rationalization* is also a noun, but it is derived from the verb *rationalize,* which means "to make rational, to interpret rationally," and "to devise self-serving reasons to justify something." Each sense of the verb thus describes a mental process, and *rationalization* commonly refers to the result of one of these processes: *Their rationalization of farm production was unsuccessful.* This meaning is not strictly synonymous with *rationale,* especially since *rationalization* commonly suggests a post-hoc, self-serving process. *A rationale for their behavior* is an actual rational basis for their actions, while *a rationalization of their behavior* suggests an attempt to defend unreasonable actions.

re–

The primary meaning of the prefix *re–,* which comes from Latin, is "again." *Re–* combines chiefly with verbs, as in these examples: *rearrange, rebuild, recall, remake, rerun, rewrite.* The prefix has been used with this meaning extensively in English since the 1600s. Sometimes it is necessary to use a hyphen with *re–* to distinguish between pairs such as *recollect* (rĕk′ə-lĕkt′) and *re-collect* (rē′kə-lĕkt′) or *recreation* (rĕk′rē-ā′shən) and *re-creation* (rē′krē-ā′shən). A hyphen may also be used when *re–* precedes a word beginning with *e,* as in *re-enact* and *re-enter.*

rear   See **raise.**

reason is because

A traditional rule holds that the construction *the reason is because* is redundant, and should be avoided in favor of *the reason is that.* The usage is well established, however, and can be justified by analogy to sentences in which *so that* follows *purpose,* as in *His* purpose *in calling her was* so that *she would be forewarned of the change in schedule.* A similar construction employs the conjunction *when* after the noun *time,* as in *The last* time *I saw her was* when *she was leaving for college.* While these constructions should be considered acceptable, they are often considered inelegant and are generally edited out of published prose.

reason why

A traditional rule states that *why* is redundant in the expression *reason why,* as in *The reason why he accepted the nomination is not clear.* It is true that *why* could be eliminated from such examples with no loss to the sense, and that *that* could be used instead of *why,* but *reason why* has been used by reputable English writers since the Renaissance, and is still in frequent use today, as this sampler will show:

> Tell me thy reason why thou wilt marry (Shakespeare, *All's Well That Ends Well* 1.03.27)

> This impossibility of making so complete and entire a separation of all the different branches of labour employed in agriculture is perhaps the reason why the improvement of the productive powers of labour in this art does not always keep pace with their improvement in manufactures (Adam Smith, *The Wealth of Nations*)

> Doubtless one leading reason why the world declines honoring us whalemen, is this: they think that, at best, our vocation amounts to a butchering sort of business . . . (Herman Melville, *Moby Dick*)

> I was within a hair's breadth of the last opportunity for pronouncement, and I found with humiliation that probably I would have nothing to say. This is the reason why I affirm that Kurtz was a remarkable man. He had something to say. He said it (Joseph Conrad, *Heart of Darkness*)

> When Newland Archer opened the door at the back of the club box the curtain had just gone up on the garden scene. There was no reason why the young man should not have come earlier, for he had dined at seven, alone with his mother and sister, and had lingered afterward over a cigar in the Gothic library . . . (Edith Wharton, *The Age of Innocence*)

> A big reason why the tech-stock sector rose so high, so fast, is that it was able to draw in so many new investors. By last summer nearly every mutual fund manager in the land had jumped into these shares (Andrew E. Serwer, "Making Sense of the Technology Stock Shakeout," *Fortune*)

> We may daily consume other animals by the billions, but we ourselves cannot be food for worms and certainly not meat for crocodiles. This is one reason why we now treat so inhumanely the animals we make our food, for we cannot imagine ourselves similarly positioned as food (Val Plumwood, "Being Prey," *Utne Reader*)

recoup / recuperate

Recoup is normally a transitive verb and takes an object. It means "to receive an equivalent for, regain" or, less commonly, "to pay back, reimburse." Thus investors usually try to recoup their losses when the stock market improves after a tumble, and debtors are obligated to recoup their creditors for their loans. The sense of recovery inherent in *recoup* has been extended to some other contexts, as when a patient recoups her health after an illness. Sometimes *recoup* is used without an object as a synonym for *recuperate*, as in *He spent six months recouping from the accident.* This usage is listed in a few dictionaries but is not widely accepted as standard.

Another confusion that occasionally arises is the misspelling of *recuperate* as *recouperate*, under the influence of *recoup;* this is not an acceptable variant.

red

Experts disagree as to why Native Americans came to be known as *red men.* One theory holds that the term was first used by early European explorers in describing the mysterious Beothuk people of Newfoundland, who were reported to paint their bodies liberally with red ocher. According to this view, the now-vanished *red men* gave their nickname to the rest of the peoples native to North America. While there is no doubt that the Beothuks did paint their bodies red, it is more likely that the adjective *red* was applied to Native Americans as a whole in the same manner in which other color labels were given to non-European peoples, in recognition of the perceived difference between the color of their skin and the paler skin of most Europeans.

As a racial label, *red* has never gained the wide acceptance of *black* and *white.* While *red* has often been used with positive connotations, particularly in the expressions *red man* and *Red Indian,* these are generally dismissed today as the romantic stereotypes of a former era when Indians were viewed as the model of the "noble savage." The term *redskin* evokes an even more objectionable stereotype—the crafty foe of pioneers and the western cavalry now further reduced to caricature status as the mascot of American sports teams. It is true that *red* has frequently been appropriated by contemporary Native Americans as an ironic or defiant term of pride, as in the Red Power movement or the title of Lakota author Vine Deloria, Jr.'s book *God is Red.* However, reference to American Indians by their purported skin color is liable to cause offense when coming from outsiders.

redundancy

A certain amount of redundancy is built in to the English language, and no one would consider getting rid of it. Take grammatical number, for instance. Sentences such as *He drives to work* and *We are happy* contain redundant verb forms. The *-s* of *drives* indicates singularity of the subject, but we already know the subject is singular from the singular pronoun *he.* Similarly, *are* indicates a plural subject, which is already evident from the plural pronoun *we.* Number is also indicated redundantly in phrases like *this book* and *those boxes,* where the demonstrative adjective shows number and the noun does as well.

But there are redundant ways of saying things that can make writing seem careless or even foolish. Many of these are common expressions that go unnoticed in casual conversation but that stick out like red flags in writing. Why say *at this point in time* instead of *now*, or *because of the fact that* when *because* will do? Something that is *large in size* is really just *large*. The trouble lies less in the expressions themselves than in their accumulated effect. Anyone can be forgiven for an occasional redundancy, since many of these are common collocations in speech, but writing that is larded with redundancies is likely to draw unwanted laughs rather than admiration.

The usages that critics have condemned as redundancies fall into several classes. Some expressions, such as *old adage*, have become fixed expressions and seem harmless enough. Others, such as *consensus of opinion, close proximity, hollow tube*, and *refer back*, can be pointlessly redundant in some contexts yet defensible in others. In these cases the use of what is regarded as an unnecessary modifier or qualifier can sometimes be justified on the grounds that it makes a real distinction in meaning. Thus a *hollow tube* can be distinguished from one that has been blocked up with deposits, and a *consensus of opinion* can be distinguished from a *consensus of judgments* or a *consensus of practice*. In other cases the use of the qualifier is harder to defend. There is no way to *revert* without *reverting back* and no *consensus* that is not *general*.

Many redundancies are discussed at specific entries in this book.

See more at **both, but, close proximity, consensus, consider as, cross section, else, equally as, free gift, hence, inside of, old adage, rarely ever, reason is because, reason why, refer back**, and **VAT tax.**

refer back

Many people consider *refer back* to be redundant, since the prefix *re–* often means "back," and the original Latin meaning of *refer* was "to carry back," and indeed, if something *refers* to something else, it points, in an abstract sense, *back* to it.

Most of the Usage Panel gives credence to this line of thinking. In our 1995 survey, 65 percent considered the phrase *refer back* redundant or inelegant. However, there may be situations in which the phrase is appropriate and justifiable: one can refer *back* to something that has already been mentioned, in contrast with *referring ahead* to something that has not yet been mentioned. Used in this manner, *refer back* should be acceptable, especially when *refer* is transitive: *We will assume this position in the coming chapters and refer the reader back to the previous chapter for arguments supporting it.*

reflection / refraction

In everyday writing, the word *refraction* occurs much less frequently than *reflection: They reflected on their achievements. This new theory was a reflection of her intelligence.* In nature, however, the process of refraction occurs just as often as reflection.

Refraction and reflection describe two different options that the front of a light wave, sound wave, or any wave can take when it encounters a boundary between two media. The media can be two dissimilar substances, such as glass and air, or they can be different regions that are in different states within a single substance, such as regions of air that are at different temperatures. *Reflection* occurs when a wavefront hits the boundary and returns to its original medium, in effect bouncing off the boundary region. *Refraction* occurs when a wavefront passes from one medium into the other, deviating from a straight-line path. For example, light passing through a prism is bent when it enters the prism and again when it leaves the prism; it is thus refracted. Light striking a mirror bounces away from the silver backing and is reflected.

The boundary between the media does not have to be abrupt for reflection or refraction to occur. On a hot day, the air directly over the surface of an asphalt road is at a higher temperature than the air further from the surface, creating enough difference in the density of the air that light passing through is visibly distorted, creating a shimmering effect. A similar effect is found in the upper atmosphere of the earth at night. The twinkling of stars is due to temperature fluctuations in the upper atmosphere and is also an example of refraction.

reflexive pronouns   See **pronouns, reflexive and intensive.**

refute

In most dictionaries, the verb *refute* has two meanings. The first is "to prove to be false or erroneous," as in *Charges of institutional bias against women were refuted by an analysis of the employment data.* In this example, it is clear that an argument was mustered to demonstrate the falsity of the charges. This usage is well established as standard.

Refute is also used to mean "to deny the accuracy of," and in this use there is no mention or implication of mustering evidence or detailed reasoning. Rather, the refutation exists as a simple statement or claim. This second use has been criticized as incorrect or inappropriate since the early 20th century, despite being common. A majority of the Usage Panel accepts the use as a synonym of *deny,* but not by a wide margin. In our 2002 survey, 62 percent accepted the example *In the press conference, the senator categorically refuted the charges of malfeasance but declined to go into details.* This suggests that many readers are uncomfortable with this usage and would prefer to see *deny* in these contexts.

Refute is sometimes used to mean "to deny the validity of, repudiate," as in *Observers are expecting the appeals court to refute the Microsoft breakup.* The Panel has scant affection for this usage. Some 89 percent rejected the example just quoted in the 2002 survey.

regard / regarding   See **as regards.**

regretful / regrettable

These words both imply that regret is involved in what is being described but they have different spheres of application. *Regretful* properly describes the emotional state of a person who is full of regret or feels sorrow:

> She peeped from the window into the garden, and felt herself more regretful at leav-
> ing this spot of black earth, vitiated with such an age-long growth of weeds, than
> joyful at the idea of again scenting her pine-forests and fresh clover-fields
> (Nathaniel Hawthorne, *The House of Seven Gables*)

Regretful can also be applied to thoughts or actions produced by this state of mind:

> "I'd like to have—seen him." It was just audible, this little regretful murmur (Booth
> Tarkington, *The Magnificent Ambersons*)

The word *regrettable* describes states of affairs and actions that are worthy of or
will likely cause regret:

> I have argued that the discontinuous gap between humans and 'apes' that we erect
> in our minds is regrettable (Richard Dawkins, *The Devil's Chaplain*)

> Dreading lest what he had heard should lead him to say something regrettable to
> her he spoke little (Thomas Hardy, *Jude the Obscure*)

The impersonal construction *it is regrettable* is often used to introduce a clause describing a situation that warrants regret:

> Both men are intellectually agile and quick witted, so it is regrettable that they did
> not sign up for a spontaneous debate (Alessandra Stanley, "Senators' Husbands in
> Velvet Gloves," *New York Times*)

Regrettable also has the virtue of being able to convey irony or implied criticism:

> . . . when she returned with her little orphaned niece, whose parents had been
> popular in spite of their regrettable taste for travel, people thought it a pity that the
> pretty child should be in such hands (Edith Wharton, *The Age of Innocence*)

regular

In grammar, the term *regular* means "conforming to the usual pattern of inflection,
derivation, or word formation in a language." For example, a plural noun that ends in
-*s* is a regular plural, and a past tense that ends in –*ed* is a regular past tense.

See more at **plural nouns** and **verbs, principal parts of.**

relative clauses

A relative clause is a dependent clause that modifies a noun. Relative clauses are often
introduced by a relative pronoun. In *The books, which I placed on the table, should be
packed up,* the phrase *which I placed on the table* is a relative clause modifying *the
books,* and is introduced by the relative pronoun *which.* Relative clauses may also be
introduced by the word *that,* or by nothing at all. In *Everything (that) you can do, I
can do better,* the phrase *(that) you can do* is a relative clause modifying *everything.*

See more at **that** and **restrictive and nonrestrictive clauses.**

relative pronouns

A relative pronoun is a pronoun that introduces a relative clause and refers to an antecedent. *Who, whom, whose, which,* and *that* are traditionally considered relative pronouns. For example, in *This proposal, which nearly everyone agreed on, was voted through last week,* the word *which* is a relative pronoun referring to the antecedent *this proposal,* and introducing the relative clause *which nearly everyone agreed on.*

See more at **relative clauses, restrictive and nonrestrictive clauses, that, which,** and **who.**

relativism / relativist

The term *relativism* refers to a related set of philosophical ideas, all of which share the core idea that there is no absolute, objective reference position from which human actions can be understood or valued. Moral relativism, for example, holds that there is no moral standard beyond the beliefs and moral evaluations of individuals or societies; thus if one society rejects a certain behavior as immoral, while another accepts it, there is no standard, in this view, by which we might judge which society is making a correct assessment. Such a position is a *relativist* position, and a person who holds such a position is called a *relativist.*

Though the term *relativity* is occasionally used to denote relativism, *relativism* is the preferred term in philosophical and ethical discourse. Einstein's theories of Special and General Relativity, aside from superficial similarities, have nothing to do with philosophical relativism (Einstein was certainly not a moral relativist), although it has been claimed that relativist thought in the 20th century was inspired by these theories.

See more at **relativity.**

relativity

Albert Einstein's theories of relativity are among the greatest achievements of 20th-century science. By virtue of this success, and of Einstein's fame, the word *relativity* is now commonly used as if Einstein were the first to make use of the concept of relative motion.

In fact, the idea of relativity is very old. Galileo effectively invoked relativity to counter the prevailing arguments that the earth did not rotate, and Isaac Newton explicitly declared a very pure kind of relativity to follow from his laws of motion. In Newton's theory, there is no absolute frame of reference, and speed is a property not of objects, but of their relation to the observer's frame of reference.

Rather than heralding an age of relativism, Einstein's theories of relativity are arguably *less* relative than Newton's. Einstein's theories assume that the speed of light is the same for any observer. This means that light is exceptional: its speed is not relative to any reference frame, but is absolute. Einstein's challenge was to reconcile this assumption with the simplicity of Newton's laws. He succeeded with his *Special*

Theory of Relativity (also called *Special Relativity*), which interestingly entails that not only speed, but also size, mass, and even the passing of time are relative to the observer. These properties, absent in Newton's more "relative" theory, capture the imagination, but also lead to the misunderstanding that Einstein invented the concept of relativity.

Einstein's *General Theory of Relativity* (also called *General Relativity*) extends the Special Theory to include cases in which bodies are accelerating due to forces such as gravity. It does not introduce any new notions of relativity itself.

Note that the names of each of Einstein's theories may be capitalized in scientific contexts.

See more at **relativism.**

relegate / delegate

Both of these terms involve assigning someone or something to a particular role or condition, and this similarity, along with their similar sound, leads to occasional confusion. *Relegate* has a physical sense, in which it means "to assign something to a position, especially an obscure or inferior position." It often seems a synonym of *banish:*

> Rice, the NFL's career leader in touchdowns, receptions and yards receiving, was a non-factor during much of the game and at times was relegated to the sidelines . . . (Dennis Georgatos, "Rice Refutes Selfish Portrayal," *Augusta Chronicle*)

Relegate also refers to categorization, where it refers to the classifying of something in a particular manner. Often the category in question is an inferior one:

> Within a few years, these human beings will be relegated to an abstract category called "the underclass" (James MacPherson, "Ivy Day in the Empty Room," *Iowa Review*)

In addition, *relegate* means to assign something, such as a responsibility, to someone for a decision or action, and here is where the word comes close to being a synonym of *delegate*:

> Nixon fought the impeachment, arguing that the Senate should not be allowed to relegate the matter to a committee (Anne E. Kornblut, "Rehnquist Has Strict View on Impeachment," *Boston Globe*)

Delegate does not have a physical sense, although the word often entails human movement. *Delegate* refers to the entrusting of a task or responsibility to another, or to the authorizing of a person to act as one's representative:

> Eisenhower learned a great deal from working under the temperamental and egocentric MacArthur, who delegated many sensitive political tasks to his discreet, persuasive, and thoroughly agreeable aide (David L. Stebenne, "Dwight D. Eisenhower," *The Reader's Companion to the American Presidency*)

> . . . waiting at the station was a teamster named Thomas J. Shaugnessey, who had been delegated by County Commissioner Hoyt to transport the two young victims (Stephen O'Connor, *Orphan Trains*)

Relegate thus commonly has the negative connotation of dismissal or even condemnation, while *delegate* is a more neutral or somewhat positive term, suggesting commitment and responsibility.

remonstrate

Traditionally this word has been pronounced (rĭ-mŏn′strāt′), with the main stress on the second syllable. Since the 1960s, the pronunciation (rĕm′ən-strāt′), with the main stress on the first syllable, has become increasingly common. This shift in stress is normal, as it has occurred in many other verbs ending in *–ate*, such as *adumbrate, contemplate, demonstrate, enervate,* and *illustrate.* In some of these words the shift is complete, and in others it is still in progress. One reason for the shift, no doubt, is the influence of the derived nouns ending in *–tion,* such as *contemplation* and *demonstration,* which are stressed on the first and third syllables. *Remonstrate* has perhaps lagged behind other verbs like it because *remonstration* is not very common.

renaissance / Renaissance

This 19th-century borrowing from French, which literally means "rebirth," is usually stressed on the first and third syllables in American English. In British English the word is usually stressed on the second syllable, which is pronounced with a long *a* sound, as (rə-nā′səns). The American English pronunciation is an approximation of the French pronunciation, while the British English pronunciation reflects the tendency in Germanic languages (of which English is one) to put the main stress on the root part of a word. Note that the word *renascence,* which also means "rebirth" or "revival," but which comes from Latin, is stressed on the second syllable.

renege

In American English *renege* is generally pronounced (rĭ-nĭg′) or (rĭ-nĕg′), with a short *i* or short *e* sound in the second syllable. The most common pronunciation in British English is (rĭ-nēg′), with a long *e* in the second syllable.

rennin / renin

Rennin is an enzyme that catalyzes the coagulation of milk and is found in the stomach of calves. In traditional farming, cheese was made by curdling milk with *rennet,* a dried extract made out of a calf's stomach lining. The word *rennet* is linked to an Old English and Old German verb meaning "to flow" or "to run." Investigators in the late 1800s discovered that rennet caused milk to curdle because of biochemical actions of the enzyme *rennin,* so named because it is a combination of *rennet* and the suffix *–in,* which designates a neutral chemical compound and commonly appears in the names of other enzymes.

While the stomach is the site of rennin production, the kidneys are the source for *renin*. *Renin*, in fact, comes from the Latin *renes*, "kidneys," to which was added the *–in* suffix. Renin is a protein-digesting enzyme that is released by the kidneys. When a major physiologic upset such as dehydration or hemorrhage causes a decrease in blood pressure, *renin* causes a series of chemical reactions that result in the release of a protein called *angiotensin II*, which causes the constriction of blood vessels and the subsequent restoration of normal blood pressure.

renown / renowned

Etymologically speaking, *renown* refers to a state of having made a name for oneself. It comes from an Anglo-Norman verb *renomer*, "to make famous," and derives ultimately from the Latin noun *nomen*, "name." Because its meaning ("the quality of being widely honored and acclaimed") implies widespread familiarity or knowledge of the person or achievement in question, many people mistakenly add a *k* to the spelling of *renown*, as if it were derived from *known*.

Renown is properly pronounced (rǐ-noun'), rhyming with *noun*, never (rǐ-nōn'), rhyming with *own*. Because of this, the word is often misspelled with a *u* instead of a *w*.

Similar spelling problems plague the adjective *renowned* and are compounded by the fact that people often reduce or drop the (d) sound at the ends of words like this in conversation. This leads to written mistakes such as *world-renown artist*, which should be *world-renowned artist*.

repel   See **repulse.**

replete

Replete means "abundantly supplied" or "satiated." It is sometimes mistakenly used as a synonym for *complete*, as in *a computer system replete with color monitor, printer, and software.*

repress / suppress

These words have similar meanings, but there are subtle differences that are worth paying attention to. Both share the general sense of holding back or subduing something, but *repress* suggests keeping something under control to maintain or regulate order, while *suppress* suggests a more active curtailment, an active fight against an opposing force. Thus, *The government repressed the rebellion* implies that the government always maintained control and that the rebellious forces never posed a serious threat to governmental power before being put down, while *The government suppressed the rebellion* suggests that a significant rebellion was under way and that the government had to react strongly to put an end to it. Similarly, one might *repress* (rather than *suppress*) a smirk in order to maintain a serious appearance, and one would take a medicine that *suppresses* (rather than *represses*) a cough in order to reduce its severity.

Both words also see use in psychology, and here a similar distinction prevails. *Repress* generally means "to exclude painful or disturbing memories automatically or unconsciously from the conscious mind." *Suppress* means "to exclude unacceptable desires or thoughts deliberately from the mind." Using *repress* to express a conscious effort, as in *For years he tried to repress his frightful memories,* is thus incorrect.

reprise

In its musical sense meaning "a repetition of a phrase or verse" or "a return to an original theme," *reprise* is pronounced (rĭ-prēz′), with its last syllable rhyming with *freeze.* However, no doubt influenced by the word *reprisal,* which has an (ī) as in *pie* in its stressed syllable, the pronunciation (rĭ-prēz′) is not uncommon but is considered by some to be a mistake. In our 2001 survey, 69 percent of the Panel reported using the (ē) pronunciation, and 31 percent reported using the (ī) pronunciation.

repulse / repel

A number of language critics have maintained that the verb *repulse* should be used only to mean "to drive away" (as in *The infantry repulsed the attack*) or "to spurn" (as in *She repulsed his rude advances with a frown*), and not "to cause repulsion in; disgust." Many reputable writers, however, use *repulse* as a synonym for *disgust,* just as the related words *repulsion* and *repulsive* are used to mean "disgust" and "disgusting." Consider the following examples:

> A bracelet of thin black leather circled his wrist, a strange touch on such a pale American. I was repulsed by his body, and when I turned away, I saw what he'd been looking at so intently while we talked (Hester Kaplan, "Live Life King-Sized," *Press*)

> The period before an attack, when the men would lie or crouch motionless for hours beside a road, was ideal for his work, and although the violence repulsed him, he couldn't deny that the sketches he had made of the Duke were some of the best he'd ever done (Peter Ho Davies, "The Silver Screen," *Harvard Review*)

> As he was saying all this, O'Kane began to laugh, and now he was in a full spate of laughter at the people looking at him, curious, appalled, while Dr. Macready tried to point out that it was not laughing laughter, that it did not mean that the young man was feeling good, far from it, that instead of being repulsed by it, they should look on it as the laughter of the damned (Edna O'Brien, *In the Forest*)

The verb *repel* is a synonym for this sense of *repulse* and is also standard when used in this way:

> But some of the time she was repelled by even the thought of her classmates, greedy and self-absorbed (Edith Pearlman, "Allog," *Ascent*)

I am repelled by her toothlessness, the brittle, crinkly parchment texture of her skin, her smell (Jessica Hagedorn, *The Gangster of Love*)

New York's executioners played a pivotal role in the state, enabling New Yorkers to support the death penalty without ever having to do the killing themselves. Each executioner came to embody the public's conflicted attitudes; people were alternately fascinated with and repelled by them (Jennifer Gonnerman, "The Last Executioner," *Village Voice*)

research

Although some language critics object to the use of *research* as a transitive verb, the usage has ample historical precedent and is common in reputable writing. In our 1988 survey, 81 percent of the Usage Panel accepted it in the sentence *He spent a week at a funeral home researching mortuary procedures for his new novel*. The past participle *researched*, when used as an adjective, was accepted by 91 percent in the sentence *The chapters on the internment are both readable and well researched*.

resource

The first *s* in *resource* is most commonly pronounced with the (s) sound, and was the preferred choice of 90 percent of the Usage Panel in our 1997 survey. Of those Panelists, 68 percent placed the primary stress on the first syllable (rē′sôrs′), 22 percent on the second syllable (rĭ-sôrs′), and 10 percent reported using both of those forms. Although pronouncing the first *s* like a (z) is also acceptable, only 10 percent of the Panel preferred saying (rē′zôrs′) or (rĭ-zôrs′).

respect   See **in regard to.**

restive / restless

The adjectives *restive* and *restless* overlap in meaning but have subtle distinctions. *Restive* usually indicates impatience or uneasiness caused by external coercion or restriction:

Surrounded by a large and restive slave population, South Carolina's leaders feared that a weakened slave economy would not survive, and that high tariffs therefore threatened slavery itself (Harry L. Watson, "Andrew Jackson," *The Reader's Companion to the American Presidency*)

Our flight remained delayed but not canceled. As time went on, many of the passengers grew restive (Robert Mayer, *Notes of a Baseball Dreamer*)

Restive also has a related sense, "stubbornly resisting control," and is sometimes applied to horses to mean "balky."

Restless can mean "characterized by a lack of rest," as in *a restless night*. It can also mean "constantly moving or acting," as in *restless seas* or *a plot hatched in his restless brain.* The confusion with *restive* arises when *restless* means "characterized by unrest, fidgety." But unlike *restive, restless* is usually not used in contexts involving external force or restriction:

> I wouldn't have her live the kind of life I had, with no use for my mind except to make me restless and bitter (Jane Addams, "The Devil Baby at Hull-House," *Atlantic Monthly*)

> The man whose future empire would be intertwined with the twentieth-century multinational corporation began by studying records of the conquistadors. The research whetted his appetite and made him restless (Adam Hochschild, *King Leopold's Ghost*)

In some cases, both restraint and restlessness are implied so that the words can be used interchangeably, as in the following quotation from the *Florida Times-Union:* "*Federal courtrooms are stodgy places except on those increasingly rare days of naturalization ceremonies. It was a noisy place Wednesday as mothers tried to quiet restive children with juice boxes and Fritos.*"

restrictive and nonrestrictive clauses

A restrictive clause is a dependent clause that identifies the noun, phrase, or clause it modifies and limits or restricts its meaning, as the clause *who live in glass houses* in *People who live in glass houses should not throw stones.* Restrictive clauses are never set off with commas, and they are not limited to relative clauses beginning with *that* or *who: She was in Paris for most of the time when she was writing her novel. They wanted to see the field where McCovey hit his last home run.*

A nonrestrictive clause (sometimes called a *descriptive clause*) does not limit the reference in this way. The noun or situation it modifies has already been identified in the text, or is unique (as a proper noun, for example), or is assumed to be unique. A nonrestrictive clause is usually set off with a comma: *The driver, who wore a mask, was not involved in the robbery. I wandered around the park until sunset, when the birds started to sing. We played at Torrey Pines, where they hold the Buick Open.*

The commas make an important distinction in meaning. Thus *the Smiths' car that is in the garage* implies that the Smiths own more than one car, and only one of them is in the garage, while *the Smiths' car, which is in the garage* implies that the Smiths own only one car.

See more at **comma** and **that.**

reticent

The noun *reticence* meaning "reluctance to speak" goes back to the early 1600s, but it was used only occasionally until the 1830s, when for some reason it caught on, along with its adjective *reticent.* More recently, however, these words have been used as synonyms of *reluctance* and *reluctant,* in contexts where communication is not involved. Some usage commentators have criticized this use, and the Usage Panel sees merit in this view. In our 2001 survey, 83 percent of the Panel found unacceptable the sentence *A lot of out-of-towners are reticent to come to the Twin Cities for a ball game if there's a chance the game will be rained out.*

This usage may have grown out of constructions such as *reticent to speak* and *reticent to talk.* Although these uses can be fairly criticized as redundancies, the communicative context seems to make some difference to the Panel, since 61 percent accepted the sentence *Whenever I fail to arrange the chairs in a circle, the students have been much more reticent to speak out.*

retro–

The prefix *retro–*, meaning "backward, back," comes from the Latin prefix *retrō–*, meaning "backward, behind." The most common English words beginning with *retro–* are derived from Latin words or elements. *Retroactive* comes from Latin *retro–* and the verb *agere*, "to drive." *Retrograde* combines *retro–* with the verb *gradī*, "to walk." *Retrospect* adds *retro–* to the verb *specere*, "to look at." The 19th and 20th centuries have seen many scientific or technical terms coined with English *retro–*, such as *retrorocket.*

revert back

The phrase *revert back* is widely considered a redundancy because the *re–* prefix means "back." As a result, *back* is usually deleted by copyeditors who encounter this construction. Unlike *refer back,* which may be justified because one can also *refer ahead, revert back* has no justification aside from its frequency of use in speech. In our 1995 survey, 78 percent of the Usage Panel considered *revert back* to be redundant.

revolve / rotate

The verbs *revolve* and *rotate* are used in everyday writing to indicate cyclic patterns. For example, *revolving debt* is debt that is carried over from one credit card statement to the next; *crop rotation* refers to the successive planting of different crops on the same land. Although the concept of revolving and rotating are treated as synonymous in everyday writing, this is not so in scientific writing. The difference between the two terms lies in the location of their central axis. If an object is orbiting another object, as the moon is earth, then one complete orbit is called a *revolution.* On the other hand, if an object is turning about itself, or rather, about an axis that passes through itself, then one complete cycle is called a *rotation.* The difference is epitomized in this statement: *The earth rotates on its axis and revolves about the sun.*

rhetoric   See **empty rhetoric.**

rheumatic / rheumatoid / rheumatism

Each of these words referring to discomfort or disability of the joints or musculo-skeletal tissues is ultimately derived from the Greek word *rheuma*, "stream, flow," since it was once thought that aches and pains were caused by a watery discharge from the body. *Rheumatic* is a general term used to refer to arthritis and other ab-normalities of the joints, as in *rheumatic fever*, an infectious disease marked by fever and painful inflammation of the joints that can cause permanent damage to the heart valves, a condition called *rheumatic heart disease*. *Rheumatoid* is a more specific reference to a type of arthritis in which chronic inflammation is caused by an au-toimmune reaction in the body. *Rheumatoid factor* refers to abnormal antibodies found in the blood of patients with rheumatoid arthritis and is used to diagnose the disease and other autoimmune conditions.

Rheumatism is a vague term used to describe various types of arthritis and other musculoskeletal conditions. Although it is still encountered occasionally in formal writing, as in the title of the medical journal *Arthritis and Rheumatism*, it is more commonly used by people outside the medical profession.

ring   See **wring**.

rise / raise

The distinction between *rise* and *raise* is straightforward: *rise* is intransitive (it does not take an object), while *raise* is transitive (it takes an object): The sun *rises*, while one *raises* the volume of a radio. In some dialects of English, however, *raise* or *raise up* has acquired an intransitive sense, as in the following excerpt of a story told by Texas blues great Lightning Hopkins: " . . . *the little boy run up there, tapped him on his back, and he raised up and said 'Hey son, why here's you again.'*" However, *raise* is not used as an intransitive verb in Standard English.

See also **rear**.

roil

The verb *roil* means literally "to make muddy or cloudy by stirring up sediment," and this meaning has given rise to a number of figurative uses. *Roil* can also mean "to be or cause to be agitated." Not surprisingly, the synonymous verb *rile* actually began its existence as a variant of *roil*.

The figurative uses appear to unsettle many Usage Panelists since several seem-ingly unremarkable examples could not elicit acceptance from more than a thin ma-jority. In our 2002 survey, the Panel was given both transitive and intransitive ex-amples. The transitive example *The lyrics of the song roiled some Asian students, who felt they were racist* was acceptable to 52 percent of Panelists. The phrasal verb *roil up*, where *up* functions as an intensifier, found even less favor. Only 44 percent accepted the sentence *The administration's comments have roiled up the university's professors, who felt the administration was declaring war on tenure.*

For intransitive uses, the Panel was no more sanguine. Some 54 percent accepted *The controversy continued to roil just two days before the primaries.* The literal use meaning "to move turbulently" found even fewer takers, with 34 percent accepting *It was like wading through surf when a mountainous breaker is roiling toward you.*

According to most dictionaries, all these uses should be acceptable. The survey results suggest then that many people are uncertain about what roil means, or they dislike the word for some reason or another and would prefer to see a synonym like *upset* or *disturb* in the transitive uses or *boil* or *roll* in the intransitive ones. *Roil* has no history of controversy in usage commentary, however, so the mixed opinions of the Panel cannot be ascribed to a legacy of criticism.

Roma / Romany

The preferred term for the people long known as *Gypsies* in English is now *Roma*, which is the plural of *rom*, the word for "man" or "husband" in the *Romany* language. (*Gypsy*, a shortening of the Middle English word for "Egyptian," is considered offensive by many Roma today; it was applied to the Roma because Europeans first believed the itinerant Roma had come from Egypt or its vicinity. The Roma are now known to have originated in northwest India, which they probably left in the 11th century.) While *Roma* is becoming somewhat more common in American English, its initial use is usually glossed in the mainstream press because many Americans are still unfamiliar with it. *Romany*, sometimes spelled *Romani*, is used as a noun in referring both to the language and to an individual member of the Roma; it is also used as an adjective, as in *Romany history* or *Romany music*. The terms *Roma* and *Romany* come from the Indic language or languages spoken by the original Roma and are unrelated to the Latin-based English words *Romania* and *Rome*.

roof

The plural of this word is *roofs*, pronounced (ro͞ofs) or (ro͝ofs) or sometimes (ro͞ovz) or (ro͝ovz). The second of these forms follows the common pattern in Modern English that changes *f* to *v* before the plural ending. This pattern is an inheritance from Old English. The Old English consonants *f*, *th* as in *thin*, and *s* remained voiceless at the beginning and end of a word, and also when they were doubled within a word, but they became voiced, that is, *v*, *th* as in *that*, and *z*, when they occurred individually between vowels. In Middle English the word for "wife," for example, was spelled *wif* and pronounced (wēf), and its plural was spelled *wives* and pronounced (wē′vĭs), with two syllables. Some Modern English words in addition to *wife* that retain this pattern of sound alternation are *thief/thieves*, *leaf/leaves*, *calf/calves*, and also *house/houses* and *mouth/mouths*. We think of these plural forms as irregular now, but they were once completely regular. Eventually, at the beginning of the Early Modern English period, the *e* in the ending *es* became silent or dropped out except after the sounds (ch), (j), (sh), (zh), (s), and (z), and English speakers began forming plurals by adding just *s* in most cases instead of *es*. While many of the words that are in the *thief/thieves* category still have their traditional plurals, some have also adopted modern plurals ending in just *s*, as *dwarf* and *roof* have. Nonetheless, the plural of *roof,* though spelled *roofs,* is sometimes pronounced (ro͞ovz) or (ro͝ovz) in some areas of the United States.

See more at **plural nouns.**

row

This word, meaning "brawl" or "uproar," is normally pronounced (rou), rhyming with *cow* and *vow*. The pronunciation (rō), rhyming with *flow* and *blow,* belongs to the homographs *row,* "line" or "succession," and *row,* "to propel a boat with oars."

run-on sentence

A run-on sentence, also called a *comma splice* or a *fused sentence,* is the improper use of a comma to join two independent clauses, as in *I was tired, he wouldn't leave* or *Listen carefully to the instructions, we will not have time to repeat them*. In edited prose, comma splices should be eliminated. In many cases, the two independent clauses may be written as two separate sentences with appropriate punctuation. *Listen carefully to the instructions. We will not have time to repeat them.* Another way to fix a run-on sentence is to insert a conjunction that makes the logical connection between the two sentences clearer. *I was tired, but he wouldn't leave.* The deliberate use of the run-on sentence can sometimes achieve special effects in informal contexts and in representations of colloquial speech. Writers should take care, however, when attempting to use run-on sentences in this way in formal contexts. These uses may easily be interpreted as mistakes or silliness.

· S ·

sacrilegious

Sacrilegious means "grossly irreverent toward what is held to be sacred." It is the adjectival form of the noun *sacrilege*. It is commonly misspelled *sacreligious* through confusion with *religious.*

safe sex / safer sex

Although the term *safe sex* is more common, *safer sex* is also used. It is advocated by some people to emphasize that the probability of acquiring or spreading a sexually transmitted disease is merely reduced and not eliminated when following recommended safeguards.

said

The adjective *said* is used primarily in legal and business writing, where it is equivalent to *aforesaid: the said tenant* (named in a lease), *said property.* Outside of these contexts *said* is usually unnecessary. Simply saying *the tenant* or *the property* will suffice.

same

The expressions *same* and *the same* are sometimes used in place of pronouns such as *it* or *one,* as in *When you have filled out the form, please remit same to this office.* As this example suggests, the usage is associated chiefly with business and legal language, and some critics have suggested that it should be reserved for such contexts. Although the usage may sound stilted, however, it sometimes occurs in informal writing, particularly in the phrase *lack of same,* as in *It is a question of money, or lack of same.*

See more at **both.**

same-sex / single-sex

Both *same-sex* and *single-sex* are adjectives used to refer to activities and arrangements that involve just one gender. The terms are used fairly interchangeably in reference to institutions such as schools, camps, gyms, or prisons. *Same-sex* has become the prevalent usage in reference to marriage or dating.

414

sarcophagi

Although this word, the Latin plural of *sarcophagus,* can be pronounced with a soft or hard *g,* as (sär-kŏf'ə-jī) or (sär-kŏf'ə-gī), the former is more common.
See more at **g.**

savings

The word *savings* usually takes a plural verb: *Your savings are safe in our bank.* Sometimes, however, *savings* is considered a lump sum and treated as a singular noun, as in *Your savings is enough to cover the down payment,* or in compound forms such as *savings account* and *savings bond.* (Note that the first word in English compounds is normally singular, as in *cinder block,* a block made of concrete and cinders.) In the United States, *savings* is also widely used as a singular noun to refer to an amount of money that is saved, as in *a savings of $2,000.* Traditionalists view this construction as illogical and prefer the form *a saving,* which is common in Britain. In American English, *a savings* is usually followed by a singular verb, as in *A savings of $50 is most welcome.* The widespread use of this construction appears to be eroding resistance to it. In our 1988 survey, 57 percent of the Usage Panel found this sentence unacceptable. This was a considerable decrease from the 89 percent who rejected *a savings* in our 1967 survey.
See more at **subject and verb agreement.**

scarcely

***scarcely* as negative adverb**   *Scarcely* has the force of a negative and is therefore regarded as incorrectly used with another negative, as in *I couldn't scarcely believe it.* For more on this problem, see **double negative** and **hardly.**

scarcely . . . than   Clauses that follow minimizers like *scarcely* and *hardly* are normally introduced with either *when* or *before.* The conjunction *than* is occasionally used here, but such use has been criticized by usage commentators as inelegant, if not unacceptable. The idea is that *than* properly introduces a comparison of some kind, and in these cases there is no real comparison being made. Note that it is fully acceptable to say *There were scarcely more than a hundred people at the meeting* and *My hometown is scarcely more than a village,* where the word *more* makes a comparison explicit. In any case, it is standard practice to say *The meeting had scarcely begun when* [or *before*] *it was interrupted,* but it may strike some readers as peculiar to say *The meeting had scarcely begun than it was interrupted.*
See more at **rarely ever.**

scarify

When readers see this uncommon word in print, they often jump to the conclusion that it is made up of the word *scar* and the verb suffix *–ify,* and so means "to cause the skin to be scarred," with the first syllable pronounced like *scar*. But *scarify* does not mean "to scar." It means "to make scratches or shallow cuts on the skin," and its first syllable is traditionally pronounced like *scare*. Since scarification can cause scarring, though, it is easy to see how *scar* and *scarify* are confused in both meaning and pronunciation.

schism

This word, which was originally spelled *scisme* in English, is traditionally pronounced (sĭz′əm). The pronunciation (skĭz′əm) was long regarded as incorrect, but it became so common in both British and American English that it gained acceptability and is now entered as a standard variant in most dictionaries. In fact, in our 1997 survey, 61 percent of the Usage Panel indicated they use (skĭz′əm), while 31 percent said they use (sĭz′əm). Another 8 percent pronounced the word as (shĭz′əm). These figures are similar to the percentages in the 1987 survey, suggesting that the two predominant pronunciations at least should continue to see widespread use for the foreseeable future. The modern spelling with the *h* dates back to the 16th century, when the word was respelled to resemble its Latin and Greek ancestors.

schizophrenia   See **multiple personality disorder.**

scone

Although this word was traditionally pronounced with a short *o*, rhyming with *gone*, it is now more commonly pronounced in the United States with a long *o*, rhyming with *stone*.

Scottish

Scottish is the full, original form of the adjective. *Scots* is an old Scottish variant of the form, while *Scotch* is an English contraction of *Scottish* that at one time also came into use in Scotland (as in Robert Burns's "*O thou, my Muse! guid auld Scotch drink!*") but subsequently fell into disfavor. To some extent these facts can serve as a guide in choosing among the many variant forms of related words, such as *Scot, Scotsman* or *Scotswoman*, or *Scotchman* or *Scotchwoman* for one of the people of Scotland; *Scots, (the) Scotch*, or, rarely, *(the) Scottish* for the people of Scotland; and *Scots, Scotch*, or *Scottish* for the dialect of English spoken in Scotland. The forms based on *Scotch* are English and disfavored in Scotland, while those involving the full form *Scottish* tend to be more formal. In the interest of civility, forms involving *Scotch* are best avoided in reference to people. But there is no sure rule for referring to things, since the history of variation in the use of these words has also left many expressions in which the choice is fixed, such as *Scotch broth, Scotch whisky, Scottish rite,* and *Scots Guards.*

sculptor / sculptress   See **feminine suffixes.**

seasonal / seasonable

Seasonal and *seasonable*, though closely related, have different uses. *Seasonal* applies to that which depends on or is controlled by the season of the year: *a seasonal rise in employment. Seasonable* applies to that which is appropriate to the season (*seasonable clothing*) or timely (*seasonable intervention in the dispute*). Rains are *seasonal* if they occur at a certain time of the year. They are *seasonable* at any time if they save the crops.

secretive

This adjective is derived from the verb *secrete*, in its meaning "to conceal in a hiding place," plus the adjectival suffix *–ive*. It makes sense, then, that the correct historical pronunciation is (sĭ-krē′tĭv), with the emphasis on the second syllable. However, more often than not this word is pronounced (sē′krĭ-tĭv), as if it were derived from *secret* plus *–ive*. This is an association that is easy to make since someone who is secretive is likely to keep secrets. Both pronunciations are standard.

seed   See **fruit.**

seem   See **cannot.**

seldom / seldomly

In the past, the word *seldom* was both an adverb and an adjective, as when Shakespeare describes the rich man who chooses not to gaze on his treasures to avoid "blunting the fine point of seldom pleasure." In contemporary English, however, the word *seldom* is an adverb only, and it needs no adverbial suffix *–ly: He seldom had the opportunity to speak his first language in his new country.* Since *seldom* often occurs alongside or in contrast to other adverbs specifying the degree of frequency of occurrence, like *commonly, habitually, rarely, usually,* and *frequently* itself, the suffix *–ly* is occasionally added to *seldom* in imitation of these other adverbs, as in the sentence *The American chestnut tree was once commonly found over much of the United States, but nowadays it is seldomly seen even in the most remote areas.* This addition of *–ly* has been criticized as a redundancy, and most dictionaries do not enter the form. Therefore, careful writers are wise to avoid it.

self–

The prefix *self–* goes back to the Old English word *self,* meaning virtually the same thing it does today. In Old English there were about a dozen compounds with *self–,* of which only one has remained common: *self-will.* In Modern English, however, the number of new compounds with *self–* has increased. *Self–* usually forms compounds with adjectives, as in *self-conscious, self-employed,* and *self-governing,* and with nouns, as in *self-confidence, self-improvement,* and *self-satisfaction.* The prefix usually indicates that the object of the action expressed or implied by the noun or adjective is the same as the one who performs the action. The prefix can also mean "automatic" or "automatically," as in *self-loading.*

self-identify / self-identified

The adjectival participle *self-identified,* with the meaning "believing or asserting oneself as belonging to a certain group or class," has gained wide currency and acceptability. The sentence *The study of Massachusetts youth found that more than 25 percent of self-identified gay teens said they had recently missed school out of fear of persecution* was considered acceptable by 87 percent of the Usage Panel in our 2002 survey. From this form, through the process known as *back-formation,* the verb *self-identify* has recently been created. It has become widely used on official forms of various kinds but may strike many readers as awkward. In 2002, 71 percent of the Usage Panel found *self-identify* to be unacceptable in the sentence *If you apply for another position within the university and you self-identify as an eligible veteran, the hiring authority must report whether you were hired in the last year.* This resistance may stem from the fact that the prefix *self–* does not freely attach to verbs. Accordingly, there are words like *self-congratulatory* and *self-congratulation,* and *self-fulfilling* and *self-fulfillment,* but no verbs *self-congratulate* and *self-fulfill.* One of the few verbs formed with *self–* is *self-destruct,* which is in fact a back-formation from *self-destruction,* just as the uncommon verb *destruct* is derived from *destruction.*

See more at **identify** and **back-formation.**

self-styled   See **so-called.**

semi– / hemi– / demi–

The prefix *semi–* means "half" or "partially." In general it combines with adjectives: *semiattached, semidry, semisweet. Semi–* also combines, less commonly, with nouns: *semidarkness, semidesert, semidome.* Alongside *semi–* there are two other similar-sounding prefixes, *hemi–* and *demi–,* that have basically the same meaning, "half." *Semi–,* however, comes from Latin *sēmi–,* meaning "half," while *hemi–* comes from Greek *hēmi–,* also meaning "half." The Latin and Greek prefixes are actually close linguistic cousins. Latin and Greek descend from the same prehistoric language, but the original *s* sound of this language, still heard in Latin *sēmi–,* changed to *h* during the development of Greek. *Demi–* is not related to the other two prefixes. It comes through French from Latin *dīmidius,* meaning "divided in half," from *dis,* "apart, asunder," plus *medius,* "half."

In American English, the prefix *semi–* has at least has three common pronunciations, depending on the word in which it occurs: (sĕm′ē), (sĕm′ĭ), and (sĕm′ī).

Hemi– has (hĕm′ē) and (hĕm′ĭ). *Demi–,* however, is usually pronounced (dĕm′ē) in American English, in such words as *demigod* and *demitasse.* The dictionary should be consulted when in doubt about the pronunciation of words containing these prefixes.

semicolon

compound sentences

1. A semicolon separates the clauses of a compound sentence when the clauses are not joined by a coordinating conjunction (*and, but, for, or, nor, so, yet*).

> Cecile will be subletting her apartment; my cousin will rent it for three months.

> The questions are provided by the analyst; the answers come from the data.

> Many industries were paralyzed by the strike; factory owners left the district, taking their money with them.

> An emphasis on universalism and "greatness" has been replaced by an emphasis on diversity and difference; the scientific norms which once prevailed in many of the "soft" disciplines are viewed with skepticism; "context" and "contingency" are continually emphasized; attention to "objects" has given way to attention to "representations" (Louis Menand, "College: The End of the Golden Age," *The New York Review of Books*)

2. A semicolon often separates the clauses of a compound sentence if the clauses are long or contain internal punctuation, even when the clauses are joined by a conjunction.

> Michael, who is interested in business, is considering schools in Rhode Island, North Carolina, and California; but his twin brother, Andrew, is going to art school in the Midwest.

> The pale end-of-winter sunlight filled the room and yellowed all their faces; and John, drugged and morbid and wondering how it was that he had slept again and had been allowed to sleep so long, saw them for a moment like figures on a screen, an effect that the yellow light intensified (James Baldwin, *Go Tell It on the Mountain*)

3. A semicolon separates the clauses joined by a conjunctive adverb (*therefore, accordingly, however, nevertheless, besides, consequently, moreover, thus, then, hence, indeed*).

> We demanded a refund; however, the manufacturer refused to give us one.

> Our account was low on funds; nevertheless, we met our payments.

> The young expatriate had a small, simply furnished room on a lively, noisy street; consequently, the roar of Parisian traffic echoed day and night (Tyler Stovall, *Paris Noir*)

series

1. A semicolon separates items of a series in which the items themselves contain commas.

The results of the election were as follows: Georgia, 12; Tim, 11; and Claudine, 5.

Among the guests were Mary Adams; her daughter, Elaine; Henry Abrams, formerly of the Redding Institute; and two couples whom I had never met.

2. If an internal comma occurs only in the last item of a series, semicolons are not necessary.

They own property in Tucson, in Palo Alto, and in Pemaquid, Maine.

with quotation marks   Unlike the comma, which is placed inside closing quotation marks, the semicolon is placed outside.

She said it in the simplest manner, as if she had said: "He's fond of wildflowers"; and after a moment she added candidly: "I think he's the dullest man I ever met." (Edith Wharton, *The Age of Innocence*)

I was termed a "bastard intellectual," an "incipient Trotskyite"; it was claimed that I possessed an "antileadership attitude" and that I was manifesting "seraphim tendencies," the latter phrase meaning that one has withdrawn from the struggle of life and considers oneself an infallible angel (Richard Wright, *Black Boy*)

---

semimonthly / semiweekly   See **bimonthly.**

---

senior

The Oxford English Dictionary traces the use of *senior* in the sense of "an older person" to the 15th century. In contemporary American English, however, this sense of *senior* is generally taken to be a shortening of the more recent *senior citizen,* and those who object to the compound may object to the shorter term as well. However, as the *OED* makes clear, *senior* has always evoked the positive qualities of aging, including wisdom, dignity, and superior position, and it is less likely to sound condescending than the obviously coined term *senior citizen.* In any case, unless humor or social satire is intended, there is often no clear alternative to *senior* other than constructions such as *older person* or *older adult.*

---

senior citizen

Some people object to *senior citizen* as a patronizing euphemism or a piece of demeaning bureaucratic jargon. However, it is not so easy to find an alternative that all can agree on. Most terms describing a person beyond middle age are generally considered too blunt (*old man, old woman*), too informal (*oldster, old-timer*), too slangy (*coot, codger, geezer*), or even more objectionably euphemistic (*golden ager*).

Senior citizen is a well-established term, first recorded in 1938, that now rarely gives real offense and that, when used appropriately, offers certain advantages over other age-related terms. Unlike expressions based on *old* or *older, senior citizen* acknowledges that age is not necessarily the only relevant factor in describing people who are advanced in years. Strictly speaking, a senior citizen is a person who has reached an agreed-upon retirement age (though who has not necessarily retired) and whose relation to society—in the form of certain benefits and privileges—has changed accordingly. Thus *senior citizen* denotes not only age but also social or civic status, making it the natural term to use when discussing older people in a political or social context. It is when *senior citizen* is used more loosely in contexts other than the societal that it draws the sharpest criticism. In those cases, a better choice might be *older person, older adult,* or simply *senior,* as in *Nearly half the members of the community choir are seniors.*

sensuous / sensual

Both of these adjectives mean "relating to or gratifying the senses." *Sensuous* can refer to the stimulation of any of the senses, but it often applies to those involved in aesthetic enjoyment, as of art or music:

> The cloven valleys of the lower world swam in a tinted mist which veiled the ruggedness of their crags and ribs and ragged forests, and turned all the forbidding region into a soft and rich and sensuous paradise (Mark Twain, *A Tramp Abroad*)

> . . . though he turned the pages with the sensuous joy of the book-lover, he did not know what he was reading, and one book after another dropped from his hand (Edith Wharton, *The Age of Innocence*)

> Ultimately, I believe, meaning has less to do with language than with music, a sensuous flow that becomes language only by default, so to speak, and by degrees (Leonard Michaels, "My Yiddish," *Threepenny Review*)

Overall, *sensual* is the more common word, and it is more likely to be applied to the physical senses or appetites, including those associated with sexual pleasure:

> He ate food with what might almost be termed voracity; and seemed to forget himself, Hepzibah, the young girl, and everything else around him, in the sensual enjoyment which the bountifully spread table afforded (Nathaniel Hawthorne, *The House of the Seven Gables*)

> The modern geisha is the aristocrat of the huge industry that has evolved through the centuries to cater to Japanese men's sensual desires (Jodi Cobb, "Geisha," *National Geographic*)

These are tendencies of usage, however, not rules. Each word can be found in well-respected writing where one might expect to find the other:

> The faces of the barmaidens had risen in colour, each having a pink flush on her cheek; their manners were still more vivacious than before—more abandoned, more excited, more sensuous, and they expressed their sentiments and desires less euphemistically, laughing in a lackadaisical tone, without reserve (Thomas Hardy, *Jude the Obscure*)

> I still remember how sensual that memoir was. Kazin wrote with his nose, making me smell what his mother was cooking for the Sabbath dinner and how his father's overalls smelled of turpentine when he came home from his job as a housepainter (William Zinsser, *Inventing the Truth*)

Such usages may move against the tide, but they should not be considered incorrect.

sentence

A sentence is a grammatical unit that is syntactically independent and contains at least one independent clause. Each independent clause in a sentence usually consists of a subject that is expressed or, as in imperative sentences, understood, as well as a predicate that contains at least one finite verb. A *simple sentence* contains a single independent clause and no dependent clauses, as in *The wind was cold* and *We built a fire*. In a command such as *Close the door!* the subject of the sentence, *you*, is not expressed, but understood. A sentence that contains one or more independent clauses, usually joined by a conjunction, is called a *compound sentence*: *The wind was cold, but the fire was warm*. If an independent clause in a sentence contains a dependent clause, then the sentence is called a *complex sentence*. *I wondered how people had survived the long winters* is a complex sentence in which *how people had survived the long winters* is a dependent clause. In edited prose, sentences should begin with a capital letter and end with a period or other final punctuation mark.

See more at **clause.**

sentence adverbs

We usually think of an adverb as a word that modifies a verb, like *beautifully* in *She sings that song beautifully*, or *clearly* in *We could see the comet clearly through the telescope*. The traditional test of an adverb is to ask a question of time, place, or manner: *when, where, how*. If the word answers a question like this, it is an adverb: *He woke up late. We walked down to the beach. The bell rang loudly.*

But certain adverbs bear no clear relationship to the verb in a sentence; instead, they modify the entire sentence. Such adverbs often appear at the beginning of the sentence, and they usually express or suggest an attitude that the speaker or writer has about the content of the sentence: *Fortunately, Higgins survived the ordeal. Frankly, the Bruins don't stand a chance in the playoffs. Disturbingly, the oversight committee was never told about the error.* Of course, sentence adverbs can also appear in other positions in the sentence, as in *Santana is undeniably the best pitcher in baseball. The candidate has, surprisingly, never run for public office before. The team has won every game, thankfully.* All of these usages are standard.

concessional sentence adverbs Bear in mind, however, that certain adverbs can introduce a note of reservation or doubt about a sentence, and they should therefore be used with care. The sentence *Santana is arguably the best pitcher in baseball* implies that others might not agree with this judgment. A sentence adverb like *admittedly* implies that the speaker or writer is making a concession to an opinion held elsewhere: *Admittedly, McGraw isn't the most effective public speaker.* Use these adverbs only if making such concessions will make the overall point more effective.

ambiguity of sentence adverbs Attitudinal sentence adverbs like *happily* and *thankfully* can sometimes be ambiguous, especially in speech, as to whether they modify the verb or the rest of the sentence. The adverb *thankfully* in a sentence like *Thankfully, Ed returned the tools* could be interpreted as describing the point of view either of the speaker or of Ed himself. Usually setting off the adverb with a comma (or commas) indicates that it modifies the whole sentence. The use of commas in *The company has, happily, launched a new venture* implies that the happy attitude belongs to the writer, not to the company. Omitting the commas implies that the company is the happy party, but assuming that the reader will share this interpretation is risky.

The widely used sentence adverb *hopefully* seems to be in a class by itself, and has become a shibboleth or, to some, a mark of poor style.

See more at **adverbs** and **hopefully.**

sentence fragments

A sentence fragment is a phrase or clause that is punctuated and capitalized as a sentence but does not constitute a complete grammatical sentence. Although the sentence fragment is traditionally seen as a fault and accordingly removed from formal edited prose, many writers have used sentence fragments to great rhetorical effect:

> She listened to Mrs. Parkes moving around the house. She looked out into the garden and saw the branches shake the trees. She sat defeating the enemy, restlessness. Emptiness. She ought to be thinking about her life, about herself (Doris Lessing, "To Room Nineteen")

> Last summer, Robin went to Richmond Hill for a month's visit. She came home early. She said it was a madhouse. The oldest child has to go to a special reading clinic, the middle one wets the bed. Genevieve spends all her time in the law library studying. No wonder (Alice Munro, "Circle of Prayer")

Such examples as these show how sentence fragments can strikingly suggest the sound of colloquial speech or the stream of a character's thoughts. Unsurprisingly, fragments are more common in narratives than in expository or argumentative prose. The expression *not that* is found at the beginning of sentence fragments that offer plausible but ultimately untrue reasons, motivations, or background conditions, often in contrast to the real reason or condition given in a subsequent clause.

> I beat Wally, and suddenly the words began to flow in the brief absence of humiliating defeat, in the brief presence of a different sport, one in which we could make a farce out of the cult of achieved masculinity. Not that I could articulate that insight at the time, but that's what we were doing. Farce is the only refuge for losers (Charles M. Young, "Losing: An American Tradition," *Men's Journal*)

Before using sentence fragments, however, writers should give careful thought to their appropriateness to the purpose at hand and to their likely effect on the intended audience, who may object to their use. In addition, overuse of sentence fragments can make a passage choppy and difficult to read.

See more at **which.**

separate

Separate, pronounced (sĕp′ə-rāt′), is frequently misspelled as *seperate,* probably by analogy with other common verbs in which the syllables (ə-rāt′) are spelled *–erate,* like *generate* and *operate.* Writers can recall the proper spelling by remembering that a *separation* often produces two or more *parts*—in fact, linguists think that the Latin words *sēparāre* and *pars,* the sources of English *separate* and *part,* respectively, may ultimately be related to each other.

series

Series is both a singular and a plural noun. When it has the singular sense of "one set," *series* takes a singular verb, even when it is followed by *of* and a plural noun: *A series of lectures is scheduled.* When it has the plural sense of "one or more sets," it takes a plural verb: *Two series of lectures are scheduled—one for experts and one for laypeople.*
   See more at **subject and verb agreement.**

service / serve

The verb *service* is used principally in the sense "to repair or maintain": *service the electric dishwasher.* Exceptions to this usage include specialized senses in finance (*service a debt*) and animal breeding (*service a mare*). *Serve* means "to supply goods or services to," as in *One radio network serves three states.*

set / sit

The verbs *set* and *sit* have been confused since the Middle Ages, so it is not surprising that they sometimes get confused today. Throughout its history *set* has been a transitive verb, originally meaning "to cause (someone) to sit" and "to cause (something) to be in a certain position." The second sense is a common meaning of the verb today: *She set the book on the table.* Since about 1300, however, *set* has also been used without an object to mean "to be in a seated position, sit." *Set* is still common as a nonstandard or regional word meaning "sit," especially in rural speech: *Stop on by and set a spell.* The most familiar intransitive use of *set* is *The sun sets.*
   Sit is mainly an intransitive verb meaning "to rest supported on the hindquarters," as in *He sits at the table.* It has other common uses, entailing occupying a location (*The house sits on a small lot*) or existing in a resting or unused state (*The skis sat gathering dust*). Nevertheless, *sit* has its transitive uses, some of which date back to the 14th century. It is more commonly used than *set* to mean "to cause (someone) to sit," as in *They sat the winning ticket holder back in his chair.* Another transitive use of *sit* is "to provide seats for," as in *The theater sits five thousand.*

sex   See **gender.**

sexist language

Some of the most interesting changes that have taken place in the English language over the last forty years have been driven by the desire to avoid, if not banish, sexism in the language. This reform movement is noteworthy for its differences from most previous reform movements, which have usually been inspired by a desire for English to be more logical or more efficient in expression. The reforms involving gender are explicitly political in intent and represent a continuing quest for ideals of gender equity to be reflected in language.

Unlike other political language reforms, elimination of sexism in language has involved basic and extensive changes in grammar, traditional grammatical rules, and common words like *man, father, male,* and *female* that have been in the language for over a thousand years. Despite this, the movement to reduce sexism in English has been remarkably successful by historical standards. It is undeniable that large numbers of men and women are uncomfortable using constructions that have been criticized for being sexist, and respected writers and speakers attempt to eliminate gender bias in language. Different people have different sensitivities, however, and not everyone agrees about what is acceptable.

Common grammatical issues that writers and speakers struggle with include the generic use of *he* or *man* to refer to a representative member of a group that includes women, the appropriateness of feminine suffixes such as *-ess,* words and metaphors with masculine connotations such as *master,* and words ending in *–man.* Also problematic are asymmetries of language, or words that single out women, such as *coed* and *shrew,* that have no masculine counterpart. Many of these words reinforce unacceptable stereotypes or judgments about sex roles, the appropriateness of certain behaviors among men or women, or the societal status of females. Words that are used only of one sex, such as *tomboy* and *sissy,* can reinforce harmful stereotypes about the nature of masculinity or femininity.

Avoiding sexist terms and constructions is just the first step in avoiding gender bias. Sexist stereotypes and assumptions can be ingrained and insidious, so it often takes real effort to uncover gender bias. For example, the English language has no shortage of terms for women whose behavior is viewed as licentious, but few comparable terms used of men. One researcher stopped counting after finding 220 such labels for women, both current and historical, while locating only 20 names for promiscuous men. Another found more than 500 slang terms for *prostitute* but could find just 65 similar terms that applied to men. While the terms applying only to women, such as *tramp, slut,* and *whore* are virtually always negative, the corresponding masculine terms, such as *stud* and *Casanova,* often have positive connotations.

Although many controversies still exist about what truly constitutes gender bias in language, striving to avoid sexist language is a worthy goal for careful writers and speakers who wish to be respectful of their subjects and audiences.

See more at **he / she, feminine suffixes, gender / sex, –man, master, shrew,** and **tomboy.**

sexually transmitted disease / venereal disease

Sexually transmitted diseases are any of various infectious diseases, including AIDS, chlamydia, and syphilis, that are transmitted through sexual intercourse or other intimate sexual contact. Historically, these have been called *venereal diseases,* derived from Latin *venus* or *vener–,* meaning "desire, love." The term *venereal disease* is becoming outdated, however, and it has been largely replaced by *sexually transmitted disease* in medical literature.

shall / will

the traditional rules   The traditional rules for using *shall* and *will* prescribe a highly complicated pattern of use in which the meanings of the forms change according to the person of the subject. In the first person, *shall* is used to indicate simple futurity: *I shall* [not *will*] *have to buy another ticket.* In the second and third persons, the same sense of futurity is expressed by *will: The comet will* [not *shall*] *return in eighty-seven years. You will* [not *shall*] *probably encounter some heavy seas when you round the point.*

the reality   Such, at least, are the traditional rules. The English and some usage sticklers are probably the only people who follow these rules, and then not with perfect consistency. In the United States, people who try to adhere to them run the risk of sounding pretentious or haughty. Americans normally use *will* to express most of the senses reserved for *shall* in British usage. Americans use *shall* chiefly in first person invitations and questions that request an opinion or agreement, such as *Shall we go?* and in certain fixed expressions, such as *We shall overcome.* In formal style and especially in legal documents, Americans use *shall* to express an explicit obligation, as in *Applicants shall provide a proof of residence* and *The Publisher shall provide the Author with an advance.* In general usage, this sense is expressed by *must* or *should.*

In speech the distinction that the English signal by the choice of *shall* or *will* may be rendered by stressing the auxiliary, as in *I will leave tomorrow* ("I intend to leave"); by choosing another auxiliary, such as *must* or *have to*; or by using an adverb such as *certainly.*

In addition to its sense of obligation, *shall* also can convey high moral seriousness that derives in part from its extensive use in the King James Bible, as in *"Righteousness shall go before him and shall set us in the way of his steps"* (Psalms 85:13) and *"He that shall humble himself shall be exalted"* (Matthew 23:12). (Note that both subjects in these quotations are in the third person.) The prophetic overtones that *shall* bears with it have no doubt led to its use in some of the loftiest rhetoric in English. This may be why Abraham Lincoln chose to use it instead of *will* in the Gettysburg Address: *" . . . government of the people, by the people, for the people shall not perish from the earth."*

See more at **auxiliary and primary verbs** and **should.**

share

When someone shares something with someone else, it is normal to assume that the shared item is the same thing. Thus, two people might share an apartment or an interest in music. But lately, *share* has been used of different things, in contexts where one might expect to see the verb *have* or *partake of.* The Usage Panel has little patience with this linguistic innovation. In our 2004 survey, 88 percent disapproved of the sentence *The two men share very different views on the acquisition of language in humans.* When people were not doing the sharing, and the meaning of the verb was "to have as a common feature or characteristic," the Panel was only slightly more tolerant. Some 77 percent rejected *Even neighborhoods twenty or thirty miles apart share differing environmental burdens.*

she   See **he / she** and **pronouns, personal.**

sheik

Recorded in English since the 16th century, this word is pronounced (shēk), rhyming with *cheek,* or (shāk), like *shake.* The former pronunciation is more usual in American English, while the latter is more usual in British English.

shell   See **orbit.**

shine

shined* and *shone   The verb *shine* has two different past tenses, *shined* and *shone,* and these forms also function as past participles. The past tense and past participle *shone* is more frequently used when the verb is intransitive and means "to emit light, be luminous": *The full moon shone brilliantly in the east.* The form *shined,* on the other hand, is used when the verb is transitive and means "to direct (a beam of light)" or "to polish," as in *He shined his flashlight down the dark staircase* or *The butler shined the silver.* Nevertheless, *shined* is sometimes used in an intransitive sense for *shone,* and *shone* is sometimes used in a transitive sense for *shined.* In the transitive meaning "to polish," however, *shined* is the only form that sounds correct: *He had never had his shoes shined* [not *shone*] *by a real shoe-shiner before.* Writers are best advised to reserve *shone* for the intransitive meaning "to emit light" and to use *shined* elsewhere.

***shine* and adverbs**   In its intransitive sense, *shine* is usually followed by an adverb to describe the intensity or nature of the illumination: *"There was a light in the front room, a slight, wavering light such as would be given by a small candle or taper. The blind was down, but the light shone dimly through"* (Sir Arthur Conan Doyle, *Beyond the City*). The form *bright* rather than the adverbial *brightly* is often seen after forms of the verb *shine*: *The sun shone bright in the sky.* *Dim, brilliant,* and other words are used in the same way, and this turn of phrase often gives an elevated air to a piece of writing: *The white walls of the city shone dim in the twilight.* In the case of adjectives of color, the construction is quite frequent and natural-sounding: *The sun shone red in the west.* Some authors, however, prefer an adverb overtly marked with *–ly* in this position: *"The air and the sky darkened and through them the sun shone redly"* (John Steinbeck, *The Grapes of Wrath*). Be aware, however, that the construction with an adjective rather than an adverb may sound precious or even ungrammatical in some contexts.

pronunciation of *shone* As both a past tense and a past participle, *shone* is usually pronounced with a long *o* sound in American English, rhyming with *stone*. In British and Canadian English, however, it has a short *o* sound, rhyming with *gone*.

–ship

The suffix *–ship* has a long history in English. It goes back to the Old English suffix *–scipe*, which was attached to adjectives and nouns to indicate a particular state or condition: *hardship, friendship*. When used to make new nouns in Modern English, the suffix is added only to nouns and usually indicates a state or condition (*authorship, kinship, partnership, relationship*), the qualities belonging to a class of human beings (*craftsmanship, horsemanship, sportsmanship*), or rank or office (*ambassadorship*).

shirk / shrink from

In contemporary English, *shirk* is usually used as a transitive verb with the meaning "to avoid," and it takes a direct object expressing the work or duty avoided: *Although the problems that teenagers face today are often difficult and embarrassing to discuss, parents who do not try to answer their children's questions directly and sincerely are simply shirking their duties as mothers and fathers.* The more general expression *shrink from* means "to recoil from" or "show reluctance to do something," as in *He shrank from all human contact* or *She did not shrink from criticizing the regime openly.* Both *shrink from* and *shirk* often take nouns like *hard work, chores,* or *required tasks* as their object.

The close similarity in sound between *shrink* and *shirk,* along with the general notion of avoidance shared by the two, has led to the occasional use of the preposition *from* with the verb *shirk*: *He did not shirk from his duty.* But this expression is widely viewed as an error and should be avoided.

Shrink from is more appropriate when emphasizing the formidable or repugnant nature of the task, while *shirk* alone, without *from,* is better when stressing the constraints imposed by social expectations or suggesting the weakness of character of those who do not meet these expectations.

shone   See **shine.**

short-lived

The pronunciation (-lĭvd) is etymologically correct since the compound is derived from the noun *life,* rather than from the verb *live.* But the pronunciation (-lĭvd) is by now so common that it cannot be considered an error. In our 1988 survey 43 percent of the Usage Panel preferred (-lĭvd), 39 percent preferred (-lĭvd), and 18 percent found both pronunciations equally acceptable.

should

should* versus *would   Just as they ignore the traditional rules governing the use of *shall* and *will,* Americans largely ignore the traditional rules governing the use of *should* and *would.* The two verbs are not always interchangeable, however. Either *should* or *would* can be used in the first person to express the future from the point of view of the past, but keep in mind that *should* sounds more formal than *would: He swore that I should* [or *would*] *pay for the remark.* The same principle applies to the verb in sentences that express a hypothetical condition or event: *If I had known that, I would* [or more formally, *should*] *have answered differently.* In the second and third persons, however, only *would* is used: *She assured us that she would* [not *should*] *return. If he had known that, he would* [not *should*] *have answered differently.*

***should* in conditional clauses**   Choosing which verb to use in conditional clauses, such as those beginning with *if,* can be tricky. In certain clauses, *should* is used for all three persons: *If I* [or *you* or *he*] *should decide to go, we will need a large car. If it should begin to snow, we will stay here tonight. Would* is not acceptable in these *if* clauses, but it does appear in other kinds of conditional clauses: *He might surprise you if you would give him a chance.* The best advice is to follow what sounds most natural. When in doubt, try a verb form in the indicative (*if it begins to snow*) or the subjunctive (*if you were to give him a chance*).

when only *should* is correct   To express duty or obligation, *should* functions as the equivalent of *ought to: I* [or *you* or *he*] *should go.*

when only *would* is correct   *Would* (and not *should*) is used to express willingness or promise (*I agreed that I would do it*) and to express habitual action in the past (*In those days we would walk along the canal at night*). *Would* also has the advantage of being a polite substitute for *will* in requests: *Would you lend me a dollar?*

should of   *Should have* is sometimes incorrectly written as *should of* by writers who have mistaken the source of the spoken contraction.

See more at **auxiliary and primary verbs, shall,** and **subjunctive.**

shrew / harpy / harridan / termagant / virago

When Shakespeare wrote about a *shrew* that needed taming, he was referring to a domineering woman with a violent, scolding, or nagging temperament. The words *harpy, harridan, termagant,* and *virago* have the same meaning. Some people consider these words to be sexist because they have no masculine counterpart and because this asymmetry implies that an overbearing nature is particularly objectionable in a female and is worth emphasizing in special terms. It has been further argued that pejorative terms like *shrew* denigrate personal qualities that are antithetical to traditional sterotypes of submissive femininity but that might be considered strong or necessary in an unbiased context or when used to describe a man.

shrink from See **shirk.**

sic

The word *sic* is used to indicate that a quoted passage, especially one containing an error or an unconventional spelling, has intentionally been retained in its original form. *Sic* is normally italicized and put in brackets, as in the following sentence:

> They thought that their candidate was a shoe-in [*sic*] to win the election, and the results were quite a shock to them.

Sic is the Latin word for "so, thus." In English, *sic* has traditionally been pronounced (sĭk), just like the word *sick.* However, a number of people pronounce the word as (sēk), like the word *seek,* using a pronunciation closer to the original Latin.

Sic, rather than *sick,* is also the preferred American spelling of the verb meaning "to urge or incite to attack," or "to set upon, attack," commonly used in reference to dogs, as in *It is dangerous to train your dog to sic on command.* The past tense and the past participle of this verb are usually spelled *sicced,* as in *He sicced his dogs on the intruders,* and the present participle is spelled *siccing.* However, the spellings *sicked* and *sicking* are also sometimes used. The word is always pronounced (sĭk), like the adjective *sick,* but interestingly it is in origin a dialectal variant of the verb *seek.*

sight / site / cite

Sight is a word with many different meanings, but two of the most common are "something seen, a view" and "something worth seeing, a spectacle," as in *the sights of London* or the cliché *a sight for sore eyes.* The word *site,* on the other hand, means "the location or setting of something," as in the phrases *construction site* or *battlegrounds and other historic sites.* Because archaeological sites and historic sites are often destinations on a sightseeing tour, the two homophones can occur in very similar contexts, and confusion is frequent. In particular, *site,* "location, setting," is often miswritten as *sight.* For example, in a sentence like *We had to walk several miles through the forest in order to reach the archaeological sight, but it was well worth the effort,* the word *sight* should be replaced by *site,* since it is the location of the remains or the ongoing archaeological investigation of the area that is the most prominent idea in the sentence. However, there may be cases in which the choice remains difficult: *Of all the sites we visited in Greece, Knossos was the most impressive.* Writers should consider carefully whether they mean "something worth seeing" or "location of an archaeological investigation" and choose appropriately.

Sight can also be a verb meaning "to take aim" and a noun meaning "a device used to assist aim by guiding the eye." Often there are two sights mounted on a firearm, and hence the noun *sight* is plural in the common idiom *set one's sights on something.* The nouns *sight* and *site* are sometimes confused in this idiom in particular, perhaps because the notion of taking aim recalls the notion of finding the proper place, or *site,* to fire. However, writers can remember to write *Once he sets his sights* [not *sites*] *on something, he'll stop at nothing to obtain it* by recalling the original metaphor behind the phrase: a hunter or soldier taking aim and looking at the target through the sights.

Cite, another homophone, is usually a verb meaning "to quote as an authority or example" or "to mention or bring forward as support, illustration, or proof." The verb is often used when specifying the exact location of a word or passage in a text, and writers should also take care not to confuse *cite* and *site* in these circumstances: *He cited* [not *sited*] *the exact place in the Constitution that restricts the power to declare war exclusively to Congress. Cite* can also be used informally as a noun in the meaning "citation."

Despite their similarity in sound, *sight, site,* and *cite* are unrelated. *Sight* comes from Old English *gesiht. Site* comes from Latin *situs,* "place, location," also the source of the English verb *situate. Cite* comes from the Latin word *citāre,* "to set in motion, summon, call upon," which is completely unrelated to *situs.*

sign   See **symptom.**

silicon / silicone

Perhaps due to the suddenness of their widespread usage thanks to technological innovations, these near look-alikes are often confused. *Silicon* is a chemical element used extensively in electronic equipment, especially in microprocessors. It is known for its unusual electrical properties (it is a *semiconductor*), which are somewhat different from both typical metals (which conduct electricity well) and typical nonmetals (which don't conduct electricity well).

Silicone is the general name for a variety of artificial compounds made out of chains of silicon and oxygen atoms. The silicon and oxygen atoms alternate along this chain, forming a polymer, with various other atoms attached along the chain. Silicones are typically colorless and odorless. They have a liquid, gel-like, or rubbery consistency, and they react poorly with organic compounds. Silicones are used especially as lubricants and sealants and are often components of medical prostheses and implants.

similar

The pronunciation (sĭm′yə-lər), which is generally not considered acceptable, is an example of *intrusion,* a phonological process that involves the addition or insertion of an extra sound. The usual pronunciation does not have a (y) sound at the start of the second syllable: (sĭm′ə-lər).

See more at **intrusion.**

simple past   See **past tense.**

simple present   See **present tense.**

simple sentence   See **sentence.**

since

As a conjunction, *since* has both a temporal sense, "after, from the time when," and a causal sense, "because, inasmuch as." In the past, some have objected to the use of *since* to mean *because.* Nevertheless, this usage is well established, and *since* provides a handy near-synonym when the word *because* has been repeated too often in a piece of writing.

Writers must take care, however, when using the word *since.* If the verb in the dependent clause following *since* is in the past tense, it may not be clear whether the temporal sense or the causal sense is intended. The sentence *Since he refused to attend, the meetings have not gone well* can have two interpretations. It can mean either *After he refused to attend, the meetings have not gone well* or it can mean *Because he refused to attend, the meetings have not gone well.* The writer should reword the sentence to specify either the temporal sense (*Since his refusal to attend, the meetings . . .*) or the causal sense (*Because he has refused to attend, the meetings . . .* or *On account of his refusal to attend, the meetings . . .*). The adverb *ever* will often suffice to bring out the temporal sense: *Ever since he refused to attend, the meetings have not gone well.*

single-sex   See **same-sex.**

singular

The singular is a grammatical form of a noun or noun phrase, usually corresponding to a single individual or a set of individuals denoted by the noun phrase. In *The girl saw the boys,* for example, *the girl* is singular, while *the boys* is plural. Note that some nouns, known as *mass nouns,* are grammatically singular but refer to a collection of things: *furniture, luggage. Collective nouns* are singular nouns that are sometimes treated as plurals: *enemy, family.*

The term *singular* also refers to a verb form that expresses the action or state of a grammatically singular subject. In *The girl sees the boys,* for example, the verb *sees* is a singular verb form, agreeing with the singular subject *the girl.*

See more at **collective nouns, count nouns, plurals,** and **subject and verb agreement.**

sink

Like the verbs *drink* and *swim, sink* is a strong verb that changes its vowel to form its past tense (*sank*) and past participle (*sunk*). Because there is so much variation in the patterns of strong verbs, the past participle is sometimes used for the past tense. These constructions are usually hallmarks of nonstandard English, but *sunk* is less strongly stigmatized in this use, and it is not uncommon to read sentences like *Mickelson sunk the putt to win the tournament* and *As he stood in the doorway, it finally sunk in: he was going to be a father* in mainstream publications.

Still, standard usage requires *sank* as the past tense. In our 2001 survey, 83 to 93 percent of the Usage Panel preferred *sank* in six different examples, in both transitive and intransitive use, such as *His failure utterly (sank/sunk) his chances for a promotion, The freighter (sank/sunk) in the storm,* and *My hopes (sank/sunk) at the dreadful news.*

See more at **strong verbs** and **verbs, principal parts of.**

site   See **sight.**

slash

1. Also called the *virgule* or *solidus,* the slash is used to separate successive divisions in an extended date. An en dash is often also used for this purpose.

    the fiscal year 1982/83 *or* the fiscal year 1982–83
    during 2004/5

2. The slash may be used with abbreviations to represent the word *per.*

    800 ft./sec. $35/hour
    4,000 gal./min.

3. A slash indicates alternatives.

    He/she must sign a waiver giving you access to his/her school records.
    Bring skis and/or ice skates if you plan to visit Vermont in the winter.

4. A slash with space on each side separates two or more lines of poetry that are quoted and run in on successive lines of text.

    The actor had a memory lapse when he came to the lines "Why? all delights are vain, but that most vain / Which, with pain purchas'd, doth inherit pain" and had to improvise.

sleight / slight

Relying upon various slights of hand in the accounting department, the corporation was able to deceive its shareholders for years. The idiom *sleight of hand* is often miswritten *slight of hand* as a result of the homophony between the words *sleight,* meaning "a trick performed so deftly that the manner of execution cannot be observed" and *slight,* meaning as an adjective "small, delicate, of little importance" and as a noun "a snub, a discourteous inattention." The mistake may also result from a notion associating dexterity with lightness of weight and thus slightness of size—an idea also suggested by the word *legerdemain,* a borrowing of the French phrase meaning "light of hand." In the past, *slight* was a common spelling for the word *sleight,* but now the two words are consistently kept apart in standardized spelling. Despite their similarity in sound, *sleight* and *slight* are different words in origin. *Sleight* is related to the adjective *sly,* from Old Norse *slœgr,* while *slight* belongs to a group of words occurring in the Germanic languages (the close relatives of English) and originally meaning "level, plain," then by extension "without note, worthless, bad," such as the German word *schlecht,* "bad."

slew / slough / slue

The noun *slew,* pronounced (slo͞o), means "a large amount or number; a lot," as in *a slew of unpaid bills.* The word is fairly colloquial and should be replaced by expressions such as "a great number" in more formal writing. The word comes from Irish Gaelic *sluagh,* "army, multitude," and is in fact one of a slew of informal English expressions of Irish Gaelic origin, such as *galore, slob,* and *smithereens.*

The word *slough* has several meanings and pronunciations. One of these is "a swamp, especially one with trees, that forms part of a bayou, inlet, or backwater." In the United States, the pronunciation (slo͞o), rhyming with *brew,* is usual in this meaning, but the pronunciation (slou), rhyming with *brow,* can be heard as well. *Slough* also has the related meaning "a hollow filled with deep mud." Frequently, *slough* is used metaphorically to indicate a state of deep despair or a place characterized by immorality, in reference to the *Slough of Despond,* where sinners become mired in the allegorical novel *Pilgrim's Progress* by John Bunyan. In this extended usage, and in the phrase *Slough of Despond,* the pronunciation (slou) is perhaps more usual. In British English, (slou) is also the usual pronunciation of the word in all senses related to the meaning "muddy terrain." The word comes from Old English *slō.*

Measures of land and geographic features are often used to specify quantities, as in the expressions like *a lot of money, a mountain of work,* and *a sea of troubles.* This tendency, as well as the homophony between *slew* and *slough* in the United States, has resulted in the misspelling of *slew* as *slough.* This frequently occurs when masses or quantities of unpleasant or tedious things are being measured, as in *I had to deal with a whole slough of problems* or *I could offer you a whole slough of reasons.* However, *slew* is the correct spelling in these instances.

Slough can also mean "a layer or mass of dead tissue," used in particular of the dead outer skin shed by a reptile or amphibian. The word also has a related verbal sense, "to be cast off or shed," as in *The snake sloughed off its skin.* In these meanings, *slough* is pronounced (slŭf), rhyming with *tough*. The spelling of this word as *sluff* is not widely accepted, even in the slang meaning of the phrasal verb *slough off*, "to be lazy, shirk," illustrated by the phrase *sluffing off at work*. The word *slough* in the sense of "to cast off" is unrelated to *slough*, "swamp," and first appeared in Middle English as *slughe*.

Slue (slo͞o) is a verb meaning "to turn sharply, veer," used in both transitive and intransitive senses: *She braked and slued the car around. The car slued around and headed back toward us with increasing speed.* It is also used as a noun meaning "a turn." *Slue* is the preferred spelling in the United States, although the spelling *slew* is usual in British usage. The origin of the word *slue* is unknown, but it is probably unrelated to the other words pronounced (slo͞o).

sloth

The traditional (and British English) pronunciation rhymes with *both*, although the word is now also commonly pronounced in American English so that it rhymes with *moth*, especially when used to refer to the sloth bear.

slough   See **slew.**

slow

Slow may sometimes be used instead of *slowly* when it comes after the verb: *We drove the car slow. Slow* is often used in speech and informal writing, especially when brevity and forcefulness are sought: *Drive slow! Slow* is also the established idiomatic form with certain senses of common verbs: *The watch runs slow. Take it slow.* In formal writing, however, *slowly* is generally preferred.

slue   See **slew.**

sneaked / snuck

The past tense and past participle *snuck* is an American invention. It first appeared in the 19th century as a nonstandard regional variant of *sneaked,* the regular form that has existed since the 1500s. But widespread use of *snuck* has become increasingly more common. It is now used by educated speakers in all regions. Formal written English is more conservative than other varieties, of course, and here *snuck* still meets with some resistance. In our 2001 survey, 61 percent of the Usage Panel preferred *sneaked* in the sentence *The pickpocket quietly (sneaked/snuck) up on his intended victim.* This was down slightly from 67 percent in our 1988 survey.

But data on frequency of use suggests that the tide is turning and that broad acceptance of *snuck* is inevitable. A 1990 review of ten thousand citations containing *sneaked* and *snuck* indicated that *sneaked* was preferred by a factor of 7 to 2. In 2004, a search of newspaper databases showed *sneaked* outhitting *snuck* by a factor of 8 to 5. In a search of the Internet in general, *snuck* was used 28 percent more frequently than *sneaked*.

See more at **dived, sink, strong verbs,** and **wake.**

SO

***so* as a connector**   As a connector, the word *so* has a number of grammatical functions. It is sometimes used as an adverb with the conjunctive meaning "consequently, therefore" (*We felt full and so stopped eating*) or "after that, then" (*By the end of the weekend, we had used up all the bread and other staples, so I drove into town to get some groceries*). It is also used as an adverbial particle to introduce certain sentences (*So what's going on here?*) and to express disapproval or sarcasm (*So this is how a boy treats his mother?*).

When functioning as a conjunction, *so* has some aspects of a subordinating conjunction and some aspects of a coordinating conjunction, much like the word *for.* Some grammar books classify *so* one way, and some another. Certainly *so* (or *so that*) has the meaning of a subordinating conjunction ("in order that" or "with the result that"): *I bought a car so I could drive to the shore. The traffic was heavy, so we arrived late.* And like a subordinating conjunction, *so* can only link full clauses, not smaller grammatical units (the way a coordinating conjunction can). But like a coordinating conjunction such as *or, so* (at least in its use expressing result) normally has a fixed position in the sequence of a sentence and can't be transposed to the front. Note that one cannot say *So (that) the floor collapsed, the house was built with shoddy materials,* much as one cannot say *Or I may play golf tomorrow, I'd like to play golf today.*

***so* or *so that* in purpose clauses**   Despite this complexity, traditional grammar has tended to view *so* solely as an adverb, and accordingly one rule stipulates that *so* must be followed by *that* in formal writing when used to introduce a clause giving the reason for or the purpose of an action: *He stayed so that he could see the movie a second time.* But since the use of *so* for *so that* is common even in formal writing, it seems best to consider the issue one of stylistic preference: *The store stays open late so* [or *so that*] *people who work all day can buy groceries.* Note that in most cases when *so* is used to express purpose, it is not preceded by a comma.

***so* or *so that* in result clauses**   It is similarly acceptable to use either *so* or *so that* to introduce clauses that state a result or consequence. Here *so* is usually preceded by a comma: *The Bay Bridge was still closed, so* [or *so that*] *the drive from San Francisco to the Berkeley campus took an hour and a half.*

***so* as a connector in a narrative**   *So the guy sits down at our table and pulls up his chair to get closer to me. So he starts telling us about his uncle . . . So* is frequently used in informal speech to string together the elements of a narrative. Readers of formal writing generally expect connections to be made more explicit, however.

***so* as intensifier**   Usage critics sometimes object to the use of *so* as an intensifier meaning "to a great degree or extent," as in *We were so relieved to learn that the dead-*

line had been extended. This may be because, unlike *very*, the word *so* presumes that the listener or reader will be sympathetic with the speaker's evaluation of the situation, and thus this use of *so* can seem out of place in formal contexts that require a more detached or neutral tone. But in certain formal situations, intensive *so* can be put to good use, as it invites the reader to take the point of view of the speaker or subject: *The request seemed to her to be quite reasonable; it was so unfair of the manager to refuse.* For *so* to be effective in this way, however, it must be used sparingly.

See more at **as.**

so-called / self-styled

Quotation marks should not be used to set off descriptions that follow expressions such as *so-called* and *self-styled,* which themselves relieve the writer of responsibility for the attribution: *his so-called foolproof method* [not *"foolproof method"*]. When used as a premodifier, *so-called* invariably indicates skepticism or disapproval on the part of the writer, but when *so called* follows the word or phrase it modifies, it is often used in a neutral manner and never has a hyphen, since it is not a compound adjective but the adverb *so* followed by the participle *called*:

> In 1862 Garibaldi, the peripatetic Hero of Two Worlds—so called because of his exploits in South America—again tried to force the king's hand by summoning his motley army of red shirts for a march on Rome (David I. Kertzer, *Prisoner of the Vatican*)

Self-styled is used in a similar fashion to imply criticism of the word it precedes, but it can also be used in a nonjudgmental way to indicate that the person has chosen a certain moniker or self-designation:

> Inside most self-styled avant-gardists is a classicist's soul, and the rule extends to underground hip-hop (Ben Ratliff, "Old-School Classicists in the Hip-Hop Underground," *New York Times*)

someday / some day / sometime / some time

The adverbs *someday* and *sometime* express future time indefinitely: *We'll succeed someday. Come sometime. Let's meet sometime when your schedule permits.* This sense can also be conveyed by *some day* and *some time.* But the open spellings are always used when *some* is an adjective modifying and specifying a more particular *day* or *time: Come some day* [not *someday*] *soon. Choose some day* [not *someday*] *that is not so busy.*

See more at **awhile** and **sometime.**

someplace   See **everyplace.**

sometime

People most often use *sometime* as an adverb meaning "at some indefinite time in the future." For when to use the single word *sometime* or the phrase *some time,* see **someday.**

Since the 15th century people have used *sometime* as an adjective to mean "former," as in *our sometime colleague.* Since the 1930s people have also used it to mean "occasional," as in *Duquette decided to trade Everett, the team's sometime star and sometime problem child.* Evidence suggests that this usage is now standard. In 1975, a majority of the Usage Panel found this "occasional" use unacceptable, but in our 2002 survey, 70 percent accepted the example quoted above.

The adverbial use of *sometime* meaning "occasionally," however, was not met with much favor. Only 19 percent accepted the sentence *The website is intended to help you navigate through the sometime confusing maze of government regulations.* In such instances, where an adjective (and not a noun) is being modified, use *sometimes* instead.

See more at **awhile.**

sonorous

The older pronunciation is (sə-nôr′əs) or (sə-nōr′əs), with stress on the second syllable. As the results from our 1995 survey indicate, however, the variant pronunciation (sŏn′ər-əs), with stress on the first syllable, is now much more common in American English. In this ballot, 84 percent of the Usage Panelists gave the pronunciation with stress on the first syllable as their pronunciation, and only 16 percent gave the older pronunciation with stress on the second syllable as their pronunciation. Two of the Panelists who are linguists noted that whereas they stress the first syllable, they pronounce it with a long *o,* as (sō′nər-əs).

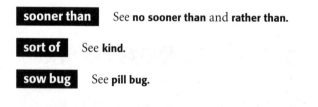

sooner than   See **no sooner than** and **rather than.**

sort of   See **kind.**

sow bug   See **pill bug.**

speak to

The phrasal verb *speak to* is sometimes used to mean "to talk about or discuss." It often occurs in the phrase *speak to the issue* (of something), as in *He encouraged the faculty to speak to the issue of student plagiarism.* This expression must be considered standard. In our 2001 survey, 81 percent of the Usage Panel accepted the sentence quoted above.

But when *speak to* is used in this way with objects other than *issue,* the Panel is split. Only 53 percent accepted the sentence *The analysts asked the CEO to speak to the company's plans for new products.* This suggests that *speak to the issue* has become a set phrase in the language, and that many people are likely to consider variations of it to be infelicitous.

species

The word *species* is used in biology for a group of organisms that have many characteristics in common and rank below a genus in taxonomy. Organisms that belong to the same species and reproduce sexually usually interbreed and produce fertile offspring (whereas organisms belonging to different species cannot produce fertile offspring). *Species* is both a singular and a plural noun: *The box elder is actually a species of maple. There are many species of hardwoods growing in the Adirondacks.*

There are two acceptable pronunciations of *species:* (spē′shēz), the choice of 49 percent of the Usage Panel in our 1996 survey, and (spē′sēz), the choice of 44 percent. (The remainder reported using both forms.)

specious

A *specious* argument is not simply a false one but one that is deceptively plausible. There is a certain contradiction, therefore, when an argument is described as *obviously specious* or *specious on the face of things.* If the fallaciousness is so apparent, the argument is not truly specious.

speed / velocity

In scientific usage, these terms are distinct from each other—in fact, they are as distinct as *distance* and *position.*

The *speed* of an object is simply the distance traveled by the object per unit time, regardless of the direction of motion. It is a *scalar* quantity, which means that it is simply a number indicating a magnitude (of some units, such as *meters per second*).

The *velocity* of an object is more complex. Velocity is a *vector* quantity, which means that it includes not just magnitude but direction. It can be represented as an arrow, pointing in the direction of motion, whose length is equal to the speed of the object. This means the speed of the object is implicit in its velocity, but its velocity is not implicit in its speed. In fact, two objects moving at the same speed can have the same velocity, the opposite velocity, velocities at right angles to each other, or at any angle in between—just as two points that are the same distance from an object could be in the same place, on opposite sides, form a right angle with the object, or any angle in between.

spelling of words with *-ie-* or *-ei-*

The spelling of words with *-ie-* and *-ei-* often poses difficulties, but there are a few general guidelines that can be followed.

1. When the two letters have a long *e* sound (as in *feet*), *i* generally comes before *e*, except after *c*: *believe, chief, grieve, niece, siege, shield*; but *either, leisure, neither, seize, sheik.*

2. After *c*, *e* generally comes before *i*: *ceiling, conceit, deceive, perceive, receive, receipt*; but *ancient, financier, specie.*

3. When the two letters have a long *a* sound (as in *cake*), a short *e* sound (as in *pet*), a short *i* sound (as in *fit*), or a long *i* sound (as in *mine*), *e* generally comes before *i*: *Fahrenheit, foreign, forfeit, height, neighbor, sleight, sovereign, surfeit*; but *friend, handkerchief, mischief, sieve.*

4. Other words spelled with *-ie-* or *-ei-* present no difficulties because the vowels are pronounced separately: *deity, piety.*
   See more at **suffixes.**

spelling pronunciation

A *spelling pronunciation* is simply a pronunciation that is based on the spelling of a word without regard to its historical or traditional pronunciation. A classic example of this is the modern spelling pronunciation (ôf′tən) or (ŏf′tən) for *often*, which for centuries has been pronounced (ô′fən) or (ŏf′ən), with the *t* silent. This particular example is so common today as to go practically unnoticed, although some people may still object to it as they feel it amounts to hypercorrection, a pronunciation produced by mistaken analogy with standard usage out of a desire to be correct. Other words with commonly heard spelling pronunciations include *alms, boatswain, comptroller,* and *forecastle.*
   See more at **pronunciation spelling.**

spinster / bachelor

The word *spinster* is usually used to describe a woman who has remained single beyond an age that is considered societally appropriate for marrying. It is objectionable to some people because it defines a woman by her marital status and assumes that being unmarried is a negative situation that a woman would never choose. *Spinster* also has the connotation of undesirability and being "over the hill." It has no masculine counterpart other than *bachelor,* which is used irrespective of age. The word *bachelor* connotes choice, freedom, and independence.

   The contrast between these two words can be demonstrated by comparing the two examples below. The first, for *spinster,* is from a Minneapolis newspaper: "[*She*] *inhabits the central role of spinster sister Lenny, conveying a pathetic loneliness as she lights a single birthday candle perched atop a lone cookie in her attempt to celebrate her 30th birthday.*" The second, for *bachelor,* comes from *People* magazine: "[*He*] *is funny and commendably restrained as . . . a 20-year-old brainiac who wants to move out of Mom's house and taste greater freedom as his bachelor uncle's roommate.*"

   When it is important to refer to the marital status of a woman who has never been married, "single woman" or "unmarried woman" are preferable terms.

split infinitive

To boldly go where no one has gone before. This phrase, so familiar to *Star Trek* fans, presents the dilemma of the split infinitive—an infinitive that has an adverb between the *to* and the verb. Split infinitives have been condemned as ungrammatical for nearly two hundred years, but it is hard to see what exactly is wrong with saying *to boldly go.* Its meaning is clear. It has a strong rhythm than reinforces the meaning. And rearranging the phrase only makes it less effective. Trekkies may also want *to go boldly where no one has gone before,* but it doesn't sound as exciting. And certainly no one wants *to go where no one has gone before boldly.* That is a different voyage entirely.

In fact, the split infinitive is distinguished both by its length of use and the greatness of its users. People have been splitting infinitives since the 14th century, and some of the most noteworthy splitters include John Donne, Samuel Pepys, Daniel Defoe, Benjamin Franklin, Samuel Johnson, William Wordsworth, Abraham Lincoln, George Eliot, Henry James, and Willa Cather. Today the split infinitive is put to effective use by a wide variety of writers. Here is a brief sample from contemporary writers:

> During the most recent eruption cycle, the smoking mountain . . . spewed enough ash and lava and mud from melted snow and ice to all but bury a nearby town (William J. Broad, "El Popo's Rumblings Draw Volcanologists to Edge of Danger," *New York Times*)

> I sometimes have the impression that to really know these weekend sailors, mountain climbers, and horsewomen, I would have to accompany them on their outings and excursions—see them in their natural habitat, so to speak (Witold Rybczynski, "Waiting for the Weekend," *Atlantic Monthly*)

> Cardiologists had long known that some people naturally form collateral blood vessels that can bypass blocked arteries, but most people do not make them or do not make enough of them to successfully divert blood (Gina Kolata, "Novel Bypass Method: A Dose of New Genes," *New York Times*)

> Still as engaging a personality as ever, Jim started making a living as a motivational speaker, encouraging people with and without physical disabilities to never accept the notion of personal limitations (Elizabeth Gilbert, "Lucky Jim," *GQ*)

None of these passages would be improved (and they all arguably would be made worse) by revision to remove the split infinitive.

The only rationale for condemning the split infinitive is based on a false analogy with Latin. The thinking is that because the Latin infinitive is a single word, the English infinitive should be treated as if it were a single unit. But English is not Latin, and people split infinitives all the time without giving it a thought. Should we condemn compound infinitives, such as *I want to go and have a look,* simply because the infinitive *have* has no *to* next to it?

Still, if infinitives split by adverbs seem jarring, they can often be avoided without difficulty. For instance, the sentence *To better understand the miners' plight, he went to live in their district* can be recast as *To understand the miners' plight better, he went to live in their district.* But as the *Star Trek* example shows, writers must be on guard not to ruin the rhythm of the sentence or create an unintended meaning by displacing an adverb.

Writers who plan on keeping their split infinitives should be wary of constructions that have more than one word between *to* and the verb. The Usage Panel splits down the middle on the one-adverb split infinitive. In our 1988 survey, 50 percent accepted it in the sentence *The move allowed the company to legally pay the employees severance payments that in some cases exceeded $30,000.* But only 23 percent of the Panel accepted the split infinitive in this sentence: *We are seeking a plan to gradually, systematically, and economically relieve the burden.* The Panel was more tolerant of constructions in which the intervening words are intrinsic to the sense of the verb: 87 percent accepted the sentence *We expect our output to more than double in a year.*

Remember too that infinitive phrases in which the adverb precedes a participle, such as *to be rapidly rising, to be clearly understood,* and *to have been ruefully mistaken,* are not split and should be acceptable to everybody. Also acceptable, even by traditional grammatical rules, are *to* constructions with a gerund, as in *He is committed to laboriously assembling all of the facts of the case.* Here what is split is not an infinitive but a prepositional phrase.

split personality   See **multiple personality disorder.**

spouse   See **wife.**

spring fever

A person who has a fever is usually listless and incapable of doing much, and the original meaning of *spring fever* (which dates back to the 1840s) was for a feeling of languor or listlessness that accompanies the warming temperatures of spring. This may be a product of an agrarian culture, in which spring usually meant a return to hard labor on the farm, and people were understandably reluctant to jump at the chance to get back at it. At least since 1945, when Oscar Hammerstein and Richard Rodgers wrote *It Might As Well Be Spring* for the movie *State Fair, spring fever* has also referred to a state of restlessness or excitement. This sense of nervous excitement, an itching to get out of the house and enjoy the weather, derives from the notion of a fever as a condition of overexcitement of bodily activity, a sense that goes back to the 1500s. It is hardly surprising that fever got tangled up with the idea of falling in love.

These two senses of spring fever are still in contention today, though some might say that they are not mutually exclusive. In our 2001 survey, 60 percent of the Usage Panel accepted both versions of the term in the following examples: *When he finally got some free time on his hands, he felt listless and lethargic from spring fever. Energized by spring fever, they spent the weekend playing Frisbee instead of studying for exams.* Since the word might be interpreted one way or the other, be sure that the context makes clear whether you mean feverish lethargy or feverish excitement.

stalactite / stalagmite

A seemingly timeless usage problem in geology is the difference between *stalactites* and *stalagmites*. They are both examples of *speleothems,* mineral deposits that form in caves. Each word is based on the Greek word *stalassein,* meaning "to drip," since the source of each in nature is the dripping of mineral-rich water within caves. The difference is in their orientation: a *stalactite* is an icicle-shaped mineral deposit that hangs from the roof of a cavern, and a *stalagmite* is a conical mineral deposit that extends up from the floor of a cavern.

stationary / stationery

Stationary is an adjective meaning "not moving" or "not capable of being moved, fixed." *Stationery* is a noun meaning "paper, writing materials, envelopes, and similar items."

These two words, which are often confused in spelling, ultimately come from the same Latin word, *statiō,* "station, fixed place of activity." However, they entered the English language by different routes. *Stationary* comes from Old French *stationnaire,* "stationary," which in turn is from Latin *stationārius,* "belonging to a military station," an adjective derived from *statiō.* *Stationery,* on the other hand, was created from the noun *stationer* in English, apparently during the 17th century. *Stationer* originally meant "a publisher, a bookseller," as well as "a merchant specializing in writing materials," and this noun too comes from Latin *stationārius,* "belonging to a station," here used to indicate a shopkeeper as opposed to an itinerant peddler. The new word *stationery* was made by adding the suffix *–y* to the end of the preexisting noun *stationer,* while the spelling *–ary* of the adjective simply reflects the original spelling of the Latin word *stationārius.* The difference in spelling results from this difference in origin, and knowledge of the history of the two words may help some writers to remember the correct spelling of *stationery* as "the stationer's ware."

Although nowadays all writers must observe the spelling distinction between *stationary* and *stationery,* spelling in general was not so fixed in the past as it is today. In fact, in some of the earliest known documents using the word *stationery,* it is "misspelled" as *stationary.*

status

In the 1997 survey of the Usage Panel, 53 percent of the Panelists preferred the pronunciation (stăt′əs), 36 percent preferred (stā′təs), and 11 percent said they use both pronunciations. The pronunciation (stā′təs) is the older, more traditional pronunciation, and it remains the most common one in British English.

staunch / stanch

Staunch and *stanch* are variant spellings of each other. *Staunch* is usually an adjective meaning "steadfast, true," as in *staunch friends,* though the spelling *stanch* is also acceptable for this usage. *Stanch* is more commonly a verb meaning *to stop the flow of*, as in *stanch the bleeding*. The spelling *staunch* is sometimes used for this verb as well.

stewardess

The word *stewardess* was once an acceptable term for a female flight attendant. The masculine form *steward* was rarely used because the large majority of flight attendants were female. Today, *flight attendant* is a widely accepted term for both male and female members of a flight crew whose main job is to interact with passengers.

See more at **feminine suffixes.**

stomp / stamp

The verbs *stomp* and *stamp* are used interchangeably in the sense "to trample" or "to tread on violently": *stomped* [or *stamped*] *the poster of the candidate, stomping* [or *stamping*] *horses.* But only *stamp* is standard in the sense "to eliminate": *stamp out a fire, stamp out poverty. Stamp* is also standard in the sense "to strike the ground with (the foot), as in anger or frustration," as in *He stamped his foot and began to cry.* Back in our 1966 survey, a large majority of the Usage Panel rejected the use of *stomp* with this sense, although it is commonly used this way, as in this newspaper quotation: *"He'll stomp his foot after a bad shot and give a steely stare when his team isn't playing up to its potential."*

The phrasal verb *stomp out* is actually more common than *stamp out* when used to mean "to walk with heavy steps," as in *He got angry and stomped out* or *He laughed and stomped out of the room,* though both verbs are standard in such uses.

straight / strait

Straight, as an adjective, means "not bent or curving, level, direct." The adjective *strait,* on the other hand, originally meant "narrow, constricted, strict." Nowadays the word is most often used in the extended sense "difficult, stressful," although in general *strait* has become uncommon as a plain adjective and occurs mostly in compounds. This unfamiliarity of *strait* has led to confusion of *straight* and *strait,* a problem that extends to the derived verbs *straighten,* "to make straight or level, extend without bending," and *straiten,* "to make narrow, confine" and also "to make difficult." In contemporary English, *straiten* is most often found as a past participle in the phrase *straitened circumstances.* Writers should be careful not to miswrite this form of the verb as *straightened: Her generosity released him from the financially straitened* [not *straightened*] *circumstances that had hindered his work on the novel.*

The adjective *strait,* when meaning "tight, confining," is often misspelled *straight* in two familiar compounds. A *straitjacket* (not a *straightjacket*) is a jacket that confines the arms. Similarly, the adjective *straitlaced* (not *straightlaced*) originally meant "having the laces of one's clothing drawn tightly," but nowadays is more often used in a metaphorical sense, "excessively strict in behavior, morality, or opinions." As the opposite of *crooked,* the adjective *straight* is also used to describe ethical and moral behavior in the senses "honest, fair-minded" and "conventional," and this may mislead writers into writing *straightlaced* for *straitlaced.*

The word *strait* is also often used as a noun meaning "a narrow channel joining two larger bodies of water." However, since straits can look straight on a map and are sometimes the most direct (or straightest) passage available to a ship, *strait* is sometimes misspelled as *straight* in such phrases as *the Straits* [not *Straights*] *of Magellan* and *desperate straits* [not *straights*].

Some writers may find that remembering the history of *straight* and *strait* helps keep the difference between the two words straight. *Straight* is a native English word descended from Old English *streht,* "stretched," past participle of *streccen,* "to stretch." *Strait* comes from Latin *strictus,* "drawn tight," by way of Old French *estreit* (Modern French *étroit*). The Latin word is also the source of English *strict,* to which other words such as *constrict* and *restrict* are related. Most of the senses of *strait* remain close to the original notion of constriction that the word conveyed.

stratum

In Standard English, the plural of *stratum* is *strata* (or sometimes *stratums*), not *stratas.*

strength   See **length.**

strong verbs

A strong verb forms its past tense by a change in the vowel of the base form and forms its past participle by a change in vowel and sometimes by adding *-n* or *-en.* *Drink, ride,* and *speak* are examples of strong verbs.

See more at **dived, sink, sneaked,** and **verbs, principal parts of.**

stupefy

The word *stupefy* and its derivatives like *stupefaction* are spelled with an *e* in the second syllable, rather than an *i.* Many English verbs are formed using the suffix *–ify,* and the frequent misspelling *stupify* is probably the result of the influence of these verbs and also of the *i* in the related adjective and noun *stupid,* which can have the meaning "stunned senseless." The verbs ending in the suffix *–ify* are often direct borrowings of Latin verbs ending in *–ficare,* like *magnify* from *magnificāre.* However, many new verbs have been invented by extracting the suffix *–ify* from words of Latin origin and attaching it to the end of other words, as can be seen in *Frenchify* from the adjective *French.* The word *stupefy,* however, comes from Latin *stupēfacere,* "to make stupid, to stun," and the *e* in the second syllable of the English word reflects the spelling of the Latin original. *Liquefy* is a similar word that has traditionally been spelled with an *e*, although the spelling with *liquify* is now accepted as a variant by several American dictionaries.

sub–

The prefix *sub–* can be traced back to the Latin preposition *sub*, meaning "under." Some words beginning with *sub–* that came into English from Latin include *submerge*, *suburb*, and *subvert*. When *sub–* is used to form words in English, it can mean "under" (*submarine, subsoil, subway*), "subordinate" (*subcommittee, subplot, subset*), or "less than completely" (*subhuman, substandard*). *Sub–* can form compounds by combining with verbs as well as with adjectives and nouns, as in *subdivide, sublease,* and *sublet.*

subconscious   See **unconscious.**

subject

In traditional grammar, the subject is the noun, noun phrase, or pronoun in a sentence or clause that denotes what is described by a following predicate. In active sentences, the subject is usually the doer of an action described by a following verb phrase; for example, in *The flowers are withering,* the noun phrase *the flowers* is the subject. In passive sentences, the subject is typically not a doer but is acted upon; for example, in *The flowers have been withered by the harsh sunlight,* the phrase *the flowers* is the subject of the sentence. Some verbs have a naturally passive meaning even when used in active constructions, such as *undergo:* in *She underwent surgery to repair her shoulder,* the pronoun *she* serves as subject. In sentences with a linking verb such as *be* or *seem,* the subject may not play any active or passive role at all, but is simply being described: The phrase *these birds* is thus a subject in such sentences as *These birds are rare* and *These birds seem upset.*

Subjects are also sometimes found within noun phrases in *possessive constructions,* where they appear in the possessive case.

See more at **object, possessive constructions, predicate,** and **there.**

subject and verb agreement

grammatical agreement   A verb must agree with its subject in person and number. Stated another way, singular subjects take singular verbs, and plural subjects take plural verbs. This oft-quoted rule generally holds true, but subject and verb agreement in English has some complications that the rule does not address.

One of the nice things about English is that its verbs do not change much to agree with a subject in number. In fact, for almost all verbs, there is only one change, adding -*s* or -*es* for third person singular, present tense. We say *He goes, She tries,* and

It matters. All other persons require no changes to the verb. We say *I play, You play, We play,* and *They play.* The past tense requires its own changes to the verb, but (except for the verb *be*) these do not involve number. Thus we say *He walked and I ran, They walked and we ran,* and so on.

The modal auxiliaries are an exception to the agreement rule. They do not change to show number. We say *I can swim, He can swim, They can swim,* and so on. The primary verb *be* is a unique case in that it has many different forms—*am, are, is, was, were*—depending on the person, number, and tense of a specific use.

notional agreement   It would be fine if this was all there was to remember, but there is more than one kind of agreement. There is *grammatical agreement,* as discussed above, and agreement in meaning, or *notional agreement.* Usually grammatical agreement and notional agreement coincide. In the sentence *He laughs,* both are singular. In the sentence *We laugh,* both are plural. But in some sentences a subject can have a singular form and a plural meaning. Thus in the sentence *Her family are all avid skiers,* the noun *family* is singular in form but plural in meaning, and the verb is plural to agree with the meaning. In other words, there is notional agreement, but not grammatical agreement, between the subject and the verb. In the sentence *Everyone has gone to the movies,* the situation is reversed. The subject *everyone* is plural in meaning and singular in form, but the verb agrees in number with the form of its grammatical subject. There is grammatical agreement but not notional agreement.

Similarly, there are some nouns like *mumps* and *news* that are plural in form but take a singular verb: *The mumps was once a common childhood disease.* Amounts often take a singular verb: *Ten thousand bucks is a lot of money.* Here again we have notional, but not grammatical, agreement—the ten thousand bucks is considered a single quantity, and it gets a singular verb.

There are a number of words in English that can take a singular or plural verb depending on how they are used. Among these are collective nouns (such as *faculty* and *family*), pronouns such as *any* and *none,* and many nouns ending in *–ics,* such as *politics.*

agreement by proximity   Certain grammatical constructions provide further complications. Sometimes the noun that is adjacent to the verb can exert more influence than the noun that is the grammatical subject. Selecting a verb in a sentence like *A variety of styles (has been/have been) in vogue for the last year* can be tricky. The traditional rules require *has been,* but the plural sense of the noun phrase presses for *have been.* While 59 percent of the Usage Panel in our 1995 survey insisted on the singular verb in this sentence, 22 percent actually preferred the plural verb and another 19 percent said that either *has* or *have* is acceptable, meaning that 41 percent overall found the plural verb with a singular grammatical subject to be acceptable.

Sometimes syntax itself makes it impossible to follow the agreement rule. In a sentence like *Either John or his brothers are bringing the dessert,* the verb can't agree with both parts of the subject. Some people believe that the verb should agree with the closer of the two subjects. This is called *agreement by proximity.* For more on this subject, see **either** and **or.**

compound subjects   In Modern English, a compound subject connected by *and* normally takes a plural verb: *Rebecca and Martha play in the same band. The house* *and the barn are on the same property. Their innovative idea, persistence, and careful research have finally paid off.* When a subject is followed by a conjoining prepositional phrase such as *in addition to, as well as,* or *along with,* the verb should be singular: *Jesse as well as Luke likes jazz. The old school along with the playground is up for sale.*

Sometimes compound subjects are governed by a sense of unity and by notional agreement take a singular verb: *My name and address is printed on the box. His colleague and friend* [one person] *deserves equal credit.* Using a singular or plural verb changes the meaning of the sentence. *Eating garlic and drinking red wine sometimes gives me a headache* means that the combination of garlic and red wine can cause a headache. With a plural verb (*give*), the sentence implies that garlic and red wine act separately; either can bring on a headache.

See more at **collective noun.**

subjunctive

the forms   *If she were coming, she would be here by now. I insist that the chairman resign! Their main demand was that the lawsuit be dropped.* These sentences all contain verbs in the subjunctive mood, which is used chiefly to express the speaker's attitude about the likelihood or factuality of a given situation. If the verbs were in the indicative mood, the first sentence would have *she was coming,* the second sentence *the chairman resigns,* and the third sentence *the lawsuit is dropped.*

English has had a subjunctive mood since Old English times, but most of the functions of the old subjunctive have been taken over by auxiliary verbs like *may* and *should,* and the subjunctive survives only in very limited situations. It has a present and past form. The present form is identical to the base form of the verb, so it is noticeable in the third person singular, which has no final *s,* and in the case of the verb *be,* which uses *be* as its subjunctive instead of *am, is,* and *are.* The past subjunctive is identical with the past tense except in the case of the verb *be,* which uses *were* for all persons: *If I were rich, If he were rich, If they were rich.*

The present subjunctive is most familiar to us in formulaic expressions such as *God help him, be that as it may, come what may,* and *suffice it to say.* It also occurs in *that* clauses used to state commands or to express intentions or necessity:

> We insist that he *do* the job properly.
> The committee proposes that she *be* appointed treasurer immediately.
> It is essential that we *be* informed of your plans.

Other functions include use in some conditional clauses (as in Shakespeare's *"For nothing can be ill, if she be well"*) and in clauses that make concessions or express purpose. In these cases the subjunctive carries a formal tone:

> Whether he *be* opposed to the plan or not, we must seek his opinion.
> Even though he *be* opposed to the plan, we must try to implement it.
> They are rewriting the proposal so that it not *contradict* new zoning laws.

The subjunctive is not required in such sentences, however, and indicative forms can be used instead (*whether he is opposed, even though he is opposed, so that it does not contradict*).

The past subjunctive is sometimes called the *were* subjunctive, since *were* is the only subjunctive form that is distinct from the indicative past tense. It appears chiefly in *if* clauses and in a few other constructions expressing hypothetical conditions:

> If he *were* sorry, he'd have apologized by now.
> I wish she *weren't* going away.
> She's already acting as if she *were* going to be promoted.
> Suppose she *were* to resign, what would you do then?

if clauses—the traditional rules   According to traditional rules, the subjunctive is used to describe an occurrence that is presupposed to be contrary to fact: *if I were ten years younger, if America were still a British Colony.* The verb in the main clause of these sentences must then contain the verb *would* or (less frequently) *should: If I were ten years younger, I would consider entering the marathon. If America were still a British colony, we would all be drinking tea in the afternoon.* When the situation described by the *if* clause is not presupposed to be false, however, that clause must contain an indicative verb. The form of verb in the main clause will depend on the intended meaning: *If* Hamlet *was really written by Marlowe, as many have argued, then we have underestimated Marlowe's genius. If Kevin was out all day, then it makes sense that he couldn't answer the phone.*

Remember, just because the modal verb *would* appears in the main clause doesn't mean that the verb in the *if* clause must be in the subjunctive if the content of that clause is not presupposed to be false: *If it was* [not *were*] *raining, I would always take the subway home rather than walk. He would always call her from the office if he was* [not *were*] *going to be late for dinner.*

Another traditional rule states that the subjunctive should not be used following verbs such as *ask* or *wonder* in *if* clauses that express indirect questions, even if the content of the question is presumed to be contrary to fact: *We wondered if dinner was* [not *were*] *included in the room price. Some of the people we met even asked us if California was* [not *were*] *an island.*

if clauses—the reality   In practice, of course, many people ignore the rules. In fact, over the last two hundred years even well-respected writers have tended to use the indicative *was* where the traditional rule would require the subjunctive *were.* A usage such as *If I was the only boy in the world* may break the rules, but it sounds perfectly natural.

subjunctive after *wish*   Yet another traditional rule requires *were* rather than *was* in a contrary-to-fact statement that follows the verb *wish: I wish I were* [not *was*] *lighter on my feet.* Many writers continue to insist on this rule, but the indicative *was* in such clauses can be found in the works of many well-known writers.

would have for had   In spoken English, there is a growing tendency to use *would have* in place of the subjunctive *had* in contrary-to-fact clauses, such as *If she would have* [instead of *if she had*] *only listened to me, this would never have happened.* But this usage is still widely considered an error in writing. In our 1995 survey, only 14 percent of the Usage Panel accepted it in the previously cited sentence, and a similar amount—but 16 percent—accepted it in the sentence *I wish you would have told me about this sooner.*

didn't* for *hadn't In speech people often substitute *didn't* for the subjunctive *hadn't* in *if* clauses, such as *If I didn't have* [instead of *if I hadn't had*] *my seat belt on, I would be dead.* This usage is also considered nonstandard, however. In our 1995 survey, 71 percent of the Usage Panel rejected it, although 18 percent felt it would be acceptable in informal contexts.

had have / 'd have / had've / had of Another subjunctive form that is sometimes used in speech but is usually edited out of Standard English is the intrusive *have* occurring after *had*, as in *If they'd have come home when they were supposed to, they would have enjoyed a good meal* and *We would have been in real trouble if it hadn't have been for you.* In speech this *have* is always reduced, as in *had' a'* or *had'n a'*, and it is sometimes rendered in writing as *'ve* or a graphical variant like *of*. The negative *hadn't have* construction often appears in conjunction with the verb *happen*, as in *If that hadn't have happened, he would not be the musician he is today*, where standard practice requires *If that hadn't happened*. The Usage Panel has little affection for *hadn't have* in these situations; 91 percent of Panelists found it unacceptable in 1995.

See more at **should** and **wish**.

subordinate clause

A dependent clause.
See **clause**.

subordinating conjunctions

Subordinating (or *subordinate*) conjunctions introduce dependent clauses, clauses that generally cannot stand alone as full sentences and depend on a main clause for completion of meaning. Subordinating conjunctions include *after, although, as, as if, as long as, because, before, if, insomuch as, since, so that, unless, until, when, whenever, where, wherever, however*, and *while*. If not attached to an independent clause, dependent clauses are considered sentence fragments. When positioned at the front of the sentence, the dependent clause is usually separated from the main clause by a comma, as in *After Desmond joined the band, he began to compose music* and *Whenever the cat got in the attic, we could hear the squirrels on the roof run away.* If the subordinate clause follows the main clause, a comma is not always required and may actually look odd in sentences like *Desmond began to compose music after he joined the band. The home team won the game because it had better pitching.* Sometimes the presence or absence of a comma can change the meaning of the sentence; for more on this, see **because.**

Subordinating conjunctions can be distinguished from coordinating conjunctions by the fact that subordinating conjunctions can only link clauses, whereas coordinating conjunctions can link shorter grammatical units like nouns and verb phrases (as in *Bob and Tom went snowboarding* and *We added the eggs but forgot to mix the batter*). In addition, the clauses introduced by subordinating conjunctions can be positioned at the front of the sentence, whereas the clauses introduced by coordinating conjunctions cannot. Thus, one can say *He planted the tree when the ground had thawed* or *When the ground had thawed, he planted the tree.* But one cannot say *And he planted the tree, the ground thawed.*

See more at **conjunctive adverbs** and **that.**

substantive

A substantive is any word or group of words that function as a noun. For example, the word *wealthy,* typically classified as an adjective rather than a noun, is a substantive in *Only the wealthy can afford to belong to that club.* The infinitival clause *to read all day long* is a substantive in *To read all day long was her idea of a vacation,* since it is acting as the subject of the sentence.

such

The adjective *such* is often followed by *that* when *such* is used to mean "of a degree or quality indicated," as in the sentence *The demand of Feinberg's specialized services is such that he commands around $200,000 a month when he gets involved in a case.* This example was acceptable to 87 percent of the Usage Panel in our 1996 ballot.

The Panel does not, however, find the phrase *such that* to be an acceptable replacement for *so that* or *in such a way that.* A mere 12 percent approve of this usage in the sentence *The products are packaged such that users can pick the components they need and add capabilities over time.*

suffixes

A suffix is an affix that is added to the end of a word, forming a new word or serving as an inflectional ending, as *–ness* in *gentleness, –ing* in *walking,* or *-s* in *sits.* Many suffixes are discussed as separate entries in this book. Adding a suffix to a base form can often require some adjustment of the word's spelling. Guidelines for making these adjustments are listed below.

adding a suffix to a one-syllable word

1. Words of one syllable that end in a single consonant preceded by a single vowel double the final consonant before a suffix beginning with a vowel: *bag, baggage; hop, hopper; hot, hottest; red, redder; run, running; stop, stopped.* There are two notable exceptions to this rule: *bus* (*buses* or *busses; busing* or *bussing*) and *gas* (*gases* or *gasses; gassing; gassy*).
2. If a word ends with two or more consonants or if it ends with one consonant preceded by two or more vowels instead of one, the final consonant is not doubled: *debt, debtor; lick, licking; mail, mailed; sweet, sweetest.*

adding a suffix to a word with two or more syllables

1. Words of two or more syllables that have the accent on the last syllable and end in a single consonant preceded by a single vowel double the final consonant be-

fore a suffix beginning with a vowel: *admit, admitted; confer, conferring; control, controller; regret, regrettable.* There are a few exceptions: *chagrin, chagrined; transfer, transferred, transferring* but *transferable, transference.*

2. When the accent shifts to the first syllable of the word after the suffix is added, the final consonant is not doubled: *prefer, preference; refer, reference.*

3. If the word ends with two consonants or if the final consonant is preceded by more than one vowel the final consonant is not doubled: *perform, performance; repeal, repealing.*

4. If the word is accented on any syllable except the last the final consonant is not usually doubled: *benefit, benefited; develop, developed; interpret, interpreted.* However, some words like *cobweb, handicap,* and *outfit* follow the models of *web, cap,* and *fit,* even though these words may not be true compounds: *cobwebbed, handicapped, fitting.* A few others ending in *g* double the final *g* so that it will not be pronounced like *j: zigzag, zigzagged.*

adding a suffix beginning with a vowel to a word ending in a silent e

1. Words ending with a silent *e* usually drop the *e* before a suffix beginning with a vowel: *force, forcible; route, routed; glide, gliding; operate, operator; trifle, trifler.* However, there are many exceptions to this rule.

2. Many words of this type have alternative forms (the preferred form is given first): *blame, blamable* or *blameable; blue, bluish* or *blueish.*

3. Many words ending in *ce* or *ge* keep the *e* before the suffixes *–able* and *–ous: advantage, advantageous; change, changeable; trace, traceable.*

4. Words ending in a silent *e* keep the *e* if the word could be mistaken for another word: *dye, dyeing; singe, singeing.*

5. If the word ends in *ie,* the *e* is dropped and the *i* changed to *y* before the suffix *–ing.* A word ending in *i* remains unchanged before *–ing: die, dying; ski, skiing.*

6. *Mile* and *acre* do not drop the *e* before the suffix *–age: mileage, acreage.*

adding a suffix beginning with a consonant to a word ending in a silent e   Words
ending with a silent *e* generally retain the *e* before a suffix that begins with a consonant: *plate, plateful; shoe, shoeless; arrange, arrangement; white, whiteness; awe, awesome; nice, nicety.* However, there are many exceptions to this rule. Some of the most common are *abridge, abridgment; acknowledge, acknowledgment; argue, argument; awe, awful; due, duly; judge, judgment; nine, ninth; true, truly; whole, wholly; wise, wisdom.*

adding a suffix to a word ending in y

1. Words ending in *y* preceded by a consonant generally change the *y* to *i* before the addition of a suffix, except when the suffix begins with an *i: accompany, accompaniment; beauty, beautiful; icy, icier, icily, iciness;* but *reply, replying.*

2. The *y* is retained in derivatives of *baby, city,* and *lady* and before the suffixes *–ship* and *–like: babyhood, cityscape, ladyship, ladylike.*

3. Adjectives of one syllable ending in *y* preceded by a consonant usually retain the *y* when a suffix beginning with a consonant is added: *shy, shyly, shyness; sly, slyly, slyness; wry, wryly, wryness;* but *dryly* or *drily, dryness.* These adjectives usually

also retain the *y* when a suffix beginning with a vowel is added, although most
have variants where the *y* has changed to *i*: *dry, drier* or *dryer, driest* or *dryest;*
shy, shier or *shyer, shiest* or *shyest*.
4. Words ending in *y* preceded by a vowel usually retain the *y* before a suffix: *buy,*
buyer; key, keyless; coy, coyest; gay, gayer, gayest; but *day, daily; gay, gaily* or *gayly*.
5. Some words drop the final *y* before the addition of the suffix *–eous: beauty, beau-*
teous.

words ending in c   Words ending in *c* almost always have the letter *k* inserted after
the *c* when a suffix beginning with *e, i,* or *y* is added: *panic, panicky; picnic, picnicker*.
This is done so that the letter *c* will not be pronounced like *s*.

suffragist / suffragette

The word *suffragist,* meaning an advocate of the extension of political voting rights,
especially to women, is used of both men and women. The word *suffragette,* which
refers only to female suffragists, became popular in the early 20th century and was
favored by many female British suffragists as well as some groups and individuals
who mocked women's attempts to gain suffrage. In the United States, however, the
word *suffragist* was preferred by advocates of women's suffrage, who regarded *suf-*
fragette as a sexist diminutive.
    See **feminine suffixes.**

superlative degree

The superlative degree is a form of adjective and adverbial expressions showing the
extreme degree of comparison. For example, the words *best* and *brightest* are the superlative degree expressions of the adjectives *good* and *bright,* respectively. Except for
some irregular cases (such as *best* above), the superlative degree forms are formed by
suffixation of *–est* (for adjectives) or modification with *most* (for adjectives and adverbs, as in *Of all the racecar drivers, Frank drives the most aggressively*).
    See more at **adjectives, adverbs,** and **comparative degree.**

suppress   See **repress.**

symptom / sign

A website about men's health asks "Is excessive flatulence a sign of disease?" It may be
a symptom, but as far as correct usage is concerned, it cannot be a sign.
    A *symptom* is a subjective indication of a disorder or disease, such as pain, nau-
sea, or weakness. It is reported by the patient to the physician or another listener. A
sign, used medically, is an objective manifestation that indicates the presence of a disorder or disease, such as abnormal laboratory test or x-ray results or specific findings
during a physical examination. Symptoms may or may not be accompanied by signs,
and signs may be present without symptoms.

syntax

The term *syntax* refers to the system of rules in a given language that governs how words are combined to form grammatical phrases and sentences. The rules of English syntax, for instance, allow words to be combined to form the sequence *the man with the yellow hat,* but do not allow those same words to form the sequence *the man with yellow the hat* or *man the with yellow hat the.*

Syntax may also refer to the specific structures of a given phrase or sentence and how they relate to each other. For example, the phrase *the man with the yellow hat* may be described syntactically as the noun phrase *the yellow hat,* which is a part of the prepositional phrase *with the yellow hat,* which in turn modifies *man,* and so on.

· T ·

tack / tact / tactic

Nautically speaking, the meaning of the word *tack* is "the position of a vessel relative to the trim of its sails" or "the act of changing from one position or direction to another." The word is also commonly used figuratively to mean "a course of action meant to minimize opposition to the attainment of a goal," as in *choosing a different tack* or *changing tack*. Although the word *tact* has an entirely different meaning ("acute sensitivity to what is proper and appropriate in dealing with others"), it is frequently used mistakenly instead of *tack,* as in these examples:

> Defensive coordinator Donnie Henderson, known as a fearless blitzer, tried a different tact, playing soft coverage (*New York Daily News*)

> Our family has taken a different tact [with holiday food preparation] for the last decade, even before my daughter became a vegetarian (*The Jerusalem Post*)

Aside from the similarity in sound between these two words, another reason for their confusion is the similarity of *tact* to *tactic,* which means "an expedient for achieving a goal; a maneuver." One can take a different tack or use a different tactic, but properly speaking, it is not possible to take a different tact.

take   See **bring.**

talk

The phrasal verbs *talk about* and (less commonly) *talk of* sometimes have a piece of writing as their subject, as in *The article talks about the humanitarian crisis in the Sudan* and *The book talks of continuing barriers to free trade.* While this usage might seem a natural semantic extension—no different, really, from the similar and widely accepted use of the word *discuss*—for many people *talk* remains primarily associated with speaking, and using it for a written medium violates a norm of standard grammar. Although the usage is not new, it appears to have been rare until quite recently: *The Oxford English Dictionary*'s sole quotation for it is from Joseph Addison in 1705. The Usage Panel, at any rate, has mixed feelings about this construction. In our 2001 survey, 42 percent rejected it in the sentence *The book talks about drugs that exist in many of our communities.* For the time being, it is probably wise to use *discuss* or another nonspeaking verb such as *argue* or *maintain* instead.

tantalize

The word *tantalize* means "to excite someone by exposing something desirable while keeping it out of reach," as in this quotation from the *Baltimore Sun:* "*But the character of Vera seems to tantalize us, asking us to wait an entire film for her to erupt, to change in some fundamental way, to grow. But she never does, leaving the audience feeling cheated.*" The word is derived from Tantalus, the king in Greek mythology who, as a result of his crimes, was condemned in Hades to stand in water that receded when he tried to drink, with fruit hanging above him that receded when he reached for it.

The use of *tantalize* has recently been broadened to refer to stimulation of the senses with no implication of frustration or being teased. In fact, the word functions almost as the opposite of its original meaning, with *delight* now being a close synonym. This new usage, exhibited in the following example from the *St. Cloud Times,* has become common enough to be listed in some dictionaries: *If you find yourself looking for a wine everyone will enjoy Thanksgiving Day, look no further. Apricot aromas will tantalize you, followed by hints of rose and citrus.* Writers who want to appear cognizant of the word's origin should avoid this usage.

tantamount / paramount

Tantamount means "equivalent in effect or value" and is followed by the preposition *to,* as in *a request tantamount to a demand. Paramount* means "first in importance, rank, or regard," as in this quotation from a letter by Abraham Lincoln to Horace Greeley: "*My paramount object in this struggle is to save the Union.*"

Writers sometimes confuse these two words probably because of their similarity in sound, as in this quotation from a review of a video game in the *New York Times:* "*Protecting your squads is of tantamount importance; if a soldier is shot, another must carry him to the nearest medic before he bleeds to death, and if two soldiers are killed the mission is aborted.*"

taut / taught / taunt

The adjective *taut* means "pulled or drawn tight; not slack," as in *a taut rope* and *taut sails.* Occasionally the sound-alike spelling *taught* (the past tense and past participle of the verb *teach*) is mistakenly used instead, as in this quotation from the *London Times:* "*There are another 21 bodies around her [a dancer] in the same pose, loose Lycra dance clothes draped around taught muscles.*"

Sometimes the spelling *taunt* (normally a verb meaning "to reproach in a mocking or contemptuous manner") is also misused for *taut,* as in this quotation from a Tennessee newspaper: "*Both horses must be facing each other with the riders' ropes pulled taunt before time is called.*"

These spellings should be kept distinct.

teach

Some grammarians object to the use of *teach* as a transitive verb when its object denotes an institution of learning, as in *My friend teaches grade school*. But this use of *teach* has been used by reputable writers since the 17th century. Here is an example from the 20th century:

> She no longer recited her lessons to the teacher she liked, but to the Principal, a man who belonged, like Mrs. Livery Johnson, to the camp of Thea's natural enemies. He taught school because he was too lazy to work among grown-up people, and he made an easy job of it (Willa Cather, *The Song of the Lark*)

temblor / tremblor / trembler

The correct spelling of *temblor,* a geological term for an earthquake, is understandably counterintuitive to an English speaker. The word suggests something that trembles, and it is often written incorrectly as *trembler* or *tremblor*. These words are related not just semantically but etymologically as well: *temblor* comes from Spanish *temblar,* "to shake or tremble," which in turn ultimately comes from Latin *tremulus,* "trembling," which is also the origin of the English verb *tremble*. Despite their similarities, the words are distinct, and only *temblor* is correct in geological contexts.

temperature   See **fever, heat.**

tenet / tenant

A *tenet* is an opinion, doctrine, or principle held as being true by a person or especially by an organization. A *tenant* is a person that pays rent to use or occupy land, a building, or other property owned by another. *Tenant* is sometimes misused for *tenet* as in this example from the *Burlington Free Press:* "*The athletic department, in consultation with students and deans, has developed a new mission statement. It supports academic excellence including a commitment to graduation while fostering the basic tenants of athletics, including sportsmanship, respect and fair play.*"

tense

A tense is a set of verb forms that indicates the time (as past, present, or future) and the continuance or completion of the action or state. See **verbs, tenses of.**

termagant   See **shrew.**

terrorism

The word *terrorism* is inherently partisan, and characterizing a violent act as an instance of terrorism usually entails siding with an established government. If soldiers in a standing army commit an egregious act of violence against civilians, it is usually called an *atrocity*, not an *act of terrorism*.

terrorism* and *terror The word *terrorism* is sometimes shortened to *terror*, especially in phrases like *the war on terror*. The difference between the two words is subtle. Dropping the *–ism* suffix changes the focus from a reprehensible method of conducting a violent conflict to a moral abstraction. Thus, *the war on terror* conjures a grave, universal conflict between good and evil, where *the war on terrorism* does not.

figurative terrorism Like the word *holocaust*, *terrorism* is sometimes extended to nonviolent situations, as in *He blocked traffic with a group of costumed actors protesting the closing of the theater—an instance of artistic terrorism*. Many people are likely to disapprove of such metaphors. In our 2002 survey, 63 percent of the Usage Panel rejected the example quoted above. The Panel was more accepting of an example that played up a conflict between parties, where the metaphor had a clearer context. Nonetheless, 51 percent rejected the example *Proponents of the theory have savagely attacked their critics and written angry letters to the journals that publish them, in what can only be called intellectual terrorism*. Be cautious in using *terrorism* in figurative contexts.

terrorist

Few words are more fiercely debated than *terrorist*, at least in its use regarding violent conflicts in specific countries. How to refer to people who use unconventional means to commit violence, often against civilians, in the name of a cause or in resisting an established government has been the subject of lively and often bitter discussion both by ordinary citizens and by the editorial boards of publications and media outlets.

People who support the use of the word *terrorist* insist that those who commit horrific acts of violence have earned this name and that to use another, less inflammatory word implicitly lends legitimacy to moral barbarism and atrocities. At the very least, in this view, avoiding the term *terrorist* suggests an unwillingness to face up to the calculated brutality involved in such acts. *Terrorist* is thus seen as the only noneuphemism available in these contexts.

Many news organizations disagree with this view and see *terrorist* and its counterpart *freedom fighter* as inherently political words. To use them as if they were neutral descriptors (whether consciously or not) is therefore to abet the propaganda of the government or other organization that has so characterized the groups in question. Among the terms that have been used instead of *terrorists* are *guerillas, rebels, outlaws, criminals,* and *disruptive elements,* and all of these have drawbacks. The term *guerilla* can be misleading in many cases, since it suggests a standing army of irregular troops (usually scattered in small bands), rather than an underground organization of secret cells. *Rebel* has traditionally been used much like *revolutionary* and usually implies adherence to a declared political philosophy of some sort. The terms *outlaw* and *criminal,* while literally accurate in most cases, lump the committers of ideological violence with burglars, car thieves, and other agents of miscellaneous antisocial behavior. *Disruptive elements* sounds very much like a bureaucratic euphemism—the kind of term that is meant deliberately to downplay the seriousness of a chaotic situation.

Many news organizations have settled on the term *insurgent* as a neutral descriptor, in the belief that the acts of such people should be evaluated on their own terms. Perhaps an even better solution is to use the name of the insurgent group itself when it is known, but in many cases the group involved in the violent act is not known, refuses to identify itself, or is one of many claiming responsibility. Certain other general terms for groups sharing an ideology, such as *white supremacist* and *jihadist* (in the post–September 11 conflicts), also offer an accurate and less inflammatory way of discussing these events.

The more general use of *terrorist*—that is, without reference to a specific conflict—is hard to dispute, since there is no good substitute for it in certain contexts, most notably when security measures are being taken to prevent attacks on civilian targets:

> [The Fire Chief] delivered a scathing attack on the mayor's policy, an attack that seemed to be grounded mainly in the Fire Department's anger over the Police Department's being given initial control of situations that might involve terrorists (Editorial, "A Rivalry and a Solution," *New York Times*)

than

Since the 18th century, grammarians have insisted that *than* should be regarded as a conjunction in all its uses. They object to constructions in which *than* is followed by the objective instead of the nominative case, since the objective case implies that *than* functions as a preposition, as in *Bob is taller than me* instead of *Bob is taller than I.* This thinking would also ban the use of *than* followed by gerunds, as in *Rather than working in the yard, we went for a walk.* But these constructions with *than* are both idiomatic in speech and are used by the finest writers. There seems therefore little reason to avoid them.

See more at **comparisons with *as* and *than;* pronouns, personal;** and **rather than.**

thankfully   See **sentence adverbs.**

that

***that / which* (restrictive and nonrestrictive clauses)**   By the traditional rule, *that* should be used only to introduce a restrictive (or defining) clause, one identifying the person or thing being talked about; in this use it should never be preceded by a comma. Thus, in the sentence *The house that Jack built has been torn down,* the clause *that Jack built* is a restrictive clause telling which specific house was torn down. Similarly, in *I am looking for a book that is easy to read,* the restrictive clause *that is easy to read* tells what kind of book is desired.

By contrast, *which* should be used only with nonrestrictive (or nondefining) clauses, ones giving additional information about something that has already been identified in the context; in this use, *which* is always preceded by a comma. Thus one should say *The students in Chemistry 101 have been complaining about the textbook, which* [not *that*] *is hard to follow.* The clause *which is hard to follow* is nonrestrictive in that it does not indicate which text is being complained about; even if it were omitted, we would know that the phrase *the textbook* refers to the text in Chemistry 101. It should be easy to follow the rule in nonrestrictive clauses like this, since *which* here sounds more natural than *that.*

Some people extend the rule and insist that, just as *that* should be used only in restrictive clauses, *which* should be used only in nonrestrictive clauses. By this thinking, *which* should be avoided in sentences such as *I need a book which will tell me all about city gardening,* where the restrictive clause *which will tell me all about city gardening* describes what sort of book is needed. But this use of *which* with restrictive clauses is very common, even in edited prose. Moreover, in some situations *which* is preferable to *that. Which* can be especially useful where two or more relative clauses are joined by *and* or *or: It is a philosophy in which ordinary people may find solace and which many have found reason to praise. Which* may also be preferable when introducing a restrictive clause modifying a preceding phrase that contains *that: We want to assign only that material which will be most helpful.*

omitting *that*   *That* can often be omitted in a relative clause when the subject of the clause is different from the word or phrase the clause refers to. Thus, one can say either *the book that I was reading* or *the book I was reading. That* can also be dropped when it introduces a subordinate clause: *I think we should try again. That* should be retained, however, when the subordinate clause begins with an adverbial phrase or anything other than the subject: *She said that under no circumstances would she allow us to skip the meeting. The book argues that eventually the housing supply will increase.* This last sentence would be ambiguous if *that* were omitted, since the adverb *eventually* could then be construed as modifying either *argues* or *will increase.*

that* instead of *who   There is a widespread belief, sometimes taught as correct usage, that only *who* and not *that* should be used to introduce a restrictive relative clause identifying a person. But *that* has been used in this way for centuries, going back to the Old English period, and has been used by the finest writers in English, as this brief sampler shows:

> The man that once did sell the lion's skin / While the beast liv'd, was kill'd with hunting him (Shakespeare, *Henry V* 4.03.94)
>
> . . . scatter thou the people that delight in war (*King James Bible,* Psalms 68:30)
>
> He that fancies he should benefit the publick more in a great station than the man that fills it, will in time imagine it an act of virtue to supplant him (Samuel Johnson, *The Rambler* No. 8)

> I wonder if I shall fall right *through* the earth! How funny it'll seem to come out among the people that walk with their heads downwards! (Lewis Carroll, *Alice's Adventures in Wonderland*)

> . . . not caring a rap whether he's the man that cleans the windows or the secretary of the navy (Mary Roberts Rinehart, *Where There's a Will*)

In contemporary usage, *who* predominates in such contexts, but *that* is used with sufficient frequency to be considered standard:

> The atoms in a diamond . . . outnumber all the people that have ever lived or ever will (Richard Dawkins, *A Devil's Chaplain*)

> It's important to realize how shocked the physicists were in the aftermath of the bombing of Hiroshima, on August 6, 1945. They describe a series of waves of emotion: first, a sense of fulfillment that the bomb worked, then horror at all the people that had been killed, and then a convincing feeling that on no account should another bomb be dropped (Bill Joy, "Why the Future Doesn't Need Us," *Wired*)

That occurs idiomatically in reference to groups (where *who* would sound peculiar):

> [He] has performed in clubs and on college campuses in New York before young, predominantly black standing-room-only crowds that cheer at the mere mention of his first name (Michael Marriott, "From Rap's Rhythms, A Retooling of Poetry," *New York Times*)

> In 1949, the man once known as Hollywood's most eligible bachelor married Gloria McLean, who had two sons, and settled into raising a family that soon included twin daughters (David Freeman, "Mr. Stewart Goes to Hollywood," *New York Times Book Review*)

Note that using *that* instead of *whom* (that is, as the object, rather than the subject, of the verb in the following clause), should presumably be unobjectionable even to those who adhere to the traditional rule discussed above. Thus constructions like *the child that the teacher spoke to* and *the teacher that the committee held up as an example* must be acceptable in all contexts. In fact, given the stilted formality that hounds the word *whom*, there is really no alternative to using *that* in such sentences.

that with the verb doubt   For a discussion of when to use *that* after the verb *doubt*, see **doubt**.

See more at **this, whatever, which,** and **who.**

that having been said / that being said / that said

Certain absolute constructions, notably *that having been said, that being said,* and *that said,* or variations such as *with all that having been said,* function as adverbial connectors similar to *however, nevertheless,* and *in spite of that.* They imply that the speaker or writer is conceding the truth about what was just said, while recognizing that the present statement is in some way at variance with it. These constructions are perfectly acceptable, though they are somewhat unusual among absolute constructions in that they occur mainly in informal or conversational settings. They are especially common in first-person accounts, as in the language of people being interviewed. In more formal writing, conjunctive adverbs like *however* and *nonetheless* are more common in these situations. Here are some examples of these constructions at work:

> This week, California oil refineries warned they will produce less and force up the price of gasoline if they don't get an exemption from any rolling blackouts. That having been said, the cost of energy in California has gone way down over the last week (David Brancaccio, "Marketplace," National Public Radio)

> I don't think that Hillary [Clinton] is a natural politician, like Bill, which is to say, someone who intuitively understands where people are coming from and what it will take to move them. I remember one night in 1992 when I was on Bill's campaign bus, and we pulled into some town in East Texas at about 11 p.m. He didn't stop shaking hands until something like 2 a.m. . . . I don't think you will ever find Hillary shaking hands at 2 a.m. That being said, she is incredibly disciplined, and what she lacks in intuition and exuberance she seems to have gone a long way toward making up through sheer hard work (Elizabeth Kolbert, "Hillary on the Hill," *The New Yorker*, Online Edition)

> We had mutual friends in sportswriters, ex-players and coaches. We were Midwesterners whose stern, honest, Republican fathers never bought anything unless they could pay for it all at once. We loved baseball, Sparky Anderson and Ted Williams. That said, we had significant differences (Dave Kindred, "Knight Acts Out a Classic Tragedy," *The Sporting News*)

Note that there is a distinction between these absolute constructions and the transitional constructions *having said that* and *having said this*. These constructions are not absolute constructions, and they often occur as dangling modifiers.

See more at **absolute constructions** and **having said that.**

the

The pronunciation of this word changes according to the sound that immediately follows it. Generally, before a consonant sound, *the* is pronounced (thə), as in *the ball, the one, the school;* before a vowel sound, *the* is often pronounced (thē) or (thĭ), as in *the apple, the hour, the opening;* and when stressed for emphasis *the* is pronounced (thē), as in *This is* the *place to live.*

See more at **definite article.**

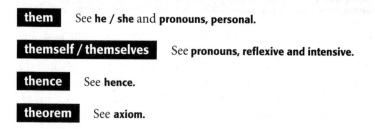

them See **he / she** and **pronouns, personal.**

themself / themselves See **pronouns, reflexive and intensive.**

thence See **hence.**

theorem See **axiom.**

there

The word *there* sometimes functions as a "dummy" or "expletive" subject, filling in the normal subject position of the sentence when the real subject follows the verb, as in *There are two people in this room* or *There came a time when I began to be interested in philosophy.* In this use *there* is distinguished from its use as an adverb indicating location, as in *Two people are there.*

According to the standard rule, when *there* is the dummy subject of a verb such as *be, seem,* or *appear,* the verb agrees in number with the following grammatical subject: *There is a great Italian deli across the street. There are fabulous wildflowers in the hills. There seems to be a blueberry pie cooking in the kitchen. There seem to be a few trees between the green and me.* But people often disregard this rule and use a singular verb with a plural subject, especially when speaking or when using the contraction *there's.* The Usage Panel dislikes this construction, however. In our 1995 survey, 79 percent rejected the sentence *There's only three things you need to know about this book.* But when *there's* was followed by a compound subject whose first element was singular, the Panel felt differently. Fifty-six percent accepted the sentence *In each of us there's a dreamer and a realist,* and 32 percent more accepted it in informal usage. The Panel was even more tolerant of the sentence *When you get to the stoplight, there's a gas station on the left and a grocery store on the right;* 58 percent accepted it in formal usage, while 37 percent more accepted it in informal usage. This usage would seem to violate the rule of subject and verb agreement, but this rule is somewhat weakened by the presence of the dummy subject *there.*

See more at **subject and verb agreement.**

thermo–

The prefix *thermo–* comes from Greek *thermos,* meaning "warm, hot." When used to form words in English, *thermo–* generally refers to heat, as in *thermodynamic,* or sometimes to thermoelectricity, as in *thermocouple.* Most of the words that begin with *thermo–,* such as *thermodynamics, thermoelectricity, thermostat,* and *thermosphere,* have only come into being in the 19th and 20th centuries. Sometimes before a vowel *thermo–* becomes *therm–,* as in *thermanesthesia,* which means "inability to feel hot or cold."

these kinds of / those kinds of   See **kind.**

 See **he / she** and **pronouns, personal.**

this

this* and *that   *This* and *that* are both demonstrative pronouns that refer to a thought expressed earlier: *The letter was unopened; that* [or *this*] *in itself casts doubt* *on the inspector's theory. That* is sometimes viewed as the better choice in referring to what has gone before (as in the preceding example). When what is referred to has not yet been mentioned, only *this* is used: *This* [not *that*] *is what bothers me: we have no time to consider late applications.*

this* as informal substitute for *a / an   *This* is often used in speech and informal writing as an emphatic substitute for the indefinite article to refer to a specific thing or person: *You should talk to this friend of mine at the Department of Motor Vehicles. I have this terrible feeling that I forgot to turn off the water.* It is best to avoid this substitution in formal writing except when a conversational tone is desired.

See more at **that.**

thrombus / embolus

The words *thrombus* and *embolus* describe two different types of abnormal blood clots and should not be used as synonyms. A *thrombus* (from Greek *thrombos,* "clot") is a blood clot formed in a blood vessel or in a chamber of the heart. It is fixed in position. An *embolus* (from Greek *embolos,* "stopper, plug") is a clot that has detached from a blood vessel or the heart and traveled through the bloodstream to another location in the body. An embolus can also be formed from other substances, such as air or fat. Both thrombi and emboli can occlude blood vessels and cause the death of body tissue, as in a heart attack or stroke.

throughout the entire

In many contexts, the word *entire* is superfluous in this expression. *The virus had spread throughout the entire population* says no more than *The virus had spread throughout the population.* But as with many apparently redundant expressions, there are cases in which the redundancy is acceptable or necessary, especially when a contrast is being highlighted. Thus, *entire* is quite legitimate in a context such as *The counterfeit bills first ended up in the local banks, spread into the eastern parts of the banking network, and ultimately began circulating throughout the entire network.* As usual, it is good to avoid redundancy, but never at the cost of precision or style.

See more at **redundancy.**

thusly

The adverb *thusly* was created in the 19th century as an alternative for *thus* in sentences such as *Hold it thus* or *He put it thus.* It appears to have been first used by humorists, who may have been imitating the speech of poorly educated people straining to sound stylish. The word has subsequently gained some currency in educated usage, but it has long been deplored by usage commentators as a "nonword." A large majority of the Usage Panel found it unacceptable in 1966, and this sentiment was echoed nearly forty years later in our 2002 survey, in which 86 percent of the Panel disapproved of the sentence *His letter to the editor ended thusly: "It is time to stop fooling ourselves."*

In formal writing, *thus* is acceptable in examples like those given above; in other styles, expressions such as *this way* and *like this* may sound more natural.

tidal wave   See **tsunami.**

tight / tightly

Both of the words *tight* and *tightly* can be used as adverbs. *Tight* follows verbs that denote a process of closure or constriction, such as *squeeze, shut, close, tie,* and *hold.* In this use it is subtly distinct from *tightly* in that it denotes the state resulting from a process whereas *tightly* denotes how the process was applied. As such, *tight* is more appropriate when the focus is on a state that endures after an activity has ended. The sentence *She closed up the house tight* suggests preparation for an impending blizzard that results in a secure state. Similarly, it is more natural to say *The windows were frozen tight* than *The windows were frozen tightly,* since it is the persistent tightness of the seal that is important rather than the manner in which the windows were frozen. *Tight* can be used only after a verb; before a verb use *tightly: The house was tightly* [not *tight*] *shut.* With a few verbs *tight* is used idiomatically and is the only correct form: *sleep tight, sit tight.*

till / until

The words *till* and *until* can be used interchangeably in both writing and speech. As the first word in a sentence, however, *until* is more common: *Until you get that paper written, don't even think about going to the movies.*

toe the line

The idiom *toe the line* means "to adhere to doctrines or rules conscientiously; conform." The phrase originated in sports in which touching a mark or line with the toe or hands signaled readiness for the start of a race. It is sometimes misspelled as *tow the line,* as in this Salt Lake City newspaper: *"Most of us have forgotten those filmstrip projectors, usually set up on a student's desk in preparation for a story with a message: how to feel safe, how to tow the line with authorities, how to get excited about the moon and outer space."* The mistake is easy to make because the image of towing a line and pulling a load fits neatly with the requirements of conformity.

together

join together   Many verbs have the sense of *together* inherent to their meanings. For example, *join* always entails a putting together of things that were previously separate. For this reason, many usage critics consider expressions such as *join together* to be outright redundancies. However, care should be taken when avoiding redundancies not to lose subtleties of meaning in the process. For example, the sentence *I joined the two straps together,* taken in isolation, contains an arguably redundant use of *together.* But in a case such as *Be sure to join the straps to the frame before you join them together,* the word *together* serves to indicate that the straps are being joined to each other. Comparable situations arise with verbs like *mix, merge, connect, combine, collaborate,* and others, as in *If we catch those spies, I'm sure they will collaborate; my worry is that they will collaborate together.* A similar situation arises in cases involving *each other,* which is also often considered redundant, but may clarify the intended meaning: *Yes, we are getting married. But we're not getting married to each other.*

together with   *Together with* is often used following the subject of a sentence or clause to introduce an addition. The addition, however, is in a prepositional phrase and is not part of the subject. The number of the verb should be governed solely by the subject: *The king* [singular], *together with two aides, is expected soon.* The same is true of *along with, as well as, besides,* and *in addition to.*

See more at **besides** and **like.**

tomato

The older pronunciation (tə-mä′tō), with an *a* like that of *father,* is the predominant pronunciation in British English. The more common pronunciation in American English is (tə-mā′tō), with a long *a.*

tomboy

A *tomboy* is defined as "a girl considered boyish or masculine in behavior or manner." The word is regarded as offensive by some people because these so-called masculine qualities often include behaviors and traits (such as being athletic, adventurous, and uninterested in decorum) that simply do not fit conventional stereotypes of feminine roles. Others consider the word *tomboy* to be an innocuous descriptor of an unconventional girl, as in this quotation from the *Cleveland Plain Dealer:* "Her late father doted on her. He explained the rules of every sport to Missy, a tomboy who loved playing tackle football with the guys and dressing in baggy clothes." In any case, *tomboy* should be used with caution.

See more at **sexist language.**

too

not too   Some people object to the use of *not too* as an equivalent of *not very,* as in *She was not too pleased with the results.* But in many contexts this construction is entirely idiomatic and should pass without notice: *It wasn't too long ago that deregulation was being hailed as the savior of the savings and loan industry. It was not too bright of them to build in an area where rockslides occur.* In these cases *not too* adds a note of ironic understatement.

cannot* . . . *too   Negation of *too* by *cannot* or *can't* may sometimes lead to ambiguities, as in *You can't check your child's temperature too often,* which may mean either that the temperature should be checked only occasionally or that it should be checked as frequently as possible.

***too* beginning a sentence**   *Too* meaning "in addition" or "also" is sometimes used to introduce a sentence: *There has been a cutback in federal subsidies. Too, rates have been increasing.* There is nothing grammatically wrong with this usage, but some critics consider it awkward.

See more at **also, of,** and **plus.**

topgallant / topmast / topsail

These nautical words are usually pronounced (tə-găl′ənt), (tŏp′məst), and (tŏp′səl), but the spelling pronunciations (tŏp′găl′ənt), (tŏp′măst′), and (tŏp′sāl′) are also acceptable.

See more at **spelling pronunciation.**

tornado / twister / cyclone / anticyclone / waterspout

The terms *tornado* and *twister* refer to the same powerful weather event, in which rotating masses of air, rising up into a large stormcloud, form into a narrow, continuous, spinning column of air at very low pressure, extending from the ground up into the storm. Their winds sometimes exceed three hundred miles per hour, and they usually display a funnel-shaped cloud that reaches from the higher stormclouds all the way to the ground.

Twister is the less formal term for this phenomenon, but it is used more commonly than *tornado* in some regions of the United States and Australia, and it is certainly not eschewed by meteorologists.

The term *cyclone* is also used colloquially to refer to tornados. Meteorologically, this is not incorrect, although a tornado is in fact only one case of a cyclone. A cyclone is simply a center of low air pressure into which winds circulate, while an *anticyclone* is an area of high pressure out of which winds circulate. In the Northern Hemisphere, the winds of a cyclone move counterclockwise, while the winds of an anticyclone move clockwise; in the Southern Hemisphere, the directions are the reverse. Occasionally, tornados form having *anticyclonic* winds (very large low-pressure weather systems, such as tropical storms and hurricanes, do not). *Cyclone* may also refer to the equivalent of hurricanes in the Indian Ocean.

A *waterspout* is technically nothing but a tornado that persists over a body of water. Most waterspouts arise under weather conditions different from those spawning tornados (generally with the formation of a large cumulus cloud over the ocean, rather than from a large thunderstorm). Thus the use of the term is better restricted to these conditions, rather than used to describe a tornado that happens to cross a pond.

tortuous / torturous / tortured

Although the adjectives *tortuous* and *torturous* both ultimately come from the Latin word *torquēre*, "to twist," their primary meanings are distinct. *Tortuous* means "twisting," as in *a tortuous road* or, by extension, "complex" or "devious," as in *a tortuous bureaucratic procedure* or *a tortuous explanation*. *Torturous* and *tortured* refer primarily to torture and the pain associated with it. However, they can also be used in the sense of "twisted; strained, belabored," as in *a tortured analogy*.

toward / towards

The difference between *toward* and *towards* is entirely dialectal. *Toward* is more common in American English; *towards* is the predominant form in British English. Both words have the same meanings.

tract / track

A *tract* is a specified or limited area of land. A *track* is a path, route, or course indicated by a mark or succession of marks left by something that has passed, as *an old wagon track through the mountains*. *Track* is often misused for *tract*, as in this obituary from the *Hartford Courant*: "He developed numerous *tracks* of land, designing and overseeing the development and construction of custom homes."

tragedy / tragic

In literature a *tragedy* is a drama in which the main character is brought to ruin because of a personal fault, a moral weakness, or an inability to cope with circumstances. Usually the character contributes in some way to his or her downfall, and the character's extreme suffering tends to outstrip the audience's sense that it was justly deserved.

But in everyday usage people often use *tragedy* and the adjective *tragic* to refer to a regrettable event or a piece of misfortune. Some people object to this extended usage, noting it distorts the true meaning of these terms. But the Usage Panel has a more tolerant view. In our 1988 survey, 80 percent accepted the example *The shooting was a tragic accident; the guard mistook the boy for a prowler.* The approval of the Panel slipped somewhat when the circumstances of the event were less dire. Seventy-one percent approved of the use of *tragic* to refer to an idealistic student's dropping out of college in despair. Some Panelists characterized this use as acceptable but hyperbolic.

trans–

The prefix *trans–* goes back to the Latin prefix *trāns–*, from the Latin preposition *trāns,* meaning "across, beyond, through." Many of the most common English words beginning with *trans–* are derived from Latin words, such as *transfer, transfuse, translate, transmit, transpire,* and *transport.* Many other words beginning with *trans–* have not borrowed directly from Latin but instead have been formed in modern times by adding *trans–* to adjectives. This group includes *transatlantic, transcontinental, transoceanic, transpacific,* and *transpolar,* with the meaning "across" or "through" a particular geographic area.

transcription / translation

Transcription and *translation* both describe genetic processes by which specific proteins are synthesized for body maintenance and growth. The word *transcription,* built from the Latin prefix *trans–,* "across," and the verb *scrībere,* "to write," refers to the process by which genetic material is copied from a strand of DNA to a complementary strand of RNA, called *messenger RNA.* In most organisms, this takes place in the nucleus.

Messenger RNA is transported across the cell's cytoplasm to the ribosome, where *translation* takes place. *Translation,* from the Latin *trāns–* and *lātus,* "brought," is the process by which a strand of messenger RNA directs the assembly of a sequence of amino acids to make a protein. The genetic "directions" in messenger RNA are interpreted by another form of RNA, known as *transfer RNA.* Each transfer RNA carries an amino acid that is positioned into a particular sequence, forming a specific protein.

transgendered   See **transvestite.**

transition

The longstanding noun *transition* has recently sprouted a verb, and like many verbs developed from nouns, it is meeting with some resistance. In our 1996 ballot, only 28 percent of the Usage Panel approved of the intransitive use in the sentence *The industry is transitioning to the Pentium processor.* Approval increased to 46 percent in a musical context, however, where the emphasis was on passage or flow, with a musician *smoothly transitioning from the clarinet's lower register to higher notes with ease.*

The Panel was decidedly less pleased with the transitive use of this verb. Only 9 percent accepted *Many chain department stores are transitioning summer stock to long sleeves and coats for fall and winter.* It seems likely, then, that in certain contexts *transitioning* will eventually become standard, but in others it will still seem jarring.

transition words

One hallmark of effective expository and argumentative writing is the organization of thoughts into a clear sequence or hierarchy that is easy to understand. Providing the reader with signposts along the way as an argument builds can turn a mediocre piece of writing into a cogent one.

These verbal signposts are usually adverbs or adverbial phrases that mark the transitions in a discourse. It is helpful to have a variety of them at one's disposal. Listed below are a number of categories of these expressions. Specific expressions that have usage problems associated with them are cross-referenced at the end.

Sequence of points: *first, second, third* or *firstly, secondly, thirdly; finally* or *lastly.*

> First, you wash your hands. Second, you grease the pan. Third, . . .

Chronology: *already, then, eventually, still, yet.*

> Then Smith, already at the point of discovery, saw the confirming data from Jones.

A change in discourse or a digressive point: *by the way, incidentally, now.*

> Now we turn to the question of Joyce's politics. Joyce was, incidentally, a mediocre student, distracted by his interest in becoming a writer.

Similarity: *by the same token, equally, in the same way, likewise, similarly.*

> Determining the sequence of proteins for the hormone was likewise difficult. Watson was similarly low on funds.

Contrast: *by comparison, by contrast, by way of comparison, contrastingly, instead, on the contrary, rather.*

> By comparison, the architecture in Back Bay is stately and historic.
> Holmes, by contrast, now had plenty of money.

Addition: *also, even, likewise, in addition, similarly, too.*

> Watson even brought some test tubes in case chemical analysis was necessary.

Result: *accordingly, as a result, consequently, naturally, of course, so.*

> Mr. Smee was well aware of his instructions. Accordingly, he logged in the time and position of the ship.

> Fussell was an opponent of the theory twenty years ago. Of course, he dislikes its reiteration under a new name.

Summary: *all in all, altogether, in conclusion, in fine, in sum, then, therefore, thus, to conclude, to sum up.*

> All in all, it is too much trouble to continue doing business this way.

Special emphasis or reinforcement: *above all, further, furthermore, in particular, moreover, to top it all off, what is more.*

> Replacing the sewer lines will prevent basement flooding. Moreover, it will dramatically improve the water quality of the river.

Concession of truth in a preceding statement in light of a contrast or qualification in this one: *admittedly, all the same, anyhow, anyway, at any rate, at the same time, despite that, for all that, however, in any case, in any event, in spite of that, nevertheless, nonetheless, of course, on the other hand, still, that (having been) said, though.*

There are many sensible reasons to preserve the estate tax. Nevertheless, many politicians oppose it.

The treatment for this disorder has many drawbacks, not the least of which is its length of necessary monitoring. Still, the treatment works and should be continued.

People who favor the project insist that the property can be developed sensibly. Of course, the environmental consultant is not among them.

See more at **adverbs, conjunctive adverbs, for, having said that, however, so,** and **that having been said.**

transitive verb   See **verbs, transitive and intransitive.**

transpire

Transpire has been used since the mid-18th century in the sense "to become publicly known," as in *Despite efforts to hush the matter up, it soon transpired that the colonels had met with the rebel leaders.* While this usage has been considered standard for generations, it appears to be on shaky ground and could be headed for obsolescence. In our 2001 survey, 48 percent of the Usage Panel rejected it in the sentence quoted above. It might be better to use a synonym such as *become known, leak out,* or *get around.*

The more common use of *transpire* meaning "to happen or occur" has a more troubled history. Though it dates at least to the beginning of the 19th century, language critics have condemned it for more than one hundred years as both pretentious and unconnected to the word's original meaning, "to give off as vapor."

But there is considerable evidence that resistance to this sense of *transpire* is weakening. In our 1966 survey, only 38 percent of the Usage Panel found it acceptable; in 1988, 58 percent accepted it in the sentence *All of these events transpired after last week's announcement.* In 2001, 66 percent accepted the same sentence. Nonetheless, many of the Panelists who accepted the usage also remarked that it was pretentious or pompous. This usage is easily avoided by saying *happen, occur,* or *take place* instead.

transvestite / transsexual / transgendered

These words all refer to individuals who adopt a physical appearance or social identity associated with the opposite sex. The words are sometimes confused, but they do have important differences of meaning. All three words can be used both as nouns and as adjectives. A *transvestite* is a person who, on occasion, chooses to dress and act in a manner traditionally associated with the opposite sex. Transvestites sometimes prefer to be called *cross-dressers.* A *transsexual* is a person who psychologically identifies with the opposite sex, wishes to be considered a member of the opposite sex by society, and adopts a corresponding appearance and lifestyle. Some transsexuals undergo sex-change operations. Those who do not are sometimes called *nonsurgical transsexuals.*

The adjective *transgendered* is sometimes used as a synonym for *transsexual* (usually referring to nonsurgical transsexuals), but *transgendered* is also used as an umbrella term for the larger community of transsexuals, transvestites, and others who manifest strong identification with the opposite sex. The corresponding noun *transgendered* is mainly used collectively (as in *public attitudes about the transgendered*). The form *transgender* is a count noun, used mainly in the plural (as in *families of transgenders*). Thus the words *transsexual* and *transgendered* sometimes overlap in meaning, and care should be taken when using these words to make clear which group is being referred to.

Note that these words do not provide any information about a person's sexual orientation, which refers to the gender to which an individual is sexually attracted.

See more at **intersex.**

trauma

This word can be pronounced (trô′mə), with the first syllable rhyming with *law,* or (trou′mə), with the first syllable rhyming with *cow.* In our 1995 survey, 56 percent of the Usage Panel preferred the former pronunciation, 41 percent preferred the latter, and a small percentage used both.

tremblor / trembler   See **temblor.**

triceps   See **biceps**

–trix   See **feminine suffixes.**

troop / troupe

The words *troop* and *troupe* both refer to groups, but different kinds of groups. A *troupe* is a company especially of touring actors, singers, or dancers. Accordingly, the verb *troupe* means "to travel with a theatrical production." *Troop* refers more generally to a group or company of people, animals, or things, especially a group of soldiers. Groups of Boy Scouts or Girl Scouts under the guidance of an adult are also called troops. The plural *troops* is often used to refer to soldiers as a collection of individuals, though the singular referring to a soldier (as in *a troop in his company*) is a rarity. *Troop* is often used as an attributive noun, with the meaning "for troops, of troops," as in *a troop ship* and *a troop withdrawal.* To troop is to move or to go as a throng.

Troop and *troupe* are sometimes confused, as in the following quotations from articles. The first (where *troop* should be used) is from a leisure and entertainment periodical: *"It's WWI, and among one troupe of soldiers appears the Angel Gabriel, only to be dismissed as a nutter whose bright white garb could get them killed."* The second (where *troupe* is called for) is from an Ohio newspaper: *"The last production will take a look at a troop of actors. . . . "*

troth

The traditional (and British English) pronunciation rhymes with *both,* although the word is now also pronounced in American English so that it rhymes with *moth.*

troupe   See **troop.**

try and

The phrase *try and* is commonly used as a substitute for *try to,* as in *Could you try and make less noise?* A number of grammarians have labeled the construction incorrect. To be sure, the usage is associated with informal style and strikes an inappropriately conversational note in formal writing. In our 1988 survey, 65 percent of the Usage Panel rejected its use in written contexts as presented in the sentence *Why don't you try and see if you can work the problem out between yourselves?*

tsunami / tidal wave

Informally, the word *tidal wave* is used as a synonym of *tsunami,* a technical term for a wave generated as a result of an oceanic event in which some sudden disturbance of the water caused by an earthquake, landslide, the impact of a meteorite, or some other powerful force creates a train of fast-moving ocean shock waves that can inundate the land. Though such waves may resemble a sudden tidal inflow more than a regular ocean wave, such waves have nothing to do with tides or tidal forces, so oceanographers and geologists eschew the term *tidal wave* when referring to such waves. Instead, they have borrowed the Japanese word for such phenomena, *tsunami.* Earthquakes are frequent in Japan, and tsunamis pose a constant threat. In Japanese, the word *tsunami* is usually written by combining the Chinese characters meaning "harbor, port" (pronounced *tsu* in Japanese) and "wave" (pronounced *nami*). In origin, *tsunami* is most often thought simply to be a compound of these two Japanese words, *tsu* and *nami,* and to mean "harbor wave, wave in a port." The word may reflect the experience of sailors and fishermen who returned to shore to discover destruction wrought by a tsunami, although they noticed no large waves while Tsunamis are not usually perceptible in deep waters without the use of special instruments, since they do not become high until they approach the land. been suggested that *tsunami* derives from the contraction of a hypothetical word *tsuyo-nami,* meaning "strong wave."

   The term *tidal wave* is reserved by scientists for the broad swell set in motion specifically by the tidal forces of the moon and sun

twister   See **tornado.**

–ty

The suffix –ty forms nouns from adjectives. The word *subtlety*, for example, means "the quality or state of being subtle." *Subtlety* ultimately comes from the Latin noun *subtilitas*, from the adjective *subtilis* ("subtle") plus the suffix *–tās*, the ancestor of our suffixes *–ty* and *–ity*. The vowel *i* usually appears before the suffix *–tās* in Latin. As Latin developed into Old French, this vowel *i* was usually lost and the suffix *–tās* developed into *–té*. The Old French form of the suffix then entered English as *–ty* as part of French loanwords. Some other English words of French origin that end in *–ty* are *certainty, cruelty, frailty, loyalty,* and *royalty*. In English the extended form of this suffix, *–ity,* is now more productive than plain *–ty* itself, as can be seen in such words as *eccentricity, electricity, technicality, peculiarity,* and *similarity*. This form of the suffix, *–ity,* represents an attempt to restore the original Latin form of the suffix, with its *i* vowel. Words ending in *–ity* are often direct borrowings of actual Latin nouns ending in *–itās,* or words recently formed in English or French from Latin elements. However, in English words borrowed directly from Latin, the Latin suffix *–itās* is always adjusted to *–ity* on the model of early borrowings of Old French words ending in *–(i)té*. The meaning of the suffixes *–ty* and *–ity* is similar to that of the suffix *–ness,* but whereas *–ty* and *–ity* come from Latin, *–ness* comes from Old English.

· U ·

ultimate   See **penultimate**.

un–

There are two prefixes spelled *un–* in English. Both go back to Old English. One has the basic meaning "not." Thus *unhappy* means "not happy." This *un–* chiefly attaches to adjectives, as in *unable, unclean, unequal, uneven, unripe,* and *unsafe.* It also attaches to adjectives made of participles, as in *unfeeling, unflinching, unfinished,* and *unsaid.* Less frequently, this same prefix attaches to nouns: *unbelief, unconcern, unrest.* Sometimes the noun form of an adjective with the *un–* prefix has the prefix *in–,* as in *inability, inequality, injustice,* and *instability.* A few stems appear with both prefixes with distinctions of meaning. *Inhuman* means "brutal, monstrous," while *unhuman* means "not of human form, superhuman." The native English prefix *un–* meaning "not" is in fact the linguistic cousin of the prefix *in–,* also meaning "not," which is derived from Latin.

When used with adjectives, *un–* often has a sense distinct from that of *non–.* *Non–* picks out the set of things that are not in the category denoted by the stem to which it is attached, whereas *un–* picks out properties unlike those of the typical examples of the category. Thus *nonmilitary personnel* are those who are not members of the military, whereas someone who is *unmilitary* is unlike a typical soldier in dress, habits, or attitudes.

The other prefix *un–* is not related, despite its origin in Old English. It forms verbs and expresses removal, reversal, or deprivation: *undress, unravel, unnerve.* This *un–* is in fact related to Greek prefix *anti–,* "against, opposite, in return," which appears in English as the prefix *anti–.*

See more at **in–** and **non–.**

unalienable   See **inalienable**.

unaware / unawares

Unaware, followed by *of* (expressed or implied), is the usual adjectival form modifying a noun or pronoun or following a linking verb: *Unaware of the difficulty, I went ahead. He was unaware of my presence. Unawares* is the usual adverbial form: *The rain caught them unawares* (without warning). *They came upon it unawares* (without design or plan).

unbeknown / unbeknownst   See **amid.**

uncharted territory

The phrase *uncharted territory* refers to a circumstance or situation that is unfamiliar or unpredictable, as in this quotation from the British periodical *Health and Medicine Week*: "*Professor Karol Sikora . . . said 'We are entering uncharted territory with the advent of molecularly targeted drugs.'*" It is frequently written or spoken as *unchartered territory,* which is incorrect. The following example of this error is from an Albuquerque newspaper: "*Under second-year head coach Phil Lopez, the Rams have rocketed right past respectability and into unchartered territory with lightning speed.*"

unconscious / preconscious / subconscious

The words *unconscious, preconscious,* and *subconscious* are used as both adjectives and nouns to refer to parts of the mind that, according to Freud's theory of psychoanalysis, contain elements that are not subject to conscious perception or control but can affect conscious thoughts and behavior. Psychological material in the unconscious is normally manifested only through dreams or certain behaviors and may sometimes become accessible to the conscious mind through the use of drugs or certain types of therapy. The word *preconscious* is used in psychoanalysis to describe mental material that has been repressed to a certain extent but that can be brought into conscious awareness with effort. The word *subconscious* is not used formally in psychoanalytic theory but is often used popularly to refer to that which is either unconscious or preconscious.

The adjective *unconscious* also refers to a physiological state in which conscious awareness is temporarily or permanently absent as a result of injury to the brain, usually caused by illness, trauma, or drugs.

under–

The prefix *under–,* which can be traced back to Old English, has essentially the same meaning as the preposition *under.* For example, in words such as *underbelly, undercurrent, underlie,* and *undershirt, under–* denotes a position beneath or below. By extension, the prefix occasionally expresses the meaning "secretly, deviously," as in *underhand. Under–* also frequently conveys incompleteness or falling below a certain standard. Some examples are *undercharge, underdeveloped, underestimate,* and *underfeed.* Note that in this sense words beginning with *under–* often have counterparts beginning with *over–: overcharge, overestimate.*

unequivocal

The adjective *unequivocal* means "admitting of no doubt or misunderstanding; clear and unambiguous," as in *There was unequivocal proof that the suspect had been at the scene of the crime* and *The play was an unequivocal success.* The word is sometimes rendered as *unequivocable,* which is not listed in contemporary dictionaries and is considered a mistake. Note this example from a music review in the *Boston Herald:* "*In the next century, one will argue about who led the straightest path from Beethoven to Schoenberg: Brahms or Wagner. The answer this evening proved unequivocable.*"

unexceptionable / unexceptional

The adjectives *unexceptionable* and *unexceptional* are sometimes confused. *Unexceptionable* is derived from the word *exception* in its sense "objection," as in the idiom *take exception.* Thus *unexceptionable* means "not open to any objection":

> The largest refreshment booth in the fair was provided by an innkeeper from a neighbouring town. This was considered an unexceptionable place for obtaining the necessary food and rest: Host Trencher (as he was jauntily called by the local newspaper) being a substantial man of high repute for catering through all the county round (Thomas Hardy, *Far From the Madding Crowd*)

> Some twenty years ago, long before Dolly showed it was plausible, a book was published claiming, in great detail, that a rich man in South America had had himself cloned, by a scientist code-named Darwin. As a work of science fiction it would have been unexceptionable, but it was sold as sober fact (Richard Dawkins, *A Devil's Chaplain*)

> . . . by the end of the 1930's . . . the prohibition against makeup had been lifted, and powder, lipstick, mascara and rouge had become unexceptionable parts of the beauty arsenal (Liesl Schillinger, "Improving Themselves," *New York Times Book Review*)

Unexceptional, in contrast, generally means "not exceptional, not varying from the usual":

> I saw my neighbour gardening, chatted with him for a time, and then strolled in to breakfast. It was a most unexceptional morning (H.G. Wells, *The War of the Worlds*)

> This paltry tale seems as unexceptional as a trip to the supermarket (Jack Todd, *Desertion*)

> His physical appearance must have been unexceptional, since few of those who knew him firsthand can recall anything about how he looked, other than the fact that he was small, "only a little man" (Daniel B. Silver, *Refuge in Hell*)

uni– / mono–

The basic meaning of the prefix *uni–* is "one." It comes from the Latin prefix *ūni–,* from the word *ūnus,* meaning "one." (Latin *ūnus* is in fact the close linguistic cousin of the English word *one.* Both descend from the word for *one* in the prehistoric language from which both Latin and English are descended.) Many English words beginning with *uni–* are borrowings of words already formed in Latin. The word *unicorn,* for example, comes from *ūni–* plus *cornū,* meaning "horn," and refers to a one-horned animal. *Uniform* comes from *ūni–* plus *fōrma,* "shape," and means "always the same" or literally "one shape." And *unison,* which comes from *ūni–* plus *sonus,* "sound," means literally "one sound." The majority of new words beginning with *uni–,* such as *unicellular, unicycle, unilateral,* and *univalent,* were coined from the 19th century.

The prefix *mono–,* which comes from Greek, is also used to express the meaning "one." (It is, however, unrelated to the English and Latin words for "one.") This prefix is especially common in compounds where the second element is also from Greek, such as *monochromatic, monologue, monopoly,* and *monotone,* but it can also be combined with elements of Latin or other origin, as in *monoculture* or *monorail.*

uninterested

The term *uninterested,* which properly means "taking no interest, not interested," is sometimes used to mean "not favoring either side, unprejudiced," where one would expect to see *disinterested* instead. The Usage Panel roundly disapproved of this usage in our 2001 survey, with 96 percent rejecting the sentence *Every historian ought to be extremely uninterested; he ought neither to praise nor to blame those he speaks of.*

See also **disinterested.**

unique

Unique may be the foremost example of an absolute term—a term that, in the eyes of traditional grammarians, should not allow comparison or modification by an adverb of degree like *very, somewhat,* or *quite.* Thus, most grammarians believe that it is incorrect to say that something is *very unique* or *more unique than* something else, though phrases such as *nearly unique* and *almost unique* are presumably acceptable, since in these cases *unique* is not modified by an adverb of degree. A substantial majority of the Usage Panel supports the traditional view. In our 2004 survey, 66 percent of the Panelists disapproved of the sentence *Her designs are quite unique in today's fashion,* although in our 1988 survey, 80 percent rejected this same sentence, suggesting that resistance to this usage may be waning.

Some criticism of the comparison and modification of *unique* no doubt stems from the word's use—and overuse—in advertising, as in *Our city's most unique restaurant is now even more unique* or in claims for an automobile that is *so unique, it's patented.* In these examples *unique* is used as a striking synonym for *unusual* or *distinctive.*

But the modification of *unique* may also be found in the work of many reputable writers, even though it is often edited out of prose before publication. Here are some recent examples:

> I am in the rather unique position of being the son, the grandson, and the great grandson of preachers (Martin Luther King, Jr., "Letter from Birmingham Jail")

> The creature is so unique in its style and appearance that the biologists who discovered it have given it not just its own species name, or its own genus or family, but

have moved way up the classification scale and declared that it is an entirely new phylum (Natalie Angier, "Flyspeck on a Lobster Lip Turns Biology on Its Ear," *New York Times*)

William Gardner Smith decided to opt for Parisian exile out of a love for French literature, especially that of Balzac and Zola, as well as a fascination with the experiences of Ernest Hemingway. Even the poverty of postwar Paris was attractive because it meant that Americans could live there very cheaply. More important, however, and more unique, was the sheer desire to escape the United States (Tyler Stovall, *Paris Noir*)

It is hard to see the modification of *unique* in these passages as a stylistic fault or a flaw of logic. Indeed, if *unique* were to be used only according to the strictest criteria of logic, it could be applied freely to anything in the world, since nothing is wholly equivalent to anything else. The word *unique*, like many absolute terms, has more than one sense and can be modified with grace in certain uses.

See more at **absolute terms, complete, equal, infinite, parallel,** and **perfect.**

unjust   See **injustice.**

up and up

The idiomatic expression *up and up,* meaning "honest, forthcoming, reliable," is used most commonly in the expression *on the up and up* with the same meaning, as in *Observers are stationed at the polling places to make sure that the election is on the up and up.* Though informal, the expression is fully acceptable, having been in use since the mid-1800s. In our 2004 survey, 88 percent of the Usage Panel accepted it in the sentence quoted above. The expression is sometimes used in Great Britain and other parts of the English-speaking world to mean "on the increase, increasing," but this usage is uncommon in American English and is likely to be considered incorrect. In 2004, only 10 percent of the Panel found it acceptable in the sentence *They had notices that part-time jobs were on the up and up as the recession lifted in the northwest.*

used to

The verb *use* is used in the past tense with an infinitive to indicate a past condition or habitual practice: *We used to live in that house.* Because the -*d* in *used* has merged with the *t* of *to* and is not pronounced in these constructions, people sometimes mistakenly leave it out when writing. Thus it is incorrect to write *We use to play tennis.* When *do* occurs with this form of *use* in negative statements and in questions, the situation is reversed, and *use to* [not *used to*] is correct: *You did not use to play on that team. Didn't she use to work for your company?*

utilize

The word *utilize* is sometimes used where the simpler word *use* might work just as well, in sentences such as *Barbara utilized questionable methods in her analysis* or *We hope that many commuters will continue to utilize mass transit after the bridge has reopened.* Some critics contend that there is no advantage to this usage, and that it is pretentious and needlessly long. But *utilize* often emphasizes the practical or profitable way in which something is used, and the word appears frequently in contexts in which a strategy is put to practical advantage or a chemical or nutrient is being taken up and used effectively:

> . . . the result of the reforms was an army with high morale and a fighting system that others emulated. Wallenstein utilized elements of the new system at Lützen; France followed suit . . . (Gunther E. Rothenberg, "Gustavus Adolphus," in Robert Cowley and Geoffrey Parker, eds., *The Reader's Companion to Military History*)

> Salesmanship, design and innovation are all utilized to attract and capture the consumer (John Kenneth, "The Myth of Consumer Sovereignty," *The Affluent Society*)

> Rainwater is absorbed by roots, transported in the vascular tissue of trees, shunted through the metabolic pathways of plants, utilized in various physiological processes, and eventually released back into the atmosphere through the leaves (David Campbell, *A Land of Ghosts*)

> If a diet contains too much phosphorus, calcium is not utilized efficiently (James Marti, *The Ultimate Guide to Diets*)

· V ·

valet

This French loan word, which has been used in English since the 16th century, was traditionally pronounced (văl′ĭt), rhyming with *pallet*. The pseudo-French pronunciation (văl′ā) has become the most common pronunciation in American English, and (vă-lā′), with stress on the second syllable, can be heard as well. Not only are both of these pronunciations acceptable, but the original pronunciation is rarely used anymore in the United States.

various of

Various is normally an adjective, but it sometimes sees use as a pronoun, as in *He spoke to various of the staff members.* Language critics have battered this usage since the 1930s as an unlicensed shift of an adjective to a pronoun. But linguistically, there is no reason to oppose it, since it is really no different than other quantifiers like *few, many,* and *several.*

Whether or not it is justifiably grammatical, the pronoun use of *various* grates on many people's nerves. In 1967, 91 percent of the Usage Panel found *various* unacceptable as a pronoun, and in 1999, 87 percent disapproved of the sentence *Various of the committee members spoke out against the measure.* Resistance to this usage was somewhat eased when it was used for inanimate nouns and was not the subject of the sentence, with 70 percent of the Panel rejecting the sentence *The tribe alleged ownership of the lake and various of its tributaries and effluents that lay within the original borders of the reservation.*

Few usage problems are more easily avoided. Simply drop *of the,* and stick with the adjectival use: *various committee members.* In fact, it's worth asking yourself whether *various* is necessary even as an adjective. It may be preferable to use *many* or *several,* unless the context calls for emphasizing the diversity of the group being specified.

vase

The usual pronunciation in American English is (vās) or (vāz), rhyming with *race* or *raise.* The pronunciation (väz) is customary in British English.

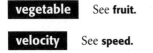

VAT tax See **ATM machine.**

vegan

The most common pronunciation of *vegan* is (vē'gən), with a long *e* in the first syllable and a hard *g* as in *goat.* In our 2004 survey, this was the preferred pronunciation of 68 percent of the Usage Panel. Other acceptable pronunciations include (vā'gən), which rhymes with *pagan,* the pronunciation of 18 percent of the Panel, and (věj'ən), which rhymes with *hedge in,* the pronunciation of 14 percent of the Panel.

vegetable See **fruit.**

velocity See **speed.**

venal / venial

The words *venal* and *venial* look and sound similar but have very different meanings. In general, *venal* refers to monetary corruption. A venal police officer is one who is given or susceptible to bribery or is otherwise capable of betraying scruples for a price. The word derives from Latin *vēnum,* "sale." *Venial,* from the Latin *venia,* "forgiveness," means "easily excused or forgiven," as in *a venial offense. Venial* is most often found in the phrase *venial sin,* which is sometimes extended to nonreligious contexts. In Catholic theology, a venial sin is one that is minor and that does not incur damnation. It stands in contrast to *mortal sin.*

Venal can be applied to both acts and people (*a venal scheme, a venal judge*), but *venial* applies only to acts, never to people. Thus *venial* is misused in phrases like *a venial official.* Similarly, the phrase *venal sin* is usually an error, although some may feel its use is justified in contexts describing greed: *venal sins of unbridled capitalism.* Even here it may well be seen as a mistake.

venereal disease See **sexually transmitted disease.**

venial See **venal.**

verbal

One meaning of the word *verbal* is "spoken, not written," as in *verbal agreement* and *verbal contract.* Though the word has been used in this way since the 16th century, some language critics have insisted that *verbal* should only be used in the sense "by means of words" and that *oral* is the proper synonym for "spoken" in these contexts. It is true that the ambiguity of the word *verbal* can cause confusion; the phrase *modern technologies for verbal communication,* for example, may refer to devices for spoken communication such as radio, the telephone, and the loudspeaker, or to all de-

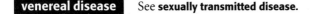

vices for linguistic communication, including the telegraph, the teletype, and the fax machine. If the context does not make the meaning clear, it is helpful to use *oral* or *spoken* to avoid ambiguity.

verbiage

The term *verbiage* has two basic meanings: "an excess of words for the purpose; wordiness," and "the manner in which something is expressed in words." It is occasionally used to mean simply "written text," especially in the context of computers and computer applications, as in *The verbiage should occupy no more than 33 percent of the screen.* However, 78 percent of the Usage Panel found this example unacceptable in a survey from 2004.

verbs

Verbs are words that express existence, action, or occurrence. In English, most verbs show tense and mood as well as agreement with their subjects in grammatical person and number. In order to do this, verbs take affixes, otherwise modify their forms, or combine with other verbs, called *auxiliary verbs.* In traditional grammar, the verb of a sentence forms part of the predicate of the sentence.

See more at **auxiliary and primary verbs** and the entries following this one.

verbs, mood of

A *mood* is a property of verbs that indicates the attitude of the speaker about the factuality or likelihood of what is expressed. The term *mood* is also applied to the sets of inflected verb forms that convey this attitude. The *indicative mood,* which is by far the most common, is used to make statements and ask questions. The verbs in the following sentences are in the *indicative mood: Wilson enjoys music. The dog ran across the street. Did the dog run across the street?*

The *imperative mood* is used to give direct commands, such as *Get out of here!* or *Stop shouting!* The *subjunctive mood* is used in a variety of contexts, including those in which the speaker expresses conditions that are contrary to fact. For example, the verbal form *were* in *If she were here, we wouldn't be in this fix* is in the subjunctive mood. The use of the subjunctive expressed by simple inflected forms of the verb, like the form *were* of the verb *be,* is very limited in Modern English compared to earlier stages of the language. In many of the roles that it formerly played in English, the subjunctive has been largely supplanted by auxiliary verbs, called *modal auxiliaries,* like *may* and *might.* Nonetheless, the subjunctive still has its uses and its usage problems.

See more at **auxiliary and primary verbs** and **subjunctive.**

verbs, principal parts of

Verbs are words that express an action or a state of being. All English verbs that are not auxiliary verbs have four principal parts: a base form (the infinitive without *to*), a present participle, a past tense, and a past participle. The principal parts are used to form tenses, and grammars usually classify verbs as regular and irregular, according to the way verbs form their principal parts. All present participles are formed by the addition of *–ing* to the base form: *making, breaking, crying*. There are several ways of forming the past tense and the past participle, however.

Regular verbs form their past tense and past participle by adding the suffix *–ed* to the base form. Thus we say *I walked, I have walked, They plodded, They have plodded, She tried, We had tried,* and so on. As these examples show, the spelling of these forms sometimes involves modification of the base form. Some rules for spelling the principal parts of regular verbs are discussed under **suffixes.**

Irregular verbs do not follow the pattern of regular verbs by simply adding the suffix *–ed*. Most change their base form—and often its vowel—to make the past tense and past participle. Here are some examples of irregular verbs showing how varied this group can be:

Base Form	Past	Past Participle
bend	bent	bent
weep	wept	wept
think	thought	thought
speak	spoke	spoken
grow	grew	grown
ride	rode	ridden
tear	tore	torn
meet	met	met
find	found	found
stand	stood	stood
begin	began	begun

English has about 180 irregular verbs, and as the chart above shows, these follow a number of different patterns. Some irregular verbs, like *burst, cast, cut,* and *split,* do not change to form the past tense and past participle (*He cut the bread. He has cut the bread*). A few verbs, like *burn* and *spell,* have both regular (*burned, spelled*) and irregular (*burnt, spelt*) past tenses and past participles. Some, like *mow* and *saw,* have both regular and irregular past participles (*mowed, mown; sawed, sawn*).

Since English has so many irregular verbs, writers should consult their dictionary when unsure about the correct form of the past tense or the past participle of particular verbs. Some forms of verbs that are commonly heard in speech in certain regions of the United States should be avoided in formal writing, since they are not acceptable in other regions. Examples of such forms include the past tense *drug* (instead of *dragged*) and the past participle *drank* for *drunk* (as in *I shouldn't have drank so much*).

Strong verbs are a group of irregular verbs that make their past tense and past participle by changing the vowel in the base form of the verb, like *sang* and *sung* from the verb *sing*. Often the past participle of a strong verb will use the suffix *–en,* or after vowels, *–n,* as in *broken* from the verb *break*. The vowel changes in strong verbs fall into a variety of patterns. In some strong verbs, for example, only the past tense shows a different vowel from the present tense, while the past participle simply has the ending typical of the strong verbs, as *threw* and *thrown,* from the verb *throw*. (The corresponding term *weak verb* refers to any verb that makes the past tense and past participle by adding a suffix containing the dental consonants *t* or *d,* like the two past-tense forms *burned* and *burnt* from the verb *burn*.) Most of the verbs that have forms made by changing a vowel of the base form are native English words that go back to Old English. Old English had seven classes of strong verbs, each with a different pattern of vowel change. This feature of English verbs goes back over six thousand years to the prehistoric language from which English and most of the other languages of Europe are descended, Indo-European, which also used vowel changes to make different forms of verbs. (The terms *strong* and *weak* do not refer to the relative rhetorical effectiveness of strong verbs as opposed to weak verbs. The terms are simply translations of German *stark* and *schwach* respectively, which were introduced by the 19th-century linguist Jacob Grimm in order to describe these two different ways—common to all Germanic languages—of forming the principal parts of verbs.) Not all verbs that have principal parts formed by altering the vowel are usually called strong verbs, however. Past tenses like *left* and *lost* belonging to the verbs *leave* and *lose* involve both the addition of a suffix with *t* and a vowel change, and verbs like these have a variety of historical origins.

Since Old English times, strong verbs have tended to become weak verbs. When children are first learning to speak, they notice the various patterns used to form the past tense, either the addition of the suffix *–ed* or the change of the vowel of the base form, but sometimes they extend the pattern properly belonging to one group of verbs to verbs that belong to a group that uses another pattern. The mistakes made by adult learners of English as a second language also illustrate the same process, and adults too may invent new forms based on analogy. For instance, several different verbs with (ī) in the base form make their past tense by changing this vowel to (ō), like *write* and *drive*. Thus the similar-sounding word *dive,* originally a weak verb, develops strong forms like *dove*. The past tense *arrove* is also occasionally encountered in speech and writing. While there are far fewer strong verbs today than there were in the past, strong verbs are still among the most frequently used verbs in English.

As a consequence of these innovations appearing over time, a great deal of variation exists in the formation of the principal parts of English verbs, with many non-standard forms arising, like *brung* for *brought* and *thunk* for *thought*. Sometimes speakers try to regularize irregular verbs by giving them the *–ed* suffix of regular verbs, as in the nonstandard past tenses *knowed* and *taked*. These forms are not crude aberrations, but the consequence of natural language change. They are attempts to establish regularity where none seems to exist.

All in all, there are about eighty irregular verbs, like *be, have, do, get, go, make, take,* and *see,* that are used with significant frequency in English, and they are likely to persist in their current forms. Even if children—or speakers in general—invent new, regular forms for these common verbs, the new forms will probably not be taken up by other speakers and become an established part of the English language. The old, irregular forms of these verbs are heard so often that language learners naturally include them as part of their mental grammars of English.

In some specialized meanings, verbs that are normally irregular require regular past tenses and past participles in *–ed*. This is the case, for example, with the verb *hang,* whose past tense and past participle is *hung* except when the verb is used transitively to describe death by hanging: *According to medieval folklore, Judas hanged* [not *hung*] *himself on an elder tree.* In other cases, as when a batter has *flied* (but not *flown*) out to end an inning, the principal parts are regular because the verbs in question are derived from nouns (as *a fly hit to the outfield*) and are not simply extended uses of the irregular verbs themselves.

verbs, tenses of

Verb tenses show time. English has present, past, and future tenses; these have three variations: simple, perfect, and progressive.

simple tenses   The simple present is formed with a present form of the verb. The simple past uses the past form. The simple future requires the auxiliary *will* or *shall* and a bare infinitive. Future time can also be expressed by certain verb phrases like *be going to* (*The tree is going to bloom soon*), *be to* (*We're to have a meeting this morning*), and *be about to* (*They are about to start the race*). Futurity is also often expressed by the simple present or present progressive tense with an adverb or adverbial as in *We leave for Portland on Tuesday* and *We are going to the beach tomorrow.*

Tense	Use	Examples
Present	current state or action	She *walks* in the park.
	habitual or repeated action	She *walks* in the park daily.
	future state or action	Her train *leaves* tonight.
		Tomorrow *is* payday.
Past	past state or action	The book *fell* on the floor.
	habitual or repeated action	We *walked* in the garden every morning.
Future	future state or action	We *will walk* in the park.
	habitual or repeated action	We *will walk* in the park every morning.

perfect tenses   The perfect tenses show a completed state or action. The present perfect is formed with *has* or *have* and a past participle. The past perfect, also called the pluperfect, requires *had* and a past participle. The future perfect uses *will have* or *shall have* and a past participle. See the table at the top of page 487.

progressive tenses   The progressive tenses show a state or action that is continuing or in progress. The present progressive is formed with *am, is,* or *are* and a present participle. The past progressive requires *was* or *were* and a present participle. The future progressive uses *will be* or *shall be* and a present participle. See the second table on page 487.

Tense	Use	Examples
Present Perfect	state or action that occurred in the past and may continue to the present	He *has walked* in the park. I *have lived* in Arizona all my life.
Past Perfect (Pluperfect)	state or action that occurred before something else in the past	He *had walked* in the park that morning. I *had lived* in Arizona before moving to Oregon.
Future Perfect	state or action that will occur before something else in the future	He *will have walked* in the park by the time we arrive. Come March, I *will have lived* in Arizona for two years.

The perfect and progressive tenses are sometimes called *aspects* instead of tenses since they show how verb action is viewed or experienced with respect to time. The perfect and progressive tenses can be combined to show action in the past that is ongoing and may continue to the point of reference: *They have been walking in the park all morning. Before we moved, we had been living in Arizona. By March, we will have been living in Arizona for two years.* The past progressive is also sometimes used as a kind of future-in-the-past: *We were flying to France the next day, so I watered the plants before going to bed.* Usually the futurity of the action or state described by the verb is made even more explicit by the use of the expression *was/were going to: Since we were going to fly to France the next day, I watered the plants.*

Tense	Use	Examples
Present Progressive	ongoing state or action	They *are walking* in the park.
	future state or action	I *am going* to the museum tomorrow.
Past Progressive	state or action ongoing in the past	They *were walking* in the park.
Future Progressive	state or action ongoing in the future	They *will be walking* in the park all day. They *will be walking* in the park tomorrow.

sequence and consistency of verb tenses   It is important to keep verb tenses in the proper sequence so as not to disrupt the coherence of time within a piece of writing. If the actions being described occur at the same time, the tenses of the verbs should represent this:

> Once Jane gets angry, it takes a long time for her to calm down.
> When the timing belt broke, the engine stopped.
> The news broke while she was sleeping.

If the actions being described occur at different times, different tenses should be used in order to make this clear:

> We didn't go to the museum on our last visit, but this time we will certainly go there.
>
> After he had eaten the soup, everyone asked how it was.
>
> Although they will soon be moving out, they have enjoyed living here.

The most common problems with tenses arise when the subject matter requires shifting back and forth between present and past tenses and when direct speech is being converted to indirect speech. The following paragraph provides an example of shifting tenses:

> I grew up in a neighborhood that surrounds a small park. We lived on a street that is lined with trees and has small, two-story houses. Many people park their cars on the street, but in the winter there is so much snow that it is difficult to find a space. My parents owned an old station wagon. Its heater had not worked for years.

In this narrative, the past events (growing up, owning a station wagon, and so on) are kept distinct from the conditions that continue into the present (the neighborhood surrounding the park, the street being lined with trees, and so on). While these conditions could have all been rendered using the past tense, the writer wants to convey a sense of continuing familiarity with the old neighborhood, and using the present tense in addition to the past makes this possible.

There are, however, many conditions that continue into the present and must be conveyed by the present tense in almost any context: *Galileo discovered that Jupiter has* [not *had*] *moons. The explorers camped on the Illinois River near where it joins* [not *joined*] *the Mississippi.*

Sometimes writers shift from past to present tense when telling a story to add vividness to the events. This legitimate tense shift is a literary device called the *historical present.* It is familiar to readers of epic poetry, but people also use it when relating everyday anecdotes:

> I was walking down Delancey Street the other day when a guy *comes* up to me and *asks* me for the time.

When writing about literature, it is especially easy to mix up tenses in a way that can confuse the reader. Take, for example, the problems in choosing tenses that a student writing a paper about Shakespeare typically faces. The student may discuss Act V of a play in the present tense and then refer back to something that happened in Act II using the past tense (after all, Act II is past in relation to Act V). Once writing in the past tense, however, the student writer may then be tempted to continue it even when discussing Act V. For this reason it is best to discuss the plot or train of events in a work of literature in the present tense—whether it is Act V or Act II that is being discussed: *Before he confronts Ophelia, Hamlet unburdens his soul in a soliloquy.* Of course, the biographical details relating to the life of the author of a literary work—how an author lived or what an author did—can be discussed in the past tense, but these subjects should be kept distinct from what the author says or attempts to do in the work of literature itself, which is eternally present. Thus a student writing about literature can say *Shakespeare portrays Hamlet as a very passionate man* and *Shakespeare presented many of his plays at the Globe Theater in London.*

When not quoting the exact words of a speaker, writers must convert direct speech in the present tense to reported speech in the past tense:

> Direct speech: "I am working for a law firm," she said.
> Indirect speech: She said that she *was working* for a law firm.

If the direct speech is in the past tense, the indirect speech must also be in the past or the past perfect:

> Direct speech: "The play opened last week," he said.
> Indirect speech: He said that the play *opened* [or *had opened*] the week before.

The second example raises the issue of whether the past perfect tense is falling out of use in such situations. The Usage Panel prefers the past perfect, but the simple past is often acceptable. In our 1995 survey, 77 percent preferred *had talked* to *talked* in the sentence *I asked if he had talked to his doctor,* leaving 23 percent for whom *talked* was unobjectionable. The Panel was even more tolerant of the simple past in an example that did not involve the problem of the conversion of direct speech to indirect speech. In *Before I was introduced to her, I (heard/had heard) the rumor about her,* 59 percent required *had heard,* while 41 percent allowed *heard.* Thus it seems likely that many readers will not notice the omission of *had*—that is, they will not notice the use of the simple past in preference to the past perfect—in these situations.

But if the direct speech is in the perfect or past perfect tense, then the indirect speech must be in the past perfect:

> Direct speech: "I have been working as a plumber for six years," he said.
> Indirect speech: He said that he *had been working* as a plumber for six years.

the past tense in conditional sentences   The past tense is also used in certain conditional clauses—specifically, those that refer to unreal or unfulfilled conditions in the present or hypothetical conditions in the future: *If he studied harder, he would receive better grades (but he doesn't study hard).* Similarly, the past perfect is used to refer to unreal or unfulfilled conditions in the past: *If he had studied harder, he would have received better grades (but he didn't study hard).*

See more at **subjunctive.**

verbs, transitive and intransitive

Most grammars classify verbs into transitive and intransitive. Transitive verbs take an object: *I read the book. She values your criticism. Priestley discovered oxygen.* Intransitive verbs do not take an object: *I sleep on a futon. She sings beautifully. The Kingsleys live in a brick house.*

Many verbs, of course, sometimes take an object and sometimes do not. In other words, they can be transitive or intransitive depending on how they are used. The verb *read,* for example, is transitive in *I read the book* but intransitive in *I usually read in the evening.*

Some basically transitive verbs, when used intransitively, still retain a sense of an implied object. For example, the verb *read,* in its intransitive use above, still implies that something is being read, even though the verb has no object describing what that something is. Similarly, the sentence *I shave in the shower* still implies that something is being shaved, namely the subject, "I."

Many verbs that describe an event intransitively have a related transitive use in which the subject of the verb causes the event to occur. For example, in the sentence *The door opened,* the verb *open* is used intransitively, while in *The butler opened the door,* *open* is a transitive verb; the butler causes the door to open.

Interestingly, many verbs classified as intransitive can be used transitively in certain very restricted contexts; for example, the verb *sleep* does not normally take an object, but it is possible to say *I slept a deep sleep,* where the object of the verb is a noun form of the word *sleep* itself. Another case is what linguists call *way* constructions, as in *I slept my way through college,* where *sleep* takes the phrase *my way* as a sort of direct object. Despite the existence of these exceptional cases, verbs like *sleep* are still considered intransitive.

Below are further examples of transitive and intransitive uses of verbs:

Transitive	Intransitive
She plays the saxophone beautifully.	She plays beautifully.
We won the game in overtime.	We won in overtime.
Jack opened the door slowly.	The door opened slowly.
We began the party with a song.	The party began with a song.

verbs, voice of

Transitive verbs have a property, known as *voice,* that allows the relationship between the subject and the action of the verb to be expressed in one of two ways. Verbs in the active voice have the performer of the action as the subject and have the person or thing that is acted upon as the object. Thus the sentences *Marty found the kitten under the couch* and *The children built a house of blocks today* have their verbs in the active voice. The performers of the action—Marty and the children—are the subjects of the sentence, and the things acted upon—the kitten and the house—are the objects.

In the passive voice this situation is reversed. The person or thing that is acted upon becomes the subject, and the performer of the action gets put in a prepositional phrase beginning with *by* or is omitted from the sentence altogether. Thus in the passive voice the sentences would read *The kitten was found* (by Marty) *under the couch* and *The house of blocks was built* (by the children) *today.*

Passive verb phrases normally consist of a form of the verb *be* followed by a past participle. Passive verbs can exist in any tense. They may or may not employ an auxiliary verb. See the table at the top of page 491.

It is important not to confuse the passive voice with a progressive form of an active or intransitive verb. Like passive verbs, progressive verbs employ a form of the verb *be,* but progressive verbs always have a present participle (ending in *–ing*),

Active	Passive
Linda drives the car.	The car is driven by Linda.
Linda drove the car.	The car was driven by Linda.
Linda was driving the car.	The car was being driven by Linda.
Linda has driven the car.	The car has been driven by Linda.
Linda may have driven the car.	The car may have been driven by Linda.

whereas a passive verb always has a past participle. Passive verbs can have progressive forms, that is, they can employ the participle *being*, but it is always followed by a past participle. Here are some examples:

Active/Progressive	Passive/Progressive
Jim is writing a book.	The book is being written by Jim.
Jim was writing a book.	The book was being written by Jim.
Jim had been writing a book.	The book had been being written by Jim.

Sometimes an adverb intervenes between the form of *be* and the participle. The sentence *Jim is carefully writing a book* still has a progressive verb in the active voice, and *The book is being carefully written by Jim* still has its verb in the passive voice.

Some passive constructions use *get* instead of *be* with a past participle. In some of these sentences the subject may have a somewhat active role even when being acted upon by the verb. Thus it is possible to say *The kitten got left in the basement,* which is no different from *The kitten was left in the basement.* But the sentence *Michelle got hired as a reporter* implies that Michelle's actions were instrumental in her securing the job. This passive with *get* is mostly limited to informal speaking and writing.

There are a few transitive verbs—called middle verbs—that cannot normally be made passive, such as *fit* (in the meaning "suit, be of the right size for"), *have, lack, resemble,* and *suit.* Thus it is possible to say *Our team lacks a good pitcher,* but not *A good pitcher is lacked by our team; That suit fits you,* but not *You are fit by that suit;* and so on. In other meanings, such as "equip with," however, the verb *fit* can be made passive: *The vehicle was fit* [or *fitted*] *with a new engine.*

Writers should be aware of the distinction between the active and passive voice in order to improve their writing. Overuse of the passive voice can lead to prose that is boring, difficult to understand, and needlessly verbose. For more on these problems, see **passive voice.**

See also **auxiliary and primary verbs, get, participles,** and **subject and verb agreement.**

vertebra / vertebrae / vertebras

The plural of the noun *vertebra,* which refers to any of the bones that make up the spinal column, is either *vertebrae* or *vertebras.* The plural form *vertebrae* is often used incorrectly as a singular, as in this example from the brochure of a medical facility: *Different parts of a vertebrae have different functions.*

The last syllable of the plural *vertebrae* can be pronounced either to rhyme with *tray* (vûr′tə-brā′) or *tree* (vûr′tə-brē′).

very and past participles

In general usage *very* is not used alone to modify a past participle. Thus, we may say of a book that it has been *very much praised* or *very much criticized* (where *very* modifies the adverb *much*), but not that it has been *very praised* or *very criticized*.

However, many past participle forms do double duty as adjectives, in which case modification by *very* or by analogous adverbs such as *quite* is acceptable, as in *a very celebrated singer* or *a performance that was quite polished*. In some cases there is disagreement as to whether a particular participle can be used properly as an adjective. In the past, critics have objected to the use of *very* by itself with *delighted, interested, annoyed, pleased, disappointed,* and *irritated*. All of these words are now well established as adjectives, however, as indicated by the fact that they are used attributively, that is, in juxtaposition to a noun they modify, as in *a delighted audience, a pleased look, a disappointed young man*.

But the situation is not always clear. Some speakers accept phrases such as *very appreciated, very astonished,* or *very heartened,* while others prefer alternatives using *very much*. Some participles can be treated as adjectives in one sense but not another, as in *a very inflated reputation* but not *a very inflated tire*. As a result, there is no sure way to tell which participles can be modified by a bare *very*. When in doubt, using *very much* is generally correct.

See more at **participles.**

victual

The modern pronunciation (vĭt′l) represents an Anglicized pronunciation of the Old French form *vitaille,* which was borrowed into English in the early 14th century. The modern spelling is a result of the fact that in both French and English the word was sometimes spelled with a *c,* and later also with a *u,* under the influence of its Late Latin ancestor *victuālia,* meaning "provisions." The word is now usually spelled *victual,* or on occasion *vittle,* but the pronunciation has remained (vĭt′l).

See more at **pronunciation spelling.**

virago See **shrew.**

virtue See **in virtue of.**

virus

A *virus* is any of a large group of submicroscopic agents that act as intracellular parasites of plants, animals, and bacteria, and consist of a segment of DNA or RNA surrounded by a coat of protein. Even though viruses are commonly described as "live" or "killed," scientists do not usually consider viruses to be living organisms. There are several reasons for this. Viruses are not cells and cannot metabolize energy. They are unable to reproduce independently but instead must inject their genetic material into a host cell that incorporates the viral genome and then produces new viruses that eventually destroy the cell.

Viruses are usually referred to as "live" when they act as pathogens or when they are used in certain kinds of vaccines, as in a news story by the Associated Press that describes *"a vaccine that is made from modified live virus and isn't considered safe for the elderly or people with medical problems."* Live viruses can replicate within host cells. The term *killed virus* refers to an inactivated virus that is used in certain vaccines. Killed viruses are chemically altered so that they can stimulate the production of protective antibodies but cannot replicate in a host cell. Other vaccines contain viruses that are "weakened," or genetically altered so that they replicate in a way that stimulates an immune response but that does not ordinarily cause disease. Using the term *inactivated* avoids the erroneous implication that a virus is a living organism.

See more at **germ.**

vitamin　　See **catalyst.**

vitiate

The word *vitiate* has a number of meanings, all of them negative. It generally means "to impair the quality or character of," as in this quotation from columnist George Will in the *Washington Post*: *"The decision to keep aircraft at 15,000 feet expressed the primary military objective of not losing pilots, even though this vitiated the stated political goal of protecting Kosovo from Serbia's marauding ethnic cleansers."* *Vitiate* can also mean "to corrupt morally," as when the librarian of the Boy Scouts of America, back in 1914, condemned the then-new Hardy Boys series of detective stories, claiming they would "debauch and vitiate" a child's imagination. In legal settings especially, *vitiate* is used to mean "to void or invalidate," as in the dictum *Contractual consent may be vitiated by error, fraud, or duress.*

A somewhat sophisticated and uncommon word, *vitiate* is sometimes misused for *mitigate* or *ameliorate*, as shown in the following examples from periodicals. The first is from *Time Out*: *"David, a boy from the posh bit of Doncaster, is staying across the tracks with his cantankerous, laid-off Uncle Robert, his long-suffering Aunt Deelie, and his cousin Charlene, who vitiates the tedium of her existence through soap opera escapism."* The second is from the *National Interest*: *"Viable, professional military and police forces must be established. . . . Dedicated fulfillment will vitiate the horrendous mistakes made a year ago, when we simultaneously disbanded Iraq's military and police, and stood by while thousands of convicts . . . were released in Saddam's last days."*

voice

Voice is a property of verbs that indicates the relationship between the subject and the action of the verb. See **verbs, transitive and intransitive** and **verbs, voice of.**

voltage

See **current.**

· W ·

wait on / wait upon

For more than one hundred years, language critics have condemned the use of *wait on* and *wait upon* to mean "await" or "wait for," as in *We are still waiting on management to approve the expenditure for new offices.* As the critics would have it, *wait on* should mean only "to serve the needs of someone." But it is hard to see why these phrasal verbs should be so restricted, especially when they have such widespread use as synonyms for *wait for* in speech and in literature:

> A committee went ashore to wait on his Excellency the Governor-General, and learn our fate. At the end of three hours of boding suspense, they came back and said the Emperor would receive us at noon (Mark Twain, *Innocents Abroad*)

> It was decided that a deputation should wait on the boy's aunt—an old maiden resident—and ask her if she would house the piano till Mr. Phillotson should send for it (Thomas Hardy, *Jude the Obscure*)

> Send word to the Captains that they shall wait on me here, as soon as may be after the third hour has rung (J.R.R. Tolkien, *The Return of the King*)

waive / wave / waiver / waver

The verb *waive* means "to relinquish a right, claim, or privilege voluntarily," as in *waiving the right to a trial*. Official permission, or a document providing such permission, is called a *waiver*. Both *waive* and *waiver* are sometimes confused with *wave* and *waver*, homophones that have entirely different meanings.

waive* mistaken for *wave   *Wave*, meaning "to move freely back and forth or up and down in the air," is sometimes confused with *waive*, especially when it is followed by a preposition such as *off* or *aside* to mean "dismiss" or "disregard," as in this example from the *Scotsman*: "*For if senior civil servants and the Executive can waive aside due legal process and parliamentary accountability so readily, why should voters believe or act differently?*"

wave* mistaken for *waive   Sometimes *wave* is miscast for *waive* in its general meaning of "relinquish." Interestingly, it is easy to imagine *wave aside* making sense in the following example from the *Calgary Sun*, where *wave* by itself is erroneous: "*Zeta-Jones says it's a tradition for performers to sing their nominated songs, and she's not about to break with that tradition even if rapper Eminem has waved the same honour.*"

495

waiver mistaken for **waver**   *Waiver* is sometimes confused with *waver*, when *waver* means "to exhibit irresolution or indecision," as in *The couple wavered over buying a house.* This mistake is seen in this quotation from an obituary in the *Boston Herald*: *"He made sure the traditions of the Boston Marathon never waivered, right down to the post-race bowl of beef stew."*

waiver mistaken for **waive**   *Waiver* is normally limited to use as a noun, and it is sometimes used incorrectly as a synonym of *waive*, as in *He waivered his privilege* or *The department waivered the requirements for several students wanting to take the course.*

waivered and **waived**   The adjective *waivered* is a recent coinage that means "permitted by a waiver." It occurs most frequently in human services, as when services not stipulated or allowed under a regulation are permitted by a waiver issued by a governmental authority. For instance, a waiver might be issued to allow support services for disabled or sick people to be provided in the home rather than in a government-supervised facility. The distinction between *waivered* and *waived* is worth observing: A stipulation in a regulation may be waived by an authority issuing a waiver. The services provided under that waiver are waivered, not waived.

wake

wake, waken / awake, awaken   The pairs *wake, waken* and *awake, awaken* have formed a bewildering array since the Middle English period. All four words have similar meanings, though there are some differences in use. Only *wake* is used in the sense "to be awake," as in expressions like *waking* (not *wakening*) *and sleeping* or *every waking hour. Wake* is also more common than *waken* when used together with *up*, and *awake* and *awaken* never occur in this context: *She woke up* (rarely *wakened up*; never *awakened up* or *awoke up*). Some writers have suggested that *waken* should be used only transitively (as in *The alarm wakened him*) and *awaken* only intransitively (as in *He awakened at dawn*), but there is ample literary precedent for using *waken* intransitively and *awaken* transitively:

> . . . something still kept insisting that I was not where I was, that I had not wakened where I seemed to be, but in the little room in Soho where I was accustomed to sleep in the body of Edward Hyde (Robert Louis Stevenson, *The Strange Case of Dr. Jekyll and Mr. Hyde*)

> There are few of us who have not sometimes wakened before dawn, either after one of those dreamless nights that make us almost enamoured of death, or one of those nights of horror and misshapen joy, when through the chambers of the brain sweep phantoms more terrible than reality itself (Oscar Wilde, *The Picture of Dorian Gray*)

> Every morning I wakened with a fresh consciousness that winter was over (Willa Cather, *My Ántonia*)

> The arrival of his breakfast awakened him into a broken and ruined world (F. Scott Fitzgerald, "Crazy Sunday," *The American Mercury*)

> One night I was awakened by a violent clap of thunder and was convinced that the world was over (Jonathan Franzen, "Caught," *The New Yorker*)

In figurative senses *awake* and *awaken* are more prevalent:

> Nor was Mr. Bumble's gloom the only thing calculated to awaken a pleasing melancholy in the bosom of a spectator (Charles Dickens, *Oliver Twist*)

> Theories, prescriptions, and discussions are forgotten, and we think only with love and reverence of this modern patriarch, so lonely amid the daily enlarging congregation of the hearts he has awakened to a sense of the mystery, the terror, the joy, the splendour of human destinies (G.K. Chesterton, G.H. Parris, and Edward Garnett, *Leo Tolstoy*)

> The women who thus cry for aid are the victims of ignorance. Awakening from that ignorance, they are demanding relief (Margaret Sanger, *Woman and the New Race*)

> Carrie looked over the large bill of fare which the waiter handed her without really considering it. She was very hungry, and the things she saw there awakened her desires, but the high prices held her attention (Theodore Dreiser, *Sister Carrie*)

woke and waked Regional American dialects vary in the way that certain verbs form their principal parts. Northern dialects seem to favor the form *woke* and *woken* as the past tense and past participle of *wake: They woke up with a start.* The past tense and past participle *waked* are heard more often in Southern dialects than in Northern dialects, as in *The baby waked up early.* However, both patterns of forming these prinicipal parts are considered acceptable.

See more at **dived, sink, sneaked,** and **verbs, principal parts of.**

wangle   See **wrangle.**

want for

When *want* means "to wish or desire," it is sometimes followed immediately by a proper noun or pronoun and an infinitive: *I want you to go to the store.* The word *for* should never precede the noun or pronoun in these constructions, as in *I want for you to go.* When *want* and the infinitive are separated in the sentence, however, *for* is required: *What I want is for you to go. I want very much for you to go.*

–ward

The basic meaning of the suffix *–ward* is "having a particular direction or location." Thus *inward* means "directed or located inside." Other examples are *outward, forward, backward, upward, downward, earthward, homeward, northward, southward, eastward,* and *westward.* The suffix *–ward* forms adjectives and adverbs. Adverbs ending in *–ward* can also end in *–wards.* Thus *I stepped backward* and *I stepped backwards* are both correct, although the forms ending in *–wards* are more common in British English. However, only *backward* (and not *backwards*) can function as an adjective: *a* *backward glance.* In order to avoid distracting the reader with inconsistencies within a single piece of writing, however, writers should avoid using adverbs in *–ward* in one instance but the equivalent adverbs in *–wards* in another instance, if no other circumstance requires that there be some variation. The use of both *–ward* and *–wards* to form synonymous adverbs goes back even to Old English, where the two suffixes had the forms *–weard* and *–weardes,* respectively.

waterspout   See **tornado.**

wattage   See **current.**

way

Way has long been an intensifying adverb meaning "to a great degree," as in *way off base* or *way over budget.* This usage is both acceptable and common but has an informal ring.

  Way is also used by many younger speakers as a general intensifier, as in *way cool* and *way depressing.* This usage remains a hallmark of the casual speech of younger people and is not appropriate for formal contexts.

way* versus *ways   In American English *ways* is often used as an equivalent of *way* in phrases such as *a long ways to go.* This usage is considered nonstandard by most editors, though it appears occasionally in less formal texts.

we

Appositive nouns or noun phrases sometimes lead writers and speakers to choose incorrect pronoun forms. Thus *us* is frequently found in constructions such as *Us owners will have something to say about the contract,* where *we* is required as the subject of the sentence. Less frequently, *we* is substituted in positions where *us* should be used, as in *For we students, it's a no-win situation.* In all cases, the function of the pronoun within the sentence should determine its form, whether or not it is followed by a noun or noun phrase.

  See more at **pronouns, personal.**

weak verbs

A weak verb is one that forms its past tense and past participle by adding a suffix that ends in *-d, -ed,* or *-t,* as *start, have,* and *send.*

  See more at **verbs, principal parts of.**

weaned on

The phrase *weaned on* is sometimes used to mean "raised on," as in *Children weaned on junk food will have difficulty switching to a healthy diet.* While this might appear to be a mistake, since *wean* refers literally to a detachment from a source of nourishment, such as breast milk, the weaning process involves a substitution of some other form of nourishment, as *At six months the baby was weaned onto solid foods.* The extension to figurative usages would seem to follow. Thus a sentence like *Paul was weaned on Dixieland jazz* suggests that Paul's exposure to this form of jazz began almost from the time he stopped nursing, that is, from a very early age. The construction thus can be used to good effect, as these examples show:

> The northerners among the refugees, who fled to South Vietnam immediately after the fall of the French at Dien Bien Phu, in 1954, were weaned on harsh weather and infertile soils and are known for their rigorous work ethic (Lowell Weiss, "Timing is Everything," *Atlantic Monthly*)

> Great War soldiers were weaned on Andrew Lang's fairy-tale anthologies and original stories such as George MacDonald's *The Princess and the Goblin* (John Garth, *Tolkien and the Great War*)

website

The development of *website* as a single uncapitalized word mirrors the development of other technological expressions which have tended to take unhyphenated, uncapitalized forms as they become more familiar. Thus *email* has recently been gaining ground over the forms *E-mail* and *e-mail,* especially in texts that are more technologically oriented. Similarly, there has been an increasing preference for closed forms like *homepage, online,* and *printout.*

well

George may look good, but he's not well. English speakers have used *well* as an adjective as well as an adverb since Old English times, and the adjective *well* continues to enjoy a healthy existence. When applied to people, *well* usually refers to a state of health. Like similar adjectives such as *ill* and *faint, well* in this use is normally restricted to the predicate, as in the example above. *Well* does see occasional use as an attributive (that is, before a noun) as in Benjamin Franklin's *"Poor Dick eats like a well man, and drinks like a sick."* It also appears in compound adjectives like *well-baby* and *well-child,* which are widely used by health-care providers and are familiar to most parents.

 Good, on the other hand, has a much wider range of senses that includes "attractive" (as in *She looks good*) and "competent" (as in *For a beginner, he's pretty good*) as well as "healthy."

feel well / feel good Some people insist that the expression *feel good* should not be used in reference to health but should be reserved for the description of a person's emotional condition. But in practice people don't often follow this distinction, and it should not be assumed that readers will be aware of it.

 See more at **bad.**

welsh

Etymologists can find no firm evidence that the verb *welsh,* meaning "to swindle a person by not paying a debt" or "to fail to fulfill an obligation," is derived from *Welsh,* the people of Wales. However, many Welsh themselves harbor no doubt on this subject and hold the verb to be a pointed slur. It makes sense then to avoid this informal term in ordinary discourse; *renege* or *cheat* can usually be substituted.

were   See **subjunctive.**

what

what as subject of a clause   When *what* is the subject of a clause, it may take a singular or plural verb, depending on the sense. *What* is singular when taken as the equivalent of *that which* or *the thing which: I see what* seems *to be a dead tree.* It is plural when taken as the equivalent of *those which* or *the things which: He sometimes makes what* seem *to be thoughtless mistakes.*

what in a clause that is the subject   When a clause that has *what* as its subject is itself the subject of a sentence or part of a linking verb construction, it may take a singular or plural verb, but determining this is more complicated. Most of these *what* clauses are singular: *What they always wanted was a home of their own.* In fact, *what* clauses are usually singular even when the verb is a linking verb, such as *be* or *seem,* followed by a plural noun or a series of nouns: *What she kept in her drawer was ten silver dollars. What truly commands respect is a large air force and a resolute foreign policy.*

In some cases, a clause with *what* as the subject may be treated as either singular or plural, depending on the intended emphasis. In *What* excite *him most* are *money and power,* the implication is that money and power are distinct elements; in *What* excites *him most* is *money and power,* the implication is that money and power are a single entity.

Notice that the verb *excite* in the above examples is singular or plural according to whether the *what* clause as a whole requires a singular or plural verb. In these cases, the word *what* agrees with the verb *within* the *what* clause as well. If the verb in the *what* clause is necessarily plural, then the whole clause similarly takes a plural verb: *What* seem *to be two dead trees* are *blocking the road.*

There are also certain sentences that have a main verb followed by a plural noun or noun phrase whose sense requires that the *what* clause be plural, as in *What traditional grammarians called "predicates" are called "verb phrases" by some modern linguists* and *What the Romans established as military outposts were later to become important trading centers.* In these sentences, the plural nouns *predicates* and *outposts* give the *what* clauses their plural meaning. Notice that in the second example, the phrase *those places (that),* clearly a plural noun phrase, could conceivably substitute for *what*: *Those places (that) the Romans established as military outposts were later to become important trading centers.*

See more at **subject and verb agreement** and **which.**

whatever

whatever* or *what ever   Both *whatever* or *what ever* may be used in sentences such as *Whatever* [or *What ever*] *made her say that?* Critics have occasionally objected to the one-word form, since *ever* in such sentences is acting as an adverb, separate from the question word *what* (as in *What were you ever thinking?*). However, many respected writers have used the one-word spelling. The same is true of the forms *whenever, whoever, wherever,* and *however.* The one-word forms *whatever, whenever,* and so on must be used when the words introduce a clause, or a noun phrase modified by a clause: *I'll leave whenever* [not *when ever*] *you leave; Take whatever* [not *what ever*] *books you need.*

***whatever* and commas**   When a clause beginning with *whatever* is the subject of a sentence, do not use a comma: *Whatever you do is right.* Otherwise, a comma is fine: *Whatever you do, don't burn the toast.*

whatever* should never be used with *that   When the phrase preceding a restrictive clause is introduced by *whichever* or *whatever, that* should not be used in formal writing. Thus *whatever book that you want to look at* is regarded as incorrect. Drop the word *that* in such cases: *Whatever book you want to look at will be sent to your office; Whichever book costs less* [not *that costs less*] *is fine with us.*

See more at **that.**

when

In informal style, *when* is often used after *be* in definitions: *A dilemma is when you don't know which way to turn.* The construction is useful, but it is widely regarded as incorrect or as unsuitable for formal discourse. In formal style, there is no alternative but to rephrase such definitions to avoid *is when.* The trick here is to make the first part of the sentence a full clause: *A dilemma is a situation in which you don't know which way to turn. You are in a dilemma when you don't know which way to turn.*

When is acceptable, however, when a noun phrase that denotes a point in time is being defined or described: *The best time to eat is when one is hungry.*

 whence   See **hence.**

whenever   See **whatever.**

where

***where* and positional prepositions**   When *where* is used to refer to a point of origin, the preposition *from* is required: *Where did she come from?* When it is used to refer to a point of destination, the preposition *to* is generally superfluous: *Where is she going?* rather than *Where is she going to?* When *where* is used to refer to the place at which an event or a situation is located, the use of *at* is widely regarded as regional or colloquial. So unless you want to convey the flavor of speech, write *Where is the station?* not *Where is the station at?*

***where* as a relative pronoun**   *Where* is also used as a relative pronoun, as in *Show me an example where government intervention in the market has worked.* The Usage Panel has mixed feelings about this. In our 2001 survey, 60 percent accepted the example just given, but only 44 percent accepted *Sometimes the discussion degenerates into a situation where each person accuses the other of being illogical.* These usages probably derive from the positional use of *where* in sentences like *He went to the house where the money was kept* and *We hid the present in the closet where we hang our coats.* These positional usages are standard, but in all of these instances, *where* can be safely and clearly replaced by *in which*.

where* for *that   *Where* is also used as a relative pronoun where *that* might normally be expected, as in *I don't see where they had much choice but to give up.* The Usage Panel has less fondness for this usage. Only 30 percent of the Panel accepted this sentence in our 2001 survey.

wherever   See **whatever.**

whet

The verb *whet* means "to sharpen, as a knife." It is also used figuratively to mean "to make more keen, to stimulate," as in whetting someone's interest or appetite for something. It is commonly misspelled as *wet,* as in this quotation from a book review in an academic journal: *"Specifically, the Editors' essay is a most concise and precise summary and evaluation of Samuels's work in all its ramifications. It is a piece that wets one's appetite for reading Samuels's publications, at least those that one has not read before."*

whether   See **doubt** and **if.**

which

***which* referring to a clause or sentence**   The relative pronoun *which* can sometimes refer to a clause or sentence, as opposed to a noun phrase: *She ignored him,* *which proved to be unwise. They swept the council elections, which could never have happened under the old rules.* Sometimes these *which* clauses are presented as separate sentences. These are technically sentence fragments, and they often pack a rhetorical punch:

> And it was then, about that time, that I began to find life unsatisfactory as an explanation of itself and was forced to adopt the method of the artist of not explaining but putting the blocks together in some other way that seems more significant to him. Which is a rather fancy way of saying I started writing (Tennessee Williams, "The Resemblance Between a Violin Case and a Coffin," *Flair*)

> The job was called a Class-A high-rise, and it was a steel building going several stories up and a few down. We were pouring decks and nonstructural beams and wrapping columns. It was in Beverly Hills, and it was on Rodeo Drive. Which sounds good but isn't (Dagoberto Gilb, "Victoria," *Washington Post Magazine*)

> I was caught for a week on the Siachen Glacier, in a giant blizzard. There is no harsher place on this earth; it belongs to no one. Which won't keep people from squabbling over it someday (Andrea Barrett, "Servants of the Map," *Salmagundi*)

While these examples are perfectly acceptable, writers who want to avoid this use of *which* and adhere to the traditional rules can usually substitute *this* for it at the start of a new sentence, though often at the loss of some dramatic flair.

Note that *which* clauses that modify whole sentences can sometimes create ambiguities. The sentence *It emerged that Martha made the complaint, which surprised everybody* may mean either that the complaint itself was surprising or that it was surprising that Martha made it. This ambiguity may be avoided by using other constructions such as *It emerged that Martha made the complaint, a revelation that surprised everybody.* Remember that *which* is used in this way only when the clause or sentence it refers to precedes it. When the clause or sentence follows, writers must use *what*, particularly in formal style: *Still, he has not said he will withdraw, which is more surprising. Still, what is more surprising, he has not said he will withdraw.*

See more at **sentence fragments, that,** and **what.**

whichever   See **whatever.**

whilst

The word *whilst* is a British variant of the word *while* and has an archaic or poetic feel in American English. While using it runs the risk of sounding pretentious, it can sometimes add a literary or ironically formal note to a piece of writing, as in these examples:

> Then there's the longtime character actor who is happily drinking himself into the poorhouse. When he copped a gig in a locally shot flick, he repeatedly held up production whilst he tried to sober up long enough to read his lines (*Boston Herald*)

> Excuse me a moment whilst I knock on wood, after characterizing what other motorcyclists do as idiotic (*Morning Call*)

Traditionally, this word is pronounced with a long *i* as in *while*.
See more at **amid**.

white

Although *white* in its racial sense has never been stigmatized in the same way as other color labels, especially *yellow* and *red*, there are many people who would prefer to dispense with all names based on skin color in favor of a more neutral vocabulary of national or geographic origin. The terms *Euro-American* and *European American* have gained some currency in recent years as an alternative to *white*, their primary appeal being their equivalence to such now-popular ethnonyms as *African American*, *Asian American*, and *Native American*. And since Europe is viewed from America as a region of many different languages and cultures, these terms can serve as a reminder that the group of people usually known as "whites" does not necessarily make up a homogeneous community. But *Euro-American* and *European American* sound artificial to many people, and the fact remains that *black* and *white* are familiar and convenient labels that are not likely to disappear from American English anytime soon.

Though *black* is sometimes capitalized when referring to African Americans or their culture, *white* is almost always spelled lowercase.

See more at **black, Caucasian,** and **Euro-American.**

who

who* and *whom The traditional rules that determine the use of *who* and *whom* are relatively simple: *who* is used for a grammatical subject, where a nominative pronoun such as *I* or *he* would be appropriate, and *whom* is used as the object of a verb or preposition. Thus, it is correct to say *The actor who played Hamlet was excellent,* since *who* stands for the subject of *played Hamlet,* and *Who do you think is the best candidate?* where *who* stands for the subject of *is the best candidate. Who* is also required when it would be part of the predicate of a linking verb construction. For example, in *She finally found out who her real friends were, who* is part of the predicate of the linking verb (its predicate nominative), while *her real friends* is the subject of the predicate.

In contrast, traditional grammar requires *To whom did you give the letter?* since *whom* is the object of the preposition *to,* and *The man whom the papers criticized did not show up,* since *whom* is the object of the verb *criticized.* These traditional rules apply in the same manner to *whoever* and *whomever.*

The rules were formulated by grammarians in the 18th century who noticed that the two words were often used interchangeably, with *whom* sometimes being used as a subject, and *who* as an object. In fact, this variation goes back to the 14th century. Today, the rules are well established as a part of formal Standard English. Nonetheless, *whom* is uncommon in speech and informal writing because of its inherently formal tone. When formality is not required, *who* generally replaces *whom.* Sentences such as *It was better when he knew who to pay attention to and who to ignore* sound perfectly natural, despite violating the traditional rules. In many contexts, *whom* sounds forced or pretentiously correct, as in *Whom do you think John's been dating?* In sentences in which *whom* is a relative pronoun, *that* can often be used instead: *The electrician that the school hired has rewired four rooms so far. The players that the coach reprimanded stayed late to work on their conditioning.*

Note that separating the word *whom* from the preposition of which it is the object is stylistically awkward. *Whom did you give your books to?* is more naturally expressed as *Who did you give your books to?* If the preposition and *whom* (or *who*) are not placed at the front of the clause, *who* is usually acceptable, at least in informal contexts: *I need to know who lied to who.* Interestingly, if both the preposition and *who/whom* are moved to the front of the clause, the form used must be *whom,* even in many informal contexts: *To whom* [not *to who*] *should we address these packages?* But note that *who* is correct when it follows a preposition as the subject of the subsequent clause: *The reporters differ as to who they think might win the nomination. I want to vote for who(ever) can best lead the country in a time of crisis.* If sentences like these seem awkward, they can be recast with nouns as the objects of the prepositions: *The reporters differ as to which candidate they think might win the nomination. I want to vote for the candidate who can best lead the country in a time of crisis.*

who in restrictive and nonrestrictive clauses The relative pronoun *who* may be used in restrictive clauses, in which case it is not preceded by a comma, or in nonrestrictive clauses, in which case a comma is required. Thus it is acceptable to say either *The scientist who discovers a cure for cancer will be immortalized,* where the clause *who discovers a cure for cancer* indicates which scientist will be immortalized, or *The mathematician over there, who solved the four-color theorem, is widely known,* where the clause *who solved the four-color theorem* adds information about a person already identified by the phrase *the mathematician over there.*

See more at **else** and **that.**

whoever   See **whatever** and **who.**

whom   See **that** and **who.**

whomever   See **whatever** and **who.**

whose

inanimate whose The possessive adjective *whose* (the possessive form of the pronoun *who*) has been used to refer to inanimate antecedents since the 14th century. It appears in the works of many illustrious writers, including literary giants like Shakespeare, Milton, and Wordsworth, and the history of English literature would be much impoverished without it. The word serves a useful purpose, since *which* and *that* do not have possessive forms, and the substitute phrase *of which* is often awkward and can ruin the flow of a sentence. In some cases, little harm is done by making such a substitution, aside from increasing syntactic complexity. A relatively simple sentence like *He pointed to a grove of trees whose trunks were coated with ice* (adapted from a story by Rick Bass) is made somewhat stilted but not unspeakable by the avoidance of *whose: He pointed to a grove of trees, the trunks of which were coated with ice.* But as sentences become more complicated, wrenching in *of which* can be especially clumsy. Consider this revision of a sentence that used *whose* in its original (penned by Natalie Angier): *The revolution in our study of how genes work began with the study of bacteria like E. coli, the DNA of which is packed very differently from that of the cells of higher organisms.* Clearly, the original phrasing (*whose DNA is packed*) is more elegant and easier to read.

In spite of its grace and handiness, inanimate *whose* has been criticized by usage commentators since the 18th century. The tradition holds that *whose* should function only as the possessive of *who,* and be limited in reference to persons. Certainly, *whose* serves this function eminently well, and in the great majority of our citations *whose* refers to a person, not a thing.

The notion of *whose* properly being a form of *who* (and not *which*) has considerable bearing on attitudes about the word. In our 2002 survey, only 44 percent of the Usage Panel approved of an example in which *whose* refers to a river: *The EPA has decided to dredge the river, whose bottom has been polluted for years.* The association of *whose* with people undoubtedly influenced the Panel's response to an example that is syntactically similar to the previous one, in which the antecedent is a book, but the subject of the *whose* clause is a person. Some 63 percent of the Panel accepted the sentence *The book, whose narrator speaks in the first person, is a mock autobiography.* Note that this still leaves almost 40 percent of the Panel in disapproval.

Because the alternative phrasing to *whose* can be so awkward, there is often no easy solution to this problem except to recast the entire sentence (and perhaps the one before it) to avoid *whose* altogether. This is one case in which the cure could be worse than the disease.

whose and **who's** Remember not to confuse *whose* with its homophonous contraction *who's* (for *who is*). This error is surprisingly common and is easy to commit when writing in a rush.

See more at **possessive constructions.**

■ **why**   See **reason why.**

wife / husband / spouse

Although it was once always true that a *wife* was the only female in a marriage and a *husband* the only male, the advent of same-sex marriage has changed this assumption. A married woman can have either a husband or a wife, as can a married man. The generic word *spouse* is always appropriate in contexts in which specifying gender is not important. When a member of a couple is defined as being a wife or husband, the other member should be referred to in parallel fashion. The traditional phrase *man and wife,* though still common, is offensive to many people. The equitably balanced phrases *husband and wife* and *man and woman* are unobjectionable.

will   See **shall.**

–wise

The suffix –wise has a long history of use to mean "in the manner or direction of," as in clockwise, otherwise, and slantwise, and these usages are fully acceptable. The suffix ultimately goes back to the Old English noun wīse, "manner of doing something," which was used to form compounds functioning as adverbs of manner. Since the 1930s, however, –wise has been used in the vaguer sense of "with relation to," as in This has not been a good year saleswise or Taxwise, it is an unattractive arrangement. If these examples sound unremarkable, this may be because –wise is used frequently in business writing and in informal speech. But in this relational usage, the suffix has never gained respectability in more formal situations and still will strike many readers as inelegant. Usually such words as saleswise and taxwise can be quite easily replaced by paraphrases such as This has not been a good year with respect to sales and As far as taxes are concerned, it is an unattractive arrangement.

wish

The verb wish is sometimes used with an infinitive as a polite substitute for want: Do you wish to sit at a table on the terrace? Anyone who wishes to may leave now. This usage is appropriate for formal style, where it is natural to treat the desires of others with exaggerated deference. Less frequently, wish is used with a noun phrase as its object, as in Anyone who wishes an aisle seat should see an attendant. Both usages may sound stilted in informal style.

See more at **subjunctive.**

with

When the subject of a sentence is followed by a noun or noun phrase introduced by with rather than and, the verb remains singular: The governor, with his aides, is expected to attend the fair.

See more at **and.**

with regard to / with respect to   See **in regard to.**

wizen

The verb wizen, meaning "to shrivel up or wither," is pronounced with a short i (wĭz′ən).

woke   See **wake**.

woman   See **girl** and **man**.

word formation   See **affixes; compound words; hyphenation; plural nouns; suffixes;** and **verbs, principal parts of.**

wordiness

Using too many words often makes it difficult to understand what is being said. The reader must work hard to figure out what is going on, and in many cases may simply decide it is not worth the effort. Verbosity also tends to sound overblown, pompous, and evasive. In general, wordy writing has three distinguishing characteristics: weak verbs, ponderous nouns, and many prepositional phrases.

One key to writing clearly and concisely is to use strong active verbs (although avoiding the passive voice as a blanket policy can lead to problems of its own; see more at **passive voice** and **verbs, voice of**). Weak verb forms such as *be, seem,* and *appear* can often be replaced with active verbs.

Wordy writing with weak verbs tends to rely on abstract nouns, often ending in *–ment, –tion,* and *–ence.* The nouns carry the semantic load and are often embedded in prepositional phrases, as in this sentence:

> It is essential to acknowledge that one of the drawbacks to the increased utilization of part-time employees is that people who are still engaged full-time by the company are less likely to be committed to the recognition and identification of problems in the production area.

With active verbs, the deletion of unnecessary words (like *it is essential to acknowledge that*), and the use of noun modifiers to do the grammatical work of the prepositions, this sentence can be compressed by about two thirds:

> Using more part-time employees often makes full-time employees less willing to report production problems.

Good writing, of course, has other virtues beside compactness. Just because a statement is concise does not make it moving. Consider the following passage from a speech by Winston Churchill voicing defiance during one of the most difficult times of World War II. It could certainly be made shorter with fewer repetitions, but it would hardly be more inspiring:

> We shall not flag or fail. We shall go on to the end. We shall fight in France, we shall fight on the seas and oceans, we shall fight with growing confidence and growing strength in the air, we shall defend our island, whatever the cost may be, we shall fight on the beaches, we shall fight on the landing grounds, we shall fight in the fields and in the streets, we shall fight in the hills; we shall never surrender.

See more at **redundancy.**

work See **force.**

would See **auxiliary and primary verbs, rather, shall, should,** and **subjunctive.**

wrack See **rack.**

wrangle / wangle

The verbs *wrangle* and *wangle* sound similar and are sometimes confused. *Wrangle* means "to quarrel noisily or angrily," as well as "to herd horses or other livestock." Thus people wrangle *with* one another or with the IRS or some other agency. The verb is also used without an object as a synonym of *argue,* as in:

> "It's funny as a crutch," he kept saying, "while we sit here wrangling under schoolmaster Wilson, John Bull's putting his hands on all the world's future supplies of oil . . . just to keep it from bolos." (John Dos Passos, *1919*)

Wangle generally means "to achieve by contrivance or manipulation," as in *He wangled a job for which he had no training* and *The reporter wangled a copy of the preliminary report from one of the committee members.* Properly speaking, one does not *wangle with* someone else.

On the other hand, most dictionaries accept that one may also wrangle something for oneself (that is, win something by argumentation), so in this sense the two words are synonyms. Thus, it is Standard English to wangle or wrangle an invitation to a party, but the latter entails putting forth a convincing argument or winning a contentious exchange of opinions, while the former entails practically any means conceivable.

Both words are sometimes used as synonyms of the verb *struggle,* in contexts where the word *wrestle* would seem more appropriate:

> A memoir of life in a foreign country . . . can be a satisfying set piece . . . The hero, always a tone-deaf boob, will wrangle with a new house and local customs, tussle with the natives, learn a language, taste the indigenous cuisine (*New York Times Book Review*)

> Although canoes can carry more, kayaks are basically closed, which means you stay drier, and so does your gear. Sea kayaks are also lighter, and thus easier to propel and wrangle in and out of the water (*New York Times*)

> Johnny Knoxville and his crew of idiots have actually earned a spot on the silver screen with their outlandish brand of antics. Caught in Japan . . . they wreak havoc on a golf course and wangle with live alligators (*Independent Weekly*)

These uses are not listed in dictionaries, however, and are considered nonstandard.

wreak / wreck

When *wreak* means "to bring about, cause," it is sometimes confused with *wreck,* "to cause the destruction of," perhaps because wreaking damage may leave a wreck. A storm can only *wreak havoc,* never *wreck havoc.*

The past tense and past participle of *wreak* is *wreaked,* not *wrought,* which is an alternative past tense and past participle of *work.* The expression *work havoc* is an acceptable way of saying the same thing as *wreak havoc.* Using the past form *wrought havoc* may cause readers to believe that *wrought* is being used incorrectly as the past form of *wreak.*

wring / ring

The verb *wring* means "to twist, squeeze, or compress, especially so as to extract liquid," and is often followed by the preposition *out: We had to wring out the towels after wiping the wet floor.* The past tense and past participle of *wring* is *wrung,* which is sometimes miscast as *wringed* or *wrang,* as in this theater review from a Texas newspaper: *"Coincidences and eerie flashbacks introduce Genny's rural past, where she wrang the necks of chickens with ominous skill."*

The sound-alike verb *ring* means "to surround" and "to move, run, or fly in a spiral or circular course." It is sometimes used erroneously instead of *wring,* as in this quotation from a California newspaper: *"'Of course, I still have moments when I want to ring his neck, and he feels the same way,' Cherie admits. 'But failure is no longer an option for us. We are making it work this time.'"*

writer   See **author.**

wrought   See **wreak.**

· XYZ ·

Xmas

The pronunciation (ĕks′məs) is the result of a misinterpretation of the abbreviation *Xmas,* where the *X* actually represents a Greek chi, the first letter of *Khrīstos,* "Christ." This pronunciation is generally only used jocularly or informally.

xylem / phloem

Both of these words refer to the vascular system that is characteristic of most plants. *Xylem* (from the Greek word *xulon* meaning "wood") refers to the sturdy tissues that conduct water and minerals upward from the roots to the stem and leaves. *Phloem* (from the Greek word *phloios* meaning "bark") refers to the softer tissues that conduct nutrients downward from the leaves to other parts of the plant. All seed-bearing plants (gymnosperms and angiosperms), along with the ferns, lycophytes, and horsetails (pteridophytes), have xylem and phloem.

ye

In an attempt to seem quaint or old-fashioned, many store signs such as "Ye Olde Coffee Shoppe" use spellings that are no longer current. The word *ye* in such signs looks identical to the archaic second plural pronoun *ye,* but it is in fact not the same word. *Ye* in "Ye Olde Coffee Shoppe" is just an older spelling of the definite article *the.* The *y* in this *ye* was never pronounced (y) but was rather the result of improvisation by early printers. In Old English and early Middle English, the sound (*th*) was represented by the letter thorn (Þ). When printing presses were first set up in England in the 1470s, the type came from Continental Europe, where this letter was not in use. The letter *y* was used instead because in the handwriting of the day the thorn was very similar to *y.* Thus we see such spellings as y^e for *the,* y^t or y^{at} for *that* (which nowadays look very odd) well into the 19th century. However, the modern revival of the archaic spelling of *the* has not been accompanied by a revival of the knowledge of how it was pronounced, with the result that (yē) is the usual pronunciation today.

yellow

Of the color terms used as racial labels, *yellow,* referring to Asians, is perhaps the least used now and the most clearly offensive. Its primary associations in contemporary

English are with the expressions *yellow horde* and *yellow peril*, references to the supposed threat posed by Asian peoples who, according to a scenario popular around the turn of the 20th century, were poised to overwhelm the rest of the world, especially whites. As with numerous other pejorative labels, *yellow* is sometimes used ironically or defiantly by Asian Americans today, as in a prominent website featuring Asian cultural links that calls itself *yellowpride.com*, but it should of course be avoided by outsiders.

yet

In formal writing, *yet* in the sense "up to now" is used with an accompanying verb in the present perfect rather than in the simple past: *He hasn't started yet*, not *He didn't start yet*. The use of *yet* with the simple past is common in speech and is often used in informal writing.

zoology

Traditionally, the first syllable of *zoology* has been pronounced as (zō), rhyming with *toe*. However, most likely due to the familiarity of the word *zoo* (which is merely a shortened form of *zoological garden*), the pronunciation of the first syllable as (zo͞o) is also commonly heard. In our 1999 survey, 88 percent of the Usage Panel found the (zō–) pronunciation acceptable, and 60 percent found the (zo͞o–) pronunciation acceptable, with 68 percent using the (zō–) pronunciation and 32 percent using the (zo͞o–) pronunciation in their own speech. Thus, while both pronunciations are acceptable, the (zō–) pronunciation is more closely associated with the word's scientific background.

In related words beginning with *zoo–*, only the pronunciation (zō), not (zo͞o), should be used: *zoogenic* (zō′ə-jĕn′ĭk), *zoon* (zō′ŏn′). The prefix *zoo–* comes from Greek *zōion*, meaning "living being" or "animal."